# NATIONAL PARK GUIDE

## 29th Edition

## Michael Frome

MACMILLAN TRAVEL • USA

Macmillan Travel
A Prentice Hall Macmillan Company
15 Columbus Circle
New York, NY 10023

ISBN 0-02-860056-8
ISSN 0734-7960

10  9  8  7  6  5  4  3  2  1

Printed in the United States of America

**Research Associate**
Brenda Cunningham

**PHOTO CREDITS**
vi: Wyoming Division of Tourism. 44: National Park Service. 48: National Park Service. 54: South Dakota Department of Tourism. 58: Natural History Association/National Park Service. 62: National Park Service. 65: National Park Service. 70: National Park Service. 74: Utah Travel Council. 78: Mark Nohl, courtesy of *New Mexico Magazine*. 82: National Park Service. 86: National Park Service. 92: National Park Service. 103: National Park Service. 108: National Park Service. 111: National Park Service. 116–117: Glacier National Park. 120: Londie G. Padelsky. 132: Wyoming Division of Tourism. 137: National Park Service. 141: National Park Service. 146: National Park Service. 151: Kay Shaw. 156–157: Kay Shaw. 160: National Park Service. 165: Michigan Travel Bureau. 172: James Gavin. 175: National Park Service. 176: National Park Service. 180: National Park Service. 183: National Park Service. 186: Kentucky Department of Travel Development. 190: National Park Service. 198: National Park Service. 204: National Park Service. 211: National Park Service. 220: National Park Service. 227: Kay Shaw. 234: Londie G. Padelsky. 241: National Park Service. 247: National Park Service. 252–253: National Park Service. 256: Kay Shaw. 260: Wind Cave National Park. 262: National Park Service photo by Richard Stenmark. 266: Wyoming Division of Tourism. 276: Yosemite Collections, National Park Service. 282: Utah Travel Council. 291: National Park Service photo by William Clark. 295: National Park Service photo by Lt. Col. M.W. Arps, Jr. 297: National Park Service photo by William Clark. 298: National Park Service. 304 (bottom left and top right): Arizona Office of Tourism. 305: Arizona Office of Tourism. 378: Photo of Florissant Fossil Beds by Tracy Harmon. 382: Photo of Great Sand Dunes by Tracy Harmon. 396: Arizona Office of Tourism. 404: National Park Service. 405: National Park Service.

All maps reproduced courtesy H.M. Gousha.

# ABOUT THIS BOOK

## The 29th Anniversary Edition

*National Park Guide* by Michael Frome is your own personal tour guide—before, during, and after your visits to the national parks.

Michael Frome, called "the voice of the wilderness," *knows* the national parks. He has explored them through the years as a camper, backpacker, canoer, and horseman. He skillfully guides you through the national parks—each brought to life with vivid portraits that reveal the park's history, geology, and unique points of interest, as well as Michael's personal observations of the parks. In this new edition, completely updated, Michael introduces readers to three great national park areas in California, established by Congress late in 1994, and also to the national parks of Canada.

Family travelers will welcome the chapter titled "Adventures for Children—Discovery and Learning." Here Michael describes how our parks provide for the special needs of children. Suggestions for activities and tips on how best to travel with youngsters are offered.

A ***Practical Guide*** within each park chapter provides vital information on park access, visitor centers, park activities (including birdwatching, hiking, bicycling, fishing), accommodations, climate, and recommended reading. Full color, detailed national park maps provide greater understanding to enhance your experience.

The Guide also devotes chapters to the many other areas administered by the National Park Service: In and Around Washington, D.C.; Archaeological Areas; Historical Areas; Natural and Recreational Areas; and Alaska Monuments, Preserves, and Historical Parks.

We are confident that you will enjoy your national parks visits with the aid of your personal tour guide to the national parks.

# CONTENTS

## THE NATIONAL PARKS

*North Cascades National Park*

## ADDITIONAL NATIONAL PARK SERVICE AREAS

## LIST OF MAPS

# PREFACE TO THE 29TH EDITION

WHEN I LOOK NORTH TO CANADA, I see one of the largest and most beautiful countries on earth, still relatively undeveloped and unspoiled. I reflect with appreciation on the idea that Canadians wisely have chosen through the years to preserve and protect examples of their diverse landscapes, along with untamed plantlife and wildlife, forests and rivers.

Even now Canadians are striving to define a comprehensive nationwide network of protected areas, including ecological reserves, national parks, provincial parks and wildlife refuges. Much of the focus is on northern Canada, with some of the largest remaining tracts of wilderness anywhere—new frontiers for travel adventure, new challenges for respect and restraint.

That is why I have chosen in this new edition of my *National Park Guide* to highlight the expanding system of Canadian national parks. Besides, I'm lucky enough to live barely twenty miles below the border of British Columbia. On many days I can see the coastal mountains of British Columbia from my window and can reach any one of half a dozen of Canada's national parks within a day or so by car.

That is why I realize the current emphasis on protection comes none too soon. In earlier years, when natural resources appeared limitless, vast unoccupied spaces were tamed. Harnessing its riches in timber, water and minerals, Canada achieved its enviably high standard of living. But the landscape changed dramatically, especially in recent years following World War II, and Canadians now strive to balance standard of living with quality of life in a wholesome environment.

For example, much of the eastern slopes of the Rockies in Alberta, where the mountains first rise from the Plains, has been greatly altered since the 1950s. Exploration roads, oil and gas wells, pipelines, stripmines and logging operations have marked the land. Consequently the Alberta Wilderness Association has proposed a network of Wildland Recreation Areas on the eastern slopes to preserve the living frontier heritage, explaining that: "Wildlands are an important link to our past and to our future. The wilderness has shaped our heritage. Our Canadian identity has been molded by the qualities of a wild and powerful land."

Even the national parks have felt the impact of modern civilization. In the early years Canadians believed their parks could serve both as resorts—

complete with hotels, golf, tennis, lawn bowling and skiing—and as wilderness nature reserves. But recently, in little more than a decade, a total of $500 million in building permits was issued in Banff National Park, leading Parks Canada (the equivalent of our National Park Service) to warn that bears and wolves, once plentiful, now are in jeopardy.

Banff is Canada's oldest and most celebrated national park. Actions to establish the world's first parks were taken at Yosemite in 1864 and Yellowstone in 1872, but Canada was close behind. In 1885, when work crews were building the trans-Canada railroad and opening new frontiers, someone had the bright idea that a part of the great land should be set aside, free of exploitation. The jewel of the Rockies was already in government ownership as "crown land," the equivalent of our public domain, and the Conservative government of Sir John A. Macdonald responded by designating Banff National Park. That was the beginning.

A few years later, in 1893, Ontario established the first provincial park, Algonquin, and in 1895 Quebec followed with Laurentides. Provincial parks and recreation areas, roughly comparable to state parks in the United States, are spread all across Canada. Newfoundland alone has more than 75, Nova Scotia about 125, Ontario more than 260, British Columbia about 300. These range from small waysides for day use only and overnight campsites up to expansive, primitive natural areas.

Parks in both countries have grown up together, ever since prime overlooks at mighty Niagara Falls in the 19th century were converted into commercialized private enterprises. Both nations learned to guard against similar encroachments at other prime points of interest. In due course Waterton-Glacier, straddling the Alberta-Montana border, became the world's first international peace park. Another was established to commemorate the favorite summer haunt of Franklin D. Roosevelt as a young man, now known as Roosevelt Campobello International Park, on Campobello Island, New Brunswick, linked to the mainland by FDR Memorial Bridge at Lubec, Maine. Quetico Provincial Park, in western Ontario, joined with the Boundary Waters Wilderness, in northern Minnesota, comprises the largest, most celebrated canoe country in the world.

One of Canada's newest national parks, Ivvavik, an arctic wilderness in the northeast corner of the Yukon, protects migration routes of more than 150,000 barren-ground caribou. The great Porcupine herd (named for the Porcupine River) travels from calving grounds on the coastal plain of Alaska each spring, protected in the Arctic National Wildlife Refuge, to winter in Canada—one of the last major wildlife migrations on earth. And in June 1993, British Columbia designated the new Tatshenshini-Alsek Wilderness Provincial Park, covering 2,367,218 acres: It links Glacier Bay National Park in the U.S. and neighboring Canada's Kluane National Park, which, in turn, adjoins Wrangell–St. Elias National Park for a total of 24,278,386 acres. The decision to safeguard the "Tat-Alsek" was made in response to a proposal for a huge open-pit copper mine, with likely serious effects on wildlife, fisheries, water quality, wilderness and recreation on both sides of the border. Now the parks will be administered cooperatively as a world wilderness reserve—the largest on earth.

We on our side of the border depend on Canada's natural riches in other ways. Eighty percent of the ducks harvested in North America are raised in the wetlands of Canada's great plains. Three major migratory flyways converge over Saskatchewan, bringing thousands of geese to feed each year. In Alberta, the delta and lowlands of the Peace and Athabasca rivers in Wood Buffalo National Park serve as the staging area for four major waterfowl flyways. In addition, the park provides summer nesting for the fabled whooping cranes, which later in the year fly south to winter at Aransas National Wildlife Refuge on the Texas Gulf Coast.

Canada's natural majesty and diversity are reflected in the cultures of its people. First came the "First Nations," the native peoples, living close to the earth when the earth was theirs to tend, and now in renaissance, with rich and distinctive ideals of spirit from which we all can learn. French and English languages and traditions derive from the historic tides of exploration and settlement, augmented in more recent times by infusion of new cultures from all parts of the globe.

Artists and writers have helped Canadians to appreciate and understand their heritage. Algonquin, best known and loved of Ontario's parks, is immortalized in paintings by the celebrated Group of Seven. In the West, Emily Carr has interpreted sacred forms in nature and in the monumental carvings of Northwest Coast Indians. Roderick Haig-Brown, the fly fisherman's fly fisherman, came from England to the Northwest, settling in the Campbell River country of Vancouver Island, where he pursued his writing career among some of the last great forests on North America. Farley Mowatt, while best known for his classic *Never Cry Wolf*, has written other important works in behalf of nature and the native people of the North. Science, too, has given voice to the voiceless. I think above all of the late Douglas H. Pimlott, professor of zoology at the University of Toronto, recipient of the 1967 Centennial Medal of the government of Canada for his heroic pioneering work.

Thanks to caring Canadians, the 1980s witnessed major advances in the parks field. In 1983 the government of Ontario established 155 new provincial parks. In 1987, Bruce Peninsula National Marine Park was established along the edge of Georgian Bay and South Moresby National Park in the Charlotte Islands off the British Columbia coast, to protect the ancient rain forest and cultural heritage of the Haida Indians. In 1988, the National Parks Act was enacted to strengthen the designation and administration of national parks.

Still more to come. Plans are underway for 18 new national parks within the next five years. Governments of both Yukon and Northwest territories are developing park systems. Parks are included in negotiations with native peoples over land administration in British Columbia, Quebec and Labrador. Here in the Northwest, the National Parks and Conservation Association and other groups are hopeful of attaining a new Cascade International Park, combining North Cascades National Park on our side with Manning Provincial Park and

Skagit Valley Provincial Recreation Area in British Columbia. Another proposal calls for a 3½-million-acre wilderness park in the Ellerslie Valley, on the central coast of British Columbia, one of the world's most mountainous and beautiful coastlines.

I wrote near the outset of this preface that current preservation efforts have come none too soon. Natural beauty is hard-pressed all across Canada. The Yukon government is involved in killing wolves by helicopter. British Columbia is "super natural," but—at Clayoquot Sound, next door to Pacific Rim National Park, the provincial government supports destructive logging of old-growth rain forest in public ownership. Wood Buffalo National Park, the nation's second largest wilderness preserve, once seemingly isolated on the Alberta–Northwest Territories border, is threatened by changing water levels at the Bennett Dam in British Columbia and by proposals to eliminate the park's herd of free-roaming bison due to the presence of brucellosis. Algonquin, Ontario's treasure, is threatened by pressures to increase rail traffic within its borders, and Kejimkujik National Park in Nova Scotia by acid rain. At James Bay, in northern Quebec, Hydro Quebec has built dams and power plants in territory never ceded nor surrendered by the native Cree, Inuit and Innu peoples, flooding ancient hunting and burial grounds, with still more projects in the works.

Nevertheless, Canada calls. I urge readers of my *National Park Guide* to go experience and absorb the world-class splendor of Canada. Allow plenty of time for national parks—as well as provincial parks. Be adventurous; there also are nearly 150 national wildlife areas and migratory bird sanctuaries. Canadians almost universally are open and friendly, and will help you with courtesy and kindness.

Please feel free to advise me of your findings, of what you like most and like least along the Canadian way. Write me to c/o Macmillan Travel, 15 Columbus Circle, New York, NY 10023. In the meanwhile, happy trails!

—*Michael Frome*

# "YOU LEARN YOU CAN DO AMAZING THINGS"

## National Parks Are for the Mobility-Impaired Too

MAJOR JOHN WESLEY POWELL showed the way. He lost one arm during the Civil War, but that didn't stop him from becoming an intrepid explorer of western frontiers—in 1869 he led the first successful expedition down the Colorado River through the Grand Canyon. Powell proved it could be done, and not only by the physically able.

Now, as then, disability need not be a barrier to making it through the Grand Canyon, nor to the enjoyment of any national park. For one thing, the parks are intended for the use of all people. Provisions for the deaf, blind, and wheel-chaired are made in the design of all buildings and facilities as well as in conducted tours. Federal law mandates equal access, leading to increased efforts to adapt to needs of the disabled.

But that is the least part of what I mean. Modern society tends to put boundaries around people and places, but when individuals push themselves, the artificial boundaries and barriers dissolve.

**Wonderful things happen.** In the summer of 1981 I went down the Colorado River in an oar-powered dory with W Mitchell. Although a paraplegic, who had lost most of his functions from the waist down, he was on his fourth or fifth trip. He would row now and then and swim. "Everybody is much closer to being equal in water," Mitchell said, expressing the sentiment of us all in the party.

Mitchell and I became good friends during the trip and later as well. I learned that he had suffered two serious accidents. In the first, a motorcycle crash in 1971, he was badly burned over 65 percent of his body. Parts of his fingers were amputated. Four years later, misfortune struck again: Mitchell broke his back in a freak airplane accident, which resulted in paralysis. But he was determined to take responsibility for his life and to rise above it. "You can still be a thinking, intelligent, active, important person," he told me. "Before, there were 10,000 things I could do, now there are only 9,000."

Mitchell loves the national parks and has done more in them than most able-bodied visitors. He's proven it can be done, and he's not the only one. Americans who are blind, deaf, limited by muscular dystrophy, spinal injuries, cerebral palsy, or impairment of sight or hearing have explored the wilderness of

1

national parks on wilderness terms. More than once I've heard such people say with pride, "You learn you can do amazing things."

**Trips for the mobility-impaired.** Of course, it requires some planning and arranging, which accounts for the emergence and growth of a new cadre of nonprofit organizations. Wilderness Inquiry of Minneapolis, for example, takes mixed-ability groups on a broad variety of guided adventures—kayaking, canoeing, rafting, hiking, climbing, and dogsledding—in Big Bend, Everglades, and Yellowstone national parks, Apostle Islands National Lakeshore, and St. Croix National Scenic Riverway.

Wilderness Inquiry began in 1978 with trips to the Boundary Waters and has expanded continually since then, with treks even to Australia and Alaska. Trips attract participants of all ages, about half able-bodied, the remainder affected by a wide range of physical challenges. The trips are real outdoor adventures, exploding the myth that wilderness discriminates against the handicapped.

**New freedoms and challenges.** For the disabled, mountains, rivers, and oceans awaken new feelings of freedom and challenge them to explore their own limits. They find the sense of fulfillment overcomes the sense of disability, invariably increasing self-esteem and confidence. The abled benefit no less, learning new lessons in caring and sharing. Adaptive equipment, such as wheelchair frames incorporated into rafts, bicycles with arm-pedals, and canoes with special seats, help the mobility impaired move themselves. Trips are often led by nurses and physical therapists. Ann Bancroft of Wilderness Inquiry struggled with dyslexia as a child. But she was with the Steger-Schurke Expedition to the North Pole in 1986.

A final word about W Mitchell. He became vice president of the National Parks and Conservation Association and a popular public speaker, with a powerful message. He does amazing things.

**Where to write.** Wilderness Inquiry is located at 1313 Fifth St. SE, Minneapolis, MN 55414; phone 612/379-3858. Other groups include the following: All Outdoors, Inc., 42 NW Greeley, Bend, OR 97701; 503/388-8103; Breckenridge Outdoor Education Center, Box 697, Breckenridge, CO 80424; 303/453-6422; Cooperative Wilderness Handicapped Outdoor Group, Idaho State University, Box 8118, Pocatello, ID 83209; 208/236-3912; and Environmental Traveling Companions, Building C, Fort Mason Center, San Francisco, CA 94123; 415/474-7662.

# ADVENTURES FOR CHILDREN—
# DISCOVERY AND LEARNING

NATIONAL PARKS ARE meant especially for children. I recall vividly the pleasures of family travel to the parks when my own two children were small. Once, in Yellowstone, I assumed we had seen enough of the geysers and thermal features and proposed we proceed to other items on our agenda. My son with all the wisdom and curiosity of a ten-year-old protested. "But, dad, each one is different." He was right, of course, and I was glad to find him so interested. Then and there I learned an important lesson: to slow down, be flexible, enjoy what's happening at the moment.

The parks provide marvelous adventures in discovery and learning. Stephen T. Mather, the first director of the National Park Service, called the parks "the most inspiring playgrounds and the best equipped nature schools in the world." I would add that in these "classrooms" children learn not only about nature but about geography, history, citizenship, and self-responsibility, while having the fun that kids deserve.

Many parks schedule activities strictly for children, conducted by personnel trained to communicate with children of various age groups. Ask about them when you first arrive, or write in advance for details. A number of parks feature a Junior Ranger program. For example:

• At Glacier National Park, Montana, junior rangers meet three times a week at Logan Pass, five times weekly at Apgar Visitor Center. The nonprofit Glacier Institute offers a special summertime program, "ABC's of Wildlife," for fourth, fifth, and sixth graders; it covers five days at a moderate cost. (Call 406/888-5441.)

• Mesa Verde National Park, Colorado, distributes a work sheet to junior rangers on their arrival, with questions to answer as they tour sites of preserved prehistoric Indian ruins (What two animals did the Anasazi domesticate? What valuable natural resource made Balcony House such a good place to live?). When the work sheet is completed, the boy or girl can return it to any park ranger station for approval and signature, and receive the official Mesa Verde junior ranger badge. It carries with it responsibility of the Mesa Verde Conservation Code: "Help keep the place you live clean, safe, and beautiful for everyone."

• Yosemite National Park, California, has conducted the Junior/Senior Ranger Program continuously since the 1930s. It now operates for three hours, 9 A.M. to noon, three days a week. Since many parents and even grandparents have been junior rangers themselves, the program is rich in tradition. The Junior/Senior Ranger group consists of forty children in two age brackets—eight- and nine-year-olds (Juniors) and ten- through twelve-year-olds (Seniors). Each group is limited to twenty, to ensure personal contact and involvement. Registration is done in advance by phone or in person on a first-come, first-served basis. A small fee is charged.

In these and other park programs children take guided nature walks and hikes, play theme games, and meet a ranger, while learning about animals, plants, history, and behavior in a group. Some programs are designed for children as young as seven, some including parents—family adventures in birdwatching, stargazing, wildlife tracking.

Wherever you go in the national parks, the following easy travel tips will help you and your children make the most of going places together. Try them and see.

• Involve the kids in planning. Discuss destinations, distances, costs. Let everyone have a say. Invariably, being partners in planning helps children cooperate throughout the trip.

• If you've never taken the kids camping before, get the feel of it with a sample in the backyard, then another somewhere close to home.

• Give each child his or her own backpack, with individual gear; keep it light for little ones, but let them share responsibility. Take time to work with them, so they understand the why as well as how of camp chores. Develop your own system of carrying plastic bags with raisins, nuts, trail food; plastic bags for litter; change of clothing in case of spills.

• Make your first trips to parks within relatively easy reach. For family travel a car is the most practical way to go. Prepare copies of maps with designated routes that kids can follow or color.

• Get a tape deck. Bring books about the parks or stories about them on cassette. Let them carry books, coloring paper, crayons, and maps in their own packs so they can reach for what they want. Bring out something extra as a surprise when you need it.

• Stop for breaks every two hours, with "free time" when you do.

• If not by car, then consider Amtrak. Kids have always loved trains. Air travel can be the most arduous, with congested airports and cramped plane cabins. Get to the airport early. Make sure of seat assignments on the plane and ask about children's meals. Bring snacks, familiar food.

• Keep a travel journal. Write it, color it, glue in souvenirs.

• Allow kids to see things their way. Don't assume they can or want to share an adult's experience. Avoid imposing your own priority, or viewpoint. Learning is great, especially when they do it at their own pace.

Many fine books on the national parks are available for children of all ages. Start them off before you go. I heartily recommend *National Park Service—Activities and Adventures for Kids*, by Bill and Jane Hallett, 32 pages with crossword puzzles, word games, drawing, and more: Look & See Publications, Box 64216, Tucson AZ 85740, $3.95.

Look for books with quizzes, puzzles, maps, and games that everybody can play. They bring the family together in fun and learning. The *Washington, D.C., Guidebook for Kids*, by Carol Bluestone and Susan Irwin, includes pages of neat quizzes, with stimulating questions like:

Who lives at 1600 Pennsylvania Avenue?
How high is the Washington Monument?
Name the only president who never lived in the White House.
Where was Abraham Lincoln assassinated?

And on another page, play the game of "Who am I?" It goes like this:

I am always remembered for my honesty. During the Civil War, I tried to keep
    the Union together. Who am I?
I am a museum that tells the story of the African people. Who am I?
I used to be called the President's Palace. Who am I?

For an entire catalogue of publications write Eastern National Park and Monument Association, 446 North Lane, Conshohocken, PA 19428. Consider especially the *Park Ranger Coloring Book* and *Kids' Birdwatcher Book*.

Then add to your collection as you travel. Almost every park offers children's books for sale at the visitor center or a building near it. In Yosemite's large bookshop, look for *Faces in All Kinds of Places*, "a worm's-eye view of flowers," and *A Kid's Guide to Yosemite*. At Yellowstone you'll find *Wolf Pack*, about the life of a wolf; *Yellowstone: A Children's Guide*, and *Family Fun in Yellowstone National Park*. Children love such books. They will read them again and again, long after you return home, learning something new each time, while recalling their adventures and discoveries in the parks.

# VOLUNTEERS IN THE PARKS

A WONDERFUL WAY to experience the national parks is to work in one as a volunteer. With the right outlook, it's even better than getting paid: doing something because you want to, out of choice rather than necessity. It's like volunteering at home to work in the local library, hospital, or animal shelter, but for a longer period, giving something of yourself and feeling better for it.

Thousands of men and women of all ages, colors and social status work as national park volunteers for periods ranging from two or three weeks to three months and more. They perform a variety of tasks that only a few years ago would have been handled by paid professionals, or that simply would not have been handled at all. "We need the volunteers because of budget restrictions," park officials will say. But I see it differently. Working as a volunteer allows the private citizen to learn how public parks are run and to make a difference in how they *should* be run. Volunteering provides the chance to give back to America for all that it has given—the chance to learn and to meet people from all over the world.

I've talked with many volunteers, without encountering a single one who did not consider the experience enriching and rewarding. Larry Requa, in his mid-80s, worked in the Needles District of Canyonlands National Park several months of each year for almost 10 years. Larry in his colorful life has been a cattle rancher in western Canada, a police officer in British Columbia, a special forces shock trooper in World War II, and a commissioner of forestry in the Yukon Territory. "I love the parks and the desert, and feel I'm doing something to preserve it," Larry told me. "I've met very nice people and made good friends." On his popular guided walks he tells visitors how he learned from an Indian chief in Canada that we are the earth, and the earth is us. Thus, as Larry puts it, "When you get out to walk, you're not conscious of your surroundings; your surroundings are you."

**How do you volunteer?** Several channels are open. Consider the route Larry Requa followed. He's classified as a VIP (Volunteer in the Park), working in the program operated directly by the National Park Service. VIPs come from all walks of life. Many are retired couples; others are students or teachers, some earning academic credits for their work.

There is no upper age limit. Applicants are required to be over 18, but even those younger may become VIPs in the communities where they live, with parental permission. Disabled persons are encouraged to apply. If you're in good health and able to perform the duties, don't hesitate to apply. You won't get paid, but some parks reimburse volunteers for out-of-pocket expenses, such as meals and uniforms, and provide housing as well.

VIPs may perform any of the following or other duties as assigned: campground host; trail crew member; backcountry wilderness ranger; park information desk clerk; carpenter; brochure writer; librarian; photographer; campfire program and guided walk leader; computer program operator; telephone operator; and wildlife aide. In looking over VIP openings at particular parks, I noted the following: Moores Creek National Battlefield in North Carolina wanted someone with knowledge of 18th century military, including use of the Brown Bess musket; San Juan Island National Historic Park in Washington needed a living history interpreter to wear 1860s military uniforms and portray camp life of the offbeat Pig War and a gardener/interpreter to help restore and interpret historic orchards and formal gardens; Antietam National Battlefield in Maryland needed hardworking people to clean Civil War headstones; and Padre Island National Seashore in Texas was looking for beach patrollers to protect endangered Kemp's Ridley turtles arriving to lay eggs in the sand.

**If you're ready to apply.** First, choose the park where you want to work, with at least two alternates.

Then call or write the VIP coordinator at those parks. (The addresses are in this *National Park Guide.*) Explain your skills, interests, and goals and ask about housing and per diems for food.

If things work out, the VIP coordinator will contact you with an agreement on duties and responsibilities. You will be given training and orientation to start you off on the right foot.

I recommend *Helping Out in the Outdoors*, a directory listing volunteer jobs in national parks, national forests and other public lands. It is published twice a year by the American Hiking Society, 1015 31st St NW, Washington, D.C. 20007. Available for $3.

**Student Conservation Association.** One of the finest volunteer groups in America, the Student Conservation Association, has collaborated with the National Park Service for more than 20 years. SCA Resource Assistants work side by side with park professionals in the field. They build trails and bridges, work at archaeological sites and offer information and assistance to visitors. Most are college students, but anyone over 18 may apply. There is no upper age limit.

Unlike VIPs, SCA volunteers receive funds to cover travel and housing, subsistence allowance for food, and uniform allowance when required. But they also work 40 hours a week for a 12-week hitch. As a university professor, I've watched students go off to SCA with enthusiasm, willingness to work, and interest in conservation—the qualities that count the most. They return with new skills of lasting benefit. Best of all, they learn to care for each other and to work together.

SCA's major single endeavor followed the 1988 fire at Yellowstone. Responding to an appeal from the National Park Service for a three-year program, the association established the Yellowstone Fire Recovery Corps. It enlisted 425 volunteers representing more than 40 states, and ranging in age from 16 to 67, to rebuild hundreds of miles of hiking trails and scores of footbridges and to revegetate more than 2,000 miles of fire lines.

Large corporations, garden clubs, and many private individuals underwrite SCA programs. For a contribution of $250 anyone can sponsor a Resource Assistant and receive correspondence from him or her. In addition to the national parks, SCA volunteers serve in federal areas administered by the Forest Service, Bureau of Land Management, and Fish and Wildlife Service and in state and local parks. For information write to the Student Conservation Association, Box 550, Charlestown, NH 03603.

**SCA high schoolers.** The growing high school program for young people 16 to 18 deserves special mention. They undertake worthwhile projects for the parks and themselves. While working at Richmond National Battlefield in Virginia, SCA high schoolers unearthed important Civil War fortifications; and at Steamtown National Historic Site in Pennsylvania, they refurbished turn-of-the-century railroad cars and cleaned up the historic rail yard. SCA has conducted projects for hearing-impaired youths at Rocky Mountain and Olympic national parks and plans more of them.

**Other volunteer programs.** The American Hiking Society sends crews each summer, winter, and spring to work in national parks, national forests, and state parks. Crews do hard work. They build and maintain trails and help to make the areas safe, attractive, and accessible. Volunteer crew members are age 16 and over and in good physical condition. Travel to and from the site is on your own. You pay a $30 registration fee, but food, training, tools, and supervision are provided by the co-sponsoring government bureau. For information and a schedule, send a self-addressed stamped envelope to AHS Volunteer Vacations, Box 86, North Scituate, MA 02060.

For many years the Sierra Club has conducted service outings, on which members do cleanup and other essential but unglamorous chores. It's not all work; half the time is free to enjoy the outdoors. Contact the Outing Department, Sierra Club, 730 Polk St., San Francisco, CA 94109.

If you want to volunteer in scientific research and can pay for it, take note of Earthwatch. This international nonprofit organization annually sponsors more than 100 projects around the world in marine studies, rain forest ecology, biology, and anthropology. It places paying volunteers as field assistants with research scientists for periods of two to three weeks.

Earthwatch receives many requests from scientists for volunteer support. Current projects include Dr. Jeff Hatfield, in Volcanoes National Park, studying exactly how introduced animal species affect native species; and Dr. Rolf Peterson has been working for years in Isle Royale National Park studying wolf/moose relationships. His findings have helped promote wolf understanding and conservation. Expedition costs range from $800 to more than $2,000, averaging about $1,300. Some scholarships are available for teachers and students. Write to Earthwatch, 680 Mount Auburn St., Watertown, MA 02272.

# ENJOY YOUR VISIT TO THE PARKS

LET'S START with the following tips to get the most from your national park travels in the 1990s:

1. Slow down. Concentrate time and energy in one or two parks, rather than rushing to see them all.
2. Make the park visitor center your first stop.
3. Drive less. Take a hike. Or a walk. Find a quiet spot to watch birds or to sit and contemplate.
4. Travel off-season, or at the beginning or end of the season. Pick weekdays instead of weekends.
5. Carry the right clothing and gear—pack with a checklist.
6. Get to your campsite, motel, or hotel early, always before dark.
7. Keep valuables locked or out of sight.
8. With children, travel at their pace. Keep them in sight while in the mountains and near streams.
9. Join a program of an educational group like the Yellowstone Institute or Yosemite Institute.
10. If you're a senior, sign up for an Elderhostel field seminar.
11. Go with an outdoors group, like the Mountaineers in Seattle. There's one near you.
12. Be a good park visitor. Take only memories, leave only footprints.

Those who try to see the maximum number of parks in the least time miss the message. They make it through the parks, touching only the centers, with little chance to explore. They are part of the crowds and congestion, ending at home in need of a break.

But you can use this book as your planning guide and return home refreshed and uplifted. Follow the slower pace to expand the dimensions of time. It isn't a question of how extensively or expensively one travels, but how intensively and perceptively. Visiting fewer parks, staying longer at each one, leads to better appreciation and more enjoyment.

Start with outlook and attitude, a willingness to adopt an unhurried approach. It's not simply a matter of where but of how—*how* to look at national parks, *how* to absorb the wonders of nature, *how* to reorient patterns of travel and thinking.

National parks are places where young and old can find inspiration. Major parks are crowded, that is true, but mostly at core areas where people congregate because they are used to urban ways. Only a short distance away lie solitude and discovery, with respite from sights, sounds, smells, and pressures of civilization.

**Proper planning.** Preparing to explore the parks can be almost as important as the trip itself. Ask yourself these questions (using a notebook to record the answers will help):

In the given amount of travel time, how much distance will I cover?

How much time will I spend in each national park I intend to visit?

Which principal sights will I see in each park and along the way? In which activities (such as hikes and float trips) will I participate?

Do I have at least a rough idea of accommodations and/or campgrounds on the itinerary? Do I have a reservation for the first night? Am I planning to arrive at a decent hour so that I can be sure of finding a place before dark?

Do I have the proper equipment—for hiking, camping, boating? Have I fully considered climate and weather?

Am I leaving home with enough money to get me there and back? Or, perhaps, should I shorten the trip, or cover less distance, to eliminate the chance of running out of funds?

Have I left word with family and friends on how to reach me in an emergency?

Figure out the answers before you leave and you won't have to worry about them later.

**Choose the season.** If you must travel in summer, try to go early or late to avoid the mid-season peak. In the parks of the northern Rockies, the best time for a wilderness trip is between July 15 and September 15. In the southwestern mountains, conditions are usually favorable from mid-June to early October.

Although summer has been accepted for years as virtually the only period to visit the national parks, more national parks are open throughout the year than most people realize. Autumn is superb. In the eastern national parks, autumn is an outstanding time for backcountry hiking. The leaves turn color; skies are clear; the sun is bright. Even in the northern parks, roads and some overnight lodgings are open until late October. The desert wilderness shows its spectacular blossoms in late winter and early spring. Best of all, the scene is natural. The animals are relatively undisturbed, the way all visitors hope to see them.

**Winter in the parks.** One way or another, winter's magic touches almost all national parks. At Mount Rainier, rangers conduct snowshoe walks, for which the Park Service furnishes snowshoes free of charge. The park publishes its own winter tabloid, *The Snowdrift*, full of news about weather, winter activities, accommodations and safety hints. At Yosemite, the Natural History Association conducts winter environmental education programs, including bird watching, field ecology and a seven-day trans-Sierra environmental ski tour.

Such programs are given all across the country. Even urban national parks take on lively winter personalities. In the National Capital Region, at Washington, D.C., you can ice skate near the Lincoln Memorial (when conditions are right), take winter bird walks, learn about winter botany at the Kenilworth Aquatic Gardens, or spend a winter afternoon at Fort Washington Park on the Maryland shore of the Potomac River. Take advantage of these activities. Parks are usually less crowded in winter.

**Lodgings in and near the parks.** Facilities on federal land in national parks are operated by private concessioners under contract to the government. My own experience shows that quality varies widely. A few—the Ahwanee in Yosemite, El Tovar at the rim of the Grand Canyon, and Caneel Bay in the Virgin Islands—are like remembrances of elegant times past; they're expensive, maybe best for a meal to celebrate. Alaska national parks are endowed with choice accommodations. Some are unusual, like Koksetna at Lake Clark, and Brooks Camp at Katmai. Glacier Bay Lodge is a top stop, too. Others that stand out in my mind include Shenandoah Countryside, a bed-and-breakfast just outside Shenandoah; Kettle Falls at Voyageurs; Rough Riders, at the edge of Theodore Roosevelt; Izaak Walton Inn, just outside Glacier; Volcano House at Hawaii Volcanoes; and Maho Bay in the Virgin Islands. These and many others are covered under individual parks in the pages that follow.

A word or two on rates and on how to save. They are always highest "in season," then generally drop 10 to 25 percent during the "off-season." For parks like Yellowstone and Glacier in the cool northern Rockies the peak season runs from late June through August. Anytime after Labor Day is definitely off-season. On the other hand, at Everglades in southern Florida winter and early spring are the in-season.

At times it's highly advisable to make reservations in advance. You're assured a bed for the night and know how much it will cost.

When making reservations at a chain hotel or motel, use the toll-free 800 number. You can obtain it easily by phoning toll-free information, 800/555-1212. Many independent hotels and large motels also have toll-free numbers. It's a good idea when you make your reservation to ask about dining hours or where the nearest restaurant may be.

Remember that owners and managers change. Last year's top hotel occasionally proves to be next year's disappointment. All efforts have been made to make these listings current and reliable. I welcome reports from readers with your compliments and complaints about facilities. Write to me c/o Macmillan, 15 Columbus Circle, New York, NY 10023.

Rates change, too. Rather than include specific prices, the Guide indicates the range: H, for High; M, for Moderate; and L, for Low. Postal zip code and telephone area code are given with the name of the community. Where street addresses are not shown, you can write a lodging facility by using the community name and zip code only.

**Camping and campground reservations.** National parks offer some of the finest camping opportunities on earth, and most varied. While camping in the parks is rich in tradition, improved equipment and accessibility have brought more campers and more demand for campsites. Most sites are still open on a first-come, first-served basis, but the most popular are now assigned by reservation.

Mistix operates a computerized reservations system for the National Park Service in assigning space at major campgrounds in certain popular parks. These include: Acadia, Maine; Assateague, Maryland; Cape Hatteras, North Carolina; Grand Canyon, Arizona; Great Smoky Mountains, Tennessee-North Carolina; Joshua Tree, California; Ozark Riverways, Missouri; Rocky Mountain, Colorado; Sequoia-Kings Canyon, California; Shenandoah, Virginia; Whiskeytown-Shasta-Trinity, California; Yellowstone, Idaho-Montana-Wyoming; and Yosemite, California.

To make a reservation at these campgrounds, call Mistix at 800/452-1111. The campsite fee ranges from $8 to $16 per night; in addition, Mistix charges $5 for handling the reservation. Visa and Mastercard are accepted for charges; otherwise, you will receive an application form to mail in with a check. You can also write Mistix, 600 W. 4th., #313, Chicago, IL 60606.

A few other park areas accept mail reservations, but not on the Mistix system. Most campgrounds continue to operate on a first-come, first-served basis—arrive early to get a better site. You may want to get a copy of *National Parks: A Camping Guide,* on sale at most parks or by sending $6.95 to Consumer Information Center, 151 W. Pueblo, Colorado 81009.

**Entrance and camping fees.** Many parks now charge entry fees, even where admission formerly was free. Congress has directed that each park's budget reflect the amount of money collected; thus, you are helping to pay for park programs and maintenance. Fees vary park by park; figure $12 or $16 per motor vehicle ($8 for bicyclists and bus riders), $30 per vehicle for highly popular parks. If you plan to visit several park areas in one year, or stay a while in any one, take advantage of a Golden Eagle Pass, a Golden Age Passport, or a Golden Access Passport, which you can obtain at any national park or national forest area where fees are charged.

The Golden Eagle Pass allows the bearer, plus all those accompanying him or her in a private vehicle, to enter all federal recreational fee areas. It costs $25 (although the charge may soon be raised significantly), and covers the entrance fee only, not overnight camping fees.

The Golden Age Passport is for senior citizens, 62 years of age or older. A $10 one-time fee is charged. The Golden Access Passport is free for residents of the United States who are permanently disabled, blind, or otherwise eligible for federal disability benefits. Both provide free admission to the parks and a 50 percent reduction on overnight camping fees at most federal camping areas. Golden Age and Golden Access Passports are readily granted to all those eligible, but applications must be made in person.

Besides the entry fees, many parks charge fees at developed camping areas. Fees for rec vehicles are naturally highest. Backcountry camping is allowed without charge.

**RV users.** Check with rangers on arrival about sites best suited for your vehicles—spaces accommodating large RVs in national parks often are very limited. You may prefer privately owned campgrounds outside the parks; many offer pools, playgrounds, laundries, convenience stores. For helpful information write National Association of RV Parks and Campgrounds, 11307 Sunset Hills Road, Reston, VA 22090. Ask the Recreation Vehicle Industry Association, Box 2999, Reston, VA 22090, for its free catalogue listing RV/camping publications; send self-addressed envelope (52 cents postage).

**Tune in to a park.** When driving through a number of national parks, you can listen to more than music on your car radio—and get some excellent information. Stations operated by the Park Service are 10-watt units usually broadcasting at 1610 on your dial.

**Birdwatching.** "Birding" is one of the best activities to bring you in tune with nature. Stop at the Visitor Center for a copy of the park checklist so you can keep notes on the birds you see. Carry along a good bird guide and binoculars. Highly recommended: *The Visitor's Guides to the Birds of the Eastern National Parks, Central National Parks*, and *Rocky Mountain National Parks*, both by Roland H. Wauer. These books culminate Ro Wauer's lifetime of love and study of parks and their birdlife. Birding is usually best in early morning and evening.

**Join a group.** A novice does well to join an outdoor or hiking club, in which he or she can benefit from trips in association with experts. Chances are there is such a club in your community or at a nearby college, sponsoring low-cost trips to national parks and other attractive areas. The Sierra Club conducts outings to national parks all over the country and around the world. The Nature Conservancy offers many trips led by experts in local natural and cultural history (703/841-3724). Check into trips organized by the Appalachian Mountain Club in Boston; Potomac Appalachian Trail Club in Washington, D.C.; Carolina Mountain Club in Asheville, North Carolina; Mazamas in Portland, Oregon; Mountaineers in Seattle, Washington, and other nonprofit groups like them.

**National forests and other areas.** National forests, administered by the Department of Agriculture, have thousands of campsites in their recreation areas. Call the National Forest Reservation Center at 800/280-2267 to reserve campsites in 156 national forests from Alaska to Puerto Rico. The Bureau of Land Management, a sister agency of the National Park Service in the Department of the Interior, has campsites and recreation areas in western states and Alaska. The Indian people have done the same on their reservations.

Consider also the facilities in state parks, recreational areas administered by the U.S. Army Corps of Engineers at major public reservoirs, and private campgrounds.

**More fun without a car.** Alternatives to private transportation—such as buses and trams—have proved successful in a number of parks. They help protect the park environment from heavy auto traffic, noise, and pollution. When operated by the government, transportation services often are free. When run by concessionaires, there usually is a charge.

Seasonal shuttles are operating at Grand Canyon, Arizona; Grand Teton, Wyoming; Mesa Verde, Colorado; Denali, Alaska; North Cascades, Washington; Zion and Bryce, Utah; Dinosaur National Monument, Colorado-Utah; Carl Sandburg Home National Historic Site, North Carolina; and Kennesaw Mountain National Battlefield Park, Georgia.

Some national parks have developed bike routes, with rentals available. In Yosemite, 150 miles of road are available for cycling, with 20 miles of level road in the valley. Grand Teton has 25 miles of white-striped four-foot-wide paved shoulders in rolling terrain between Jenny Lake and Jackson Lake Lodge for the use of cyclists and pedestrians. You can also bike at Mesa Verde, Glacier, and Grand Canyon. The new off-road touring bikes enlarge opportunities, but create problems in resource protection. Check park regulations and live up to them.

Bike routes are installed at some national parks in the East also. You'll find them at Cape Cod National Seashore, Massachusetts; Fire Island National Seashore, New York; and the Chesapeake & Ohio Canal National Historical Park, which extends 185 miles from Washington, D.C., to Cumberland, Maryland. In the Washington, D.C., area, bike paths are extremely popular with visitors and residents alike. Ask for a copy of the *Bike Guide to Washington Area National Parks*, which shows bike routes and rental locations.

For long-distance biking between the parks, consult Adventure Cycling Association (formerly Bikecentennial), Box 8308, Missoula, MT 59807; 406/721-1776. It offers conducted tours as well as a set of cycling maps that cover the country. Of special value are Great Parks North Bicycle Route, Great Parks South Bicycle Route, and Southwest America Bicycle Trail.

**Getting there on public transportation.** Bus companies offer low per-mile fares to large and small towns across the continent, as well as discount plans that allow unlimited riding for a week to a month. Air fares are a bargain on high-volume, competitive routes, but they are expensive when flying to small towns, including national park gateways. Amtrak rail fares generally are more expensive than motor coach for the same distance, but less than regular air fares. Watch them all for discounts and excursions.

Most intercity bus lines, trains, and airlines have facilities for handling backpacks and skis. However, aluminum frame backpacks are apt to receive harsh treatment on the planes. You can haul more gear with less strain on a bus or train.

Keep in mind that once again you can ride the rails to the Grand Canyon. Service was resumed in 1990 after a long hiatus. Ride from Williams, Arizona, to the South Rim in passenger cars restored in 1920s style—pulled by steam engines, of course. (See the Grand Canyon section for details.)

A low-cost alternative way to tour the national parks is the Green Tortoise, a no-frills travel adventure for young at heart. Although the bus operates on a fixed schedule, there is room for seeing the sights your own way. Many routes take in a few national parks, together with several interesting and lesser known scenic spots. Write Green Tortoise, Box 24459, San Francisco, CA 94124; 800/227-4766.

**Photography.** Plan to bring back a picture record of your travels, but don't let picture taking get in the way of personal observation. The best wildlife picture is one of an animal in its natural habitat—feeding, resting, or whatever—and unaware of the photographer. Don't crowd animals; allow them to act naturally by using a long telephoto lens. Be patient; be safe. Good photographs are the product of time.

Use a tripod whenever possible; a steady camera improves photo sharpness. Have plenty of film to allow bracketing and to catch combinations of action and scenery.

Permits generally are not required for either commercial or noncommercial photography, but they may be required in cases involving the use of models, sets, or props, or when it might cause damage to the resources or disruption of normal visitor use. Common sense and courtesy make the best guides.

**Pets.** Your dog or cat is welcome to join you in visiting the national parks, but it must be kept in your car, on a leash, or caged at all times. Animals are not permitted in public buildings or on trails—with the exception of guide dogs for persons who are blind or deaf. Remember not to leave a pet in a car on a hot day—it may suffer heat stroke, even with the windows open.

**Backcountry use permits.** These are now required extensively at heavily used fragile mountain areas and whitewater rivers.

Permits and reservations are free. They generally cover specified trail or boat access camping areas in remote portions of the parks.

For additional information on backcountry permits and reservations, address Backcountry Information at the park you plan to visit. For whitewater permits, write River Trips at the park of your choice.

In addition to backcountry use permits, several parks soon may require mountain climbers to carry insurance to pay the cost of rescue operations. This policy is being considered for Mount Rainier and Denali. If you are planning a technical climb in any park, contact the backcountry office for information about permit requirements and insurance.

**Equipment and clothing.** Your choice of equipment and clothes can mean the difference between an enjoyable trip and an ordeal. Learn the temperature range in the part of the country you're visiting and dress accordingly. Use the "layer system," wearing extra garments as you need them, then peeling them off as the weather moderates. Wear a pair of good boots (broken in) and heavy socks to prevent blistering. Have confidence in your sleeping bag to keep you warm in the weather you're facing or change your plans. A tent protects you in bad weather, but its added weight and bulk must be considered. Because open fires are forbidden in some areas, a stove may be necessary.

Always carry water when hiking. On a day trip, travel with a fanny pack or light knapsack, containing the basics: water bottle, camera, sunscreen, insect repellant, and raingear. Develop your own equipment checklist to match conditions of the area. Make sure it includes the following:

## Equipment

| | |
|---|---|
| backpack | small flashlight & lantern |
| pack raincover | long cord (for hanging food at night) |
| tent | |
| groundcloth | extra plastic bags |
| sleeping bag | waterproof matches |
| sleeping pad | sunscreen & lip balm |
| fanny pack (for day trips) | insect repellant |
| stove and fuel bottle | first-aid kit, moleskin |
| cooking gear | toilet articles & tissue |
| cup, bowl, eating utensils | water filter |
| plastic water bottles | binoculars |
| Swiss army knife | map, compass |
| sunglasses | field guide |

## Clothing

insulated underwear
wool outerwear: shirt, sweater, pants, cap
sun hat, T-shirt, shorts
insulated inner gloves, wool mittens
hiking boots, sneakers for camp
insulated inner socks, wool outer socks (with extra pair)
rain gear: parka, pants

Make sure you're prepared for whatever the weather may offer. Such items as wool shirt, heavy sweater, down vest, parka shell, and rain pants will come in handy at one point or another. Don't cut corners. Purchase good quality equipment—you're investing in comfort and safety.

**Park roads.** The routes in a park are not expressways, so take it easy and concentrate on driving. Enjoy the view from overlooks and parking areas. Then make caution your constant companion when leaving the car.

**Lyme disease alert.** It's something new, caused by tick bites. You'll see warning signs posted in parks where the disease has been found. Best prevention is protection against ticks: use tick repellant; wear long pants; undress and check for ticks. Lyme disease is treatable with antibiotics.

**Value your valuables.** And they will always be yours. Of all your fellow park visitors, 99 percent are as honorable and trustworthy as you. But watch out for that other 1 percent! Thieves visit national parks and look for easy prey.

When away from your car, lock everything of value in the trunk, or put it out of sight. Lock all doors and windows. Wherever you stay, keep your radios and cameras out of sight. Thieves look for easy pickings along main park roads where people congregate. You can help the rangers by advising them of suspicious-looking persons in campgrounds and parking areas. Vacationers in the outdoors are in a relaxed frame of mind. Keep your guard up, practice precautions, and you won't be sorry later.

**Some words of caution.** National parks are governed by rules and regulations; they must be, considering the heavy volume of visitors and the need to protect their resources. But rules involve simple courtesy and common sense. They add to your safety and enjoyment. Use only the designated campgrounds, which are developed for your convenience. Please maintain quiet from 10 P.M. to 6 A.M. Build a fire only in a campground fireplace and extinguish it completely when you leave. Do not smoke on the trail. If you feel you must, stop in a cleared area. Carry out all burned matches, ashes, and butts. When driving, use your ashtray. Report fires immediately to a park ranger.

**Attention foreign visitors.** Ask at park information stations for translated editions of park brochures and other services. Ask also about foreign-language speakers; carry a bi-directional dictionary just in case.

Because public transportation is limited in this country, many foreign visitors find it necessary to rent a vehicle. Before driving long-distance to a remote park, make sure the fuel tank is full and the car is running properly.

**Tread softly, tread lightly.** National park use has risen dramatically. Backpackers and day hikers number at least 30 million and are growing by 10 percent annually. Wilderness use in the Grand Canyon alone has increased more than 300 percent in a decade. This kind of growth can't help but have an adverse impact on fragile nature. Try for minimum impact. It costs you nothing. It takes only common sense. The following few tips may help.

• Stay on the trails. They lead to your destination via the best route and are marked and designated for your protection. Cutting across switchbacks looks easier, but it can prove dangerous and contributes to erosion.

• Use designated campsites where provided, or sites previously used, or sites least damaging to vegetation. Choose a location a reasonable distance away from water to prevent pollution and to allow access for wildlife. Avoid making "improvements," like trenching around tents.

• Eliminate need of fires. Campfires are likely to kill vegetation at the site, change soil chemistry and alter ecosystems. Use lightweight backpack stoves. In the hot summertime, it's a good idea to carry meals that require no cooking.

• Wash—yourself, dishes, clothes—away from streams and lakes. Carry water to your campsites for these jobs. Use biodegradable soaps (such as Ivory or castile products). Dispose of wastewater away from water sources.

• Use toilets where provided. Otherwise, when nature calls, choose a spot away from trails, campsites, and water sources—preferably in rich soil. Dig a hole about 6 inches deep; when through, cover it with soil removed. Natural decomposition will do the rest.

• Refuse to leave refuse. Pack out what you packed in, crushing cans for compactness. Use emptied food containers for leftovers or messy liquid garbage. If you find somebody else's litter, pack it out, too. Many parks now have recycling stations; do your share to help. We know Indians by their arrowheads—should we be known by our beer cans?

• Tread safely. Going alone is officially and properly discouraged, but absolutely meant for some people, at certain times. Keep within the range of your physical capability. Allow about one hour for each 2 miles covered, plus an additional hour for each 1,000 feet of altitude gained. Let someone know your plans.

• Lakes, streams, and springs look appealing, but the water in them may carry contaminants that can make you sick. Guard against giardia, a protozoan that causes "backpacker's diarrhea." Boil water on the trail for one minute or use a filtration kit. And guard against hypothermia, the number one killer of outdoor recreationists. Dress properly to stay dry and warm. Avoid challenging stormy weather. Take along and nibble on high-energy foods.

• At the first sign of trouble, rangers check the trail registers—use them. When lost, try to retrace your steps to where you left the trail. If that fails, don't panic! Find shelter; mark your location (make a large "X" on the ground with clothes and gear so it can be seen from the air). Stay in one place—you'll be found more quickly.

• Children on an outing are eager to explore new surroundings, so keep an eye on them. A child can become confused only a few yards from a trail or camp

# NATIONAL PARK SYSTEM

ONE INCH EQUALS APPROX. 240 MILES

© The H.M. GOUSHA Co.

and can easily be lost. Don't let them play near mountain streams unattended at any time, especially during spring runoff.

• Fill out the trail registers. This safety measure pinpoints your location, and helps park personnel learn from your answers how better to care for the backcountry. Before you go, study park maps and plan your itinerary carefully. Discuss your trip with park personnel at a visitor center or ranger station. Ask about weather and trail conditions.

• Treat all animals as wild. Park regulations that prohibit feeding of bear or deer and the molesting of any animal are enforced on your behalf, as well as the animals'. Remember that national parks are meant for wild animals to roam free in *their* native habitat. Some knowledge of wildlife habitats will help you find the animals, and so will a good pair of binoculars. The best approach is to rise with the sun and to hike through forest and meadows. By 8 or 9 A.M., many animals are in seclusion, not seen again till dusk.

• Respect the bears. If one approaches your car, stay in it with windows closed until the bear goes on its way. Even though bears appear tame, they may turn impulsively and inflict serious injury. Do not feed, tease, or frighten them in any way. While hiking in bear country, whistle, talk, sing, or carry a cowbell so you don't surprise the animals. If you see a bear at a distance, make a wide detour. When camping, avoid the use of odorous foods and suspend your food between trees high off the ground. Cook away from your sleeping area, where possible, and keep your possessions clean.

• Keep a record of what you see and where; take pictures and pleasant memories to your home. Leave only your footsteps for your family to retrace another day.

**Bouquets and brickbats.** Take a few minutes when you return home to dispatch letters of praise or complaint. These are *your* national parks and you're entitled to the last word. If you find campgrounds closed and educational and recreational programs reduced and inadequate, the best single individual to write to is your congressman or congresswoman. He or she should welcome your views. Write a letter to the editor of your hometown newspaper, too. Let everyone know how you found the parks and how you feel about them.

# CANADA'S NATIONAL PARKS

CANADA IS CLOSE at hand and accessible, sharing with the United States the longest unarmed border in the world. It is, however, a different country, with its own distinct history, its own diverse traditions and cultures. Some sections convey the French feeling, not exactly of France, but of French Canada, while other sections convey the English heritage enriched in the New World. Canadians across the continent reflect origins the world over, just as Americans do. In areas of Canada, Native peoples prevail, living in a modern world yet nurturing their world view, their ancient connection with earth, water, sky.

Canada's national parks are diverse too, extending from the eastern edge of North America across the lakes, plains, and prairies of mid-continent and the Rocky Mountains to misty islands off the Pacific Coast and to reaches of the Arctic near the top of the world. The older parks are developed with resort enclaves; the newer ones generally emphasize the natural and simple, free of urban amenity.

Several Canadian national parks have been designated by the United Nations as world heritage sites and biosphere reserves, but all of them are world class. So try to do them right, perhaps concentrating on one or two or three, with planning and pre-trip reading. The more time you invest beforehand, and the more focused your goal, the more satisfying the trip will be. Patience pays dividends. Heed the words of Emily Carr, one of Canada's finest artists and observers of nature:

> *Everything is alive. The air is alive. The silence is full of sound. The green is full of colour. Light and dark chase each other. Here is a picture, a complete thought, and there another and there. . . . There are themes everywhere, something sublime, something ridiculous, or joyous, or calm, or mysterious. Tender youthfulness laughing at gnarled oldness. Moss and ferns, and leaves and twigs, light and air, depth and colour chattering. . . . You must be still in order to hear and see.*

Sound advice wherever you go! Now these tips to help you on your way.

**Entrance Fees.** An annual permit to the national parks costs $25, for vehicle and all passengers. Daily permit averages $4, four-day fee $9. Canadian citizens 65 and over can obtain free annual permits at any park entrance where fees are collected.

**Seasons, clothing, shoes.** Summer days can be warm and bright, especially bright at high elevations, but you never can be sure. Bring a bathing suit, sunglasses, sunscreen, and broad-brimmed hat or cap, but sweater and waterproof gear too. Rely on warm layered clothing, including wool cap, wool sweater, polypropelene long johns, wind jacket and pants, gloves, insulated boots. Bring insect repellant to cope with possible black flies in late spring–early summer. June is a choice month, when everything is fresh, days are long, and crowds still light even at popular spots. September and early October often are mild, clear, rich in color, peaceful. Review and use your maps; carry binoculars.

**Lodgings and food.** Campgrounds are plentiful and strategically sited, in national parks, provincial parks, and in private developments in and around communities. For roof overhead, generally you can find whatever you want, low-cost to luxury, but the farther from cities the simpler accommodations will be—accept and enjoy simplicity. Bed-and-breakfast, hostels, farm-and-country lodgings are plentiful in key areas. Take advantage of local cuisine, notably in French Canada, but wherever you go.

**Prices and admission fees** are quoted in Canadian dollars. The exchange rate fluctuates, but the U.S. dollar definitely goes farther in Canada, to your advantage. Almost all establishments will accept your U.S. currency at the official exchange rate. Credit cards work, with the same advantage. You will be charged a Goods and Services Tax (GST), but keep your papers and get a rebate at Canadian duty free shops when you leave. Gasoline prices are significantly higher. The Canadian gallon is based on the Imperial quart, ⅕ larger than the U.S. quart. (One Canadian gallon equals 4.5 litres; one U.S. gallon equals 3.8 litres.) Your own stamps won't work for a letter home. Postage to the U.S. is 49 cents Canadian for card or letter.

**Distances and dates.** One kilometer equals ⅝ of a mile; calculate simply by figuring 100 km equals 60 miles (actually 62, but round it off). One hectare equals 2.5 acres. Major holidays you may face include Victoria Day, May 24, or the preceding Monday; Canada Day, July 1; Thanksgiving, second Monday in October; Christmas Day and Boxing Day, December 26. For a simple way to convert temperature from Centigrade (which Canadians favor) into Fahrenheit, double the Centigrade figure and add 30 (6 Centigrade equals 42 Fahrenheit).

**Entering Canada.** It's easy, though lines at highway border crossings sometimes can be long, so allow time for it. Carry a passport, driver's license, or voter registration card for identification and proof of citizenship. Dogs and cats need certification of rabies vaccination in the past three years.

**Transportation.** You don't have to go all the way by car. Call VIA Rail Canada for information about service and schedules (800/361-3653). If you want to go in convenience and comfort, major tour operators offer packages to the popular parks; travel agents can help. Some national parks are beyond highways, but commercial airlines provide scheduled service to gateways, where bush pilots take over.

**Guidance and help.** You're never far from it. Visitor information centers (centres, as Canadians spell it) are widespread in cities, towns, and recreation areas across Canada. Provincial and territorial governments will send materials to help in planning. Addresses and phone numbers are provided in the following pages.

# NEWFOUNDLAND

At the eastern edge of the continent, Newfoundland and Labrador comprise the tenth and newest Canadian province, officially established in 1949. Come to see icebergs floating south after breaking off from glaciers in the far north, and seabirds in great numbers—including about 95 percent of all North America's puffins, together with gannets, kittiwakes, murres, auks—breeding in midsummer in cliffside colonies along the coasts.

GROS MORNE, on the Gulf of St. Lawrence in western Newfoundland, was established in 1976 to protect dramatic cliffs, fjord valleys, coastal bogs, and glacial lakes. At the visitor center, near Rocky Harbor off Highway 430, videos tell the story of Gros Morne ("big lone mountain"), the largest of Canada's maritime national parks, and how to enjoy it. Make the most of your visit by climbing the James Callaghan Trail to the summit of Gros Morne Mountain (seven hours round-trip) for vistas of mountains, lakes, fjords, and the Gulf of St. Lawrence. Take the boat cruise, daily from Rocky Harbour, through Western Brook Pond, a freshwater fjord in the Long Range Mountains, northernmost branch of the Appalachian chain. Cliffs tower almost 2,000 feet, with waterfalls cascading from the heights. Camp at any of five principal and other accessible backcountry sites. Find lodgings in nearby communities. Address: Gros Morne National Park, Box 130, Rocky Harbour, Newfoundland, Canada AOK 4NO; 709/458-2066.

TERRA NOVA. Canada's easternmost national park, along Bonavista Bay on the Atlantic Ocean, may be where John Cabot made his landfall in 1497 to claim this newfound land for England. Now it's the place to see migrating birds like the arctic tern during spring and fall and permanent residents, including eagles, ospreys, ptarmigans, chickadees, and jays. Start at the Newman Sound visitor center just off the Trans-Canada Highway, which runs through the park. Join the naturalist-led summer bird walk to the mounted telescope overlooking the mud flats. Board a summer cruise to see icebergs, and possibly whales, in

Bonavista Bay, then hike a section of the Coastal Trail to see where you've been. The park contains an 18-hole golf course, if that's your pleasure, but you can also canoe and fish freshwater streams and sheltered saltwater inlets. Camp in developed areas at Newman Sound or Malady Head, or in primitive sites along the coast. Lodgings and supplies are available in Glovertown, Traytown, Terra Nova, and other Eastport Peninsula communities. Address: Terra Nova National Park, Glovertown, Newfoundland, Canada AOG 2LO; 709/533-2884.

**SEE ALSO.** Castle Hill National Historic Park, at Placentia, dating from the 17th century, when the French selected a small fishing village here as headquarters for their Newfoundland fishing fleet. For birders: Cape St. Mary's Ecological Reserve, home of one of the largest colonies of gannets on the continent, plus other species.

**GETTING THERE.** By car, Marine Atlantic car ferries from North Sydney, Nova Scotia, to Port aux Basques; in summer, a second ferry to Argentia. By plane, scheduled service from Montreal to Halifax.

**FURTHER INFORMATION.** Tourism Branch, Box 2016, St. John's, Newfoundland, Canada A1C 5R8; 800/563-6353.

# PRINCE EDWARD ISLAND

Life in Canada's smallest province is centered around farming and fishing, but Prince Edward Island is also the playground province of Atlantic Canada, with almost 500 miles of sand beach and saltwater swimming.

**PRINCE EDWARD ISLAND.** The national park extends along the northern shore of the Gulf of St. Lawrence coast only 24 miles from Charlottetown, capital of the province. Start at the visitor center, at the intersection of Highways 6 and 13 in Cavendish, from which you can follow hiking trails along sweeping sand dunes, red sandstone cliffs, and salt marshes. Look for eagles and ospreys overhead, cormorants, gannets, gulls, and guillemots offshore. The park is the site of the two-story cottage that inspired "Anne of Green Gables," now a popular stop, especially in summer. From one of the three campgrounds you can easily cycle the Gulf Shore Parkway and swim from the park's saltwater beaches. Other facilities include golf and tennis. Overnight lodgings are available in and near Cavendish. Address: Prince Edward Island National Park, Box 487, Charlottetown, PEI, Canada C1A 7L1.

**SEE ALSO.** Province House National Historic Site, next to the Confederation Centre of the Arts in Charlottetown, site of meetings leading to Canada's confederation in 1867.

**GETTING THERE.** Take the ferry from Cape Tormentie, New Brunswick, across 8.7-mile Northumberland Strait to Borden. Another ferry runs from Cariboo, Nova Scotia, to Wood Islands. It's an easy drive from either terminal.

**FURTHER INFORMATION.** Visitor Services, Box 940, Charlottetown, PEI, Canada C1A 7M5; 800/565-0267 from the U.S.

# NOVA SCOTIA

Virtually surrounded by water, the Nova Scotia peninsula and adjacent Cape Breton Island are rugged outcrops of the Appalachian chain. The province is steeped in history dating from early settlement, and in Scottish and Acadian legacy.

**CAPE BRETON HIGHLANDS.** Stretching across part of the northern tip of Cape Breton Island, the park was established in 1936, the first in maritime Canada. It borders the Atlantic Ocean on one side and the Gulf of St. Lawrence on the other, with one of the most beautiful drives in North America, the historic Cabot Trail, now a paved highway, winding and climbing along three sides of the park, and opening spectacular vistas from coastal headlands. Stop first at Cheticamp information center for details on park activities and facilities. If you don't bring your own bicycle you can rent equipment here. Cycle clockwise, to take advantage of prevailing wind. Hiking trails of various length, from easy to strenuous, lead from the Cabot Trail to the interior forest, stronghold of lynx and moose, and to the coast. You'll find several campgrounds along the Cabot Trail and lodgings convenient to both entrances. Address: Cape Breton Highlands National Park, Ingonish Beach, Nova Scotia, Canada B0C 1L0; 902/285-2691.

**KEJIMKUJIK.** Call it "Keji" for short. The southernmost maritime park (about 250 miles directly east of Acadia National Park in Maine) was established as a wilderness park. You can follow historic canoe routes and portages with primitive backcountry campsites, swim and hike the rolling wilderness landscape of lakes and rivers in the footsteps of Micmac (Mi'kmaq) Indians. The Mersey Meadows Trail at park headquarters makes a good opener; look for scarlet tanager, great crested flycatcher, and other rare species. The Seaside Adjunct, near White Point Beach, attracts waterfowl and shorebirds including the endangered piping plover. The gateway to the park, off Highway 8 at Maitland Bridge, is about 100 miles southwest of Halifax. The park is open all year, with cross-country skiing in winter. Stay overnight at nearby Annapolis Royal, a prime Canadian historic beauty spot. Address: Kejimkujik National Park, Maitland Bridge, Nova Scotia, Canada B0T 1N0; 902/682-2770.

**SEE ALSO.** Fortress of Louisbourg National Historic Site, largest historic reconstruction in Canada, as it was in 1744, with buildings and streets faithfully recreated; also, Alexander Graham Bell National Historic Site, in Baddeck, where Bell conducted experiments that changed the world.

**GETTING THERE.** Highways join the Trans-Canada Highway from New Brunswick into Nova Scotia. Better yet, take a cruise on the *Bluenose*, six hours from Bar Harbor to Yarmouth, or on the *Scotia Princess*, 11 hours from Portland. Or you can fly from major cities to Halifax, and rent a car. Cape Breton Island is regularly served by Canadian airlines.

**FURTHER INFORMATION.** Nova Scotia Information and Reservations, Box 130, Halifax, NS, Canada B3J 2RS. Call from U.S. 800/341-6096, from Canada, 800/565-0000. (Ask for a copy of *Nova Scotia Back to Nature*; it's free.) Cape Breton Island, 800/565-9464.

## NEW BRUNSWICK

The largest maritime province borders the state of Maine, but otherwise is ringed by 1,400 miles of coastline, facing the Bay of Fundy on the south, Gulf of St. Lawrence on the east, and Bay des Chaleurs on the north. New Brunswick is the only officially bilingual province, with approximately 35 percent of its population French-speaking.

**FUNDY.** Visitors come from all over the world to witness the famed high tides rise and fall (twice daily, approximately every 12 hours and 30 minutes) in the funnel-shaped Bay of Fundy. But there's a lot more to it, particularly since the tides influence all life within the park. Be sure to walk the tidal flats during low tide to see barnacles, anemones, and periwinkles under the rocks. Rangers at the information stations at Wolfe Lake and Alma Beach entrances will tell you the best times and places. Hiking trails lead through wooded hills and alongside rushing streams and waterfalls to scenic cliffs above the Bay of Fundy. Combine nature and history going through the Pointe Wolfe covered bridge. The park was established in 1948 with a range of facilities from overnight lodgings, saltwater pool, golf course, bowling green and tennis courts to canoeing, camping, and beach swimming. You can also stay in Alma, at the edge of the park. Captain's Inn, B&B, is tops. Address: Fundy National Park, Box 40, Alma, Canada EOA 1BO; 506/887-2000.

**KOUCHIBOUGAC.** Say it Koo-she-boo-gwack; it's from the Mic-Mac, for "river of long tides," for the river running through the heart of the park. Reach it via Highway 11 on New Brunswick's northeastern coast. The Information Centre inside the main gate will help you on your way to varied beach, salt marsh and woodland trails, hiking, canoeing, bicycling, and primitive campsites. You can swim from Kelly's Beach on Northumberland Strait, sheltered from the sea by sand dunes, or rent a kayak to explore rivers and lagoons. The Kelly's Beach area has a boardwalk over a salt marsh alive with birds on summer mornings. Address: Kouchibougac National Park, Kent County, New Brunswick, Canada EOA 2AD; 506/876-2443.

**SEE ALSO.** Roosevelt Campobello International Park, on Campobello Island, linked to the mainland by FDR Memorial Bridge at Lubec, Maine, and by ferry from Deer Island. Tie it in with a visit to Acadia National Park in Maine.

**GETTING THERE.** Fundy National Park is reached via the Trans-Canada Highway between Moncton and Saint John onto Route 114 or Highway 2 from Quebec. Kouchibougac is off Route 11 near Chatham.

**FURTHER INFORMATION.** Tourism New Brunswick, Box 12345, Fredericton, NB, Canada E3B 5C3; 800/561-0123.

# QUEBEC

Canada's largest province extends from the edge of the Arctic to Appalachian highlands in the Laurentides (or Laurentians), embracing caribou country, isolated fishing villages, and the St. Lawrence River running through the province. Prepare for *Cuisine Quebecoise*, and enjoy it.

**FORILLON.** At the northeast tip of the Gaspé Peninsula, or *Gaspesie*, where cliffs and the forested Chic-Choc Mountains plunge into the sea, you can see a summer spectacle of thousands of nesting kittiwakes, cormorants, guillemots and other seabirds, seals on offshore rocks, and possibly whales as well. The park is 15 miles northeast of Gaspé via Highway 132. As Quebec's first national park, established in 1970, Forillon protects headlands, cliffs, dunes, salt marshes, arctic-alpine vegetation, lakes and streams. You may see deer, moose, bear, fox, and beaver along the many hiking trails. You can swim from pebble beaches or the sandy beach at Penouille and take a guided boat tour from Cap-des-Rosier along the cliffs to Cap Gaspé. Three campgrounds are located within the park, while lodgings and meals are available in nearby Gaspé towns. Address: Forillon National Park, Box 1220, Gaspé, Quebec, Canada G0C 1R0; 418/368-5505.

**LA MAURICIE.** Quebec's largest national park is bordered by even larger wildlife reserves, Mastigouche and St. Maurice, thus protecting a significant portion of rolling hills, mountains, lakes, rivers, and forests in the heart of the Laurentides. Starting from the Saint-Jean-des-Piles interpretive center, take to the trails on foot or bicycle, scenic drives by car, or water trails by canoe. Look for moose and bear, possibly lynx if you're lucky, and nesting birds. Park campgrounds and Wabenaki and Andrew lodges are open all year; cross-country skiing and snowshoeing are popular in winter. La Mauricie is easy to reach from Montreal, via Trois Rivières, then north along the Saint-Maurice River north on Highway 55. Address: Box 758, Shawinigan, PQ, Canada G9N 6V9; 819/536-2638.

**MINGAN ARCHIPELAGO.** Off the north shore of the St. Lawrence River, in the Jacques Cartier Strait between Longue-Pointe and the Aguanus River, this new park of the 1980s encompasses 40 islands covered with boreal forest and rocky outcrops. Boats to the islands leave from Havre-St-Pierre, passing rock formations in stratified limestone, sculpted by waves and currents; reservations are strongly advised. Bring binoculars to view Atlantic puffins on rocky islands and islets, possibly whales offshore; a plant guide will come in handy, too, to help identify rare flowering plants. Reach the park by driving northeast of Quebec on Highway 138 via Tadoussac and to the top of the Gulf of St. Lawrence. Stop at visitor centers at Longue-Pointe-de-Mingan and Havre-St-Pierre for information about wilderness camping. Lodgings are in nearby communities. Address: Mingan Archipelago National Park, Box 1180, Havre-St-Pierre, PQ, Canada GOG 1PO; 418/538-3331.

**SEE ALSO.** Forges of St-Maurice National Historic Park, eight miles north of Trois Rivières, site of Canada's first ironmaking village, which operated for more than 150 years.

**FURTHER INFORMATION.** Tourism Quebec, Box 20,000, Quebec, Canada G1K 7X2; 800/363-7777. Ask for *Activities and Services*, about provincial parks and wildlife reserves.


# ONTARIO

Second in size among provinces only to Quebec, Ontario borders four of five of the Great Lakes (all except Lake Michigan). It shares with the U.S. natural features from Niagara Falls in the east to the Quetico-Superior canoe country in the west.

**BRUCE PENINSULA.** The national park protects cedar swamps, woodlands and rocky barrens on the peninsula between Georgian Bay and Lake Huron, one of the last remaining wild areas in southern Ontario. From the visitor center and campground at Cyprus Lake, follow trails winding through cedar and birch forests, carpeted with rare orchids, wildflowers and ferns, and skirting dramatic cliffs along Georgian Bay. The park is open all year, with cross-country skiing in winter. Lodgings and meals are available in Tobermory, at the tip of the Bruce Peninsula, and other local communities. The park is a four-hour drive from metro Toronto to Owen Sound, then Highway 6 on the peninsula. Address: Bruce Peninsula National Park, Box 189, Tobermory, ON, Canada NOH 2RO; 519/596-2233.

**FATHOM FIVE NATIONAL MARINE PARK.** Canada's first national marine park was established in 1987 as a companion piece to Bruce Peninsula National Park—it memorializes marine history between the islands off the Bruce Peninsula and Manitoulin Island, and also embraces nearby islands with spectacular limestone cliffs, caves, and grottoes. More than two dozen wrecks that sank in fierce gales remain preserved in the cold, clear waters of Georgian Bay, 19 of them within park boundaries. Glass-bottom tour boats from Tobermory offer excellent views of the *Sweepstakes* and *Grand Rapids* in Big Tub Harbor. Park waters are open to scuba diving among the wrecks. For another rewarding activity, take a water taxi (during summer or fall) to Flowerpot Island, to walk among rock chimneys and caves. Address: Fathom Five National Marine Park, Box 189, Tobermory, ON, Canada N0H 2R0; 519/596-2233.

**GEORGIAN BAY ISLANDS.** On the lower east coast of Georgian Bay (across the water from the Bruce Peninsula), the national park includes 59 scenic islands. Activity centers on the largest island, Beausoleil, easily reached on a 15-minute water-taxi ride from Honey Harbor. Best start first, however, with a stop at the park visitor center on Muskoka Road in Honey Harbor for maps and guidance. Once on Beausoleil, set up camp at one of the primitive sites, then swim, snorkel, scuba dive, or fish. Walk the trails from Cedar Spring to view wetlands, meadows, and remnants of ancient forests. It's an easy drive north from Toronto on Highway 400, then west just above Waubashene and Victoria Harbor on Highway 5 to Honey Harbor. Address: Georgian Bay Islands National Park, Box 28, Honey Harbor, ON, Canada P0E 1E0; 705/756-2415.

**POINT PELEE.** The southernmost tip of Canada, 35 miles southeast of Detroit, is a birder's paradise. Point Pelee is a small park, covering only 3,500 acres reaching into Lake Erie, but a key resting stop for birds in migration on both Atlantic and Mississippi flyways—over 300 species have been counted. Come spring or fall to walk the boardwalk winding through the marshland to watch them by the thousands (mid-September for Monarch butterflies migrating from Mexico). Be sure to see the sunset from Pigeon Bay on the west side. The park and its trails are open year-round; canoes and bicycles are available for rental April through October. From Detroit, enter Canada through Windsor, drive southeast on Highway 3 to Leamington, then continue south to the park visitor center. Address: Point Pelee National Park, R.R. 1, Leamington, ON, Canada N8H 3V4.

**PUKASKWA.** On the eastern shore of Lake Superior, largest and purest of the great lakes, Pukaskwa (pronounced Puck-a-sah) preserves a sample of Canadian Shield wilderness, with spruce, fir, birch, and aspen covering the underlayer of ancient Precambrian rock. Leave your car behind and take to the Coastal Hiking Trail, winding through the boreal forest and over rocky ridges, with time to observe arctic plants and heron rookeries, and overnighting at primitive campsites. Or bring a canoe for whitewater adventure on the White and Pukaskwa rivers. From the U.S., drive north on Highway 17 from Sault Ste. Marie through Lake Superior Provincial Park—with time to see the Indian rock art at Agawa Indian Rock—to Marathon, then to the Hattie Cove gateway via Highway 627. From the west, the park lies 200 miles east of Thunder Bay. Address: Pukaskwa National Park, Highway 627, Heron Bay, ON, Canada P0T 1R0; 807/229-0801.

**ST. LAWRENCE ISLANDS.** Between Kingston, at the eastern edge of Lake Ontario, and Brockville, upstream on the St. Lawrence, the park contains 21 widely scattered units of the fabled Thousand Islands. Most of the Thousand Islands—which actually number 1,700—have long been developed privately, but the islands and rocky islets of the park are yours to visit and enjoy. Take a water taxi to see wildflowers or to camp at primitive sites accessible only by boat. Or join a boat tour from one of the resort towns for a tour of the Thousand Islands. From the U.S., drive north on Interstate 81, across Wellesley Island into Ontario, then a few miles northeast to park headquarters and visitor center at Mallorytown Landing, complete with campground and beach. Address: St. Lawrence Islands National Park, Box 469, Mallorytown, ON, Canada K0E 1R0; 613/923-5261.

**SEE ALSO.** Algonquin Provincial Park, Canada's oldest provincial park (established in 1893), with a thousand miles of canoe routes, overnight hiking loops, lodges, and campgrounds.

**FURTHER INFORMATION.** Tourism Ontario, Queen's Park, Toronto, ON, Canada M7A 2E5; 800/ONTARIO (668-2746).

# MANITOBA

Canada's heartland prairie province extends from North Dakota at the U.S. border north to Hudson Bay. Ernest Thompson Seton, pioneer naturalist and author, found inspiration for some of his finest work in Manitoba.

**RIDING MOUNTAIN.** Rising out of a sea of farmland, the park contains representative forest, grassland and meadows, lakes and streams, with varied foot and horse trails. Visitors can see a herd of bison near Lake Audy, a memorial to the prairie past. The visitor center on the south shore of spring-fed Clear Lake provides exhibits and interpretive programs. Facilities and activities in the park include golf, tennis, boating, and camping; hotel and motel lodgings are available. Check dates for the Summer Arts Program. From the east, turn off the Trans-Canada Highway, west of Winnepeg, at Portage la Prairie on Route 16, then to Highway 10 at Minnedosa. Address: Riding Mountain National Park, Wasagaming, MB, Canada R0J 2H0; 204/848-2811.

**SEE ALSO.** The International Peace Garden, northeast of Minot, North Dakota, on Highway 10 and US 281. Or take the train from Winnepeg to Churchill (two nights) on Hudson Bay, where Cape Churchill and Cape Tatnam Wildlife Management Areas cover almost six million acres to protect coastal and tundra ecosystems for polar bears, woodland caribou, and 200 species of birds.

**FURTHER INFORMATION.** Travel Manitoba, 155 Carlton Street, Winnipeg, Manitoba, Canada R3C 3H8; 800/665-0040.

## SASKATCHEWAN

Ancient homeland of the Plains Indians, now Canada's breadbasket, the province attracts waterfowl by the thousands to feed and breed in and around ponds and potholes.

**GRASSLANDS.** This new park in southwestern Saskatchewan is being developed to preserve and interpret a fragment of land history. At the Val Marie-Killdeer area, you can turn back the clock in short-grass prairie, complete with prairie dog, antelope, prairie falcon, and golden eagles, and find opportunity for wilderness camping. At adjacent Wood Mountain Post Historic Site, buildings on the site of an early North West Mounted Police post recount the history of the Sioux and Mounties; the Rodeo Ranch Museum includes exhibits on Indians, ranching and saddle making. The park lies north of Malta, Montana, via US 191 and Highway 4. If you're traveling west on US 2 to Waterton-Glacier, take time for a side trip to Grasslands. Address: Grasslands National Park, Box 250, Val Marie, SK, Canada S0N 2T0; 306/298-2257.

**PRINCE ALBERT.** Nearly a million acres of boreal forest, prairie grassland, and aspen parkland are preserved within this national park. Established in 1927 as "southern edge of the Great Northern Forest," it includes the busy townsite of Waskesiu, with park visitor center, hotel and motel, golf, lawn bowling, outdoor theaters, the Waskesiu International Hostel, and two major campgrounds. Beyond the resort hub lies the backcountry of deep woods, with lakes, streams, and ancient bogs. Hike the Elk Trail or Hunters Lake Trail, or rent a canoe to make your way to primitive campgrounds. By all means make a pilgrimage by foot or canoe to the cabin called Beaver Lodge and grave of Grey Owl—the Englishman Archibald Belaney, adopted by the Ojibway Indians—on the shore of Ajawaan Lake, where the celebrated conservationist worked to protect this choice wild country as sanctuary for caribou, deer, bear, elk, beaver, bison, and 227 recorded bird species. Prepare by reading his book, *Tales of an Empty Cabin*. The main entrance is 50 miles north of the city of Prince Albert, off Highway 2. Address: Prince Albert National Park, Box 100, Waskesiu Lake, SK, Canada S0J 2Y0; 306/663-5322.

**SEE ALSO.** Clearwater River Provincial Park, Saskatchewan's first wilderness provincial park, a Canadian Heritage River between the outlet of Lloyd Lake and the Alberta border, a challenge for skilled canoeists and backpackers.

**FURTHER INFORMATION:** Tourism Saskatchewan, 191 Saskatchewan Drive, Regina, SK, Canada S4P 3V7; 800/667-7191.

# ALBERTA

The province is largely a rolling plateau rising to the most dramatic sections of the Rocky Mountain chain. Its renowned national parks are popular in winter as well as summer, with some of the world's best skiing.

**BANFF.** Canada's first national park, dating from 1885, encompasses scenic snowy mountains, valleys, glaciers, forests, alpine meadows, lakes and wild rivers. In the bustling town of Banff, start at the Parks Canada information office to learn everything you can see and do in the way of auto touring, hiking over more than 800 miles of trail, canoeing, camping, climbing, cycling, fishing, riding, and how to budget your time. Get a permit here (free) for backcountry use. Yes, you can drive from Banff to Lake Louise between breakfast and lunch, but allow for hikes, whether short or long, into quiet valleys and alpine meadows. Go see the crown jewel, Lake Louise, and the Chateau Lake Louise, a landmark of the Rockies, built like an English manor house. Stop at Moraine Lake, reflecting the Valley of Ten Peaks. If you come in August, take in the festival at the Banff Centre School of Fine Arts. Consider coming in autumn, after summer crowds. Address: Banff National Park, Box 900, Banff, AB, Canada TOL OCO; 403/762-1550.

**GETTING THERE.** By car, through Calgary, 86 miles from Banff on the Trans-Canada Highway; north from Waterton-Glacier on Highway 2 to Calgary. Major airlines fly to Calgary, where you can rent a car or join an all-inclusive guided tour. VIA Canada Rail provides direct service, featured on various guided tours. For economy, check Rocky Express, six-day tours departing from Banff International Hostel.

**JASPER.** The largest of Canada's Rocky Mountain parks and Banff's northern (and less crowded) neighbor is accessible by car from Banff over the scenic Icefields Parkway, passing towering peaks and more than 100 glaciers. Virtually all of Jasper lies beyond the road, a wilderness sanctuary for bighorn sheep, bear, moose, elk, wolves, and caribou. The park includes Mount Columbia, 12,294 feet, the highest point in Alberta. Visit the park information center, or ask a ranger, about the many ways to explore the park, either alone or with a group. Daily bus tours operate from Jasper. If you're driving, take a side trip east on Yellowhead Highway 16 to see Punchbowl Falls, tumbling through a narrow crevice in a steep limestone cliff, then head for nearby Miette Hot Springs, run by the Canadian Parks Service. You can also join a raft tour on the Athabasca River. Accommodations in Jasper range from the historic Jasper Park Lodge to chalets with kitchen to campsites. Jasper lies 220 miles west of Edmonton on Highway 16, 172 miles north of Banff, 250 miles northwest of Calgary, 520 northeast of Vancouver. You can fly direct to Edmonton, rent a car or join a tour there. Address: Jasper National Park, Box 10, Jasper, AB, Canada TOE 1EO; 403/852-6161.

**ELK ISLAND.** Alberta's smallest national park was established in 1906 in the Beaver Hills, traditional hunting lands of the plains Indians. Though only a half-hour drive east from Edmonton, Elk Island is surprising, for its herds of elk and bison, its beaver and other mammals, and more than 200 species of birds. You can hike on 60 miles of trail, camp in aspen and mixed-wood forest, canoe on chain lakes, and climb the bird birding tower to see some of the best for yourself. Address: Elk Island National Park, RR 1, Fort Saskatchewan, AB, Canada T8L 2N7; 403/992-6380.

**WATERTON LAKES.** The Canadian section of Waterton-Glacier International Peace Park was established first, in 1895, fifteen years before its companion piece to the south. Taken together, the area, ancient homelands of Kootenai and Blackfeet, has been called the "crown of the continent." In the early Canadian park tradition, the Waterton townsite provides golf, tennis, and swimming in a heated outdoor pool, and accommodations at Lake McDonald Lodge, built in 1913, and Prince of Wales Hotel, built in Bavarian style in 1927 on a hilltop overlooking Waterton Lake. Stop at the park information center for details on guided walks and talks, narrated boat cruises on Waterton Lake, with mountains rising 3,000 to 4,000 feet above. Ask about wilderness trails and backcoun try campsites. Whether camping or not, take to the trails to appreciate the "land of shining mountains." (See the section on Glacier National Park elsewhere in this book.) Address: Waterton Lakes National Park, Waterton Park, AB, Canada TOK 2MO.

**WOOD BUFFALO.** The park was established in 1922 in subarctic wilderness astride the Alberta–Northwest Territories border to protect the largest herd of free-roaming bison in the world. It embraces boreal forest, sand dunes, lakes, and the delta and lowlands of the Peace and Athabasca rivers—staging area for four major waterfowl flyways. Wood Buffalo provides summer nesting critical to survival of the fabled whooping crane. The park's gravel roads are open May 1 to November 1, when you can join guided nature and canoe programs. Reach the area by car through Slave Lake on Highway 35, then Highway 68 to Peace River, or by bus from Edmonton. Check into offerings of tour companies and outfitters for bicycling, canoeing, climbing, and rafting packages. Address:

Wood Buffalo National Park, Box 750, Fort Smith, NWT, Canada XOE OPO; 403/872-2349.

**SEE ALSO.** Dinosaur Provincial Park, northeast of Brooks off the Trans-Canada Highway, containing the most extensive dinosaur fields in the world, accessible on interpretive hikes and bus tours given frequently during the day.

**FURTHER INFORMATION.** Alberta Tourism, Box 2500, Edmonton, Alberta T5J 2Z4; 800/661-8888.

# BRITISH COLUMBIA

British Columbia, Canada's western frontier, extends from the Rockies to the North Cascades, the Coast Range, and to Pacific islands off the coast and north to border Alaska and the Yukon. Its heritage includes the rich culture of Northwest Indians.

**KOOTENAY AND YOHO.** These two national parks adjoin each other on the western slope of the Rocky Mountains and share boundaries with Banff National Park as well. In fact, with Jasper National Park they were declared in 1985 a comprehensive World Heritage Site. Though less renowned than their Alberta neighbors, Kootenay and Yoho are beauty spots in their own right. For Kootenay, take the Banff-Windermere Highway, Highway 93. It runs the full length of the park, about 70 miles south to north through valleys of the Vermillion and Kootenay rivers, passing towering summits, hanging glaciers and mineral pools. At Radium Hot Springs, near the west entrance (the southern end) you can take to the trails, rent a canoe or rubber raft, join a bike tour, and then bathe at Radium Hot Springs. At the other end, see the Paint Pots, where Blackfoot and Kootenay Indians used the bright colored muds to stain their bodies and decorate their tepees. Yoho is on the Trans-Canada Highway, where it crosses Kicking Horse Pass, the crest of the Rockies, then descends between mountain slopes and rock walls and waterfalls of Yoho Valley. Be sure to see the Burgess Shale Fossils, a fossil bed of more than 120 species, some dating back 500 million years. At Emerald Lake you can rent a canoe or rowboat. Lake O'Hara, another beauty spot, is the site of the 1930s showpiece log-cabin Lake O'Hara Lodge. Addresses: Kootenay National Park, Box 220, Radium Hot Springs, BC, Canada VOA 1MO; 604/347-9615. Yoho National Park, Box 99, Field, BC, Canada VOA 1GO; 604/343-6324.

**GLACIER AND MOUNT REVELSTOKE.** For anyone coming to see the Canadian Rockies these two parks are well worth adding to the itinerary. They're not part of the Rockies, but of the Selkirks to the west (which extend south into Idaho). Glacier and Revelstoke are only 10 miles apart from each other, linked by the

Trans-Canada Highway and Canadian rail between Calgary and Vancouver. The most spectacular features are the more than 400 glaciers scattered through the parks in steep, wild mountain terrain. Approaching from the east, stop at Rogers Pass for panoramic viewpoints into the heart of the park. Allow time at the information center for exhibits and films on railroad history. You will learn how, in 1910, 62 men were killed by an avalanche while clearing snow from an earlier slide in trying to build the railroad. (Ultimately efforts were abandoned and the railroad was tunneled under Mount McDonald and along Summit Road.) Trails follow the railroad's progress past the ruins of a 19th century resort hotel and stone pillars that once supported railroad trestles. You can also hike trails across wildflower-carpeted meadows to the glaciers. By car, the scenic Summit Drive goes to the summit of Revelstoke, overlooking peaks and steep valleys of the Selkirk Mountains. Once at the summit, take the Mountain Meadows Trail, keeping an eye for golden eagles overhead. You'll find two campgrounds in Glacier, none in Revelstoke, and overnight lodgings at Rogers Pass. Address: Glacier and Mount Revelstoke National Parks, Box 350, Revelstoke, BC, Canada V0E 2S0; 604/837-7500.

**PACIFIC RIM.** On the windswept western shore of Vancouver Island, Canada's first national park on the Pacific is composed of deep-green headlands, great forests, rocky islands, and sandy beaches, with choice birding and whale watching. Three separate units include: Long Beach, a seven-mile sweep of sand and driftwood between the towns of Ucluelet and Tofino, popular with surfers and beachcombers; Broken Islands in Barkley Sound, ideal for kayakers; and the West Coast Trail, 48 miles between Bamfield and Port Renfrew, moderately tough but with rewarding coastal scenery. (Note: the trail is so popular that hikers are required to reserve starting times, sometimes weeks in advance.) To reach the park from the mainland, take a B.C. ferry from either Tsawwasswen, on the southern edge of Vancouver, or Horsehoe Bay, on the north side, to Nanaimo on Vancouver Island. Then head north on the Vancouver Island Highway, and across the island on Highway 4 toward Ucluelet and Tofino. Stop at the Long Beach visitor center and also at the Wickanninish center for an introduction to open ocean seabirds and to gray whales that feed in summer in Wickanninish Bay. From Port Alberni you can take the all-day trip aboard the passenger-freighter *MV Lady Rose* as it journeys through the Broken Islands to deliver mail and cargo to Bamfield and Ucluelet, sometimes with porpoises and whales off the bow. At Tofino, hire Dutch to take you in his skiff to see the marvelous rain forest of Clayoquot Sound, now threatened by logging. Accommodations and meals are available in towns bordering the park. The park has two campgrounds, at Green Point and Schooner Cove, but remember that it rains here. Address: Pacific Rim National Park, Box 280, Ucluelet, BC, Canada V0R 3A0; 604/726-4212.

**SOUTH MORESBY.** On one of the southernmost islands of the Queen Charlotte chain in the northern Pacific, this new park of the 1980s preserves ancient rain forest, islands, lakes, coastline, a fragment of the sacred homeland of Haida Indians, and a marine reserve. South Moresby is about 120 miles from the north end of Vancouver Island, and is accessible by plane from Vancouver and Prince Rupert or by B.C. Ferries from Prince Rupert, northern terminus of B.C. Ferries.

**SEE ALSO.** Tatshenshini-Alsek Wilderness Provincial Park, the great new park established by British Columbia in June 1993, not only encompasses 2,367,218 acres—which makes it larger than Yellowstone—but it links Glacier Bay National Park and neighboring Canada's Kluane National Park, which in turn adjoins Wrangell-St. Elias National Park, for a total of 24,278,386 acres. Wildlife watching, hiking, climbing, and river rafting all are outstanding. The trip down the "Tats-Alsek" is considered the finest wilderness trip on the continent.

**FURTHER INFORMATION.** Tourism British Columbia, Parliament Buildings, Victoria, BC, Canada V8V 1X4; 800/663-6000.

# NORTHWEST TERRITORIES

Five times the size of Texas, the Northwest Territories cover one-third of the land mass of Canada, but with about 63,000 people, or less than 1 percent of the population. The landscape, much of it in arctic tundra, appears infinite, inspiring, harsh. Five national parks have already been established, while potential additions, along with migratory bird sanctuaries and heritage rivers, are under study.

**AUYUITTUQ.** Canada's first national park north of the Arctic Circle was established on Baffin Island, the fifth largest island in the world, north of Labrador and uppermost Quebec, to protect a vast wilderness of the Penny Ice Cap, glaciers, jagged mountain peaks, deep valleys and fjords, and marine coastal wildlife. Here is a place to meet Inuit, Dene, Metis and Inuvaluit, native peoples living close to the earth, eating meat of caribou, muskox, arctic char, and muktuk (whale skin with blubber attached). To reach Auyuittuq—in Inuit "the land that never melts"—fly to Iqaluit, on Frobisher Bay, then on a smaller plane for the one-hour flight to Pangnirtung, or "Pang," just below the Arctic Circle. Outfitters provide a variety of services, including dropoffs and pickups, guided fishing, canoeing, and backpacking.

**NAHANNI.** Centered around the South Nahanni River in the Canadian Northwest, roadless Nahanni embraces waterfalls twice the height of Niagara, sulphur hot springs, and wilderness habitat for abundant moose, trumpeter swan, black bear, grizzly, and Dall sheep. It's a long way to the park, from wherever you are. You can drive to Fort Nelson, British Columbia, then via the Liard Highway to Fort Simpson, which began as a Hudson's Bay trading post and is now the gateway to Nahanni. Outfitters will take you in for canoeing and fishing on the South Nahanni or for day trips hiking into the Ragged Mountain Range. Address: Nahanni National Park, Box 300, Fort Simpson, NWT, Canada XOE ONO.

**AULAVIK.** On Banks Island in the far north, the park landscape ranges from lush vegetation and prime muskox habitat in the watershed of the Thomsen River to tundra on the northern coast on Castel Bay, an area frequented by polar bears. Outfitters offer naturalist-led tours of one to five days flying from Inuvik, the site of park headquarters on the mainland north of Fort McPherson. Inuvik is reachable by car from Dawson over the Dempster Highway and by plane. Address: Aulavik National Park, Box 1840, Inuvik, NWT, Canada XOE OTO; 403/979-3248.

**NORTHERN ELLSMERE.** On Ellsmere Island, almost touching Greenland across the Robeson Channel, Canada's newest and northernmost national park embraces mountain ranges, (including Mount Barbeau, 8,544 feet, highest mountain in eastern North America), glaciers, and fjords. Outfitters offer escorted backpacking across the tundra, with camping at the shore of Lake Hazen, largest lake north of the Arctic Circle.

**WOOD BUFFALO.** See Alberta.

**GETTING THERE.** Parks of the Northwest Territories are distant, but flights from Edmonton, Calgary, Vancouver, Winnipeg, Ottawa, and Montreal on major airlines connect with regional scheduled service and local charters.

**FURTHER INFORMATION.** Tourism Division, Government of the Northwest Territories, Box 1320, Yellowknife, NWT, Canada X1A 2L9; 800/661-0788.

## YUKON TERRITORY

In Canada's most northwestern corner the Yukon is endowed with lofty mountains, great forests and rivers, and legends of the Klondike Gold Rush.

**IVVAVIK.** An arctic wilderness bordering the Beaufort Sea in the northeast corner of the Yukon, Ivvavik protects the migration routes of more than 150,000 barren-ground caribou, the great Porcupine herd (named for the Porcupine River) traveling from and to calving grounds on the coastal plain of Alaska— one of the last major wildlife migrations on earth. Access to the park is by charter plane. Nearby Herschel Island/Qikiqtaruk Territorial Park preserves the site of an old arctic whaling station and ancient Inuvialuit hunting camp. Address: Ivvavik National Park, Box 1840, Inuvik, NWT, Canada XOE OTO; 403/979-3248.

**KLUANE.** Together with bordering Wrangell-St. Elias National Park in Alaska (the largest U.S. national park), Kluane constitutes a wilderness preserve of more than 20 million acres, a complex of tundra, glaciers, and massive mountains rising to Mt. Logan, 19,550 feet, the second highest peak in North America. The park is one of the last strongholds of grizzly bears, wolves, caribou, and other wilderness-dependent species. You won't find roads, except on the eastern and northern edges, but you can still enjoy the park on its own terms. Mountaineering, fishing, and ski touring are prime activities. Float the Alsek River past the snout of Lowell Glacier, where it sets blue icebergs adrift. Or join a guided trek into the Donjek Valley, with vistas of rock and ice of the Donjek Glacier, and of caribou, sheep, and possibly grizzlies. You *can* drive to park headquarters and the visitor center at Haines Junction, at the junction of the Haines and Alaska highways, and chart your activities from there. Pitch your tent in the campground near Elias Lake, then hike along old mining roads. Join a guided walk over the 12-mile Auriol Interpretive Trail, through moose country laden with fireweed, mossberries, dewberries, and Labrador tea. At nearby Burwash Landing, visit the Kluane Museum of Natural History, to see the exhibits on Yukon wildlife. Address: Kluane National Park, Box 5495, Haines Junction, YT, Canada YOB 1LO.

**SEE ALSO.** Hike through history on the fabled Chilkoot Trail that drew thousands in the 1898 Gold Rush. The 32-mile trail starts from Dyea, near Skagway, Alaska, climbing into Chilkoot National Historic Site, the largest one in Canada. It's still a challenge, demanding preparation, stamina and three to five days.

**FURTHER INFORMATION.** Tourism Yukon, Box 2703, Whitehorse, YT, Canada Y1A 2C6; 800/661-0408 in Yukon Territory. Or 403/667-5340.

# CALIFORNIA'S NEW NATIONAL PARKS

WITH PASSAGE of the California Desert Protection Act in 1994, Congress established two major new national parks and a new national preserve. In total size, they cover more than 9 million acres—an area eight times the size of Yosemite. The new Death Valley National Park, with 3.3 million acres, now becomes the nation's largest national park outside of Alaska.

Both Death Valley and Joshua Tree, known and loved as national monuments, have been enlarged and reclassified as national parks. Mojave, the country's newest national preserve, covers 1.4 million acres of prime scenery and ecological value east of Barstow. It was formerly administered by the Bureau of Land Management (BLM), a federal agency in charge of millions of acres of federal domain throughout the West with a mandate for multiple uses.

Why these new national parks? Why now? The action was taken because 25 million acres of federal lands in California's desert have been subjected to intensive use from urbanization, mining, livestock grazing, hunting, and off-road vehicle travel. Recreational use has skyrocketed—for hunting, hiking, horseback riding, motorcycling, nature study, photography, enjoyment of quiet. Fragile desert soils over wide areas have been eroded, compacted, and degraded. The desert tortoise, an "indicator species" of land health, has declined by 90 percent within the past half century.

Couple such considerations with rising awareness of desert beauty, history, and scientific values. The new parks include ancient dinosaur tracks, petroglyphs carved thousands of years ago, waterfalls, mountain ranges up to 8,000 feet and habitat essential for rare and endangered wildlife. The time proved right to protect these resources, to identify them as national treasures.

National park designation will permit appropriate vehicle access, camping, hiking, and scientific and educational activities. Grazing will continue in the Mojave, and so will hunting under regulation. The new law specifies that more than six million acres of the desert national parks will be components of the National Wilderness Preservation System, left in their natural state, to be visited, enjoyed, and protected as wilderness.

In addition to establishing the national parks, the act designates more than 4 million acres in 69 separate areas of BLM land as wilderness, including the pinyon-clad Inyo Mountains, Cadiz Dunes, and Mecca Hills badlands. The desert is a wonderland of adventure and discovery: Go to isolated waterholes

and moist shady canyons for choice birding opportunities; visit sites like Panamint City, Randsburg, Calico, the Saline Salt Tram, and Twenty Mule Borax
Road for vestiges of western settlement and the gold rush. To learn more about
the desert and how you can help, write the California Desert Protective Council,
3750 El Canto Drive, Spring Valley, CA 92077.

NOTE: Accommodations in park profiles are identified by price range with the
following symbols: **H** = High priced; **M** = Moderately priced; and **L** = Low priced.

# ACADIA NATIONAL PARK

## MAINE

### ESTABLISHED 1919

IN TRAVELING THE NEW ENGLAND COAST, I found the finest surviving fragment of unspoiled nature on Mount Desert Island, far north in Maine. We are lucky to have it preserved and protected, a treasure in a thousand and one ways, with surf-splashed cliffs rising to the highest point along the Atlantic and crowned with cool mountain forests.

The beauty of Acadia has long been recognized by artists and writers and by wealthy families in the choice of their summer retreats. I find it fascinating to read how individuals with vision worked to make it a national park. Thanks largely to the efforts of George B. Dorr, a man of means and conscience, a portion of the area was proclaimed Sieur de Monts National Monument in 1916. It was changed to Lafayette National Park in 1919 and, enhanced with bequests of land from John D. Rockefeller, Jr., to Acadia National Park in 1929. The preservation work they started still continues, now led by Friends of Acadia, Box 725, Bar Harbor, ME 04609.

Acadia, 47 miles from Bangor, Maine, is the only national park in the northeastern United States. It is small as national parks go, fewer than 40,000 acres, but with unending variety.

Watching cormorants and gulls as they congregate on a rocky shoal reminds me of the importance of islets, islands, and undisturbed seacoast as nesting grounds for sea birds. The Maine coast, centered in Acadia and Mount Desert Island, has some of the most vital sites for a large variety of North Atlantic sea birds. More than 275 species of birds inhabit the park during the course of a year.

Here I can understand that ours is a nation born of the sea, bred on salt spray, and nurtured with adventures of the deep. The waters of bays and harbors around Acadia are speckled in summer with sails of pleasure yachts, and in every direction the sea roars against the rocks. Champlain sailed this way on his 1604 exploration of the French province of Acadia, and the Jesuits established a short-lived settlement. In time, schooners and brigs were built in every cove, while offshore great fishing fleets would rendezvous and whiten the horizon with hundreds of sails.

In the interior, the landscape of deep-blue lakes shielded by steep slopes tells the story of ancient glacial action. Massive sheets of ice moved down from the

frozen north, piling rock, gouging lakes, and shaving peaks to bare granite. Now this land remains under snow each year until April, when the delicate trailing arbutus signals the beginning of spring, first in a procession of 500 varieties of wildflowers. In the low wetlands ducks nest, persistent beavers build their dams, and migratory wading birds, like the magnificent great blue heron, poke their bills underwater searching ceaselessly for fish, frogs, or tadpoles.

A month-long fire in 1947 claimed 10,000 acres, including prime forest and homes of the age of opulence. But natural fire, like glaciers and the sea, plays its part in the cycles of nature. It's fascinating to return periodically to witness the process of plant succession and emergence of a new virgin forest. Once the fire stopped, small plants took hold, building soil texture and nutrients. They were succeeded by berries, then by birch, aspen, and sumac, pioneering the new forest, and ultimately replaced by spruce and firs, a pleasure to behold.

## THE PRACTICAL GUIDE

The heart of the park is on **Mount Desert Island,** easily reached from the mainland via the Thompson Island Causeway, but there are two other important sections: rocky little **Isle au Haut,** affording a distinctive, simple island experience, and the **Schoodic Peninsula,** the only portion of the park on the mainland. It takes a little effort to reach it, but Schoodic Point is one of the most beautiful places you'll ever see. The best way to approach Acadia is on Route 3 from Bangor.

BACKGROUND. After passing through Ellsworth, the mainland town closest to the park, stop at the **Hulls Cove Visitor Center.** On reaching Mount Desert Island, the **Thompson Island Information Center** will be helpful too. You'll find other sources of guidance at Bar Harbor, the largest resort community on Mount Desert.

By car (bus and taxi tours available from nearby towns) follow the 27-mile **Park Loop Road** for the sound and smell of the sea and the lick of the waves, and to view **Great Head,** a promontory above the surf.

Allow plenty of time to stop at scenic overlooks and to walk the trails. Observe where waves at work have tunneled 85 feet into granite cliffs. Pools glisten from a profusion of

rockweed, algae, kelp, flowering anemone, and that brightly colored sea snail called dog whelk.

At **Otter Point,** a trail winds through spruce and fir to the shore, where wild roses meet salt spray. Many arctic plants grow in the cool ocean fringe. Offshore, cormorants and gulls congregate on a rocky shoal, while small lobster boats are seen hauling in their pots—a reminder that in America the delectable lobster grows only in the cold waters off northern New England. When you reach the windswept summit of **Cadillac Mountain,** 1,530 feet, magnificent vistas unfold, from the open sea to Mount Katahdin far inland.

**Somesville,** the site of Mount Desert Island's first permanent settlement (1761), lies on the loop road at the head of a steepsided fjord called Somes Sound. **Beech Cliff,** several miles south, is reached on a five-minute walk through a spruce-fir forest. It overlooks Echo Lake. Stop for the breathtaking view of water, beach, mountains, and fir forests.

**Nature walks** are conducted by members of the park staff from July 1 to Labor Day. Approximately 150 miles of footpaths reach every mountain summit and transverse every valley; they are designed for all types of walkers and hikers. The **Nature Center** at

ACADIA
NAT'L PARK
MAINE

0   1   2   4
ONE INCH EQUALS APPROXIMATELY 6 MILES

M-9-ZM-924-C          © The H.M GOUSHA Co.

Sieur de Monts Spring contains displays on
nature and history; the adjacent **Abbe Museum** houses Indian Stone Age relics. Evening campfire programs are held in summer.

**Naturalist sea cruises** are conducted
among the islands of Frenchman Bay. One of
the best, the *Sea Princess*, leaves from Northeast Harbor. It stops at Little Cranberry Island, with time ashore to visit the Islesford
Historical Museum, truly a treasure. Check
into the wide variety of trips available—
sailing, whale watching, birdwatching, seabird watching.

**Isle au Haut,** the least-known part of Acadia, takes planning and preparation to reach
but is well worth it for camping, hiking, and
birding. The island is reached from Ston-
ington, on the mainland, via a 45-minute ferry
trip. Write park headquarters for details. (See
address under "For Further Information.")

**Schoodic Peninsula,** the only mainland
section of the park (about an hour and a half
by car from Bar Harbor), offers a good

daylong side trip. A one-way road leads
around the peninsula, and a gravel road leads
to the top of Schoodic Mountain. Allow plenty
of time to absorb the seascapes.

**ACTIVITIES.** Acadia offers other activities besides nature walks and sea cruises. Have
lunch, tea or dine at the *Jordan Pond House*,
on the Park Loop Road just north of Seal
Harbor—an activity in itself. **Bicycling** gives
an interesting view of the park. Pick up a free
copy of the *Bicycle Guide to Acadia National
Park* and follow the old carriage trails. Sea
kayaking is popular, too. Rentals and guided
trips, by bike or kayak, are available in Bar
Harbor.

**Swimming** is popular from Sand Beach
(with those who like their ocean water cold)
and inland at Echo Lake Beach and Lake-
wood. **Fishing** is permitted inside the park,
both freshwater (state license required) and
saltwater from the rocks.

A network of carriage paths, affording scenic views of mountains, lakes, and sea, has
been set aside for **ski touring** and **snowshoeing.** Several shops in Bar Harbor rent equipment. Prepare for the sound of snowmobiles;
Acadia is one of the few national parks where
these machines are allowed.

**ACCOMMODATIONS.** More than 2,500 guest
rooms are available in Bar Harbor alone,
which means that in summer it can be a typically crowded, bustling resort; for calm and
quiet you may want to locate at Northeast
Harbor or Southeast Harbor. For July and August make reservations early, particularly for
those handsome old summer cottages converted to B&Bs. Try this selection:

**Briarfield Inn,** 60 Cottage Street, Bar Harbor, ME 04609. Refurbished in Victorian style
as B&B, with handy access to downtown Bar
Harbor. 800/228-6660, or 207/288-5297.

**Claremont Hotel,** Southwest Harbor, ME
06479. Gracious old estate on the National
Historic Register, hotel, cottages and dining
room on Somes Sound. 207/244-5036. M-H.

**Collier House,** Route 102, Mt. Desert, ME

04660. B&B six miles from Bar Harbor, in converted farmhouse and three separate buildings on 30 acres. Cross-country ski trails in winter. 207/288-3162. M.

**Kimball Terrace Inn,** Northeast Harbor, ME 04662. Overlooking municipal pier, with balconies or patios, and pool. Open year-round. 207/276-3383. M.

**Edgewater Motel and Cottages,** Box 566, Bar Harbor, ME 04609. Small motel and cottages on the water at Salisbury Cove outside Bar Harbor; boats available. 207/288-3491. M.

**CAMPGROUNDS.** Two campgrounds inside the park, **Blackwoods** and **Seawall,** are usually filled by noon in July and August. These are supplemented by private campgrounds in the towns.

You can be sure of a site at Blackwoods by making a reservation through Mistix. Seawall continues to operate on a first-come, first-served basis. Maximum stays are 14 days between May 15 and October 15 at Seawall, all year at Blackwoods.

**Lamoine State Park** lies less than 15 miles away, with screened sites, a small beach, and boat landing.

**SEASONS.** Most visitors come in summer, although campgrounds, picnic areas, and other facilities are open from about May 10 to Octo-ber 15. June is a good month for fishing, bird-watching, and nature walks. It's also the best month to see land birds in the spruce-fir and hardwood forests. Shore birds and pelagic species are most numerous in the outer islands in late July and August. September is marked by mild weather, fall colors, and crisp air. Snow and ice keep the park road system closed December through April. Be sure to bring warm clothing and a raincoat; evenings are cool even in summer, and rainy days occur in any season.

**NEARBY.** Bar Harbor is the starting point of the international motor ferry operating daily to **Yarmouth, Nova Scotia,** so that can well figure in your trip planning. The trip takes about six hours. Reservations are recommended in summer.

Bar Harbor and other towns offer deep-sea fishing trips, boat rentals and windjammer cruises on old handcrafted schooners. Write Maine Windjammers Association, Box 317B, Rockport, Maine 04856.

**RECOMMENDED READING.** *The Story of Mount Desert Island,* by Samuel Eliot Morison (Boston: Little, Brown & Co.).

**FOR FURTHER INFORMATION.** Write Superintendent, Acadia National Park, Box 177, Bar Harbor, Maine 04609. 207/288-5456.

# ARCHES NATIONAL PARK

## UTAH

ESTABLISHED 1971

EARLY COWBOYS had their own name for it—Schoolmarm's Bloomers. But to me the official name, Delicate Arch, seemed right. There it was, the most famous landmark in the park, balanced precariously atop its base.

Then I realized it was the setting that counted even more, the wind-swept mesa at the edge of the precipitous red cliffs and massive domes of slickrock, a great natural theater more dramatic than any players walking across its stage.

Erosion and weathering have produced more giant stone arches, windows, pinnacles, and pedestals in the red rock here than in any other section of the nation. More than 200 arches have been discovered, with Delicate Arch alone vaulting to a height greater than that of a seven-story building.

Exactly what forces, I wondered, fashioned these formations and the spectacular towers, sweeping coves, balanced rocks, and the figures resembling humans and animals in the red-rock country? Geologists say the earth's crust first warped upward to form an anticline, an arch of stratified rock some 30 miles in length. Then the crest of the huge fold sank in, forming what are now known as Salt Valley and Cache Valley. Water entering cracks in the rock dissolved some of the cementing material, then running water and wind removed the loose sand, forming thin fins of soft sandstone. More rapid weathering of areas in vertical walls resulted in undercutting, while carving by water and frost continue to our day and will beyond it.

Arches is part of a large area, one of the most awesome on earth. The park should never be viewed, or considered, alone, but always within the context of the colorful canyonlands of southern Utah and the upper Colorado River region, where the erosion of nature over aeons has dissected the anatomy of the earth and left it exposed.

I like to compare the stone archways and fins of Arches with the unique formations of nearby Canyonlands National Park. At Arches, the rock was deposited as sand about 150 million years ago, during the Jurassic period. This 300-foot layer, called the Entrada sandstone, lends itself to a cycle of erosion that results in a graceful, smoothly contoured natural arch. Canyonlands has some great arches, too, such as Druid Arch and Angel Arch, but they are found mostly in the Cutler Formation, which tends more toward the development of standing rocks (for which Canyonlands is famous) and apparently lacks the arch-forming capability of the Entrada.

Some arches, such as Delicate Arch, have been left isolated by erosion of surrounding fins. In due course, the continued thinning by weather will result in their collapse. The visitor can observe all stages in the process of development and decay.

Soil, grasses, and trees are scant in this setting. The sparse pinyon-juniper ecosystem prevails, though the land is by no means barren. The desert has a beauty all its own. If I slow down and stay put, I can see a variety of birds as well as ground squirrels, rabbits, kangaroo rats, and other rodents. Deer, coyote, and foxes are present, too, but are most active at night.

Arches was proclaimed a national monument in 1929 in order to preserve its great scenic and scientific values. It was enlarged and boundaries were changed several times until the park was established in 1971. The park now has a total of 73,379 acres. I wish it could be enlarged again to embrace additional adjacent areas of geologic significance.

## THE PRACTICAL GUIDE

The park lies only 5 miles from Moab, a logical base of operations for both Arches and Canyonlands. Arches is divided into six distinct sections, with roads and hiking trails twisting through each area. You can't do justice to it by road, so try to allow at least one day for a good hike to see some of the most impressive features in each section.

BACKGROUND. The **Visitor Center** is just off US 191, and you'll find excellent pictures, displays, and explanations of the landscape. Even if you're driving through and have only an hour, it is worth a stop. The main park road starts from here. It winds to the top of the slickrock plateau, then to **Courthouse Towers** for exciting views over the outlying mountains. Take the 1-mile hike from the parking area through **Park Avenue,** a narrow corridor where sandstone walls rise vertically 150 to 300 feet.

Continue over the paved road to **The Windows,** where you can see and photograph eight immense arches, as well as many smaller formations. After another 2½ miles northeast you come to a junction with a graded road leading to viewpoints of **Delicate Arch,** the "Crown Jewel of Arches National Park." Geologists have calculated that it took at least 70,000 years for combined forces of frost, wind, and rain to fashion the trimly tapered freestanding arch. Take the 1½-mile foot trail to the arch itself, for the view of the Colorado River gorge and the snow-peaked La Sal Mountains.

There is history here, too, as you'll discover on the trail to the **Wolfe Ranch,** settled in 1888 by a Civil War veteran, John Wesley Wolfe. He tested himself and the elements for more than 20 years before recognizing the land was too tough. But the corral, root cellar, and cabin of 1906 endure to tell the story of Wolfe and his family.

Then drive past **Fiery Furnace,** a series of parallel fins that provide an interesting excursion for hikers. But this area can be a nightmare of passageways—only ranger-conducted tours are allowed. These leave each morning at hours noted at the Visitor Center. At **Devils Garden,** 9 miles north of Balanced Rock, the road ends. A 2-mile trail leads to beautifully sculptured arches—Pine Tree, Partition, Double O, and Dark Angel. **Landscape Arch,** the longest known natural stone arch in the world, is also along this trail. By turning off on the graded road at **Skyline Arch** and driving 8 miles across Salt Valley, you reach the **Klondike Bluffs,** a rugged section with a 1-mile hiking trail to **Tower Arch.** Before attempting to explore the bluffs, or any section of the backcountry, notify a park ranger. The ranger will furnish latest road information plus briefing on backcountry travel.

**BIRDWATCHING.** About 130 species of birds have been recorded in Arches. Although essentially a desert area with relatively little vegetation, the three habitats, or life-communities—desert scrub; pinyon-juniper, or pygmy, forest; and riparian woodland—reveal much of interest to the birder. **Courthouse Wash,** in the riparian woodland, is the most productive birding area, especially during spring and fall migrations, when species the birder doesn't expect to see bathe and rest in washes beneath cottonwood, tamarisk, and willow. **Devils Garden** is the best breeding area in the pygmy forest for birds such as ash-throated flycatcher, hairy woodpecker, gray vireo, titmouse, jay, and black-throated gray warbler. During warmer months, the black-throated sparrow is the typical bird of the desert scrub.

**TOUR OPERATORS.** Outfitters at Moab feature a variety of trips, including the following: for river-running and day river trips on a paddlewheel riverboat, **Tex's Tour Center** (Box 67); for jeep tours, **Tag-a-Long Tours** (Box 1206); for horseback trips, **Bob's Trail Riders**

(435 North Main). The zip code for Moab, Utah, is 84532.

**ACCOMMODATIONS.** There is camping in the park, but no lodgings. See the section for Canyonlands National Park for motels in nearby Moab.

**CAMPING.** A modern campground for tents and trailers is located at **Devils Garden,** an excellent base in the park interior. Campfire talks are given nightly during summer.

**SEASONS.** It's dry desert here. (See reference to weather under "Seasons" in Canyonlands section.) Spring and fall are the best times to visit. Summer is hot. From May to August, except in abnormally dry years, you can expect colorful displays of wildflowers in the moist places, particularly in Salt Valley. Winter is cold but comfortable.

**NEARBY.** The companion piece to Arches is **Canyonlands National Park,** a fantasy of red-rock gorges, canyons, and sheer cliffs. This is the "standing up country," an explorer's delight on foot, horse, or jeep. **Behind the Rocks,** the red-rock escarpment on the northern boundary of Moab, has only been penetrated in the past decade but is becoming a high point for jeep tours.

Twenty-five miles southeast of Arches, **Fisher Towers,** a tall group of pinnacles, guard the entrance to **Castle Valley,** a beautiful area of meadows and pastures banked on one side by red rock and on the other by 12,000-foot peaks of the La Sal Mountains.

**FOR FURTHER INFORMATION.** Write Superintendent, Arches National Park, Box 907, Moab, UT 84532. 801/259-8161.

# BADLANDS NATIONAL PARK

## SOUTH DAKOTA

ESTABLISHED 1978

ON VISITING the Badlands in 1986, I thought about the name and whether it was well applied. To the Sioux this strange, arid, contorted fragment of fantasy in southwestern South Dakota was *mako sica,* or "bad land." Early French traders and trappers agreed, calling it *les mauvaises terres à traverser.* I could understand why in their day it was "bad land to cross." But I saw something different in the varicolored formations resembling spires, towers, and pinnacles in the ridges, low hills, and cliffs between the White and Cheyenne rivers. Kevin Costner introduced this country to millions of moviegoers in "Dances With Wolves."

I saw the evidence of incredibly abundant fossils that scientists have been studying for more than a century and relatively undisturbed prairie plants that are scarce elsewhere. I saw a bison herd and pictured what life was like when they were plentiful across the plains. And I saw too the great historic sites of the Oglala Sioux. So I perceived the Badlands as good lands, rich in natural and cultural heritage.

The land of White River, as I learned, at one time was part of a shallow inland sea. Then, about 60 million years ago, the Rockies and Black Hills pushed up through the earth's crust, leaving the sea bottom a plain of mud. Streams cut downward, meandering and widening their floodplains. Unceasing wind, rain, water, and frost removed and rearranged the soft fragments of rock. The process still continues—few landmarks long remain in the same form or dimension.

While still a marshy plain, the region was inhabited by forms of wildlife now unknown. With the discovery of fossils unearthed from tombs of mud and clay, paleontologists have identified remains of the three-toed horse, saber-toothed cat, oreodont, and early ancestors of the hog, camel, and rhinoceros. The Badlands are widely known today as a rich repository of fossils of the Oligocene epoch.

Along with change in geology over millions of years, the climate changed, too. With dry winds from the north and diminishing rain, grasslands replaced swamps and silted marshes. Today the annual precipitation is about 16 inches and prairies persist. The mixed-grass prairie with its many species of plant life is one of the most fascinating (though overlooked) aspects of the Badlands. In spring the ground is bright with wildflowers. Early summer finds a covering of big bluestem, needle-and-thread, little bluestem, blue gamma, and buffalo grasses, all bending and dancing in the wind.

The first people to see this region were the native Arikara Indians, who were displaced by the Sioux in the late 1700s. The national park, in fact, is deep in modern Sioux heartland. In the winter of 1890, the fateful year of the Wounded Knee Massacre, a band of more than a thousand Indians fled to the Badlands for refuge, dancing the Ghost Dance atop the Stronghold Table, hoping to invoke the spirits to restore their freedom to roam. But it was not to be.

Then came the homesteaders and ranchers, striving to contend with a harsh natural environment of dry alkaline soil, where droughts are common and where winter lasts half a year and summer temperatures are in the 90s or higher. In 1929 Congress authorized establishment of Badlands National Monument and, with the Dust Bowl days of the 1930s, many homesteaders and ranchers were glad to sell their land for this new federal venture and to move. The monument was officially proclaimed in 1939. With the addition in 1976 of 133,300 acres (formerly used as an air force gunnery range), the monument was more than doubled in size to its present 243,500 acres. Then in 1978 Congress voted to redesignate the area a national park.

That major 1976 park addition, known as the South Unit, lies within the Pine Ridge Indian Reservation. It assures that the spiritual sites of the Sioux are respected. I find it a moving experience to visit the spectacular overlooks and ponder the words of Red Cloud: "Riches would do us no good. We could not take them with us to the other world. We do not want riches, we want peace and love. I never want to leave this country; all my relatives are lying here in the ground and when I fall to pieces I am going to fall here."

## THE PRACTICAL GUIDE

The national park is easily reached from I-90. Turn off the interstate on South Dakota 240, which makes an arc through the park, between the towns of Cactus Flat and Wall. You can get an introduction to the Badlands in this 40-mile scenic loop.

**BACKGROUND.** The center of activity is **Cedar Pass Visitor Center,** near Interior, where naturalists will help you get oriented and answer questions. See the orientation slide program, the museum collection of fossils and Indian artifacts, and the "touch room."

The **White River Visitor Center,** located in the South Unit, is south of the town of Scenic. It features Indian cultural exhibits and a videotape program on the history of the Oglala Sioux.

**Nature walks and talks** are given daily during summer months at the Cedar Pass area, particularly during early morning, late afternoon, and at night, the best times to observe plants and wildlife.

**TRAIL ADVENTURES.** You can walk anywhere you like in the Badlands (but be careful on the edge of the crumbly formations). Trails are best, however, if only because of the excellent markers that interpret nature at work. **Fossil Exhibit Trail,** for instance, is a ¼-mile walk that shows fossil replicas, like those embedded in soft rock for 35 million years. **Door Trail** is an easy ¾-mile walk starting from the north end of the Windows parking area and leading through a natural doorway into the Badlands formation. You can backpack anywhere in the park and be out of sight just over the ridge crest from the road. Ask a ranger about **Sage Creek Wilderness.** The rolling prairie, with grassy hills and wooded draws interspersed with badlands, is a place to see pronghorn an-

telope, bison, badgers, and prairie dogs and to hear the song of the coyote at night.

There is no permit required for backcountry camping but plan on carrying drinking water (at least one gallon per person per day). Best hiking hours in summer are in early morning and evening to escape midday heat.

Be sure to wear proper footgear. Sturdy boots or shoes in summer will help ward off injury from cactus spines and prairie rattlesnakes. Warm, sturdy, waterproof gear in winter will help reduce exposure to the weather.

Always apply common sense when navigating slopes, since soils can be slippery, especially in rainy weather.

**BIRDWATCHING.** Plenty of distinctive birds frequent the Badlands. The prairie horned lark is one of the first to nest in the spring. The western meadowlark arrives early in March and lingers until a severe autumn storm drives it southward. Look for the western nighthawk (just before sunset, especially in fall migration), marsh hawk, sparrow hawk, and the little western burrowing owl. Pick up a copy of the bird checklist at a visitor center.

**ACCOMMODATIONS.** In addition to lodging in the park, motels are located in Kadoka, eastern gateway to the Badlands, and at Wall, farm and ranch center widely known for the Wall Drug Store. The town of Interior, two miles southwest of park headquarters, has gas stations, store, cafe and commercial camping with a few motel units. Obtain information on the State of South Dakota by calling toll-free 800/843-1930 (800/952-2217 in South Dakota).

**Cedar Pass Lodge,** Badlands National Park, SD 57750. Operated by the Oglala Sioux as a park concession, it offers rustic, comfortable cabins and dining room; open May to mid-October. 605/433-5460. L to M.

**Sundowner Motor Inn,** Kadoka, SD 57543. Heated pool. 605/837-2296. M.

**Kings Inn Motel,** Wall, SD 57790. Children under 12 free. 605/279-2178. M.

**West Motel,** Kadoka, SD 57543. Family rates. 605/837-2427. L.

**CAMPING.** You can camp year-round at Cedar Pass, with 110 campsites and developed facilities, and at Sage Creek if you're prepared to rough it. Reservations are required for groups. Bring cookstoves for hot meals, since fires are prohibited throughout the park.

**SEASONS.** Though summer is most popular, the park is open all year. Spring has generally clear, cool days, with occasional snows in April. Summer can be extremely hot. Fall, with a long Indian summer, is enjoyable. A visit in winter, when peaks are mantled in snow, can also be rewarding, though blizzards may temporarily block roads.

In whatever season you plan to visit, be ready for sudden, drastic weather changes. Summer storms frequently bring lightning, hail, and high winds. Be on guard against heat exhaustion in the summer and exposure in the winter.

**NEARBY.** A visit to the Badlands is easily linked with a trip to **Wind Cave, Jewel Cave,** and **Mount Rushmore,** all units of the National Park system. In Rapid City, visit the **Museum of Geology** and **Sioux Museum.**

**FOR FURTHER INFORMATION.** Write Superintendent, Badlands National Park, Box 6, Interior, South Dakota 57750. 605/433-5361.

# BIG BEND NATIONAL PARK

## TEXAS

### AUTHORIZED 1935/ESTABLISHED 1944

TEXANS CAN CLAIM almost anything about the mighty Big Bend and will be speaking modestly. This wilderness park presents an opportunity for a desert experience unequaled in its region and perhaps in the nation.

The heart of the 802,541-acre park lies 410 miles west of San Antonio and 300 miles southeast of El Paso but is worth all efforts to reach it, if only for the majesty of its vastness and the opportunity to absorb the adventurous, lonely frontier above the Rio Grande. In 1989, the Harte brothers, Ed and Houston, donated their large ranch to the park, adding 100 square miles of desert, mountain, and prairie.

In driving from the nearest towns, Alpine and Marathon, each more than 70 miles away, I thought there must be a greater population of jackrabbits and deer than people in between. The approach through vast ranch country provides a fitting foreground to this masterpiece of Southwest desert landscape, dominated by the upthrust of the massive Chisos Mountains.

I marvel at the geologic history of the park. Millions of years ago an inland sea covered the Big Bend. Sediments of mud, sand, and lime on the floor of the sea later hardened into rock; traces of shells and fossils are still found embedded over the area. During a later period dinosaurs and giant crocodiles (possibly 50 feet long) roamed through dark marshes and tropical forests. Then came volcanic activity and mountain building, followed by millions of years of erosion, and castles and cathedrals were carved in rock.

The waters of the Rio Grande have played their part in the carving process. The river extends for 118 miles along the boundary of the park—which also is the boundary between the United States and Mexico—on its great U-shaped bend. Three times on its course the river cuts through massive, dramatic canyons: Santa Elena, Mariscal, and Boquillas, which provide sightseeing adventures for every visitor.

In 1975, in *Science* magazine, two scientists reported the discovery in Big Bend National Park of bones of the largest flying creature ever known. Douglas Lawson, a doctoral candidate at the University of California, and Dr. Wann Langston, director of the Vertebrate Paleontology Laboratory, University of Texas, said the bones were those of the pterosaur (sometimes called the pterodactyl), a flying reptile with a wingspan of 38 feet. The pterosaur became extinct about 60 million years ago.

Human history is part of the treasure of the Big Bend. Bandits took refuge behind its rocky barricades. Comanche warriors passed through on their way into Mexico. Mexican revolutionaries invaded the United States into the Big Bend in 1916. Before the park was established, large livestock herds grazed where visitors now may enjoy wilderness camping.

I enjoy Big Bend as a place to absorb the richness of the awesome desert. The park contains more than a thousand different plants, including rare species that grow only here.

The beginning and end of the day are the best times to see the park's wide range of animals. Among them are the coyote, ringtail, and possibly the rare kit fox in Tornillo Flats—sometimes the sleek pronghorn will be seen here, too. Mule deer and collared peccary, or javelina, are apt to be in the Grapevine Hills. Lizards and snakes are not uncommon, but they are anxious to give humans a wide berth. Once I saw a tarantula on the hiking trail, but this giant spider was not unfriendly. I looked him over respectfully, from a distance, and then we each went our separate ways. It is wise to travel with a good bird guide, for nearly 400 species of birds have been seen in the park. These include the rare, lyric-voiced Colima warbler, whose only known nesting places are here and in Mexico.

## THE PRACTICAL GUIDE

Allow at least three full days to explore the Big Bend, though a full week will occupy any visitor's time usefully, exploring by car, raft, afoot, and on horseback.

Approaching from the west, El Paso lies 328 miles from Big Bend. You can reach the park by driving to Van Horn and Marfa, then south to Presidio and the Maverick entrance—it's the long but scenic route, including the River Road along the Rio Grande. You can also head due east from Marfa to Alpine, then south to the Maverick entrance. Or from Alpine continue to Marathon, then south to the Persimmon Gap entrance the distance is longer but it takes less time. If traveling from and to the west, try to make a loop trip. From the east, Big Bend lies 405 miles from San Antonio, 251 miles from Del Rio, via Persimmon Gap.

**BACKGROUND.** From the entrance to the park at Persimmon Gap, 39 miles south of Mara-

thon, it is 29 miles to park headquarters at Panther Junction in the foothills of the Chisos. Use the giant relief map at the Visitor Center there to chart your course, and ask for current information on river and road conditions.

Principal roads in the park are paved. Improved dirt roads normally are in good condition except following rainstorms.

Get out of your car and hike the trails. You have more than 350 miles of them.

Allow the better part of a day for the trip to **Santa Elena Canyon,** a massive boxlike gorge carved through limestone cliffs. It lies 45 miles from the center of things at Chisos Basin. From the picnic area at the river shore, a footpath leads along a rocky ledge into the heart of the canyon. On the way there or back, stop at **Castolon,** where adobe houses reflect pioneer settlement by Mexican farmers, the U.S. Cavalry, and rugged cattlemen. You can purchase items of food or clothing at the historic Castolon Store, which has been in business since 1919. Nearby, the river is so narrow that you can cross by rowboat to the Mexican village of **Santa Elena.**

Spend part of another day at **Boquillas Canyon,** the longest of Big Bend's famous gorges, where the floodplain of willows and cottonwoods is frequented by many birds, particularly spectacular with late afternoon sun on the canyon walls. It lies 35 miles from Chisos Basin. Be sure to take in the nature trail at Rio Grande Village, to learn about this life-community and enjoy the views above the river. Then visit a village out of yesterday, **Boquillas,** across the "border without barricades." You will pay to ride across the river in a skiff, then on a burro for 1 mile to the village, but the modest fee is well worth it.

If you are in good physical condition (not necessarily an expert rider), the daylong horseback trip to the **South Rim** is one of the finest experiences available in any national park. It reveals the full sweep of the nature community, upward through pinyon, oak, and juniper, through an "island forest in the sky" more like the North woods than Southwest desert. The greatest reward is the view from the crest, more than 7,200 feet high, of the silvery Rio Grande, the tawny desert, and rugged Mexican Sierra del Carmen extending to the horizon. A shorter trip leads to the **Window,** a great gap in the mountains, ideal for picture taking.

**Lost Mine Trail** from Panther Pass is the most popular hiking route; it takes three to four hours to make the 5-mile round trip to Lost Mine Peak.

**Old Ore Road,** running north from Rio Grande Village to the yucca forest on Dagger Flats, is an interesting off-the-beaten-path primitive route. It parallels the old stage road to Boquillas across desert flats and arroyos. Hikers can use it to reach the Telephone Canyon trailhead, intersecting the Strawhouse and Marufo Vega trails, the major network on the east side of the park. Almost all dirt roads in the park are primitive.

**HIKING GEAR.** Wear hiking shoes or boots, not sneakers, in this country to avoid painful contact with thorny mesquite, prickly pear, and catclaw. Wide-brimmed hats are most practical. Don't plan any longer hike across the harsh desert lowlands than you feel sure you can make. Carry plenty of water.

**BOATING.** This a choice experience on the Rio Grande—for experts. Inflatable rubber rafts are recommended for float trips. Some portaging may be necessary due to shallow water. If the river is above the 5-foot level, special restrictions are enforced. Water conditions are difficult to predict. From October through March the level is low but stable, and the weather is pleasant. The summers are definitely hot on the river. No boats or accessory equipment are available for rent or loan inside the park. A permit must be obtained at park headquarters or a ranger station.

Rubber-raft trips are offered by private outfitters headquartered at Terlingua and other nearby towns. Check at park headquarters or any ranger station for information. Two-day raft trips include a chance to camp overnight on a sandbar in Boquillas Canyon or Santa Elena Canyon. Mariscal Canyon is a good one-day trip. The Lower Canyons trip lasts six days, covering rugged, isolated country with major rapids and natural hot springs. Experts call it one of the nation's most exciting river runs. Contact Far Flung Adventures, Box 31, Terlingua, TX 79852; Outback Expeditions, Study Butte, TX 79852; Big Bend River Tours, Lajitas, TX 79852; Rough Run Outfitters, Marathon, TX 79842; or Whitewater Experience, 3835 Farnham, Houston, TX 77098.

**PHOTOGRAPHY.** Early morning is best at Santa Elena Canyon; by noon there is little or no sunlight on the walls. Boquillas Canyon, in shadow until noon, improves in the afternoon. Sunset through the Window makes a colorful study from almost any point. You get best results with long shadows early or late in the day.

**BIRDWATCHING.** Big Bend is one of the finest of all birding parks. It furnishes habitat for many Mexican birds found nowhere else in the United States. Most celebrated are Colima warblers, rare sparrow-sized songsters that divide their seasons between south-central Mexico and the Chisos Mountains. Here also is the greatest concentration of breeding peregrine falcons remaining anywhere in the United States. Pick up a copy of *Naturalist's Big Bend*, a handbook by Roland H. Wauer, which features a significant chapter on birds. It is published by Texas A & M Press, College Station, Texas, and is available at the Visitor Center. Following wet summers, lowland flats along the Rio Grande are apt to contain vast arrays of wintering sparrows. Big Bend National History Association offers educational programs of one to three days on birds, wildflowers, and archaeology and geology. Write Seminar Coordinator, Box 68, Big Bend National Park, TX 79834.

**ACCOMMODATIONS.** National Park Concessions, Inc. operates a lodge and trailer sites in the park. Lodgings and private campgrounds outside the park are located at Study Butte and Lajitas, west of the park; Terlingua, the western boundary; and Alpine, center of ranching and a college town, where you can visit the Museum of the Big Bend on the campus of Sul Ross University.

**Chisos Mountain Lodge,** Big Bend National Park, TX 79834. Motel and stone cottages, dining room, campground, and supply store, are located at the center of activity for most of the year. Reservations essential year-round. 915/447-2291. M.

**Cavalry Post Motor Inn and Badlands Motel,** Terlingua, TX 79852. Styled as frontier fort and western town, facilities include riding, tennis, swimming, and dining. 915/371-2471. M.

**Sunday House Inn,** Alpine, TX 79830. Two-story motel with pool. Under 12 free and senior citizen rates available. 915/837-3363. L to M.

**Indian Lodge,** Box 786, Fort Davis, TX 79734. State-owned and operated pueblo-style lodge in Davis Mountains State Park, 31 miles northwest of Alpine, with handy access to Fort Davis National Historic Site. Swimming pool and scenic walking trails. Under 12 free. Closed two weeks in mid-January. 915/426-3254. L.

**CAMPING.** Big Bend provides a variety of opportunity. The two major campgrounds are at **Chisos Basin** (62 sites) and **Rio Grande Village** (99 sites). Chisos is most popular Easter through Thanksgiving, but when it grows cool at the basin it is still shirt-sleeve weather in the desert around Rio Grande Village. Facilities there include a trailer park, large campground, and supply store. There is also a smaller campground at **Cottonwood,** near Castolon, with less-developed facilities. Primitive camping is available along backcountry roads, with a permit obtained from any ranger station. Carry plenty of water and be sure to prepare for potential emergencies.

**SEASONS.** Sunshine is abundant all year. Snow is light and rare in the mountains. Winter is nippy at higher elevations but pleasant in the lowlands (70 and 80 degrees Fahrenheit even in January), and an ideal season here. Spring arrives early. The desert blooms from late February through April; some years Dagger Flat, in the northeast part of the park, presents a rare spectacle of thousands of giant dagger yucca (Yucca carnerosana) unfolding massive clusters of creamy blossoms. Summer is hot (100 degrees) in desert and river valley, but pleasant at Chisos Basin and the best time of year for the mountains.

A good time to walk the desert is at twilight, the witching hour when deer feed on open hillsides and coyotes begin their nocturnal serenade. Be on the lookout for rattlesnakes out to feed on rodents. They won't strike if you keep your distance, so avoid sitting on rocks or logs they're likely to shelter under, and keep your eyes open. Don't worry about giant tarantulas you may meet; they're relatively harmless.

**NEARBY.** The **Black Gap Wildlife Management Area,** near the Persimmon Gap entrance, covers 100,000 acres, with fishing opportunities on a 20-mile stretch of the Rio Grande. **Fort Davis National Historic Site,** on the road down from Carlsbad Caverns, New Mexico, is a restoration of the most impressive old frontier fort in the Southwest. It adjoins **Davis Mountains State Park,** a combination of scenic peaks and canyons, with modern overnight lodge accommodations and recreation facilities. Motels are located in the towns of Alpine and Marathon, between Fort Davis and Big Bend. At Alpine, visit the fascinating **Museum of the Big Bend** on the campus of Sul Ross State University. You'll learn about the history and settlement of the country. County Route 170, the scenic **Camino del Rio,** leads northwest from the park through the mining ghost towns of Study Butte and Terlingua, noted as the scene of the annual International Chili Cookoff in early November, and on to Presidio, a gateway into Mexico via Ojinaga and Chihuahua.

**RECOMMENDED READING.** *The North American Deserts,* by Edmund C. Jaeger (Stanford, CA: Stanford University Press) and *The Big Bend Country: Facts, Stories & Legends,* by Ross Maxwell (Big Bend, TX: Big Bend Natural History Association)

**FOR FURTHER INFORMATION.** Write Superintendent, Big Bend National Park, TX 79834. 915/477-2251.

# BISCAYNE NATIONAL PARK

## FLORIDA

ESTABLISHED 1980

LATE IN AUGUST 1992, the eye of unforgettable Hurricane Andrew took perfect aim at the offshore islands, waters, and mainland section of the national park and first struck the United States here. On the islands, or keys, mahogany, gumbo limbo, and *lignum vitae* forests were either stripped bare of lush green foliage or their trees were broken. Only four people are known to have stayed along the keys during the storm. Three were in a boat and two of them died.

The park's new administration building, nearing completion when Andrew hit, was built to withstand winds up to 130 miles per hour. It did that and more, sustaining only minor damage. A temporary visitor center tells the story of the storm and interprets its long-term effects on flora and fauna.

The northernmost living coral reefs in the continental United States extend from the national park south to Key Largo National Marine Sanctuary. Pounding waves generated by the hurricane damaged the reefs, but not nearly as extensively as first feared. The worst deep-water damage was at Triumph Reef, off Elliott Key, but the violence of the storm may have even helped by cleaning reef patches of harmful algae. As scientists say, the reefs have evolved through hurricane cycles of damage and recovery; their concerns center on human-caused decline in water quality and reef infections.

Although Biscayne Bay's northern half, bordering Miami and Miami Beach, has long been developed (if not overdeveloped), the southern half in the 1960s still remained a rich breeding ground for corals, sponges, shellfish, and fish.

Biologists, engineers, sportsmen, and conservationists rallied to defend the bay against a proposed refinery on the mainland and subdivision on the keys. They warned that it is an enclosed body where prevailing winds blow onshore and that industrial wastes could turn the whole bay into a stagnant, oily pool, damaging parks, yacht clubs, homes, and hotels. They had little idea of exactly how to save the bay, but studied one legal and legislative potential after another.

As the controversy heightened, the developers showed their defiance by bulldozing a path the entire length of Elliott Key, barely missing a stand of rare palm trees. But public support for preservation was growing, leading to the establishment in 1968 of Biscayne National Monument.

People began to sit up and take notice of this jewel of nature. They found the islands and islets, numbering about 30, support stands of rare mahogany and *lignum vitae,* and species of ferns and palms that had been thought extinct. The tropical forests shelter migratory birds.

As a result, in 1980 the monument was significantly enlarged to cover approximately 181,500 acres and reclassified as a national park. The additions include islands and mainland mangroves that serve as nurseries for marine life. The national park is enhanced by the nearby Key Largo Coral Reef National Marine Sanctuary, which has 100 square miles of underwater life. Biscayne has been a haven for boaters, birdwatchers, fishermen, snorkelers, and scuba divers and likely will be again.

The **Visitor Center** is located at Convoy Point, on Biscayne Bay east of Homestead. It's easy to reach by car from anywhere in the metro Miami area. There are boat launch ramps at Homestead Bayfront Park and Marina next to Convoy Point.

Biscayne National Underwater Park Co., the concession at Convoy Point (305/247-2400), has canoe rentals available. You can join a narrated glass-bottomed boat tour or a snorkel/scuba trip. Reservations are required and a fee is charged. Call first.

**Elliott Key** is easily reached across the Intracoastal Waterway. The visitor center and restrooms remained intact through Hurricane Andrew. A ranger is stationed here who will furnish helpful guidance.

**SNORKEL AND SCUBA.** Much of the area is so shallow you normally can see abundant tropical fish, corals, and sponges simply with mask, snorkel, and fins, but some reefs may be covered with silt as a result of the 1992 hurricane. On the eastern edge of the shelf, however, the outer reef drops to depths of greater than 100 feet. Behind the outer reef, in sheltered lagoonlike waters, small patch reefs rise to the surface, affording novice and intermediate divers an opportunity to become acquainted with Florida's coral reefs. While at park headquarters, check on current conditions. Be sure to display a dive flag and tie it to a buoy to prevent damaging the reef with your anchor.

**FISHING.** In the reefs, fishing for grouper and snapper is popular; you can try your luck for the big ones—marlin, kingfish, dolphin, and sailfish. Bear in mind that Florida law prevails. The bay and creeks are closed to lobstering.

**SPECIAL NOTE.** Possession, disturbance, or removal of corals, sea fans, sea feathers, tropical fish, shells, historical artifacts, and natural features is prohibited. These are all best left in place for others to enjoy.

**ACCOMMODATIONS.** The campground on Elliot Key is available to boaters and via concession-operated tour boat, Biscayne Aqua-Center, Inc., Homestead, FL 33030. 305/247-2400. Look for accommodations in the Miami area or south of Homestead in the Keys. See listings under Everglades National Park.

**NEARBY. John Pennekamp Coral Reef State Park,** first undersea park in the continental United States, lies directly south. On shore the park includes a campground and a marina. **Everglades National Park** is 30 minutes west.

**FOR FURTHER INFORMATION.** Write Superintendent, Biscayne National Park, Box 1369, Homestead, FL 33090-1369. 305/247-2044.

# BRYCE CANYON NATIONAL PARK

## UTAH
### AUTHORIZED 1924

ALL OF SOUTHERN UTAH—the "Color Country"—might qualify as a national park. Perhaps it all can't be one, but there is no doubt about Bryce Canyon. It is not very large, only 37,102 acres, but it includes some of the most colorful and unusual erosional forms on earth.

The heart of the park is but a short, narrow strip along the jagged edge of the Paunsaugunt Plateau, one of the seven great "tables" dominating southern Utah. Below the plateau rim stand cathedrals, palaces, chessmen awaiting the next move, and entire miniature sculptured cities. Many formations are named, such as Thor's Hammer, Queen's Castle, Gulliver's Castle, Hindu Temples, and Wall Street, but you will find plenty that may suggest names of your own.

These are colored variously pink, iron-red, and orange, blended with white, gold, and cream, and here and there striped with lavender and blue. All of this spreads out from the amphitheaterlike rim as far as the eye can see until, far in the distance, it blends into the expansive Utah-Arizona landscape of plateaus dark with evergreen forests.

Only a few, if any, places in the world provide better opportunity to realize the power and persistence of forces that have shaped the earth's surface than Bryce Canyon. Geology of the last 60 million years began with layers of sediment being deposited by inland lakes, followed by mountain building caused by powerful pressures coming from within the earth. Huge blocks were broken off and raised higher until they formed distinct plateaus, or tablelands. Then over the centuries rain, frost and thaw, running water, plant roots forcing themselves deeper into the cracks, and chemicals in the air have exercised their influences through alternate layers of harder and softer rock.

This country was known to Indians and favored by the Paiutes, who described the formations as "red rocks standing like men in a bowl-shaped canyon." It was they who named the Paunsaugunt Plateau, which means "home of the beaver," a reminder that many species of wildlife dwell on this high, cool plateau.

Adventurous trappers and prospectors may have visited the area during the period from 1830 to 1850, and Mormon scouts searching for fields and pastures may have reached the south base of the Paunsaugunt Plateau between 1850 and

1866. It was the intrepid Major John Wesley Powell who initiated the scientific investigation of the valleys and plateaus of southern and central Utah, in 1871. His route began at Kanab, ascended Johnson Canyon, then crossed the many deeply trenched streams rising in the plateau walls of what is now the national park. One early settler, Ebenezer Bryce, pushed farther upstream than the others and tried raising cattle, but gave it up and departed, leaving only his name.

J. W. Humphrey, forest supervisor of the Sevier Forest, headquartered at Panguitch, was largely responsible for making the exquisitely scenic area of Bryce Canyon available to the public. He not only publicized its attractions in the local newspaper but pressed for the development of primitive roads.

The Bryce fever caught hold. In 1919, the Utah legislature memorialized Congress, urging the establishment of a national monument to be called Temple of the Gods. The effort was rewarded in 1923 when Bryce Canyon National Monument was designated by presidential proclamation, then was given even greater recognition the following year when Congress raised the status of the area, naming it Utah National Park. In subsequent years the park was enlarged, its name changed once again.

Bryce Canyon was advertised far and wide during the halcyon days of trail travel to the national parks. Those days have long ended and other national parks have been established in southern Utah, but Bryce Canyon remains a jewel among them.

## THE PRACTICAL GUIDE

The park is small enough so that you can cover the full drive along the high rim and back, a distance of 34 miles, in less than three hours, but plan to stay much longer. Scenic overlooks provide broad perspective before seeing the formations at close range from hiking and riding trails.

The approach roads to Bryce are deceptive: 4,000 feet in elevation are gained in the last 60 miles. This is high country, ranging from 8,000 to 9,000 feet above sea level, and it demands a leisurely pace, particularly for anyone with a heart condition. Allow extra time for everything, including eating and hiking.

**WITHOUT A CAR.** Color Country Tours provides transportation by motor coach three times weekly from Cedar City. This is designed primarily as a one-day tour with stops at Zion Canyon Overlook, **Cedar Breaks National Monument,** and Navajo Lake before reaching the park Visitor Center. However, one-way transportation is offered, including pickups at Cedar City Airport (served by Sky West from Salt Lake City). You can also reach Cedar City via Greyhound or Trailways.

**BACKGROUND.** Located at the park's entrance, the **Visitor Center** contains orientation exhibits on geology, biology, and archaeology. Illustrated talks are presented daily in summer. For an introduction to the park, take a van trip from Bryce Canyon Lodge to Bryce Point, Inspiration Point, and Paria View. Then prepare to walk.

**Main Bryce Amphitheater,** between **Boat Mesa** and **Bryce Point,** a distance of 4 airline miles, contains a concentration of sights. In this compact area are 21 miles of trail and spectacular vistas. You can see how the vegetation changes with elevation. Sagebrush claims the valley floors below. The slopes up to 7,000 feet are covered with pinyons, junipers, and Gambel oaks. Above and below the rim, between 7,000 and 8,500 feet, are ponderosa, limber, and bristlecone pines, and Douglas fir.

Navajo Loop, most popular hike (about 1½ miles and 1½ hours), starts from the inspiring setting of **Sunset Point.** It begins with a gradual 521-foot descent into the canyon, then winds among an outstanding array of formations, with time for rest and picture taking en route. The last lap is an amazing series of stairlike switchbacks. Guided walks are given daily.

**Under-the-Rim Trail,** completed in 1965, offers 23 miles of hiking into quite wild country, with opportunities for solitude and exploration. Yet it parallels the main park road, so it can be taken conveniently in sections; you can reach it from three spur trails. Extending from Bryce Point to the south boundary at **Rainbow Point,** this trail opens the heart of the Pink Cliffs scenery. The traveler who is concerned with preserving park features for the future will stay on the trails. The traveler who is concerned with his or her children's safety will be sure they do the same.

**HORSEBACK RIDES.** These afford the least strenuous way of probing the canyon trails, on a morning or an afternoon trip from Bryce Canyon Lodge. There is a lot of variety to enjoy, riding through cool and shadowed canyons, over switchbacks and ridgetops, and along the base of cliffs. For reservations, call 801/834-5219; be prepared for large groups and steep, narrow trails.

**PHOTOGRAPHY.** Opportunities are limitless. Use your imagination to bring home more than a visual record of where you have been; shoot your own interpretation of what you have seen. In Bryce Canyon you can experiment with sidelighting and backlighting, using the brilliant landscape to your advantage. Be careful to shade your lens when shooting toward the sun. The deeper the blue of the sky, the more intense will be the coloring of the rocks. Telephoto and wide-angle lenses are helpful but not essential. **Yovimpa Point** is the best place to catch the setting sun's rays on the Pink Cliffs; it is unsurpassed for beauty.

**BIRDWATCHING.** Three distinct habitats support varied birdlife. Good birding is found in the pinyon pine–juniper–Gambel oak areas of Jolley Hollow, the Mossy Cave area, and along the trail from Sunset Point to the town of Tropic. You're likely to find scrub and pinyon jays, black-throated gray warblers, and Cassin's kingbirds. In the ponderosa pine and sage areas, best bets are in the meadows around the Visitor Center and around Sunrise and Sunset viewpoints; you're likely to see bluebirds, tanagers, warblers, olive-sided flycatchers, and Townsend's solitaires. Then in the Douglas fir and white fir forest, observe closely at Rainbow Point, where you may see Williamson's sapsuckers, hermit thrushes, and ruby-crowned kinglets. Naturalist-led bird walks are given occasionally and an evening program on birds about every two weeks.

**ACCOMMODATIONS.** Lodging and camping are available in the park, as well as at Panguitch, Cedar City and other nearby communities.

**Meaudeau View Lodge,** Cedar City, UT 84720. Distinctive log inn, 9 rooms and suites, all with private bath, at 8,400 feet in Dixie National Forest. Offers trout fishing and cross-country skiing in winter. 801/648-2495. M to H.

**Bryce Canyon Lodge,** Box 400, Cedar City, UT 84720. Operated as a concession inside the park, by TW Services, Inc., the 70-unit motel and refurbished rustic cabins offer meals, campers' store and laundry. Some cottages are without bath. Open mid-May to October 2. 801/586-7686. M.

**Best Western Rubys Inn,** Rubys Inn, UT 84764. Located 1 mile north of park entrance. Horseback riding, indoor pool, square dancing, winter snowshoeing and cross-country ski trails. Trailer park as well as lodge. 801/834-5341. M.

**Knell and Knell Annex,** Cedar City, UT 84720. Some rooms at the Annex are equipped with refrigerators. 801/586-6566 (or 9487). L to M.

**CAMPING.** Two campgrounds are located inside the park near the Visitor Center; a grocery store is available with limited supplies. The camping limit is 14 days. This area requires permits for backcountry use.

**SEASONS.** If you come in late spring or summer, wildflowers alone will make your trip worthwhile, including paintbrush, columbine, yarrow, and penstemon. Temperature, like vegetation, varies with altitude.

Between April and October, days are warm, with occasional thundershowers, followed by cool evenings.

The lodge is open from mid-May to the end of September only; all park roads are kept open during winter, when white snow contrasts with the brilliant colors of the Pink Cliffs. Skies are deep blue and haze free.

**NEARBY.** The **Dixie National Forest** encircles the park. The nearest recreation area, at Pine Lake, elevation 8,200 feet, has fishing, boating, camping. **Red Canyon** campground is located midway between Bryce and Panguitch, off Utah 12. **Panguitch Lake,** in addition to forest camping, has boat rentals, cabins, and fishing. Panguitch, 27 miles west of Bryce, is an interesting ranching community. East on Utah 12 at Cannonville is the turnoff for Kodachrome Basin State Park, with colorful sandstone formations, campsites with showers. Call 801/679-8562 to check condition of entry road. **Escalante Petrified Forest State Reserve,** 50 miles east of Bryce Canyon on Utah 12, has self-guiding nature trails and a campground. To hike the spectacular Escalante Canyons along the Escalante River, stop at the Bureau of Land Management office in Escalante to obtain a backcountry permit.

Consider a side trip to **Capitol Reef National Park,** a 20-mile uplift of sandstone cliffs, near Torrey. East of Cedar City, a short side trip will take you to Cedar Breaks National Monument, a natural amphitheater in the Pink Wasatch Cliffs.

**Bryce Canyon, Zion,** and **Grand Canyon** national parks are intimately related geologically. A visit to all three of these parks is like a tour through gigantic galleries of 600 million years of the geologic past. Farther along Utah 12, near Boulder, Anasazi State Park marks the largest Anasazi settlement west of the Colorado River.

**FOR FURTHER INFORMATION.** Write Superintendent, Bryce Canyon National Park, Bryce Canyon, UT 84717. 801/834-5322.

# CANYONLANDS NATIONAL PARK

UTAH

ESTABLISHED 1964

IN THE FALL of 1985 I went camping and hiking with friends in the section of Canyonlands called the Needles, so named for its thousands of red-and-white rounded pillars, spires, and balanced rocks, some rising as high as 30-story buildings. One day we hiked to the confluence of the Green and Colorado rivers, entrenched in their deep, winding gorges, from which benches of land spread outward to meet cliffs of orange-red sandstone. It was a dramatic, wild setting, out of the fictional pages of Zane Grey and the real-life pages of John Wesley Powell, who explored the full length of the Colorado River.

Days were warm, though not uncomfortable. Nights were cool to chilly. We were alone most of the time but did encounter a few parties on the trail. They were composed of older people, cheerful hikers traveling with pocket guides and binoculars. They did not want things to be easy in the wilderness.

Until recent years the Canyonlands region was little known outside of southern Utah. A few dirt roads penetrated the edges, but most of it was inaccessible. Since 1964, when it became a national park, the world has been learning of the flaming color and rocky landscape.

Here the Colorado and Green rivers sliced through layers of rock and stripped them back to raveled ancient edges. Tributary streams, rain, and frost then carved the details. The puzzles of how and when these events happened are part of the enchantment.

The elevations in the park range from 3,600 feet in low-lying basinlands to plateaus and mesas of almost 7,000 feet, with unending variety in landscape.

Though portions of the 337,570-acre national park are still unexplored, evidences of prehistoric humans have been located in ruined villages and in petroglyphs chipped nearly a thousand years ago.

Native plants and animals are typical of the arid pinyon-and-juniper community, except for the cottonwoods and water-loving plants around the seeps and springs. Deer, coyotes, and foxes are among those present but rarely observed. A local native population of desert bighorn inhabits a portion of the park. From May to August, except in extra-dry years, wildflowers carpet the moist locations.

Most roads are unpaved. Portions of the backcountry can be seen only by four-wheel-drive vehicle, boat, horseback, or afoot. Yet visitors can get a generous sampling of the area with time and patience.

**BACKGROUND.** Two approaches are available by passenger car to the Canyonlands frontier. The northern gateway is the old pioneer Mormon town of **Moab,** where Zane Grey set many of his novels—in the days before uranium, oil, and potash. A graded, dry-weather road off Utah 313 leads to the **Island in the Sky** section of the park. Dominating the land between the two rivers, the tip of this mesa, **Grandview Point,** affords a spectacular rimrock view of the park with its red-hued cliffs, buttes, and mesas. At the end of a short hiking trail, **Upheaval Dome,** a mysterious fragment of geology, is a deep, vertical-walled

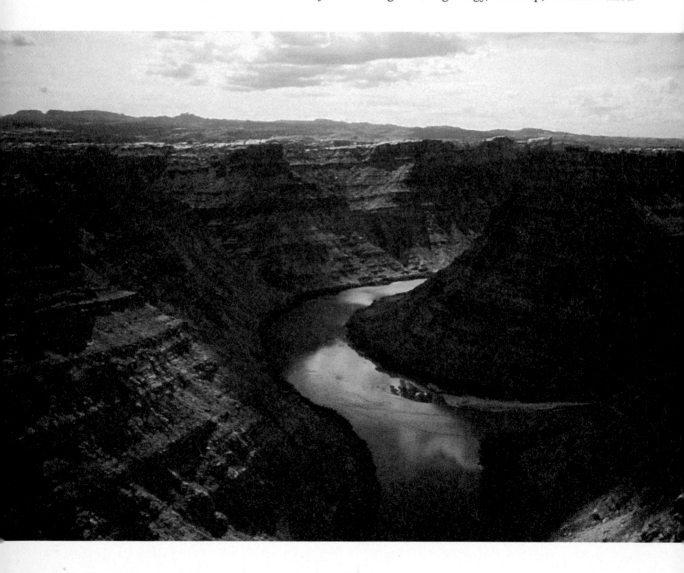

crater with a cream-colored mass of stone upthrust through surrounding red-tinged sandstone.

From the southeast gateway, **Monticello,** at the foot of the Abajo Mountains, US 191 travels north 15 miles to Church Rock. Paved Utah 211 leads first to the landmark known as **Newspaper Rock,** in Newspaper Rock State Park, where a series of petroglyphs were chipped into the cliffside by prehistoric and historic Indians. The ranger station just inside the park is a good place to learn about park programs and facilities. Passenger cars find it passable to **Squaw Spring** and Squaw Flat Campground, about 3 miles beyond the ranger station. But a four-wheel-drive vehicle is essential to reach **Elephant Hill,** at the brink of the spectacular **Needles** area.

**Four-wheel-drive vehicles** afford opportunities to explore more of the park. A challenging jeep trail heads west from Squaw Flat into the Needles and **Chesler Park** along **Devil's Lane** to the confluence of the Green and Colorado rivers.

**TOUR OPERATORS.** Jeep tours are conducted by local experts into the Needles and also deeper into the backcountry to see such features as **Angel Arch,** a sandstone span guarded by an angellike figure. Angel Arch and surroundings were first discovered and named as recently as 1955. Outfitters also run guided pack trips for hikers and horseback riders. A list of the outfitters is available by mail from the park.

Adventures are offered by the **Canyonlands Field Institute** during spring, summer, and fall "for those who wish to understand, not just to see." These include guided trips, seminars, photo workshops, and programs for children. Write Canyonlands Field Institute, Box 68, Moab, Utah 84532.

**BICYCLING.** The country around Moab has become a powerful destination for mountain bikers—not only Arches and Canyonlands, but the backcountry administered by the Bureau of Land Management. Spring and fall are best seasons. (Summer's too hot, winter's chilly.) Find maps at local bike shops and Back of Beyond Bookstore. Carry plenty of water, tools, parts. To help protect the desert, ride only on roads, trails, slickrock.

**BOATING.** Access to portions of the park is feasible from two directions. One is from the town of **Green River,** which is the starting point of the annual 196-mile Friendship Cruise and Motorboat Marathon to Moab every May and June. The other direction is from **Moab** on the Colorado River to the confluence of the two rivers. Boat tours are run frequently, giving a new dimension to the Canyonlands experience. Wild **Cataract Canyon,** below the junction, is known as "the explorer's nightmare and modern river runner's challenge." Commercial river trips with proper boats and expert rivermen are the best way to view these rapids.

In big-water rapids like Cataract Canyon small boats are often lashed together, side by side, to form a "G-rig," named for Georgie White, the woman who invented this kind of arrangement for floating the once-mighty waters of the Colorado River in Grand Canyon.

If you are capable of going on your own, you must apply for authorization and a required permit. However you go, count on viewing abundant and varied birdlife, from ouzels along the rocks to high-flying golden eagles. Be sure to plan your trip with a copy of *Canyon Country Paddles*, by Verne Huser (Salt Lake City: Wasatch Publishers, Inc.).

**ACCOMMODATIONS.** The park has no overnight lodgings, food, or gasoline facilities. Motels are located in Moab, Monticello, and Green River. Camping supplies are available in these towns. For help, stop at Moab Visitor Center, 805 N. Main, Moab, UT 84532, or call 800/635-6622.

**Apache,** 166 S. 4th East St., Moab, UT 84532. Pool and playground. Senior citizen rates are available. 801/259-5727. M.

**Triangle 44 Motel,** 164 E. Central, Monticello, UT 84535. 801/587-2274. M.

**Best Western Gateway,** Blanding, UT 84511. En route to Glen Canyon National Recreation Area, with access to Natural Bridges and Hovenweep national monuments. Under 12 free and senior citizen rates available. Pool. 801/678-2278. M.

**CAMPING.** Inside the park, campgrounds at **Squaw Flat** and **Willow Flat** are equipped with tables, fireplaces, and pit toilets; there is a 14-day limit. Firewood is not available, so bring your own fuel as well as water. This area requires permits for backcountry use. Primitive camping is permitted at designated locations in the **Island in the Sky** section and in the backcountry. Plan to carry extra water at all times. State park campgrounds are located at **Indian Creek,** near the Needles area, and at **Dead Horse Point,** south of Moab. Good campgrounds are located in timbered **Manti– La Sal National Forest,** one section of which is just south of the park; another, east of Moab.

**SEASONS.** This is desert country, where daily, as well as seasonal, temperature changes can be extreme: hot days in summer get up to a maximum of 110 degrees Fahrenheit, cooling rapidly after sundown to a low shortly before sunup, then rising rapidly again. The average annual temperature is from 50 to 55 degrees Fahrenheit, but there are lows of 20 below zero. Some snow falls on the rims during winter. Spring and autumn are mild and pleasant. The average annual precipitation is 5 to 9 inches, much of the moisture coming in late-summer thundershowers.

**NEARBY.** The companion piece to Canyonlands, **Arches National Park,** outside of Moab, contains an overwhelming concentration of red-rock arches, immense windows, and pinnacles.

Within 25 miles of the heart of Canyonlands, the Monticello and Moab districts of **Manti–La Sal National Forest** provide the contrast—high cool woodlands rising to summits of the La Sal and Abajo mountains, more than 11,000 and 12,000 feet, with fishing, camping, and scenic drives. Downstream on the Colorado lies **Glen Canyon National Recreation Area,** where Lake Powell, a major watersports center, is formed behind the third highest dam in the world. Near Blanding and Bluff, **Natural Bridges National Monument** contains three huge sandstone bridges, magnificent canyons, and ancient Indian ruins. **Hovenweep National Monument** embraces a chain of well-preserved but isolated prehistoric Indian towers in the famed Four Corners region of the Southwest, near the point where the boundary lines of Colorado, Utah, Arizona, and New Mexico converge.

Southwest of Bluff, the town of **Mexican Hat** is gateway to fantastic **Monument Valley,** a land of buttes and mesas, where the Navajo Indians are developing visitor facilities astride the once-remote Utah-Arizona desert boundary.

**FOR FURTHER INFORMATION.** Write Superintendent, Canyonlands National Park, 446 South Main Street, Moab, Utah 84532. 801/259-3911.

# CAPITOL REEF NATIONAL PARK

## UTAH

ESTABLISHED 1971

I LOOKED AWAY from the scenery of tilted cliffs and rainbow rock layers in south-central Utah, a strange and still little-known land, to read an excerpt of the 1880 description of it by Clarence E. Dutton, a pioneering geologist. The year was 1880. "The colors are such as no pigments can portray," he wrote. "They are deep, rich and variegated; and so luminous are they that light seems to flow or shine out of the rock rather than to be reflected from it."

His words are still valid. Here I explored the Waterpocket Fold, a strip of colorful rock layers almost 100 miles long (72 miles within the national park), formed from a buckling or wrinkling of the earth's crust. At Cathedral Valley, in the northern end of the park, I saw spectacular monoliths 400 to 700 feet high, of reddish brown sandstone capped with grayish yellow strata—many free-standing on the valley floor.

Capitol Reef itself, a segment of the Waterpocket Fold, is a 20-mile-long uplift rising 1,000 feet above the Fremont River (roughly midway between Canyon-lands and Bryce Canyon national parks), embracing the beauty Mr. Dutton described; but this is only a portion of the new park. It now includes nearly all of the most spectacular, readily understood monocline in the United States. Exposed and eroded rock layers laid down more than 125 million years ago stand on edge like pages of a gigantic geology book.

Due to its isolation and difficulty of access, the Capitol Reef country actually was undiscovered by whites and unexplored until comparatively recent times. The earliest inhabitants apparently were prehistoric Indians who arrived during the Basket Maker III period, dating back to about A.D. 700, and who remained until not later than 1275 (when the great 25-year drought began). These people left reminders of their occupancy in the form of large, distinctive petroglyphs, some of which are found near Fruita and on Pleasant Creek.

The first white people of record to see any part of this area were members of the William Wolfskill party of 1829. On his celebrated voyage down the Colorado River in 1869, John Wesley Powell discovered the Dirty Devil River, which he later renamed the Fremont and revisited on his expedition of 1871.

Soon afterward, Professor A. H. Thompson, Powell's geologist, explored and mapped the area, applying names to various features, which are still in use.

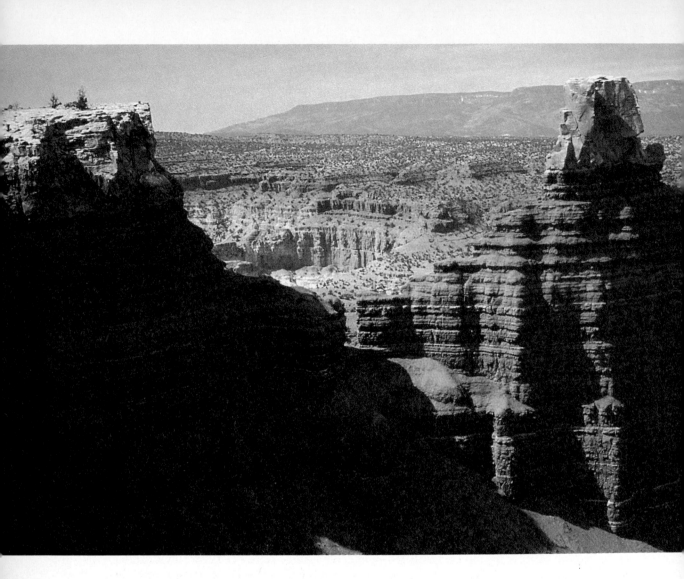

Other geologists followed, including C. E. Dutton, who looked down on Capitol Reef and described the Waterpocket Fold.

At the Grand Wash I observed another kind of history. Climbing a steep and strenuous trail to the high cliffs, I came to Cassidy Arch, named for Butch Cassidy, the outlaw, who may have used the area as a hiding place. If so, he certainly knew how to pick his out-of-the-way spots.

In 1937, a scenic spur of this huge monocline was proclaimed Capitol Reef National Monument. Later enlarged to 241,865 acres that take in the entire Waterpocket Fold running north to south and striking downward west to east, the area was made a national park in 1971. It presents a complete geological story, enhanced by its isolation.

The main access to the park is via Utah 24, an all-weather road connecting with I-70 on the northeast (near Green River), on the northwest with US 89 (near Salina). Though the road cuts through the northern portion of the park, this area is most enjoyed by hikers and backpackers.

**BACKGROUND.** Before taking to the trails, see a "new" side of the park at the one-room **Old Fruita School House,** the first building restored (in 1984) under a Park Service program for preserving this area's unusual history. Fruita, settled in the 1870s and 1880s, was a farming outpost at the edge of dry desert. Miners, cowboys, outlaws, and explorers found it a welcome oasis in their travels. Park headquarters now occupies the former townsite. Besides the schoolhouse, the restoration program features part of the original orchards, a pioneer dwelling, barn, and smokehouse.

A number of trails, ranging from easy to strenuous, provide opportunities for everyone. Serious distance hikers need to recognize possible problems of lack of water or too much of it. The arid climate makes the park susceptible to long droughts that dry up seeps, springs, and water pockets. Then, a sudden shower may send tons of water hurtling down a narrow canyon. Always check with park rangers on water and weather conditions.

The road entering from the west passes a series of scenic viewpoints—**Chimney Rock, Panorama Point,** and **Goosenecks**—opening on footpaths of varying lengths. Goosenecks Overlooks face the deep zigzag canyon carved by Sulphur Creek. You'll find others en route east, notably **Hickman Bridge** and **Behunin's Cabin.**

Six miles from the park's west boundary, the modern **Visitor Center** features displays of the area's first inhabitants, pre-Columbian Indians of the Basket Maker period, and of the 19th-century Mormon settlers. Check out the bookstore. The orientation program will help prepare you to tour the park's roads and hiking trails. Observe Park Service precautions about flash floods: never park in a shallow lowland area or enter a gorge while it's raining.

On this route **Grand Wash** affords a fairly easy hike of 2¼ miles along the bottom of the wash. You'll pass between sheer canyon walls displaying unusual rock formations. There is another trail, more strenuous, climbing steeply to the high cliffs and **Cassidy Arch.** Four miles south a spur road leads to **Capitol Gorge,** passing thousands of "solution pockets" (or potholes) carved by wind and water, and the start of a hiking trail to the base of the **Golden Throne,** a massive butte providing spectacular views over the entire canyon. Inside the gorge you'll find Indian petroglyphs, names of pioneers carved into the rock, and enormous natural water tanks.

For years Grand Wash and Capitol Gorge were the most popular attractions of the national monument, but there are many more accessible now, particularly for those with four-wheel-drive or high-clearance vehicles. **Cathedral Valley** is one such section, a good day's trip from the Visitor Center. Rock formations bear such names as Temple of the Sun, Temple of the Moon, Gypsum Sinkhole, and Glass Mountain. Going north into Cathedral Valley, it is first necessary to pass through the **Valley of Decision,** a narrow gap where a driver must choose whether to proceed or, in the face of clouds and threatening skies, turn back. The roads into Cathedral Valley are unpaved, and travel can be difficult, or impossible, if rain does occur. But it may well be worth it for the chance to see and photograph the sandstone buttes against the background of towering Thousand Lake Mountain. Check at the Visitor Center for latest information on road conditions.

The **Waterpocket Fold** derives the first part of its name from the shallow depressions that sometimes collect rainwater and hold it for long periods as a boon to human and animal alike. **Burr Trail,** a 66-mile old cattledrive route, is the only way to go east-west across the fold in the southern end of the park; the first 29 miles, from the town of Boulder, have been smoothed and widened—the rest of the road is usually suitable for auto traffic but not recommended for heavy trailers. Before entering the park, you'll pass through a 30-mile stretch of public domain land and find plenty of spectacular sandstone country, everything from near-white buff to deep red. From the top of Burr Trail, you come to the junction with **Muley Twist Canyon,** running north and south. North are several arches, accessible by jeep or foot traffic, while to the south you will find choice wilderness backpacking country.

**ACCOMMODATIONS.** Besides the park campground, western-style lodgings are close at hand at Torrey, and 19 miles west at Bicknell.

**Rim Rock Resort Ranch,** Torrey, UT 84775. Two miles west of the park boundary. Facilities for trailers. Offers four-wheel drive tours through portions of the park. 801/425-3843 or 800/243-0786. M.

**Capitol Reef Inn and Cafe,** Torrey, UT 84775. Small and satisfying, a winner with views from the Kiva. 801/425-3271. M.

**CAMPING.** Capitol Reef's campground is a mile south of Utah 24. It has campsites, water, and toilets, plus pump station, and is open all year for 14-day stays.

**SEASONS.** Summer daytime temperatures at the Visitor Center (elevation 5,418 feet) are in the 80s and 90s; nights are generally cool. spring and autumn are mild, with cold weather lasting from mid-December through February. An abundance of insects and birds brings new life to spring. In the lowlands of Cathedral Valley, desert plants turn glorious shades of red and gold in autumn.

**NEARBY.** At Boulder, on the site of an Indian ruin dating back nearly 1,000 years, **Anasazi State Park** gives an introduction to the Anasazi—the Ancient Ones—who roamed the Southwest. **Calf Creek Recreation Area,** between Boulder and Escalante, run by the Bureau of Land Management, provides good camping facilities and a 5½-mile round-trip scenic trail to Calf Creek Falls. **Escalante Canyon,** portions of which are accessible by car or jeep, is explored best on backpack trips of two to four days. Escalante country, wild and beautiful, combines deep, narrow canyons, river-cut cliffs, natural bridges, hanging gardens, and waterfalls—one of the finest unprotected wilderness areas in America. Best months for hiking the canyons are April, May, September, and October. In the **Henry Mountains,** rising to more than 11,000 feet on the east side of the Waterpocket Fold, the Bureau of Land Management has developed four recreation sites with access to hiking.

**FOR FURTHER INFORMATION.** Write Superintendent, Capitol Reef National Park, Torrey, Utah 84775. 801/425-3791.

# CARLSBAD CAVERNS NATIONAL PARK

## NEW MEXICO

### ESTABLISHED 1930

I WOULD NEVER have expected (if I hadn't known what was coming) to find such a display beneath the foothills of the tawny Guadalupe Mountains in southern New Mexico, a few miles north of the Texas border. Aboveground, desertlike flatlands and mountains swept away to remote horizons. Below, however, a whole new world would unfold.

Although other cave systems are known to be deeper and a few have more miles of surveyed passageway, none surpasses Carlsbad in the immensity of its chambers. The famous Big Room is considered the largest underground room in the world.

I found that immensity is not Carlsbad's only distinguishing quality. The formations of limestone are of endless variety and beauty. Some of the inverted spires known as stalactites are shaped like fragile chandeliers. Stalagmites grow from the floor like massive domes or frozen waterfalls of stone. In some cases, stalagmites and stalactites are joined, forming monumental columns and pillars. Yet alongside may be densely clustered growths called helictites, phenomenal for their delicate appearance.

The limestones in the caverns are very old. They formed about 200 million years ago, during the Permian period, from a reef bordering an inland sea. In a process that began less than 60 million years ago, these caverns were hollowed out by underground water slowly dissolving its way through cracks in the earth. In more recent times, the inside water has drained away and another stage of formation has begun. Slowly and carefully, nature builds anew on drops of rain and snow seeping down from the surface. Each drop carries a tiny amount of dissolved limestone. The water passes on, leaving its cargo of minute increments to cavern formations.

During the 1880s ranchers and settlers of New Mexico referred to the cavern as Bat Cave. They were content to let the bats have it as their special place. Soon after, however, the deposits of bat guano attracted attention. Within a few years thousands of tons were extracted by a mining company. Early in this century a local boy, James Larkin White, went exploring, armed only with a kerosene lamp. His reports on the marvels found in the cave attracted the interest of others, notably Robert Holley of the General Land Office and Dr. Willis T. Lee of

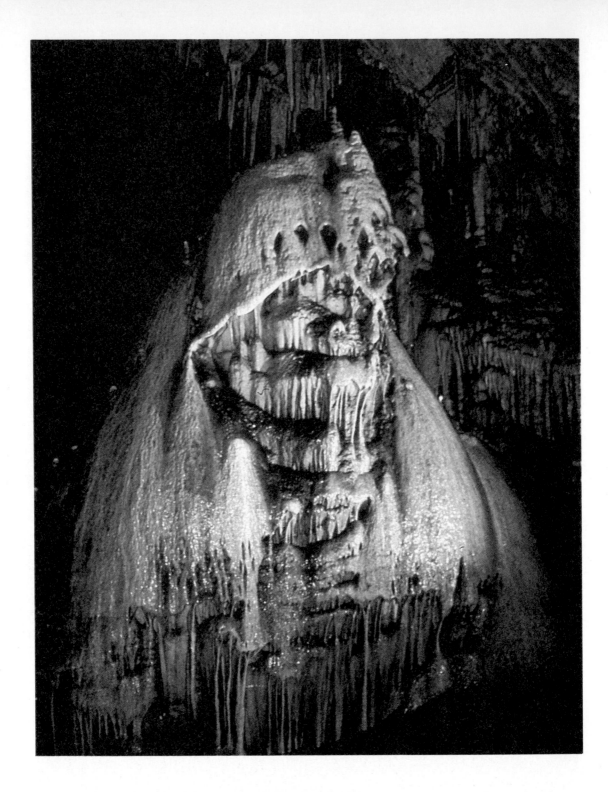

the United States Geological Survey. On October 25, 1923, President Calvin Coolidge proclaimed Carlsbad Cave a national monument, embracing 719 acres.

With national publicity, Carlsbad became famous. Visitors thronged to this remote attraction, even though (in those pre-elevator days) entrance to it was via a miner's bucket lowered by windlass almost 200 feet to the cavern floor. Carlsbad remained a national monument for only seven years. In 1930, a bill to make it a national park passed Congress without opposition and was approved by President Herbert Hoover.

More than 70 caverns lie within the 46,753-acre park, but development has been limited to the largest and most easily accessible of these, the mighty Carlsbad Cavern, in which the famous Big Room has a ceiling as high as a 60-story building and a floor space large enough for 14 football fields.

## THE PRACTICAL GUIDE

You can stop off to view the cave and the aboveground environment in half a day with ease. During most of the year, you may enter at any time during operating hours to spend as long, or as short, a period as you wish on self-guided trips underground. Ask one of the rangers for advice. A nominal fee is charged for entry into the cavern.

Two traditional trips are available. The long one requires approximately three hours with 3 miles of walking, starting with a relatively steep descent down switchback trails to a depth of 829 feet. The shorter tour requires about one hour and covers 1¼ miles of mostly level trail in the Big Room, 750 feet below. It begins at the Visitor Center; descent is by elevator. Visitors in wheelchairs can travel into the Big Room.

From early June through Labor Day, the caverns are open 7:30 A.M. to 6 P.M. During the rest of the year hours are from 8:30 A.M. to 3:30 P.M.

Guided trips are conducted four times daily during portions of December, January, and February.

BACKGROUND. The **Visitor Center** lies at the end of the 7-mile drive from the park entrance. Stop here first to see the displays on the history of the caverns. You'll find a restaurant at the Visitor Center; lunches and refreshments are also available when you reach the Big Room underground.

The **cave walk** begins at the natural entrance, through an arch 90 feet wide and 40 feet high in its greatest dimensions. National Park Service rangers are in charge. They will probably call attention to the infrared detection system; it sounds an alarm if you try to touch limestone formations or wander off the trail. The caverns' temperature remains at 56 degrees Fahrenheit throughout the year; carry a sweater or wrap. The trail extends a mile downward through the main corridor, with high ceilings and large passages, through the **Green Lake Room,** named for a small green pool, into the **King's Palace,** which many visitors consider the most ornate of all chambers. Electric illumination reveals the circular form of the palace and its curtains of glittering cave onyx. The trail leads through a series of brilliantly scenic rooms. The **Queen's Chamber** is adorned with formations so translucent that a light placed behind them brings out faint tints of pink and rose.

The **Papoose Room** is a beautiful little chamber, its low ceiling gleaming with stalactites. All of these are only a prelude to the **Big**

Room. After a luncheon stop and rest, the walk continues to the vast chamber where the ceiling arches 255 feet overhead. One formation poised over the path is aptly named Sword of Damocles. It is followed by totem poles, snowbanked forests, the celebrated Rock of Ages in a dark central alcove, and the Giant Dome. All trips end with a welcome elevator ride to the Visitor Center at the surface.

New Cave, a cave in another area of the park, was opened to the public in 1974. Guided lantern tours, limited to 25 persons, are conducted through this large, undeveloped cave. Reservations are required for the challenging New Cave trips, scheduled daily during summer and weekends only in winter. New Cave is accessible only by walking up a steep ½-mile primitive trail from the mouth of Slaughter Canyon. The cave was discovered in 1937 by a goat herder, Tom Tucker, searching for lost animals. It was used in 1950 as the setting for the film *King Solomon's Mines.*

Bat flights can be observed every evening from May through October, as bats spiral outward for their nightlong feeding on insects in the surrounding valleys. Despite age-old superstitions, the bats of Carlsbad Caverns reveal themselves to be fascinating creatures: alert, great divers and flyers, and useful to people by feeding on destructive insects. Once numbering 7 to 8 million but now only about half a million, they spend the day hanging head downward in dense clusters from the walls and ceilings. At night they zoom out, 5,000 a minute, on the trail of moths and other insects. A park naturalist explains the bat flight each evening at the cave entrance, just before the flight begins at sunset.

Aboveground the surface of the national park conserves an attractive display of semi-arid vegetation and wildlife. Mule deer are frequently seen from the park road in the morning and evening. Fawns of the mule deer arrive into the world in late June and early July. Lizards of many kinds perch on top of rocks while sunning themselves and watching for food or enemies. Stroll along the self-guiding nature trails, if only to learn the identifying names of cacti and other plants that clothe the desert of the Southwest.

Guided nature walks are conducted over the **Oak Springs Trail.** An observation tower atop the Visitor Center provides the best view of the vast Delaware Basin. On a clear day you can see Guadalupe Peak, highest point in Texas.

Off-trail hiking and backpacking opportunities are plentiful. Elevations range from 3,600 feet to 6,300 feet atop Guadalupe Ridge at the park's western boundary. If you want to hike the backcountry, register first at the Visitor Center. Trails are poorly defined but can be followed with a topographic map. There is no water available in the backcountry, so don't plan a trip without adequate preparation.

**PHOTOGRAPHY.** You will probably do most of your shooting in the Big Room. It will be helpful to learn in advance the equipment and exposures to use below; also to identify the principal features, such as Hall of the Giants, Giant Dome, Temple of the Sun and Rock of Ages. Don't overlook the four scenic rooms on the first part of the long trip. Photos may be taken at will, the only restriction being that visitors are not permitted to leave the paved trails.

**WITHOUT A CAR.** T.N.M. & O. coaches make a round trip daily to Whites City, at the park entrance, from El Paso, Texas, and from Carlsbad, New Mexico. Bus service is available from Whites City to the park Visitor Center four times daily.

**ACCOMMODATIONS.** There are no overnight facilities in the park; however, there is a nursery for children too young to undertake the cavern tour. Families traveling with pets will be pleased to find kennels available at the park. Motels, hotels and campgrounds are located in Whites City, near the park entrance, and in Carlsbad, 27 miles from the park. The Living Desert State Park, an unusual indoor/outdoor museum, is in Carlsbad.

**Best Western Cavern Inn,** Whites City, NM 88268. Virtually at the entrance to the national park, with heated pool, steambaths, and playground. 505/785-2291. M.

**Carlsbad Inn,** Carlsbad, NM 88220. Pool. Family rates. 505/887-3541. M.

**Motel 6,** Carlsbad, NM 88220. Pool. 505/885-8807. L.

**CAMPING.** Five overnight private campgrounds with full facilities are located in Carlsbad.

**SEASONS.** The park is open every day of the year except Christmas Day. Winter temperatures are mild, snow and ice rare. Spring and fall are excellent times to visit, when desert flowers bloom. Summer days are hot, but the cool caverns provide welcome relief, and during the evening temperatures drop.

**NEARBY.** Tie in a visit to **Guadalupe Mountains National Park** in Texas for good hiking and surprising mountain vistas.

**FOR FURTHER INFORMATION.** Write Superintendent, Carlsbad Caverns National Park, 3225 National Parks Highway, Carlsbad, NM 88220. 505/885-8884.

# CHANNEL ISLANDS NATIONAL PARK

## CALIFORNIA

ESTABLISHED 1980

I'VE BEEN to the Channel Islands twice, marveling every minute at this natural wonderland so close to the Southern California megalopolis. The rocky beaches and outcrops provide important breeding and resting areas for sea birds. The islands are a stronghold for seals and sea lions, including the only breeding colony of northern fur seals south of Alaska. Waters around the islands are on major migration routes of whale species—including not only the familiar gray whale, but the blue whale, the world's largest mammal.

It didn't take me long on arrival to determine why the Channel Islands have been left largely to their own. Wind and fog are common, storms likely. But weather creates a mood to match the raucous cries of the sea lions and landscape of untamed seas.

Between Point Conception and the Mexican border, off the coast of California, the eight Channel Islands lie in two groups, 10 to 70 miles from the mainland. The park consists of five of them, plus 125,000 acres of surrounding submerged land and water. The northern quartet of islands, all in the park, was once an extension of the Santa Monica Mountains, broken away by the sea in geologic history. The islands were discovered by the intrepid Juan Rodriguez Cabrillo in 1542, when they were still inhabited by the seafaring Chumash Indians.

Rocky beaches teemed with fur seals, sea lions, and elephant seals, and the offshore kelp beds with sea otters. The cliffs and beaches were dense with birds, including colonies of auklets, cormorants, murrelets, and pelicans. Then the Spanish began taking eggs and seal meat. They were followed by the Russians in their massive quest for fur, and ultimately by the Americans, who came to exploit whatever fur sources remained and to introduce cattle, sheep, and hogs.

Of the southern Channel Islands, offshore between Los Angeles and San Diego, San Nicolas and San Clemente have been administered by the U.S. Navy as bombing-range and missile-tracking stations. Santa Catalina, privately owned, is developed as a well-known resort and ranch, presently accessible to the public through the Santa Catalina Island Conservancy and Los Angeles County Department of Parks and Recreation.

Since 1938 two of the islands, Anacapa and Santa Barbara, with their cliffs, beaches, mountains, and canyons, have been protected as a national monument. With the 1969 oil spill off the coast of Santa Barbara, concern arose for these and the other islands and the waters around them. Consequently San Miguel, the westernmost island (administered by the navy), was added to the monument in 1976. And in 1980 the new national park was established, with provisions for acquiring Santa Rosa and a portion of Santa Cruz.

The islands continue to become more accessible and their special values better known and understood. Geologists are intrigued by the earthquake faults, freshwater springs, mountain ranges and valleys, as well as the varieties of rock. It is also a treasure of flora, with more than 600 plant species, including some that grow nowhere else in the world.

Archaeological values are high on all the islands. Midden and village sites of the Chumash people on Santa Rosa and San Miguel are especially significant because of their antiquity and abundance. Charred remains of dwarf mammoth associated with island sites have tentatively been dated at about 40,000 years old, indicating one of the earliest evidences of people in North America.

I came away with a delightful memento purchased at the park Visitor Center, an "audio postcard," a tape with the sounds of birds and gulls, of pinnipeds, and of waves in the intertidal zone. Not as good as the real thing, but it helps to remember a choice place in the sea around us.

## THE PRACTICAL GUIDE

A stop at the park Visitor Center is worthwhile. Follow the signs to the end of the harbor in Ventura. Exhibits and slide shows furnish an introduction to the islands. Island Packer Cruises (1867 Spinnaker Dr., Ventura, CA 93001; phone 805/642-1393), located adjacent to park headquarters, provides tours to Anacapa Island and transportation to Santa Barbara Island, most frequently June to September, with special whale-watching trips in winter. Two weekends a month Island Packers dispatches a 35-passenger boat for a daylong trip to the century-old Scorpion Ranch at the east end of Santa Cruz Island, 23 miles off the coast. Bring your own lunch and drinking water and dress warmly.

Transportation, on an irregular basis and by charter, is available from other ports. For those traveling in personal boats, be warned that Santa Barbara Channel is subject to afternoon rising sea and high wind. Anchoring at either Santa Barbara or Anacapa can be hazardous, and you need a skiff or small boat to go ashore. Only expert boaters should try to make it to San Miguel Island, which is usually subject to rough conditions. You are well advised to visit park headquarters first, at the Ventura Marina.

BACKGROUND. Closest to the mainland (about 11 miles south of Oxnard) and most accessible is **Anacapa Island,** really composed of three separate islets covering a total of 700 acres. Best anchorages include East Fish Camp and Frenchy's Cove (the latter named for "Frenchy" LeDreau, who lived

peaceably in a shack on the island from 1928 to 1956). The National Park Service utilizes a cluster of old Coast Guard buildings, where personnel were stationed until 1969 to operate the lighthouse and horn. East Island Campground has fireplaces and tables, but you must bring your own water and fuel. Campground reservations are required; they may be obtained by contacting park headquarters (or call 805/644-8262). Though beaches on the island are few, cliffs rise 250 feet above the sea. You'll see many birds, including Brandt's cormorants, double-crested cormorants, gulls, and oystercatchers. West Anacapa has been set aside as a sanctuary for brown pelicans, a species rebounding from the brink of extinction—landings are prohibited. Following the 1½-mile nature trail on East Island, you will pass unusual plants and animals as well as spectacular scenery, 150 feet above the waterline. On land, the giant coreopsis, a striking treelike sunflower, grows in dense stands, producing yellow flowers in early spring.

**Santa Barbara,** the smallest island, lies 38 miles west of San Pedro Harbor in Los Angeles. It takes a steep climb of more than 100 feet from Landing Cove to the small primitive camping area. Though vegetation has suffered due to past grazing, because of Santa Barbara's isolation sea mammals abound—sea lions along the rocky south shore, harbor seals and bull elephant seals weighing up to 8,000 pounds.

**San Miguel,** westernmost island, and little **Prince Island** cover a little less than 10,000 acres. Fog and wind are common. In fact, wind-driven sand covers much of the island, with caliche forests in the dunes. There are more species of pinnipeds found on San Miguel than in any other single location in the world. Mating, giving birth, and/or hauling out are California sea lions, northern elephant seals, Steller sea lions, harbor seals, northern fur seals, and Guadalupe fur seals. These furred mammals once were found in great numbers along the mainland coast, but today breed and pup almost exclusively in the Channel Islands. Access to San Miguel is by permit only; check at park headquarters. One-day trips, camping trips, and two-day excursions landing on both San Miguel and Santa Rosa are available.

**Santa Cruz,** the largest island, covers 60,500 acres with peaks over 2,000 feet, rugged slopes and steep shoreline. A large part of the island is administered by the Nature Conservancy, which welcomes a certain degree of public use. Check with them at 213 Stearns Wharf, Santa Barbara, CA 93101, about naturalist-led day trips to Pelican Bay. Island Packers can arrange for stays at refurbished but simple Smuggler's Cove Ranch at the east end of Santa Cruz. **Santa Rosa,** covering 53,000 acres, is still worked as a cattle ranch. Visitors can camp on Santa Rosa or explore the island on day trips. Rangers lead trips to significant points on the island.

**DIVING AND FISHING.** With caves, coves, and shipwrecks, the Channel Islands offer some of the best diving off the West Coast. Divers also like to bring back abalone, lobster, and scallops. Rockfish, perch, and sheepshead are among major targets for anglers. Special restrictions do apply. Check with park headquarters.

**ACCOMMODATIONS.** In addition to the island accommodations listed below, excellent motels in a wide range are located at Ventura, Santa Barbara, and nearby communities.

**Christy Guest Ranch,** Channel Island Adventures, 305 Durely Ave., Camarillo, CA 93010. Rustic, renovated ranch house and tents at Christy Beach on Santa Cruz Island are accessible on 20-minute flight from Camarillo. Packages include airfare, meals, and four-wheel drive land excursions. 805/987-1678.

**Smuggler's Cove Ranch,** Island Packers Co., 1867 Spinnaker Dr., Ventura, CA 93001. Bed down in a recently refurbished historic adobe at the east end of Santa Cruz Island. Solar panels provide electricity for hot water and showers. Bring your own bedding and food. 805/642-1393 or 800/243-0786.

**CAMPING.** Camping is available on Anacapa and Santa Barbara islands. Many park visitors stay on their own boats.

**NEARBY.** For camping near park headquarters, try **Emma Wood State Beach,** 3 miles north of Ventura on US 101, and **McGrath State Beach,** 3 miles south on Harbor Boulevard. You can learn a lot about the Channel Islands at the **Santa Barbara Museum of Natural History,** which displays a replica of a Chumash dugout canoe and charred dwarf mammoth taken from Santa Rosa.

**FOR FURTHER INFORMATION.** Write Superintendent, Channel Islands National Park, 1901 Spinnaker Dr., Ventura, CA 93001. 805/658-5700.

# CRATER LAKE NATIONAL PARK

OREGON

ESTABLISHED 1902

I HAD HIKED the 2½ miles on fairly gentle grade to the fire tower at the summit of Mount Scott. It was the highest point in the park, 8,926 feet, almost 2,800 feet above Crater Lake, the jewel of southern Oregon. The color of the lake was the deepest, most brilliant blue—resulting from the reflection of sunlight on waters more than 1,900 feet deep. I was struck also by the setting, the green Cascadian forest of pines, fir, and hemlock, fitting to the jewel.

It was a clear day, and to the south, 100 miles distant, I saw the great snowy cone of Mount Shasta, 14,000 feet high. It made me think of what Crater Lake was like—in the time before the lake.

It was only yesterday, as time beyond our own time is measured, 10,000 years ago, when Mount Mazama, a 12,000-foot volcanic peak, rose above the green crest of the Cascades, along with her neighbors, mounts Shasta, Adams, Hood, St. Helens, Rainier and Baker—all mighty sentinels of the Northwest range. Then about 6,840 years ago Mazama erupted with violence.

The mountaintop collapsed, forming an immense crater 20 square miles in area, surrounded by towering walls. This masterpiece of nature's creation is known as a caldera. Now I could take in the entire lake, cradled in the extinct volcano, at one time from the rim of lava cliffs, a spectacle hard to match.

This scenic wonder apparently was discovered in 1853 by John Wesley Hillman, one of a party of miners searching for the Lost Cabin Mine near the headwaters of the Rogue River. He and his friends voted to name it Deep Blue Lake, but the discovery was not made public for 31 years. The first official exploration was conducted in 1883 by Dr. J. S. Diller, a geologist, who conducted a sounding of the lake and recorded its depth at 2,008 feet. A century later, scientists have still found surprises in the depths, such as mats of bacteria and lake-bottom hot spots, which may indicate ongoing geothermal activity.

William Gladstone Steel, a transplanted Kansan, who first saw Crater Lake in 1885, is credited as "Father of the Park." His determined crusade began with a petition to President Grover Cleveland that all lands around Crater Lake be withdrawn from homesteading and other claims; this was granted February 1, 1886. From then on he fought an uphill battle until Congress voted to establish the national park, with an act which President Theodore Roosevelt approved on May 22, 1902. Steel was appointed the second superintendent in 1913. Two years later he presided over the opening of Crater Lake Lodge, which cost about $50,000 to build. In 1995, after three years of rehabilitation costing $50 million the lodge reopened.

At 1,932 feet, Crater is the deepest lake in the United States. In the Western Hemisphere only Great Slave Lake in Canada is deeper. While the lake is the focal point, the 183,180 acres of green meadows and forests inside the park serve as a sanctuary for species of wildlife under harsh attack elsewhere. The badger, coyote, bobcat, and mountain lion are rare but do exist; more common is the beautiful red fox. The yellow-bellied marmot usually can be found in the rockslides. Golden-mantled ground squirrels make their appearance at every parking turnout. I saw California gulls frequently over the lake, even bald eagles and a high-flying golden eagle. Jays and nutcrackers were common along the rim, experts in poaching the tourist circuit. Juncos, chickadees, and nuthatches made good companions on the hiking trails. Each traveler becomes conscious of his or her own favorites.

## THE PRACTICAL GUIDE

Plan enough time at Crater Lake to be there at sunrise, when the calm, mirrorlike water reflects the high peaks with sharp clarity. Late afternoon is a choice time, too, especially to see deer in the meadows.

Approaching from Klamath Falls (57 miles away) via the south entrance, or from Medford (69 miles) via the west entrance, note the action of Annie Creek, Castle Creek, and other streams carving their vertical-wall canyons ever deeper in the channels where glaciers once flowed.

**CRATER LAKE NATIONAL PARK**

0    2    4    6
ONE INCH EQUALS APPROXIMATELY 6.6 MILES

© The H.M GOUSHA Co.    M-9-ZM-874-S

Kerr Notch), are spires and fluted columns formed when loose volcanic fragments solidified around gas and steam vents.

A number of trails lead from the drive to other views. The end of **Discovery Point Trail** is near the spot where the young miner Hillman and his friends first spotted the incredible sight of what he called Deep Blue Lake. **Garfield Peak** is one of the best vantage points, with a clear view of **Wizard Island,** actually a small volcanic cone produced by seething fire within the caldera after destruction of Mount Mazama.

**Pumice Desert,** produced by ancient volcanic action, lies along the north entrance road leading to Diamond Lake (4 miles north) and Bend (92 miles north). The lodgepole pine has gained a precarious foothold on the desert floor in nature's mission of clothing old devastation with a new forest.

**TOUR OPERATOR.** A 2½-hour launch trip around the lake, accompanied by a park naturalist, from the boat landing at the foot of Cleetwood Trail will afford an intimate perspective of the inside of a volcano and its multicolored lava cliffs. The concession-operated launches run from late June through Labor Day, 9 A.M. to 3 P.M. The trail is the only access to the water. It is only 1.1 miles, but allow plenty of time; carry water and limit gear to essentials. It is steep going down, steeper on the return. It is well worth the effort to observe the vistas of Wizard Island and Phantom Ship.

**HIKING TRAILS.** The varied types of trails provide the chance for exercise and intimate contact with nature. More than 100 miles of trail through evergreen forests are open to hikers. The leisurely trail through **Castle Crest Wildflower Garden** presents orchids, violets, columbine, asters, and a host of others, identified by plant labels. A 2½-mile trail from Rim Drive leads to the fire tower at the summit of **Mount Scott,** above Cloudcap. For serious backcountry travel, buy a trail guide at park headquarters or the Visitor Center. Permits (free) are required for overnight stays.

**BACKGROUND.** The **Visitor Center** is conveniently located at Rim Village, between the cafeteria and Crater Lake Lodge. Interpretive displays will answer many questions, and rangers will help to start you right. The broad terrace of **Sinnott Memorial,** outside the exhibit building, is an excellent orientation point, where talks on the geologic origin of the lake are given several times daily.

From the Visitor Center at Rim Village begin **Rim Drive,** a 33.4-mile trip around the lake. At Cleetwood Cove, halfway around the lake, the road merges into one way. From this point all vehicular traffic must travel in a clockwise direction. Buses operate from Klamath Falls in summer, and scenic bus tours around the drive are scheduled daily. **Cloudcap,** among the snowbanks and whitebark pines, provides a sweeping vista that complements the one at Sinnott Memorial. Hikers may want to follow the 2½-mile trail to the fire tower at the summit of Mount Scott. **The Pinnacles,** 6 miles off Rim Drive (from

**CAMPFIRE PROGRAMS.** These are held every evening at Mazama Campground. Indoor campfire programs are conducted in Rim Center building.

**BICYCLING.** Riding is feasible but challenging, with long, steep grades. Rim Drive is narrow, without shoulders; half of it is open to one-way traffic only in a clockwise direction from Cleetwood Cove. Be sure to carry water; Rim Village is the only source along the rim.

**ACCOMMODATIONS.** The historic **Crater Lake Lodge** at Rim Village was refurbished and reopened in summer 1995, definitely more upscale than ever. 503/594-2511. M-H.

**Mazama Village,** Crater Lake Lodge, Box 7, Crater Lake, OR 97604. A new facility operated by Crater Lake Lodge, with 40 motel-type units and camper store, just 7 miles from the lake, adjacent to the park campground. Reservations are strongly advised for the short summer season. 503/594-2511. M.

**Diamond Lake Resort,** Diamond Lake, OR 97731. Located 22 miles from the park, with 40 motel rooms and 40 cabins. 503/793-3333. M.

**Thompson's Bed and Breakfast,** 1420 Wild Plum Court, Klamath Falls, OR 97601. Choice for canoeing and birding on Upper Klamath Lake. 503/882-7938. L.

**Prospect Hostel,** 480 Mill Creek Dr., Prospect, OR 97536. Located 40 miles from Crater Lake, with a unisex dormitory. It provides access to the wild Rogue River. 503/560-3795. L.

**CAMPING.** Two campgrounds in the park operate first-come, first-served. **Lost Creek,** on The Pinnacles spur road from East Rim Drive, has 12 sites for tents only; no fees are charged. It opens in late July. **Mazama Campground,** operated by the park concession (fee charged), has no hookups, but provides fresh water, flush toilets, and dump station. Other campgrounds are in surrounding national forests.

**SEASONS.** Lodge and cabins are open from about June 15 to September 10, and campgrounds from July through September. Weather during the short two-month summer is unpredictable, with warm days and chilly nights. The north entrance is usually closed by snow until late June, and Rim Drive till late July; but the south and west entrances are open all year. From late October through May heavy snowfalls create a glistening attraction, with reflections of high peaks in the mirrorlike water.

**NEARBY.** The **Cascade Mountains** surrounding Crater Lake comprise one of the finest recreation areas of the Northwest. Four miles north of the park, **Diamond Lake** lies within **Umpqua National Forest,** with campgrounds on the east shore and miles of forest trails to **Mount Bailey, Mount Thielsen,** and along the Pacific Crest Trail. **Lake of the Woods** is one of the most attractive areas of Winema National Forest, with good fishing for rainbow trout and camping near the base of Mount McLoughlin. The **Ashland Loop Drive** passes through stands of Douglas fir and ponderosa pine within **Rogue River National Forest.** So does the **Pacific Crest Trail,** running from Washington to the California border. **Ashland** is the scene of the Oregon Shakespearean Festival, mid-July to early September. If driving up from the west coast of California, be sure to stop at **Redwood National Park,** between Orick and Crescent City, California, and at **Oregon Caves National Monument,** a limestone and marble cavern with formations of unusual beauty. If coming from the south, visit **Lava Beds National Monument,** California, a scene of ancient volcanic activity that became a battleground in the Modoc Indian War of 1873.

**FOR FURTHER INFORMATION.** Write Superintendent, Crater Lake National Park, Box 7, Crater Lake, Oregon 97604. 503/594-2211.

# DEATH VALLEY NATIONAL PARK

## CALIFORNIA

### ESTABLISHED 1994

I NEVER SAW anything like those giant golden-white sand dunes until I came to Eureka Valley, but there they were, fully a mile wide, three miles long, and nearly 700 feet high. I can't imagine anything like them anywhere else, at least not in America. Fortunately, the Eureka Dunes are among the key additions that now constitute Death Valley National Park and that make it even more inviting, exciting, and comprehensive than in its previous history as a national monument.

In observing the dunes, canyons and mountain walls, I reminded myself that Death Valley is one of the world's most colorful places. I watched colors and hues change with shifting sunlight across a land with few signs or marks of humankind. Yet Death Valley and environs are famous in western history. Records of Indians go back thousands of years. Death Valley gained its name as an obstacle to '49ers in the California gold rush. Roads were built in the 1880s for "Twenty Mule Teams" hauling borax from desert mines. Later, "Death Valley Scotty" built his celebrated Mediterranean-style castle at the northern boundary.

I can find here more than 600 different species of plants, from the pickleweed, growing at Badwater, well below sea level, to bristlecone pines thousands of years old, on Telescope Peak, above 11,000 feet. No fewer than 21 species of plants are endemic to the valley, while four, possibly five, species of fish are found only here. One of the most unusual sites I've ever seen is the 40-acre hillside called Devil's Hole, the limestone cavern home of the entire population of *Cyprinodon diabolis*, one type of desert pupfish, living in what likely is the most restricted environment of any animal in the world.

In 1933 Death Valley was proclaimed a national monument, covering more than a million acres of some of the hottest, driest desert and the lowest point in the Western Hemisphere, 282 feet below sea level. The additions of 1994, besides Eureka Valley, include Saline Valley, treasure chest of the Great Basin on the northwest border of Death Valley, vast and varied, with a forest of Joshua trees; portions of Panamint Valley, and of the Owlshead Mountains, low, rugged, with stunning views of Death Valley and the Amargosa River; and Greenwater Valley, a jagged range with rock shelters and petroglyphs.

**BACKGROUND.** For Death Valley, along the Nevada border east of Owens Valley, climate is a key factor. Remember this is one of the hottest places on earth, with summer temperatures sometimes reaching 130-plus degrees and little nighttime cooling. A summer visit is definitely *not* recommended. For all its past remoteness, however, the park is readily accessible. One gateway is via Route 127 (off Interstate 15), then on Route 190 at Death Valley Junction (Amargosa). Or take Route 190 off Route 395 through Panamint Springs.

**ACTIVITIES.** Check at Furnace Creek Visitor Center, which features exhibits, slide shows and conducted walks. **Trail trips.** Fine short and long hikes are available in all parts of the park. Among the long trips, a 7-mile trail leads to the top of **Telescope Peak** from Mahogany Flat Campground, at the head of Wildrose Canyon. Start in early morning, allowing six to eight hours. When temperatures top 90 degrees, however, stay in the shade till another day. Carry your hiking boots, plenty of water, and topographic maps for all-day or overnight trips. **By road.** Outstanding views are accessible, including scenic 9-mile Artists Drive, **Zabriskie Point, Titus Canyon,** the **Salt Pools, Badwater, Dante's View,** and **Devil's Golf Course. Bicycles** are available for rental at Furnace Creek.

**Birding and Wildlife.** With its long north-south valley, the park serves as a funnel for migrating birdlife both spring and fall. Despite low average rainfall (1.76 inches per year) and high temperatures, some streams run year-round. You'll be surprised at the birds stopping for a short time at water holes and moist canyons—not simply desert birds, but Canada geese, snow geese, many kinds of ducks, egrets, herons, ibis and sandhill cranes. Keep your eye open for desert bighorn sheep in the rugged mountains, as well as coyote, deer, fox, and badger.

**Scotty's Castle,** one of a kind, handsomely furnished and decorated, was built by a legendary nabob who brought luxury with him to his desert retreat. The admission charge is well worth it.

**CAMPING.** Nine campgrounds in the park range in elevation from sea level (Furnace Creek and Texas Spring) to 7,500 feet and higher (Thorndike and Mahogany Flat).

**ACCOMMODATIONS.** Furnace Creek Inn and Furnace Creek Ranch are both operated by Fred Harvey, Inc. (Death Valley, CA 92328; 800/622-0838 or 619/786-2345). Stovepipe Wells Village has motel-style accommodations and trailer park (Death Valley, CA 92328; phone 619/786-2387). Accommodations near the park are at Beatty, Shoshone, and Trona.

**NEARBY.** If you're going to (or coming from) Las Vegas, take the side road (178 into 372) through scenic **Toiyabe National Forest.**

**SEASONS.** Climate is ideal November through April, when daytime temperatures are mild and only a few winter nights are below freezing. Holidays like Thanksgiving, Christmas and Easter, and Death Valley Encampment (early November) are busy times.

**FOR FURTHER INFORMATION.** Write Superintendent, Death Valley National Park, Death Valley, CA 92328. 619/786-2331.

# DENALI NATIONAL PARK

## ALASKA

ESTABLISHED 1917

EARLY ALEUT INDIANS knew Mount McKinley as *Denali*, "the high one." To others it is simply *the* mountain. However you look at it, Mount McKinley constitutes a massive monument to the forces of nature.

The overpowering feeling is one of largeness and naturalness, which is Alaska's special gift to the nation. "Can one describe such a scene and such an environment to wander about in?" once wrote the master of wilderness, Olaus J. Murie. He could find no words, except to add that for him this region comprised the greatest scenic experience on the North American continent.

When I come to Denali I wish that I had more time to wander in this wonderful national park and preserve of 6 million acres, an immense sanctuary of glaciers, forests, tundra, blue lakes, and wildlife roaming free. But time seems in short supply, despite all the conveniences of the age. I realize the need to concentrate on perception in order to understand and fully appreciate Denali. In early territorial days this was rough, untracked country, testing the skills of sourdough prospectors, hunters, geologists, and naturalists. Those people had the time to take it all in. Even after establishment of the national park in 1917 as a great wilderness reserve, it remained inaccessible. But since 1957, with completion of the Denali Highway, the park is easy to reach from Anchorage and Fairbanks—so easy that the wilderness would be overrun without some measure of control. Instead of allowing private vehicles, the park provides free bus transportation—and that's a blessing.

In 1980 Congress voted to enlarge the park to almost 4,700,000 acres, bordered by a new national preserve of 1,330,000 acres. The addition includes the southern half of the mountain and spectacular peaks of the Kichatna Mountains. Congress also voted to change the name to Denali—from Mount McKinley—National Park, adopting the ancient Indian name for the mountain.

The park terrain rises from about 1,400 feet to 20,320 feet, the highest point on the continent, at the summit of Mount McKinley. There are other major peaks, like Mount Foraker, or "Denali's Wife" (called Sultana by early Indians), at 17,400 feet also taller than anything in the "lower forty-eight"; Mount Silverthrone, 13,220 feet; and Mount Russell, 11,670 feet. Many glaciers, up to 30 and 40 miles long, are still active on these and other mountains inside the park.

One of them, Muldrow Glacier, the largest northward-flowing glacier in Alaska, stretches from the summit of Mount McKinley's twin peaks to within a mile of the park road. The whole landscape is influenced by glaciation of the past and present, with broad, U-shaped valleys, small kettle lakes, old and new moraines.

White and black spruce are the chief evergreens growing in the park, with cottonwood and willow along the streambeds, dwarf birch on the lower mountain slopes, quaking aspen and Alaska birch interspersed with the spruce. Most of the park, however, lies above timberline, which varies from 2,500 to 3,000 feet. The vegetation becomes alpine tundra—lichens, mosses, tough grasses, sedges—a variety of dwarfed, matlike plants capable of surviving in severe climate and also of producing a surprising display of delicate blossoms.

Lichen proves useful in this setting, maybe not immediately to humankind, but as a food source to the wildlife community that humankind protects. Caribou, the most numerous large animal in the park, feeds on such humble plants during its annual stay here, but the concentration of caribou in great herds has not been evident in recent years.

Seen with the naked eye, or even binoculars, the Dall sheep, a species of bighorn, looks like a white speck on the higher slopes, as it safeguards itself by climbing to crags beyond the reach of predators like the wolf. It is fascinating to watch the Dall's short, springy, and muscular jumps when running over the flats. The Dall is obviously unsuited to level terrain, in contrast to its efficiency on the cliffs.

Since the "1910 Sourdough Expedition," Mount McKinley has been successfully climbed by mountaineers from all over the world. Despite technological advances in equipment and conditioning of modern climbers, McKinley remains a difficult challenge. The weather is unpredictable and severe. The mountain has claimed its share of casualties.

Mount McKinley rises nearly 17,000 feet above the surrounding country, and all above 7,000 feet is enveloped by snow and ice—tough for climbers, spectacular for scenic enjoyment. The mountain has two peaks: South Peak, the upper portion, 20,320 feet, and North Peak, 19,470 feet, two miles away. It is so brilliant a landmark that it can be seen on clear days from Anchorage and Fairbanks, when not obscured by low-hanging clouds.

## THE PRACTICAL GUIDE

You'll have 16 to 20 hours of daylight during summer; use them all. Some of the best weather is in early morning, about 3 A.M. Many visitors spend one night as part of an Alaska tour and then depart the next day. However, this great park is worthy of at least two or three days in order to really catch the flavor of the arctic wilderness, wander over the tundra, the vast river bars, and through the spruce forests. Binoculars are essential to observe animals. Insect repellent is advised for anyone planning a hike.

**ACCESS BY CAR.** Arrive via George Parks Highway and Denali Highway, Route 3, extending from Paxson (at Milepost 185.5 on Richardson Highway) to Cantwell (Milepost 209.9 on Parks Highway). The park road extends 90 miles from its connection with Denali Highway, but during summer months private vehicles beyond Savage River check station (Milepost 12.0) are restricted to those people with camping reservations. Once at designated campsites they, and others, must use the free shuttle-bus system. The gravel, curving park road does not lend itself to a heavy volume of traffic, and protection of the environment is an even more important factor. Restricting auto traffic enables visitors to view wildlife, which otherwise would be driven away. Call 800/622-7275 to take advantage of the advance reservation system for three campgrounds and the shuttle system. Up to 25 percent of campsites and seats are set aside for visitors who plan in advance. A $4 service fee is charged per seat and/or campsite, in addition to park admission and user fees for campsites and buses (credit cards accepted). Remaining bus seats and campsites can be reserved in person, up to two days in advance, at the Denali Visitor Center. Shuttle-bus service begins at the Riley Creek Campground and runs all the way to Wonder Lake. During the summer season, shuttle buses operate outbound from Riley Creek from 6 A.M. to 5 P.M. and inbound from Wonder Lake from 8:30 A.M. to 6:20 P.M. Buses drop off and pick up visitors at many points along the highway. Carry your food with you; there is no service beyond the entrance area.

TRAINS, PLANES, BUSES. The Alaska Railroad provides daily service in summer from Fairbanks (four hours) and Anchorage (eight hours). In 1985 Tour Alaska introduced the Midnight Sun Express, restored superdome cars. These are the last two cars of the express train, with a dining room beneath the dome lounge. In summer, planes fly at least twice weekly, connecting Anchorage and Fairbanks with the park airstrip. Buses run on daily schedules and on sightseeing tours.

BACKGROUND. Eielson Visitor Center, 65 miles west of the entrance, is at an elevation of 3,730 feet. Glass-enclosed exhibit rooms face Muldrow Glacier and the towering twin peaks. The displays interpret glacial geology and the mountain-climbing history of the park. The first climbers were sourdoughs impelled by the urge to see the top.

**McKinley Park Station,** gateway to the park, includes a service station, store, campground, hotel, and park headquarters. The mountain becomes visible, on clear days, about 8 miles farther on.

**Teklanika River,** 27 miles from the entrance, typifies glacial rivers flowing north from the Alaska Range over numerous channels and wide gravel bars, creating a braided course. The milky cast derives from glacier-ground rock flour.

**Igloo Canyon** is an excellent locale for animals, particularly Dall sheep. Learn to spot animals by looking for contrasts of color and form in the landscape.

**Sable Pass,** elevation 3,900 feet, is the best place to observe grizzly bears browsing on lush grass or ripping tundra for its succulent roots. Though most common here, bears may be seen anywhere in the park, roaming the spruce forests, the aspen thickets, the bare mountain slopes. A feeding grizzly is not impressive looking, seemingly slow moving, but it can run faster than a horse and demonstrates pride in being called *Ursus arctos*. He's powerful—stay away. The best place to see moose is in the **Savage River area,** though they may appear anywhere along the road. They spend a great deal of time in lakes and ponds searching for summer food and should not be approached closely, either.

At **Highway Pass,** the most breathtaking view of the mountain—to the snow plume of the **South Peak**—bursts upon the motorist coming over the rise. For the rest of the way you are almost constantly in view of the peaks, always changing, but always dominating the landscape. Caribou are common from this pass westward.

Wildflowers spread across the fields of **Stony Hill Overlook** in June and early July—which here means springtime. These include the state flower, forget-me-not, as well as arctic poppy, densely carpeted white dryas, white and pink pyrolas, and heather. Take time for at least a short walk from the overlook parking lot. Many birds nest on the surrounding tundra. A search with binoculars may reveal a wildlife spectacle: grizzlies on nearby hillsides, caribou feeding on the lowlands, a wolf on a hunting trail.

You can photograph and dream over reflections of the mountain at **Wonder Lake.** It was near here that Olaus Murie, while exploring with another distinguished biologist, his brother, Adolph, discovered his "greatest scene." He wrote: "We looked before us, across the wide valley to the white Denali and the snowy Alaska Range rising high on the horizon. To be on that ridgetop, to look at what was before us!"

The southern side of the 1980 **park addition** is generally accessible from Parks Highway, which runs between Fairbanks and Anchorage. Scattered motel and commercial campground accommodations are located along the way, with a fine campground available at Byers Lake in **Denali State Park.** Access to the northern portion is possible by charter flights to **Lake Minchumina.** Backpacking and wilderness camping opportunities are plentiful for those who can take care of themselves. Be sure to get a backcountry-use permit.

**TO SEE THE MOUNTAIN.** The view of Mount McKinley is one of the world's truly spectacular sights, but thick clouds frequently obscure it from visitors. The mountain can be seen clearly fairly often in the early morning and late evening hours, but seldom at noon. Studies over a two-year period indicate that the view is best during the morning hours, and that August is by far the best month.

**HIKING AND BACKPACKING.** Register at the Riley Creek Information Center and obtain a backcountry-use permit for off-highway camping. No fires permitted; use gas stoves. Always check with the information center or with a ranger for current information on wilderness travel. Certain areas may be restricted due to critical wildlife habitat. Cross-country travel is complicated by heavy patches of brush, tundra, marshes, and streams.

**FISHING.** Licenses are not required. Despite the wide renown of Alaska's fishing streams fishing in the park is poor because most rivers are silty and ponds are shallow. Count on far better luck at the Brooks Camp in Katmai National Park.

**MOUNTAINEERING.** Mount McKinley is climbed by many parties each summer. Most attempts are made from the south side of the mountain with Talkeetna as the jump-off. Park personnel will assist in briefing all mountaineering parties wishing to climb McKinley or other peaks within the park; in fact, regulations require advance registration with the superintendent. Mountain Trip (907/345-6499) offers guided climbs and climbing seminars.

**Cathedral Spires** comprise a fantastic landmark of the new addition, visible from the air. They are a challenge to the most indomitable of mountain climbers. Kichatna Spire, the highest of the Cathedrals (8,985 feet) was first climbed only as recently as 1966. The spires are rated as North America's greatest single stand of vertical rock.

**TOUR OPERATORS.** The Denali National Park Hotel runs bus tours daily during summer as far as the Toklat River, starting at 4 A.M., 6 A.M., and 3 P.M. A box lunch is furnished. The driver stops briefly for good views of wildlife and accommodates photographers as much as the schedule permits before returning to make connections with the train to Anchorage.

**PHOTOGRAPHY.** Long hours of daylight provide plenty of time for picture taking. Days are often cloudy, obscuring the mountain, but cloudy days can be excellent for wildflower photography. Try to interpret the three life-communities of the park: northern forest (or taiga), tundra, and perennial snowfield.

Professional wildlife photographers prefer late summer and early fall, when many animals are at their prime in appearance. In summer, large mammals generally wear scruffy, matted coats; moose and caribou have only partially formed antlers.

**ACCOMMODATIONS.** In addition to several facilities in the park, there are accommodations just outside the park on the George Parks Highway and in the communities of Cantwell and Healy. A recreational vehicle campground in Healy offers hookups, groceries, showers, and coin laundry. Write Denali Park Central Reservations, Box 200984, Anchorage, AK 99520.

**Harper Lodge,** McKinley Park, AK 99755. A large hotel (150 rooms) a mile from the park entrance, opened in 1987 by Princess Tours, with Jacuzzi-equipped deluxe rooms. 800/426-0442. H.

**Denali National Park Hotel,** ARA/Outdoor World, Ltd., McKinley Park, AK 99755. Located near the entrance station; naturalist-guided walks and lectures are given daily in the area. The breakfast of sourdough hotcakes, eggs, and bacon will soften the blow of rising at 2 or 3 A.M. Open late May to mid-September. 907/683-2215. (Winter, 825 W. 8th Ave., Anchorage, AK 99501; 907/278-1122.) M to H.

**Camp Denali,** Box 67, McKinley Park, AK 99755. A wilderness retreat with tent cabins equipped for housekeeping and rustic chalet cabins with family-style meals in the dining room. Classic views of Denali above Wonder Lake. Sourdough Vacation packages include guided day hikes, canoeing and optional campouts. Open June to mid-September. 907/683-2290. (Winter, Box 216, Cornish, NH 03746; 603/675-2248.) M to H.

**North Face Lodge,** c/o Camp Denali, Box 67, McKinley Park, AK 99755. Reached by the park road to Wonder Lake and Kantishna, it offers wilderness stays of 1 to 2 days early June to early September. 907/683-2265. M to H.

**McKinley Wilderness Lodge,** McKinley Park, AK 99755. Motel units, cabins, RV parking, and dining room at Milepost 224 on the Parks Highway, open mid-May to mid-September. 907/683-2277. M.

**CAMPING.** The park now takes reservations by phone for about 25 percent of its campsites and round-trip seating on park shuttles. A reservation fee is charged, but it's worth it. Call 800/622-PARK. The remainder of spaces are held for walk-in two-day advance reservations at the visitor center. Six campgrounds are well spaced along the park road; one is off the highway by trail. The closest to the McKinley railroad station is **Morino** (⅛ mile by trail), then **Riley Creek** (1½ miles), **Savage River** (12 miles), **Sanctuary River** (22 miles), **Teklanika** (29 miles), **Igloo** (33 miles), and

**Wonder Lake** (84 miles). Motorists may drive in their own vehicles without a permit to Riley Creek (100 sites) and to Savage River (29 sites). The controlled-access areas are beyond the Savage River Bridge: Sanctuary River (7 sites), Teklanika (50 sites), Igloo (7 tent sites), and Wonder Lake (20 tent sites).

Permits to camp beyond the Savage River Bridge are available at the Riley Creek Information Center. All stays are limited to 14 days. The park requires permits for backcountry use.

Warm clothing, waterproof shelter, and mosquito repellent are important. Firewood can be purchased in the park.

**SEASONS.** Spring arrives late, in June and early July, with wildflowers, nesting birds, 24 hours of daylight—and mosquitoes. After August 15, you have a share of two seasons. The atmosphere is crisp and clear; animals appear in their glossy winter coats, and mosquitoes are gone. Leaves of the very few hardwood trees turn gold and orange, while the alpine tundra turns into a vast Persian carpet of gold, red-orange, purple, brown, and green. Nights at this season are dark and invariably chilly. Summers are moderately warm, wet, cloudy. Come prepared with clothing for temperatures from freezing to 80 degrees Fahrenheit. For comfort, dress in layers.

The park road and public facilities are usually open from mid-May to mid-September. Morino and Riley Creek campgrounds are open all year.

Though most public facilities are closed in winter, the park is open to dog mushing, ski touring, and snowshoeing. Trails are established through much of the park, but check at headquarters for weather and trail conditions.

**RECOMMENDED READING.** *Two in the Far North,* by Margaret Murie (Edmunds, WA: Alaska Northwest) and *Denali: The Story Behind the Scenery,* by Steve Buskirk (Las Vegas: KC Publications).

**FOR FURTHER INFORMATION.** Write Superintendent, Denali National Park, Box 9, McKinley Park, AK 99755. 907/683-2294.

# DRY TORTUGAS NATIONAL PARK

FLORIDA

ESTABLISHED 1992

THE RECEPTION COMMITTEE proved to be everything promised, everything hoped for. I mean that it was made up of birds by the thousands, high flyers, divers, birds clustered in the trees on shore, birds crowded on the beaches. Like others on board, I watched them through binoculars and through the charter boat's telescope, thankful for being in the Dry Tortugas in May, virtually at the height of the nesting season and before tropical storms. The Tortugas, sandy coral keys extending into the Gulf of Mexico beyond the Florida keys, provide nesting and breeding grounds for sea birds—sooty tern, noddy tern, brown pelican, frigate bird, and masked booby—plus resting sites for hundreds of thousands of birds headed for summer nesting across the United States and Canada.

I found the Dry Tortugas definitely off the beaten path. The cluster of seven tiny islands lies seventy miles from Key West, removed from television, telephones, and fresh water. But that does not diminish their importance or appeal. The islands were discovered by Ponce de Leon in 1513, then used as a pirates' hideaway during the colonial period. President Theodore Roosevelt in 1908 declared the area a wildlife refuge in order to protect the birds; in 1935 President Franklin D. Roosevelt declared it a national monument to protect Fort Jefferson, a massive all-masonry fortification, the largest of its kind in the Western world. Late in 1992 Congress voted to reclassify and rename it as a national park to reflect the significance of the least disturbed coral reef system in the United States.

On shore, while taking the self-guided tour of the old fort, I marveled at the brick arches and thick walls extending fifty feet from foundation to crown. Construction began in 1846, with materials brought from Florida, as part of the chain of seacoast defenses strung from Maine to Texas. Fort Jefferson was never really finished, never saw action, but served as a federal military prison during and after the Civil War. The most prominent prisoner, Dr. Samuel Mudd, the physician who set the broken leg of John Wilkes Booth, the assassin of President Lincoln, spent four years at Fort Jefferson; his work in behalf of victims of a yellow fever epidemic earned commutation of his life sentence.

**ACCESS.** Check Key West Chamber of Commerce for information on air taxis (flight time, twenty minutes) and charter boats. Most visitors arrive by seaplane early in the day and return to Key West late afternoon, but they miss the glorious subtropic sunset and sunrise.

**ACCOMMODATIONS.** Camping is allowed at ten sites, equipped with picnic tables and grills. And that's all. There are no amenities, food, motel, or water, except for water fountains and salt-water flush toilets. Private boaters can anchor and camp overnight on the beach. Charter boats provide simple accommodations for about forty-five passengers.

**ACTIVITIES.** Bring snorkel and scuba gear to explore coral reefs and wrecked ships in clear, shallow water; fishing, birding, photography.

**SEASONS.** Between April and September seabirds land by the thousands for nesting; Spring is best.

**FOR REEFWATCHERS.** Make a loop starting south of Miami with Biscayne National Park, Pennekamp State Park, Florida Keys National Marine Sanctuary, then including Buck Island Reef National Monument and Virgin Islands National Park. Get a copy of the *Greenpeace Book of Coral Reefs*, by Sue Wells and Nick Hanna.

**FOR FURTHER INFORMATION.** Write Superintendent, Dry Tortugas National Park, Box 279, Homestead, FL 33030. 305/246-2521.

# EVERGLADES NATIONAL PARK

## FLORIDA

### AUTHORIZED 1934/ESTABLISHED 1947

THE HEART of the Everglades was directly in the path of Hurricane Andrew when it struck Florida in 1992. Damage was extensive, but principally to buildings and facilities. In one sense, the park wilderness weathered the storm better than cities and farms around it. Hurricanes, after all, are not new, and nature has its own way of adjusting to such seeming violence, even benefiting from it. Thus the post-hurricane visitor will see a different park, a landscape in the process of change.

A trip to the Everglades will be an exciting, revealing experience. Look for lessons to be learned. Most park personnel were left homeless; they will have stories of caring and sharing in the midst of hardship. Andrew swept through the center of the park like a tornado 20 to 30 miles wide. In its wake it left a gash of uprooted coastal mangroves, snapped and broken pines, and flattened thick tropical hardwoods. Scientists can only monitor change and speculate the long-term results. Although experts initially expressed grave concern for the park wildlife, days later they reported that bears and panthers had hunkered down or run for cover. Migrating shorebirds, such as willets and avocets, returned. Flocks of ibis and egrets brightened the skies. Herons calmly fed on fish in the sawgrass again. Scientists forecast optimistically that bird populations should not be affected negatively, that woodpeckers, in fact, will prosper from an abundance of bug-infested trees, while large waders, like spoonbills and woodstorks, might well find new nesting trees. Time alone will tell.

When I was in the Everglades in 1991, a little more than a year before Andrew, I saw that the River of Grass was slowly drying and dying, largely because of diversions for agriculture and homes. Dirty water flowing into the park from the north and intrusive non-native plants threatened to undermine and radically alter the Everglades as they have been known and loved. The aftermath of Hurricane Andrew provides a choice opportunity to stop, look, and listen, and to make new plans for the future.

But certainly all Americans have benefited from saving this bit of wonderland at the southern tip of the Florida peninsula. Development in South Florida unfortunately has caused great damage to the Everglades ecosystem. Park interpreters explain to visitors cause and effect and actions now being taken to rescue a refuge for beautiful tropical birdlife found hardly anywhere else on earth.

The Everglades constitute a refuge for humans, too—a place at booming Miami's doorstep to find inspiration from the unimproved works of nature. The Everglades themselves, and some of the birds, reptiles, and mammals, are either rare or cannot be seen elsewhere in the nation. Here are the wood storks (the only storks in the United States), huge birds whose pure white feathers contrast with their jet-black wing tips. Along the palm-fringed shoreline, brown pelicans may be seen gliding or flapping their wings while flying in formation to a distant rendezvous. Over the mangrove swamp inland, yellow-crowned and black-crowned night herons soar over the trees. Elsewhere are the roseate spoonbills, big pink birds with crimson splashes, and the great white herons spreading their immense wings seven feet from tip to tip. Four species of kite can be seen here, three of which nest in the park. Many species of hawk winter here, including some rarely found elsewhere in the East.

These birds and others, colored blue, green, black, yellow, red, and several shades in between, gather by the thousands to build their nests and bring their young into the world. Their refuge in the Everglades, covering 1,506,539 acres, is larger than the state of Delaware.

Long before the European explorers arrived, aboriginal Indians, the Calusa and Tequesta, were attracted to this region by its abundant resources—the great beds of conchs, oysters, and clams. They made their homes on the islands or on the riverbanks and hammocks nearby, utilizing the fish, game, and plant foods around them. The modern Indians—Miccosukees and Seminoles—arrived in Spanish Florida after the American Revolution. Many Creeks of Georgia and Alabama, crowded by the invading white settlers, fled to the Florida peninsula. They were forced continually southward, finally retreating to the Everglades, where deer, fish, and fruit were plentiful. They traded alligator hides, otter skins, and egret plumes with the white settlers.

At the turn of this century the Everglades area was known as the home of many varieties of birds of striking beauty; some, like the egrets, were prized for plumes on women's hats. They were shot on a large scale and even then threatened with extinction. The National Committee of Audubon Societies raised funds in 1902 to engage a warden, Guy Bradley, but he was murdered in 1905. It was a tragedy that gave impetus to both the bird conservation movement and to the preservation of the area.

Sparked by the Florida Federation of Women's Clubs, Royal Palm State Park was established in 1916. Five years later, in 1923, Stephen T. Mather, director of the National Park Service, declared, "There should be an untouched example of the Everglades of Florida established as a national park." The Tropical Everglades National Park Association, headed by Dr. Harold Bailey and Ernest F. Coe, was founded to lead the citizen movement to achieve that goal.

Action, however, was slow, even though in 1934 Congress voted to establish an Everglades National Park, for opponents in the House tacked on a provision that no money be appropriated to purchase land for five years. Fortunately,

Governor Spessard Holland worked with citizen groups to get the money for Florida's share of the land purchase. In 1946 the state legislature provided $2 million for the purchase of private lands in the area, clearing the way for the park's establishment.

Everglades National Park was dedicated December 6, 1947, by President Harry S Truman. Leaders in the effort, besides Coe and Bailey, had been Spessard Holland, who had gone from the governor's chair to the United States Senate, and John D. Pennekamp of the *Miami Herald*. Marjory Stoneman Douglas helped the cause further with her powerful book *The Everglades: River of Grass*.

The true everglades were called by the Indians *Pahay-Okee*, the "grassy waters," or "river of grass," but the park is a many-sided spectacle of unusual plant communities and wildlife. Clusters of trees and dense vegetation in the open glades form islands called hammocks, with hardwood trees that are common in the West Indies, including the mahogany, strangler fig, and coppery-barked gumbo-limbo. In other sections are bald cypress and pine forests of the southern swamps. Hundreds of interesting plants grow from the edge of Florida Bay and the Gulf of Mexico into the wilderness: from graceful, towering royal palms to delicate lilies and ferns. Many of the big trees unfortunately were lost during the 1992 hurricane.

The Everglades teem with life—from fish, crustaceans, and shellfish to snakes, deer, raccoons, and possums. The park is the last major sanctuary of the Florida panther. The lagoons provide a pasture for Florida's unusual, air-breathing, vegetarian sea cow, the manatee. The most celebrated swamp dwellers are the blunt-nosed alligator, who sticks to fresh water, and the rare long-snouted crocodile, who prefers its water salty. The crocodile once ranged as far north as Jacksonville but now is rarely found anywhere but in Florida Bay and the national park. These values make the Everglades worth saving.

Since 1948, however, massive dikes and drainage canals constructed around the park to divert water for the benefit of large-scale agriculture and real estate have severely disturbed the natural balance. The reduced water flow has seriously restricted aquatic and bird life, so steps have been taken to reverse course. Establishment of Big Cypress National Preserve in 1974 helped safeguard the natural flow of fresh water. Then in 1989 Congress voted to acquire and add 108,000 acres to the national park to further improve the water supply. The Florida Panther National Wildlife Refuge, covering almost 25,000 acres, was established in the same year to help a species down to dangerously low numbers.

Farther north, the Corps of Engineers, which once converted the 98-mile-long Kissimmee River into a wide, deep channel, is now working to return the Kissimmee to its original meandering bed. Much of this progress is due to the efforts of former governor, now senator, Bob Graham, who has declared: "By the year 2000 the Everglades will look and function more like they did at the turn of the century than they do today." Learning the lessons of Hurricane Andrew may make this even more likely.

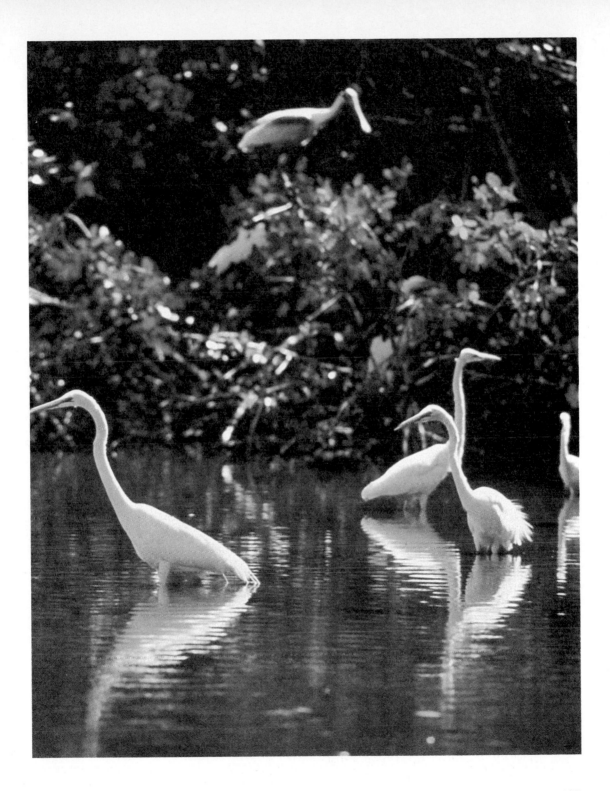

It is possible to get a peek at the Everglades even in a few hours. If you are driving down to Key West, or vacationing in Miami, go through Homestead into the park for at least a little while. Bear in mind that Homestead and neighboring Florida City were flattened by the hurricane, their schools and homes blown apart. The Florida Keys, however, suffered minimal damage. Naples and the Gulf Coast part of the park were left in good shape—when Andrew reached the west coast its winds had weakened.

This is a park of wonderful watery boulevards and byroads for boaters. In fact, the Western Water Gateway at Everglades, southeast of Naples, provides access only by boat. Visitors traveling by boat are well advised to obtain a set of navigational charts.

**BACKGROUND.** Approaching from Homestead, the **Visitor Center** at the main park entrance was very badly battered. Check at the entrance station and temporary visitor center for latest information on park programs and trail conditions. The **Anhinga Trail** has been completely rebuilt. The **Gumbo-Limbo Trail,** a popular half-mile introductory walk that was left an impassable thicket of branches and roots, has been cleared and reopened.

**Flamingo,** 38 miles from the park entrance, at the subtropical tip of the mainland, is the main center, converted from an old fishing village. It was undamaged by the hurricane, which missed the southern half of the park, including Cape Sable and Florida Bay. This is your base for exploratory trips into the wilderness of Whitewater Bay and hundreds of miles of winding mangrove rivers, the channels and keys of Florida Bay, the Gulf area, the mangrove coast, and tropical beaches of Cape Sable. Flamingo features a concession-operated motel, dining room, screened-in pool, housekeeping cabins, and lounge. These facilities were occupied by park personnel, dispossessed from their own homes. Accommodations may be difficult to obtain. The Visitor Center provides a graphic history of the park and serves as a springboard for sightseeing and exploration. Facilities at Flamingo include a 57-slip marina with diesel and gas fuel, tackle, live bait, and general store; canoes and 14-foot skiffs are available for rental. Guides and charter boats are on hand for sportfishing, birdwatching, and photography trips.

**Canoe trails** vary in length, so you can paddle for any length of time from an hour to a week. Check for an update before starting. The five trails are Noble Hammock, Hells Bay, West Lake, Bear Lake, and, longest of all, the Wilderness Waterway. Primitive campsites are located on most trails; be sure to get a backcountry use permit. The Wilderness Waterway is a well-marked 100-mile route between Everglades City and Flamingo through creeks, rivers, and open bays. Backcountry campsites are available along the way, but there is no water.

Study *Guide to the Wilderness Waterway of the Everglades National Park* by William G. Truesdell (University of Miami Press) before your trip.

**Cape Sable** is tucked away on the southernmost point of the continental United States. Experienced canoeists, traveling inland waters, can reach it in four to six hours from Flamingo; motorboats take about 45 minutes. The Cape has beautiful white beaches and desertlike vegetation—yucca, century plants, prickly pear cactus. Obtain a permit and camp at one of the primitive sites.

**TOUR OPERATORS.** Boat tours are offered from Everglades City by a national park concessioner, Sammy Hamilton, a native of the area. From Flamingo the one-hour sunset cruise affords a spectacular view of roosting grounds of thousands of birds in the shallow waters of Florida Bay. The Whitewater Bay cruise, conducted three times daily, is a two-hour excursion among mangroves, with plenty of chances to view birds and wildlife.

The park also offers naturalist-led canoe excursions. Check locally for commercial guide and outfitting services. Canoeists can rent craft or bring their own; you need to provide your own life jackets, food, and water—bring cameras, too, for excellent photo opportunities. North American Canoe Tours can also help with canoe rentals, shuttle service, and guided expeditions; write them at Everglades City, FL 33929, or call 813/695-4656 in season, 203/739-0791 in summer.

**TRAM TOURS.** Depart in winter season from **Flamingo.** They are designed to interpret plant and birdlife of the wilderness area. Early in this century, egrets and spoonbills were slain and whole rookeries destroyed in hunting for plumes for women's hats; at one period these beautiful birds almost disappeared, but now they display their plumage for admiration, not exploitation.

**Shark Valley** open-air tram bus tours originate at a parking area just inside the park entrance, 30 miles west of Miami on the south side of the Tamiami Trail. The trip parallels a canal to the Shark Valley Observation Tower, which affords an excellent view. The two-hour tram tours generally leave every hour on the hour during the winter season and at two-hour intervals during the summer season. The Shark Valley tram service operates year-round; a fee is charged. Reservations are recommended—305/221-8455.

**NATURALIST PROGRAMS.** Included are daily talks and walks and evening campfire programs during the winter season. The Visitor Centers at Flamingo and Parachute Key house displays on natural and human history, from the era of the ancient Indian Mound Builders to the age of the modern bird conservers.

You may also want to contact Wilderness Southeast, a private institute that organizes educational excursions in the Everglades and elsewhere. Write 711 Sandtown Rd., Savannah, GA 31410.

**FISHING.** The waters offshore are famous for sea trout, tarpon, redfish, snapper, and other fish. Fully equipped charter boats run from Flamingo and Everglades. Freshwater fishing with rod and reel requires a Florida fishing license; licenses are also needed for saltwater fishing.

**ACCOMMODATIONS.** Lodgings are available in the park and in the communities of Homestead, Key Largo, and Islamorada. Also look into Florida's state parks—40 of them have camping facilities, and several have vacation cottages at reasonable rates, all located in attractive natural settings. Write for a copy of *Florida State Parks Guide*, Department of Natural Resources, 3900 Commonwealth Blvd., Tallahassee, FL 32303; 904/488-7326.

**Cheeca Lodge,** Box 527, Islamorada, FL 33036. A beachfront complex with lodge rooms and cottages, some with kitchens; pool, tennis, par 3 golf; dining room with ocean view. Under 18 free; family rates. 813/664-4651 and 800/327-2888. M to H.

**Flamingo Lodge, Marina and Outpost,** Box 428, Flamingo, FL 33090-0428. Operated as a park concession by TW Services, Inc., it offers housekeeping cottages for families, in addition to motel-type rooms, dining room, cafeteria and swimming pool. Rates are lower between April 15 and December 15 than during the winter peak. 813/695-3101. M.

**Coral Roc,** 1100 N. Krome Ave., Florida City, FL 33034. Pool, picnic tables. Some rooms with refrigerators. Under 12 free. 813/247-4014. M.

**CAMPING.** Campgrounds are located at Long Pine Key (6 miles from park entrance), Chekika and Flamingo. Stays are limited to 14 days between November 1 and May 1, to 30 days the rest of the year.

Camping is permitted in the backcountry if you first obtain a permit at park headquarters or a ranger station. Camping facilities near the park are located at Collier-Seminole State Park, 19 miles north of Everglades, on the Tamiami Trail, and at private campgrounds north of Homestead.

**SEASONS.** Winter and early spring are ideal for watching birds and wildlife—because animals concentrate around the few remaining water areas. The weather is usually mild enough for shirtsleeves. Mosquitoes can be a problem in late spring and are likely to become fierce by summer. From June until August giant loggerhead turtles crawl onto the beaches at Cape Sable to lay their eggs.

**NEARBY.** Two outstanding areas are **Big Cypress National Preserve** and **Biscayne National Park** (see separate listing). Showpiece of the Seminole country is the **Dania Indian Reservation** at Hollywood with an outstanding arts and crafts center and display of Seminole life. The Seminole campground, open to the public year-round (fee charged), is a base for airboat and swamp-buggy tours.

For a naturalist's tour south of Miami, start with the beautiful **Fairchild Tropical Garden** in Coral Gables, displaying palms, cycads, an amazing rain forest and desert forest. Include a stop at **Redland Fruit and Spice Park,** a center of tropical plant culture, north of Homestead. Coming down the west side of Florida, start at the **Thomas A. Edison Botanical Gardens and Laboratory,** where the wizard of electricity maintained his winter home amid 14 acres of rare trees, ferns, and flowers. The **Everglades Nursery,** 6 miles southwest, one of the largest nurseries for palms and tropical plants, presents a bougainvillea exhibit every February. On the way south, **Everglades Wonder Gardens,** at Bonita Springs, display over 2,000 specimens of native wildlife. In Naples, the **Caribbean Gardens** contain an outstanding collection of orchids, bromeliads, and air plants—plus a large assortment of waterfowl—on their 30 subtropical and tropical acres. From mid-January to May 1, you can take an all-day combination tour of the gardens and the National Audubon Society's **Corkscrew Swamp Sanctuary.** Corkscrew, a wildlife sanctuary of 6,000 acres, is truly the companion piece to the Everglades. Containing our country's largest remaining stand of virgin bald cypress, many towering 130 feet, it is 35 miles from Naples and is reached on station-wagon tours.

South of the park on the sparkling overwater road to Key West, **John Pennekamp Coral Reef State Park,** in the Atlantic Ocean off Key Largo, is the first undersea park in the continental United States—a fantasy-land of coral beauty, protected as the breeding ground of fish, shellfish, and turtles. You can explore the park by glass-bottomed boat and see brilliantly colored fish swimming among old wrecks caught in the reef. Onshore the park has a campground, nature trail, wading area, and marina (rental boats and diving gear available). Another state park, **Bahia Honda,** south of Marathon, has facilities for fishing, picnicking, boating, camping, and an excellent beach for swimming.

In Key West, a visit to the **Audubon House** is appropriate, for it is restored to its appearance of 1832, when it was occupied by America's greatest nature painter; it was he who discovered the great white heron that now finds its refuge in the national park.

Finally, the land runs out, but 70 miles west of Key West lies **Fort Jefferson,** a 19th-century coastal fort in the newly designated (late 1992) Dry Tortugas National Park, famous for reef islands with their rich bird, plant, and undersea life.

**RECOMMENDED READING.** *The Everglades: River of Grass*, by Marjory Stoneman Douglas (St. Simons Island, GA: Mockingbird Books).

**FOR FURTHER INFORMATION.** Write Superintendent, Everglades National Park, Box 279, Homestead, FL 33030. 305/242-7700.

# GATES OF THE ARCTIC NATIONAL PARK

## ALASKA

ESTABLISHED 1980

FLYING INTO THE BROOKS RANGE from Fairbanks and Bettles, I was struck by the dramatic scene, larger than life, of granite peaks and knifelike ridges intersected by long valleys, many highlighted by sparkling lakes and rivers. The immensity of the country was overwhelming.

The entire national park lies above the Arctic Circle, about 200 miles northwest of Fairbanks. It embraces 7,952,000 acres on Alaska's North Slope. To give an idea of its dimensions: Gates of the Arctic park is almost four times the size of Yellowstone National Park, in the Rockies. It is, in fact, the second largest national park in the world, exceeded in size only by Wrangell–St. Elias National Park, in southeastern Alaska. Its river courses flow through some of the largest untouched basins in America.

This region has long been regarded as worthy of protection. From 1929 to 1939 Robert Marshall, scientist, explorer, and conservationist, conducted research around the headwaters of the Koyukuk River. Tracking up the North Fork, he observed two facing peaks, which he named Frigid Crags and Boreal, collectively, Gates of the Arctic. It was Marshall who suggested that the 600-mile-long Brooks Range, from the Yukon to the Arctic Sea, be designated a wilderness area.

As Eskimo tribes, the Inuit people of the North, have known for centuries, the Brooks Range is richly endowed with wildlife. Here I saw a portion of the great Western Arctic caribou herd that migrates hundreds of miles each year, pouring back and forth through the passes between northern calving and feeding grounds to the winter range south of the mountains, feeding on moss and lichens of the tundra. Many species find their niches: black bear in spruce lowlands of the south; Dall sheep on windswept mountainsides; moose among the willows; wolverines, wolves, lynx, grizzly, eagles, falcons, and many migratory birds.

# THE PRACTICAL GUIDE

A number of guides lead trips into the Brooks Range in summer. Outfitters can supply all the necessary equipment—though visitors in this terrain should be experienced hikers and campers and be trained in survival skills. Be sure you and your equipment are up for it. Fairbanks has a complete range of merchandise and services. Bettles, about 50 miles south of the park, is reached on scheduled airline service and is the jump-off for small-plane charter flights into the park.

**ACCOMMODATIONS.** Several private lodges are available throughout the park and adjacent preserve. These include:

**Walker Lake Lodge,** 930 9th Ave., Fairbanks, AK 99701. Rafting, sailing and sportfishing. 907/452-5417. M.

**Wiseman Lodge,** Box 10224, Fairbanks, AK 99701. Historic lodge, adjacent to North Slope Haul Road, offers backpacking, fishing, trail rides, and natural history tours June to September. Private rooms, family-style meals. M.

**HIKING AND BACKPACKING.** The best plan is to be dropped off and picked up by chartered aircraft. Be sure to pick a competent, experienced bush pilot; these pilots can land on lakes, rivers, or river bars, as well as airstrips. Higher elevations provide excellent hiking, usually combining open tundra, sparse shrubs, and occasional woodland.

**FLOATING AND FISHING.** Among the rivers, the pristine **Noatak** rises in the central Brooks Range and then flows for almost 450 miles to Kotzebue Sound, on the Arctic Ocean. A large part of its journey is through the new Noatak National Preserve. Other key rivers are the **Alatna, John, North Fork** (of the Koyukuk River), **Nigu-Itivilik,** and **Kobuk.** Fishing is good within the park. **Walker Lake,** a 13-mile-long jewel, and other lakes and rivers within the park contain grayling; you will also find lake trout and char. **Anaktuvuk Pass,** a village within the park, is the home of a Nunamiut Eskimo group noted for the ceremonial masks made of animal skin (usually caribou) and fur trim they make and sell here.

**SEASONS.** Midsummer temperatures along south slopes occasionally reach the 80s and, once in a long while, the 90s during the day. Highlands are generally cooler, with freezing temperatures at night on the north slopes by mid-August or early September. Weather can change abruptly at any time during the summer, so pack rain gear. Prepare for insects: first mosquitoes, then gnats later in the summer, especially on the vegetated west lowlands.

**RECOMMENDED READING.** *Alaska Wilderness: Exploring the Central Brooks Range,* by Robert Marshall (Berkeley: University of California Press).

**FOR FURTHER INFORMATION.** Write Superintendent, Gates of the Arctic National Park, Box 74680, Fairbanks, Alaska 99707. 907/456-0281.

# GLACIER BAY NATIONAL PARK

## ALASKA

ESTABLISHED 1980

SKIES WERE OVERCAST and a light rain fell, typical southeast Alaska weather, but virtually all of us passengers on the *Spirit of Glacier Bay* were on deck with our binoculars. The waters of Glacier Bay were flecked with icebergs and dotted with islands and rocks teeming with birds—cormorants, guillemots, horned and tufted puffins, gulls, and eagles. At least half a dozen humpback whales made their presence known, breaking the surface, blowing, then diving out of view. We saw hundreds of seals, a black bear with cub along the beach, and mountain goats on the high crags. All told, a superlative wildlife show.

The changing coastline, visible from the *Spirit*, was forested by vegetation ranging from spruce-hemlock rain forests to small pioneer plants claiming a foothold in recently exposed glacial slopes. Glaciers were in every stage of development, from actively moving ice masses to those nearly stagnant; I recalled that as recently as 250 years ago the entire bay was covered with an ice sheet 3,000 feet thick. At narrow, fjordlike inlets we approached ice cliffs up to 200 feet high and observed icy blocks "calving," crashing into the sea and causing huge waves.

John Muir publicized Glacier Bay and made his way into the heart of that distant, dazzling glacial world. Muir went near the end of October 1879 when, as he wrote, "young ice was beginning to form in the branch inlets occupied by the glaciers, and the mountains were mantled with fresh snow all the way down from the highest peaks and ridges of the Fairweather Range nearly to the level of the sea."

Why had Glacier Bay not been found earlier, since its surroundings in southeast Alaska were known? The answer is uncomplicated: when Captain George Vancouver sailed through the waters of Icy Strait, in 1794, Glacier Bay was little more than a dent in the shoreline. A towering wall of ice completely filled the broad, deep basin. That wall actually was the seaward outlet of an immense glacier.

By Muir's time the ice front had retreated 48 miles. A tall spruce-hemlock forest had begun to take its place, while tidewaters had invaded the basin and filled the deep, narrow fjords. Based on what he saw and learned, the great naturalist produced some of his finest writing. For example: "Here one learns that the world, though made, is yet being made; that this is still the morning of creation; that mountains long conceived are being born, channels traced for coming rivers, basins hollowed for lakes; that moraine soil is being ground and spread for coming plants . . . on predestined landscapes, to be followed by still others in endless rhythm and beauty."

The glaciers kept receding. By 1916, Tarr Inlet was free of ice, and the terminus of Grand Pacific Glacier stood 65 miles from the mouth of Glacier Bay. Nowhere else on earth have glaciers receded at such a rapid rate.

Glacier Bay was set aside as a national monument in 1925. Congress voted in 1980 to declare it a national park, with considerable enlargement. The park covers a little more than 3,220,000 acres, bordered by a national preserve of approximately 55,000 acres and a wilderness area of more than 2 million acres. It is now a World Heritage Site, joining one other national park (Wrangell-St. Elias) and two Canadian parks as the largest joint protected area in the world.

By plane, you can fly from Anchorage or Juneau via Alaska Airlines or from Juneau via LAB, a commuter line. Flight time from Juneau is about 30 minutes. Planes land at Gustavus Airport, about 10 miles from Bartlett Cove, center of activity in the park, reached by bus. Cruise liners traveling the Inside Passage from Vancouver and Seattle visit Glacier Bay, but their time is limited. Yacht trips or combination fly/cruise tours from Juneau and Gustavus to Glacier Bay are available, with overnight accommodations on land or aboard ship. Check with your travel agent before leaving home.

**CRUISING THE BAY.** From the center of activity at Glacier Bay Lodge, the concession-operated cruise boat, *Spirit of Adventure,* makes daytime excursions up the bay. The *Wilderness Explorer,* more like a floating hostel than a hotel, combines sea kayaking with cruising on trips of three to eight days. Call Glacier Bay Tours and Cruises, 800/451-5952.

**ACCOMMODATIONS.** Lodgings are available in the park and at nearby Gustavus.

**Glacier Bay Lodge,** Gustavus, AK 99826. The park concession, with modern rooms and meal service at Bartlett Cove, is the starting point of naturalist hikes and other programs. It serves as an excellent base for fishing, with panoramic views of Lower Glacier Bay, the Beardslee Islands, and the Fairweather Range. Tour packages assure reservations during popular, short season from mid-May to late September. Dormitory rooms each accommodating up to eight persons (men and women separately) are available at lower rates. 907/697-3221 or 800/426-0600. (Winter, 1500 Metropolitan Park Bldg., Seattle, WA 98101; 206/624-8551.) M to H.

**Gustavus Inn,** Gustavus, AK 99826. A small family-run inn outside the park, features charter fishing and kayaking. 907/697-3311. M.

**CAMPING AND KAYAKING.** A campground at **Bartlett Cove** is open May to September. **Sandy Cove,** about 20 miles up the bay, is a popular anchorage (bear activity sometimes closes it to camping); wilderness camping is available throughout the park. The cruise boat will drop off and pick up hikers at points en route for an additional fee. Kayaking is increasingly popular. The cruise vessel is equipped to carry kayaks. Rentals and guided trips are available; make arrangements in advance. You can make a pleasant one-day trip from Bartlett Cove out among the Beardslee Islands; pack a picnic lunch and insect repellent.

**SEASONS.** At Bartlett Cove summer temperatures range from 55 to 75 degrees Fahrenheit. Prepare for periods of mist and moisture, interspersed with clear and warm days. Remember that summer days in Alaska are long, with only brief darkness.

**FOR FURTHER INFORMATION.** Write Superintendent, Glacier Bay National Park, Bartlett Cove, Gustavus, AK 99826. 907/697-2230.

# GLACIER NATIONAL PARK

## MONTANA

### ESTABLISHED 1910

FROM AVALANCHE CAMPGROUND I followed the two-mile trail to Avalanche Lake, an easy walk that anyone could enjoy. The trail ran along a stream scoured by stones swirling in the torrent of milky glacial water from Sperry Glacier. It led me to thinking of how glaciers and streams had shaped the peaks and valleys, gouged out the lakes, and sculpted rich land formations of the northern Rockies.

I looked up to see a great natural amphitheater, a glacial cirque; a thin knife-edge of rock, an arête; and a towerlike sentinel gouged by two or more glaciers, a horn. But I saw much more: the telltale signs of grizzly droppings on the trail and claw marks on the trees; a red-tailed hawk wheeling overhead, and a slate-gray water ouzel, shaped like a chunky wren with short tail, bathing in the stream. As a wilderness sanctuary of 1,013,598 acres, Glacier is one of the last strongholds of the grizzly, along with bighorn sheep, mountain goats, mules, deer, moose, and elk—at least 57 species of mammals and 210 species of birds.

Feeling that hardly any area of its size concentrates as much rugged mountain splendor as Glacier National Park, I came ultimately to Avalanche Basin, where waterfalls plunge over 2,000-foot-high rock walls.

The scenery of its thousand waterfalls tumbling from glacial snow masses into sparkling lakes and streams, surrounded by primitive forests, is overwhelming to everyone who comes this way. Yet the experience here is intimate, for the visitor can walk in the company of wildflowers up to the frozen rivers themselves and spend a cool summer's night in a chalet within easy walking distance of a glacier.

This mighty place is more than one nation's park. Its proper name is Waterton-Glacier International Peace Park, a reminder that it not only lies astride the Continental Divide but spills over the Montana border of the United States into the southwest part of Alberta, Canada. Through a sanctuary of nature two countries commemorate the spirit of good will.

Few areas in the West produce a more comprehensive show of trees, plants, and wildflowers. Glacier is a rendezvous of a thousand species of the South, East, West, and even the Arctic. In the valleys on the east side are stands of Engelmann spruce, subalpine fir, and lodgepole pine, but across the western slopes, where moisture is heavier, the forests are more luxuriant with groves of ponderosa pine, Douglas fir, larch, hemlock, and western red cedar. Beneath these trees and across the open meadows a colorful display of wildflowers stands out everywhere as one of the park's major attractions. The showiest one to me is bear grass, a misnamed member of the lily family, while other flowering plants include the glacier lily along the edge of snowbanks, Indian paintbrush, fireweed, gentians, and asters.

# THE PRACTICAL GUIDE

Seven days, or even 14, are not too many to spend in this park with its superb 700-mile network of hiking and riding trails.

If you are on a Northwest tour, Glacier deserves three full days and two nights. If you're traveling by Amtrak's Empire Builder, arrange to stop over and tour the park. The Empire Builder stops daily at both Belton (West Glacier) and East Glacier (late April through late October) or Browning (the rest of the year).

You can reach the park by bus as well. Rocky Mountain Stage makes six trips weekly from Great Falls to East Glacier from May 1 to October 1. Shelby, Kalispell, and Great Falls are served by Intermountain Transportation, which connects with Greyhound and Trailways.

**BACKGROUND.** A full range of exhibits, information and introductory programs is available at the major **Visitor Centers** at Apgar, St. Mary, and Logan Pass.

The **naturalist program** includes accompanied boat and trail trips, evening campground programs, and slide talks in the hotels. **Glacier Institute** offers outdoor courses of one to five days for credit or noncredit. Courses include color photography, alpine ecology, grizzly ways. The institute's address is Box 1457, Kalispell, MT 59903.

**Going-to-the-Sun Road,** the 50-mile link between St. Mary Lake on the east side and Lake McDonald on the west side of the park, crosses the Continental Divide at Logan Pass (elevation 6,664 feet), where springtime pre-

vails and alpine flowers reach their height of bloom as late as August. One of the outstanding scenic routes in the world, open from mid-June until mid-October, Going-to-the-Sun climbs gently above treeline while it unfolds vistas of lakes, waterfalls, and high cliffs. Portions of the Going-to-the-Sun Road are closed to bikes 11 A.M. to 4 P.M., June 15 through Labor Day, due to heavy motor traffic.

Vehicles more than 20 feet long are not allowed on the road. Width is limited to 7.5 feet, including mirrors or extensions. Park trailers and oversized vehicles can be parked at the Avalanche and Sun Point parking areas and take the shuttle bus. **Chief Mountain International Road** is an outstanding park-to-park highway on the eastern flank of the mountains, through the Blackfeet Indian Reservation and around the base of Chief Mountain, with a view of the Great Plains bending eastward, then through a beautiful spruce and fir forest. It crosses the Canadian border with a clear view of Mount Cleveland, Glacier's highest peak (elevation 10,448 feet). **Waterton Lakes National Park,** on the Canadian side, receives half as many visitors as Glacier, but is a jewel in its own right. When going to Canada you need to pass through customs.

**TOUR OPERATORS.** All-expense tours ranging from one to ten days may be arranged by travelers arriving by bus or train with Glacier Park, Inc., the principal concessioner.

**TRAIL RIDES.** Saddle horses are available at Apgar Corral, Lake McDonald Lodge, and Many Glacier Hotel. A popular all-day trip leads from **Many Glacier Valley** over scenic Swiftcurrent Pass. Other trips range from two-hour and half-day tours for novices to longer climbs for experts.

**HIKING TRAILS.** The trails fan out in all directions from hotels, chalets, and campgrounds. From Logan Pass on the Going-to-the-Sun Road, take the Alpine Meadow Walk through a lush garden bordered by massive mountains with endless vistas of wilderness. The wooden walkway enables visitors to see and enjoy the scenery while protecting fragile tundra vegetation. Another popular easy walk, the **Avalanche Lake Trail,** leads from Avalanche Campground, off the Going-to-the-Sun Road, to Avalanche Basin, a good route on which to carry a picnic lunch and fishing gear.

For serious overnight hiking, obtain topographic or hiking maps and guidebooks available at Visitor Centers. Park officials advise against trying to cover too much country in a day, or crossing glaciers, which can be treacherous. Hikers must register at a ranger station and obtain a free, but required, backcountry permit for overnight trips. Mountain climbing is ill advised because of fragile rock, unpredictable weather, and hidden glacial crevices. **Sperry Chalet,** reached only by trail from Lake McDonald or Sun Point, and **Granite Park Chalet** have been closed subject to environmental review.

**BEAR FACTS.** Bears wander, covering a lot of territory in search of food. A bear will claim any it finds; so keep a clean camp, store your food suspended high in a tree, and sleep well away from it. A considerate camper and good conservationist will dispose of garbage in a bearproof garbage can or pack it out of the backcountry—and never bury it. Though normally shy, grizzly bears can be a problem in the backcountry when approached without warning. Hikers do well to carry a bear bell, or rocks in a can, to make their presence known on the trail.

At Avalanche Campgrounds and Many Glacier, the Park Service allows camping only in hard-sided vehicles. You may elect to stay in the park's protected camping area, or "bear cage"—a link fence, barbed-wire enclosure, accommodating 12 campers at a time.

**LAUNCH TRIPS.** These are operated on Lake McDonald, the largest lake in the park, on the west side; Two Medicine Lake, in the southeast corner; St. Mary Lake, surrounded by soaring peaks, waterfalls, and primitive forest; and on Swiftcurrent and Josephine lakes, in the Many Glacier region, to view spectacular glacier-carved scenery. Photo trips on launches are offered. Small boats and fishing tackle are available for rental.

**FISHING.** The season extends from the third Saturday in May through November 30. Be sure to obtain your permit (no fee). Seasonal migrations of native cutthroat, bull trout, and Kokanee on the west side provide much sport, but mackinaw, or lake trout, are taken in the larger lakes. The pygmy whitefish is the most unusual, but rare, found only in a few widely scattered localities in North America. Fly casting with artificial fly is generally practiced; using live or dead fish for bait is not permitted.

**BIRDWATCHING.** Of special interest to birders is the high-altitude alpine environment from mid-June to early September. Watch especially for white-tailed ptarmigan, golden eagle, blue grouse, water pipit, Clark's nutcracker, mountain bluebird, and gray-crowned rosy finch. Each fall Kokanee salmon and bald eagles migrate to Lower McDonald Creek, where they produce an unforgettable wildlife spectacle (best viewed from the Apgar Bridge). While the salmon spawn, the eagles feed on the salmon. The peak usually comes around mid-November. The eagles begin to feed each day about 30 minutes before sunrise, continuing for two hours. Then many spend the rest of the day perching in large trees, as many as 30 or more eagles per tree.

**BICYCLING.** The Going-to-the-Sun Road is challenging but popular. During peak hours of motor traffic the road is closed to bikers. Specially designated campsites are available at Sprague Creek Campground. You can rent a bike at Village Inn, Apgar.

**RAFT TRIPS.** West Glacier outfitters conduct raft trips daily during summer on the Middle Fork of the Flathead River, scenic, splashy, and safe. They take half day or full day (with lunch included).

**SKIING.** This sport is growing in popularity. Get a copy of the Ski Trails brochure published by the Glacier Natural History Association, outlining 14 marked trails in the park, rated beginner, intermediate, and advanced. Trails are designated with orange metal markers. Izaak Walton Inn, at Essex, features 30 miles of groomed trail just outside the park.

**ACCOMMODATIONS.** Extensive facilities are operated on concession by Glacier Park, Inc. These include lodging in many historic structures at strategic locations, meals, camper supplies, boat rentals and launches, bus transportation, and bicycle rentals. Information and reservations for the following lodgings can be obtained through Glacier Park, Inc., East Glacier, MT 59434; 406/226-5551. (During summer in Montana only call 800/332-9351 and from late September to mid-May the address is Greyhound Tower Station #5185, Phoenix, AZ 85077; 602/248-2600.) Reservations are necessary.

**Many Glacier Hotel.** Overlooking Swiftcurrent Lake in the Many Glacier region; a 5-story hotel (no elevator) with a variety of rooms and suites (including "family rooms" of two rooms with connecting bath). Bighorn sheep sometimes are seen on the lawn. Services include coin laundry, barber, and beauty shop. M to H.

**Glacier Park Lodge.** In a beautiful setting just outside the southeast corner of the park, the building reflects an earlier day. It rises 4 stories (without elevator) and includes pictur-

esque lobby, swimming pool, and 9-hole golf course, as well as barber and beauty shop. M.

**Lake McDonald Lodge.** Built about 1914, the lodge is on the shore of Lake McDonald, just off the Going-to-the-Sun Road. The dining room, in rustic motif, has a choice view of the lake. Under 12 free. M.

**Apgar Village Inn.** Also overlooking Lake

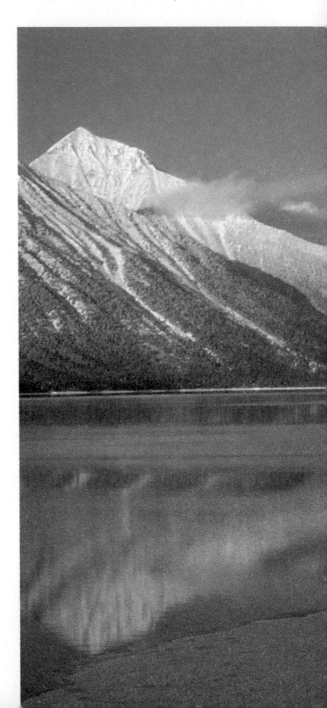

McDonald, the inn has access to the beach for swimming. Some rooms have kitchens. Open summer only. 406/888-5484. M.

**Swiftcurrent Motor Inn and Cabins.** A trail center for hikers, this complex ranges from motel rooms with full bath to cold-water cabins without bath. L to M.

**Rising Sun Motor Inn and Cabins.** Near the St. Mary entrance, eastern gateway to Going-to-the-Sun Road. L to M.

**St. Mary Lodge,** East Glacier, MT 59434. Motel units and cabins along a rushing creek between East Glacier Park and Many Glacier; open summer only. 406/732-4431. M.

**Izaak Walton Inn,** Box 653, Essex, MT 59916. Unusual spot, classy without luxury, on

# GLACIER
## NATIONAL PARK
### MONTANA

0        4        8        12
ONE INCH EQUALS APPROXIMATELY 10.4 MILES

Trails
Inquire at Ranger
Station before using

M-9-ZM-1330-S          © The H.M. GOUSHA Co.

US 2 southeast of West Glacier; with early–20th century railroad atmosphere (and reachable by Amtrak). Popular for cross-country skiing and hiking. 406/888-5700. L to M.

**North Fork Hostel and Cabins,** 80 Beaver Dr., Box 1, Polebridge, MT 59928. The hostel embodies simplicity, with wood heaters and cooking range (and no electricity) complementing its natural setting between the national park and Flathead National Forest. 406/888-5241 or 800/775-2938. L.

Additional accommodations are available on the east side at East Glacier, Browning, St. Mary; on the west side at Apgar, West Glacier, Hungry Horse, Whitefish and Kalispell.

**CAMPING.** Major campgrounds are located around St. Mary, Rising Sun, Apgar, and Two Medicine. Smaller, less developed facilities should not be overlooked. **Kintla Lake** campground, for instance, is an isolated beauty spot in the North Fork Valley near the Canadian border, with wonderful hiking along the lake. Attractive campsites can be found along the North Fork of the Flathead River in **Flathead National Forest** and southeast of the park in **Lewis and Clark National Forest.** Canadian campgrounds are different from those in the United States, being equipped with community kitchen shelters. **Glacier** requires permits for all backcountry use. There are 70 backcountry camps. Camping permits for these particular camps cannot be obtained more than 24 hours before starting your trip, for a maximum of six days, with no more than three consecutive nights in any one campground.

**SEASONS.** Going-to-the-Sun Road is usually closed by snow from mid-October until early June. Naturalist-conducted activities run from about June 15 to Labor Day. Accommodations inside the park are open mid-June to mid-September. Still, early June has its spe-cial appeal, with light crowds, freshness of spring, and wealth of flowers. So has September (even the end of the month). With the coming of autumn, scarlet berries and yellow and orange leaves make the park a colorful panorama. The golden-yellow needles of the larch, a strangely behaved conifer, stand out in bright contrast against a background of its green neighbors. During summer, days are warm, evenings chilly. Warm clothing is essential for hiking in the high country; so is a raincoat to cope with thundershowers.

**SHOPPING.** In Apgar village, **Montana House** is a showcase of arts, crafts, and handmade clothing of the entire state. The **Northern Plains Indian Crafts Association** has a trading center at St. Mary, just outside the park. Shops at Waterton sell English woolens, Eskimo sealskin slippers, and wildlife prints.

**NEARBY.** Close to the western entrance to the park, **Kalispell** and **Whitefish** provide motel accommodations and access to camping, fishing, boating, and hiking in **Flathead National Forest** and state parks. At Kalispell, visit the restored **Conrad Mansion,** an authentic example of luxurious living and architecture in the Northwest at the turn of the century. **Flathead Lake,** south of Kalispell, is the largest natural freshwater lake west of the Mississippi (28 miles long, 10 miles wide), bordered by the mighty Mission Mountains and the forested foothills of the Salish Mountains. At Browning, 12 miles from East Glacier Park, the **Museum of the Plains Indian,** near the center of the million-acre Blackfeet Reservation, interprets the ancient customs of the Indians of the Great Plains. The excellent exhibits and displays of early wood carvings and frescoes make the visit worthwhile.

**FOR FURTHER INFORMATION.** Write Superintendent, Glacier National Park, West Glacier, MT 59936. 406/888-5441.

# GRAND CANYON NATIONAL PARK

## ARIZONA

ESTABLISHED 1919

AFTER HIS FIRST TRIP to the Grand Canyon in 1903, President Theodore Roosevelt urged that nothing be done to mar its grandeur: "Keep it for your children and your children's children, and for all who come after you, as one of the great sights which every American if he can travel at all should see."

On every visit I make to the Grand Canyon, I can understand why he said that. The first sight of it excited my appetite to see more; the first answers to my questions stimulated my curiosity to ask a thousand more questions. I recall being at the rim before daybreak to watch the first rays of the sun illuminate the walls, and then again at dusk to watch darkness reclaim the scene. I felt humbled, cleansed of self-interest, swept up by the spirit of what John Burroughs called "the world's most wonderful spectacle, ever changing, alive with a million moods."

One winter I came to spend Christmas at the Grand Canyon. It was a very different place, uncrowded, peaceful, the white of snow softening the reds of ancient rock. My friend and I enjoyed our Christmas dinner at El Tovar, the great old hotel at the canyon rim. A Christmas to remember.

Another time, in summer, I went down the Colorado River in a wooden dory, plunging through the great rapids, camping on the sand beaches, and thinking of John Wesley Powell. In 1869, he made the first daring voyage through the canyons of the Green and Colorado rivers in just such a dory, a modern odyssey of a thousand miles, worthy of the ages. Motor trips in big rubber rafts cover the 277 miles of Colorado River through the Grand Canyon in 7 to 12 days. The dory trip took 18 days, without a single moment of boredom.

In form, size, glowing color, or geological significance, nothing approaches the Grand Canyon of the Colorado River. President Theodore Roosevelt recognized its value to the nation by proclaiming Grand Canyon National Monument in 1908. It became a national park in 1919. Congress nearly doubled the size in an act signed by President Gerald Ford on January 3, 1975. The expansion increased the park acreage from 783,561 acres to 1,218,375.

The park now extends from the mouth of the Paria River to the Grand Wash Cliffs. The Marble Canyon absorption adds the upstream 50 miles of the Grand Canyon, with rapids and 3,000-foot canyon walls. This addition completes protection of the 277-mile water route extending from historic Lees Ferry, where river runners start downstream, to the Grand Wash Cliffs, overlooking Lake Mead.

From rim to rim, the canyon varies in width from .1 mile in Marble Canyon to 18 miles farther downstream. Measured from the North Rim developed area, which is 1,200 feet higher than Grand Canyon Village on the South Rim, it is 5,800 feet deep—substantially more than 1 mile straight down.

The North and South rims are only 9 miles apart (214 miles by road), but they are distinctly different—two of many worlds within the universe of the Grand Canyon. The North Rim extends into the Canadian zone of climate and plant life and, at 9,000 feet, into the subarctic Hudsonian zone. The famous blue spruce on the heavily forested North Rim is not seen at all on the other side of the canyon, which is more typical of the arid Southwest. Nor is the white-tailed, black-bodied Kaibab squirrel. On the other hand, the Abert squirrel, grizzled gray of body and tail, with white underparts, is strictly a South Rim dweller. The two color phases of the tassel-eared squirrel never meet.

How old is the Grand Canyon and how, actually, was it formed? Century after century, the walls have weathered, crumbled, tumbled their shreds of sand, gravel, mud, and rock into the water and have given the river tools for scouring and gouging. The canyon widens and changes constantly. Its appearance varies with the hour of the day.

The rock layers exposed to view are pages in the textbook of earth's history, spanning 2 billion years. The uppermost strata, the Kaibab and Toroweap formations of Permian age, were formed approximately 250 million years ago. Below them lies the Coconino sandstone, the solidified remains of sand dunes, in which fossilized footprints indicate a lizard type of life. Next are the Hermit shale and the Supai shale and sandstone, with traces of amphibians and fossil ferns. The course of history can be traced through one layer to another to the tilted layers of late Precambrian rocks, perhaps a billion years old. The rocks at the bottom of the Inner Gorge are among the oldest exposed rocks on earth, the hard black rocks of the Precambrian age.

The down-cutting process began somewhere between 6 and 25 million years ago. At first, geologists thought that the ancestral Colorado River meandered over a broad plain until a general rising of the land caused it to flow more swiftly. Instead of being displaced, it cut downward. According to the traditional theory, the slow rise was concurrent with the lifting of the Rocky Mountains, which gave the river greater runoff and consequently more carrying and cutting power. As the Colorado deepened its course, the canyon walls grew steadily higher. A recent theory, endorsed by many experts on the Colorado Plateau geology, declares that the Colorado River once drained eastward and was separated by the Kaibab Plateau from another drainage to the west. Then the land uplift near the present Arizona–New Mexico border blocked the flow of the Colorado, forming a large lake. When the western drainage eroded toward its source, it tapped the waters of the lake, and the period of canyon cutting began.

Any theory must account for water flowing through a hill, rather than around it. Water runs downhill. Why didn't it flow around the hill instead of through it? Or was the river here first? And did it continue to cut down as the hill was uplifted? Or did a stream flowing off the top of the hill cut down through the hill and capture an ancestral Colorado River ponded to the east? Or is the story even more complex, involving several periods of uplift and possible damming of the Colorado River to the east of the canyon?

We may never know all the answers. Certainly human knowledge and human affairs are dwarfed by these older natural forces. We can, however, trace Indian occupation of the canyon back 4,000 years. The record of Europeans dates only to 1540, when the Spaniard Don Lopez de Cardenas was led by Hopi Indians to the great gorge. Essentially it was John Wesley Powell, geologist, explorer, and chronicler of the arid West, who made Americans aware of it.

A few entrepreneurs, who felt the Grand Canyon should be exploited for its resources, endeavored to block establishment of the national park. Others have wanted to control a tourist toll road on Bright Angel Trail, or to string a cable car into the canyon. To this day proposals are advanced to mine the region and to dam the Colorado River. But most people support Theodore Roosevelt's idea: to do nothing to mar its grandeur.

## THE PRACTICAL GUIDE: SOUTH RIM

This side is easier to reach, more heavily visited. Stay at least two days here, if only to watch the magic change between dawn and dusk. Do the usual things if this is your first visit, but then go on to the unusual opportunities available to explore Grand Canyon. **Main gateways to the South Rim** are Williams and Flagstaff, less than two hours by car. Bus lines run limited schedules from these two cities; Amtrak arrives at Flagstaff and connects with bus service to the canyon. Airlines serve Grand Canyon directly by means of an airport 10 miles south of the park; each flight is met by a bus from Grand Canyon Village.

**BY RAIL.** Take the Grand Canyon Railway from Williams; a 1910 steam engine pulls 1920s coaches year-round on trips of 2¼ hours ending on the South Rim at the last log railway station still standing in the United States.

Reservations suggested; 800/843-8724. Once at the depot, you can take a driver-guided motorcoach excursion offered by Fred Harvey Transportation Company.

**BACKGROUND.** The **Visitor Center,** at the east end of the village, is an important stop for orientation exhibits and dioramas. For times and places of all interpretive programs, check the free park newspaper, the Grand Canyon *Guide.* **South Rim drives** from Grand Canyon Village give the introduction, covering 33 miles with excellent views and linking the main focal points. The West Rim is closed to private cars from Memorial Day through September. However, the free Canyon Shuttle minibuses operate at frequent intervals, with stops at the key points along the 8-mile route from the Bright Angel Lodge to Hermits Rest. Visitors are encouraged to get off the shuttle buses in order to gain different views. The West Rim Shuttle operates from 7:30 A.M. to sunset, Memorial Day through Labor Day. The West Rim Drive leads 8 miles to **Hermits Rest,** passing excellent lookouts and the head of Bright Angel Trail; it is a pleasant summer bicycle route.

The Main Village Shuttle provides regular service from early morning through late evening, Memorial Day through September, between the Bright Angel Lodge and Maswik Lodge area (bank, general store, post office, and Yavapai Lodge office), Yavapai Observation Station, the Visitor Center, El Tovar Hotel, and back to the starting point.

**Yavapai Observation Station** is ½ mile east of the Visitor Center. Farther east, the East Rim Drive leads to **Tusayan Ruin,** a small prehistoric pueblo with a museum, which tells the story of Pueblo people who inhabited and left Grand Canyon before the Europeans came; **Lipan Point,** with a view of the winding river and the San Francisco Peaks to the south; and the **Watchtower** at Desert View, perched on the brink of the canyon, 25 miles from the village, with telescope views of the Painted Desert, Kaibab National Forest, and the surrounding Indian country. Bicyclists will find spectacular views along the narrow road to Desert View, but may have to contend with traffic.

**DAY HIKES.** Even short in duration, day hikes can be rewarding and revealing, giving a feeling for the immensity and natural beauty of the canyon. Hiking here is the reverse of mountain climbing. The downhill part comes first, then the upward climb, which takes more time—and more energy. So decide in advance how many hours you wish to hike. When one-third of your time has elapsed, turn around and start back. The two best trails for day hikes, particularly for hikers new to the canyon, are South Kaibab and Bright Angel. Limiting yourself to walks along the rim is a good idea until you become used to the thin air at this elevation.

On the steep **South Kaibab Trail,** the hike to Cedar Ridge—which offers magnificent scenery—covers 1½ miles each way. It takes about 2½ hours round trip. On the **Bright Angel Trail** (originally used by Havasupai Indians to gain access to Indian Garden, you can descend from the South Rim just west of Bright Angel Lodge and head for Mile and a Half Resthouse or Three Mile Resthouse (water in summer). The trip to **Indian Garden** covers 4½ miles each way, or at least 9 miles round trip. This oasis lies 3,060 feet below the rim. Allow ample time to return before dark.

Permits are not required for day hikes, but it is always a good idea to discuss your plans with a ranger.

**ACCOMMODATIONS.** Grand Canyon National Park Lodges, the principal South Rim concessioner, offers a wide range of accommodations. Reservations for the following lodgings are necessary. Box 699, Grand Canyon, AZ 86023, 602/638-2401, for advance reservations or 602/638-2631 for same-day reservations.

**El Tovar.** A showpiece hotel of the national parks, built in 1905 and restored in the early 1980s, El Tovar has a lovely dining room overlooking the canyon. H. **Kachina Lodge.** Next to El Tovar on the canyon rim, it has a variety of motel rooms and suites. Register at El Tovar. M.

**Bright Angel Lodge and Cabins.** Well located in the park, Bright Angel provides hotel rooms and cabins, some with canyon views. Ask about historic cabins with fireplace. Adjoining are the Bright Angel Restaurant and Arizona Steakhouse. M. **Thunderbird Lodge.** Register at Bright Angel Lodge. Under 8 free. M to H.

**Yavapai Lodge.** Opposite the park visitor center, this large facility has a cafeteria offering fast-food service. M.

**Maswik Lodge.** It offers more than 287 rooms; 37 cabins; and has a cafeteria. Under 8 free. L to M.

**EATING—SOUTH RIM.** There are many beautiful viewpoints for sunrise and sunset picnics, but be sure to carry out trash. Food and picnic supplies are available in the park and in the surrounding area, but prices are high; you may want to shop for them in Flagstaff. **El**

GRAND CANYON NATIONAL PARK
ARIZONA

NORTH RIM
Mid May to
Mid October

SOUTH RIM &
DESERT VIEW
Open All Year

Grand Canyon Lodge-Store
Campground-Cafeteria
Information

Travel across Canyon by foot,
mule-back or airplane only

GRAND CANYON
Hotel—Lodge—Cabins—Store
Post Office—Campground
Garage—Clinic—Park Hdqtrs.
Trailer Village

Travel into Havasupai
Indian Reservation by
advance reservation only.

--- = Trails
☐ = Inquire at Ranger
Station before using

ONE INCH EQUALS APPROXIMATELY 7.5 MILES
0   1   2   4   6   8

© The H.M GOUSHA Co.

M-9-ZD-1228-S

NAVAJO INDIAN RESERVATION

KAIBAB NATIONAL FOREST

HAVASUPAI INDIAN RESERVATION

Tovar, built in 1905 to celebrate the railroad bonanza, has a lovely dining room overlooking the South Rim. Arrive early to get a table near the window. The **Arizona Steakhouse,** adjoining Bright Angel Lodge, is a cheery modern steak house. **Bright Angel Restaurant,** near the rim, and Moqui Lodge, outside the park, offer casual dining. **Yavapai** and **Maswik Lodge** cafeterias have fast-food service.

**SEASONS.** Facilities on the South Rim are open all year. While the summer is crowded and reservations are imperative, during the winter the park is congestion free. Temperatures drop well below freezing at night but are warmer during the day.

**NEARBY.** A trip outside Grand Canyon National Park to the **Havasupai Indian Reservation** is a separate excursion from the generally visited South Rim area. This is an attraction unique in the United States, a desert oasis with the turquoise-blue waters of Havasu Creek cascading in spectacular waterfalls. It is a 190-mile drive from the South Rim Visitor Center to the end of the road at Hualapai Hilltop, the point of entry. Access from there to the town of Supai, 2,000 feet below, is over a precipitous trail. The 8 miles must be covered on horseback or on foot. Havasu Canyon is of special interest to geology students, botanists, birdwatchers, and anthropologists. All campers are required to call the campground reservation office in Supai, Arizona, 602/448-2141, to make or confirm reservations before leaving the rim at Hualapai Hilltop. Reservations must be made through the Havasupai Tourist Enterprise, Supai, AZ 86435. The Tribal Council assesses an entry fee, payable at the Tourist Office. There is a seven-day limit and an additional charge for camping.

There are two tourist lodges with kitchen facilities in the village. The Havasupai operate a village cafe; you can also purchase groceries in the tribal store. Arrangements for horses and lodging also must be made in advance, by telephoning or writing Havasupai Tourist Enterprise.

## THE PRACTICAL GUIDE: INNER CANYON

The Inner Canyon may be reached by foot, muleback, or boat. Summer heat is brutal. Winter temperature extremes between rim and canyon floor are severe. Spring and fall are ideal times to descend into the Grand Canyon's desert. Some of North America's wildest scenery makes effort and discomfort worthwhile.

**ACCOMMODATIONS. Phantom Ranch.** This small guest facility, alongside Bright Angel Creek, is reached by hiking or mules only. It consists of 11 cabins and 4 dormitories capable of sleeping 92. Each cabin has four beds, a good desk with a light, a heater, toilet, and key to the bathhouse where you can get a hot shower. Overnight packages are offered, but reservations are essential. Grand Canyon National Park Lodges, Box 699, Grand Canyon, AZ 86023; 602/638-2401.

**CAMPING.** Camping below the rims is a rewarding experience, if planned with plenty of time. Hikers can be accommodated at **Phantom Ranch** or at numerous primitive campsites (reservations are required). Going on foot is challenging to those in excellent physical condition. On the **Bright Angel Trail,** water is available in summer at two points between the South Rim and Indian Garden; from there to the river, the hottest part of the trip, none is available. From Bright Angel Lodge it's 9½ miles to Phantom Ranch. The serpentine trail descends 4,600 feet, passing layers of sedimentary rock.

On the steeper **South Kaibab Trail,** 6½

miles to the river from the rim at Yaki Point, no water is available. Summer temperatures in the canyon are extremely high. Study preventive measures and treatment of heatstroke and exhaustion. Plan to carry an adequate water supply, a gallon a day per person. And drink it! The toughest part comes at the end with the uphill climb. If you have the stamina, consider the cross-canyon hike from Phantom Ranch to the North Rim on the **North Kaibab Trail** (approximately 14 miles).

Hikers planning to camp in the Inner Canyon must obtain a permit or reservation at the Backcountry Office or the North Rim Ranger Station. To be assured of campsites, consider it mandatory to make reservations. You can't count on finding one of the campsites below the rim open when you want it.

The backpack trip from the North Rim to Phantom Ranch is filled with superb scenery, passing aptly named **Ribbon Falls,** 4,560 feet below the North Kaibab Trailhead. The last 5 miles are the hottest, but under partial shade following the course of Bright Angel Creek.

**Bright Angel Campground,** adjacent to Phantom Ranch and Bright Angel Creek, requires a backcountry permit. Reservations are required: contact Backcountry Office, Box 129, Grand Canyon, AZ 86023.

**WHITE-WATER ADVENTURE.** There are many ways to see the Grand Canyon, but perhaps none as thrilling as from a rubber raft or wooden boat, navigating the turbulent Colorado River. Campsites are usually on white-sand beaches.

Eighteen concessioners are licensed by the National Park Service; write the Park Superintendent for a complete list (see address under "For Further Information"). Write several of them for literature and check them out to be sure you get the trip you want. A motor-powered raft will get you through faster, but that's not how John Wesley Powell did it.

Lees Ferry, at Page, Arizona—just below Glen Canyon Dam—is the usual launching site for Grand Canyon river trips. You can travel the river for about 277 miles, running 160 recognized rapids, all the way to Lake Mead, though most parties end at Mile 225 at Diamond Creek. Motor trips take 7 to 12 days; oar-powered rafts 10 to 12 days; and wooden dories 18 days. Options are available for partial trips of 3 to 8 days, beginning or ending at Phantom Ranch.

Boaters wishing to raft the Colorado on their own must apply long in advance for a permit. Address inquiries and applications to the Park Superintendent (address under "For Further Information").

**SEASONS.** Temperatures in the canyon in summer commonly rise as high as 110 degrees Fahrenheit. Heat exhaustion is a real possibility. Hiking conditions are best in spring and autumn when weather is mild on the rims and within the canyon.

**TOUR OPERATORS.** Going by muleback to Plateau Point is a one-day trip that provides a popular way of viewing the canyon from the ground up. The trip from the South Rim begins on the celebrated twisting **Bright Angel Trail** at the west end of Grand Canyon Village and goes to the Tonto Platform and Plateau Point.

Even more adventuresome is the two-day trip into the Inner Gorge, stopping overnight at the small guest facility, Phantom Ranch, alongside Bright Angel Creek. The ride down over switchbacks cut into the sheer cliffs seems forbidding, but the surefooted mules haven't lost a rider yet in more than 50 years. Riders must be over 4 feet 7 inches tall, weigh under 200 pounds, and be conversant in English. After lunch at Indian Garden, a cottonwood oasis, the trail reaches the level of the roaring Colorado, crosses the narrow Kaibab Suspension Bridge, and continues a mile farther to the ranch. The schedule includes a period of relaxation before dinner. The temperature is 20 degrees warmer here than on the South Rim, 4,600 feet above. The next morning, you start the return trip by the **South Kaibab Trail,** equally colorful but a little shorter, reaching the South Rim at Yaki Point, 3½ miles east of the village, in time for lunch.

Confirmed reservations for muleback trips are necessary. Write Grand Canyon National Park Lodges, Box 699, Grand Canyon, AZ 86023. If you do not have a reservation, make it your first point of business on arrival in the park.

The **North Rim muleback trip** into the canyon is a one-day outing on the North Kaibab Trail, cut from solid rock, to **Roaring Springs.** For reservations, write to Grand Canyon Trail Rides, Box 1638, Cedar City, UT 84720.

## THE PRACTICAL GUIDE: NORTH RIM

Being less accessible, this side is less congested. It affords different views and a different feeling. The vistas are spectacular, and the cool Kaibab Plateau is covered with beautiful forest, where families of deer roam late in the day and flowers of mountain and field meet.

**BACKGROUND. The Gateway to the North Rim** is Jacob Lake, Arizona, where a 44-mile paved road leaves US 89A taking visitors to the Grand Lodge on Bright Angel Point.

**Cape Royal Drive** from Grand Canyon Lodge extends 20 miles to **Cape Royal,** with choice stopping places en route. **Point Imperial,** 3 miles off the main road, is the highest point of the entire canyon rim, at 8,803 feet, with excellent views over the Painted Desert, Marble Canyon and the Little Colorado River. Along the last part of the drive, the roadway is bordered with fragrant locust. Inquire at the NPS Information Desk about current access to Point Sublime; there the Inner Gorge is closer than at any other spot along the North Rim.

**Bright Angel Point** is the tip of the promontory jutting a mile into the canyon, flanked by Roaring Springs Canyon and the Transept. A self-guiding nature trail from Grand Canyon Lodge is an easy walk of ½ mile. Good roads and less traffic make the North Rim best for bicycling.

**NATURALIST PROGRAM.** The daily schedule includes geology talks at Cape Royal, evening campfire programs at the campground on Bright Angel Point, and other programs. For a complete schedule check at the information desk in the lobby of the lodge.

**TUWEEP.** The western portion of the national park is the area formerly included in Grand Canyon National Monument, which contains remote portions of the Grand Canyon and is an ideal target for the rugged traveler.

The most outstanding location is at **Toroweap Overlook,** 2,800 feet above the snakelike Colorado River, on a sheer, vertical wall. It is reached by driving 9 miles west from Fredonia, Arizona, into the Kaibab Indian Reservation, then turning south onto a 50-mile graded road to Tuweep, and then an additional 5 miles on an unimproved road. A small campground is on Toroweap Overlook, but there is no water or gasoline, and the last food available is at Fredonia, and the road is impassable when wet.

**ACCOMMODATIONS. Grand Canyon Lodge.** Modest cabins and motel units on pine-shaded grounds provide magnificent canyon views. Dining room and cafeteria are part of the complex; open summer only. For reservations, write TW Services, Inc., 451 N. Main St., Cedar City, UT 84720; 801/586-7686.

**Kaibab Lodge,** North Rim Rural Route, Fredonia, AZ 86002. Less than 20 miles north of the North Rim in Kaibab National Forest, it offers motel rooms and rustic cottages. 602/638-2389. M.

**CAMPING.** A campground (with showers) is located near the ranger station. Stays are limited to seven days.

**SEASONS.** The North Rim is open mid-May to late October if weather permits. Evenings are cool even during the summer. During winter, heavy snows close the access roads. From September until mid-October, days are mild and clear, and golden-leaved aspen mantle the hillsides.

## THE PRACTICAL GUIDE: IN THE REGION

Adjacent to both North and South Rim are units of the **Kaibab National Forest,** with many recreation areas. The North Kaibab contains an abundant and famous herd of mule deer.

**Bryce Canyon** and **Zion** national parks are related geologically to the Grand Canyon and are linked by highway with the North Rim. Phases of the Colorado River story unfold upstream at **Glen Canyon National Recreation Area,** on the Utah-Arizona border, and downstream at **Lake Mead National Recreation Area,** where Arizona, Nevada, and California come together. Driving south on US 89, the traveler can visit **Wupatki National Monument,** preserving prehistoric Indian pueblos, and **Sunset Crater National Monument,** a volcanic crater active as recently as A.D. 1065.

**Flagstaff,** at the foot of the San Francisco Peaks, is a growing, changing city of the West. The **Museum of Northern Arizona** is a companion piece to the Grand Canyon, the one physical and visual, the other devoted to arts, anthropology, and the study of natural sciences. Flagstaff is also gateway to the **Navajo** and **Hopi reservations** that border the Grand Canyon to the east.

**Lowell Observatory,** where U.S. moon astronauts trained, offers guided tours at 1:30 P.M. weekdays, holidays excepted. During summer months, visitors can obtain tickets from the Flagstaff Chamber of Commerce to peer through the powerful Lowell telescope on Friday evenings.

**VISITING THE RESERVATIONS.** Full guest accommodations are available at Cameron, Tuba City, Kayenta, and the Hopi Cultural Center at Second Mesa—a good place to buy Hopi arts and crafts.

**RECOMMENDED READING.** *Exploration of the Colorado River and Its Canyons,* by John W. Powell (New York: Dover Publications); *Grand Canyon,* by Joseph Wood Krutch (New York: William Morrow & Co.); and *A Field Guide to the Grand Canyon,* by Stephen Whitney (New York: William Morrow & Co).

**FOR FURTHER INFORMATION.** Write and request a Trip Planner from Superintendent, Grand Canyon National Park, Box 129, Grand Canyon, AZ 86023. 602/638-7701.

# GRAND TETON NATIONAL PARK

## WYOMING

ESTABLISHED 1929

THE GUIDE SAID that he normally was an English teacher in Jackson, but he most certainly was an expert in piloting the rubber raft down the Snake River and pointing out the highlights along the way. We drifted silently past wildlife—coyotes, elk, ducks, herons, bald eagles feeding their young in a high nest—with plenty of chances for photography. The boatman reminded us in a pleasant way always to give wildlife a break, wherever we might be, by keeping a respectable distance. He felt a responsibility, which he clearly wanted to share.

It was a leisurely trip. The Snake was mostly calm and quiet, providing the opportunity to shift my attention to the 40-mile-long cluster of huge peaks dominating the landscape. Some mountain ranges are taller and more massive, but the Tetons rise, without foothills, boldly and abruptly from the earth. From the west side, in Idaho, I had seen them like towering spires parading against the sky. From their bases within the park they spread their images across large, forest-bordered lakes. On the mountain trails along their flanks, they become a network of rock gardens filled with glaciers, waterfalls, and wildflowers.

We stopped for lunch at a beautiful picnic area on Deadman's Bar. The boatman and I talked a while. His name was Vern Huser and we became friends. It was a long time ago, and Vern since then has gone on to write books about running rivers all over the country. So it's not only the places that make the national parks, but the people you meet in them.

The frontispiece of the sheer, jagged peaks, the high basin known as Jackson Hole, is part of the treasure of the 310,418-acre national park. John Colter, who in 1806 left the Lewis and Clark expedition to trap beaver and explore the country, may possibly have been the first white man to come this way, where only Indians had passed before to hunt elk. Then followed the mountain men, the traders, trappers, and the cattlemen. In the 1880s the homesteaders arrived, but they learned the country was too high, cold, and barren for successful farming.

The valley, about 50 miles long, varying in width from 6 to 12 miles, is rimmed by mountains—the high plateaus of Yellowstone National Park on the north, and the Mount Leidy Highlands and Gros Ventre Range on the east and south. It is bisected by the Snake River flowing through Jackson Lake, then through sagebrush meadow and finally through forest and between steep bluffs.

Moose, the largest and least wary member of the deer family, are often seen. Antelope, bison, elk, and mule deer—the wildlife for which Jackson Hole has been famous since the era of the mountain men—are as large as life.

Streams and lakes abound in fish and waterfowl. The trumpeter swan, largest of all swans, once reduced to near extinction, has made a healthy comeback, thanks to its sanctuary in the Tetons.

The story of the park is hardly complete without reference to the late John D. Rockefeller, Jr. He first came to visit this country in 1926. Encouraged by Horace M. Albright, then superintendent of Yellowstone National Park, Mr. Rockefeller in years that followed purchased more than 30,000 acres of the Jackson Hole Basin and presented them to the government for preservation. In the face of extensive local opposition to the park, it wasn't easy. But I can't imagine anyone regretting it today.

# THE PRACTICAL GUIDE

You can see the mountains on a breezy drive-through, but you can do the same from the pages of a picture book with less effort. Give yourself a chance to really appreciate this park; even on a short tour, plan to spend at least one full day. **Signal Mountain Overlook,** accessible by automobile, provides the best orientation to the mountains. Turnouts along the way up offer picture-taking vistas. The summit commands a panoramic view over the Snake River valley. It lies off the **Teton Park Road,** which leads to campgrounds, fishing sites, and most mountain trails. The **Rockefeller Parkway,** parallel to the Snake River, is one of America's most scenic roads, with wayside turnoffs and displays; it is part of the valley motor loop.

**NATURALIST PROGRAMS.** The Tetons are filled with the widest range of activities, whatever your interest may be. These will contribute to the enjoyment and appreciation of the park. Illustrated talks are presented in the campgrounds each evening during the summer and three times weekly at Jackson Lake Lodge. Guided nature walks are conducted every day, and all-day hikes, two days a week. The two Visitor Centers complement each other in telling the story of the Tetons: **Moose,** the fur-trading era (open year-round); **Colter Bay,** Indian Arts Museum, displaying the varied art forms of the American Indian from the David T. Vernon collection, including intricately carved pipes, masks, and weavings (open mid-May to mid-October). Pick up a printed copy of the naturalist programs in the park newspaper.

At Jackson Lake Lodge, square dance programs are held every Wednesday during summer.

**SUMMER SEMINARS.** Most are five days long, conducted in the park by the Teton Science School. Subjects covered include geology, photography, wildlife, and techniques of wilderness living. Participants are free to stay in group campgrounds or hotels. For information write Teton Science School, Box 68, Kelly, Wyoming 83011.

**HIKING TRAILS.** The trails are the means to fully exploring and appreciating the Tetons. Short hikes of half-day or all-day duration are rewarding and worthwhile. A good get-acquainted hike will take you to **Hidden Falls.** It can begin and end with a boat trip across beautiful **Jenny Lake,** at the foot of the Cathedral group, to Cascade Canyon. Overnight trips permit leisurely viewing of mountain flora, varied wildlife, and expansive mountain vistas. The well-conditioned person has no difficulty hiking from the 6,500-foot valley floor to the **Teton Crest Trail,** about 4,000 feet higher, where it becomes possible to make a loop trip completely encircling the Grand, Middle, and South Tetons and adjacent high peaks. The **Paintbrush Canyon Trail** climbs from the south end of Leigh Lake to the upper end of Paintbrush Canyon, bordered with paintbrush and other wildflowers, and with fine views of the lakes beyond the mouth of the canyon. More than 200 miles of trail furnish a wide variety of hiking—through the valley to high mountain lakes and craggy passes above timberline. Watch for sparrow hawks, prairie falcons, and golden eagles, soaring and wheeling on rising air currents above the cliffs and peaks. One part of the Teton Range, from **Leigh Canyon to Berry Creek,** is wilderness in the truest sense,

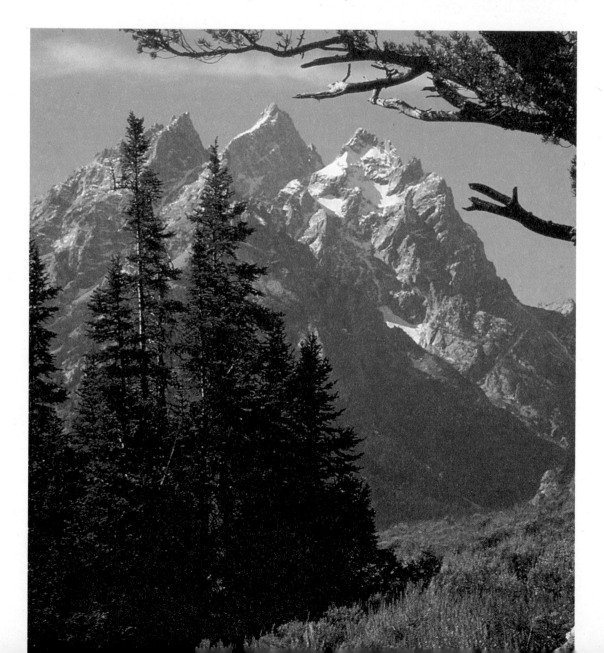

being almost devoid of trails. Expert hikers who want to test their skill in this area can obtain helpful advice from the Colter Bay or Jenny Lake ranger stations. Be sure to obtain a backcountry camping permit—it is required. Warm clothing, comfortable hiking shoes, and a good sleeping bag are all essential for overnight hikes; water-repellent clothing and equipment are useful in the event of sudden summer squalls.

**HORSEBACK RIDING.** Opportunities are available at various levels of ability. Children can enjoy an hour or two on a saddlehorse trip around the lakes, starting from the park concession corrals at Colter Bay, Jenny Lake, or Jackson Lake Lodge. Better riders can spend a full day on the high trails or arrange pack trips through the concessioner or guest ranches in the valley.

**MOUNTAINEERING.** Mountain climbing begins where trail hiking leaves off. The Exum Mountain Guide Service (Box 56, Moose, Wyoming 83012), headquartered at Jenny Lake, and Jackson Hole Mountain Guides (Box 547, Teton, Wyoming 83025) offer training for beginners. Even on the first day you practice crawling upward like a spider and swinging from a clifftop in a 20-foot rappel. Two days of instruction are required to go on the guided overnight climb of Mount Owen, Mount Moran, or the Grand. In a single year about 2,000 climbers make the ascent of the Grand, over at least 16 basic routes, ranging from relatively easy (with guides) to some of the finest rock-climbing in the nation. Mountaineering, however, can never be taken lightly. All climbers are required to register in person at the Jenny Lake Ranger Station. The summer climbing season usually extends from June 15 to September 15, the brief summer season at high elevations between snows and storms.

**FISHING.** In wild streams and lakes, fishing is typical of recreational angling in the northern Rockies. Cutthroat and native trout may be taken with an artificial fly during most of the summer and autumn, but mackinaw trout in Jackson and Jenny lakes can best be caught by trolling with heavy tackle. A Wyoming license can be obtained at tackle shops for the season or a five-day period.

**PHOTOGRAPHY.** Wildlife shooting—with camera. One of the great sports in the Tetons is observing animals in their natural state. These creatures are part of the rich legacy of the West, and pictures of them are among the best possible souvenirs. It will help to have a telephoto lens. For safety's sake, keep your young photo fans (and grown-ups) a considerable distance from all animals. More than 100 species of birds inhabit the park. Look for the huge trumpeter swans in flight over the lakes or building their mounded nests, sometimes over the lodges of muskrat and beaver.

Near the south entrance to the park is the **National Elk Refuge,** which is maintained primarily for the winter care of the Jackson Hole elk herd. Most of the flock of this handsome native deer, second largest to the moose, spend the summer grazing in the high range beyond view. Moose can be seen at any season in the early morning and at dusk along river bottoms and in fragrant meadows. There aren't many mule deer in the park, but hikers may see them, or their tracks, along the trails. The sleek pronghorn sometimes appear in small bands on Antelope Flats. A herd of bison runs free in the park. One of the great prizes of the bird watcher and photographer is the shy and rare trumpeter swan, sometimes seen in the elk refuge and other times on Christian Pond east of Jackson Lake Lodge.

**FLOAT TRIPS.** Snake River trips give a sample of adventure on a western stream. Rubber rafts, piloted by expert guides, make a four-hour trip from Pacific Creek every day during the summer, with a stop for lunch at Deadman's Bar. Two-hour trips are also available. You can put a canoe into the water at **String Lake** and be immersed in solitude, free of outboard motors. Canoe rentals are available at Pelican Bay Marina, Colter Bay Village, and Signal Mountain Marina.

Scenic boat rides are operated on **Jackson Lake,** the valley's largest and deepest body of water, to the far shore, where you look deep into wilderness country. Regularly scheduled, narrated scenic cruises, conducted by Grand Teton Lodge Company, include the Fire Cruise, which provides insight into the "Let-the-fire-burn" policy successfully practiced in various national parks. The Sunday evening "Steak Fry Cruise" leaves in late afternoon from Colter Bay Village in a 50-passenger cruiser for Elk Island. Visitors often observe sandhill cranes at close range. Steaks are barbecued and served around sunset. You can also rent rowboats and canoes on the lake. And on Jenny Lake, rental boats are also available. If you bring your own boat, you must obtain a permit at park headquarters; motor-propelled craft are allowed only on Jackson, Jenny, and Phelps lakes. For strictly boating recreation, larger and better bodies of water are located within driving distance, outside the national park.

**Menor's Ferry,** near park headquarters, is a reconstruction of the pioneer vessel that began operating across the Snake River in 1892. Exhibits tell about the settlers and their early transportation. When water level of the river permits, ranger-naturalists conduct demonstration rides.

**ACCOMMODATIONS.** The largest concessioner, Grand Teton Lodge Company (Box 240, Moran, WY 83013; 307/543-2811), provides not only lodging and meals, but guided bus tours, horse trips and float trips, and recreational vehicle camping with full hookups. Two major seasons are summer and winter. In winter months deep snow usually makes for excellent skiing. Reservations are advisable. Grand Teton Lodge Company's overnight accommodations are:

**Jenny Lake Lodge.** In a shaded setting, one- and two-room log cabins are furnished in taste and sophistication. The Sunday buffet dinner is one of the dining treats of Wyoming (reservations advisable). H.

**Jackson Lake Lodge.** In the center of park activities, this large lodge consists of motel rooms, some with excellent views and some otherwise. The lobby is a well-known rendezvous, marked by picture windows facing the lake and the Tetons beyond. Facilities include dining room, coffee shop, picturesque bar, pool, beauty and barber shops. M to H.

**Colter Bay Village.** Distinctive log cabins, originals of pioneer settlers, have been assembled in one area and furnished with appropriate, but modern, facilities. Grocery and coin laundry are located in the village. L to M.

**Colter Bay Tent Cabins.** These combine log and canvas and are equipped with screen door and bunks, affording a touch of comfort to outdoor living. L.

Other lodgings are available in nearby Moose, Jackson, and Teton Village, and in Driggs, Idaho, on the west side of the Tetons. They include the following:

**Lost Creek Ranch,** Box 95, Moose, WY 83012. A superlative resort with picture view of the mountains. Most cabins with fireplace and private patio. Riding, swimming, tennis. 307/733-3435. H.

**Dornan's Moose Enterprises,** Box 39, Moose, WY 83012. Kitchen-equipped cabins and restaurant at a convenient location on the Snake River near Jenny Lake. 307/733-2415. M.

**Flagg Ranch Village,** Grand Teton National Park, WY 83012. On the Rockefeller Memorial Parkway, near the southern entrance to Yellowstone National Park, well-known Flagg Ranch has motel rooms and cabin units (with and without bath), grocery store, and recreational vehicle camping with utilities. Activities include horse rides and float trips. 307/543-2861 and 733-8761 or toll-free outside Wyoming 800/443-2311. L to M.

**CAMPING.** Five public campgrounds are maintained by the Park Service: **Colter Bay** (largest and most developed, with coin laundry, general store, restaurant), **Lizard Creek, Signal Mountain, Jenny Lake,** and **Gros Ventre.** In addition the concessioner-operated **Colter Bay Trailer Village** has trailer sites with power, water, and sewer connections. Limit of stay at all campgrounds is 14 days, except at Jenny Lake, where the limit is 10 days. This park requires permits for backcountry use and accepts reservations for backcountry camping. Twelve developed campgrounds in adjacent **Teton National Forest** are part of the total camping complex.

**TRANSPORTATION.** Most visitors arrive by car, but there are other ways, too. Greyhound operates bus service to Idaho Falls, Idaho, with connections to Jackson by Star Valley Stage. Air service on Trans Western and Western airlines reach Jackson from Idaho Falls, Idaho, and Salt Lake City, Utah, all year. Buses run by the Grand Teton Lodge Company meet each flight and connect with Jackson Lodge, Colter Bay Village, and Jenny Lake Lodge. Cars are not essential inside the park. Daily guided tours cover the most important scenic areas (and also include Yellowstone National Park on separate schedules). There is convenient interpark service to hiking and fishing trailheads, and bicycles are now available for rental.

**SEASONS.** Most activities are concentrated in the months of July and August, although the naturalist program begins in early June. Jackson Lake Lodge is open mid-June to mid-September and is least crowded before July 4 and after Labor Day. Colter Bay has a longer season, late May to October 1. Flower months are June and July in Jackson Hole, July and August in the high country. Fishing is best in September, when days are sunny and clear, though snows may swirl around the summits. In autumn, elk are most easily observed and most exciting to watch. At this time of year, when golden aspens glitter on the hillsides, the mature bulls round up their harems of cows. The area about Signal Mountain and Burnt Ridge is the best part of the park from which to watch their activity and to hear the challenging bugle of the bull elk. This alone is worth the visit.

Winter is a season of majesty, undreamed of by the nearly 4 million visitors who come this way in summer. Roads are open from Jackson through the park and over Togwotee Pass, affording vistas of the mighty Tetons rising stark and white between the snow flats and a clear sky. In early winter, depending on snow and weather, large bands of elk move across the open flats to their wintering area south of the park. During a severe winter as many as 11,000 elk have concentrated in the refuge, part of an old migration route, which is now critically blocked from further southward movement by the settlement of man. To winter visitors, the spectacle of this mass of wild animals, many still bearing enormous racks, is the thrill of a lifetime. The public is invited to ride horse-drawn sleds (small fee) into the midst of the herd to see and photograph the animals.

**SKI TOURING.** This sport is increasingly popular, and the eastern part of the park has four marked trails. Each is about 8 to 10 miles long. Park concessioners offer rental equipment and instructions.

**NEARBY.** The national park is part of an immense western outdoor recreation region. It includes Yellowstone National Park; John D. Rockefeller, Jr. Memorial Parkway; Bridger-Teton, Shoshone, and Targhee national forests. The closest, the Bridger-Teton National Forest, encompasses three sides of Jackson Hole, with elevations up to 12,165 feet, plus the headwaters of the Yellowstone River and the South Fork of the Snake. Swimming is available at **Granite** and **Astoria Hot Springs,** both south of Jackson. **Jackson** itself, a historic western supply point, still has its wooden boardwalks leading to restaurants, saloons, and craft shops. This is a year-round vacation crossroads for dude ranchers, fishermen, campers, and for hunters and skiers. Don't overlook **Driggs, Idaho,** 40 miles from the south entrance to the park. It's the Targhee side of the Tetons, with choice hiking, backpacking, and skiing, as well as motels and resort lodgings.

**RECOMMENDED READING.** *One Day at Teton Marsh,* by Sally Carrighar (Lincoln: University of Nebraska Press); *Across the Wide Missouri,* by Bernard De Voto (New York: AMS Press); and *Teton Trails,* the park trail guides.

**FOR FURTHER INFORMATION.** Write Superintendent, Grand Teton National Park, Box 170, Moose, Wyoming 83012. 307/733-2880.

# GREAT BASIN NATIONAL PARK

## NEVADA

### ESTABLISHED 1986

THE GREAT BASIN is one of the most lightly populated and least-known parts of our country, but no less worthy than any other part. So I found myself thinking while driving almost 500 miles from Salt Lake City west across the open frontier. It was June 1987, only a few months following action by Congress to establish our newest national park, the first one in Nevada.

The region called Great Basin has been derided as a desert, but not as I saw it. It extends from the Wasatch Mountains in Utah to the Sierra Nevada in California, and from Idaho south to Arizona, landlocked, with no outlet to the sea. It is dry and arid, blocked from moist Pacific winds by the high Sierra peaks, but is never dull. I stopped again and again to admire the hardy vegetation—sagebrush, rabbit brush, grass saltbush, pinyon, juniper, grasses, and sedges—that survive and thrive in a harsh environment, and mountain peaks rising like sentinels here and there above them. Flowers, including primroses, buttercups, phlox, paintbrush, and beautiful coral mallow, flash in springtime. The Great Basin is marked by the remnants of Pleistocene lakes, like Lake Bonneville, an ancient inland sea in northwest Utah, and Great Salt Lake.

It's a long way between post offices in the Great Basin. I'm glad there still are such regions, where this generation can envision the openness of times past. To locate the new park properly, it lies on the eastern edge of Nevada, near the small town of Baker a few miles south of US 50. It is 70 miles east of Ely, on the route to Reno, and 290 miles north of Las Vegas (via US 93).

The park embraces 77,100 acres, a relatively small parcel considering the grandeur of the country. The highlights are Lehman Cave, one of the largest limestone caverns in the West (formerly protected as a national monument), and Wheeler Peak, 13,063 feet, one of the highest points of the Great Basin. Between cave and summit, the park embraces everything from sagebrush to alpine meadows, glacial lakes, aspen forests, and stands of venerable bristlecone pines, 4,000 years old, among the oldest living things on earth.

The park is new, but the idea of a national park dates from early in the century. Mining and ranching influences blocked it, but conservationists never quit. In the 1950s, Weldon Heald, a well-known Arizona writer, championed the concept. In the sixties, Darwin Lambert, then a newspaper editor in Ely, organized the Great Basin National Park Association, enrolling members in many states. They spread the gospel, leading ultimately to the park's designation in 1986.

## THE PRACTICAL GUIDE

You will undoubtedly have traveled a long distance to reach Great Basin National Park, so consider it an important destination and allow ample time to do it right. If you're camping, you can spend two or three days or longer to advantage. If driving on a timetable, plan at least the better part of a day here.

**BACKGROUND.** The **Visitor Center** is the first structure on entering the park. It was built to serve the former Lehman Caves National Monument and is well established, with wall maps, introductory film, historic displays, and literature. Spend an hour at the center. Talk with the ranger on duty; he or she will suggest the best ways to spend your time and

will help with travel information. Don't miss the chance to learn about history: of how Jedediah Smith explored the Great Basin, to be followed by early adventurers, surveyors, and gold seekers; and of how Wheeler Park was named for Lieutenant George Wheeler, who led a survey party in 1869 and again in 1879.

**LEHMAN CAVES.** Take the naturalist-led tour starting from the Visitor Center. (A fee is charged.) It takes about 1½ hours to walk two-thirds of a mile underground. You'll see huge fluted columns, curtains of stone, color-splashed ceilings, twisting helictites, and other unusual formations found in few other caves. Compare the formations you see here with those in other western national parks and monuments (such as Wind Cave, South Dakota; Carlsbad, New Mexico; Timpanogos, Utah; and Oregon Caves, Oregon), and Lehman will rank high by any standard. Temperature in the cave averages about 50 degrees Fahrenheit, so *wear warm clothing*. The ticket for the tour carries a minimap showing the **Gothic Palace, Lodge Room, West Room, Grand Palace,** and **Talus Room**—ask the naturalist to sign and date it and you have a neat memento.

**WHEELER PEAK SCENIC DRIVE.** This extends 12 miles on a steep winding grade to the 10,000-foot level. Stop along the way for unfolding vistas of the Great Basin. You'll see **Baker Creek** and **Lehman Creek** flowing out of the glaciated canyons of snowy Wheeler Peak. The road ends at Wheeler Peak Campground, where further adventure begins, now on foot.

**HIKING TRAILS.** Well developed and attractive, the trails lead through aspen groves and along bubbling high mountain creeks. In spring and summer many kinds of wildflowers—lupine, yellow aster, larkspur, columbine, and others—bloom along the trail, advancing higher up the mountain with the season. With good luck you may catch sight of wildlife—mule deer, bobcats, bighorn sheep, or a mountain lion. But don't be surprised to see cattle grazing, since Congress chose to allow it here, unlike in other national parks.

Take one of the easy trails to **Stella Lake** or **Teresa Lake.** If the snow has melted, take the spur trail near Teresa Lake for the 1-mile side trip to the forest of bristlecone pine, embracing some of the oldest trees in the world. They have made it through many centuries on these quartzite ridges, gnarled and wind bent, each tree a living lesson in survival. With time and

planning and favorable weather conditions, hike up the talus ridges to the windy summit of **Mount Wheeler,** 13,063 feet, the highest mountain peak entirely in Nevada. But be sure to carry water wherever you hike, and protect yourself against the possible stomach upset of giardia from drinking untreated water.

**SEASONS.** For half the year the slopes are covered with snow. Lehman Cave is open all year, but the upper trails may not be accessible until late June or July.

**ACCOMMODATIONS.** The little town of Baker, 5 miles from the park, has two small motels, likely with more to come, while Ely, 70 miles west, has a full range of overnight and eating facilities.

**Silver Jack Motel,** Baker Ave., Baker, NV 89311. Tree-encircled, rustic character. 702/234-7323. M.

**Jailhouse Motel,** Fifth and High, Ely, NV 89301. Have some fun in rooms called cells (the motel is on the site of the old-time jail). Dining room and its menu are "cellular," too. 702/289-3033. M.

**Copper Queen Motel,** 701 Avenue I., Ely, NV 89301. Ask for room in wholly adequate, older unit; it costs less and you'll still have access to pool and all the rest. 702/289-4884. M.

**CAMPING.** The park has four **campgrounds (Baker Creek, Lower Lehman, Upper Lehman, Wheeler Peak),** all with trailer spaces and access to good hikes.

While the park itself offers camping only, the concession-operated **Lehman Caves Cafe and Gift Shop** at the Visitor Center merits a special word for its old-fashioned fountain, homemade soup, and Native American crafts.

**FOR FURTHER INFORMATION.** Write Superintendent, Great Basin National Park, Baker, Nevada 89311. 702/234-7331.

# GREAT SMOKY MOUNTAINS NATIONAL PARK

## NORTH CAROLINA – TENNESSEE

### AUTHORIZED 1926/ESTABLISHED 1934

IT WAS an adventure I'll never forget. I expected spring in late March, but it was strictly winter in the Smokies. Where wildflowers should have been bursting with color, the ground was mantled with snow, and, in places, with ice. Consequently, it took a while to get organized with the right gear for the weather, and it was after midday before we started up the trail to Mount LeConte, one of the favored vista points in the park, especially for sunset watching.

I confess that my friend, Mack Prichard, state naturalist of Tennessee, carried the heavy pack. We followed a stream thickly bordered by laurel and rhododendron. The sky was generally clear, though scattered clouds, typical of the Smokies, hung low about the mountaintops and in the valleys. We saw forests dusted white with snow extending in rolling waves—it was reminiscent of a picturebook scene of Bavaria or the Black Forest. The higher we climbed, the colder it became. As we passed under the rocky outcrop of Alum Cave Bluff, the tree limbs were weighted with glistening icicles, which now and then broke loose with thundering pops. We made it to the mountaintop and huddled all night in the old stone shelter, built for summer use and downright breezy in winter. Looking back, I realize it was well worth the effort.

Astride the common border of North Carolina and Tennessee, unbroken for a distance of 70 miles except for one transmountain road, the Smokies stand as the masterwork of the Appalachian highlands. Fed by the fertile land and nourished by rain and rushing streams, plant life is luxuriant and varied, with more kinds of trees than in all of Europe. Most of it was logged before the coming of the park, but not LeConte, whose great trees we saw covered with snow.

The park covers 517,014 acres, embracing some of the oldest mountains on earth. Their foundations were laid on the floor of a shallow sea over 500 million years ago. The loftiness of the mountains was produced during a long period of earth upheavals called the Appalachian Revolution, about 200 million years ago. The Smokies escaped the icy tongue of glaciers and gave sanctuary to many plant species fleeing the frigid North. As a result, it is today the meeting ground of northern and southern types of forests.

I find the history of the region as fascinating as its natural endowments. For hundreds of years, the Smokies were part of the mountain empire of the Cherokee Indians, which at its height extended from Virginia south to Georgia and Alabama. They lived in harmony with nature in small communities along the streams, but once the advancing colonists—moving in one direction inland from Charleston, South Carolina, and in another down from Virginia and Pennsylvania—pressed their settlements into the hills the Indians were doomed.

At first, settlers took up the generous valleys and coves. On the North Carolina side, John Jacob Mingus settled in the Oconaluftee Valley in 1792. He may have been the first white man to live in what is now the national park. Others followed in the 1800s, living in isolation, moving into the subvalleys, along creek branches and up the steep hillsides to scrabble for a hard living. They grew almost everything they ate and made almost everything they wore.

The national park was a long time in coming to the Great Smoky Mountains. The idea was first advanced by Dr. Chase Ambler of Asheville, North Carolina, who organized the Appalachian National Park Association in 1899. It was renewed in 1923 by Mr. and Mrs. Willis P. Davis of Knoxville, Tennessee. But establishing a national park in the southern Appalachians, or anywhere in the East, demanded a different approach than in the West. Essentially, western parks were carved out of land already owned by the federal government as part of the vast public domain. But in the Smokies, 85 percent of the total acreage was owned by 18 timber and pulpwood companies, while the remaining 15 percent was divided among a multitude of 6,000 small farmers and owners of summer homesites.

In 1924, however, the Secretary of the Interior appointed a special committee to survey the entire mountain region for the best location for a national park. Finally the committee reported that: "The Great Smoky Mountains easily stand first because of the height of the mountains, depth of valleys, ruggedness of the area and the unexampled variety of trees, shrubs and plants." In 1926 legislation was enacted by Congress to establish three national parks: Shenandoah, Smoky Mountains, and Mammoth Cave national parks.

The Smokies lie about one hour's drive from Asheville, North Carolina, or from Knoxville, Tennessee. They are within a day's driving time of almost all the large cities of the East and Middle West. Hikers may follow approximately 900 miles of winding trails along clear streams and waterfalls. The Appalachian Trail follows the mountain crest the full 70-mile length of the park, with a chain of overnight trailside shelters. I've also enjoyed short trails passing forest giants hundreds of years old, and valleys alive with spring wildflowers and blooming summer plants. Road viewpoints unfold the vista of wilderness—the peaks rising above 6,000 feet and extending to the horizon like green waves, and the valleys screened by bluish or smokelike mist, from which the mountains derive their name.

Plan for at least two days, or take to the trails for a longer stay. Avoid the mistake of trying to "see" the Smokies only by driving over the transmountain road (US 441) on your way to another destination.

**BACKGROUND.** When approaching from Tennessee, through Gatlinburg or Townsend, stop first at **Sugarlands Visitor Center** near park headquarters. On the North Carolina side, stop at the **Oconaluftee Visitor Center** to obtain information and to see the 19th century farmstead. Nearby **Mingus Mill** presents a water-powered, turbine-driven gristmill as another page out of the past. Along US 441, a major viewpoint is at **Newfound Gap.**

**Cades Cove** is one of the choicest spots of any national park. Drive the 11-mile loop road past fields, frame churches, and pioneer homesteads. May through October, the miller grinds corn at the Cable Mill and you can purchase a bag at Cades Cove Visitor Center.

**ACTIVITIES. Hiking.** A number of trails begin from US 441. From Alum Cave parking area, you can hike to **Alum Cave Bluffs** (five miles round trip), where rose-purple rhododendron bloom in mid-June. The stronger hiker may climb the **Chimney Tops** (four miles and three hours round trip), a high, rocky perch. The **Cove Hardwoods Trail** is an easy one. It passes through an area where settlers once cultivated the land; then plunges through virgin forest. From Newfound Gap, you can sample the Appalachian Trail.

Many visitors enjoy hiking short distances on the **Appalachian Trail,** either from Davenport Gap at the eastern boundary; Fontana Dam, the southwest terminus; or from Clingman's Dome. The full distance takes six to eight days, with shelters spaced about a day's journey apart; each shelter provides bunks for at least 12 persons and is restricted to one night's use. Be sure to pick up a backcountry permit at any Visitor Center or Ranger Station.

**Bicycling.** Though much of the park terrain is too steep, the 11-mile loop through Cades Cove is ideal for cycling, and bicycles are available for rent at the Cades Cove Campground Store. Check with rangers for other routes suitable for cycling.

**Bird watching.** More than 200 species have been recorded in the park. Spring migration and summer nesting season are generally the best times for bird observation. While hiking the trails, watch hardwood forests and rhododendron thickets for nesting sites. Pick up a copy of *Notes on the Birds of Great Smoky Mountains National Park,* by Arthur Stupka.

**Naturalist Programs.** These are conducted by park personnel during the summer season. For more serious activity, Great Smoky Mountains Institute at Tremont offers two one-week summer courses on topics such as wildlife, mountain storytelling, and cultural history. Write the Great Smoky Mountains Institute, Route 1, Box 700, Townsend, TN 37882.

**Fishing.** Fishing is permitted year-round in open waters. Some 600 miles of streams flow through the park, many offering opportunities for rainbow and brown trout. The possession of any brook trout is prohibited. Certain streams are closed to fishing, as protection for the brook trout. A Tennessee or North Carolina fishing license is required. Inquire at the Ranger Stations or Visitor Centers for a free copy of park fishing rules and regulations.

**ACCOMMODATIONS.** A wide range of lodgings are plentiful around the park. Principal concentration on the Tennessee side is at Gatlinburg and Pigeon Forge—handy, but crowded. Simple overnight accommodations are provided in the park by a single concession:

**LeConte Lodge,** Box 350, Gatlinburg, TN 37738. Atop Mount LeConte, reached by foot or horse trail only; a favored outdoors rendezvous for years. It is open April through October. 615/436-4473. L.

**Cataloochee Ranch,** Box 500, Route 1,

Maggie Valley, NC 28751. Distinctive, tastefully furnished lodge and cabins at 5,000 feet elevation operate on Modified American Plan mid-May to late October. Tennis and riding. 704/926-1401. M to H.

**River Edge Motor Lodge,** 948 River Rd., Gatlinburg, TN 37738. Rooms with balconies. Heated pool. 615/436-9292. M.

**Fontana Village Resort,** Fontana Dam, NC 28733. This family resort includes 250 housekeeping cottages of 1 to 3 bedrooms, 2 pools, par 3 golf, tennis, square dancing and crafts. Rent a boat and cross Fontana Lake to Hazel Creek or hike the Appalachian Trail in the national park. 704/498-2211. M.

**Bell's Wa-Floy Retreat Hostel,** 3610 E. Pkwy., Gatlinburg, TN 37738. For those who manage on their own; with swimming pool and volleyball. Open year-round. 704/436-5575. L.

**CAMPING.** During summer months, the three major campgrounds (Elkmont, Smokemont, and Cades Cove) are on a computer reservation system operated by HSN Mistix. Reservations are required May 15 through October 31. Call HSN Mistix at 800/365-CAMP. A free permit is required for all backcountry camping. Pick up yours at any visitor center or ranger station. Campgrounds are also located in communities near the park.

**SEASONS.** Spring weather can begin as early as January or as late as March. Hikers and campers should bring warm clothing for cool weather until May. Wildflowers usually are outstanding for the Spring Wildflower Pilgrimage, held annually at Gatlinburg the last weekend of April, with wildflower and botany lectures, photography seminar, bird walks, and field trips in the park. The lowlands in summer are warm; the summits are always cooler. Rainfall and thundershowers are likely, making raingear a must. For a rewarding experience, hike to Gregory's Bald in late June, when spectacular masses of wild azaleas bloom along the edges of this hillside meadow. During the last weekend of September and the first weekend of October, sorghum making is demonstrated alternately at Cades Cove and Oconaluftee Farm Homestead in the manner handed down from generation to generation.

**NEARBY.** Just outside the park, in North Carolina, the **Oconaluftee Village** and **Qualla Crafts Shop** display the handicrafts and history of the Cherokee people. They serve as a fitting prelude to an evening performance of the outdoor drama, "Unto These Hills." The **Blue Ridge Parkway** provides motoring adventure and picnic areas at high, cool elevations, with expansive vistas of the Smokies and other ranges. **Pisgah National Forest** includes 80 miles of the Appalachian Trail and the site of the historic "Cradle of Forestry in America" at the Pink Beds south of Asheville. **Nantahala National Forest,** the Cherokee "land of the noonday sun," has facilities for fishing, camping, hunting, and the beautiful Joyce Kilmer Memorial Forest, with towering giants 500 and 600 years old. **Fontana Lake** is the largest of a network of TVA and other reservoirs providing water sports. On the Tennessee side, the **Cherokee National Forest** has many camping sites, plus nature trails and scenic drives. Enthusiasts of handicrafts will want to attend the **Craftsman's Fairs,** held at Asheville in July and at Gatlinburg in October.

**RECOMMENDED READING.** *Strangers in High Places* by Michael Frome, *Our Southern Highlanders* by Horace Kephart, and *Hiker's Guide to the Smokies* by Dick Murlless and Constance Stallings.

**FOR FURTHER INFORMATION.** Write Superintendent, 107 Park Headquarters Road, Great Smoky Mountains National Park, Gatlinburg, TN 37738. 615/436-1200.

# GUADALUPE MOUNTAINS NATIONAL PARK

## TEXAS

AUTHORIZED 1966/ESTABLISHED 1972

I VISITED the Guadalupe Mountains before they were designated as a national park, in the company of J. C. Hunter, Jr., who made the national park possible. "I hold title to the land," he said, "but how can anyone consider himself owner of this magnificent country, when these mountains have stood alone here for millions of years?"

Actually, the first proposal for a park of some kind was made by his father, Judge J. C. Hunter, of Culberson County, Texas, in 1925.

Judge Hunter purchased one section of land in remote West Texas and had prospects of donation of an additional 6,000 to 8,000 acres from other owners for park purposes, but that initial project fell through. He continued to acquire land during the 1930s and '40s. The judge and his son used this territory west of the Pecos as a ranch for angora goats to produce mohair wool, but were careful to avoid overgrazing the land, in anticipation of it one day becoming part of a national park. Even after the death of the judge in 1945, his son continued to expand the "Hunter Lands" in the Guadalupe Mountains.

New impetus was given in 1958 when Wallace E. Pratt offered to donate his ranch lands, which included the mouth and north fork of McKittrick Canyon, an area rich in natural values. Pratt had been associated with Humble Oil Company as chief geologist and vice president until his retirement in 1945. His donation of 5,632 acres was completed in 1961. Then J. C. Hunter, Jr., moved to offer 72,000 acres around McKittrick Canyon at a price of $1.5 million. When Congress, spurred by Senator Ralph Yarborough of Texas, authorized establishment of the park in 1966, it picked up one of the greatest land bargains in history—a national park at $21 per acre. Following acquisition of mineral rights from the State of Texas and other sources, the park was formally established and dedicated on September 30, 1972.

I rode a mule, surefooted and determined, rather than stubborn, up the rugged, brushy slopes. The foot of the mountains I found landscaped with agaves and cacti, but with rising elevation the vegetation changed to pines,

**145**

alligator juniper, even Douglas fir in favorable settings. I learned that on the highest peaks, some spots show decidedly alpine characteristics.

The Guadalupe Mountains stand like an island in the desert, 110 miles from El Paso and barely below the border that Texas shares with New Mexico. The most prominent feature of the 86,416-acre national park is El Capitan, a sheer, thousand-foot, whitish-colored cliff. Directly north of it, Guadalupe Peak, 8,749 feet, is the highest point of the Lone Star State.

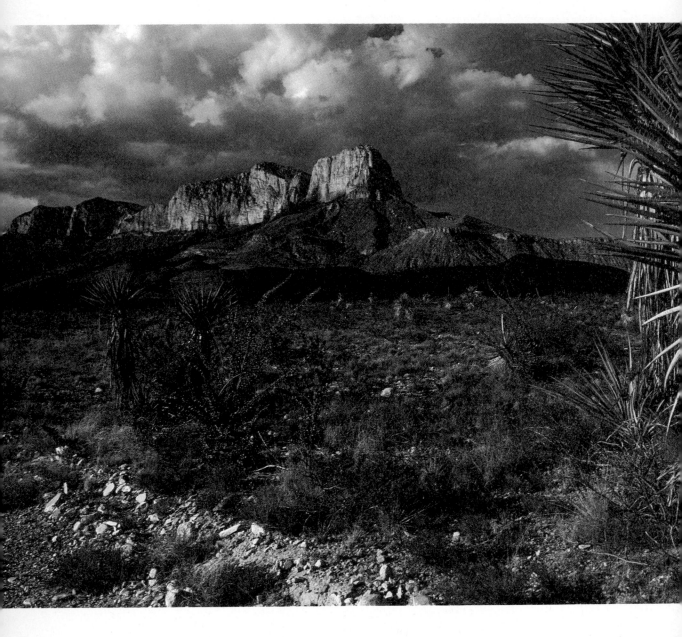

Geologically speaking, they are a spectacular exposure of one of the world's most extensive and significant fossil reefs. They date from the Permian period, between 230 and 280 million years ago, when a vast saltwater basin occupied a large part of present Texas and New Mexico. In the shallower water, marine organisms and waterborne minerals formed a limestone reef similar to the one that shelters the coastland of Queensland, Australia, today. Also of major geological interest is the tremendous earth fault on the abrupt west side of the park.

Prehistoric Americans evidently occupied these canyons as early as 12,000 years ago. Many pictographs are found in caves and rock shelters.

Roasting pits found at all elevations indicate that early inhabitants followed the ripening of native plants from the valley floor in spring to the highest ridges in autumn. The first references in history were written by the Spanish conquistadors in the course of their journeys north from Mexico. They found Mescalero Apaches living in the area.

I saw hawks, hummingbirds, vireos, and warblers, among the 200-plus species of birds found in the canyons and over clifftops. I wish that I had caught a glimpse of a mountain lion, bear, or wild turkey. With luck, you might succeed where I failed.

## THE PRACTICAL GUIDE

Roads cross only limited portions of the park, but more than 80 miles of rugged, scenic hiking trails provide broader access. Several scenic sites, including the remains of a stage station on the Butterfield Stage Line, are accessible by car.

BACKGROUND. Center of activities, the new **Visitor Center** is located at Pine Springs, Texas, 55 miles southwest of Carlsbad, New Mexico. It is on US 62/180 and is open 7 A.M. to 6 P.M. in the summer and 8 A.M. to 4:30 P.M. in the winter. The Visitor Center houses a natural history museum. Be sure to see the slide show in the auditorium; it concentrates on the park wilderness. A self-guided, 2-mile hike to Smith and Manzanita Springs can be made at any time. Self-guided nature trails are available at McKittrick Canyon, Main Visitor Center, and Dog Canyon.

A paved road leads to the **McKittrick Canyon** contact station, at the mouth of McKittrick Canyon. Allow time to see the exhibits and self-starting slide program. This area is open for day use only; the road is closed each evening. You will see rare plant communities on the lower floor of the canyon. The walls reveal the Capitan Reef and fore-reef and back-reef marine deposits. The trail covers 3½ miles along the bottom of the canyon before beginning a steep four-mile climb to the top of McKittrick Ridge. Some parts of McKittrick Canyon are designated Research Natural Areas and are closed to all entry.

HIKING. Trails are available for both experts and novices. Unless experienced in this type of country, content yourself with one-day hikes. Trails are rocky and often steep. Weather conditions are apt to change rapidly. The hike to **Devil's Hallway** leads up the floor of Pine Canyon; it takes about six hours. Watch for the rare spotted owl, which has been seen on many occasions along trails into the high country.

Hikes in the high country afford spectacular sights of the Chihuahan Desert and salt flats spreading out below. You'll see historic sites, including the "Pinery" stage station, Frijole and Williams ranch houses, and the Pratt Lodge stone cabin.

**ACCOMMODATIONS.** Other than camping, there are no overnight facilities in the park. The nearest are at Whites City (35 miles northeast) and Carlsbad (55 miles northeast), both in New Mexico; these are listed under Carlsbad Caverns National Park. Nearest facilities in Texas are at Van Horn, 65 miles south.

**Best Western Inn of Van Horn,** Van Horn, TX 79855. Pool, 9-hole golf privileges. 915/283-2410. L to M.

**Ranch,** Van Horn, TX 79855. Some kitchen units. Pool. Family rates available. 915/283-2225. L.

**CAMPING. Pine Springs Campground,** a short drive from the information station, is at the entrance to the Pine Springs Canyon. It offers 24 tent sites and space for 17 recreational vehicles, water, and modern restroom building. A fee is charged per night per vehicle.

**Dog Canyon Campground** and trailhead are reached from New Mexico. Dog Canyon lies 70 miles from Carlsbad via US 285 and New Mexico 137 through Lincoln National Forest. The campground, 1 mile inside the park boundary, contains 18 tent sites and five spaces for self-contained vehicles. At 6,300 feet elevation, summer is comfortable and pleasant. This is a good place to start either a day hike or backpack, since you don't have the steep climb on the eastern escarpment near Pine Springs. You can have a good hike to Lost Peak, 2½ miles south over a well-marked trail. You can bring private horses to Dog Canyon, but you must have feed and water for them.

In addition to the campgrounds in the park, several private campgrounds are located at Whites City and in the city of Carlsbad. If you are planning to camp in the backcountry, register at the Information Station, where you can purchase a good topographic map of the high country and obtain a permit for one of the designated camping areas. Be sure you have proper equipment, including sturdy boots, map, head cover, and adequate water. Watch out for rattlesnakes, especially during their early morning and evening feeding hours.

**FOR FURTHER INFORMATION.** Write Superintendent, Guadalupe Mountains National Park, HC 60, Box 400, Salt Flat, TX 79847-9400. 915/828-3251.

# HALEAKALA NATIONAL PARK

## HAWAII

### AUTHORIZED 1916

IT WAS one of those typically clear Hawaiian days. From the observatory at the summit of Haleakala crater, I looked across the waters of the Pacific. The Big Island of Hawaii rose boldly against the sky, while in the opposite direction, northwest of where I stood, were the neighboring islands of Lanai, Molokai, and Oahu. All of them, I thought, are like children of the sea, raised from the earth's crust by repeated volcanic action.

The Hawaiian islands, with their distinctive birds, plants, and Polynesian culture, are as much a part of the United States as any part of the mainland, yet they add extra dimensions to the character of the nation. Where else could I stand in the "House of the Sun," or Haleakala, where the demigod Maui held the sun prisoner in order to give his people more daylight hours? And whether legend or not, I saw where the sun has helped produce unusual native plants among the multicolored cones, cinders, pumice, and ash.

Maui, the "Valley Island," on which Haleakala is located, was formed, so they tell us, by two volcanoes rising from the sea. In one million years or so, a small part of the island has been tempered into fertile fields, now growing sugarcane and pineapple, but the mammoth Haleakala bears eloquent witness to the volcanic explosions of the Pacific.

Haleakala was a spiritual and cultural focal point of Hawaiians for perhaps a thousand years before Captain Cook arrived in the islands. In fact, while hiking within the park, I saw the remains of an ancient hand-laid stone and learned that some archaeologists suspect that Hawaiians have occupied the crater for religious purposes.

Missionaries, seafarers, and surveyors visited Haleakala in the 1800s. The most famous American to describe it was Mark Twain, in *Roughing It*. He was so enthusiastic about this site that in 1881 he wrote to Charles Warren Stoddard: "If the house would burn down, we would pack up the cubs and fly to the isles of the blest, and shut ourselves up in the healing solitudes of the eroded valley of Haleakala and get a good rest. . . ."

It was Lorrin A. Thurston, grandson of missionaries and publisher of the *Pacific Commercial Advertiser*, who led the effort to establish a national park of Hawaii's volcanoes. In 1907, the Hawaii legislature invited no fewer than 50 members of Congress and their wives to see the proposed park area firsthand. Their visit included a fancy dinner cooked over hot lava vents at the edge of Halemaumau. In 1912, Dr. Thomas Jaggar, lately hired as director of the Hawaiian Volcano Observatory, joined the campaign. He and Thurston were tireless boosters of the park idea. In 1916, with little controversy generated, Congress voted to authorize the new Hawaii National Park, consisting of three separate sections: Kilauea, Mauna Loa, and Haleakala. In 1960, Haleakala was established as a park in its own right, giving official sanction to what had been a sacred, unspoiled wilderness for perhaps 1,400 years.

Early in 1969, major portions of Kipahulu Valley became part of the national park. The addition includes the beautiful pools of the 'Ohe'o stream and 54 acres fronting on the ocean. The Kipahulu Valley, on the east slope of Haleakala volcano, provides ancient forests, waterfalls, lava pools, and many cultural sites.

The park covers 28,665 acres, but when I reached the rim, I realized that most of it is contained within the valley; it is 7½ miles long, 2½ miles wide, and 21 miles around. The floor of the valley, the heart of the park with its richly colored cinder cones, lies 3,000 feet below the summit, covering an area of 19 square miles. The last volcanic action on Maui occurred in the 1790s (outside the park), but earthquake activity is still recorded and felt here.

I marveled at the unusual life of the park. The plant most characteristic of Haleakala is the rare, yucca-like silversword, which grows as a mass of silvery, saberlike leaves; when full grown its flower stalk produces a hundred or more vivid purplish blooms. As soon as the seeds of this bloom mature, the plant dies.

I caught sight of a nene, a Hawaiian goose hawk, and several honeycreepers. It was not surprising to learn that 70 different birds indigenous to the island are unlike any others in the world, and that a few of them live only in Haleakala.

## THE PRACTICAL GUIDE

ACCESS. Passenger planes make several flights daily (20 minutes) from Honolulu to Maui. Arrangements for tours can be made at Kahului Airport or at Maui hotels. Some visitors come by rental car. The park is reached on the highest paved road in the mid-Pacific, often with clear views of the ocean and at other times with flowing mists and cloud banks, creating a variety of Pacific moods. For the full enjoyment of the park, plan two or three days, and stay overnight in the cabins within the park, which are reached only by hiking or on horseback. Reservations for the cabins must be made three months in advance.

The real adventure is within the eroded valley itself. There are no roads, but 30 miles of well-marked trails show how plant life increases as you descend and move eastward. Here you find rare birds like the Hawaiian goose, or *nēnē*. Though it has entirely forsaken the water, its feet retain some webbing. This native bird was reintroduced to the island near Paliku Cabin in 1962, in a cooperative project by the State of Hawaii, the U.S. Fish and Wildlife Service, and the National Park Service. To protect rare and endangered species, pets are not allowed in the crater.

**BACKGROUND.** Park headquarters are located 1 mile beyond the entrance. A ranger can help you plan your visit. Even if your time is limited, he will suggest a drive to the crater rim viewpoints, which rise steadily upward to the summit. **Kalahaku Overlook** contains an area of silversword, enclosed to protect them from troublesome goats roaming loose and from thoughtless visitors, but even here roots have been damaged by overeager amateur photographers. This striking, unusual plant once flourished so abundantly that the park near the summit appeared bathed in moonlight from the glow of its silvery leaves. But by the beginning of this century human vandalism and unchecked livestock grazing brought the silversword to the edge of extinction. Plants are still found on the slopes of cinder cones. Depending on weather, as many as 100 plants flower in a good season. Each plant flowers but once, a bright yellow and reddish-purple, then dies slowly as seeds mature.

From the Visitor Center near the summit, a trail goes up 380 yards to White Hill, a formation lighter in color than most Hawaiian lava.

**ACTIVITIES. Hiking.** If you plan to hike any of the trails, remember the difference in altitude here; if you are accustomed to the atmosphere at sea level, take things easy and settle for a sample.

**Red Hill Overlook,** the highest point of the rim (and on the island), affords an excellent vantage for picture taking.

**Two hiking trails** lead into the eroded valley, **Halemauu** at 8,000 feet and **Sliding Sands** at 10,000 feet. Most persons enter via Sliding Sands and return via Halemauu, and are encouraged to do so. For safety reasons, a permit is required for all overnight trips.

The hike down Sliding Sands, across the floor and out on Halemauu covers about 12 miles. You can do it in a day. En route you'll see a variety of native shrubs with unusual flowers or berries; Hawaiian snow, a lichen, the first plant to appear after a lava flow in higher altitudes; sandalwood trees; and mountain pili, distinct from the lowland variety once used for grass houses.

**Paliku** is a lush oasis deep inside the northeast corner of the park. Clouds moving up the windward slopes and spilling over the rim have furnished the moisture. Here the nene feeds upon grasses, leafy plants, and berries in open or semiopen areas.

**Bottomless Pit** lies along the Halemauu Trail. Keep away from the crumbly edges of

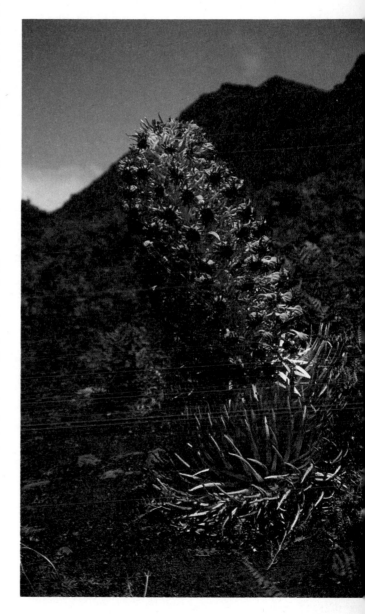

this old spatter vent, since the bottom is 65 feet down. Nearby are Pele's Paint Pot, a colorful pass between cinder cones and Pele's Pig Pen (reached on a cross trail), a half-buried spatter vent. Near Holua Cabin you'll cross the Silversword Loop Trail.

For comfortable hiking, wear sturdy boots, and carry a canteen. Be sure to have a light raincoat and a sunhat. If you haven't been out in the sun lately, use suntan lotion liberally.

**Botany, Bird watching.** Hawaii provides habitat for plants and birds found nowhere else in the world, and to many others of the tropics alone. Visit the two national parks, Haleakala and Hawaii Volcanoes, for about a thousand different kinds of flowering plants, ferns and fern allies. Get a copy of *Trailside Plants of Hawaii's National Parks* by Charles H. Lamoureux (professor of botany at the University of Hawaii) and be on the lookout for species like the ti, a member of the lily family, and the noni, a small tree that is a member of the coffee family, probably introduced by early Polynesian settlers. Both are near the Kipahulu. Among the birds, the parks shelter rare and lovely species like the nukupuu, a honeycreeper long thought extinct, and the brilliant iiwi, with bright scarlet body and black wings and tail. Travel with your own copy of *Hawaii Birds*, published by the Hawaii Audubon Society.

**Whale watching.** Waters stretching between the islands of Maui, Molokai, Kahoolawe, and Lanai are favored courting, birthing, and nursing grounds of the magnificent humpback whales. Usually they appear about mid-December through April, bearing and nursing young in comparatively quiet inshore waters. Though humpbacks once numbered about 100,000, their worldwide population is now estimated at 5,000. Besides the playful humpbacks, most graceful of the great whales, you are also likely to see groups of pilot whales, spinner porpoises, and bottlenose dolphins.

The **Kipahulu** and **Wailua Cove** are major scenic attractions along an unspoiled section of the Maui coast. A slow, winding road, Hawaii 36, circles east Maui, providing access to several small villages. Driving time from the Wailuku-Kahului area should be between three and four hours, but allow the better part of a day for stops at scenic state parks and freshwater pools where you can take a dip. At Keanae, drive down to the little settlement along the coast to see the century-old church and the surf pounding lava outcrops. There are several resorts and campgrounds in the Hana vicinity to use as a base to visit beautiful beaches, gardens, and the national park. Try to hike some of the upper jeep roads and trails that lead to exciting views of several waterfalls. The two-mile hike up Pipiwai Valley passes ancient Hawaiian farmsites and goes through an extensive bamboo forest to Waimoku Falls.

**RIDING.** Guided saddle tours into the crater, passing cinder cones and lava fields, are offered by nearby commercial stables. Riding may be easier than hiking, but with thin air, sun, and wind, it still takes stamina. Contact Pony Express, Box 535, Kula, HI 96790 (667-2200) or Thompson Ranch, RR2, Box 203, Kula, HI 96790 (878-1910).

**ACCOMMODATIONS.** The sole accommodations in the park, other than campgrounds, are three cabins within the crater reached by trail. None is closer than 4 miles from the rim. They are equipped with bunks, cookstove and firewood. There is a maximum stay of two nights in each cabin. Because of their popularity, a lottery for reservations is held the first day of each month for two months ahead. For details, write Superintendent, Box 369, Makawao, Maui, HI 96768. On Maui itself, phone park headquarters, 808/572-9306.

Outside the park, in Kula, center of Maui's vegetable and flower growing, and in Hana there is a range of accommodations available.

**Kula Lodge,** Kula, HI 96790. Mountain hideaway, with chalets and restaurant. A good base for hiking and riding in Haleakala. 808/878-1535. H.

**Waianapanapa State Park,** Division of State Parks, Box 1049, Wailuku, HI 96793. At the edge of Hana, the state park maintains kitchen-equipped rustic cabins sleeping four to six. Reservations required well in advance. 808/244-4354. L to M.

**Aloha Cottage,** Hana, HI 96713. Perched above Hana Bay, kitchen-equipped cottages are popular and in demand. 808/248-8420. L.

**CAMPING.** One campground is located near the park entrance in the **Hosmer Grove,** surrounded by introduced trees and native shrubs. Backpack camping is allowed at two designated areas—**Holua** and **Paliku,** by permit only. You can obtain a permit at park headquarters. Camping is limited to two nights at either site and to a maximum of three nights per month. Hikers are asked to pack out all refuse and to be self-contained, because of the fragile environment of the crater. At **Kipahulu** an undeveloped campground is located in an open pasture southeast of the Ranger Station, near the ocean. Neither firewood nor drinking water is available. A camping permit is not required, but camping is limited to three nights per month. Check the bulletin board at Kipahulu Ranger Station for a list of guided hikes, Ranger talks, and cultural demonstrations.

**SEASONS.** Rarely does temperature on Maui fall below 55 or rise above 90—rarely above 80 in the mountains. Come prepared for cool, windy weather at the high park elevation. Summers usually are clear; winters are more cloudy and rainy. At night, temperatures will drop into the low 40s, or high 30s, even during summer.

**NEARBY.** Maui has become a bustling resort center with a variety of oceanside hotels, motels, and apartments. A few small inns, such as Kula Lodge and Silversword Inn, are located in the high valleys en route to the park. Camping is permitted without charge in public parks, with four-day limit; permits are obtained by writing Superintendent, Maui County Department of Parks, 1580 Kaahumanu Avenue, Wailuku, Maui, Hawaii 96793.

Seven parks are located on beaches along the shoreline, including **Waiehu Beach Park,** with excellent shelling and fishing. The drive between **Hana** and **Wailuku,** on the coast below Haleakala, offers unusual beauty among heavily foliaged gorges, fishing settlements, and small villages. You can fly direct to Hana from Honolulu in a little under one hour. Hotel Hana-Maui is one of the finest resorts anywhere in the islands. **Waianapanapa State Park,** just outside "heavenly Hana," offers camping and kitchen-furnished cabins (requiring reservations well in advance). Visit the little Congregational church facing the sea chosen by Charles A. Lindbergh as his final resting place. In a setting of flowering oleander and plumeria the simple burial stone bears this memorable inscription; "...If I take the wings of the morning and dwell in the uttermost parts of the sea."—C.A.L.

**FOR FURTHER INFORMATION.** Write Superintendent, Haleakala National Park, Box 369, Makawao, Maui, Hawaii 96768. 808/572-9306.

# HAWAII VOLCANOES NATIONAL PARK

## HAWAII

ESTABLISHED 1916

I COULD hardly believe that I was climbing to the summit of Mauna Loa, but there I was on the world's largest volcano, a mountain built by layer upon layer of lava, rising from about 20,000 feet below the sea to 13,677 above. It was 1985, though my mind traveled back to the early Hawaiians making their way to the top without shoes, backpacks, or freeze-dried food, perhaps without warm clothing, living close to nature as they were meant to.

My companion and I hiked upward through a forest of 'ōhi'a, the pioneer tree of fresh lava flows. "The invincible 'ōhi'a," Mark Twain called it after observing its trunks emerging like spears of grass from volcanic crevasses. Hawaiians of other days fashioned spears, mallets, and bowls from its hard wood. Though we hadn't heard many sounds since starting from the trailhead, we suddenly became aware of a whirring of wings and stood very quietly. Joe, my companion, a national park ranger, said it was an *apapane,* the most common surviving species of Hawaiian honeycreeper, flitting from tree to tree to feed on nectar from 'ōhi'a blossoms. We could not catch sight of this striking bird, but were lucky enough to hear its rambling, rolling song.

Everything natural and native about Hawaii—its birds, insects, plants, ferns, and trees—seems so distinct and luxuriant, explaining why native Hawaiians speak of "Aina," the traditional love of land, or reverence for life. Their poetic oli, or chants, and the hula recount traditions that weave humankind into the universe. The summit of Kilauea, for instance, is considered the sacred palace of the goddess Pele. As daughter of Earth Mother and Sky Father, Pele came to Hawaii in flight from her cruel older sister, goddess of the sea. She found her refuge in the volcano, where she has prevailed ever since as goddess of fire.

Our climb took the better part of two days—we spent the night at a shelter cabin conveniently sited at the 10,000-foot level, but I made it to the top of mighty Mauna Loa. Its lava flows occupy more than 2,000 square miles of Hawaii, the "Big Island." Its 1949 eruption continued for almost five months. A year later it spewed one of the most voluminous flows in history, producing about 600 million cubic yards of lava in 23 days.

Mauna Loa then slumbered for 25 years, until July 5, 1975, when it erupted in a six-mile curtain of fire at the Mokuaweoweo Crater and a two-pronged lava flow from Pohaku Hanalei. The eruption wiped out the upper portion of the trail to the summit. Earthquakes were continuing at the rate of one or two a minute five days later. Mauna Loa erupted again on March 25 to April 15, 1984.

Neighboring Kilauea has been more active, erupting 50 times since 1980. Repeated eruptions in 1983 and 1984, continuing into 1985, provided awesome views and extensive property damage along the park's eastern boundary. This eruption created a new cone over 700 feet high. In 1989, the Wahaula Visitor Center was destroyed by a Kilauea surface lava flow. Whenever a new eruption occurs, Hawaii residents rush out to view the magnificent fiery display. Parking lots on the rim are quickly filled and airplanes buzz overhead.

Kilauea and a portion of the flank and summit of Mauna Loa are within the 229,117-acre national park. These young volcanoes, which may have been formed only within the last million years, grow with energy, keeping ahead of the ever-present agents of erosion.

Fortunately, despite their seeming ferocity, Mauna Loa and Kilauea are relatively gentle giants that seldom become dangerously explosive even while liberating tons of molten rock from vents and cracks.

I have never, on any of my several visits, seen an eruption in progress, but the signs of geologic upheaval and earth-building are everywhere—in hissing fumaroles, smoldering firepits, pungent sulfur banks gleaming against black moonscapes and once-molten lava still showing the patterns in which it was spewed. Climbing to the top and looking over it all certainly proves a superlative national park adventure.

## THE PRACTICAL GUIDE

ACCESS. Passenger planes make frequent flights daily from Honolulu to the Big Island. Direct flights also operate to and from Kona and the mainland.

The national park is included in the itinerary of guided motorcoach and bicycle tours. Cars can be rented either at General Lyman Field, Hilo or at Kailua-Kona.

BACKGROUND. Park headquarters is off Hawaii 11, the Mamalahoa Highway, connecting Kona and Hilo. Allow ample time for the Thomas A. Jaggar Museum, on the volcano's rim. Completed in 1987, it is one of the finest museums in any national park. It contains maps, models, and paintings on the story of the park; color films of recent eruptions are shown hourly each day. It is named in memory of Dr. Thomas A. Jaggar, who established the Hawaiian Volcano Observatory in 1912. The Wahaula Visitor Center, destroyed by lava in 1989, was replaced by a moveable information booth at the coast.

Crater Rim Drive, covering 11.1 miles, provides the best orientation to the park. It leads from park headquarters to the Thurston Lava Tube, formed when the outer crust of lava hardened and the inner portion flowed away. You can explore the tunnel-like formation for a distance of about 500 feet. Nearby thrives the glorious **Tree Fern Forest.** Rains average about 100 inches annually, sustaining a growth of many varieties of ferns, over-towered by a dense growth of tropical 'ōhi' a trees. Whenever the 'ōhi' a blooms, one finds the apapane, a small nectar-sucking bird as red as the lehua (the feathery 'ōhi'a blossom), but with black wings and gray belly. Equally abundant in the forests is the 'amakihi, a small yellow-green insect gatherer, and the 'el-epaio, a perky flycatcher. The road dips into the crater to a parking area at the brink of the **Halemaumau pit.**

Northwest of the Hawaiian Volcano Observatory, in the direction of Mauna Loa, lies **Kipuka Puaulu,** or "Bird Park," a typical "is-land" of old surface surrounded by young lava flows. A nature trail leads into a forested sec-tion, an arboretum of 40 varieties of trees, some peculiar to the island of Hawaii. A few are the only living representatives of their van-ishing species. On fresh rock surfaces of the younger lava flows the sturdy 'ōhi'a, the color-ful 'ali'i and pūkiawe shrubs pioneer a new forest. Perhaps the final point of interest on Crater Rim Drive is **Devastation Trail** at Kilauea Iki crater overlook, scene of the 1959 eruption. From this viewpoint you can look across the crater and view the cinder cone, part of the main caldera, and, on a clear day, Mauna Loa.

**Kau Desert,** the leeward slope of Kilauea Crater, also on the rim road, receives very lit-tle rain from the trade winds but is soaked occasionally by a heavy general storm. The Southwest Rift is marked by a great crack area.

**ERUPTION NEWS.** You can get the latest with a phone call. On the Big Island, dial 967-7977. From Oahu and the other islands, dial 1-967-7977.

**ACTIVITIES. Hiking. Mauna Loa Trail** pro-vides one of the most unusual hikes in the Na-tional Park system. The route to the summit, at 13,677 feet, is 18 miles one way. Allow at least three days and plan very carefully with a copy of Lisa Peterson's excellent *Mauna Loa Trail*

*Guide,* which you purchase at the Visitor Cen-ter. From the mountain parkland the trail rises through the fringe of straggling mamanis and railliardias. Above 10,000 feet, it enters the vast expanse of barren lava fields, winding be-tween pumice cones and along lava-splattered cracks. Ice lingers in the cracks most of the year. Hikers can stay overnight at park cabins at Red Hill, 10,000 feet, and on the summit. Another good backcountry trip is the **Halape Coastal Hike,** about 8 miles one way to the coastal section of the park, with camping near a fine white sand beach. Even if you don't go the whole length, drive out to Hilina Pali, reached from a turnoff halfway down the Chain of Craters Road. Then walk out at least a little way for the marvelous views of the untouched and still forming southeast coast. Few visitors take the trouble to visit this point, though they are missing one of the finest ocean views on the island. Actually, the park has over 150 miles of foot trails.

**Photography.** Park headquarters area receives about 100 inches of rain yearly. This

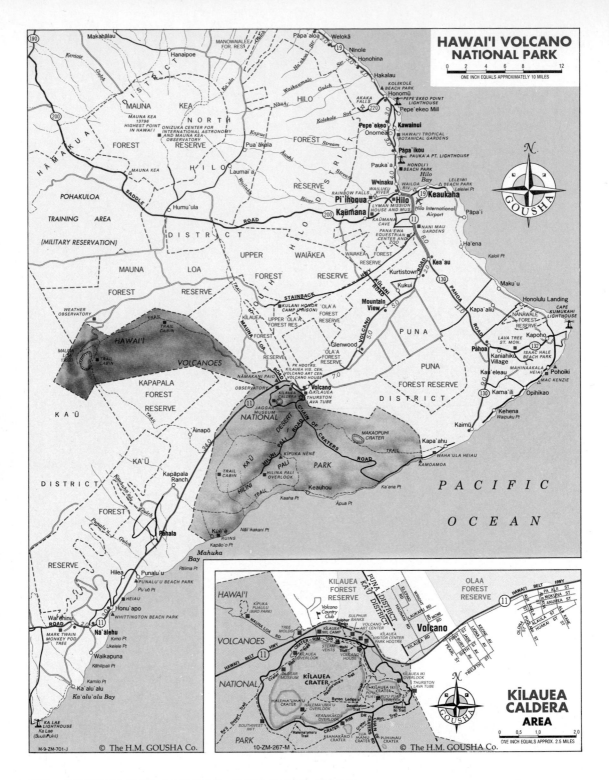

means many days are overcast and dark. Fortunately, a rough pattern is predictable—most early mornings are clear and bright, but by noon the northeast trade winds have blown in a dense cloud cover. If you are fortunate enough to arrive during an eruption, you will find high-speed color film and a telephoto lens useful.

**ACCOMMODATIONS.** There is only one lodge inside the park, Volcano House. Outside the park lodgings of varying size and quality are at vacation centers such as the Kona Coast and Hilo. Many are large, chain-operated. Others are locally owned. For a list of B&Bs, write Hawaii's Best Bed and Breakfasts, Box 563, Hawaii 96785; 808/885-4450.

**Volcano House,** Hawaii Volcanoes National Park, HI 96718. At 4,000 feet elevation on the rim of Kilauea, it is a modern, comfortable lodge, a good stop for lunch or overnight. It is within easy walking distance of the park visitor center and headquarters. A sauna bath, supplied by natural volcanic system steam vents, is available 24 hours a day. Volcano House derived a large part of its character from the personality of the late George Lycurgus, who acquired the earlier Volcano House in 1904 and established it as a "celebrity" inn. He died in 1960, at the age of 101. The original Volcano House, adjacent to the visitor center, was built in 1877 and used continuously until 1939. It was refurbished and reopened in 1975 as the new Volcano Art Center, an excellent place for shopping. It is listed on the National Register of Historic Places. 808/967-7321. M.

**Manago Hotel,** Captain Cook, HI 96726. Family-run, friendly, and old-style excellent cooking. It is near Kealakekua Bay and Pu'uhonua o Honaunau National Historical Park (City of Refuge). 808/323-2642. L.

**Shirakawa's Hotel and Motel,** Naalehu, HI 96772. Midway between Kona and Hilo, the southernmost hotel in the country is set in a lush area 1,000 feet above sea level. New motel units apart from the main house have private baths; some have kitchenettes. 808/929-7462. L.

**CAMPING.** The park concessioner operates 10 tiny, unfurnished A-frame cabins in a koa and eucalyptus forest 3 miles from park headquarters, which places you near the 100-acre Bird Park, a green island amid stark lava flows. Each cabin sleeps four. Community rest rooms have hot and cold water. A modest charge is made, and linens are extra.

The national park itself has two cabins for hikers to the summit of Mauna Loa. One, near 10,000 feet elevation, sleeps nine persons; the other, at 13,250 feet, the southwest edge of the summit caldera, sleeps eleven. Both are free, but expect company of other hikers. You'll find a water catchment and pit toilets. Bring food, flashlight, bedroll, parka, water, and gas stove. No reservations are taken; when registering at the Kilauea Visitor Center you'll learn the number of hikers already on the trail.

**SEASONS.** Seasons are not pronounced in semitropical Hawaii, but the weather can be cool at any time at the high elevations in the park. Rainwear will be essential, as heavy precipitation can be expected frequently.

**NEARBY. Pu'uhonua O Honaunau National Historical Park** (formerly City of Refuge National Historic Park), on the Kona coast, which became part of the national park system in 1961, contains an ancient burial temple of Hawaii's kings and interprets the story of the early Hawaiian settlers. An interesting horticultural area, **Akaka Falls State Park,** distinguished by its varied tropical plants, trees, and shrubs, is located north of Hilo near the sugar fields of Honomu.

A visit to Hawaii Volcanoes should be linked with a stop at Maui to see **Haleakala National Park;** together these areas formerly constituted Hawaii National Park.

**FOR FURTHER INFORMATION.** Write Superintendent, Hawaii Volcanoes National Park, HI 96718. 808/967-7311.

# HOT SPRINGS NATIONAL PARK

## ARKANSAS

ESTABLISHED 1921

WALKING DOWN BATHHOUSE ROW in downtown Hot Springs, I let my imagination lead me into the past. I pictured the scene in the 1930s and '40s—the baths filled with pilgrims seeking relief from the aches and pains of arthritis, gout, and assorted other diseases. I tried to visualize American life in the age before vaccines and the modern miracle drugs we now take for granted.

Hot Springs is a bit of a ghost of itself. From a million baths in 1946, it's down to about 100,000 baths a year now. Still, it holds a special charm, maybe like the beginning of the hot tub. The Indians had the right idea—it was a sacred place for them. Then Hot Springs was discovered by French trappers and explorers in the 1700s. I would like to have been with them when they watched the vapors rising from the valley and felt the healing properties of the springs. Ultimately, the federal government in 1832 established the springs as a federal reservation. I wonder if anyone back then could possibly have envisioned that action as the first step leading to the national park.

In the 19th century, resorts with medicinal bathing ("spas") were extremely popular. The idea of the bath as a recreational pursuit goes back in history to the ancient days of the Greeks, Romans, and Saxons. In fact, Bath, the most famous spa in England, had its beginning when the Romans discovered the healing qualities of the waters; the remains of the luxurious baths are now Britain's most significant Roman relic. From Europe, the spa idea was transplanted to America as a mark of culture.

Virtually all spas were reserved for the wealthy and aristocratic. Establishment of the Hot Springs Reservation on behalf of the people was a fitting action in a growing republic. Nevertheless, the area remained largely in private holdings, with titles in litigation for years. In 1870, Congress set up legal procedure for settling titles and claims to titles. The national park was established in 1921, through the influence of Stephen T. Mather, as a successor to the reservation that had existed previously. It's very different from all other national parks, covering only 4,860 acres. But it tells a particular story told in no other park.

The park's 47 hot springs are along a fault, or ancient break, in the earth's crust. The water from two springs can be seen emerging naturally. The water from the upper springs is collected and released near the Arlington Lawn in a water display to one side of a massive tufa surface. The water from other springs is collected in a 300,000-gallon reservoir for use in the bathhouses.

With so many developments in modern medicine, notably cortisone, antibiotics, and painkillers, the demand for therapeutic bathing has declined. Eight historic bathhouses are still preserved along Bathhouse Row, but only one, the Buckstaff, remains open. The full treatment, including hot packs, steam cabinet, and needle shower, lasts 90 minutes. Many swear there is nothing more relaxing.

Civil War veteran Colonel Samuel Fordyce, who believed he owed his life to the healing waters of the hot springs, built the elaborate Fordyce Bathhouse. Today the Fordyce serves as the park visitor center, complete with fountains, stained-glass windows, and authentic furnishings. In recent years art galleries have sprouted along Central Avenue.

Because the park is small and nearly surrounded by a busy resort city, the 24-mile network of hiking trails and the undisturbed woodland are a pleasant surprise to those who find them. I like to walk in the dense forest that covers the steep, rocky hills of the park, with wildflowers blooming seasonally. Nearly 150 species of birds have been identified. The altitude of the park varies from 600 feet on the valley floor to 1,400 feet on the summits. It reminds me of how much there is to absorb without covering any great distance.

## THE PRACTICAL GUIDE

**BACKGROUND.** Two open hot springs have been set aside for viewing purposes. Visit **Display Springs,** which are not sealed and still emerge naturally, located adjacent to the **Grand Promenade,** a landscaped, brick-paved walk.

A daily summertime tour, "Hot Prospects among the Thermal Features," includes the underground Indian Spring and other sites associated with the geology of hot water. It starts from the south grounds of Quapaw Bathhouse. For a glimpse of the golden age of the bath, be sure to stop in the Visitor Center in the restored Fordyce Bathhouse.

The rugged hill country around Hot Springs abounds in hunting, fishing, canoeing, and hiking opportunities. Three manmade lakes are in the area, lakes Ouachita (Wash-i-taw), Hamilton, and Catherine.

**ACCOMMODATIONS.** Hotels, motels, and tourist homes are abundant in the city. Several of the hotels have their own bathhouse facilities.

**Williams House,** 420 Quapaw, Hot Springs, AR 71901. This historic, well-furnished inn, within walking distance of Bathhouse Row and park visitor center, includes full American breakfast in the rate. 501/624-4275. M.

**Shorecrest,** 230 Lakeland Dr., Hot Springs, AR 71901. On Lake Hamilton, it provides kitchen-equipped cottages, marina, and pool. 501/525-8113. M.

**CAMPING.** The 47-site Gulpha Gorge Campground is set in a beautiful valley 2 miles from the center of Hot Springs, at the foot of Hot Springs Mountain. During summer, there are outdoor evening programs in the amphitheater. The campground is an excellent place for birdwatching, especially during winter. Pick up a copy of the park's bird checklist, which includes nearly 150 species. The park's forest of shortleaf pine, oaks, hickories, and gum, along with the dense ground cover, provides choice habitat for a variety of birds. Keep your eyes open for the small animals abundant in the forest.

For another worthwhile attraction, visit the Hot Springs Mountain Observation Tower.

**SEASONS.** The season at Hot Springs covers the entire year. Winters are mild, allowing for outdoor activities. Spring and fall offer special features for nature lovers and photographers. Fall colors abound in October, especially along the West Mountain Scenic Road.

**FOR FURTHER INFORMATION.** Write Superintendent, Hot Springs National Park, Box 1860, Hot Springs, AR 71902. 501/624-3383.

# ISLE ROYALE NATIONAL PARK

## MICHIGAN

### AUTHORIZED 1931

IT WAS SO QUIET and solitary on the trail that I paused for a moment, sure that I could have heard the orchids poking up through the forest litter if only I listened hard enough, if only I would be still and attentive to them. Then I wandered on toward Mount Franklin. It was not very high, only 1,074 feet, but it provided wonderful vistas of forested wilderness, fjordlike harbors, lakes, rugged waveswept shores, surrounding islets, and the waters of Lake Superior extending to the distant horizon in all directions.

Isle Royale National Park, covering 571,790 acres, is the largest island in Lake Superior, the largest and cleanest of the Great Lakes. In the summer of 1986, I drove completely around Lake Superior and learned something of its marvels, like the Apostle Islands off the coast of northern Wisconsin, Pictured Rocks on the Upper Peninsula of Michigan, and Pukaskwa National Park in Ontario. Then I went to Isle Royale, out in the heart of Lake Superior, where there are no cars, no roads, and the only loud noise was the sound of an outboard motor offshore.

The only way to reach Isle Royale is by seaplane or boat, but it attracts creatures that can fly, swim, or drift across the water barrier.

Beaver, muskrat, mink, and weasel are residents. So are the snowshoe hare, squirrel, and red fox. The bald eagle, osprey, pileated woodpecker, 25 kinds of warblers, and, most frequently seen, the herring gull, have made their way across 42 miles of water from the nearest Michigan shore, 13 miles from the Minnesota shore, or 14 miles from Canada. But not so for the deer, bear, porcupine, and skunk, unable to bridge the water.

Moose, which I saw along streams and on the shores of inland lakes, were not known on the island before 1900, but when the lake froze in about 1912, a number of them may have ventured over the ice, or they may have swum across. In the winter of 1948–49, wolves made their way across, arriving at a time when the moose herds had grown overabundant. The wolves have since played their role in the balance of nature. I wish that I had caught sight of a wolf, or heard a wolf howl. The wolves were "out to lunch," but I felt their presence, which heightened the experience of being there. I learned with sorrow that during the 1980s the wolf numbers were low—below two dozen—for reasons scientists could not explain.

Studies of the wolf-moose relationship at Isle Royale have achieved much recognition in the world of biology, reminding me that parks are much more than playgrounds; they are also laboratories of learning.

At various locations in the park, I saw ancient Indian mining pits, and learned that radiocarbon tests date these pits back 3,800 years or more. I learned also that copper mined by hammerstone in the prehistoric age was used on the trading trails throughout the Great Lakes.

I came to Isle Royale on the six-hour boat crossing from the Upper Peninsula of Michigan, filled with anticipation. The promise was wholly fulfilled; the park experience amounts to relaxed isolation, with plenty of healthy exercise. A chain of campgrounds extends almost the full 45-mile length of the island and across its 9-mile width. Attractive and comfortable accommodations are provided at Rock Harbor, with many opportunities for photography, fishing, and the study of nature in all its moods.

One thing I learned is that rain on the trail is a strong likelihood. Another lesson, a bit of incidental intelligence, has stood me well in the game of trivia. What is the name of the largest island in the largest lake on the largest island in the largest lake in the world? Isle Royale is the largest island in Lake Superior. Now, find the rest.

## THE PRACTICAL GUIDE

About 16,000 visitors make the crossing from mainland Michigan or Minnesota each year during the May-September season. They stay an average four days either at the full-service lodge or the backpacking campsites. By contrast, the average stay in Yellowstone or the Grand Canyon is four hours. At Isle Royale, a week is even better.

ACCESS. The "main highway to the park" is *Ranger III*, the National Park Service motor ship, 165 feet long, which makes two round trips weekly. It sails from Houghton on Michigan's Upper Peninsula, 70 miles away, returning one day later. The crossing aboard this 650-ton ship takes about 6½ hours. A Park Service program is delivered aboard in both directions, but carry a good book to help pass the time. There is a snack bar, so you won't go hungry. The *Ranger* delivers you to Rock Harbor, the main center of activity. Advance reservations should be made by writing the park.

The park is served by ships other than the *Ranger*. The privately owned *Isle Royale Queen III* makes a round trip daily from Copper Harbor to Rock Harbor. From the west, the *Wenonah*, operated by Grand Portage–Isle Royale Transportation Lines, Inc., makes a round trip daily from Grand Portage to Windigo, a distance of 20 miles, leaving 9:30 A.M. June 20 to Labor Day. This trip gives you the opportunity for a one-day excursion, with time ashore for a hike at Windigo. The 63-foot *Voyageur II* makes a two-day trip from Grand Portage to Windigo and Rock Harbor each Monday, Wednesday, and Saturday at 9:30 A.M. The vessel remains overnight at Rock Harbor. Boat operators will transport your small runabout or canoe. Gasoline may be purchased at Rock Harbor and Windigo marinas. A seaplane operates out of Houghton mid-May through September, daily except Wednesdays.

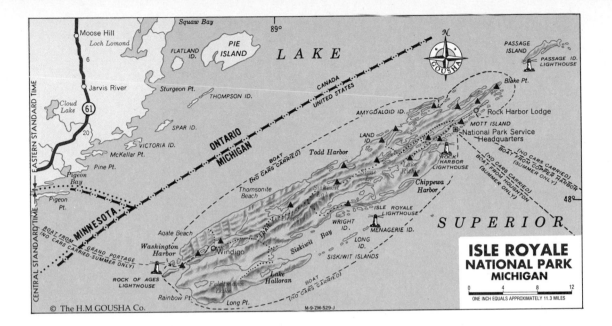

Map labels: Moose Hill, Loch Lomond, Squaw Bay, PIE ISLAND, 89°, L A K E, FLATLAND ID., PASSAGE ISLAND, PASSAGE ID. LIGHTHOUSE, Jarvis River, Sturgeon Pt., THOMPSON ID., CANADA, UNITED STATES, AMYGDALOID ID., Blake Pt., Rock Harbor Lodge, Cloud Lake, 61, EASTERN STANDARD TIME, ONTARIO, MICHIGAN, MOTT ISLAND, National Park Service Headquarters, SPAR ID., LAND ID., 20, VICTORIA ID., McKellar Pt., Pine Pt., BOAT (NO CARS CARRIED), Todd Harbor, Stone, Lake Richie, ROCK HARBOR LIGHTHOUSE, BOAT FROM COPPER HARBOR (NO CARS CARRIED) (SUMMER ONLY), BOAT FROM HOUGHTON (NO CARS CARRIED) (SUMMER ONLY), Pigeon Bay, Thomsonite Beach, Siskiwit, Chippewa Harbor, 48°, Pigeon Pt., MINNESOTA, TRAIL, ISLE ROYALE LIGHTHOUSE, S U P E R I O R, Agate Beach, WRIGHT ID., MENAGERIE ID., Washington Harbor, Windigo, Siskiwit Bay, LONG ID., CENTRAL STANDARD TIME, BOAT FROM GRAND PORTAGE (NO CARS CARRIED-SUMMER ONLY), ROCK OF AGES LIGHTHOUSE, SISKIWIT ISLANDS, Feldtmann Lake, Lake Halloran, BOAT (NO CARS CARRIED), © The H.M GOUSHA Co., Rainbow Pt., Long Pt., M-9-ZM-529-J

**ISLE ROYALE NATIONAL PARK MICHIGAN**

0  4  8  12
ONE INCH EQUALS APPROXIMATELY 11.3 MILES

**ACTIVITIES. Hiking.** The national park is laced with 166 miles of foot trails. The **Greenstone Ridge Trail** extends 40 miles from Rock Harbor Lodge to Washington Harbor, following the backbone of the island. The trip should be planned to cover several days.

Even if you don't go all the way, you can get a good sample by hiking to Mount Franklin, then continuing to **Ojibway Lookout,** with a superb view of the Canadian mainland standing out 15 miles north. There are other fine trails as well. One leads to mellowed and restored **Rock Harbor Lighthouse,** built in 1855 to guide boats into the harbor during the early copper mining days. Another goes to **Monument Rock,** a towering 70-foot pinnacle carved by waves and ice, then continues past ancient beaches and a copper mining site, used by prehistoric Indians, to **Lookout Louise,** for one of the most beautiful views in the park.

**Windigo Mine.** This old copper pit was mined by white men until about 1899. A fine trail leads from Washington Creek along the river to the mine ruins.

**Fishing and Boating.** Motor launch trips can be arranged at Rock Harbor Lodge. Boats and canoes can be rented. A modern marina for small boats and private cruisers is located at Rock Harbor. About 50 kinds of fish are found on inland streams, bays, and lakes and in Lake Superior. No fishing license is required for inland waters of the park. With its numerous lakes, deep bays, and offshore islands, Isle Royale provides many miles of waterways for the canoeist and kayaker. Use caution, however, respecting the chance of sudden winds and rough waters. Canoeing here is definitely not recommended for beginners. You can get water taxi service from Rock Harbor to any dock on the northeast half of the island.

**Naturalist Program.** Interpretive Ranger-guided walks are conducted from Rock Harbor and Windigo. Illustrated talks on various topics are conducted each evening at 8:30 at both of these places, and at Daisy Farm Campground twice weekly.

**TOURS.** A good way to make the round trip over the whole island is to go one way by trail and the other by boat. The *Voyageur,* privately owned, circumnavigates the park three times weekly. You can board it at Rock Harbor Lodge and travel to Windigo, or vice versa; or you can arrange to have it pick you up at lakeside camps. Write Grand Portage–Isle Royale Transportation, Inc., 1507 North First Street, Superior, Wisconsin 54880.

From Rock Harbor Lodge you can take a half-day sightseeing trip aboard the *Sandy*, operated by the park concessioner. With a park naturalist aboard, the boat visits important landmarks like Lookout Louise, Edison Fishery, Daisy Farm, Raspberry Island, and the historic Rock Harbor Light House.

**ACCOMMODATIONS.** The only accommodations available on the island are at the concession-operated lodge. Accommodations en route to the park are at Houghton and Copper Harbor, Michigan, and Grand Portage, Minnesota.

**Rock Harbor Lodge,** c/o National Park Concessions, Inc., Box 405, Houghton, MI 49931. The lodge has 20 attractive twin-unit housekeeping cabins, suitable for families, plus 60 lodge rooms. Dining room and snack bar are open to the public. The atmosphere is friendly and informal. Other services offered at this facility include a marina, groceries, canoe and boat rentals, and guided fishing trips. Make reservations well in advance for the short season, June through Labor Day. 906/337-4993; winter 502/773-2191. M.

**CAMPING.** This is a great park for camping, if you plan carefully and come fully prepared. On arrival, register and get a permit. The best type of facility for the first night is one of the three-sided shelters (capacity six persons).

Then take off for the tent sites. Keep in mind that long-term campground stays are not available. Camping supplies are sold at Rock Harbor and Windigo, but you'll be wise to bring your own.

**SEASONS.** The weather is cool and the travel season short—from mid-June until shortly after Labor Day. Fog is common during June and early July. Mosquitoes, blackflies, and deer flies can be a problem early and midsummer, although shelters are screened. Temperature during the day seldom rises above 80 degrees, and nights always are cool. Warm clothes are important.

**NEARBY.** Michigan's Upper Peninsula is the center of an old copper mining industry. The **Museum at the Michigan Technological University** at Houghton contains a large collection of minerals. **Fort Wilkins State Park,** northeast of Copper Harbor, contains restored buildings and historical museum relating to a remote army post established in 1844. Anyone coming from Grand Portage should visit the **Grand Portage National Monument,** on the site of the "great depot" of the fur trading days.

**RECOMMENDED READING.** *The Wolves of Minong,* by Durward Allen. The Isle Royale National History Association offers a wide variety of reading material—write for their list.

**FOR FURTHER INFORMATION.** Write Superintendent, Isle Royale National Park, 800 E. Lakeshore Drive, Houghton, Michigan 49931-1985. 906/482-8753.

# JOSHUA TREE NATIONAL PARK

## CALIFORNIA

ESTABLISHED 1994

I CONCENTRATED my attention on a single Joshua tree, almost 40 feet tall, in full bloom, with densely clustered, sharp-pointed leaves, and long greenish-white blossoms. I recognized that it was not a tree at all, but *Yucca brevifolia*, a many-armed giant species of yucca. Then the thought crossed my mind that cactus, ocotillo, palo verde, yucca, and other native plants lend character and quality to the special deserts where they grow, in the same sense as trees do to their respective forests—and how fortunate we are to have them protected in national parks, monuments, and other public lands.

For example, the Saguaro, *Cereus giganteus*, giant of the cactus family, reaching 35 or 40 feet, unique to the Sonoran desert of southern Arizona and northwestern Mexico, luckily is safeguarded in Saguaro National Monument at the edge of Tucson, enabling springtime visitors to enjoy its beautiful creamy white flowers. Then there's the distinctive organ pipe, in Organ Pipe National Monument, in southwestern Arizona along the Mexican border—the second largest cactus, without arms like the Joshua tree, producing a cluster of stems that suggest the name given to it. The Joshua tree, for its part, found only in the arid lands of California, western Arizona, Nevada, and southern Utah, was named by the Mormons, who found in its angular branches resemblance to the outstretched arms of Joshua leading the Israelites into the Promised Land.

The national park is like a modern Promised Land, a choice parcel of the steadily diminishing Southern California desert, abounding in varieties of flora growing among striking granite formations, and providing refuge for desert bighorn sheep, bobcat, badger, and coyote. It was first set aside as a national monument by presidential proclamation in 1936, largely through the interest and effort of Mrs. Sherman Hoyt, of Pasadena, "friend of the desert." But mining interests in 1950 succeeded in lobbying elimination of fully one-third of the 825,340-acre national monument. Now, at long last, the expanded new national park embraces such prime areas as the Coxcomb Mountains, in the northeast corner, where granite jumbles, spiky peaks, and winding canyons provide habitat for desert tortoise, bighorn sheep and burro deer, and Eagle Mountain, in the southeast, with hidden valleys, web-like washes, and rare Alverson's foxtail cactus.

**BACKGROUND.** The park is at the edge of the popular booming resort and retirement region centered around Palm Springs, Rancho Mirage, and Palm Desert. It lies less than 150 miles east of Los Angeles via Interstate 10. Reach the north entrance on Route 62 to Twentynine Palms, the south entrance 25 miles east of Indio via Interstate 10, and the new Eagle Mountain district another 25 miles to Desert Center.

**ACTIVITIES.** Begin at the Visitor Center at Twentynine Palms, and chart your course into the northern and western sections, where you'll find the largest stands of Joshua trees and the rock formations of monzonite. Plan to join a guided spring walk and guided car-caravan tour to Desert Queen Ranch (also called Keys Ranch), a fascinating little-known landmark. The **Jumbo Rocks** and **Hidden Valley** offer exceptional scenery and photo opportunities. From **Key View Point,** look down over Coachella Valley, including Indio, Palm Springs, and the Salton Sea.

**Birdwatching.** Bring binoculars to view desert birds, and more besides. Landlocked Salton Sea, southwest of the park, provides some of the most unusual bird records in Southern California, including seabirds at various times of year.

**Seasons.** Joshua trees and other vegetation reach their peak of bloom March through May; nearly 40 percent of all visitors come during these three months. Temperatures can be low and conditions chilly December to early April.

**ACCOMMODATIONS** are plentiful in nearby communities. If you need help, call Palm Springs Reservation Center, 800/4458-4373, or Palm Springs Condominium and Hotel Reservations, 800/323-4SUN.

**CAMPING.** Nine primitive campgrounds are located in various sections of the park. Prepare to carry wood, gas and supplies to all of them and water to all but Cottonwood and Black Rock. Make reservations for Black Rock through Mistix, 800/452-1111.

**NEARBY.** The largest state park outside of Alaska, **Anza-Borrego State Park,** embraces a thousand square miles of mountain and desert, with hiking, backcountry camping, archaeology, plant and animal study. **Salton Sea,** one of the world's largest inland bodies of salt water, south of Indio, offers camping, hiking, swimming, saltwater fishing.

**FOR FURTHER INFORMATION.** Write Superintendent, Joshua Tree National Park, 74485 National Monument Drive, Twentynine Palms, CA 92277. 619/367-7511.

# KATMAI NATIONAL PARK

## ALASKA

### ESTABLISHED 1980

KATMAI was the scene of a violent eruption in 1912, which turned a nameless green valley on the southern shore of the Alaska Peninsula into the Valley of Ten Thousand Smokes, but I remember it most as the place where I watched an Alaska brown bear, otherwise known as a grizzly, and her two cubs feed on migrating salmon in the Brooks River. Katmai takes some effort to reach, but superlative Alaska wilderness scenery makes it an excellent choice on any itinerary. As for the ten thousand smokes, there are no longer active fumaroles in the valley, but the signs of live volcanoes are evident on surrounding mountains.

Katmai was designated a national monument in 1918. In 1980, Congress voted to enlarge the area to 3,669,000 acres and reclassify it as a national park, bordered by a national preserve of 423,000 acres.

Of many lakes, one of cobalt blue color fills the crater of Mount Katmai. Sportsmen know Katmai for some of the best trophy sportfishing in Alaska. Whether catching fish or absorbing lakes, rivers, glaciers, and waterfalls, Katmai is the trophy in itself.

## THE PRACTICAL GUIDE

**ACCESS.** Take a scheduled jet from Anchorage on a spectacular 290-mile flight passing over great volcanoes and glaciers to King Salmon on the park's west side, then a commercial flight (June through Labor Day) or air charter to Brooks Lodge.

**ACCOMMODATIONS.** Two concession facilities in the park, operated by Katmailand, Inc.,

are open mid-June to early September, which makes reservations important. Package tours including air transportation and meals are a good bet. Consult a travel agent or Katmailand, Inc., 455 H Street, Anchorage, AK 99501; 800/544-0551.

**Grosvenor Camp.** Located on a channel connecting Lake Colville and Lake Grosvenor, this fly-in lodge is favored by sportfishermen.

It accommodates eight in rustic comfort. Rates include guide service, boat/motors. H.

**Brooks River Lodge.** The center of activities in the park, located at the mouth of the Brooks River. Starting point of daily tours to the Valley of Ten Thousand Smokes. M to H.

**CAMPING.** Start by setting up headquarters at the campground on the shore of Naknek Lake near the Brooks River Lodge. Check with the rangers about backcountry travel. With a permit you can camp anywhere, but prepare for the pesky white Fox in mid- to late summer.

Canoeing and kayaking on the Grosvenor and Savanoski rivers are worthwhile activities. The country is rough but rewarding.

If you visit beaches in the park, you may see signs of oil from the tanker *Exxon Valdez,* which ran aground in Prince William Sound in 1989. Heroic efforts by the National Park Service couldn't stop oil from fouling much of the shoreline and killing scores of seabirds and sea otters.

**BEARS.** From late July to September dozens of bears gather to feed on sockeye salmon. A viewing platform near Brooks Falls allows you to observe bears up close. Otherwise, keep a respectable, safe distance. The Alaska Department of Fish and Game operates another bear-viewing area on the McNeil River. For information on the lottery system used to grant permits on this popular site, write the department at 333 Raspberry Rd., Anchorage, AK 99518.

**SEASONS.** The travel season runs from mid-June to mid-September. The temperature is usually mild, but rain is always a possibility, so carry raingear.

**FOR FURTHER INFORMATION.** Write Superintendent, Katmai National Park, Box 7, King Salmon, AK 99613. 907/246-3305.

# KENAI FJORDS NATIONAL PARK

## ALASKA

ESTABLISHED 1980

I DROVE south from Anchorage to the Kenai Peninsula. Seward, the only town on the east coast of the peninsula and gateway to Kenai Fjords, is only 127 miles from Anchorage. I found the entire trip a delight, like a prelude to the natural wonder of the national park. The Seward Highway follows the shore of Turnagain Arm (which Captain Cook mistook for a river leading to the Northwest Passage), through Chugach State Park, one of the largest in the country, and Chugach National Forest, with broad vistas of the Kenai Mountains. The peaks and ice fields form the spine of the peninsula, and I felt as though I was driving across Switzerland—but Alaska, I daresay, is more expansive.

Seward proved a fitting gateway, cradled between mountain ranges, yet a harbor at the edge of the sea. This was only the beginning. A full-day cruise showed what surely must be one of the most beautiful marine environments on earth. This area was little known until establishment of the national park in 1980. Its 580,000 acres embrace rugged cliffs, mist-shrouded fjords, and a massive icefield, with mountaintops rising thousands of feet above it.

Harding Icefield, the dominant feature, covers 300 square miles, with its outflowing glaciers about 1,100 square miles. The central ice core is a rare example of Pleistocene ice masses that once covered half of Alaska. It rises above the landscape and seascape, with its mountaintops fittingly called *nunataks*, the Eskimo word for "lonely peaks."

During the course of the cruise, I learned that the fjords of the park were formed when the ancient ice cap flowed down to the sea and then retreated, leaving behind deep inlets—which world travelers will at once compare with the fabled fjords of Norway and New Zealand. Icebergs from calving glaciers provide ideal refuge for harbor seals, while the rugged coastline provides habitat for nesting birds. I saw and heard many sea lions raucously expressing themselves on sheltered islands and islets.

Back on shore, I drove to Exit Glacier, one of several rivers of ice flowing off the ice field. This retreating, yet active, glacier provides an excellent setting to explore. Newly exposed scoured bedrock, mountain goats, and a regime of plant succession from the earliest pioneer plants to the mature forest of Sitka spruce and western hemlock are part of the Exit Glacier setting.

Kenai Fjords is becoming one of the principal highlights of any Alaska itinerary. It lies less than 50 miles from Prince William Sound, where the *Exxon Valdez* ran aground in 1989, spewing 11 million gallons of oil into the sea. Kenai Fjords was impacted to some degree, but from all reports visitors are still treated to spectacular vistas. Next time in Alaska I plan to see for myself.

## THE PRACTICAL GUIDE

**ACCESS.** The 127-mile Seward Highway is fully paved from Anchorage and marked with mileposts. Train service is available May 27 to September 4 on Friday, Saturday, and Sunday, and occasionally during the week, leaving Anchorage at 7 A.M., arriving in Seward at 11 A.M. Scheduled bus service and commuter flights (35 minutes) are available between Seward and Anchorage. The Alaska Marine Highway connects Seward with Homer via Kodiak, and also provides service to Valdez and Cordova.

**BACKGROUND.** The park **Visitor Center,** on Fourth Avenue, Seward, should be your first stop if you're arriving by car. It is open 8 A.M. to 5 P.M. daily in summer. From here head for the most accessible of the park's glaciers, Exit Glacier. Turn at Milepost S3.7 on the Seward Highway, then follow Exit Glacier Road for 9 miles. From here you can follow a ½-mile walking trail to the face of the glacier. Allow plenty of time to stop at the Exit Glacier Ranger Station and picnic area a mere ¼-mile from the glacier.

About 40 miles of shoreline in Kenai Fjords were fouled by oil from the 1989 *Exxon Valdez* tanker spill in Prince William Sound. The National Park Service worked to protect the Alaskan parks from the spill, and probably saved them from much worse damage. You may not see oil along principal tour boat routes—but remember the spill as sobering evidence of the power of man to pollute or preserve the environment.

**ACTIVITIES. Sightseeing.** Daily charter sightseeing cruises of full-day and half-day are offered from Seward. You can arrange an overnight charter for a more extensive trip. Be sure to bring binoculars. Bring warm clothes and raingear. While there are only a few landing sites, you'll see a magnificent vista from the boat: rock rising from sea level thousands of feet to snowy peaks, and rock fins, sea arches, caves, and cliffs that are being constantly reshaped by the pounding energy of incoming tides. In **Resurrection Bay,** largest of the fjords, keep a sharp watch for whales, porpoises, harbor seals, and sea otters.

**Birdwatching. Aialik Bay** and **Harris Bay** harbor immense concentrations of sea birds—puffins, murres, kittiwakes, and auklets. Nearby **Chiswell Island,** part of the Alaska Maritime National Wildlife Refuge, is another great spot for sea birds and marine mammals, which seek out these small islands because the fractured ledges seem to suit their needs.

**Sea Kayaking.** Bring your own kayak or rent one at Seward. You can join a guided trip even if you haven't had experience. Consider the 3-day, 2-night trip to Holgate Arm, viewing whales, sea lions, and sea bird rookeries, with camping on the beaches. Write Alaska Treks and Voyages, Box 625, Seward, AK 99631.

**Fishing.** This is popular along the coastal area. Resurrection Bay is known for silver salmon up to 20 pounds and halibut up to 200 pounds. Other fish include lingcod, a variety of rockfish, as well as chum and pink salmon.

**Sailing.** This is another top sport. You'll find charter operators able to provide everything you need.

**ACCOMMODATIONS.** There are no accommodations in the park, but a full range of services is available in Seward, including motels, RV parks, and bed and breakfasts.

**Marina Motel,** Seward, AK 99664. A small facility with rooms in view of the bay; picnic area and tandem bikes available to guests without charge. 907/224-5518. M.

**Van Gilder Hotel,** Seward, AK 99664. In the heart of Seward, this hospitable old-timer is listed on the National Register of Historic Places. The restaurant (like virtually all of them here) specializes in seafood. 907/224-3079. M.

**CAMPING.** A 10-site walk-in campground is located at Exit Glacier. Two municipal campgrounds in Seward are open when free of snow, which is usually from about March to November.

**SEASONS.** Summer temperatures reach into the 50s and 60s. The climate can be very wet, so prepare accordingly. In September begins the wet, steamy fall, the end of the tourist season. Exit Glacier is open to winter visitors.

**NEARBY.** Take the walking tour of picturesque Seward, nestled between mountain ranges. A number of homes and shops date back to the early 1900s. Visit the small-boat harbor, port to fishing boats, charter boats, and sailboats. Make a stop at the Seward Museum, operated by the Resurrection Bay Historical Society. Exhibits and films are on display at the Institute of Marine Science Building. Several Forest Service campgrounds are located along the Seward Highway leading from Anchorage.

**FOR FURTHER INFORMATION.** Write Superintendent, Kenai Fjords National Park, Box 1727, Seward, AK 99664. 907/224-3175.

# KOBUK VALLEY NATIONAL PARK

## ALASKA

ESTABLISHED 1980

I WAS 40 miles north of the Arctic Circle with a friend, Bob Belous of the National Park Service. He had spent considerable time in the Arctic and knew the country well. We were on the Kobuk River, an ideal stream for easy canoeing and kayaking. The vegetation was tundra type, the kind that reveals an intimate beauty when examined closely. Bob mentioned that the dry, cold climate supports a remnant flora that once characterized the tundra bridge over which prehistoric men and women crossed from Asia to Alaska. He was especially interested in showing the Great Kobuk Sand Dunes spread over 25 square miles, with rolling dunes rising to heights of 100 feet—a rare spectacle.

In striking contrast is Onion Portage, the site where for thousands of years caribou have crossed the Kobuk River and where Eskimo and their predecessors have camped to hunt them. Uncovering layers upon layers of artifacts has brought to light a sequence of cultural development spanning 10,000 years; as my friend mentioned, Onion Portage has been called "the most important archaeological site ever found in the Arctic."

The national park covers 1,710,000 acres, the basin of the broad, gently winding river rimmed by mountains. It provides summer breeding habitat for more than 100 species of birds coming from all over North and South America and from lands bordering the Pacific Ocean. Twice yearly, thousands of caribou funnel through passes of the Baird Mountains between northern calving grounds and southern wintering grounds, foraging while in the Kobuk's tundra plains, in company with grizzly and black bear, wolf and fox.

## THE PRACTICAL GUIDE

**ACCESS.** Regular jet service connects Kotzebue, one of Alaska's oldest and largest Eskimo communities, with Anchorage and Nome. Chartered light aircraft and scheduled bush air carriers serve several Eskimo villages, particularly **Kiana** and **Ambler,** strung along the Kobuk River.

**ACTIVITIES. Backpacking and Canoeing.** The Kobuk River is almost 300 miles long, flowing from the south flank of the Brooks Range and picking up the waters of at least 50 tributaries before emptying into Kotzebue Sound and the Chukchi Sea. Within placid Kobuk Valley, about 150 miles inland from Kotzebue, the river seems like a series of lakes to the canoeist. Bring fishing gear; the Kobuk specialty is the Shee fish. You can head out from Ambler or Kiana, which have small stores and simple facilities operated by Eskimos.

Terrain in most areas is good for hiking. You can reach the sand dunes on an easy hike from the river.

**Camping.** There are no campgrounds. Camp anywhere except in the archaeological zones or any private property along the river.

**ACCOMMODATIONS.** The national park is essentially undeveloped, meant for wilderness camping. A few simple facilities are emerging in villages along the Kobuk River. Otherwise, the only accommodations offering convenience are at Kotzebue, Alaska's largest Eskimo village.

**Nul-Luk-Vik Hotel,** Kotzebue, AK 99752. Operated by the NANA regional native corporation, the hotel overlooks Kotzebue Sound on Arctic Bay. Though constructed as a modern facility, open year-round, service and upkeep are erratic. 907/442-3331. H.

**SEASONS.** Summer temperatures often reach the 80s during the day, then drop sharply at night. June and July are the clearest months, followed by rainy August and September. Mosquitoes reach their peak in June, but you're apt to find gnats and other insects later in the summer.

**NEARBY.** Kotzebue is the commercial center of Northwestern Alaska, gateway to **Bering Land Bridge National Preserve** and **Cape Krusenstern National Monument,** as well as Kobuk Valley National Park. It is essentially an Eskimo community, where the Fourth of July features traditional native games. During the Arctic Trade Fair, the week following, people from throughout the region trade handicrafts and participate in traditional dances and feasts. There are no sidewalks in Kotzebue and there is only a short stretch of paved street, near the airport.

The **Museum of the Arctic** is the principal attraction, featuring wildlife dioramas, Eskimo dancing for tour groups, and demonstrations of Eskimo skills. The west end of the building houses the National Park Service information center, open 7 A.M. to 9 P.M.

**RECOMMENDED READING.** *Coming into the Country,* by John McPhee.

**FOR FURTHER INFORMATION.** Write Superintendent, Kobuk Valley National Park, Box 1029, Kotzebue, AK 99752. 907/442-3890.

# LAKE CLARK NATIONAL PARK

## ALASKA

ESTABLISHED 1980

MY FRIENDS, Chuck and Sara Hornberger, operate Koksetna Camp, a lovely little lodge at the edge of Lake Clark that scarcely intrudes on the wilderness around them. They exemplify harmony in life, with nature, each other, and their guests. Sara grows her own vegetables, no small feat in Alaska, while Chuck guides visitors on intimate excursions through the country he knows and loves.

He can't possibly show it all, of course. The national park and preserve cover a little more than 4,045,320 acres in the heart of the Chigmit Mountains, where the mighty Alaska Range meets the Aleutian Range. Here is a composition of wilderness peaks, glacial valleys, sparkling lakes, waterfalls, and streams, plus towering semiactive volcanoes that show how this portion of the earth is still in the process of formation.

Though roadless, the national park lies only 150 miles from Anchorage and is readily accessible by plane. The flight itself gives an inspiring overview. Lake Clark Pass and Merrill Pass, the main routes through the mountains, open up vistas of hanging glaciers lining the valley walls. The coastal region of the park, bordering the western shore of Cook Inlet, is highlighted by the fuming volcanoes, Mount Iliamna and Mount Redoubt, both rising more than 10,000 feet above their bases at sea level.

I've been to Koksetna twice, in summer, but I've listened to Chuck and Sara describe the quiet adventure of winter on Lake Clark. It sounded appealing, a time of peace, when nature rests, which some winter I hope to experience.

## THE PRACTICAL GUIDE

**ACCESS.** Air charters are available from Anchorage and Kenai. It costs less, however, to take a scheduled commercial flight to Iliamna, 35 miles west of the park, and charter from there.

**ACCOMMODATIONS.** Several small lodges are located along the lakeshore on private land inside the park, close to the villages of Nondalton and Port Alsworth. These are reached by air taxi, most inexpensively from Iliamna.

179

Lodges offer boats, fishing tackle, and other outdoor gear. In addition to the following, there are other accommodations in Iliamna and on Lake Iliamna.

**Alaska's Wilderness Lodge,** 7320 6th Ave., Tacoma, WA 98406. Features fly-out fishing (for salmon, rainbow trout, lake trout, char, grayling and Dolly Varden). Family rates available. 206/564-6682. M to H.

**Koksetna Wilderness Lodge,** General Delivery, Port Alsworth, AK 99653. Rustic, comfortable cabins and family-style meals match the wilderness setting. Bird and wildlife observation on the Chulitna River are features. 907/781-2227. (September–May, 1425 5th St., Colusa, CA 95932; 916/458-7446.) M.

**ACTIVITIES. River-Running and Fishing.** The Chilikadrotna River offers an excellent white-water experience for rafters and kayakers. The Chilikadrotna flows out of Twin Lakes in a good steady current, past the Bonanza Hills and through a spruce-hardwood forest. The four-day float to the Mulchatna River takeout provides plenty of opportunity for fishing and hiking. You could also start from Turquoise Lake and float the Mulchatna for two days to the end of Bonanza Hills.

Grayling are easy to catch. Around mid-July rivers and creeks become choked with spawning bright-red sockeye salmon. Several species of salmon, as well as trout, northern pike and char, are in the lakes and streams.

**SEASONS.** Between June and August temperatures in the eastern portion of the park average between 50 and 65 degrees, but the western and interior portions are warmer, reaching as high as 80. Autumn, though cold, is an attractive time. A few lodges stay open year-round for those interested in ice fishing, winter camping, and sheer solitude with nature.

**FOR FURTHER INFORMATION.** Write Superintendent, Lake Clark National Park, 222 West 7th Avenue, Box 61, Anchorage, AK 99513. 907/271-3751.

# LASSEN VOLCANIC NATIONAL PARK

## CALIFORNIA

### ESTABLISHED 1916

I ARRIVED in June (of 1987) and it was barely summer. The nighttime temperature in the campground was still around freezing. No wonder the park was so
thoroughly uncrowded. But that's what I like about Lassen. It lies within a day's
drive of the San Francisco Bay area, but is lightly used, except for the peak of
summer.

It is truly a jewel, though, with much to offer. Lassen Volcanic is the smallest
(106,372 acres) of the five national parks on the California mainland, but a
beauty spot nonetheless, being in the heavily wooded northeast part of the state
where the Sierra Nevada meets the Cascades.

One of the most recently active volcanoes in the United States forms the core
of this national park where snow sometimes falls lightly in summer on blue
lakes and evergreen forests. In January, cross-country skiers take to the high
slopes and visit steaming fumaroles, hissing hot springs, and boiling mud pots.
Thus, visitors can enjoy the park and learn about volcanism in any season.

The towering mass of Lassen Peak, 10,457 feet, is the southernmost of the
chain of volcanoes in the Cascades that stretch nearly 700 miles north to British
Columbia. Arrayed in stately single-file rank, they form part of the Pacific "Ring
of Fire" that arcs from South America to Alaska, Japan, and Indonesia and
includes three-fourths of the world's active volcanoes.

The violent eruption of Mount St. Helens in 1980 came as a reminder that the
Northwest has been the scene of earthly cataclysms over millions of years. St.
Helens, most symmetrical of Cascade volcanoes, has seldom gone more than
100 to 150 years without an eruption. Mount Baker, in northwest Washington,
came close to erupting in 1975, and Mount Rainier shows steam vents and
warm caves along the rim of its crater and has a history of massive mudflows.

At Lassen, the last series of eruptions began in the spring of 1914, after at least
400 years of quiet slumber, and continued over a period of seven years. In 1915,
red tongues of lava spilled through a notch in the crater rim, flowed down the
western slope 1,000 feet and hardened in place. But on the northeast flank, hot
lava melted the deep snowpack, causing a mammoth river of mud to rush
downhill carrying 30-ton boulders in its path. Three days later, a column of
vapor and dust rose more than five miles in the sky, while a low-angle blast

struck the northeast flank again, widening the path of destruction to more than a mile, mowing down trees and all life in its path for a length of five miles. It was these eruptions that drew nationwide attention.

The geology of the volcano had been studied for more than 30 years (notably by J. S. Diller of the U.S. Geological Survey) before establishment of the park. In 1907, President Theodore Roosevelt signed a proclamation setting aside Cinder Cone and Lassen Peak as national monuments. Then, following the eruptions of 1914–17, Lassen Volcanic was established as a national park. The park carries the name of Peter Lassen, a Danish pioneer who, during gold rush days, boarded emigrants and guided them across the mountains, but he had no connection with the purpose of the park or the volcanism for which it is known.

Lassen is now dormant, but scientists believe that future eruptions are possible. In the meantime, it is a pleasure to experience the deep forest, rushing streams and waterfalls, the alpine meadows, and the best bubbling mud pots, sulphur springs, and other thermal features west of Yellowstone.

## THE PRACTICAL GUIDE

**BACKGROUND.** Many important scenic and volcanic features can be seen from the 30-mile-long Lassen Park Road, which half encircles Lassen Peak, so it can easily be included as a half-day side trip while driving north or south on I-5 (California 99) or US 395. Most of the eastern half of the park is superb for hiking and camping. More than 150 miles of marked trails lead to old volcanoes, thermal features, lakes, and other natural features.

**Manzanita Lake,** near the northwest boundary, is rimmed with firs and pines. At least six types of pines are found in the park: Jeffrey, ponderosa, sugar, western white, and lodgepole at lower elevations, plus white-bark pine, which climbs and struggles to survive at 10,000 feet. Willows and thin-leafed alder dip their roots into the clear waters of the lake. For information, stop at Park Headquarters, on California Route 36, near Mineral, *outside* the park (on the road from Red Bluff), or at Manzanita Lake Visitor Center, on the Lassen Park Road.

**Chaos Crags** and **Jumbles** are along the Park Road. The Crags, like Lassen Peak, are towering, plug-like masses pushed up through vents a few thousand years ago.

Rocky avalanches from the Crags created the Jumbles. The small coniferous trees growing around them are known as the Dwarf Forest. You can see a young pine forest taking hold of the soil while you drive 2½ miles through the **Devastated Area,** which was denuded of all vegetation in the volcanic blast of 1915.

**ACTIVITIES. Hiking.** Lassen Peak Trail starts from near the summit of the Park Road at 8,512 feet elevation. The climb is 2½ miles and takes four to five hours round trip, but the view from the summit is worth the effort. Overlooking craters, blue lakes, and forests, this is the high point of a visit to Lassen Volcanic.

The trail from **Kings Creek Meadows** to the falls, 1.3 miles, shows Lassen's wildflowers at their best, including crimson snow plant, leopard lily, paintbrush, lupine, penstemon, and bleeding heart.

**Bumpass Hell** is the destination of a 1.5-mile walk worth taking for the name alone. It leads from the Park Road through an alpine wildflower area to the largest display of hot springs in the park, with bubbling mud pots testifying to underground turbulence. It was named for an early hunter, whose tragic mistake in placing one leg into a boiling pool should be fair warning to stay on trails and skip the shortcuts.

**Sulphur Works** is 2 miles from the southwest park boundary. A self-guiding trail leads through an area of seething gases and heat emitted from the central vent of Mount Tehama.

**Cinder Cone** is one of the outstanding volcanic features of the park, which justified its separate establishment as a national monument in 1907. It is believed to be the source of "fires" and "flaring lights" in 1850–51, which were seen as far off as 160 miles. Black in color, bare of vegetation, it lies surrounded by multicolored heaps of volcanic cinder and ash, called the Painted Dunes, and looks as though it was formed yesterday. Cinder Cone is reached by hiking from Summit Lake or from **Butte Lake** in the northeast corner of the park. Fantastic Lava Beds is a mass of lava flows that originated from the base of Cinder Cone.

**Winter Sports.** Downhill skiing is available at concession-operated Lassen Park Ski Area, just inside the southwest entrance. Facilities include one triple-chair lift and two rope tows, plus day lodge with ski rental. Heavy snow closes the main highway November to June, but the entire park is open to cross-country skiing. Trails starting from Manzanita Lake and Lassen Chalet are marked according to skill levels. The trip between the lake and chalet covers about 30 miles. The park staff conducts snowshoe hikes, winter wildlife programs, and winter survival workshops. Call park headquarters at 916/595-4444. Lodgings are available outside the park.

**Fishing and Boating.** Rowboats and canoes can be used on most lakes (except Reflection, Emerald, Helen, and Boiling Springs). In the spirit of backcountry recreation, motorboats are prohibited on all lakes in the park. Many lakes and streams have rainbow, brook, and brown trout; remember that a California fishing license is required.

**Naturalist Programs.** Check the schedule at Manzanita Lake Visitor Center or at any entrance station. Guided walks and hikes are held every day in summer. Start with the Early Bird Watch and end with the Star Watch. Campfire programs are conducted during the summer at Manzanita Lake and Summit Lake. Visit the historic *Loomis Museum*, reopened in late 1993 after ten years of closure.

**ACCOMMODATIONS.** There is only one overnight facility in the park; however, lodge and resort accommodations are available nearby on California 36, 44 and 89. Winter resorts in Tehama County, south of the park, are easily reached from Chico or Red Bluff.

**Drakesbad Guest Ranch,** California Guest Services, Inc., Mineral, CA 96063. A concession-operated facility of lodge and cabin rooms and bungalows, with thermally heated pool, serves as a base for riding and pack trips. The concession also provides horses, camper store services, and winter ski rentals. Mid-June to mid-September 916/595-3306; year-round 916/529-1512.

**Lassen Mineral Lodge,** Box 160, Mineral, CA 96063. Motel complex (kitchenettes available) with pool, restaurant, general store, tennis, and ski rentals. 916/595-4422. M.

**Childs Meadow Resort,** Route 5, Box 3000, Mill Creek, CA 96961. Ringed by mountains nine miles from the park on California 36, it features cabins and motel units, some with kitchenettes; a haven for nordic skiers. 916/595-4411. M.

**CAMPING.** Campgrounds below 6,000 feet are generally open mid-May to October; those above 6,000 feet may not open till mid-June. Campgrounds at Manzanita Lake, Crags, and Summit Lake on the Lassen Park Road have spaces for trailers and some modern conveniences, but no hookups for electricity, water, or sewage. The Southwest campground has modern conveniences also, but you must walk about 100 yards from the parking area to the site. Summit Lake is best for backcountry hiking. Other campgrounds are at Lost Creek, Juniper Lake, Warner Valley, and Butte Lake, on dead-end spur roads. Camping is permitted June to October, depending on weather. The camping limit is seven days at Summit Lake and Lost Creek, 14 days at all other sites. This area requires permits for backcountry use.

**SEASONS.** Summer is the main season. Overnight accommodations in the park are open mid-June to mid-September. Wildflowers burst into bloom in early summer, but the show continues until September. Lassen's annual snowfall is between 400 and 700 inches; winter sports programs are offered at the northwest and southwest entrances.

**NEARBY.** Many campgrounds and recreation areas lie within the 1,147,000 acres of **Lassen National Forest.** A major campground is located southeast of the park on the west shore of **Lake Almanor** (elevation, 4,550 feet), one of the largest artificial bodies of water in California, noted for its abundant trout. Other camping and picnic areas are conveniently located north of the park along **Hat Creek.** At **McArthur-Burney Falls Memorial State Park,** 11 miles north of Burney, Burney Falls is a cataract of singular beauty.

**FOR FURTHER INFORMATION.** Write Superintendent, Lassen Volcanic National Park, Box 100, Mineral, California 96063. 916/595-4444.

# MAMMOTH CAVE NATIONAL PARK

KENTUCKY

AUTHORIZED 1926/ESTABLISHED 1941

I TRIED to imagine what Mammoth Cave was like 4,000 years ago, when, according to bits of evidence (implements, clothing, several natural mummified bodies), it was first inhabited by primitive people seeking shelter, flint, gypsum, and other materials. The national park is relatively new, but the cave is ancient, and I find much of its appeal in history. Electrification began only in the 1920s. On my first visit, in the 1950s, rangers would still demonstrate the old lighting technique: heaving torches of wood or cloth into receptacles, or baskets, high in the cavern chambers.

Discovered by white settlers sometime before 1799, this great cave was destined to become an attraction of wide renown and lasting appeal. Edwin Booth, the Shakespearean actor, once recited from Hamlet's soliloquy in an underground room now called Booth's Amphitheatre. Ole Bull, the celebrated Norwegian violinist, performed here in 1851—the same year Jenny Lind, the Swedish Nightingale, shattered the subterranean stillness with her golden voice. Those were thrilling days, when visitors eagerly toted whale-oil lamps, and ladies were advised that "bloomers or Turkish dress" constituted proper attire, and many came from afar to explore "the greatest cave that ever was."

Mammoth Cave still provides a full quota of thrills. Although Carlsbad Caverns National Park in New Mexico contains the largest single chamber, Mammoth Cave is recognized as having the most extensive cave system in the world. It consists of more than 300 miles of charted passageways filled with spectacular rock formations and domes, though nobody knows how large it really is. Several levels have been explored, but many underground streams are still at work, shaping more passages.

The national park, about 90 miles from Louisville and the same distance from Nashville, covers 52,369 acres. It lies near Bowling Green in south-central Kentucky, where the limestone terrain is pitted by depressions called sinkholes. Some geologists call the area the Southern Sinkhole Plain, but local people are apt to refer to it as the "Land of 10,000 Sinks." Walking through the portions of the cave open to public view, chambers and passageways bearing such names as "Grand Central Station," "Wright's Rotunda," and "Cleveland Avenue," I marveled at the formations of travertine, or cave onyx, in thousands of intricate and

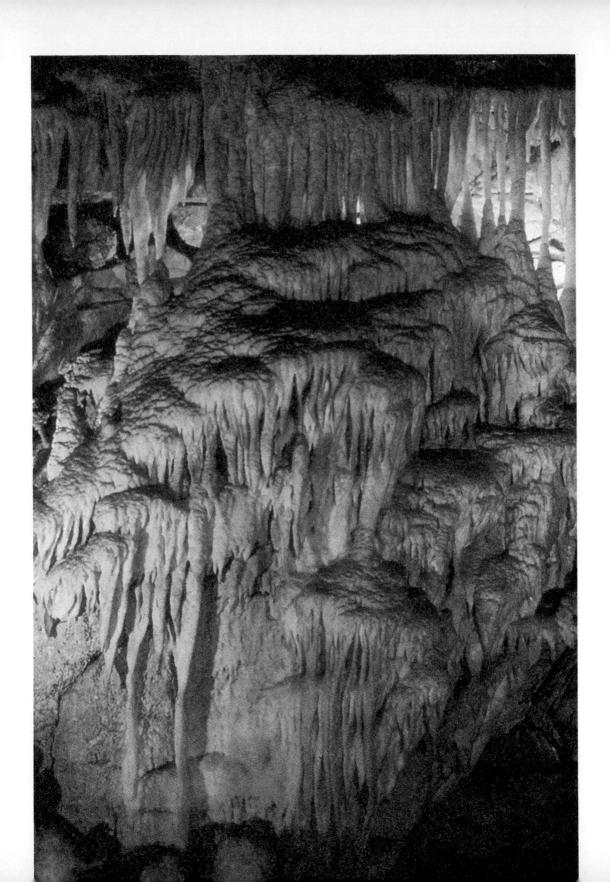

artistic patterns, including stalagmites, stalactites, draperies, and cascading flowstone. Mammoth Cave was the first-known cave to contain gypsum, restricted to drier portions, where slow leaching of calcium sulfate through porous limestone forces the gypsum crystals outward into the cave.

These subtle processes of nature have been under way for a period longer than humans can imagine. They continue to form new caves, to decorate the older ones, and to enhance the visual beauty of the mammoth underground that has delighted visitors since its discovery. For many years, the cave was in private hands; the country is fortunate that it is now protected as a public trust.

There is more to the park than the underground. I particularly enjoy the scenic hills and valleys on the surface. A wide variety of birds and wildflowers enliven the forest of hardwood trees. White-tailed deer, woodchucks, cottontails, and squirrels are likely to be encountered.

The Green River, joined by underground streams, winds 25 miles across the park. It is the key to the active circulation of underground and surface waters, assuring that new passages will continue to be formed at the lower levels of Mammoth Cave for a new world of hidden beauty.

## THE PRACTICAL GUIDE

You can see the cave on one of the guided tours conducted every day, ranging from one to six hours, and then be on your way. But don't overlook the good overnight accommodations and campgrounds, and the opportunities for hiking, boating, and fishing on the Green and Nolin rivers.

Watch the road signs carefully when approaching this park. There are several commercial caves in the area. Don't confuse them with the national park.

**BACKGROUND AND TOURS.** Tours into the cave are conducted every day of the year except Christmas Day. Reservations for all cave tours are available through Mistix Corporation. Reservations for all tours are available at the Visitor Center. Only persons accompanied by a National Park Service ranger may enter the cave. Most trails are solid and reasonably smooth. The temperature is 54 degrees all year; carry a sweater or jacket. Low-heeled shoes are a must for comfort; do not wear sandals. The pace underground is leisurely, with frequent rest stops, but if you have any doubts about your endurance, settle for one of the shorter trips. A tour is conducted for mobility-impaired visitors in wheelchairs.

**Frozen Niagara Tour** (three-fourths mile, two hours) displays a variety of formations. Among them is Frozen Niagara, the largest travertine formation in the cave, a fine example of flowstone, formed through centuries of deposition from water flowing over rock formations instead of dripping from them. Then you look down at Crystal Lake, a pool formed by a stalagmite dam.

**Historic Tour** (two miles, two hours) is self-guided. Enter through the natural opening near the Visitor Center, then see the **Rotunda,** scene of saltpeter mining during the War of 1812, and Indian artifacts. The trip continues to **Mammoth Dome,** aptly named. The eyeless fish from underground streams are seen along the route.

**The Half-Day Tour** (four miles, four and a half hours) takes you to some beautiful gypsum formations. The group stops for lunch 267 feet underground in the **Snowball Room,** with its clusters of gypsum that resemble snowballs on the ceiling. Then it passes through **Frozen Niagara,** the spectacle in travertine.

**Lantern Tour** (three miles, three hours) is unique. It gives the thrill of times past, before the cave was electrically wired. Trips are scheduled regularly throughout the summer and are limited to 60 persons.

**Wild Cave Tour** (five miles, six hours) is scheduled during summer and weekends during spring and fall. This rugged spelunking adventure, which extends through crawlways and unimproved passages, requires the aid of hard hats and headlamps. Participants must be at least 16 years of age. Advance reservations are required: contact Mistix Corporation by phone (1-800/967-2283).

**Tour for mobility-impaired visitors** (one-half mile, one and one-half hours) is available.

**Green River Cruise.** The *Miss Green River II*, a twin diesel-powered cruiser, makes several cruises daily. The twilight cruise reveals not only the forests along the riverbanks, but deer, beaver, turtles, and a snake or two, all completely at home. Cruises last one hour. The ticket office is in the Visitor Center.

**Cave Island Nature Trail.** It begins and ends near the Historic Cave entrance, winding through the woods for about a mile. In addition, there are more than 7 miles of hiking trails keyed to geology, botany, and zoology. Guided walks are conducted daily during the summer.

**ACTIVITIES.** During summer months and spring and fall weekends, evening programs are given nightly at either the campground or the amphitheater.

**Hiking.** If you want to avoid crowds, take to the back country, where you can hike and camp for as long as three days without crossing your own trail. A network of meandering trails leads along high ridges and through steep, scenic valleys.

**Fishing** is permitted all year with throw lines, pole and line, rod and reel. No license is required. Swimming conditions are unsafe along the river.

**Craft Shop** features outstanding weaving, pottery, metalcrafts, baskets, brooms, and wood carvings. Here you can acquire a dulcimer.

**ACCOMMODATIONS.** National Park Concessions, Inc. (Mammoth Cave, Kentucky 42259; 502/773-2191) operates the only lodgings in the park. These are:

**Mammoth Cave Motel.** This older facility of 108 rooms and nearby cottages is the center of activity. M.

**Sunset Point Lodge.** Consists of newer motel units. M.

**Woodland Cottages.** Older units, economy-style. L.

Outside the park there are many types of accommodations in the nearby communities of Cave City, Park City, and Horse Cave.

**Best Western Park Mammoth Resort.** Park City, KY 42160. A resort-like inn on spacious grounds offers 18-hole golf, lighted tennis, hayrides, mini-train rides and indoor-outdoor pool. 502/749-4101. M to H.

**Barren River Lake Lodge,** Lucas, KY 42156. Located at Barren River State Park, it provides lodge rooms, kitchen-equipped cottages, tent and trailer sites. Pool, lighted tennis, 9-hole golf, swimming beach, and fishing on reservoir. 502/646-2151. M.

**Jolly's,** Cave City, KY 42127. Pool. Family rates available. 502/773-3118. L.

**CAMPING.** The campground of 110 sites, southeast of the Visitor Center, is adjacent to laundry, supply store, and showers, which are open during the summer. There is a limit of 14 days all year.

**SEASONS.** In spring, the hardwood forest is filled with wildflowers. Autumn is the time of brilliant color changes, when the days are mild and clear and the nights are crisp and chilly.

**NEARBY.** Ten miles north of the national park, **Nolin Lake Reservoir** formed behind Nolin Dam, completed in 1963, has over 6,000 acres of boating and fishing waters.

North and east of Mammoth Cave lie **Abraham Lincoln Birthplace National Historic Site** and the **Bluegrass** country around Lexington.

**FOR FURTHER INFORMATION.** Write Superintendent, Mammoth Cave National Park, Mammoth Cave, Kentucky 42259. 502/758-2251.

# MESA VERDE NATIONAL PARK

I DROVE across the Four Corners country, coming northeast from the Grand Canyon. It was winter, a few days after Christmas. The weather outside was quite cold and the landscape stark, a combination of mountain and desert, with little vegetation. It was magic in a way, a world of endless horizons, free of cities and modern structures. It was Indian country, settled first two thousand years ago, and still Indian country.

From the main highway, I reached at last the narrow mountain road, with sharp curves and steep grades, leading to Mesa Verde.

The tableland runs 15 miles long and 2,000 feet above the valley to the north. Its rimrocks command the horizon for more than a hundred miles, up through the purple Rockies and down across the stark desert of the Four Corners. On its south side, this table mountain is honeycombed with deep canyons. In long crannies and huge arching caves within these canyons and on the mesa tops stand hundreds of villages. They bespeak a lost world that struggled to survive in a harsh environment, flourished for a time, and was abandoned two centuries before Columbus.

Although it was winter, there were plenty of visitors in the park (though nowhere near the crowds of summer). Our fascination with Mesa Verde lies in its mysteries. Enthusiasts sometimes ascribe to these cliff dwellings superlatives such as "the largest," "the earliest," or "the most important." All of these may be true, and none may be true, for the only constant in history, as in nature, is change. From these ruins, archaeologists have given their best interpretation of a creative chapter in the story of prehistoric America, but their evaluations change as they acquire new knowledge.

The park covers 52,036 acres in the southwestern tip of Colorado. The region initially was occupied about the beginning of the first century A.D. by nomadic hunters turning to the land. At first they seem to have ignored the Mesa Verde, choosing instead the stream valleys for their villages. During the sixth century, however, they took up residence among the heavy forests of juniper and pinon on the mesa tops. They found a permanent supply of water, arable soil, and shelter. These Indians remained for 800 years, during which they advanced and refined arts, architecture, agriculture, and industry. From pithouses and crude pueblos, they progressed to great structures in the sheer rock, to which we have assigned such names as Cliff Palace and Balcony House—towers, terraces, whole towns built in the caves. Toward the end of the 13th century, they left their houses empty in the cliffs, their Temple to the Sun unfinished, and wandered away to search for water and to mingle with other tribes in the Southwest. Their bloodlines could well be carried down to many of the modern Pueblo Indians along the Rio Grande in New Mexico and west to the Hopi country in northern Arizona. As to why they deserted their villages, there is no simple answer. The abandonment was gradual, over a long period of time; the precise reasons are part of the puzzle of archaeology and history.

The early period of exploration to unravel the mysteries began in 1859, with a series of geological surveys. In 1874, William H. Jackson, the famous frontier photographer of the Hayden Survey, visited, photographed, and named Two Story House in Mancos Canyon, at the southern tip of Moccasin Mesa. B. K. Wetherill and his five sons became intimately familiar, through their cattle-herding activities, with Mesa Verde and its treasures. In 1888, Richard Wetherill and Charles Mason discovered Chapin Mesa. In 1891, Baron Gustavus Nordenskiold, of Sweden, guided by the Wetherills, recorded 22 cliff dwellings and performed major excavations; some of the materials he took to Europe now form part of the collection of the Finland National Museum. Indeed, some of the choicest prehistoric American artifacts are housed in European museums.

As the ruins became known, they were increasingly ravaged by cowboys and adventurers in search of salable artifacts. In protest against the vandalism, scientific and educational institutions urged that protective measures be taken. In 1891, the Colorado legislature petitioned Congress for the establishment of a national park on a part of the Ute Indian Reservation. Legislation to achieve that goal was introduced but continually failed (partly in dispute over whether mining should be permitted) until 1906, the same year that saw passage of the Antiquities Act. Unfortunately, the new park included almost none of the ruins it was supposed to preserve. The most valuable, including Cliff Palace, were on Ute deeded lands. In 1906, the Secretary of the Interior called for an archaeological survey, to be conducted by the Smithsonian Institution, to determine exactly what ruins situated on Ute lands should be embraced in the park and what the boundaries and acreage should be. But the Utes refused to trade until 1913, when they finally agreed to accept a much larger acreage of their own selection. The boundaries were again changed in 1931, 1932, and as recently as 1963 to ensure protection of the mesas and their ruins.

Concerned citizens and scientists prominent in the early history of the park included Mrs. Gilbert McClurg, who organized and promoted the Colorado Cliff Dwelling Association; Dr. J. W. Fewkes, of the Smithsonian Institution, who conducted extensive excavations and repairs over a period of years; and Dr. Jesse Nusbaum, who served as a young photographer on the 1906–07 Smithsonian survey, and who later became superintendent of Mesa Verde National Park.

A great deal has been learned about the changes in the ways of people while they dwelt here. Life at Mesa Verde is divided into four ages. The first is called the Basketmaker Period, when shallow caves furnished shelter and corn and squash were raised in small fields on the mesa top. Basketry, the earliest American craft, characterized this era, and woven baskets, bags, sandals, and containers of all sorts were created. Sometime after A.D. 450, their culture advanced into the Modified Basketmaker Period, when their architecture included development of the pithouse, a semi-subterranean room with low walls and a flat roof of mud-covered poles and sticks.

There were all sorts of variations in the shape of the pithouse—circular, D-shaped, square with rounded corners; antechambers with doorways; ventilator tunnels with vertical shafts; and ladders giving access through a smokehole in the rooftop. The Modified Basketmakers replaced some of their baskets with pottery, which enabled them to cook in fireproof vessels.

The Developmental Period, a time of experimentation, saw the emergence of a new type of house, a rectangular structure with vertical side walls and flat roofs. Houses were joined to form compact groups around open courts, where daily activity went on. Instead of pithouses, people built underground pitrooms in the courts, stylized ceremonial rooms called kivas, which are still used by Pueblo Indians. This was a period of expansion, flourishing arts and crafts, and the introduction of cotton, along with the use of the true loom. The people of this period built an ingenious chain of ditches to conserve water atop Chapin Mesa and to save the time it took to haul water from springs below.

Then came the climax of Mesa Verde culture, the golden age called the Classic Pueblo Period, from A.D. 1100 to 1300. Nearly all house walls were double, with massive outer walls. It was the sophisticated age of fine craftsmanship, beautiful black-on-white pottery made without the aid of a wheel, turquoise jewelry, and woven cloth. In the last phase, the twilight of Mesa Verde, architectural monuments were constructed in the most spectacular locations, on the cliff ledges and in the caves. Walls of houses and kivas occasionally were covered with handsome designs, sometimes colored red, white, yellow, and black.

Of hundreds of silent cities in the cliffs, actually few have been scientifically studied. A major archaeological project started in 1958 on Wetherill Mesa, one mile wide and 10 miles long, has finally been completed. It was opened to visitors in 1972—the first new area since the park was established in 1906.

Mesa Verde is the best-known archaeological monument in the Southwest, but I like to view it in a context with others, like Canyon de Chelly, Chaco Canyon, Bandelier, and Hovenweep. They fit together, unfolding a story, offering a common lesson about the past, and perhaps about the future as well.

## THE PRACTICAL GUIDE

**BACKGROUND.** During summer, since large crowds jam the park, several ruins are open on a first-come, first-served basis, with numbers limited. Stop at the Far View Visitor Center for details and guidance. Park roads, designed as scenic drives with reduced speed limits, will take longer than normal highway driving.

From the park entrance, the center of activities lies 21 miles ahead. This is the place to decide whether to make overnight reservations in the park (if there are vacancies), to head for the campground, or to spend a few hours and travel on.

**Park Point Fire Lookout** is one of five numbered stops at points of interest along the entrance road. At 8,572 feet above sea level, this is the highest elevation in the park. It opens views into Arizona, Utah, New Mexico, and Colorado, the states sharing the Four Corners. The mighty landmark of the desert, Shiprock, on the Navajo Indian Reservation, rises 1,400 feet. Viewed at sunset, it shimmers in the alpenglow, looking more like a ship than a rock.

**Park Museum.** A series of outstanding dioramas, accompanied by baskets, feather cloaks, and jewels found during excavations, reveals the successive cultures of the cliff dwellers. At the museum visitors learn the ground rules for visiting the dwellings, which have been dangerously weakened by time. Obtain tickets (no charge) to visit Cliff Palace and Balcony House, the most popular sites; these cliff dwellings are visited only with rangers on guided trips, or when marked "open for visitation" with a ranger posted on duty; mesa-top ruins, which are less susceptible to damage, may be visited unaccompanied, 8 A.M. to sunset.

**Ruins trip on Chapin Mesa.** Check the museum for the daily schedule. This is your chance to enter the inner sanctum of the American Stone Age. The trips are self-guiding in summer, led by a ranger in other seasons. **Spruce Tree House,** best preserved and one of the largest cliff dwellings in the park, contains 114 living rooms, of which 8 are kivas. **Cliff Palace,** the largest and most famous community dwelling, was discovered by Richard Wetherill and Charles Mason in 1888. Built under the protection of a high, vaulted alcove roof, it contains more than 200 rooms, of which 23 are kivas. Houses rising in some sections to four stories were home to as many as 200 persons. **Balcony House,** in a high cave on the west wall of Soda Canyon, demonstrates architectural detail and construction skills in a choice defensive setting.

**Ruins Road drive.** Two self-guiding loops cover 12 miles and provide views of many cliff dwellings with roofs still intact after a thousand years. Ten excavated mesa-top ruins may be visited. They demonstrate the entire range of architectural development in the sequence in which they were constructed, starting with a Modified Basketmaker pithouse of the late 600s. The road passes **Square Tower House** (not open), with a tower rising to a height of four stories, built against the near-perpendicular wall of Navajo Canyon, with the cliff forming its back wall. **Sun Point Pueblo** is interesting because its inhabitants, in the late Classic Pueblo Period, deliberately tore down the roofs and walls and used them to build a cliff dwelling in a nearby canyon. The last stop is **Sun Temple,** a great ceremonial structure also of the late Classic Pueblo Period, built on a promontory over Cliff and Fewkes canyons. No part of the building was roofed, and only some stone-working tools were found within.

**Wetherill Mesa** is second only to Chapin Mesa for the impressive concentration of cliff dwellings. Wetherill is spectacular but fragile. At the Far View Visitor Center, you can board a free bus for the 12-mile ride to Wetherill. Then you switch to an open-sided minitrain for a leisurely trip along a narrow path through the pinon-juniper forest to see the impressive ruins dating from the 12th and 13th centuries. Private autos are allowed to visit the site. The road from Far View Visitor Center includes 12 miles of pulloffs with exhibits and spectacular views. Be sure to stop to visit Step House and Long House.

**TOURS.** Conducted bus trips of two or three hours around the ruins are run by Far View Lodge.

**ACTIVITIES. Hiking.** This activity is restricted in Mesa Verde because of the fragile nature of the ruins. Petroglyph Point Trail leads from the museum around the base of the cliff on the east side of Spruce Tree and Navajo canyons, but you must obtain a written permit from the chief ranger's office. Longer trails are located in Morefield Canyon. Hiking is best done in areas outside Mesa Verde, and visitors should acquaint themselves with the Federal Antiquities Act and the Archaeological Resource Protection Act, prohibiting "pot-hunting" and vandalism in this and similar areas. Under this act, it is a federal offense to remove, injure, damage, or destroy "any historic or prehistoric ruin or monument, or any object of antiquity" situated on federal lands. Children should be advised firmly that every piece of pottery, bone, and stone plays a part in telling the story and that regulations are strictly enforced.

**Evening campfire programs** are presented nightly at the Morefield campground amphitheater, 9 P.M. from June until Labor Day.

**Photography.** The cliff dwellings are best photographed in the afternoon, for most caves face west-southwest. Large mesa-top ruins are good any time of day. Excellent scenic views are obtained from Mancos and Montezuma Valley overlooks and Park Point.

**ACCOMMODATIONS.** In the park modern motel-type accommodations are operated by a concessioner, the Mesa Verde Company. Other facilities are plentiful at Mancos, 7 miles east; Cortez, 10 miles west; and Durango, 38 miles east. The concessioner also operates grocery stores accessible to campgrounds.

**Far View Lodge,** Mesa Verde Company, Box 277, Mancos, CO 81328. It is appropriately named considering the distant vistas of the Four Corners. Open mid-May to mid-October. Smaller rooms cost less. In season 303/529-4421; rest of year 303/533-7731. M.

**Lake Mancos Guest Ranch,** Box 218, Mancos, CO 81328. This distinct mountain resort has rooms and cabins with private patios (but no room phones). Pool and children's program. Open summer only. Weekly rates available. 303/433-7900. M.

**Teller House Youth Hostel,** Box 457, Silverton, CO 81433. Here's the chance to stay inexpensively in a famed old mining town. Hostelers won't find a kitchen, but the rate includes an American breakfast. 303/387-5423. L.

**CAMPING. Morefield Canyon Campground,** five miles from the park entrance, at 7,800-feet elevation, has modern campsites, most of which accommodate trailers. The campground runs on first-come, first-served basis, with a 14-day limit. Morefield Village, operated by the park concessioner, includes supply store, coin-operated laundry, showers and carry-out snack shop. Service stations are located at Far View and Morefield Village.

**SEASONS.** Accommodations are provided about May 15 to October 15 (limited basis after Labor Day), but an interpretive program is presented year-round, with trips scheduled to at least one cliff dwelling, weather permitting. The park is open all year; after October 15 you may visit the museum and drive one loop of the ruins road, viewing cliff dwellings from canyon rims and visiting the mesa-top ruins. Summer days are warm, evenings chilly. Freezing weather arrives early at this high elevation.

Airlines operate daily flights to Durango, where rent-a-car service is available.

**NEARBY.** For a new, off-beat travel adventure, visit Ute Mountain Tribal Park, covering about 125,000 acres of cliffs, mesas, and canyons, with hundreds of ruins in various degrees of stabilization, along a 25-mile stretch of the Mancos River, just south of Mesa Verde National Park. The season opens in May, or possibly June, depending on weather and road conditions.

**San Juan National Forest** to the north offers excellent fishing, hunting, backcountry trails, and numerous small campgrounds, all within two hours drive of Mesa Verde. Check for locations at ranger offices in Durango and Marcos.

Durango is the starting point of a ride on the historic **Durango and Silverton Narrow Gauge Railroad.** The train runs daily, except Christmas. From mid-May through October the train makes a round trip each day from Durango to the old mining town of Silverton, a journey through the deep canyons of the Animas River. The rest of the year the trip is from Durango to the Cascade Canyon. From late June through August, reservations are necessary. Phone 303/247-2733 for more information.

Mesa Verde was isolated and hard to reach for many years, but modern paved highways have shortened the driving time to one day from Denver and Salt Lake City. Grand Canyon is a six and one-half hour drive, and Santa Fe approximately six hours. Road improvement across Monument Valley, Arizona, links Mesa Verde, via US 160, with spectacular frontier scenery of the Four Corners country.

Mesa Verde will be appreciated more when you visit and compare it with national monuments of the region. A dry climate and the use of stone and adobe by ancient architects have combined to produce extremely well-preserved ruins. Because of the excellent stage of preservation and the impressive structures, more archaeological sites have been incorporated in the National Park system in the Southwest than in any other part of the country. National monuments in the vicinity of the Four Corners are **Aztec Ruins,** New Mexico, a great prehistoric American town of the 12th century; **Chaco Canyon,** New Mexico, representing a high point of the ancient Pueblo civilization; **Hovenweep,** a network of towers and pueblos spread across Colorado and Utah; **Navajo,** Arizona, three of the largest, most elaborate cliff dwellings; and **Canyon de Chelly,** Arizona, fantastic ruins in red cliff and cave country, where modern Navajo Indians have homes and farms.

**FOR FURTHER INFORMATION.** Write Superintendent, Mesa Verde National Park, Colorado 81330. 303/529-4465.

# MOJAVE NATIONAL PRESERVE

## CALIFORNIA

ESTABLISHED 1994

HEADING EAST past Barstow, the freeway leads to Las Vegas, but I turned off at Baker into the desert to explore a region destined to become America's newest national park. I found once again that the desert is friendly; it invites exploration. The Mojave is a wonderland of salt flats, dry lakes, volcanic craters, lava flows, mountain ranges, sand dunes, Joshua tree forests, cinder cones, ancient rock art, and uncounted remnants of early Indian life.

But however did it become a national preserve? That's part of history, too. I remember when a caring group of Californians organized the Mojave National Park Coalition. That was in 1976, the year Congress passed legislation mandating a long-term management plan for 25 million acres of the California Desert Conservation Area. The act required that desert lands be managed "in a manner that will protect the quality of scientific, scenic, historical, ecological, environmental, air and atmospheric, water resources and archaeological values." It called for treating the California desert as a total ecosystem, "extremely fragile, easily scarred, and slowly healed."

In 1980 the East Mojave National Scenic Area of 1.5 million acres was designated administratively, under jurisdiction of the Bureau of Land Management. But public pressure for a national park continued, the proponents citing evidence of erosion caused by off-road vehicles, desert intaglios rutted with wheel tracks, and prehistoric pictographs desecrated. Thus in 1994 Congress acted to establish the new national preserve. It differs from the national parks, in that hunting and livestock grazing are permitted under regulation in certain areas. Otherwise, preservation is the prime purpose, and the beautiful lanfair valley is protected.

The Mojave merits this recognition, if solely for the opportunity to observe and absorb the miracles of desert life. Plants, for example, endure long periods without water, then take advantage of brief but violent rainstorms. The creosote bush spreads roots close to the surface to catch moisture before it evaporates. Most cacti use green stems, instead of leaves, to produce food. Most animals are nocturnal in their habits—wise enough to stay under cover during the heat of the day—but are wondrous and varied in form, function, and color. The little kangaroo rat spends its whole life without taking a drink. The once common but now rare desert tortoise, cousin to the celebrated giant tortoise of the

Galapagos Islands, moves slowly over the desert on blunt club-shaped feet. Watching a red-tailed hawk filling its niche by feeding on rodents and rabbits or a Swainson's hawk soaring high on wind currents reminds me that birds, of all wildlife, are most easily seen in daytime.

## THE PRACTICAL GUIDE

**BACKGROUND.** The park occupies a large triangle in southeastern California between Interstate 15 leading from Barstow to Las Vegas and Interstate 40 from Barstow to Needles and Lake Havasu, with US 95 as base of the triangle to the east. A few major paved roads lead into the park, joining gravel and dirt roads. Be sure to fill your tank.

**ACTIVITIES.** Hiking, backpacking, rockhounding, birding, wildlife watching, photography, nature study, archaeology, and history are all choice pursuits in the Mojave. Horseback riding too, though horses are not permitted at developed campsites. Commercial cattle ranching is still allowed.

The Kelbaker Road, south from Baker (on I-15) provides access to key points in the park, including the **Cima Dome,** a mass of once-molten granite-like monzonite, called the most symmetrical natural dome in the United States, and the historic town of **Kelso,** site of a classic Union Pacific railroad depot. On the Cima Road, south from I-15 at Valley Wells, take the 2-mile Teutonia Peak Trail, meandering through the world's largest and densest Joshua tree forest—trees are more than 25 feet high and several hundred years old—to a lookout over Cima Dome. Then scramble over the rocks a quarter mile to the top of Teutonia Peak, 5,755 feet. Ivanpah-Lanfair Road, between Nipton near I-15 and Goffs near I-40, leads through Ivanpah Valley, one of the likely places to see the desert tortoise, and then a cluster of old mines.

**Birdwatching.** Some of the best places are in the New York Mountains along the Ivanpah-Lanfair Road. Moist shady canyons attract orioles, golden eagles, white-throated swifts. Isolated waterholes draw Gambel's quail, roadrunners, and migrating buntings and other species. The best birding is sitting patiently next to a small desert waterhole.

**ACCOMMODATIONS.** Bun Boy Motel in Baker (20 units, 619/733-4363) may be closest to the park. Barstow, gateway to the Mojave from the west, has a variety of chain and independent lodgings.

**CAMPING.** Principal sites, simple and semi-developed, are at Mid-Hills and Hole-in-the-Wall, but primitive camping is allowed almost anywhere along the roads—but not within 600 feet of a watering spot.

**SEASONS.** Pick your time carefully. Best months are October through May. Don't take winter for granted—heavy rain, even snow at higher elevations, is always a possibility. Best time to come is spring, especially April, when the Joshuas bloom, adding white flowers to their photogenic forms. Summer at low elevations can be a sizzler; though the country is dry, a summer storm likely leads to flash floods. Whenever you come carry plenty of water.

**NEARBY. Providence Mountains State Recreation Area,** on an all-weather road 17 miles east of Essex on I-40 displays high desert tableaus framed by red volcanic peaks. Tours are conducted to limestone Mitchell Caverns. At Barstow, check the **California Desert Information Center** for related points of interest.

**FOR FURTHER INFORMATION.** Write Superintendent, Mojave National Preserve, Desert Information Center, 831 Barstow Rd., Barstow, CA 92311. 619/256-8313.

# MOUNT RAINIER NATIONAL PARK

## WASHINGTON

ESTABLISHED 1899

I MADE IT TO CAMP MUIR, at 10,000 feet, in a little over four hours. I went with a light day pack, starting from Paradise, the center of activity in the park, at 5,450 feet. The forest of Douglas fir at the lower elevation yielded to trim alpine fir and grassy highland meadows flecked with wildflowers. I hiked alone at my own pace, stopping where I wished to watch the wonderful white and green world of the Cascades unfold. At Pebble Creek, the sign said Camp Muir was only 2.4 miles, but it was steep and tedious, virtually all on snow. Above the flower fields, Rainier became a complex of cliffs, ridges, canyons, and cascading glaciers, such as long, narrow Nisqually Glacier bordering the route on the west.

Camp Muir was as far as I went. It was enough for me. I rested and ate my pack lunch at this cluster of stone shelters, the gateway to the summit at 14,410 feet. Climbers start from here as early as 1 A.M., roped together, hoping to reach their goal and back before the sun brings ice-fall dangers, returning all the way to Paradise by late afternoon. It is a challenge under the best of conditions, with weather, snow, and ice, variable and unpredictable, adding to the mystery and magnetism. As John Muir wrote in 1888, after reaching the site now named for him (then known as Cloud Camp): "The night was like a night in Minnesota in December."

The trip down from Camp Muir was effortless, sheer pleasure; it was almost as easy to roll as to walk. I marveled at the great mountain above me.

About 40 square miles of icy, glacial rivers cap Mount Rainier, the loftiest volcanic peak of the Cascade Range. They flow downward from the 14,410-foot summit of Columbia Crest to timberline, at about 6,500 feet, and contribute to lakes and waterfalls in the midst of flowering meadows. In the valleys around the base of the mountain, heavy precipitation spurs the growth of dark, cathedral-like forests of the mighty and wonderfully proportioned Douglas fir, Western hemlock, Western red cedar, Sitka spruce, Pacific silver fir, and other giants of the Northwest.

Rainier is a gleaming landmark visible for hundreds of miles in all directions when the weather is clear. It is the fifth highest peak in the United States south of Alaska, rising higher above its base than any other in the "lower 48." Nearby Mount St. Helens was another prominent feature of the Northwest—until its explosive eruption in May 1980. Now it is administered as a "national volcanic monument," a contrasting companion piece to Rainier.

The broad dome of Mount Rainier is a kingdom of glaciers. The Emmons Glacier, about 4.3 miles long and 1 mile wide on the northeast flank, is the largest glacier by overall size in the United States south of Alaska, while the Carbon Glacier, on the north face of the mountain, is the longest—6 miles. The glacier system of Rainier, though a mere remnant of its former size, is recognized as the country's most extensive "single peak" glacial system outside of Alaska. It contains a total of 26 named glaciers and 50 small, unnamed glaciers and ice patches.

In this national park, which covers 235,404 acres, the visitor can learn some of the simple truths that are known about glaciers and their behavior. On the Nisqually Glacier, the body of ice has been determined to move from 50 to over 400 feet per year at the 6,000-foot level. Movement varies within each glacier; the masses of ice move downward by virtue of their own weight, faster at the center than along the edges, and are influenced by the steepness of slope. Most glaciers of the world have been receding and growing shorter, as the case had been at Mount Rainier from the late 19th century until recent years. Slowly, vegetation crept into the barren areas. In recent years, however, the major glaciers on Rainier have reversed the trend and expanded, advancing downhill.

I picture Mount Rainier as a glacial laboratory in which I can watch the rivers of ice in action and the effects of their movements. The glacier churns and moves the earth's mantle and pieces of bedrock; it rasps the firm rock in its path, leaving it smooth; it carries away the plowed-off and filed-off debris, plus rock fragments fallen from the mountain slopes. Around the base I can identify glacial moraines, representing the accumulation of earth and rock dust where they are finally deposited. Then I observe how glacial debris, plucked and scoured from the mountain cone, is transported downstream.

Climate is a major influence upon Mount Rainier. It becomes more severe with rise in elevation, so that Longmire, elevation 2,760 feet, receives about one-third as much snow as Paradise, elevation 5,500 feet, which has averaged about 575 inches a year. The snow feeding Mount Rainier's glaciers originates as clouds over the Pacific Ocean. Rising to pass over the mountains, westerly winds are cooled, and the condensing moisture falls as rain and snow.

I find much to enjoy at lower elevations, where heavy moisture produces a luxuriant growth of trees and wildflowers, equally as lovely as the more celebrated flowers of the mountain meadows. The species of the deep woods, such as the three-leaf anemone, long tube twinflower, Pacific trillium, calypso, and spring beauty, actually outnumber those typical of the higher elevations. But almost anywhere I go there are blossoms, right up to the edge of the snowbank and sometimes up through the snow. The entire experience is enriched by the sight and sounds of more than 50 species of mammals and 130 species of birds. I look for mountain goats in bands along the rocky crags between 6,000 and 9,000 feet during summer and for closeups on the trail of the hoary marmot, a large furry rodent, sunning himself on rocky slopes from 5,000 feet to timberline. Elk migrate into the park each spring and remain until late fall.

## THE PRACTICAL GUIDE

**ACCESS.** Mount Rainier National Park is a good one-day automobile trip from Seattle or Tacoma, both about two hours driving distance. Hikers, mountain climbers, and campers enjoy longer stays. Each year, more than two million people visit the park, mostly in summer. Snowfields are enjoyed by 35,000 winter visitors; it's a good time to come.

**TOURS.** One-day bus tours leave Seattle daily before 9 A.M. and return by 6 P.M. They're easy to arrange through most Seattle hotels or by calling the Gray Line office.

**BACKGROUND.** The four Visitor Centers of the park are at Longmire, Paradise, Sunrise, and Ohanapecosh.

**ACTIVITIES. Hiking.** Mount Rainier is a hiker's park, offering more than 300 miles of trail. You can hike for an hour or a day, or spend two weeks backpacking while absorbing breathtaking views and experiences to remember.

Note especially that the famed Blue Ice Caves have been closed due to excessive melting, which has weakened and collapsed the ceiling of ice.

Try to take at least one of the easy trails, no matter how short your time in the park. In the Longmire area, the **Nisqually River Trail** makes a pleasant two-mile family hike from Cougar Rock Campground down to the Visitor Center. The **Silver Falls Loop,** from Ohanapecosh Campground and Washington

123, is a good low-level destination when storms sweep the high country; the three-mile loop rises only 300 feet through the forests along the Ohanapecosh River. With more time, make a full-day hike to such places as **Panorama Point,** on a four-and-a-half-mile loop from Paradise parking lot, with a climb of 1,400 feet, and **Van Trump Park,** a climb of two and a half miles and 1,900 feet from Christine Falls parking lot (10 miles up Paradise Road from Nisqually entrance) to beautiful Comet Falls. **Skyline Trail,** a five-mile loop above the tree line that begins just west of Paradise Ranger Station, has been rebuilt to help control erosion; enjoy views of surrounding peaks and Nisqually Glacier, and admire the hand-built stone stairs.

A backcountry use permit is required for all summer overnight camping. If headed for a popular area on a summer weekend, you'll be wise to reserve a campsite in advance. Contact Hikers' Center, Mount Rainier National Park, Ashford, WA 98304 or call 206/569-2211.

**Wonderland Trail** offers one of America's top hiking experiences. It completely encircles the mountain, a distance of 93 miles, with campsites spaced about 8 to 12 miles apart. It travels through dense forests, climbs to alpine meadows, and passes close to glaciers. It requires preparation and proper gear. It's a long 93 miles, with plenty of steep climbs and descents, so plan for at least 10 days and count on more like 14.

Parts of the trail can be enjoyed a day or two at a time, or even on a half-day hike, being linked with spur trails to the park road system. The 30-mile section between **Paradise** and **Sunrise** passes lakes, waterfalls, and the glacial-formed Box Canyon of the Cowlitz River. From Sunrise to **Carbon River,** 16½ miles, hikers enter the deep backcountry to see Winthrop Glacier, Mystic Lake at 5,800 feet, and through Moraine Park at the foot of Carbon Glacier. From Carbon River around to **Longmire,** the trail crosses one stream after another while passing the Mowich Glaciers, Golden Lakes, and wanders between the fingers of Tahoma Glacier.

**Northern Loop Trail,** a branch off the Wonderland Trail, winds from Sunrise, at 6,400 feet elevation, through the meadows of Berkeley Park, carpeted with paintbrush, lupine, mountain buttercup, and other flowers, across the southern tip of the beautiful Chenuis Mountain to **Ipsut Creek Campground** on Carbon River, a distance of 17½ miles.

**Driving. Stevens Canyon Road,** completed in 1957 as part of the 117-mile road network in the park, is an outstanding scenic drive of the Northwest. The park has five approaches: via the **Nisqually,** or southwest entrance; **Carbon River,** or northwest entrance; **Ohanapecosh,** or southeast entrance; **Chinook Pass** entrance, on the crest of the Cascade Range at the east boundary; and **White River** entrance, off the beautiful Mather Memorial Highway from the northeast. An attractive route for motorists leads from the Nisqually entrance to **Longmire,** then 13 miles past Cougar Rock campground and Christine Falls to **Paradise Valley,** with subalpine fir, mountain hemlock, and fields of wildflowers. Continuing east from Paradise, Stevens Canyon Road passes beautiful Reflection and Louise lakes, with vistas of the rugged Tatoosh Range and Mount Adams. It intersects the East Side Road north of Ohanapecosh; you can turn north to Tipsoo Lake near Chinook Pass or continue north to the White River entrance, leading into Sunrise, the highest point reached by improved road in the State of Washington, facing Emmons Glacier.

**Mountain Climbing.** This is one of the thrills of this national park, which served as training grounds of the 1963 American Mount Everest expedition. The concession guide service conducts a varied program for both novices and experienced mountaineers. The best is the climb to the summit, a long, strenuous ascent over moderately difficult terrain. It takes serious training and conditioning. Part of the pleasure of the trip is just participating in the snow- and ice-climbing school (one day). The climb takes two days. Climbing gear is available for sale or rent at Paradise. Contact Rainier Mountaineering, Inc., Paradise, WA 98397; phone 206/569-2227. In the winter, write to 201 St. Helens Ave., Tacoma, WA 98402 or phone 206/627-6242. About 4,500 climbers reach the summit each year over several routes. But it takes an expert guide or leader to spot treacherous crevasses and crumbling lava. Routes are officially open all year, but weather is best from late spring to early fall.

**Winter Sports.** Snows blanket the high country. Paradise is closed in winter, but snowshoeing and cross-country skiing, with supervised and prepared tube runs, are available on weekends until snow forces road closures—usually in mid-November. The Visitor Center, in fact, offers guided snowshoe walks and winter interpretive programs during this time. Major ski developments with mechanical lifts are located nearby in the **Snoqualmie National Forest.**

**Fishing.** All waters are open, except those posted, without a license. Special restrictions exist for several areas in the park. Lakes normally are open July 4 to October 31, but snowpack may delay opening until late July or even early August; stream fishing conforms to the state fishing season. Glacial streams and upland lakes are generally too cold to support much aquatic life, but some remote lakes and clear streams provide fair to good trout fishing. Boats without motors are allowed in most lakes. Swimming conditions are poor.

**Naturalist Programs.** Guided nature walks and evening illustrated talks are conducted at Paradise, Longmire, Sunrise, Ohanapecosh, and Ipsut Creek. "The Ecology of Birds of Mount Rainier" is the theme of weekend and weekday workshops in July, jointly sponsored by the National Park Service and Central Washington State College at Cispus Environmental Learning Center. Field trips and classes focus on identification, behavior, and natural history. Accommodations are in Cispus dormitories. For information write Department of Biology, Central Washington State College, Ellensburg, WA 98926.

**Wildlife Watching.** Many, and varied, species of birds frequent the park—because of its environmental diversity. Look for hawks and golden eagles in subalpine meadows, Canada geese and pintail ducks on the lakes, passing through on migration. Almost 150 species have been recorded during one season or an-

other, so carry a good bird guide. Mammals on the park checklist total about 50. Deer are mostly seen in high forests and meadows during summer. They come into lowlands for the winter, and fawns are dropped during May and June. The best place to find elk is on Shriner Peak, reached by trail from Ohanapecosh. Best places for goats are Van Trump Park, Emerald Ridge, and the Colonnades and Cowlitz Chimneys. When traveling in high country you won't have to look for marmots—they'll be there. Carry a good pair of binoculars and scan the cliffs as you hike. Avoid feeding wildlife; they become dependent on panhandling and can't make it on their own through rough winters.

**ACCOMMODATIONS.** Concession-operated lodgings in the park are located at Longmire, near the Nisqually entrance, and at Paradise, at higher elevation. For reservations, write Mount Rainier Guest Services, Star Route, Ashford, WA 98304; 206/569-2275. Concession operations are:

**Paradise Inn.** In a scenic alpine setting at

5,400 feet, the oldest part dates from 1916 and is listed on the National Register of Historic Places. The inn has undergone extensive refurbishment. Some rooms are with shared bath, and cost less. Full-service dining room, lounge, and snack bar. Open late May to mid-October. M to H.

**National Park Inn.** Adjacent to Hikers Information Center at Longmire, elevation 2,700 feet, the inn reopened following major remodeling. The hotel was built in 1916 and is listed on the National Register of Historic Places.

Outside the park, lodgings are located near Enumclaw and Buckley, 20 to 25 miles from the Carbon River entrance, and, on the east side, in the vicinity of White Pass and Packwood on Washington 123, near the southeast entrance.

**Old Mill House B&B,** 116 Oak St., Eastonville, WA 98328. On the west side of the park, a converted mansion recreates the classy style of the 1920s. 206/832-6506. M.

**Lodge Youth Hostel,** Box 86, Ashford, WA 98304. A mere quarter-mile outside the Nisqually entrance, it is close to the trails, whether for summer hiking or winter skiing and snowshoeing. 206/569-2312. L.

**CAMPING.** The main campgrounds inside the park are at Cougar Rock, Ohanapecosh, and White River. Sunrise is a pleasant walk-in campground. For those who want solitude and more primitive conditions, small Class B campgrounds are at Sunshine Point and Ipsut Creek. Limit is 14 days, no trailer utilities. Camping is permitted in remote areas of the park. From June 15 through September 30, a backcountry use permit must be obtained. Other campgrounds are adjacent to the park in Snoqualmie National Forest.

**SEASONS.** Views of the mountain and glacier are obscured much of the year by clouds and fog, but warm, clear weather may be expected during the height of the summer season from about July 1 to early September. Two wildflower climaxes occur, one in early July and the other during August. Indian summer weather sometimes continues well into October. Most roads, including Stevens Canyon, are closed for the winter after the first heavy snowfall, usually about November 1. The road from the Nisqually entrance is open all year, although snow conditions may cause it to be closed for short periods. In winter, the road deadends at Ohanapecosh and no services are available.

The weather conditions can be uncertain during late winter and early spring. Snowstorms are interspersed with many clear, warm days. Be prepared for a sudden snowstorm. Be sure to carry tire chains.

**NEARBY.** Named in memory of the first director of the National Park Service, Mather Memorial Highway, a 50-mile scenic drive on Washington 410, starts at the boundary of the Snoqualmie National Forest southeast of Enumclaw, continues through the park to Chinook Pass, then down the American River. **Federation Forest State Park,** 15 miles north of the White River entrance on Washington 410, contains a museum and interpretive center on the natural history of White River Valley. Allow at least half a day to visit Mount St. Helens National Volcanic Monument, a part of Gifford Pinchot National Forest. Join interpretive programs and trail walks to relive the incredible power unleashed on May 18, 1980. Permits are required for climbs above 4,800 feet. Call the climbing Hotline, 206/247-5800, or write Mount St. Helens National Volcanic Monument, Rt. 1, Box 369, Amboy, WA 98601.

**RECOMMENDED READING.** *Exploring Mount Rainier,* by Ruth Kirk, and *50 Hikes in Mount Rainier National Park,* by Ira Spring and Harvey Manning. For climbers: *Cascade Alpine Guide—Columbia River to Stevens Pass,* by Fred Becky, and *The Challenge of Rainier,* by Dee Molenaar.

**FOR FURTHER INFORMATION.** Write Superintendent, Mount Rainier National Park, Tahoma Woods, Star Route, Ashford, WA 98304. 206/569-2211.

# NORTH CASCADES NATIONAL PARK

## WASHINGTON

ESTABLISHED 1968

FROM Bellingham on the coast, my friends John and Rotha Lou and I drove southeast to Sedro Woolley, stopping at the North Cascades Visitor Center (operated jointly by the National Park Service and U.S. Forest Service). We picked up maps, asked a few questions and headed east on State Route 20, the North Cascades Highway, one of the most scenic roads in America. We drove only to Marblemount, forking onto the Cascade River Road to the trailhead at the base of Cascade Pass. It was a brilliant, sunny day in the summer of 1987. I would not say the trail was crowded, but a good number of people were out to stretch their legs and to enjoy a day in the mountains.

The trail was laid out in relatively easy switchbacks that almost anyone could handle. John had been over this route many times. As a hiker, climber, skier, and historian, he knew the North Cascades intimately. Now and then, he would cite bits of history and lore, but he was absorbed with the show of wildflowers sprinkling the hillsides and meadows. We hiked leisurely for about two hours to reach Cascade Pass (elevation 5,384 feet), a vantage point for viewing steep rock ridges, glaciers, snowfields, and cascading waterfalls, a setting to compare with the most spectacular mountain scenery on earth.

In order to protect it for posterity, Washington's third great national park was established in 1968. The region is often called the "American Alps," and is one of the last of our primeval landscapes. The most prominent structural features of the Cascades—the volcanoes—are considered the largest freestanding objects in the contiguous United States.

This country had long been known to the Indians. The first white men who ventured into the North Cascades undoubtedly were trappers and hunters. In addition to a great variety of furbearers and game animals, they found a breathtaking land of alpine scenery, snow-capped peaks, cascading streams, and western foothills covered with dense softwood forests. In 1814, Alexander Ross, backed by fur-trading interests, went over Cascade Pass in search of a short route to the Pacific.

Sometime prior to 1850, gold and other metallic ores—including silver, copper, lead, mercury, iron, and chromium—were discovered. Prospectors and fortune-seekers were immediately attracted to the region, although the only

profits were made by those selling food and equipment to the miners. The net effect was to stimulate river transportation, trail improvement, and settlement by hardy souls. Lucinda Davis, who had mining claims up the Cascade River, moved to Cedar Bar in 1897, near the present town of Diablo, opened an inn and became the first woman to climb Sourdough Mountain and Davis Peak. The harvest of timber from the dense Cascade forests also began around the mid-1800s, but it was decades later that large-scale commercial logging became important.

An abundance of high-quality water, stemming partly from melting snowfields and glaciers, was another resource to be recognized. In 1919, Seattle City Light started its hydroelectric developments, which led eventually to the construction of the towns of Diablo and Newhalem.

In 1899, Mount Rainier National Park was established out of the old Mount Rainier Forest Reserve. During the following years, many proposals were advanced for additional areas of national forests in the North Cascades to be transferred to the National Park Service. The critical need for action did not become obvious, however, until the 1950s. In his classic work, *The Wild Cascades*, Harvey Manning recalls that as recently as 1948, he and other outdoorsmen felt "the wilderness was inexhaustible, and if one valley was logged, or two or three or a dozen, we could always escape to what seemed uncountable virgin valleys remaining." Then the growing infiltration of bulldozers, chain saws, and logging trucks changed everything.

The North Cascades Conservation Council, headed by Patrick D. Goldsworthy, and the Sierra Club, led by David Brower, mounted a major national campaign. In January 1963, the Secretaries of Interior and Agriculture (responsible for parks and forests, respectively) agreed to form a study team to review administration of the North Cascades. Despite the political power of the timber industry and resistance of the Forest Service, the study team report of October 1965 recommended establishment of a new North Cascades National Park, though not as large as conservationists had wished and with some key features, such as Mount Baker, omitted. In February 1966, appropriate legislation was introduced in both houses of Congress. Hearings were held in Washington, D.C., and Washington State in 1967 and 1968, and in the latter year, the bill was passed, establishing a national park and two national recreation areas, Ross Lake and Lake Chelan, totaling 674,000 acres.

I marvel at the North Cascades as a range of giant faults and massive overthrusts, a thoroughly complex geology. Formed of weather-resistant rock, the high stretch of the Cascades intercepts some of the continent's wettest prevailing winds. The resulting precipitation has produced a network of hanging glaciers and icefalls, ice aprons and ice caps, hanging valleys and waterfalls. Works of ice make the North Cascades a rough, tall country, and a steep one from valley to summit. Some of the finest mountaineering opportunities in the United States are found here.

Between the moisture-laden west side and the dry east slopes, plant communities show a tremendous variation, ranging from subalpine conifers, green meadow, and alpine tundra, back down to pine forests and sunny-dry shrub lands. They combine to form a vast array of unimpaired wilderness life communities; the national park was established to keep them free.

On a backpack trip I made in 1985, hiking to Cascade Pass from Stehekin, on the east side, I saw many deer on the trail. A pair of spotted fawn poked their inquisitive noses into my campsite at Basin Creek, while a hummingbird flitted among the shrubs. I hiked for a time with a young woman, Irene, who knew her plants and gave me a field lesson identifying yarrow, thimbleberry, elderberry, serviceberry, and other plants and flowers that flourish during the brief summer.

On another trip, in winter, I floated the Skagit River in a rubber raft from Marblemount to Rockport, a few miles from the edge of the park, counting more than thirty bald eagles roosting in the trees and feeding on salmon in the stream.

Mountain goats, deer, and black bear are frequently seen in the wilderness. Other wildlife include the wolverine, marten, fisher, grizzly bear, cougar, and moose. White-tailed ptarmigans and a host of smaller birds and mammals make this harsh land their home.

The national park covers 504,780 acres in two units, each with a major wilderness as its core; Ross Lake National Recreation Area separates the two. The northern unit, bordering Canada, includes Mount Shuksan and the Picket Range, composed of glaciers, granite peaks, high lakes, and remote valleys. The southern unit includes the "Eldorado high country" and the Stehekin River valley, one of the finest glacier-carved canyons in the Cascades.

The Ross Lake Recreation Area covers 117,574 acres between the Pasayten Wilderness of the Forest Service and the two units of the national park. Lake Chelan National Recreation Area consists of 61,890 acres at the head of the lake and in the lower Stehekin Valley.

## THE PRACTICAL GUIDE

**ACCESS.** The major access to the park is on Washington 20, the North Cascades Highway, a link between Okanogan and US 97 in north-central Washington and Mount Vernon on I-5 on the Pacific coast.

Slow down to enjoy the vistas; the road is not meant for speeding. The highway was dedicated in 1972 as "the most scenic mountain drive in Washington." Points of interest include (coming from the east) Early Winters Information Station (operated by Okanogan National Forest and the National Park Ser-

vice); Washington Pass, the highest point on the highway (with picnic area and scenic overlooks); Rainy Pass, with picnic area and day hikes on the Pacific Crest Trail; Ross Lake Recreation Area, and the new park visitors center at Newhalem.

Besides the cross-park route, access to the periphery is possible via Washington 542 from Bellingham on the west, Highway 3 in Canada from the north, and by boat or float plane service daily from Chelan (north of Wenatchee on US 97) at the southern end of

55-mile-long Lake Chelan. There are almost 360 miles of trails in the park and adjacent recreation areas.

**Ross Lake** is one of three lakes formed by dams on the Skagit River, which starts in Canada and flows through the Ross Lake National Recreation Area. The lake is 1,600 feet above sea level and extends 1½ miles into Canada, collecting water from a 1,200-square-mile watershed. The reservoir, completed in 1950, is in the center of a region with 150 active glaciers and hundreds of jagged peaks. Drainage from these perpetually snow-covered peaks makes Ross Lake quite cold even in August.

Access to Ross Lake is gained via a 3½-mile trail starting at the Diablo Lake Resort or from the Ross Dam powerhouse at the head of **Diablo Lake** along a 1-mile gravel road. At the Ross Lake Resort you can stock up on gas and ice, or rent boats, motors, and cabins. The lake is 24 miles long and 2 miles across at its greatest width. It takes strong paddlers to canoe on Ross Lake. Boaters can't put ashore just anywhere, because of steep canyonlike walls ringing the lake. The gorgelike terrain creates hazardous gusts of wind, which can be counted on to whip up every afternoon and early evening. Large boats should have poles aboard to push them off from shore should they experience power failure in the wind; small-craft owners need to be alert to winds that can blow them onto the rocks.

**ACTIVITIES. Backpacking.** This is a favorite sport in the Ross Lake country. On the west rise the peaks of the Picket Range; farther north, Little Jackass Mountain and the Canadian peaks beyond the head of the lake. Most of this country can be hiked, but don't try the rugged ridges unless you have a rock-climbing background. From the town of Diablo, a strenuous 7-mile hike leads to Sourdough Mountain, looking up at towering peaks and glaciers. Rangers at Hozomeen, just below the Canadian border, can give directions to smaller lakes overlooking Ross Lake. By all means travel with a good topographical map.

**Hiking.** About 360 miles of hiking and horse trails exist throughout the four units of the North Cascades complex. North from Diablo Lake you can go up Big Beaver Creek to Whatcom Pass and the high lakes—this trip does not require rock-climbing experience, nor does the hike to Ruby Mountain.

Going into Hozomeen, allow time in Skagit Valley Recreation Area (a British Columbia provincial park) to walk the Chittenden Meadow Interpretive Trail, named for Curley Chittenden, a key figure in the fight to save Skagit Valley from being flooded for the Ross Lake reservoir. Then hike from the camping area up to Hozomeen Lake, an alpine jewel.

**Diablo Lake,** northeast of Newhalem in the Skagit Valley, lies between the north and south units of the park. An impressive trip to the south—not strenuous, but two or three days for most walkers—leads up **Thunder Creek** and over **Park Creek,** then down to **Lake Chelan.** This trip passes close to spectacular glaciers and the lofty peaks of the Eldorado wilderness, such as Eldorado, Forbidden, Buckner, and Goode.

An alternative to this route is to drive from the west to Marblemount on the Skagit River, then 22 miles along the Cascade River, stopping 2 miles short of Cascade Pass in the scenic climax of the range. The short hike to the pass takes one through an alpine world of flowering meadows, sheer cliffs, and glaciered peaks, and the headwaters of two wild rivers flowing east and west. Cascade Pass is one of the most popular areas.

**Lake Chelan** furnishes the classic approach to the range. The passenger ferry *Lady of the Lake II* and the faster *Lady Express* operate daily in summer. Lake Chelan, set in a glacial trough, is about 1,500 feet deep at its deepest point and varies from ¼ mile to 2 miles wide, flanked by forested slopes and wilderness peaks.

The trip by ferry from Chelan to Stehekin takes about 4 hours. Do as the locals do: Drive to Fields Point, about 15 minutes by car above Chelan, where you can park and leave your car in safety and board the ferry. You will save an hour and still see the best of the lake. For a faster trip across the lake, board the smaller *Lady Express*, for which advance tickets are advised. Write or call Lake Chelan Boat Company, Box 186, Chelan, 98816; 509/682-2224.

You can also fly from Chelan to Stehekin by float plane via either of two local carriers: Chelan Airways, 509/682-5555, or Stehekin Air Service, 509/682-5065. A good idea is to fly one way and take the ferry the other.

Stehekin is gateway to a wilderness wonderland, a delight for backpackers and day hikers. You can camp in the valley or find comfortable bed-and-board if you wish.

Wherever you stay, be sure to go to dinner one evening at Cascade Corrals; it has been operated for many years by the Courtney family.

Park Service and private vans provide transportation up the Stehekin Valley for a fee. You can get off at any of a number of trailheads; however, reservations should be made for transportation to any of the trailheads above High Bridge. Space in the vans is limited, so be sure to call the park for more information if your trip depends on this service. Between arrival and pickup, a party may walk along forest trails, climb peaks, or fish the rivers and lakes. Take the shuttle 23 miles to the last stop at **Cottonwood Camp** and hike to **Horseshoe Basin,** one of the great spectacles of the Cascades. Or head up the switchbacks to **Cascade Pass,** and down to the Johannesberg parking lot on the Cascade River Road from Marblemount. It takes planning, but it is well worth the trouble.

**Field Classes.** The North Cascades Institute (2105 Highway 20, Sedro Woolley, WA 98284) conducts a popular series of two-day and three-day courses on botany, ecology, history, archaeology, and history during the summer. Winter seminars cover birding, edible and medicinal plants, and weather watching. Contact the Mountaineers, 300 3rd Ave. W., Seattle, WA 98119, for information on naturalist outings, snowshoeing, backpacking, and other outdoor activities.

**Eagle Watching.** One of the country's largest winter concentrations of eagles descends on the Skagit River between Marblemount and Rockport. Try the Washington Eddy lookout, one mile east of Rockport. Best time is mid-January when up to 300 eagles come to feed on salmon. The Skagit River Bald Eagle Natural Area is administered by the Nature Conservancy and Washington Department of Wildlife.

**Fishing and Hunting.** Besides the two big lakes, many small lakes and countless streams tempt the fisherman with rainbow, eastern brook, cutthroat, and Dolly Varden. Be mindful of special regulations when fishing Ross Lake. The season usually opens in late June or early July; for exact dates, check with the Washington State Game Department or park rangers. Several areas closed to fishing are well marked. These include spawning grounds at the north end of the lake. Fishing in the Canadian part of Ross Lake and the Skagit River requires a British Columbia license. Lightning Creek, to the south, and Little Beaver, to the north, provide some of the lake's choice fishing. So does the channel alongside Cat Island.

Hunting is permitted within the two recreation areas, in accordance with state laws, but not in the park.

**ACCOMMODATIONS.** Two concessions provide lodging in the national park complex, one each on Ross Lake and Lake Chelan. In addition, facilities are available on private land in Stehekin and at the communities of Marblemount and Concrete to the west, Chelan and Winthrop to the east.

**North Cascades Lodge,** c/o Lake Chelan Boat Company, Box 186, Chelan WA 98816. Accessible via Chelan by float plane or by the *Lady of the Lake* tour boat. The lodge was completely refurbished in 1994; some units include kitchens. Food service, groceries and boat rental. 509/682-4584. M.

**Ross Lake Lodge,** Rockport, WA 98283. Housekeeping units, sleeping one to four persons and completely furnished, are classed as: Modern Units, with shower, toilet, and electric or propane cooking; Rustic Units, with wood-burning stove and community sanitary facilities; and Modern Bunk Units, with shower, toilet, wood heat, and propane cooking. Rental boats, canoes and kayaks; transportation service provided from Seattle City Light Boat Dock. 206/397-7735 (Newhalem via Everett operator). L to M.

Among private facilities in Stehekin are the following:

**Cascade Corrals,** the Courtney Ranch, Stehekin, WA 98852. Simple tent-cabins with canvas roofs and kerosene lamps. The Courtneys also feature guided hiking and horse trips and winter cross-country skiing. 509/682-4677. M.

**Silver Bay Lodging,** Box 43, Stehekin, WA 98852. Attractive B&B and two guest cabins in romantic lakeshore setting, with hot tub, bikes, canoes. 509/682-2212. M-H.

In Chelan, **Campbell's Lodge,** Box 278, Chelan, WA 98816, has motel and cottage units overlooking Lake Chelan. Pool and sand beach. 509/682-2561. M.

For information about Winthrop and the Methow Valley, east of the park, write Methow Valley Central Reservations, Box 505, Winthrop, WA 98862.

**CAMPING.** There are several campgrounds in the area: at North Cascades National Park, Lake Chelan National Recreation Area, and Ross Lake National Recreation Area. All have 14-day limits. North Cascades requires permits for backcountry use.

**SEASONS.** At lower elevations and on the big lakes, the season extends from early April to mid-October, at higher elevations from mid-June to mid-September. The western side of the range receives more rain and has more lakes and streams; consequently, days are cooler. On the east side, the combination of more sunshine, warm rock surfaces, and sparse vegetation makes for warm days and cool nights.

The North Cascades Highway is generally closed by snow for part of each winter. However, you can still reach Stehekin Valley by ferry (or float plane), and take in cross-country skiing, which is becoming increasingly popular here.

**RECOMMENDED READING.** *The Wild Cascades*, by Harvey Manning. *Cascade-Olympic Natural History—A Trailside Reference*, by Daniel Mathews.

**FOR FURTHER INFORMATION.** Write Superintendent, North Cascades National Park, 2105 Highway 20, Sedro Woolley, WA 98284. 206/856-5700.

# OLYMPIC NATIONAL PARK

## WASHINGTON

### ESTABLISHED 1938

I WALKED along Shi Shi Beach, just below Neah Bay, and listened to chattering seabirds. The Northwest is endowed with many miles of scenic beaches, of which Oregon's are the best known. Admiring the spectacular rock formation at Shi Shi known as Point of Arches, I felt that Washington's coast may be the most underrated along the entire Pacific. The coastal wilderness certainly adds a great deal to Olympic National Park; I was glad I wasn't taking it for granted. Wild and beautiful Shi Shi has always been there, to be sure, but only in 1976 did Congress vote to include it in the national park, and then it took nine years—until 1985—to complete the transfer of the land from state to federal ownership.

While wading around the Shi Shi tidal pools, I looked up at the Olympic Range. The mountains and the rain forests beneath them are the companion pieces to the ocean strip. They fit together in nature's pattern. The mass of peaks embraces the moisture-filled Pacific winds, wringing from them rain, snow, and mist.

From glaciers and snowfields, water flows downward through rushing streams, over forest slopes and outward past a sandy beach, returning to its source and a renewed journey. Along the course of the water cycle, momentous happenings combine to tell the story of 908,720-acre Olympic National Park.

The finest results of heavy precipitation are represented in the valleys along the Pacific, the Bogachiel, Hoh, Queets, and Quinault, the serene botanical gardens called rain forests, comprising the entire sweep of plant progression from fungi, mosses, and lichens to immense trees 300 feet high and a thousand years old. Similar forests parallel the ocean from Alaska to California, but no forests are more luxuriant than those here.

The Olympic Peninsula, the "upper left-hand" corner of the West, lies in semi-isolation, bordered by the waters of the Pacific, the Strait of Juan de Fuca, the clustered cosmos of Puget Sound and the Hood Canal. It presents a marvelous geological story, with about 60 living glaciers in the high country. Six major glaciers, some blue, some white, are on 7,965-foot Mount Olympus alone. It gets the greatest precipitation of any spot in coterminous United States, perhaps 200 inches, most of it in the form of snow. I've learned never to visit the Olympics without raingear.

Below the glaciers, the alpine meadowlands on the northern side of the park, a mile above the sea, are especially rich in mountain wildflowers, including glacier and avalanche lilies, lupine, white buckwheat, columbine, asters, Indian paintbrush, and others. According to the experts, eight species of herbaceous flowering plants are found in these high mountains and nowhere else.

Growing conditions in the moderate climate have been so favorable since the last glacial age that the Olympic Peninsula, below the meadows, has bloomed into a forest of evergreen giants. Within the national park are record-making trees, or near-record-making trees, of the "big four" Olympic species. Western red cedar, growing largely in moist valley bottoms, reaches heights of 175 feet. It has a cinnamon-red, fibrous bark and flat, lacy sprays of almost fernlike leaves. Western hemlock, a little smaller, grows at elevations up to 3,000 feet, a tree of dark russet-brown bark, showing abundant, very short cones at the end of its branches. Then, in the rain forests, the energetic, lordly Sitka spruce towering over most other trees is easily recognized by its sharp, silvery-green needles. The mightiest of the big four is the Douglas fir, exceeded only by the redwood and giant sequoia in size of all trees on the continent. This stately, wonderfully proportioned tree grows to heights of 250 feet and sometimes 300 feet. In age,

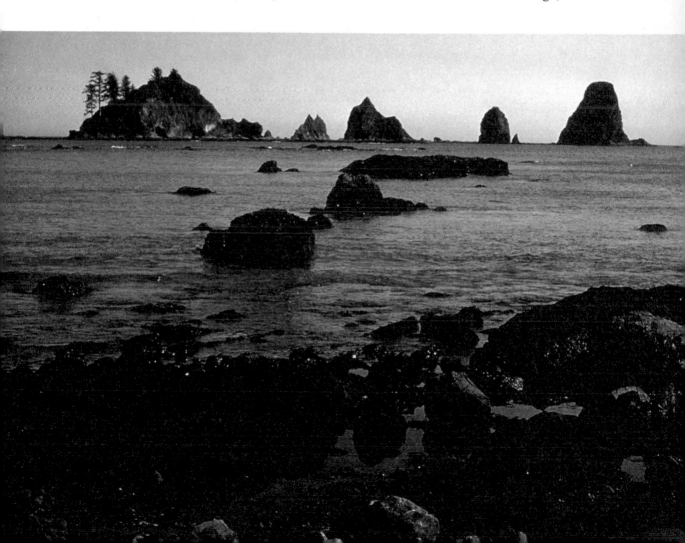

the larger trees may be from 400 to 1,000 years old. The Douglas fir was discovered by Dr. Archibald Menzies, in 1791, on the west coast of Vancouver island, but was named for David Douglas, the roving Scottish botanist who brought a specimen back to England. The big trees of the Olympic Peninsula have been the source of controversy for many years. Only a few of the great stands are protected in the national park, while heavy logging of old-growth forests continues on private timberlands and on areas administered by the U.S. Forest Service.

The Olympic area first received national recognition because of its wildlife, particularly the Roosevelt, or Olympic, elk. These large members of the deer family grow as heavy as 900 to 1,000 pounds. Between 4,000 and 5,000 live in the park, mostly on the west side, constituting the largest remaining herd of their kind anywhere in the world. Though many of them migrate in summer to the high country, I noted in the forest much evidence of their presence— footprints in the hardened mud and telltale elk pellets scattered in clusters over the ground.

Of more than 50 different species of wild mammals, black-tailed deer are frequently seen in the lowlands as well as in mountain meadows. Birds include the rare spotted owl.

I saw wildlife of another sort along the 50-mile-long coastal portion of the park called the Pacific Coast Area. Four species of seals, sea lions, and whales, the flippered animals, frolic in the offshore waters or on the rocks. Thousands of marine birds nest on small islands, and the strip lies within one of the major flyways of migrating birds. I watched persistent waves and the encroaching sea continue the endless process of sculpture—carving seascapes on tree-studded islands, rocky arches, and crescent beaches.

## THE PRACTICAL GUIDE

Spend at least two days seeing the highlights of the park as part of a tour of the Olympic Peninsula. You can combine it with ferry cruises across Puget Sound and to Victoria, British Columbia. Check with Washington State Ferries (206/464-6400).

**BACKGROUND.** Principal Visitor Centers are at the **Pioneer Memorial Visitor Center and Museum** located at the southern edge of Port Angeles, gateway to the most accessible portions that lie along the north side, and at the **Hoh Rain Forest** on the west side. From Port Angeles, start the **Heart O' the Hills Road,** leading to **Hurricane Ridge Road,** 18 miles of paved road from sea level to 5,229 feet. Trailers should not try to make it beyond the campground, 5.4 miles from US 101. Halfway up, at **Lookout Rock,** vistas unfold across the Strait of Juan de Fuca; on a clear day you can see the snowy mass of Mount Baker in the northern Cascades.

**ACCESS.** Without a car, from Port Angeles take the Clallam Transit System to Lake Crescent Lodge, Fairholm Campground, and Sol Duc Hot Springs Resort (daily during the summer). Reach Port Angeles by Greyhound from Seattle. Or, from Olympia take Washington Coast Lines to Lake Quinault, southwest entrance to the park.

**TOURS.** Scheduled and charter tours are offered during the summer by Gray Line of Port Angeles and Evergreen Trailways, Seattle.

**ACTIVITIES. Hurricane Ridge** is the upper terminal of the main road. Superb views of the Olympic Mountains are framed through the windows of Hurricane Ridge Lodge. The **Big Meadow Nature Trail** is a leisurely walk that anyone can take and enjoy. Or, drive 8 miles more on a narrow, unpaved road (open during summer only) to **Obstruction Point,** elevation 6,450 feet, which places you at the threshold of the heart of the high country, with the best view of mighty Mount Olympus available by road. This is the starting point of fine hiking trails, including one to **Deer Park Campground,** passing wildflower meadows—with a good chance to observe Columbian black-tailed deer and Olympic marmot. Fifteen roads enter the park like the spokes of a wheel, but none is permitted to penetrate the core of wilderness. "Where the roads end," according to park enthusiasts, "trails begin." Over 600 miles of trail thread the park, permitting short, easy trips of a day or less and more difficult hikes of a week and more. Trailside shelters are now few and far between, so bring your own tent or shelter material—and be sure to carry rain clothing.

**Lake Crescent,** the largest lake in the park, is nestled between the forested slopes of Pyramid and Mount Storm King. US 101, west of Port Angeles, follows the shore of the lake for 10 miles. From the western end of the lake, a road follows the Sol Duc River to **Sol Duc Campground,** the beginning of trails to **Seven Lakes Basin,** in the subalpine zone, and other high country of exceptional beauty.

**Rain Forest Nature Trails** are at the end of Hoh River Road on the west side of the park. The river is often swollen with "milky" silt from the glaciers on Mount Olympus, but it is only one feature of the forest, where precipitation averages 140 inches yearly. This forest is a complex community of many living things. The forest litter contains a thriving population of mice, shrews, salamanders, and insects. Sitka spruce is the most characteristic large tree of the rain forests, and here it reaches its greatest size; one of the largest anywhere (though the record holder is outside the park), 41 feet, 8 inches in circumference, is located about 3½ miles up the trail from the Hoh Rain Forest Visitor Center. At least 70 kinds of mosses are present, some covering rocks, others growing like air plants from the limbs of trees, draped in fragile beauty like mysterious poetry of the forest. Roosevelt elk are sometimes seen in the vicinity of the Visitor Center and along the trails.

**Kalaloch** borders Washington 101 at the southern end of the park's coastal strip. Seven short trails lead from the highway to the beach, where ocean waves have worn back the land. In this laboratory of life between the tides, colorful hydroids, sea urchins, and anemones thrive in pools where the shore is rocky and protected from strong waves. Densely clustered mussels and barnacles cling to rocks near shore, while crabs scurry for shelter beneath them. Other creatures prefer the sandy beaches. On a weekend in clam season, when the tide is low, Kalaloch Beach becomes pockmarked with holes and bumpy with piles from the "guns" (spades with long, narrow blades) of clam diggers in quest of Pacific razor clams (*Siliqua patula*), a delectable, meaty shellfish that grows from California's Pismo Beach to the Aleutians. On a hike along the shore, a bald eagle might be seen flying from a nest in the top of a tall snag; other birds are always present, including gulls, crows, oyster catchers, and cormorants.

**Three Indian villages** are encompassed by the Pacific Coast Area, while a fourth abuts it on the south. A few of their fishermen still use dugout canoes hewn in traditional fashion from single cedar logs. The $2 million Makah Cultural and Research Center, opened in 1979, traces five centuries of Makah cultural history. The museum was built after tidal erosion exposed the ruins of an ancient Indian settlement near Lake Ozette. The exhibit hall includes a replica of a traditional Makah long-house.

**ACTIVITIES. Hiking.** Ozette is about 68 miles west of Port Angeles. Two routes lead to North Wilderness Beach: the 3⅓-mile Indian Village Trail to Cape Alava and 3-mile Sand Point Trail to the beach south of Alava. You can hire an outfitter at Lake Ozette Resort to boat you and gear to either the Ericson Bay Trail or Allens Bay route. You can also reach North Wilderness Beach via La Push. From just south of La Push, several trails reach out to secluded beaches, often heavily used in summertime. To the north of La Push, Rialto Beach is a popular day-hike area, and a jump-off spot for the 3-day hike up the coast to Cape Alava. Another route to the Pacific beaches is from Neah Bay south.

Bring a tide table. If you miscalculate, you're apt to be trapped by incoming tides. Pick up a wilderness permit to camp on the beach, but prepare for rain at any time with durable tent and raingear.

**Naturalist Programs.** The three Visitor Centers (Pioneer Memorial Visitor Center and Museum in Port Angeles, Kalaloch, and Hoh Rain Forest) offer an important introduction to the park—enhancing one's understanding as well as enjoyment. July 1 through Labor Day, terrace talks and short walks are conducted daily by naturalists, most often at Hurricane Ridge, the Hoh Rain Forest, and along the coastal beach. Excellent evening programs, illustrated with slides or movies, are given at the eight major campgrounds after the sun goes down.

**Fishing.** The extensive streams and lakes contain rainbow, brook, cutthroat, and the anadromous steelhead trout. No license is required, but check regulations.

**Field Seminars.** Olympic Park Institute offers an extensive schedule of courses in such topics as wildflowers, tidal pools, Indian basketry, and geology. Write the institute at HC 62, Box 9T, Port Angeles, WA 98362.

**Birdwatching.** With its great coastal and inland features—from glaciers and snow-fields to lush rain forests—Olympic is outstanding for birders in the Northwest. Seabirds nest on offshore rocky islands, and migratory birds make this a rest stop along the Pacific flyway.

**ACCOMMODATIONS.** A variety of motel-type lodges and housekeeping cabins are available at several locations inside the park. In addition, there are hotels, motels, and resorts in Port Angeles and elsewhere on the peninsula. For information, write the Resort and Hotel Association, Seattle Ferry Terminal, Seattle, WA 98104.

**Kalaloch Lodge,** Star Route 1, Box 1100, Forks, WA 98331. Rooms at the Lodge, log cabins, and Sea Crest House Motel vary in size and price. Operated by ARA Leisure Services, the lodge offers meals and groceries. 206/962-2271. M.

**Log Cabin Resort,** 6540 E. Beach Rd., Port Angeles, WA 98362. Lakeshore resort with motel, chalets, rustic housekeeping cabins (without cooking or eating utensils), RV sites with hookups, campground with central water supply, and restrooms. Dining room, beach, and boat dock on Lake Crescent. 206/928-3325. M.

**Lake Crescent Lodge,** HC 62, Box 11, Port Angeles, WA 98362. Cottages and motel units, some with views of lake and mountains, 20 miles west of Port Angeles. Dining room, coffee shop, and rowboat rental. 206/928-3211. M.

**Sol Duc Hot Springs Resort,** Box 2169, Port Angeles, WA 98362. This varied complex near the park campground includes modern furnished cabins, rustic woodstove-heated cabins, kitchenette motel units, unfurnished plain camping cabins and RV sites with hookups. It features hot mineral baths and warm mineral swimming pool (additional charge). Dining room, groceries, and camping supplies. 206/327-3583. L To M.

**Lake Quinault Lodge,** Quinault, WA 98575. Beautifully sited in the rainforest of Olympic National Forest on the southwest border of the national park, it is now operated by ARA Leisure Services. Some rooms have fireplaces and balconies. Indoor pool. Dining room specializes in Northwest seafood, with expansive view of Lake Quinault. 206/288-2571. M to H.

**Manitou Lodge,** Box 600, Forks, WA 98331. The refurbished log fishing lodge in an old timber town makes a good B&B base for exploring the west-slope Olympic rainforests. 206/374-6295. L.

**Fort Worden Youth Hostel,** Fort Worden State Park, Port Townsend, WA 98368. The hostel is 63 miles from the national park, in an historic Victorian port town worth seeing in its own right. 206/385-0655. L.

**CAMPING.** Campgrounds are maintained near the end of, or adjacent to, nearly all the entrance roads in the park. Most have complete camping facilities during the summer. All major park campgrounds have sanitary dump stations, but they lack hookups. Camping near the beaches of the Pacific Coast Area is pleasant during dry weather. Other campgrounds can be found on the peninsula in state parks, the Olympic National Forest and on private lands.

**SEASONS.** This park has special features to admire in every season of the year, even though snow covers high country roads and trails from late fall to early spring. Port Angeles and the northern side of the peninsula are served by bus throughout the year from Seattle; San Juan Airlines operates daily flights during the summer; rental cars are available; and ferry service is maintained across Puget Sound. Winter is best for spotting elk, and for quiet walks along the ocean beach (where lodgings are open all year). Hurricane Ridge is open weekends for skiing (with the aid of two rope tows and Pomalift). Naturalists conduct snowshoe walks (snowshoes provided), cross-country ski tours, demonstrations of winter skills, and informal fireside talks. Most popular snowshoe and ski route on Hurricane Ridge is the 1.5-mile Hurricane Hill Road. You can also ski from Hurricane Ridge down to Mt. Angeles, a distance of 3 miles. Hurricane Ridge Road is open daily as far as conditions permit; the road opens at 9 A.M., then closes to uphill traffic at 4 P.M. For current weather and trail information call the Port Angeles Visitor Center (206/452-9235).

Come prepared with proper clothing and repair equipment for skis and snowshoes. By late May all accommodations and most of the developed campgrounds are open, and by June wildflowers start marching up the mountains.

Summer is mostly cool and sunny, though rainproof garments are a must for hikers and campers. September and October are often delightful, with Indian summer; in early fall spawning salmon may be seen in many rivers, performing the grand and final act of their lives. In this normally misty land, mid-autumn is often clear and cloudless for days on end.

**NEARBY.** US 101, the broad Olympic Highway, nearly encircles the peninsula. It begins at the southern tip of Puget Sound, in **Olympia,** where the state capitol is handsomely landscaped and restaurants are famous for oyster dinners. Along the way campgrounds and scenic areas in **Olympic National Forest** unfortunately are interspersed with heavy logging. In the southwest corner of the national forest, along the shores of Lake Quinault, are three campgrounds, summer homes, and the Lake Quinault Lodge, with fishing, boating, and swimming enhanced by the surrounding dark forests. Within walking distance is the rain forest of the Quinault Natural Area, including the famous "Big Acre," the greatest known stand of Douglas fir in the United States. **Port Angeles,** Washington, fishing center and northern crossroads of the peninsula, is linked by ferry with **Victoria,** British Columbia, a city with gardens that are almost as lovely as nature's botanic splendors in the Olympic wilderness.

**RECOMMENDED READING.** *Olympic Battleground,* by Carsten Lien and *Cascade-Olympic Natural History—A Trailside Reference,* by Daniel Mathews.

**FOR FURTHER INFORMATION.** Write Superintendent, Olympic National Park, 600 E. Park Ave., Port Angeles, WA 98362. 206/452-4501.

# PETRIFIED FOREST NATIONAL PARK

## ARIZONA
ESTABLISHED 1962

DRIVING across the high plateaus of northeastern Arizona, it was hard for me to believe that once a forest grew here. Yet, dense beds of ferns, mosses, and trees thrived in marshlands and along streams. Conifers once flourished in scattered groves on hills and ridges above the water.

That was about 225 million years ago, in the Triassic period, when the continents were still locked together in a single landmass we now call Pangaea. The park we know today was a low-lying swamp basin located near the equator. The scene has changed since then. The land now receives fewer than ten inches of moisture yearly. Most plants I saw were small and inconspicuous (though many have delicate, beautiful flowers), with only occasional junipers and cottonwoods.

This was, however, the Painted Desert, a wide arid land of plateaus, buttes, and low mesas—low in water and plant growth, but lavish in displaying many hues in bands of sandstones, shales, and clays. Logs of petrified wood are often brilliant and vivid, leaving little doubt about the ancient forest.

Indian ruins and petroglyphs show that ancient people dwelled in these environs. The Anasazi, prehistoric farmers who inhabited the area from about 6000 B.C. until A.D. 1450, shaped the petrified wood into tools and weapons and used the brilliantly colored pieces as trade items.

Curiously, Spanish explorers showed no interest in the petrified wood, probably because it lacked valuable minerals. Early traders and fur trappers repeatedly crossed the area, but they also showed no interest in the fossil wood. The first written reports of note apparently were made by American military and railroad surveys following the Mexican War. Still, the area remained almost unknown until the coming of the railroad and settlers late in the last century. Then began a rush for riches by souvenir hunters, gem collectors, and commercial jewelers that might have destroyed in two or three decades the treasures that nature had taken millions of years to create. Large quantities of wood were either dynamited for gems or freighted to stations at Adamana and Billings (Bibo) for shipment to the East. The erection of a stamp mill to crush the logs into abrasives stirred public opinion into demanding federal regulations to protect these fossil deposits.

Though Arizona was not yet a state, its territorial legislature petitioned Washington in 1895 to have Chalcedony Park, as the Petrified Forest was then called, set aside as a national preserve. With persuasion from the naturalist John Muir, who located fossil bones in the area in the early 1900s, President Theodore Roosevelt responded to the plea by declaring the area a monument. In 1962, private land holdings within the boundaries were acquired and Petrified Forest was made a national park.

The national park of 93,533 acres consists of six separate "forests," with great logs of agate and jasper lying on the ground, many of them broken into fragments. It is believed the trees were transported by flooding streams from the surrounding highlands and buried under mud and sand, then covered over by layers of silica-rich volcanic ash. Traces of iron, manganese, and carbon stained the silica to form the present rainbow colors.

That life once thrived in this arid, isolated land seems difficult to accept. Yet, fossilized plants, fish, invertebrates, and primitive dinosaurs have been found. You can view life-sized reconstructions of three ancient, giant reptiles at the museum. They are the only reconstructions of these animals anywhere, the product of exhaustive detective work into the mysteries of Petrified Forest.

## THE PRACTICAL GUIDE

ACCESS. Main points of interest lie along a 28-mile road running north-south through the park between I-40 and US 180. Short drives to several places back from the main road may increase the distance of the complete trip to about 34 miles. You can see the main features and wayside exhibits within one and a half to three hours. If you are driving west, there is no need to double back, for the town of Holbrook lies 26 miles from the north entrance and 19 miles from the south entrance. Eastbound parties should simply reverse the order, leaving I-40 at Holbrook and proceeding to the south end of the park via US 180. After driving north through the park, rejoin I-40 from the north boundary. Gallup, New Mexico, lies 70 miles east.

ACTIVITIES. Rainbow Forest Museum. Exhibits at the museum include outstanding specimens of polished petrified wood, fossils, minerals, and diagrams explaining how wood becomes petrified. A spur road to the Long Logs reveals the "logjam" character of deposits, with logs piled helter-skelter upon one another. A partially restored pueblo, the Agate House, built centuries ago of petrified wood chunks, overlooks the Rainbow Forest at the end of a foot trail.

Rainbow Forest is near the south entrance. Many trunks exceed 100 feet in length; the ground is strewn with chips of onyx, agate, carnelian, and jasper.

Jasper Forest was named for the opaque colors of some of the petrified wood here. A parking viewpoint located on a ridgetop faces great masses of log sections strewn on the valley floor. Nearby Agate Bridge is a mammoth single log, with over 100 feet exposed and both ends encased in sandstone. A deep ravine has gradually been carved into the sandstone, leaving the log looking like a natural bridge. North along the park road lies the beautiful Blue Mesa. Colorful banded buttes, mesas, and cones clearly reveal the ancient layers of marsh. Erosion nibbling at the soft earth has left some petrified logs stranded in unusual postures on slender pedestals.

**Newspaper Rock,** a massive sandstone block, is filled with picture writings of prehistoric Indians. The signs and symbols have never been interpreted, but probably represent clan symbols, religious symbols, and simple doodling. Nearby lies the **Puerco Pueblo Ruin,** the remains of a pueblo occupied in the 14th century. The pueblo consisted of about 75 rooms, which surrounded a large courtyard.

The 6-mile **Rim Drive** along the desert rim has nine overlooks that offer spectacular views and photographic opportunities. The most amazing property of the Painted Desert is the ever-changing quality of its colors. Minute quantities of iron oxide have stained the layers of land many shades, ranging from harshly gaudy red to softly soothing blue. Colors are most vivid after a rain in early morning or late evening. **Pilot Rock,** 6,235 feet, the highest point in the park, lies to the northwest. **Black Forest,** a concentrated deposit of dark petrified wood, is not accessible except by hiking—try it only if you are conditioned to the desert, and first notify a ranger of your plans.

Stop at the old **Painted Desert Inn Museum.** The inn was built as a hip-roofed stone trading post. Between 1937 and 1940 workers of the Civilian Conservation Corps added the fine beam ceilings, hand-carved corbels, buttresses, and other features. In 1948, when the building was a Fred Harvey inn and restaurant, Fred Kabotie, noted Hopi artist, painted the murals. The Inn Museum, 2 miles north of the Visitor Center just off I-40, is open year-round.

Be sure to stop at the Administration Building, near the north entrance, to see the displays and orientation film.

**Souvenirs for Sale**. Samples of polished petrified wood, found on private land *outside* the park, may be purchased at the Painted Desert Oasis and Rainbow Forest Lodge. These establishments, about 26 miles apart, are located near the park entrances. Both are open every day of the year (except Christmas

Day and New Year's Day) to sell souvenirs and refreshments. The Painted Desert Oasis also offers lunches and gasoline. Or you can hunt your own fossilized wood souvenir at Petrified Forest Gift Shop, on US 180 near the south entrance of the park; here you can collect wood from privately owned fields littered with petrified logs, and purchase your specimens by weight. The gift shop is open daily, about 19 miles southeast of Holbrook, and offers free, primitive camping. Children should be restrained from attempting to pick up loose petrified wood in the park; if each youngster took one piece, there would be little left in 20 years for *their* children to see and enjoy. Though commercial exploitation has been halted, theft by park visitors poses a threat just as dangerous. For this very reason, federal law prohibits removal of any petrified wood from the park, no matter how small the piece. Obey the numerous warning signs; don't run the risk of being arrested, with the possible fine or even jail sentence that would result.

**Photography.** Colors are most vivid to record after a rain. Early or late in the day are the best times for pictures, because shadows provide contrast, and the warmer light intensifies the red colors of the soil.

**ACCOMMODATIONS.** There are no overnight lodgings in the park; however, there is a concession-operated lunchroom. Approaching from the west, motels are located at Holbrook, 19 miles from the park. If you are traveling north across the Navajo Reservation, facilities are at Ganado and Chinle.

**Best Western Arizonian Inn,** 2508 E. Navajo Blvd., Holbrook, AZ 86025. Pool. 602/524-2611. M.

**Best Western Chieftain,** Chambers, AZ 86502. Twenty-three miles from the park. Pool. 602/688-2754. M.

**Arizona Rancho Motor Lodge,** Box 698, Holbrook, AZ 86025. Hostel. 602/524-6770. L.

**SEASONS.** This is high country, ranging from 5,300 to 6,200 feet in elevation. During the winter, be alert for icy spots on the highway. During spring, the showy blossoms of yucca, cactus, and mariposa lily will be on display, followed by blooms of paintbrush, aster, and other plants during the summer.

**NEARBY.** There are no overnight facilities inside the park, and backpacking camping is available in wilderness areas only (permit required). Campgrounds are in the **Sitgreaves National Forest,** over 50 miles south; **Coconino National Forest,** nearly 100 miles to the west; and in the Indian lands to the north. Motels and restaurants are located at Holbrook and other nearby communities. The closest to the park, coming from the east, is at Navajo, 15 miles away. Ask a park ranger about road conditions and facilities on Arizona 63 to **Ganado** and **Chinle** in the heart of the Navajo Reservation. **Canyon de Chelly National Monument,** near Chinle, is one of the fantastically beautiful areas of the Southwest. Inquire also about conditions on Arizona 77 across the Five Buttes into **Keams Canyon Campground** on the Hopi Reservation. About 100 miles due south of the park, **Hawley Lake** on the Fort Apache Reservation provides motel facilities, fishing, and recreation.

**FOR FURTHER INFORMATION.** Write Superintendent, Box 2217, Petrified Forest National Park, AZ 86028. 602/524-6228.

# REDWOOD NATIONAL PARK

## CALIFORNIA

ESTABLISHED 1968

With friends I walked the Tall Trees Trail, winding down to Redwood Creek and then alongside it. The setting was misty and moody, a world of rich alluvial soil and deep shadows among giants. It was mid-February 1986 and raining steadily, which only added to the mystery of the scene. I stood beneath the tallest tree, 367.8 feet, a monument in itself, a testament to life, yet helpless and dependent.

The Redwood Empire is a shrunken kingdom as compared with a century, or even a quarter century, ago. Establishment of Redwood National Park in 1968 gave national recognition and protection at last to one of the natural wonders of the United States and the world. It assured the preservation of an area representative of the finest remaining virgin growth of redwoods, with the incomparable scenery of the tallest trees on earth.

The coastal redwoods constitute a special province. In early geological times, these trees were widely spread across North America. Today, they are found only in a narrow band along the moisture-rich northern coast of California. As a living tribe, the redwoods are remnants of the age of dinosaurs; as individual creatures, some have been growing a thousand years or more.

The redwood is the earth's tallest living tree, commonly growing more than 200 feet high, occasionally more than 300 feet. Trunks are 15 to 20 feet in diameter, with exceptional specimens up to 25 feet.

The first successful redwood preservation effort came in 1902 with establishment of Big Basin Redwoods State Park in the southern redwood belt near Santa Cruz. The establishment of Muir Woods, just north of San Francisco, followed in 1908 as a gift of land from Congressman William Kent to the federal government in honor of John Muir.

In 1918, the Save-the-Redwoods League was formed. In half a century, with matching funds provided by the State of California, it placed large acreages of primeval redwood forest in the California State Park System. Three of these parks—Jedediah Smith, Del Norte Coast Redwoods, and Prairie Creek Redwoods—form the core of what is now the park.

In 1963 and 1964, the National Park Service made a survey of the redwood region. Of the original growth forest of almost two million acres, only 15 percent remained. Of this volume, only two and one-half percent, or approximately 50,000 acres, was protected in state parks. At the annual rate of redwood logging, it was estimated that virtually all old-growth redwoods not protected in parks would be gone within 20 or 30 years.

Although the national park was established in 1968, critical problems remained unsolved. Logging practices of large timber companies around the borders of the park threatened erosion of the famous Redwood Creek watershed, site of the world's tallest trees. As a consequence of erosion, streambeds rose and great old trees were literally drowned. In 1978 Congress expanded the park by an additional 48,000 acres, bringing the total size to 106,000 acres.

The expansion area is composed mostly of cutover lands—with 200 miles of logging roads, 3,000 miles of skid trails, and thousands upon thousands of burnt stumps of what were once magnificent redwood trees. I visited this area during my 1986 trip and saw a major rehabilitation effort: seeding logging roads, reshaping contours to cope with gullies and landslides, and planting young forests. I see it as an expression of faith in the future. One day giant redwoods may grow here again.

On another day, my friends and I hiked in the rain on trails in Prairie Creek Redwood State Park. There were towering, overpowering redwoods, but also the thick understory produced by abundant winter rain: rhododendrons 40 feet tall, red-barked madrone, alder, oak, maple, azalea, and skunk cabbage. One friend, Lucille Vinyard, spoke of the springtime beauty of the redwood forest, but I was absorbed with the ferns, waist-high around me: lady ferns, large and delicate; sword ferns, with leaflets resembling miniature swords complete with hilts; giant horsetail, so named for the tufts growing from the main stem; and the five-fingered fern, whose black stems the Indians favor to create designs in basketry. Ferns are among the most ancient living creatures; where others evolve, ferns survive. Painters, photographers, and poets, I thought, come to the forest to transpose nature into art; what they find is art in nature.

## THE PRACTICAL GUIDE

**BACKGROUND.** Of the national park's 106,000 acres, about 40,000 acres are considered "old growth," with trees of 400 years and older. Some of the finest stands are in three California state parks, which lie within the national park and which eventually will be transferred to the federal government.

These three parks provide camping for tenters and small trailers. During the summer the campgrounds fill early. Fees are charged and sites may be reserved through any Mistix outlet (800/444-7275), $6.95 reservation fee.

National Park information offices are located at Hiouchi, Orick, and Crescent City. At these sites, learn where and how to join interpretive programs, which during summer range from guided tide pool walks to recreations of pioneer history. Allow time to learn the differences between the coastal redwood and its cousin, the giant sequoia (see Sequoia National Park and Yosemite National Park chapters for references to the latter). At the Orick center, on the west side of Highway 101 near the mouth of Redwood Creek, buy a ticket for the shuttle service operating during summer to within a mile of the Tall Trees Grove on Redwood Creek.

**VISITOR CENTER.** Stop at the Newton B. Drury Center, headquarters of the National Park at Crescent City (24 miles south of the Oregon border). Evening programs are scheduled during the summer months.

**ACTIVITIES.** **Field seminars** on birds, photography, and park ecosystems are conducted summer weekends; a small fee is charged. Write Redwood Field Seminars, Redwood National Park. Motels are available.

**Orick,** a small town close to the Pacific Ocean and 330 miles north of San Francisco (or about 40 miles north of Eureka), is the southern gateway to the park. About ½ mile north, turn onto Bald Hills Road, which passes through a towering stand of redwoods. Park your car 2 miles up and start to walk the **Lady Bird Johnson Grove Trail.** The loop is a mile in length and takes an hour to walk, passing the site where the park was dedicated on August 27, 1969.

**The Tall Trees Grove,** containing some of the tallest trees on earth, is accessible via private vehicle or shuttle service (no RVs) during summer. The 16-mile ride takes about 30 minutes. The walk from the trailhead to Redwood Creek is mostly downhill, so allow twice the time to hike back. You may want to hike the entire trail, which is one of several backpacking opportunities in the park. The trail is flat and easy, running mostly along Redwood Creek. You can make the round trip in a long day, but you'll get more out of it in two days, with time to look up to treetops more than 300 feet high. Camping is allowed in the streambed. The trail crosses the creek at several points on footbridges in place during summer months only. Obtain a backcountry permit at the trailhead.

Continuing north, **Prairie Creek State Park** presents a superb botanical garden combining great coastal redwoods, Douglas fir, Western hemlock, and Sitka spruce knit together with broad-leafed trees and many flowering plants. Visit the lovely grove dedicated in June 1979 to the memory of Newton and Aubrey Drury, the two brothers who worked tirelessly in the campaign to save the redwoods. The park is almost a rain forest, with up to 100 inches of rain falling mostly in the winter months. More than 20 hiking trails wind among the redwoods here. At least half begin at the trail map at park headquarters. Two campgrounds, Elk Prairie and Gold Bluffs Beach, provide a total of 100 sites (reservations through a Mistix outlet).

The 1,100-acre Madison Grant Forest lies within the park boundaries. Here about 200 Roosevelt elk roam free. They make excellent picture subjects, but avoid getting too close—for your own good.

The park ranges in elevation from 1,500 feet to sea level. The western slopes drop off abruptly at the **Gold Bluffs,** fronting the Pacific, an area of sand flecked with gold, rugged promontories, and huge waves breaking over the smooth sand beaches. When visiting the ocean section of the national park, always respect the tide, the heavy undertow, and the rocky shoals that make the beach one for watching rather than swimming and surfing. In summer a naturalist program is presented at Prairie Creek.

Driving north on US 101, the Redwood Highway passes through many miles of redwoods. Klamath, midway between Orick and Crescent City, is famous for its steelhead and salmon runs on the Klamath River. Look for the start of the **Coastal Trail** at Lagoon Creek. The trail winds south along the bluffs, through spruce forests, ending high on Requa Hill overlooking the mouth of the Klamath River. This is a choice route for birdwatching, so carry binoculars. You're likely to see cormorants, oystercatchers, several species of gulls, possibly a great blue heron, and little birds called turnstones.

**Klamath Beach Road,** 8 miles long, covers some spectacular scenery. Fishermen can also try their luck in the numerous streams of **Del Norte Coast Redwoods State Park,** 8 miles south of Crescent City. Del Norte contains four groves of redwoods, with steep slopes bearing the trees almost to the ocean shore. It is one of the rare places where the natural ecological transition from virgin redwood growth down to a wild ocean shoreline remains essentially undisturbed. Follow Damnation Creek Trail to see this at its best. The park is noted also for the profusion of rhododendron blooming in May and June, in areas easily reached by foot trails. Del Norte has excellent camping facilities at Mill Creek Campground, 1 mile east of US 101. Reservations can be made through Mistix. Mill Creek, running through the campground, is pleasant for swimming, wading, and trout fishing in season.

A number of small beaches are unsafe for swimming, although the rocky coast, marked by heavy surf, does not discourage surf casters.

The northern boundary of the national park lies on the beautiful Smith River above Crescent City. In **Jedediah Smith State Park** is an outstanding dense forest of redwoods along Mill Creek. Because of its location at the northern edge of the coast redwood belt, this park contains an interesting array of coastal and inland trees, including ponderosa pine, with a lush underbrush of rhododendron, azalea, fern oxalis, salal, and huckleberry. The entire park is laced with trails. **Stout Memorial Grove** has the largest trees in the park, including the 340-foot Stout Tree, which is a giant among giants.

The Smith River in Jedediah Smith State Park has a very long sandy beach for bathing, with a picnic area nearby. To get campsites in the park during summer, arrive early.

**Fishing** is good for rainbow trout and cutthroats in spring and summer, then for large steelhead and salmon running from October to the end of March.

**Bicycling.** Located 60 miles south of the park, **Avenue of the Giants** is the most popular route for cyclists, a scenic alternative for US 101. It extends 28 miles from the Phillipsville exit of US 101 in the south to Pepperwood in the north.

**ACCOMMODATIONS.** Lodgings are principally located in Crescent City, northern gateway to the national park, and Eureka, 40 miles south of Orick, southern gateway to the national park. (Eureka is about 290 miles north of San Francisco.)

**Requa Inn,** 451 Requa Rd., Klamath, CA 95548. Country inn at the edge of the park, freshly refurbished and overlooking Klamath River. 707/482-8205. M.

**Eureka Inn,** Eureka, CA 95501. A classic four-story building of 1922 in Tudor decor, with rooms remodeled; a National Historic Landmark. Pool and sauna. Under 16 free. 707/442-6441 or 800/862-4906. M.

**Klamath Redwood Hostel,** Eureka, CA 95501. New facility in restored 19th-century home, at the mouth of Wilson Creek near the coast. Families accommodated in the same room. 707/482-8265. L.

**SEASONS.** Campgrounds in Prairie Creek State Park usually are filled in summer; a choice time to visit is from Labor Day through early November, when the deciduous trees change color. Try whale watching in spring and fall. Birdwatchers should bear in mind that the redwoods lie in the Pacific Flyway, attracting migrants to stop off during spring and autumn migrations. Horseback riding facilities operate April through October. Winter has a special appeal; the moisture-drenched redwoods seem most natural.

**FOR FURTHER INFORMATION.** Write Superintendent, Redwood National Park, 1111 Second St., Crescent City, CA 95531. 707/464-6101.

# ROCKY MOUNTAIN NATIONAL PARK

## COLORADO

### ESTABLISHED 1915

I LIKE to travel in Rocky Mountain National Park with Enos Mills as my guide. He was more responsible for the park's establishment in 1915 than any other person. He knew and loved the park. He was "the John Muir of the Rockies," spreading national park sentiment everywhere in the country. At the ceremony dedicating the park (September 4, 1915), which Mills organized and supervised, notables and nature enthusiasts were abundant. The event, according to the *Rocky Mountain News*, inspired a rendition of the national anthem "probably never given by so many voices at so high an altitude before."

Two years later, in 1917, Mills published his guidebook, *Your National Parks*. "Magnificent mountains in the sky, peak after peak along the horizon—an inspiring skyline—such is the setting of Rocky Mountain National Park," he wrote. "From one hundred miles distant, out on the plains of Colorado or Wyoming, these snowy, rugged mountain-tops give one a thrill as they appear to join with the clouds and form a horizon that seems to be a part of the scenery of the sky."

The scenery of the sky still prevails. The park embraces the untamed portion of the Front Range, one of the highest regions of the country—rough, spectacular, and noble, deriving its name as the first wave of the Rockies to rise from the central Great Plains.

The valleys are about 8,000 feet above sea level, but within the park are 59 peaks 12,000 feet in elevation or higher. Perpetual snows mantle the highest summits and valley walls, while small glaciers still decorate the heads of some of the high mountain canyons. Highest of all towers Longs Peak, 14,255 feet. A variety of trails make this a "climbing and hiking park." And when you drive to the summit on Trail Ridge Road, in the section between Lava Cliffs and Fall River Pass, you are at a lofty 12,183 feet, as high as a motorist can go anywhere in the national parks.

The park covers about 265,700 acres, although Mills wanted it to be much larger. I marvel, on each visit, at the geologic story. One hundred million years ago a great sea covered much of this area, with subtropical forests lining the shores. Gigantic forces within the earth caused an uplifting of the land under the sea. During a long period of upheaval and erosion, another series of uplifts,

40 to 60 million years ago, raised the mountain range still higher, giving the streams vigor to carve deep, sharp valleys. Then, about a million years ago, the Ice Age began and glaciers carved their characteristic U-shaped valleys. They left enormous moraines—deposits of loose rock material—and other evidence of their work. As Mills noted, nowhere in America are glacial records of such prominence more numerous, accessible, and easily read.

At least a thousand years ago Indians passed through, leaving arrow points, hand hammers, and even fragments of crude pottery. Within the past two centuries the park was the haunt of the Utes, then of the Arapahoes, who left their mark in trails still in use.

After the United States acquired the region through the Louisiana Purchase, explorers and adventurers passed near the park. The intrepid John C. Frémont made two expeditions, in 1843 and 1844, and Francis Parkman was there in 1846. In 1859, during the Colorado Gold Rush, Joel Estes visited the area and the following year settled his family in the grassy meadow now known as Estes Park. An Irish nobleman, the Earl of Dunraven, fell in love with this magnificent country in 1872 and resolved to build a great estate and game preserve. Through his feudal regime, many beauty spots were preserved. He publicized the region and entertained Albert Bierstadt, the celebrated artist of classic Rocky Mountain landscapes. During the 1880s a mining boom occurred in the area that is now the west side of the park; prospectors filed claims and operated out of little settlements like Lulu City, Dutchtown, and Teller, but they found little pay dirt, and the boom soon collapsed.

Forests and wildflowers on the mountain flanks reflect the story of the struggle of earth forces and the adjustment to varied environments. At the summits, tiny dwarf plants of the alpine tundra, like those of the arctic tundra in Siberia and northern Alaska, cluster densely together and carry the banners of life high above tree line. Far below, pines, blue spruce, and aspen thrive in the sheltered valleys.

Between the two extremes, some 750 kinds of plants are spread over the wide range of elevations, soils, and exposures to the sun and moisture.

The lofty rocks are the natural home of bighorn, or mountain, sheep—powerful, agile animals that symbolize Rocky Mountain National Park. You may also see elk, beaver, golden eagles, and hawks, depending on where you are and how perceptively you look. Bear in mind that the mountains are still their dwelling place and humans the outsiders.

I enjoy looking for different species of birds in different sites and different seasons. The rose-finch and ptarmigan live year-round near the snow line above the limits of tree growth. During flower-filled, sun-flooded days of June, while evening shadows cross the openings, the beautiful silvery notes of the hermit thrush mingle with the wild surroundings. In June, too, the cheerful water ouzel carols intensely by its chosen home along the mountain streams. It's wise to carry a bird guide, considering that about 150 species dwell in, or visit, the park.

And there are butterflies, too. On a recent summer while coming down a trail in the tundra, hikers were excited by a number of "black butterflies." It proved to be a swarm of Magdalena Alpine, *Erebia magdalena*, the only pure, velvety black butterfly in North America, known to frequent high, precarious rock-slides above timberline (usually over 10,000 feet) in a few western states. Collectors and watchers travel many miles, sometimes risking their lives while treading treacherous scree, to encounter these black beauties. While *Erebia magdalena* is normally a rare sight, denied to all but the agile, here was a swarm flitting from rock to rock within 10 feet of a parking lot.

## THE PRACTICAL GUIDE

**BACKGROUND.** Stay three or four days to sample the highlights, longer for a mountain vacation, at one of the campgrounds or resorts in the area. However, if you are in Denver (65 miles away) with time to spare, take a bus tour (or rent a car) and head for the gateway of Estes Park and the Trail Ridge Road.

Gear your pace to change in elevation. At high altitudes the atmosphere is thinner than at sea level, increasing the work of heart and lungs. Motoring and normal sightseeing cause little problem, but strenuous hiking and climbing can, unless you are in prime condition. If you have a heart condition, do not overexert. Even climbers should start slowly, acclimating to 7,500 and 8,500 feet before heading for 12,000.

**Trail Ridge Road** climbs 5,000 feet on its winding course from Estes Park, at the east entrance, to the crest of the Front Range, then descends 4,000 feet to Grand Lake at the west entrance; yet this modern, high 44-mile road, following an ancient Indian trail over the Continental Divide, is comfortable and safe all the way. Dress warmly; while the air is light and dry, you are entering a cold-climate zone. Allow a minimum of three hours for the drive.

However you travel, whether by car, foot, or horseback, take note of changes in plant life from the valleys to the high peaks. At lower elevations the climate is relatively warm and dry. Open stands of ponderosa pine and juniper grow on slopes facing the sun, while on the cooler north slopes Douglas fir is mixed with them. Along the streamsides you'll see blue spruce. On drier sites you'll see dense stands of lodgepole pine. Look for the lovely groves of aspen, with leaves that tremble in the wind and turn a golden yellow in autumn. Allow plenty of time to walk trails in meadows and glades where wildflowers carpet the ground, among them Rocky Mountain iris, pasque-flower, and penstemon.

Above 9,000 feet or so, cool dark forests of Engelmann spruce, subalpine fir, and limber pine dominate the scene, while luxuriant wildflower gardens spread over the forest floor. The beautiful blue Colorado columbine is particularly abundant in this subalpine zone, especially on rockslides (although found in all zones of the park). Unfortunately, the columbine has become scarce in many areas of the state through thoughtless picking and digging, which is now prohibited by law. As you near timberline, where cold winds constantly blow, note how the trees became twisted, bending with the wind and hugging the ground.

Presently trees give way to alpine tundra, open expanses of grasses, mosses, and lichens characteristic of the Arctic. These plants grow close to the ground, their way of surviving the desiccating winds. They flower brightly and produce seeds quickly during the brief summer, then take on autumnal colors of choice beauty. Trail Ridge Road takes you through 11 miles of the tundra world above tree line.

VISITOR CENTERS. Approaching from Estes Park, the **park headquarters,** a beautiful low building of reddish-pink stone, houses an audio-visual program and relief model of the park. If coming from the west, start at the **Public Information Building** or the **Kawuneeche Visitor Center** near the Grand Lake entrance. These are both open all year. Two others (Moraine Park Museum on Bear Lake Road and Alpine Visitor Center on Trail Ridge Road) are open summers only. **Lily Lake Visitor Center,** opened in 1991, is located along Highway 7, seven miles south of Estes Park. Scenic Lily Lake is just across the highway.

ACTIVITIES. **Sightseeing.** From park headquarters you may decide to go up the old **Fall River Road,** narrow, winding, and completely safe if you stick to the 15-mile speed limit; it is intended for sightseeing and picture-taking at a leisurely pace. It joins the main road at Fall River Pass (so you can make a loop tour from Estes Park). If you go the main route, from Many Parks Curve you see the whole central and eastern portions, dominated by Longs Peak. From **Rainbow Curve,** the Mummy Range is visible to the north and the Great Plains to the east. Soon you rise above timberline where fir, pine, and spruce covering yield to rock and tundra, and reach the 4-mile section above 12,000 feet—one of the world's unforgettable motoring experiences. From **Rock Cut,** you get superlative views of glacial-carved peaks along the Continental Divide. From the lower end of the parking area, take the one-hour round trip by trail to the **Toll Memorial,** in the center of tundra meadowlands.

Continuing on the western side, at **Milner Pass,** 10,759 feet, you cross the Continental Divide, the backbone of North America. From Kawuneeche Valley, the road follows the Colo-

rado River to **Grand Lake,** largest natural lake in Colorado.

**Living History.** In 1974 the nationally famous Never Summer Ranch, one of Colorado's first dude ranches, became the first living history exhibit in the park. At the end of 1973, John G. Holzwarth, Jr., the popular proprietor, closed the 800-acre ranch and sold it to the government for a modest price, rather than make an easy fortune from developers. The ranch lies 9,000 feet high in the Kawuneeche Valley between the Continental Divide and Never Summer Mountains. When you visit the homestead you'll be walking 50 years into the past. Another worthwhile site, the **Old MacGregor Ranch,** is on a scenic easement to the park, at the edge of Estes Park. Lurilla MacGregor willed, when she died in 1970, that the ranch continue raising cattle as "an educational and charitable institution." Here visitors can see a vignette of the past, while black angus cattle graze in a mountain meadow.

**Hiking and Climbing.** Over 300 miles of trail thread the park to the famous and lesser-known scenic points. Some are designed for a half-hour's leisurely walk, others for strenuous exploring. Get a copy of "Short Hikes in Rocky Mountain National Park," available at vistors centers.

The **Five Senses Trail,** built by the Youth Conservation Corps at the edge of Sprague Lake, makes a lovely scene accessible to the handicapped; it also encourages sensitivity and observation by everyone.

The energetic hiker who wants to become a climber does well to take a few lessons from the Colorado Mountain School, an approved park concession (351 Moraine Ave., Estes Park, CO 80517). For any hike to the summit of Longs Peak (8 miles from Longs Peak Campground), check first at the Longs Peak ranger station and be sure to sign out and in on the trail register. A bivouac permit must be obtained at park headquarters or the ranger station by all planning overnight climbs. Severe storms come quickly in the mountains, surprising climbers unused to the Rockies. Rangers require that you never climb alone,

always attempt routes within your ability, and turn back when adverse weather or exhaustion threatens. Following this advice assures that you will climb again.

Five small glaciers still exist in the park as a result of strong winter winds from the west, which drift dry, powdery snow into the heads of canyons on the east slope, where they accumulate. These drift glaciers are different from the large alpine glaciers of Mount Rainier, Olympic, and North Cascades National Parks in Washington State, where the snowfall is heavy; but they do move at the rate of about three feet a year and develop crevasses late in summer.

**Andrews Glacier** can be reached by a fairly strenuous hike of about 4 miles; Andrews Tarn, at the foot of the glacier, is milky in appearance because of the pulverized rock carried by meltwater. The other glaciers can't be reached by trail, but take the 5-mile hike from Bear Lake to Flattop Mountain to view Tyndall Glacier, which lies between Hallett Peak and Flattop.

**Trail Riding.** Most trails in the park can be traveled on horseback, including the **Flattop Trail,** a good day's ride across the Continental Divide between Estes Park and Grand Lake. A number of livery stables adjacent to the park have horses and guides available for pack trips in the high country. Horses may also be rented from a livery concession at Glacier Basin and Moraine Park within the park.

**Naturalist Program.** To see the fascinating natural history of these mountains, join one or more of the many hikes led by ranger-naturalists. These trips range from two hours to all day and open a new world of understanding. The naturalist will show where and how to look for beavers building dams, help identify some of the birds of the park, and try to bring you within sight of mule deer grazing at the edge of forest or on the tundra. Campfire programs, usually illustrated with slides or film, are held at the main campgrounds and park headquarters. Moraine Park and Alpine Visitor Centers have interpretive museums. The building at Moraine Park is worthy of attention in its own right. Dating from 1923, it was part of a popular summer resort, one of a number scattered over the mountains that have been acquired by the national park.

**Summer Seminars.** Sessions from one day to one week in ecology, geology, botany, photography, archaeology, and biology are conducted in cooperation with Colorado State University and the University of Northern Colorado. These are professionally taught and offered for college credit (Rocky Mountain Nature Association, Inc., Rocky Mountain National Park, Estes Park, CO 80517-8397; 303/586-1265).

**Birdwatching.** Conducted bird walks, talks, and evening programs for beginning birdwatchers are scheduled regularly three or four times weekly on the east and west sides of the park. Take advantage of these opportunities. June is a choice month to watch birds, since they are breeding and establishing territories. Pick up a copy of *Birds of Rocky Mountain National Park*, by Allegra Collister.

**Bicycling.** Three routes are open from the end of May to mid-October: Bear Lake Road (8 miles); Trail Ridge Road (18 miles); and Horseshoe Park/Estes Park Loop (16 miles). Trail Ridge is the toughest, but all have steep uphill climbs. Auto exhaust fumes can be a problem, especially in late afternoon. Keen cyclists will find challenge and reward.

**Fishing.** Fishing season is open year-round, except as posted. A Colorado fishing license is required, but special fishing regulations apply in the park. Familiarize yourself with these before you fish.

**Photography.** The most spectacular scenery of snow-crowned mountains faces the east, so morning light is best at most locations. The west side is good for pictures of streams, lakes, and ranches.

**TOURS.** Circle bus trips are conducted from Denver during the summer travel season by Estes Park Bus Company. The most popular is the 240-mile, two-day loop to Estes Park, over Trail Ridge Road to Grand Lake (overnight stop), then returning to Denver over Berthoud Pass, twice crossing the Continental Divide. This company also makes connections at Denver with airlines, railroads, and buses for service to the park area. Sightseeing trips in the park are scheduled daily during summer by the Estes Park Bus Company and the Rocky Mountain Park Company.

**ACCOMMODATIONS.** The two principal tourist centers are the villages of Estes Park and Grand Lake, which provide a full range of hotels, motels, and cottages. If you want to try the informal ways of the Rockies, you may want a dude ranch vacation. For a list of ranches near the park, write Colorado Dude and Guest Ranch Association, Box 6440, Cherry Creek Station, Denver, CO 80206.

**Stanley Hotel,** Estes Park, CO 80517. It's the most famous hotel in town, an old-timer built by the Stanley Steamer twins, and inspiration for Stephen King's novel *The Shining*. 303/586-3371. M.

**Western Riviera,** Grand Lake, CO 80447. A lakefront location, with picnic tables, playground, and pleasant views. 303/627-3580. M.

**Dougal's Mountain Inn,** Grand Lake, CO 80447. This hostel constructed of log in authentic style is 1 mile from the park entrance. 303/627-3385. L.

**Estes Park Center, YMCA of the Rockies,** Estes Park, CO 80511-2800. Covering 1,400 acres and bordered on three sides by the national park, it includes rustic, but modernized rental cabins and lodges, plus varied recreation facilities and activities.

**CAMPING.** Campgrounds have seven-day limits, except Longs Peak, where the limit is three days. No electric or shower facilities are available. The largest and most developed are at Glacier Basin, Aspenglen, and Moraine Park on Bear Lake Road. Timber Creek Campground, on the western slope, has similar facilities (fireplaces, flush-type comfort stations, running water, picnic tables). Longs Peak is popular with those who plan to ascend the mountain. Trailers are permitted in all but Longs Peak, which is for tent camping only. There are numerous trail camps. Permits are required for backcountry camping and bivouac climbs.

Glacier Basin campsites are available for summer use, through Mistix outlets.

**SEASONS.** Spring reaches the lower altitudes in late April and advances upward in ensuing weeks. The scheduled official opening of Trail Ridge Road is Memorial Day. Sometimes it opens earlier, sometimes on that day, but then may be closed for a week by snow. Summer is the peak season, the time to enjoy the high country with its brilliant skies, warm sun, and sparkling streams. The state flower, Colorado columbine, is found in bloom June through August, depending on location, amidst a myriad of other wildflowers. September is a superb month in the Rockies, a time of clear, crisp days when aspens glitter golden on the hills. With good fortune you may hear a bull elk bugling and catch a glimpse of one on a hilltop with his handsome rack sharply outlined against a blue sky. Reduced rates are offered during autumn at many ranches. In winter, join ranger-guided snowshoe hikes Saturday and Sunday and Saturday evening programs.

**Ski Touring.** The three most popular areas are Bear Lake, the glacier basin of Sprague Lake, and Wild Basin. Detailed maps are available from park rangers or in Estes Park. Ski rentals, instruction, and guide service are provided by Colorado Mountain School (351 Moraine Ave.), Rocky Mountain Ski Tours (156 Elkhorn Ave.) and elsewhere in Estes Park and other communities.

**NEARBY.** Bordering the park on the east, northeast, and south, **Arapaho-Roosevelt National Forest** comprises almost 800,000 acres, with good campgrounds, choice lake and stream fishing, and active glaciers accessible by trail. Unique off-the-highway tours operate from Estes Park in four-wheel-drive vehicles to the forest observation tower at Panorama Peak, overlooking the Great Plains and mountain ranges extending from Wyoming to New Mexico. Big Thompson Canyon lies on US 34, the main road from Estes Park to Loveland; for 16 miles the road is flanked by a foaming, roaring stream and rugged rock walls. Across the Divide, bordering the southwest corner of the park, **Arapaho National Recreation Area** complements majestic natural beauty with a scenic lake and mountain playground. Formerly known as Shadow Mountain National Recreation Area, it was administered by the national park until 1979. It is now a unit of Arapaho-Roosevelt National Forest. Man-made reservoirs, Lake Granby and Shadow Mountain Lake, are linked by channel to Grand Lake to form the "Great Lakes" of Colorado. This area offers camping, riding, swimming, fishing, boating, and sight-seeing boat cruises. Guided tours at the **Granby Pumping Plant** on Lake Granby unfold the story of the Colorado/Big Thompson Project, which diverts water via 13 miles of tunnel from the western slope under the great peaks of the park for irrigation and hydroelectric power in eastern Colorado; power lines and terminals of the tunnel were kept outside the park.

**FOR FURTHER INFORMATION.** Write Superintendent, Rocky Mountain National Park, Estes Park, CO 80517-8397. 303/586-2371.

# SEQUOIA and KINGS CANYON NATIONAL PARKS

## CALIFORNIA

### ESTABLISHED 1890 AND 1940

MY FRIEND Marvin Jensen and I headed by car for the trailhead at Mineral King. It was only 25 miles from Three Rivers, but a long drive, winding and climbing along the East Fork of the Kaweah River, on a road built by miners over a century ago. We stopped for lunch at Silver City, a little settlement at 6,900 feet, a gateway to the high valley that recalled the early days. For a few short years in the late 1870s Mineral King promised to become another Comstock Lode, a mountain of rich silver ore. Prospectors scrambled over the peaks and staked their claims, without finding much metal.

But I found what I was looking for—a thoroughly challenging and stimulating national park experience, hiking and backpacking in an area only recently added to Sequoia National Park. A little strange, perhaps, considering that Sequoia, the second oldest national park (second only to Yellowstone), was established in 1890. Both Sequoia and adjacent Kings Canyon were set aside to preserve groves of giant sequoia trees, the largest of living things, remnants of once widespread forests that covered a great portion of the Northern Hemisphere. The two parks, which are administered as one, do much more. Stretching 65 miles from north to south, they protect an unbroken wilderness of granite peaks, gorges, rockbound glacial lakes, flowering alpine meadows, and virgin forests. The parks comprise, for me, the heart of the Sierra Nevada, the country's highest mountain range this side of Alaska, a jagged crest extending from the Cascades southward for some 400 miles, with elevations from 7,000 to 14,000 feet.

In 1978 Congress added Mineral King Valley to Sequoia National Park. The beautiful alpine valley's high peaks, lakes, and clear streams are protected and preserved; so are its rare wildlife species, including peregrine falcon, bighorn sheep, spotted owl, and pine marten.

It was now June 1985. A few years before, I traveled with my friend Marv down the Colorado River through Grand Canyon National Park, when he was stationed there. He was strong, agile, and tireless. Once we took off from the Mineral King trailhead at 7,500 feet, the steep climb, high elevation, and loaded pack meant nothing to him. There was no easy route to the alpine lakes basin, but he chose the toughest unmaintained trail leading to the Mosquito Lakes. We reached the first lake, surrounded by a red fir forest, and kept climbing the chaparral slopes flecked with wildflowers, finally stopping to camp on the rocks overlooking the middle lake, the second of three.

Next morning Marv proposed climbing the trailless flank of the high ridge between the Mosquito Lakes Basin and the Eagle Lake Range. It was a forbidding challenge that I would never attempt on my own; with a patient guide and friend, however, I dared to meet the challenge. Besides, the country was irresistible—with granite peaks, gorges, canyons, and meadows, expansive and wild. Once on top, we dropped our packs and advanced up the rocky, knife-edged ridge. Marv indeed knew where we were going, for presently we intercepted the trail to Eagle Lake, at about 11,000 feet. Descending from the ridge on the Eagle Lake side, after picking up our packs, should have been easier, but the slope was steep and rocky, with narrow ledges and loose, sliding material. Yet there was chaparral in the rock, abundant with blooming wildflowers, including rein orchis, Indian paintbrush, shooting stars, and leopard lily.

During our pilgrimage of two nights and three days, we saw few people. Perhaps that's how it should be. That country needs to be used lightly to be understood and loved, to impart the feeling of freedom, and the confidence and control that I shared with my friend on the trail.

I spent another day on my own, revisiting well-established portions of the park. Before walking the easy trails in Giant Forest, I read a few pages of John Muir's *Summering in the Sierra*. It recounted his adventures of 1875, when he studied the sequoia belt. Muir faced hard mountaineering before the winter storms, but was confident. "I will make a way, and love of King Sequoia will make all labor light." With Muir as guide and companion, the mind becomes receptive to more than the eyes can see. At Giant Forest, I recalled Muir's description of "giants grouped in pure temple groves." These trees grow naturally in about 75 separate locations along the western Sierra slope, but Giant Forest is the largest of them all, enhanced by mild winters and gentle terrain. The giant sequoia (*Sequoiadendron giganteum*) and its relative the coastal redwood (*Sequoia sempervirens*) are the last surviving species of a large genus of ancient times. The redwood, growing near the Pacific Ocean in a more or less continuous belt 450 miles long, is the world's tallest tree, with a relatively slender trunk, while the giant sequoia is the world's largest tree in *volume*, with an immense trunk and very slight taper. In fact, the entrance to the finest part of Giant Forest is guarded by the General Sherman Tree, the world's largest living creature, at least 2,500 to 3,000 years old, 272 feet tall, and at least 32 feet in diameter at the base.

Beneath the giant sequoia, the forest floor is often covered with lupine, dogwood, hazelnut, chinquapin, and willow, creating a contrast of color in dark groves. Magnificent stands of sugar pine, sometimes attaining a base diameter of 11 feet with finely tapered trunk rising more than 200 feet, ponderosa and Jeffrey pine, white and shasta fir, and incense cedar also thrive here. But the sequoias, massive and vigorous, tower above all as patriarchs of the forest community. They can be seen now as John Muir found them here.

The high country constitutes a vast region of unbroken wilderness, providing one of the outstanding experiences of the National Park System. Motorists can glimpse the wild country from overlooks, but by foot or horse trail you put yourself into the midst of canyons, rivers, lakes, and meadows, as well as high on the Sierra Crest, ranging in elevation from 11,000 feet to the 14,495-foot summit of Mount Whitney. The hiker's principal boulevard is the John Muir Trail, which runs 218 miles from Yosemite Valley down through two national parks and three national forests. These areas preserve the feeling of the original California, the country where Indians roamed and fished, and where the Spaniards gazed on the plunging waters of the Kings River and named it *Rio de los Santos Reyes*—River of the Holy Kings.

**BACKGROUND.** You can hike or ride for days on end without retracing your course. However, Sequoia and Kings Canyon offer choice opportunities to get started in wilderness backpacking on weekends. Even if you're not going to the backcountry, allow at least two or three days.

Note the four key centers of activity and plan activities at and from them: **Giant Forest/Lodgepole,** in Sequoia National Park; **Grant Grove,** preserving the General Grant Grove of sequoias in Kings Canyon National Park; **Cedar Grove,** where the South Fork of the Kings River flows between massive granite walls, also in Kings Canyon National Park; and **Mineral King,** at the end of a long, winding road in Sequoia National Park, definitely for the backcountry traveler.

**ACCESS.** From mid-May to late October, Guest Services provides bus transportation from Fresno airport, rail, and bus depots. Stops in the park are at Grant Grove, Lodgepole, and Giant Forest (phone 209/565-3373).

**VISITOR CENTERS.** If you must approach via the Ash Mountain entrance, the first center is one mile east, a good spot to get your bearings. During your stay, allow time to visit the Grant Grove and Lodgepole Visitor Centers and absorb the displays on the story of the trees and the geology of the parks. Make the most of guided walks and talks.

**BACKGROUND. Giant Forest** embraces all phases of the giant sequoias within a small area, from tiny saplings to giants that have lived their lives and now, toppled by some wintry blast, lie with roots uptorn. The growth is dense: eight sequoias can be counted within a radius of 50 feet, and four others, perhaps four feet in diameter, within a radius of 25 feet.

**General Sherman Tree,** the largest of living trees, is in Giant Forest near the Generals Highway. It is approximately 275 feet tall and 102.6 feet in circumference; there are taller trees, but none of such bulk. To protect the tree, the Park Service has built a wooden fence around it, a gentle reminder that damage possibly can occur from heavy human impact. Actually, the beauty of the tree is best appreciated when viewed from a point where the visitor's eye can encompass its great size. Trees such as this continue to reproduce themselves, and thousands of young sequoias grow in favorable localities throughout the park, their lovely cone-shaped forms seeming like a mass of Christmas trees.

Within easy driving or walking distance of Giant Forest are a number of notable sights. **Moro Rock,** 2 miles by road or trail, is one of the great monoliths of the Sierra Nevada. From its top, or even its slopes, you can see both the ridges of the Sierra's backbone at the horizon and the silvery Kaweah River, 4,000 feet below and almost straight down. Not far away, in **Crescent Meadow,** an easy trail leads to **Tharp's Log,** headquarters of the pioneer white man of Giant Forest, Hale Tharp, who had been guided up the mountains by Indians. He built a cabin in a fallen sequoia log, which Muir called a "noble den." Make it to **Beetle Rock** and **Sunset Rock** at sunset for views to remember. If you don't mind a ½-mile downhill hike from the parking area, and back up again, you can visit **Crystal Cave,** a small but beautiful marble cavern, open during the summer. Tours are provided.

**Generals Highway,** a scenic drive worthy of the superb country, connects the two parks, running 47 miles from California 198 at Ash Mountain in Sequoia to California 180 at Grant Grove in Kings Canyon. It is open all year.

**General Grant Tree,** from which Grant Grove takes its name, is second in size to the General Sherman, measuring 267 feet tall with a circumference of 107.6 feet. The **Robert E. Lee Tree** in the same grove is almost as large. A few minutes' drive leads to **Big Stump Basin,** filled with ghostly reminders of early logging. The **Hart Tree** (277.9 feet tall), stands in the **Redwood Mountain Grove,** west of the Generals Highway.

**Cedar Grove,** center of activity in Kings Canyon, is reached from General Grant Grove, on California 180, on a 28-mile drive through Sequoia National Forest and along the South Fork of the Kings River. The road descends through open country and past hillsides, then into the river canyon. From an overlook you can watch the brawling waters of the South and Middle Forks form their junction. Beyond, one canyon vista succeeds another until the highway crosses the river at Boyden's Cave; then the route closely follows the foaming river. Six miles past Cedar Grove Ranger Station, the road ends at Copper Creek, or Roads End, beneath solid granite walls, one of the take-off points for the great expanse of high mountain country, which makes up more than four-fifths of the area of these two parks.

**ACTIVITIES. Hiking.** Trips of a single day and outstanding character can be made from Giant Forest, Crescent Meadow, Lodgepole Campground, Dorst Campground, and Roads End. **Twin Lakes,** reached from Lodgepole, are famous for their unsurpassed setting at an elevation of 9,500 feet; if you have the time, Silliman Pass is worth the extra climb.

**Bearpaw Meadow,** elevation 7,800 feet, is the destination of a choice overnight trip from Giant Forest, a distance of 11 miles over the **High Sierra Trail,** a close rival of the John Muir Trail for outstanding scenery. Travel light and rent a tent cabin with meals provided (advance reservations), or pitch your own tent. The High Sierra Trail joins the John Muir Trail at Wallace Creek, 37 miles east of Bearpaw, offering many possibilities for side trips into the Great Western Divide country—Big Arroyo, Kern Canyon, and Mount Whitney.

**Mineral King Valley** is 25 miles east of Three Rivers. Facilities are rustic and limited; trails rise sharply from the valley floor—already 7,500 feet above sea level. Its timberline peaks, subalpine meadows, and surrounding lake reward you with astonishing beauty.

**Backcountry** is accessible over about 800 miles of trail, via 28 trail entrances. Travel leisurely; relax, fish, and enjoy nature along the way. By so doing you avoid overexertion in the rugged terrain and high altitude. Most backcountry trails are snow-covered until late May. Wilderness permits are required for overnight camping and some trails have limited access. Plan your trip and make reservations at least two weeks in advance. Before starting out, check with a ranger so that someone knows where you are and when to expect you back.

**Horseback trips** over the hundreds of miles of pack trails are popular. Saddle horses are for rent in Giant Forest, General Grant Grove, Cedar Grove, Owens Valley, and Mineral King.

Many people enter the high country from Owens Valley, east of the Sierra. From Lone Pine, a road leads to **Whitney Portal,** elevation 8,367 feet, closest point by road to Mount Whitney, and the location of a pack station. The trail up is considered fairly easy, but it is a long trip. The Mount Whitney Trail is limited to 75 persons a day; reserve space in advance (Mount Whitney Ranger District, U.S. Forest Service, Box 8, Lone Pine, CA 93545; 619/876-5542). Many other mountains in the two parks are popular with climbers, too, but consult with a park ranger before starting; hikers can become injured, or get seriously ill from altitude sickness.

**Fishing.** There are 800 miles of streams and 500 lakes, many with rainbow and eastern brook trout. The headwaters of the Kern are the native habitat of the highly prized California golden. Buy a state fishing license at stores.

Streams are usually very cold, swift, and powerful, and surrounding rocks are slippery; therefore, **swimming** can be dangerous. Be especially careful of children, who tend to underestimate the power of moving water.

**Skiing.** Giant Forest Village and Grant Grove Village are the main centers of cross-country ski activity. A favorite trail for skiers and snowshoers follows an unplowed road from Giant Forest Village to sequoias in Crescent Meadow, with a stop at Moro Rock on the way. Temperatures are just above freezing during the day. Ski shops have rental equipment.

**ACCOMMODATIONS.** Accommodations in these twin parks are concession-operated by Sequoia Guest Services, Box 789, Three Rivers, California 93271. The reservations number is 209/561-3314. Additional lodgings are at Three Rivers, western gateway to the park.

**Cedar Grove Lodge.** Thirty miles east of Grant Grove, this motel unit is open mid-May to October. Fast food service, market, gas station, and bicycle rentals. M.

**Giant Forest Lodge** in Giant Forest Village. Year-round facilities include motel with bath, cabin with bath, rustic room with bath, and rustic semihousekeeping with central bath. L to M.

**Stony Creek Lodge.** Open year-round, cottages and rooms with and without bath. Rustic semihousekeeping canvas-topped cabins are heated by wood stove. Meal service and groceries. L to M.

**Bearpaw Meadow Camp.** Summer only. A chance to break away and yet have a little tent-cabin comfort. Breakfast, dinner served family-style and box lunches available. L.

**Buckeye Tree Lodge,** Three Rivers, CA 93271. One-half mile from the park entrance; small motel, friendly service on the bank of Kaweah River. 209/561-4611. M.

**M Bar J Guest Ranch,** Badger, CA 93603. Features trail riding into the park, square dancing, and meals cooked with local foods. 209/337-2513. M.

**CAMPING.** Campgrounds at Lodgepole, Dorst Creek, Grant Grove, and Cedar Grove are well developed. Lodgepole is best suited to trailers, though it has no electric or sewer connections. Occupancy is limited to 14 days, and in summer it operates on a strict reservation basis. Reservations are available through Mistix for Lodgepole; all others operate on a first-come, first-served basis.

**SEASONS.** Most accommodations in the park are open mid-May to mid-September and some until late October. Limited facilities are open at Giant Forest and Grant Grove all year. Entrances to the high mountain passes are seldom open before July 1, but the General Grant Grove section and Giant Forest area are open all year, and roads generally are kept clear in winter. In winter the giant sequoias are draped with snowlike candelabra and express a liveliness that contrasts with their somber summers. Though most visitors come during the summer, an equally good time to visit is in April and May, when the foothills are covered with flowering redbud, buckeye, and laurel. However, spring weather is very changeable. Storms can bring fresh snow in mid-May. If heading for the high country, prepare for everything from sunshine to blizzard. During autumn, dogwood, aspen, and oak enliven the landscape with their brilliant foliage.

**NEARBY.** More than 50 camping and picnic sites are located in **Sequoia National Forest,** which lies adjacent to the two national parks on the west. **Hume Lake,** on CA 180 north of General Grant Village, offers recreational facilities, including swimming. **Stony Creek Campground,** lodge, and service station are convenient to Kings Canyon National Park, south of Grant Grove on the Generals Highway. High mountain lakes and streams noted for golden trout enhance the forest's beauty. On the east side of the park, **Inyo National Forest** has nearly 900 natural lakes set among granite peaks towering from 12,000 to 14,000 feet. From **Big Pine** a road leads west to Palisades Glaciers, a mass of living ice flush against Bishop Pass in Kings Canyon. In contrast to this high, cool country, only 80 miles to the east of Mount Whitney is the lowest point in the Western Hemisphere, Bad Water, in **Death Valley National Monument** astride the California–Nevada boundary.

**RECOMMENDED READING.** *Summering in the Sierra,* by John Muir; *Starr's Guide to the John Muir Trail* and *Backpacking in the Sierra Nevada; Discovering Sierra Trees,* by Stephen F. Arno.

**FOR FURTHER INFORMATION.** Write Superintendent, Sequoia and Kings Canyon National Parks, Three Rivers, CA 93271. 209/565-3341.

KINGS CANYON
AND SEQUOIA
NATIONAL PARKS
CALIFORNIA

0    4    8    12
ONE INCH EQUALS APPROXIMATELY 9.8 MILES

© The H.M GOUSHA Co.

M-9-ZM-1504-S

# SHENANDOAH NATIONAL PARK

## VIRGINIA
### AUTHORIZED 1926/ESTABLISHED 1935

I WAS overnighting at Skyland, once a private resort and now part of the concession operation in the national park, and I thought of how particular individuals had influenced the park. That afternoon, I had stopped at the Harry F. Byrd, Sr., Visitor Center, named for the prominent Virginia governor and U.S. senator who knew Shenandoah National Park intimately. Byrd was a self-avowed mountain lover. He climbed every peak in the park, and his favorite peak, Old Rag, once a year. "In the tragedies and other strains of our modern world," he wrote, "generations to come will receive a peace of mind and new hopes in lifting their eyes to the peaks and canyons of the Shenandoah National Park."

That prophecy has already come true. Shenandoah National Park is a natural refuge of hills of hardwood and pine forests, and open meadows, with vistas of gentle valleys and mountains beyond them. Though deep in the Blue Ridge Mountains of Virginia, the park lies but 75 miles from the nation's capital, and less than one day's drive from New York, Cleveland, or Charleston, SC. To the populated East, it provides the chance to find peace of mind and inspiration.

Sixty mountain peaks, ranging from 2,000 to over 4,000 feet, reach up to blend their gentle summits with the billows of bluish haze that give the mountains their name.

While at Skyland, I thought of the alliance between Byrd and George Freeman Pollock, the colorful owner of this mountaintop resort. Pollock, a born naturalist, had come to the Blue Ridge from Washington, DC, in the 1890s, starting with a tent camp, then log cottages. Byrd first came to Skyland in 1907, when it could only be reached by horseback or buckboard. His father owned a cottage there, which he gave the future governor as a wedding present. Without the love and concern of these two men for the mountains, the national park might never have come into being.

When Pollock Knob was dedicated in October 1951, the *Washington Evening Star* editorialized: "Mr. Pollock loved the Appalachians and it was his vision of their permanent value to successive generations that finally led to the Shenandoah Park's being set aside as a permanent recreational property of the whole Federal commonwealth."

The highlands of Shenandoah are part of the same Appalachian range that stretches to the Acadian hills of the Northeast. Skyline Drive is a lofty vantage point for viewing the panoramas of the Shenandoah Valley, or Valley of Virginia, to the west, and the rolling hills of the Piedmont Plateau to the east. For a distance of 105 miles, this scenic route stretches like a ribbon down a bright tapestry, crossing and recrossing the ridgetop. In precolonial times, game and Indian trails ran along this crest, and by the time of the Revolution, the beauty of the Shenandoah area in the Blue Ridge was known to Americans. The nine years of labor that went into construction of the drive forged the first link of a longer mountaintop boulevard that continues southward for almost 500 miles over the Blue Ridge Parkway to the Smokies.

Though the land is ancient, establishment of the national park is fairly recent. Shenandoah was first approved by Congress in 1926, when Acadia was the only national park east of the Mississippi. But complete acceptance depended upon the people of Virginia's acquiring the land and deeding it to the federal government. Unlike the western parks, these were not public lands, but privately owned, mostly by struggling mountain folk. It took almost ten years, but individuals like Pollock sparked enthusiasm and energy to make this beautiful highland a gift to the nation. Even a president's personal landholding—Herbert

Hoover's fishing camp on the Rapidan—became part of the park. And another benefactor, the Richard King Mellon Foundation of Pittsburgh, announced in 1990 it would donate nearly 1,300 acres to the park to guard Shenandoah from encroaching development.

I like to hike to Camp Hoover from Big Meadows wayside (a little more than six miles round trip, but easy and scenic all the way). The camp is surprisingly simple, but it served Hoover's purpose. He enjoyed the region, where he could fish the quiet pools and riffles in the streams. Today the park is a hiker's paradise, with 500 miles of trails, including part of the Appalachian Trail. It is a delight for birdwatchers, who can find more than 200 species at one time or another during the year, and for wildflower enthusiasts, who may identify as many as 80 flowering plants in a day's walk.

## THE PRACTICAL GUIDE

**BACKGROUND.** You could easily cover the full length of Skyline Drive in a day, but you would miss the meaning of it. Stay at least one or two nights at a lodge, motel, or campground. Drive within the speed limit (35 mph) for both touring enjoyment and safety. Allow time to stop at overlooks and to sample the trails.

**ACCESS. Four main entrances** lead to the park and Skyline Drive, including the north entrance at Front Royal; Thornton Gap, between Luray and Sperryville; Swift Run Gap, between Stanardsville and Elkton; and the south entrance, the link with the Blue Ridge Parkway, at Rockfish Gap, between Charlottesville and Waynesboro. Seventy-five parking overlooks give plenty of opportunity to observe the mountain slopes and surroundings in all their moods. From **Hogback Overlook,** on a clear day, you can count 11 bends in the Shenandoah River.

**VISITOR CENTERS.** If you enter from the north, stop at **Dickey Ridge Visitor Center,** where exhibits describe park attractions and facilities. Also visit the **Byrd Visitor Center** at Big Meadows. It interprets the culture of the colorful, hardy mountaineers who lived in the park area.

**ACTIVITIES. Trail trips.** A variety of short trail trips enables intimate contact with park features. From Skyland, you can hike the 1½-mile round-trip **Stony Man Nature Trail.** This leisurely path leads through a cross section of the nearly 100 species of trees in the park. It ascends the slopes of Stony Man Mountain to its craggy 4,010-foot summit. The 5-mile hike (allow half a day) to **Whiteoak Canyon** begins just south of Skyland, taking visitors through an ancient hemlock forest into a wild, water-splashed garden of rock, vines, and shrubs. Five miles farther south, the **Hawksbill Mountain Trail** (2 miles round trip) leads to the highest point in the park, 4,049 feet above sea level, clothed in remnants of a spruce-fir forest. From Big Meadows, trails lead to waterfalls and other points of interest. The trail to **Old Rag Mountain** leads to the most spectacular, fascinating peak in the park. It lies east of the main Blue Ridge chain, an imposing mass of granite, with a rocky, boulder-strewn ridgecrest nearly 5 miles long. Hikers love it because of unique Ridge Trail, which winds around massive boulders for more than a mile, and even through a cave, before reaching the summit with expansive views in all directions. The 7.7-mile circuit hike is tough and takes a full day.

The starting point for the hike, at the little town of Nethers (near Sperryville), is a drive of 30 miles from Skyland, 40 miles from Big Meadows. To reach **Hoover Camp** on the Rapidan River, where the president's old lodge and a caretaker's cabin have been restored, start at Big Meadows wayside, just past Milepost 51. The circuit hike, a little over 6 miles long, is easy and scenic.

**The Appalachian Trail** follows the mountain crest for 94 miles through the park, with numerous spur trails. It is possible to take the trail in large or small measure. Park your car at a picnic area, overlook, or parking area on Skyline Drive and you can hike for an hour or a half-day. For overnighting in the backcountry or designated wilderness areas, secure a free camping permit at a ranger station. Five locked cabins are furnished with mattresses, blankets, stove, cooking utensils, and dishes (for reservations, write the Potomac Appalachian Trail Club, 118 Park Street, SE, Vienna, VA 22180).

**Riding and Cycling.** Horses can be rented at Skyland for an hour, half-day, or all day. Heading to Whiteoak Canyon will give the taste of a wilderness trail ride, but the horses are gentle enough for children. Bicycling is welcomed on Skyline Drive and the public roads in developed areas.

**Fishing** for native brook trout is good in a number of beautiful mountain streams, April to mid-October. A Virginia license is required (three-day nonresident trout license is available at all major concession facilities). Rapidan and Staunton rivers and their tributaries are "fishing-for-fun" streams.

**Naturalist Program.** Guided hikes are conducted daily, mid-June to Labor Day, to major points of interest. Campfire programs are given at Skyland, Loft Mountain, Big Meadows, and Lewis Mountain.

**Birdwatching.** At the height of spring migration you are likely to spot 100 different species (though the park is visited by twice that number during the year). Woods are filled with songbirds—listen for wrens, warblers, thrashers, and tanagers. With good fortune, especially in the northern part of the park, you are apt to spot a wild turkey. Common ravens, uncommon in the eastern United States, are residents of Shenandoah. Look up and you'll see the soaring birds—hawks, vultures, and ravens—riding air currents over mountaintops and valleys.

**Events.** Mountain Heritage Days in July feature arts and crafts, music, food, and mountain dancing. Hoover Days, held the weekend closest to Hoover's birthday, August 10, include programs and exhibits at the Byrd Visitor Center and guided tours of Camp Hoover.

**TOURS.** Motorcoach tours run through the park, spending at least one night at Skyland or Big Meadows. Itineraries usually include other highlights of Virginia, such as the Caverns of Luray, Charlottesville, and Staunton. The tours are available from most major cities in the East.

**ACCOMMODATIONS.** ARA Virginia Sky-line Company operates concession lodges, dining rooms, grocery and camper stores, and coin laundries at key locations along Skyline Drive. The company address: Box 727, Luray, VA 22835; 703/743-5108 or 800/999-4714. Accommodations are:

**Skyline Lodge and Cabins.** A few miles below Thornton Gap entrance station (Route 211), the season here runs from early April to early November. New units have the view of Shenandoah Valley from the ridge crest; older units have the rustic feeling and cost less. L to M.

**Big Meadows Lodge.** About midway between Thornton Gap and Swift Run Gap entrance stations, handy to Byrd Visitor Center. Motel rooms with private balconies and a few housekeeping cabins. Open May to November. M.

**Lewis Mountain Cabins.** Southernmost accommodations, housekeeping cabins and tent cabins from May to late October. L.

Nearby accommodations are at Front Royal, Luray, New Market, Harrisonburg, and Waynesboro. Charlottesville, Staunton, and Lexington definitely are within easy driving

(continued next column)

range. Motels in various price ranges are plentiful. Resort-type lodgings include:

**Boar's Head Inn,** Charlottesville, VA 22905. Designed around an 1834 gristmill, rooms at this sophisticated resort have private patios or balconies. Facilities include pool, lighted tennis, golf privileges, and jogging trails. 804/296-2181. H.

**Shenandoah Countryside,** Rt. 2, Box 377, Luray, VA 22835. Outstanding B&B accommodations with magnificent vistas, plush organic flower and veggie gardens, wood-fired sauna, and use of bicycles. 703/743-6434. M.

**CAMPING.** Campgrounds in the park are located at Big Meadows, Lewis Mountain, and Loft Mountain. Most operate on a first-come, first-served basis, with a 14-day limit. Big Meadows and Loft Mountain have supply stores, pay showers, coin laundries, ice, and wood. Campers who fail to keep food (including ice chests) locked in car trunks may expect company—black bears. There are no utility connections for trailers, but sewage disposal stations are located at Big Meadow and Loft Mountain.

Shenandoah requires backcountry use permits and accepts reservations for backcountry camping. Big Meadows campsites can be reserved through Mistix.

SEASONS. Skyland opens in late March, Big Meadows Lodge opens in May, and both remain open till late October or early November. Big Meadows wayside and campground are open March through November; the other campgrounds are open from mid-April or May to mid-October. The park itself is open all year, except when severe ice or snow storms close Skyline Drive for short periods. The beauty of winter in the highlands is a special treat. Ski touring is often practical, especially on old roads. Rangers will suggest the best areas. On cold, crisp days evergreens stand out boldly against the snowy white mountain background. Icicles cascade over the cliffs, presenting opportunities for unusual photography. Winter walkers should stay on the designated trails, wear adequate clothing, and not push their physical endurance while walking through snow. Motorists should carry a good set of chains and have adequate ventilation while the car motor is running. The park remains cool until June, though spring flowers and budding trees—hepatica, red maple, and bloodroot—begin their show in late March. In mid-April the magenta flush of redbud floods the valleys, followed by the creamy white of dogwood. In succession come azalea and black locust, then the pink and white mountain laurel—a profusion of flowers during most of June. In summer, temperatures are a comfortable 15 degrees lower than in the valley below. You can usually count on mid-70s by day, mid-40s at night. This is the peak period for visitors, though crowds are fairly light in midweek. By mid-September, foliage begins its autumn color change, gradually flowing downward from the mountain tops to coves and hollows. There are several color peaks; the most luxurious displays among non-oak species usually occur between October 10 and 20. Yet there is still new blossoming of yarrow, asters, and witch hazel. In spring and fall, naturalists present illustrated evening talks at the Byrd Visitor Center at Big Meadows.

NEARBY. Both the Piedmont and Shenandoah Valley are rich in Civil War battle sites. **Lexington,** in particular, is associated with Robert E. Lee, who served as president of Washington and Lee University, and Stonewall Jackson, who left for the war from the faculty of Virginia Military Institute (VMI). **New Market Battlefield Park,** a surprising and outstanding area, depicts Jackson's valley campaign and the role of VMI cadets. The national park is flanked by **George Washington National Forest.** Its largest recreation area, **Sherando Lake,** 14 miles south of Waynesboro, provides a campground, sand beach, bathhouse, and naturalist program. An unusually interesting area, **Elizabeth Furnace,** in the Massanutten Mountains near Front Royal, has camping and a nature trail winding through an old iron furnace community.

FOR FURTHER INFORMATION. Write Superintendent, Shenandoah National Park, Rt. 4, Box 348, Luray, VA 22835. 703/999-2243.

# THEODORE ROOSEVELT NATIONAL PARK

## NORTH DAKOTA

ESTABLISHED 1978

THE Badlands, I felt sure, looked much to me as when Theodore Roosevelt first saw them more than a century ago—wild, untamed, composed of what he called a "curious, fantastic beauty." My hunch is the Badlands remain wild today because the pioneers couldn't subdue them. The climate is severe in both winter and summer, and the soil resists cultivation. I studied the contrasting bands of light and dark in the buttes and bluffs, the mesas, washes, and sharply eroded valleys—all reminders of the ancient past, when broad rivers deposited thick layers of sediment on a plain. At Scoria Point, I saw massive bluffs capped with red scoria, where a vein of lignite burned and baked sand and clay into natural brick. Doubtless there is some commercial value to it, but this country is better admired than exploited.

Theodore Roosevelt learned that lesson the hard way. He first came to the Badlands in the fall of 1883 to hunt buffalo. Though still in his early 20s, he was already a Harvard graduate, deeply interested in history, adventure, and the outdoors. In this primitive frontier country, a strange region of buttes, gorges, and canyons carved by the Little Missouri River, Roosevelt found a "postgraduate course" in life itself.

On that first trip, he and his guide camped beneath the stars or found shelter, on occasion, with friendly ranchers. He was so impressed that he bought a share in his first cattle ranch. From then until the end of the century, he made a career of ranching, full-time in some years, part-time in others. "There are few sensations I prefer," he wrote in this period, "to that of galloping over these rolling limitless prairies, rifle in hand, or winding my way among the barren, fantastic and grimly picturesque deserts of the so-called Bad Lands." As a result of a bitter winter, Roosevelt lost more money than he made in ranching, but he learned the need for protecting natural resources from indiscriminate use and later became the "conservationist president."

Roosevelt, like many others, was fascinated by the weird erosional patterns carved by the restless Little Missouri. Where a huge section of the bluff has slipped to the valley floor, bands of color once horizontal are now perched at almost any angle. "Viewed in the distance at sunset it looked exactly like the ruins of an ancient city," wrote General Alfred Sully after viewing the Badlands in 1864.

In that year Sully led 2,000 men into western Dakota Territory on a military expedition against the Sioux, the nomadic native people who ranged over a vast domain in the heartland of the continent. Sully's troops pushed west across the Little Missouri and routed the Sioux near Square Butte, 7 miles from the present site of Medora. Though he withdrew and the Sioux regained control of the area, their independence was short-lived. By 1880 all organized Indian resistance on the northern plains was broken.

Then came cattlemen after free rangeland and hunters after abundant game. The great buffalo herds were eradicated from the plains and their place was taken by livestock. Before long, the grasslands were overstocked and over-grazed. Ranchers suffered crippling losses when cattle perished by thousands during harsh winters. Following the turn of the century, small farms and ranches dominated the scene, but they fared little better. Hard times in the 1930s forced many residents to pull up stakes and let their submarginal holdings of land revert to the government.

The idea of setting aside a portion of the North Dakota Badlands in honor of Theodore Roosevelt was first advanced by local friends soon after he died, in 1919. A national memorial park, the only one of its kind, was established by Congress in 1947 to cover 70,000 acres. It was reclassified in 1978 as a national park, to serve as a natural sanctuary linking humanity to all things of past and present.

## THE PRACTICAL GUIDE

**ACCESS.** The park is located in western North Dakota, with its headquarters at Medora, 17 miles west of Belfield (138 miles west of Bismarck) and 62 miles east of Glendive, MT. It can be reached easily via I-94, which runs east-west. Coming from the south, US 85 intersects I-94 at Belfield.

Medora is the gateway to the South Unit of the park. The North Unit is reached by continuing north on US 85, which provides direct access to it. A third unit, the site of Roosevelt's Elkhorn Ranch, is difficult to reach; for directions, check at park headquarters.

**South Unit.** Start at the Visitor Center to see exhibits covering Roosevelt's early life and the cattle industry, as well as the natural history of the Badlands. Visit the restored **Maltese Cross Cabin** directly adjacent. This was Roosevelt's first home in the Badlands, moved here from its original site 7 miles away; though it may seem simple now, it was luxurious in its day.

While in the South Unit, drive the scenic loop road to **Wind Canyon,** probably the best example of Badlands erosion accelerated by the force of wind. It affords a spectacular vista of weird and brilliantly colored tablelands, buttes, and other formations. **Buck Hill Overlook,** the highest formation in the Painted Canyon, gives the broadest panoramic view. **Petrified Forest,** an area of ancient conifer stumps (which may have been a species of Giant Sequoia), with diameters of 6 and 8 feet, can be reached on foot or horseback—it's a round trip of 16 miles.

**North Unit.** Take the drive of about 13 miles for breathtaking views of bluish bentonitic clay and the weird erosional patterns carved by the meandering Little Missouri. Note that cottonwoods are first to grow in newly deposited sediment along the river's edge, stabilizing the soil and providing shade. This creates an environment for less hardy trees like ash and juniper, which eventually supplant the cottonwoods.

**ACTIVITIES. Hiking.** Opportunities are extensive and varied. Both units have short, self-guiding nature trails readily accessible and longer routes for those who want to get off the beaten path. Pick up a copy of the free *Backcountry Guide.* Hikers are not restricted to existing trails, but exercise caution by picking areas with good footing; soil can be slippery when wet and crumble under you when dry. Wear a cap to protect you from the sun and a pair of good hiking boots. Talk to the rangers about precautions for rattlesnakes and bison.

**Horseback riding** is popular in the vicinity, and you'll find a number of opportunities to join trail rides. A horseback riding concession is located at **Peaceful Valley Ranch** in the

South Unit; other trail rides operate outside both units.

**Floating.** Canoeing on the Little Missouri affords an ideal way to explore the Badlands. You can put in at the South Unit of the park (at old US 10), journey through remote country, pass the site of Roosevelt's Elkhorn Ranch, camp in cottonwood groves, and take out at the North Unit about four days later. Actually, you could travel much farther, since the Little Missouri State Scenic River covers 274 miles from the southwest corner of the state (near Marmath) to Lost Bridge on North Dakota 22, close to the state park at Little Missouri Bay.

**Birdwatching** is a choice experience. Among more spectacular birds are the golden eagle, the great horned owl, and the sandhill crane. The park is frequented by ducks, geese, and other migratory species traveling the Missouri River flyway.

**ACCOMMODATIONS.** In Medora, there are modern motels and the refurbished Rough Riders Hotel, where Teddy Roosevelt stayed. Other motels are located at Watford City, 15 miles from the entrance to the North Unit, and Dickinson, 38 miles east of Medora.

**Rough Riders Hotel,** Medora, ND 58645. The small hotel, where Theodore Roosevelt stayed, is one of a kind, almost part of the park itself. The dining room specializes in western cooking, serving fresh walleye, trout, and chopped buffalo steak. 701/623-4433. M.

**Best Western Prairie Winds Inn,** Dickinson, ND 58601. In a lively city that hosts the annual Roughriders Days Celebration, four days over July 4, this motel has a pool and children under 13 stay free. Senior citizen rates available. 701/225-9123. M.

**Super 8,** Watford City, ND 58854. Fifteen miles from the entrance to the North Unit of the park. 701/842-3686. L to M.

**CAMPING.** Two excellent campgrounds are located in the park (limit 14 days). Sites cannot be reserved, but arrive by early afternoon and you will probably find an attractive location. If you plan to camp in the backcountry, check with a park ranger for tips on camping spots—and be sure to register. There are campgrounds in **Custer National Forest,** which surrounds the national park. **Sully's Creek State Park,** located south of Medora, provides primitive camping along a tributary of the Little Missouri.

**SEASONS.** Summer is the most popular time, though the park is scarcely overrun with visitors. Summer greens soften tones of the stark Badlands. In autumn, too, trees and shrubs cover the river bottom with harvest hues. The first snows of late September signal the coming of winter. The park is kept open all year, and the South Unit road from the Visitor Center to Wind Canyon is plowed in winter. In the North Unit, the road is plowed from the entrance to the Caprock Coulee trailhead.

**NEARBY.** The little town of Medora is linked intimately with the park. The **Chateau de Mores,** a lavish two-story mansion, was built by the founder of Medora, the Marquis de Mores, a contemporary of Roosevelt. The **Museum of the Badlands,** located just outside the park entrance, houses an outstanding collection of relics of early frontier life.

**FOR FURTHER INFORMATION.** Write Superintendent, Theodore Roosevelt National Park, Box 7, Medora, ND 58645. 701/623-4466.

# VIRGIN ISLANDS NATIONAL PARK
## VIRGIN ISLANDS
### AUTHORIZED 1956

SNORKELING in the clear, sunlit waters of Leinster Bay, I felt as though I was traveling in some other world. Coral of many hues rose like trees, mountains, and spires in the underground forest, while schools of brilliantly colored fish rested lazily on stony branches or glided in and out among rocks and plants. Lacy purple sea fans swayed in the gentle current, and delicate anemones carpeted the reef like flowering shrubbery in full aquatic bloom.

On each visit to the Virgin Islands, I realize anew that here is one of the smallest, yet most beautiful, national parks. It covers just over half of the island of St. John, which itself is only nine miles long and five miles wide. The park occupies 12,900 acres, including 5,600 acres of offshore water and reefs. Yellowstone, by contrast, occupies more than 2.2 million acres.

This doesn't make our little park in the Caribbean any less appealing or less of a treasure, for coral reefs are to the Virgin Islands what geysers are to Yellowstone and granite domes are to Yosemite. Few areas span so wide a range of life, from the underwater coral to sea grape shading the strand of white sands along indented bays, and from tropical flora clothing the valleys to green mountaintops opening vistas of neighboring islands and the distant sea.

The park was established in 1956; none too soon, considering that the past few years have seen the unending discovery and commercial development of one "unspoiled" West Indies beach after another. In time, St. John may be one of the few areas left to show sparkling beaches, tropical forest, Danish ruins, and coral reefs in their untouched state.

The course of its history began more than 100 million years ago, when volcanoes erupted deep in the ocean and the buckling crust of the earth raised rock islands above the surface of the sea. Ever since, the beaches of St. John have been a zone of arriving life, with ocean currents and each new tide delivering animals and plants, insects, eggs, seeds, and seedlings to form new colonies here. Meanwhile, the coral reefs have formed a world of flowers that are not plants but tiny animals of the subtropic seas. The coral gardens derive their varied and vivid colors from the myriad tiny organisms living within them.

While hiking the island trails, I found the pattern of life changing upward from the sea. The pale strand is shaded here and there by a seagrape tree, its large leaves tinged with red, and with small purple fruit. Heading to the rainy mountaintops, I observed a swift transition in vegetation, and was glad to have a tropical plant guide in my pocket.

Nature operates on its own timetable. Hurricane Hugo struck the island in September 1989, damaging corals, scouring seagrass beds, uprooting mangrove trees, and stripping leaves and branches from the forests. Hugo is a reminder of natural forces still at work, shaping and reshaping the island.

Humans have lived in the Virgin Islands for several thousand years. Among the earliest were the Arawaks and the Caribs, who left petroglyphs behind. Christopher Columbus touched St. Croix, the largest island, on his second voyage, in 1493 (the beginning of European contact), but it was the Dutch and the Danes who shaped the colonial culture. Denmark acquired the Virgin Islands in the 1700s; its nationals established sugar plantations, imported slaves, and built their estate houses on high, breezy hills. They prospered until the mid-19th century, when sugar prices fell, the slaves were freed, and the old plantations were left to become shadowy ruins of history. The United States bought the islands in 1917. The other islands, St. Croix and St. Thomas, developed much more rapidly, happily for St. John.

## THE PRACTICAL GUIDE

**ACCESS.** The Virgin Islands are only four hours from New York, and less from Miami. Flights go to St. Thomas, the capital. Take a taxi from the airport to Red Hook, for the ferry ride across Pillsbury Sound to Cruz Bay, the main community on St. John. You can also take a ferry from downtown Charlotte Amalie (on St. Thomas); it's a longer trip, but very pleasant, and you will avoid the congested traffic to Red Hook. Another possibility is to fly to San Juan, PR, then go directly to St. John via flying boat.

If you plan to stay on St. Thomas, take one of several excellent one-day package tours to the park, which include the ferry trip, guided shuttle tours, swimming, snorkeling, and lunch. If you come over independently on the ferry to the park entrance at Cruz Bay, taxis with guides offer worthwhile tours. You can rent a jeep, but it's not really necessary, since open-air vans run around the island frequently.

Dress casually and comfortably, but respect local customs—for example, refrain from strolling through town in a bathing suit. Bring walking shoes, cool clothing, swimsuit, snorkel, sunscreen, and insect repellant.

**VISITOR CENTER.** Start early at the park visitor center at Cruz Bay for information, maps, and exhibits of the park's many features. Check here for the schedule of naturalist-conducted historic and nature walks and the evening programs at Cinnamon Bay Campground.

**ACTIVITIES. Sightseeing. Centerline Road,** the main road of St. John, climbs over the heights to the harbor of Coral Bay on the east. The road winds up past buildings of the 1700s, including the Moravian Bethany Church. From a distance, the wooded hills resemble the New England countryside, but there are fruit trees like the soursop and mango; little plants and vines bearing local botanical names such as clashie melashi, eye bright, and better man better; and exotic trees like the gnarled, strangely shaped silk cotton, which produces kapok in its seed pod. Avoid eating strange wild fruits—some are poisonous.

From the overlook near **Mamey Peak,** elevation 1,147 feet, islands of the American and British Virgin Islands spread over the brilliant blue sea around Coral Bay.

**Reef Bay Trail** is of special interest to the visitor who wants to hike or find subjects for sketching and/or photography. From the top of Centerline Road, the 2½-mile trail winds down (a descent of about 800 feet) on an old Danish carriage road, through a moist, then dry, forest. A short side trip leads to undeciphered petroglyphs dating from Arawak and Carib days at the base of a waterfall. Another side trail leads to the Reef Bay estate house, once the center of a flourishing plantation. The trail ends on the sand beach. A park naturalist leads a scheduled trip, returning to Cruz Bay by boat (a fee is charged; reservations are required).

**Snorkeling.** Anybody who can swim can snorkel, and equipment can be rented at the Cinnamon Bay Dive Shop and Trunk Bay Snack Bar, or at St. Thomas. If you're a beginner, join the guided snorkel tour at Cinnamon Bay. It starts with the basics of snorkeling. Never snorkel alone. Test the snorkel gear in shallow water. If it leaks, don't use it. Respect submerged features—avoid standing on or touching coral formations.

**Trunk Bay Beach** leads to the **underwater self-guiding trail,** which reaches a depth of only 10 feet. Most visitors can read the labels etched on submerged glass plates.

**Swimming,** with or without a snorkel, is one of the pleasures of the park, but the safest places to swim are where lifeguards are on duty.

**Boating and Fishing.** Sailboats and other boats are available for rent on St. Thomas and St. John. On your first experience, it pays to engage a skipper. Bear in mind that dropping anchor in the reefs damages the coral, so avoid it. Saltwater fishing is equally good in all seasons. Three bonefish flats are near St. John. Charter boats are available in Cruz Bay and St. Thomas for offshore marlin, tuna, sailfish, wahoo, and others. Spearfishing in waters of the park is prohibited. You can help protect fish, shellfish, and lobster by leaving them undisturbed.

**Annaberg Ruins.** A self-guiding trail helps recapture the story of the sugar estates at these ruins on the North Shore, which the Park Service has stabilized as a protection against further weathering. Cane grown on the hillsides was carried by mules, donkeys, or oxen to be crushed in the windmill or on the grinding platform.

**ACCOMMODATIONS.** In addition to the concession-operated beach cottages in Cinnamon Bay Campground, accommodations are available on private land within the national park and at several resorts at Cruz Bay.

**Caneel Bay, Inc.,** Cruz Bay, St. John, VI 00830. Opened in 1956 by Laurance Rockefeller, Caneel Bay became one of the Caribbean's finest resorts. Expansion and various changes over the years have somewhat dulled the early image. Reservations during the winter peak are sometimes hard to get; package plans in effect May 1 to November 1. Make reservations through a travel agency or Rockresorts, New York. 800/223-7637; New York only 800/442-8198; New York City 212/586-4459. H to H+.

**Maho Bay Camps,** 17 E. 73rd St., New York, NY 10021. On private land within the park, a choice place to stay and absorb the treasures of the area. Kitchen-equipped tent cottages are set in the woods overlooking the curved sand beach of Maho Bay, with access to community showers, toilets, camp store, and moderately priced restaurant.

Maho Bay has added a new facility, Harmony, with apartment-type accommodations in the forest above the beach. Harmony is constructed largely of recycled materials and uses sun and wind power; guests are encouraged to monitor energy use and efficiency. A seven-day minimum stay requirement year-round at Harmony and at Maho Camp between December 15 and April 30. 212/472-9453 or 800/392-9004. M to H.

**CAMPING.** Cinnamon Bay Campground facilities include bare sites for tent camping; prepared sites with tents; and modest beach cottages with cots, bedding, linen, and cooking utensils. All are in great demand, so write far in advance for rates and reservations (Cinnamon Bay Campground, Box 720, Cruz Bay, St. John, VI 00830; phone 800/223-7637). The camping limit is 14 days. There are no chiggers, but ticks, mosquitoes and sandflies are sometimes present, especially after rainfall and relative calm. The camp sells groceries and supplies and has an excellent restaurant.

**SEASONS.** Peak periods of use for campsites and beach cottages are November to March and June to August. Peak popularity of the Virgin Islands in general, as a refuge from winter cold, extends from December to March. April and May are very attractive months. The climate is equable year-round, with an average annual temperature of 79 degrees. The lowest recorded temperature is 61 degrees; the highest is 98 degrees. The water temperature is delightful for swimming.

**NEARBY.** Both St. Thomas and St. Croix are popular Caribbean resorts, landscaped with bright hibiscus, oleander, and bougainvillaea. At Charlotte Amalie, the capital city, visited by many cruise liners, the 25 shops between Queen's Street and Waterfront Promenade feature merchandise from all over the world—because St. Thomas is a duty-free port. St. Croix, 40 miles south, clings to its Danish colonial architecture and history. **Christiansted National Historic Site,** along three waterfront blocks of the main city, encompasses an old fort and public buildings. **Buck Island Reef National Monument,** a mile and a half off the coast of St. Croix, is regarded as one of the finest marine gardens in the Caribbean; it is visited on boat cruises from St. Croix and provides snorkelers with an underwater nature trail. **Salt River Bay National Historical Park and Ecological Preserve** is the site of a visit from Columbus and artifacts from earlier peoples.

**FOR FURTHER INFORMATION.** Write Superintendent, Virgin Islands National Park, Box 7789, Charlotte Amalie, St. Thomas, VI 00801. 809/775-6238.

# VOYAGEURS NATIONAL PARK

## MINNESOTA

### AUTHORIZED 1971

I SPENT a day following foot trails on the Kabetogama Peninsula in Voyageurs National Park and that day was all too short. The park includes large lakes— some of the largest in the upper Midwest—on which motorboating is allowed, but once away from the powerboat lanes, I found the Peninsula filled with fresh, sparkling, and intimate scenes. The boreal forest, though broken here and there by bogs, surprising palisades, and sand beaches, for the most part reached to the water's edge. Wild rice grew in shallow bays and streams. I saw part of a chain of interior lakes well suited for canoeing.

On the trail into Agnes Lake, I heard a rustling in the brush. At first it sounded like the wind, but the air was calm. It proved to be a bear cub that I had disturbed, scampering up a tree. The beaver ponds I saw were habitat for aquatic plants, which fed insects, which in turn fed fish and birds. Across the water, I observed a loon scanning the scene, then diving for lower depths as suddenly as it had appeared.

Minnesota's national park embraces a choice portion of the forested lake country on the northern border, once the setting of an epic chapter in American history. For a century and a half, French-Canadian voyageurs plied this net- work of lakes and streams in sturdy canoes, transported trade goods, explorers, missionaries, and soldiers to the West, and returned to Montreal with vast quantities of furs.

Sentiment for preserving this area had been felt and expressed in Minnesota for many years. In 1962, Governor Elmer L. Andersen and state officials toured the area with major landowners and representatives of the National Park Ser- vice; they issued a joint memorandum recommending field studies as soon as possible. In 1965, Andersen's successor, Karl Rolvaag, and 5,000 fellow Minne- sotans signed a petition at the State Fair urging establishment of Voyageurs National Park. And in 1967, a third governor, Harold LeVander, committed the "full force" of his administration to establishment of the park. During the same year, the National Park Service reaffirmed its choice of Kabetogama as "the outstanding remaining opportunity for a national park in the northern lake country of the United States." The entire Minnesota delegation, led by Repre- sentative John Blatnik and Senator Walter Mondale, then introduced legisla-

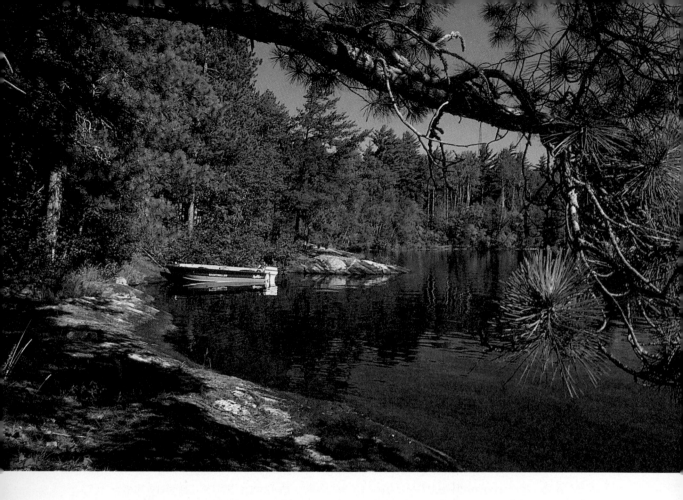

tion in Congress, which acted favorably. The bill authorizing the new park was signed in January 1971.

Sigurd Olson—author, naturalist, and a living Minnesota legend—played a major role in the park movement, making countless presentations in his home state and Washington. Voyageurs National Park Association, headed first by Judge Edwin P. Chapman, labored toward making Minnesota's first national park a reality.

Although the log forts and other physical traces of the *coureurs du bois* and voyageurs have long since vanished, it is still possible to capture a sense of solitude and challenge. The park has all the wildness and immense scale associated with the northern shield region—a surface shaped by continental glaciation into an endless system of internal waterways. Of the park's 218,000 total acres, 84,000 acres are water. Nature is still at work here, revealing its handiwork of times past while constantly changing it. The landscape is marked by 30 lakes and a tangle of streams. Smooth, polished, and grooved rock surfaces are visible on many islands—they are the tops of rocky crags the glacial ice failed to remove.

It requires no scientific analysis, however, to enjoy or appreciate the Voyageurs country of today. Stands of fir, spruce, pine, aspen, and birch reach to the water's edge, broken here and there by bogs, cliffs, and sand beaches. Wildlife species such as deer, moose, and black bear remain. This is one of the few places in the country outside of Alaska with a pack of timber wolves. Beavers thrive among the aspen. Throngs of birds indigenous to the area and numerous varieties of waterfowl make their nests and feed in the peninsula's many bays and lagoons.

I found a choice bit of cultural history here, too, at the Kettle Falls Hotel, at the extreme east end of Rainy Lake. Built in 1913, the hotel served trappers, traders, fishermen, and lumberjacks. It reopened in 1988 after a $2.5 million restoration. It's a treasure to enjoy, worthy of the north woods around it.

# THE PRACTICAL GUIDE

**BACKGROUND.** Lying east of International Falls, the park is irregular in shape, measuring about 40 miles from east to west and varying in width from 3 to 15 miles. It includes numerous islands and 30 lakes. The main body of land, Kabetogama Peninsula, covers 75,000 heavily forested acres, relatively undeveloped and accessible principally by water. Surrounding the peninsula are waters ranging from narrows less than 100 feet wide to lakes several miles across, dotted with islands accented with rocky points. Four lakes dominate the area within the park: **Namakan, Kabetogama, Rainy,** and **Sand Point.** Rainy Lake, the largest, covers 350 square miles, three quarters of it in Canada.

**ACCESS.** The primary access to the park is via US 53, extending from Virginia, MN, north to International Falls. County and state roads lead from US 53 to Crane Lake, at the eastern end of the park; the south shore of Lake Kabetogama; the Ash River and Rainy Lake's Black Bay. There are no roads into the interior of the park.

**Crane Lake Gorge,** lying just to the west of the park, is one of the spectacular scenic wonders of Crane Lake, where the Vermillion River tumbles through a narrow chasm between vertical rock walls before it flows into the lake. There are trails on both sides of the canyon and many plants and mosses on the moist forest floor. Wild rice grows in shallow bays and streams, and cranberry bogs are common.

**TOURS.** Tour boats are an important part of the interpretive program. Visitors are able to drive to the visitor centers at the park edges, but access to the interior is by boat. Tour boats feature interesting narration by a park naturalist or boat operator. The *Pride of Rainy Lake,* departing from the Rainy Lake Visitor Center, is the largest jet-powered passenger boat in Minnesota, carrying 49 passengers. Voyageurs National Park Boat Tours offers rides from the new Kabetogama Lake Visitor Center. The *Locator Lake Adventure* combines a two-mile naturalist hike and canoeing on Locator Lake with the boat trip. Another option is the sunset cruise.

**Historic values** are high. Underwater archaeologists have recovered parts of voyageur canoes, muzzle-loading rifles, beads intended for Indian trade, and other artifacts. An existing link to a more recent era is the **Kettle Falls Hotel,** "Minnesota's most remote resort," a choice spot for a meal, even if you can't stay over. There was a brief gold rush in the early 1890's at **Rainy Lake City.**

**ACTIVITIES. Boating and Canoeing.** State regulations apply. Boaters not familiar with these waters should obtain the services of a guide (through a local resort or hotel) or obtain charts. Large lakes are formidable and can become suddenly rough. Small boats and canoes should prepare to wait out rough water; there are several points in the park. Better yet, plan a course that avoids wide expanses.

**Fishing.** The four large border lakes—Rainy, Sand Point, Namakan, and Kabetogama—are popular with walleye anglers; they are also rich in northern pike and smallmouth bass. Shoepack Lake on the peninsula is known for its muskellunge.

**ACCOMMODATIONS.** Clustered mostly at Crane Lake, Kabetogama Lake, Ash River, and Rainy Lake, 60 resorts lie near the park, offering everything from housekeeping cabins, hotel rooms and houseboat rentals to guide services and charter trips by boat or floatplane. In addition, there are two hotels operated as concessions in the park. They are:

**Kettle Falls Hotel,** Orr, MN 55771. One of the country's most unusual hostelries, it dates from 1913 when it was built to provide meals and lodging for workers constructing dams at Kettle Falls and Squirrel Narrows. Open mid-May through September, and late December through March. 800/322-0886. M.

**Whispering Pines Resort,** Orr, MN 55771. Family housekeeping cabins, fully equipped (and boat furnished with each cabin), comprise this resort at the narrows between Kabetogama and Namakan Lakes. Accessible via the Ash River Trail to the central entrance of the park. 218/374-3321. M.

**Thunderbird Lodge,** Route 8, International Falls, MN 56649. Three-story lodge and cottages on Rainy Lake. Pool, tennis and 9-hole golf privileges. 218/286-3151. M.

**Nelson's,** Crane Lake, MN 55725. Founded by the Nelson family in 1931 on spacious grounds fronting Crane Lake, it offers furnished housekeeping cabins and resort dining. 218/993-2295. M.

**CAMPING.** National Park Service island campsites are available without charge. The state of Minnesota and several resorts provide camping spots near the park. Along both the north and the south shores of Kabetogama Peninsula are many places with smooth, glaciated rock that are well suited for camping and picnicking. The peninsula's interior holds a number of lovely lakes that can be reached only by foot.

The park has small campgrounds at King Williams Narrows and Mukooda Lake, accessible only by boat.

Private campgrounds are located in each of the four resort communities.

**SEASONS.** Summers are cool. Warm clothes and insect repellant are important. September, when aspen and birch change colors, can be a beautiful month.

**NEARBY.** East of the park lies the renowned **Boundary Waters Canoe Area Wilderness** in the **Superior National Forest.** The wilderness is adjacent to **Quetico Provincial Park** across the border in Ontario. Main gateways are at Grand Marais, Ely, and Crane Lake. **Fort Frances,** Ontario, linked by bridge with International Falls, was the site of Fort St. Pierre, built by Pierre de la Verendrye, the explorer, in 1731.

**RECOMMENDED READING.** *The Singing Wilderness*, by Sigurd Olson; *Rainy River Country*, by Grace Lee Nute; and *Voyageur Country*, by Robert Treuer. Additional suggested reading: *Voyageurs National Park*, by Greg Breining; *Kettle Falls, Crossroads of History*, by Shannon King; and *Gold Town to Ghost Town*, by David Perry.

**FOR FURTHER INFORMATION.** Write Superintendent, Voyageurs National Park, 3131 Highway 53, International Falls, MN 56649-8904. 218/283-9821.

# WIND CAVE NATIONAL PARK

## SOUTH DAKOTA

### ESTABLISHED 1903

I WATCHED two prairie dogs, standing upright like furry little men or women. They advanced toward each other, embraced in greeting like family or friends, then went their separate ways. One of them scooted into its hole, and I wished that I might have peeked into that underground house, which is said to be the most complex, elaborate dwelling constructed by a North American mammal.

The colonies of prairie dogs at Wind Cave comprise, for me, one of the treasures of the National Park system. For one thing, they typify the prairie, or what remains of it. At one time, prairie dogs numbered in the millions. Their "towns" were surprisingly huge—one, in Texas, was estimated in 1900 to cover 25,000 square miles and to contain 400 million animals. Now they are found only in a few places, mostly in sanctuaries like Wind Cave.

I enjoy this national park as a prairie vignette. I watch the seas of grass ripple in the wind, short and medium grasses sprinkled with wildflowers. The sleek pronghorn, alone or with a mate, roves across the hillsides. Small herds of huge, shaggy bison lumber slowly, following ancient pathways. The animals are remnants of great herds that once covered the mid-continent. I wish there were more—more animals and more prairie saved—but at least there is this much to yield the feel and flavor of original America.

The park contains 28,059 acres, a relatively small area. Yet it includes not only a prime example of mixed-grass prairie, but a meeting ground of eastern and western flora. Here I can see the stately American elm and burr oak from the East merging with ponderosa pines of the western mountain forests and with yucca, cactus, and cottonwood from the arid Southwest.

Below the surface, the Wind Cave was formed in one of the thick limestone formations that underlie a large part of the Black Hills. It derives its name from strong currents of air that blow alternately in and out, believed to be caused by changes in atmospheric pressure outside.

Development of the cave began in the 1890s with the "Wonderful Wind Cave Improvement Company." Passages were opened and stairways built, leading to galleries decorated with unusual crystal formations. These were formed when cracks in the ancient limestone were filled with calcium carbonate deposits.

In 1902, legislation was introduced to set aside Wind Cave as a national park.

It was enacted that year and signed by President Theodore Roosevelt on January 9, 1903. Wind Cave thus became the first cave park to be established in the National Park system.

I still favor the park aboveground, where I observe dominant grasses of both the true prairie and shortgrass plains. In spring and summer, I look for pasqueflower (South Dakota's state flower), scarlet globemallow, prairie coneflower, mariposa lily, and prickly poppy. I watch elk, buffalo, and pronghorn. And prairie dogs, of course. They're not really dogs, but burrowing ground squirrels that rely on keen hearing, excellent eyesight, and a community warning system for protection. Like all wild creatures threatened by the advance of civilization, they have not had an easy time of it, yet they enrich the landscape by being part of it.

## THE PRACTICAL GUIDE

**BACKGROUND.** Wind Cave is a lightly visited national park, thus increasing its charm to the visitor who prefers elbow room. It makes for a very pleasant natural interlude amidst the Black Hills. Conducted tours of the cave, requiring one to one and a half hours, are given year-round.

**VISITOR CENTER.** Open daily except Thanksgiving Day, Christmas, and New Year's. Travel information and educational publications are available. A concession-operated lunchroom is located here; food service is available late spring, summer, and fall.

**ACTIVITIES.** **Cave trips** are led by uniformed guides of the National Park Service, using either the walk-in entrance or elevator. Trails are hard-surfaced. Low-heeled, rubber-soled walking shoes are best for comfort and safety. Temperature year-round is approximately 53 degrees; wear a light sweater or jacket. Besides the regular trips, **candlelight tours,** reminiscent of the turn of the century, are held several times daily during summer (limit 10 persons per party). **Spelunking tours** are conducted daily in summer, with spacecrawling into a primitive section of the cave (limit 10 persons).

**Rankin Ridge Nature Trail** leads to the highest point in the park (elevation 5,016 feet). The trail is 1¼ miles long and takes about an hour. Binoculars are useful in getting a panoramic view of the Black Hills from the observation tower.

**Wildlife** is wonderful to watch and photograph, from a respectable distance. Do not approach bison on foot; even a young bison may inflict serious injury. Early morning and evening are good hours for viewing elk and deer. Cliff swallows, golden eagles, bald eagles, and several varieties of woodpecker are often spotted here. The white-winged junco can be seen only in the Black Hills.

**Naturalist Program.** Activities will keep you on the go from morning till after dark. Campfire programs are held each evening on many subjects, and naturalist-led activities will acquaint visitors with other aspects of the park.

**ACCOMMODATIONS.** Camping and concession-operated lunchroom are located in the park. Adjacent community of Custer offers camping (Custer State Park, Custer, SD 57730), plus lodging facilities.

**State Game Lodge,** Custer, SD 57730. Once used by Calvin Coolidge as summer White House, it includes lodge rooms, furnished cabins, restaurant, and playground. The lodge is a good place to have a sizzling buffalo steak, or "buffalo burger." Open early May to late September. 605/255-4541. M.

**Best Western Inn by the River,** Hot Springs, SD 57747. On the southeast edge of the Black Hills, Hot Springs lies 12 miles south of the park. Pool. 605/745-4292. M.

**Blue Bell Lodge,** Custer, SD 57730. Kitchen-equipped cottages, restaurant, and store are open mid-May to early October. 605/255-4531. L to M.

**CAMPING.** One-half mile north of the headquarters area, **Elk Mountain Campground** provides camping and trailer sites from mid-May through mid-September, but electric, water, and sewer hookups are not available. There are numerous private and public campgrounds in the area.

**SEASONS.** Cave tours are conducted year-round, except major wintertime holidays. Tourist centers in the Black Hills are jammed in midsummer. Early summer wildflowers and autumn foliage make these attractive seasons. In May, prairie dog pups emerge from their holes for the first time. You can see the "booming," or courtship dance of the sharp-tailed grouse. In June, bison and elk calves, deer fawns, and pronghorn kids are first seen, while spring flowers are abundant. September and October are excellent months for wildlife watching, with elk and deer mating and pronghorns grouping together.

**NEARBY.** Within easy range are **Mount Rushmore National Memorial** and **Jewel Cave National Monument,** a series of chambers and limestone galleries with sparkling crystal-lined walls. **Custer State Park,** adjacent to the national park, contains a very large bison herd.

Campgrounds are located in **Black Hills National Forest** and **Custer State Park.** The state park contains several overnight lodgings, including **State Game Lodge.**

A word of caution: the Black Hills contain a heavy concentration of commercial tourist attractions advertising "fun for the entire family" and "education" for your youngsters. Choose carefully, particularly if you are on a close budget.

**FOR FURTHER INFORMATION.** Write Superintendent, Wind Cave National Park, Hot Springs, SD 57747. 605/745-4600.

# WRANGELL–ST. ELIAS NATIONAL PARK

## ALASKA

ESTABLISHED 1980

I CHECKED the map as my friend Paul and I drove east from Anchorage. The country all around us looked as though it would easily qualify as national park land. It was expansive, natural, and free of settlement. We stopped for lunch at Glennallen, the hub of the Copper River frontier and gateway to the Wrangells. While the countryside was relatively flat, with small lakes and streams, I could see clearly the great peaks ahead—Sanford, Drum, Wrangell, and Blackburn—that make the Wrangells a special place.

North America's "mountain kingdom" embraces the greatest concentration of high peaks on the continent, including Mount St. Elias, at 18,008 feet the second highest (after Mount McKinley), plus several others rising above 14,500 feet. Covering 12,318,000 acres, Wrangell–St. Elias is the largest park in the National Park system, yet larger still when considered together with bordering Kluane National Park in the Yukon Territory of Canada. Together they have been placed on the United Nations' World Heritage List of outstanding natural areas.

Glaciers and snowfields of these massive mountains dominate the landscape. More than 100 major glaciers constitute the largest ice field in the world below the polar region. One glacier alone, the celebrated Malespina, is larger than the entire state of Rhode Island.

Paul and I spent our time exploring the Chitina Valley, the heart of the park, drained by the Chitina River, one of a dozen major rivers flowing down from the rugged mountain. We saw Dall sheep abundant on the rocky ledges and signs of grizzly along the trails. The park also includes coastal beaches on the Gulf of Alaska, which I hope to visit soon.

We also found human signs, at the old mining towns of McCarthy and Kennicott, focal points of activity within the Chitina Valley portion of the park. These towns were born in the early 1900s, when the Kennicott Copper Company began mining and milling one of the world's richest copper deposits. In its heyday, McCarthy had more than 1,000 residents, compared with the handful there today who relish its isolation. With this setting, I could hardly blame them.

# THE PRACTICAL GUIDE

**ACCESS.** The easiest way to arrive is flying by charter service direct from Anchorage, or from Glennallen or Chitina. The flight affords spectacular views of glaciers, mountains, and roaring rivers. It is also feasible to go by car. Allow a full day from either Anchorage or Fairbanks. Drive to Glennallen and then south on the Richardson Highway to the Edgerton Highway into Chitina, at the confluence of the Copper and Chitina Rivers. From there the 63-mile "McCarthy Road" follows the roadbed of the Copper River and Northwestern Railway. Check road conditions; it can be rough or slippery following rain. A four-wheel-drive vehicle is highly desirable.

McCarthy is reached by hand-operated cable tram across the Kennicott River. Bring thick gloves to make pulling easier.

**ACTIVITIES.** There are lots of opportunities for hiking and backpacking, with routes including those on the Hanagita Valley, Nikolai Pass, Jacksina Creek drainage, and the demanding Chitistone Canyon. Mount Drum and Mount Sanford, in the Wrangells, and Mount St. Elias are among the most challenging peaks known to climbers. The Bremner, Chitina, and Copper rivers offer excellent rafting with all classes of water. For a thrilling four-day trip, put in on the Kennicott River, near the glacier, and float down through the Nizina River Canyon and into the Chitina, which joins the mighty Copper River at the town of Chitina.

**ACCOMMODATIONS.** This huge, diverse park, still little known, is hardly the place to expect luxury or creature comforts. Several lodges, as well as campgrounds, are most easily accessible by air taxi service to landing strips and lakes in the park. You can drive to accommodations in McCarthy, in the park interior, but the last 65-mile stretch from Chitina is strictly for four-wheel-drive vehicles. Accommodations are also located on the Tok Cutoff, in Glennallen, and in Chitina, en route to McCarthy. The old company town of Kennicott makes a good base from which to explore the area. Dominated by a 14-story copper processing plant, it consists of about 40 buildings, all painted red with white trim. From McCarthy or Kennicott, you can hike on the Kennicott Glacier or explore the old mines. During summer, wildflowers and berries cover the countryside. Dall sheep, caribou, and moose often are seen crossing the hills and occasionally black bear and brown bear.

**McCarthy Lodge,** Wasilla, AK 99687. An historic facility near the old Kennicott copper mine is open May through September. M.

**Kennicott Glacier Lodge,** Box 103940, Anchorage, AK 99510. Five miles uphill from McCarthy (they will come get you), the lodge is near the center of the original boomtown, now a National Historic Landmark, and at the edge of the mountain wilderness. 907/258-2350. M.

**McCarthy Wilderness B&B,** Box 11241, Anchorage, AK 99511. Simple, no frills, run by St. Elias Alpine Guides for outdoors people. 907/277-6867. L to M.

**SEASONS.** July generally has the best weather, with clear, warm days. Otherwise, the Wrangells can be cool, cloudy, and wet. Autumn is an attractive time, mosquito-free. So is winter, with plenty of opportunity for cross-country skiing in dazzling settings.

**FOR FURTHER INFORMATION.** Write Superintendent, Wrangell–St. Elias National Park, Box 29, Glennallen, AK 99588. 907/822-5234.

# YELLOWSTONE NATIONAL PARK

## WYOMING · MONTANA · IDAHO

### ESTABLISHED 1872

Soon after the great Yellowstone fires of 1988, I met my friend Russell E. Dickenson, a former Director of the National Park Service (from 1980 to 1985), at a conference in Washington State. "The Yellowstone you and I knew for those many years," he said rather ruefully, "will never be the same." That is true. Visitors now see a new and different Yellowstone. But the more I consider it and discuss it with experts, the more convinced I become that Yellowstone emerges better than ever.

I revisited Yellowstone in June 1989, and found life after fire, a rebirth, the continuation of a life cycle that visitors can observe, absorb, and appreciate. The damage of 1988, unquestionably extensive, in a sense was more commercial than ecological. Concession-operated accommodations in the park were evacuated for a time, then closed earlier than normal. Tourist trade in nearby communities was affected. But there is more to fire than the charred forest, hotel evacuation, and commercial loss. And in a national park, above all other places, there should be more.

Prepare to see evidence of the Big Burn. It will be extensive, but not solid. Some areas remain untouched. About 45 percent of the park was affected to some degree, although the flames skirted many popular scenic vistas. Within the burns, large sections remain unaffected. The heaviest fires were in stands of aging lodgepole pine, waiting to be ignited to make way for new growth. Wildlife, in the long run, benefits. Plants, insects, fish, and wildlife find new food sources. Visitors have the chance to examine the greatest example of Yellowstone fire in 300 years: to look, listen, and learn.

Covering 2,221,773 acres, Yellowstone embraces vast distance without factory fumes or firearms. Its spaciousness is a stronghold for wildlife—the grizzly bear, elk, bighorn, and bison, noble creatures that must have roaming room to live and perpetuate their species; so too for majestic winged animals of the wilderness: the bald eagle, trumpeter swan, raven, and great gray owl. Of all native species, only the wolf has been missing from the scene, exterminated in the onrush of civilization. But plans and studies are now under way to bring the wolf home to Yellowstone.

Old Faithful, spouting hot water jets, and more than 10,000 other geysers, hot springs, and bubbling mud volcanoes make it the most extensive thermal area in the world—but they are only the beginning of the park's wonders. Here are the Grand Canyon of the Yellowstone River, where brawling waters rush through twisting rock walls, and Yellowstone Lake, famed for its scenic beauty and its fighting cutthroat trout, and as a gateway to backcountry canoeing. Here are innumerable plants, trees, and wildflowers of stream and lake, sagebrush desert, open meadow, and high forest.

Millions of years ago, this region was submerged beneath an inland sea. During a period of internal upheaval, the earth pushed its crust upward and the water receded. Then followed a sequence of volcanic explosions and lava flows over the Yellowstone plateau. The earth's crust fractured, great faults developed, and mountain ranges arose. In time came falling temperatures and the age of the glaciers.

Glaciers modified the hot-spring basins, which are remnants of volcanism—

an expressive link between the ancient age and our own. Cold ground water, trickling downward, strikes vapors rising from seething super-hot magmas perhaps a mile down. The water boils upward, emerging at the surface as steam, causing caverns in soft rock below and terraces above.

Geyser activity varies greatly. During 1978, Steamboat Geyser, which had been bubbling quietly for almost a decade, blew its stack twice, raising spectacular columns of water 350 to 400 feet high. It thus became "the largest active geyser in the world," dwarfing Old Faithful, which rises to an average of 130 feet. However, while Steamboat is irregular and unpredictable, Old Faithful erupts with some regularity. The interval between eruptions lengthened following large earthquakes in and near Yellowstone in 1959 and 1975. Old Faithful's average interval after the 1983 earthquake at Mt. Borah, Idaho, increased from about 69 to 78 minutes. By late 1989 the interval had stretched to 85 or 95 minutes. Nearby geysers are erupting with greater frequency. Another major geyser, Giant Geyser, located near Old Faithful, exploded in 1978 for the first time since 1955. The park is home to over 300 geysers.

John Colter, who took leave of the Lewis and Clark expedition in 1806 to do some independent exploring, is believed to have been the first white man to see and report on this wondrous place. Among trappers and explorers who followed, Jim Bridger ("Old Gabe") added, with some exaggeration, his version— which became known as "Jim Bridger's lies." In 1859, Bridger guided the first government expedition into the area—the Army Corps of Topographical Engineers, with F. V. Hayden as geologist. Other expeditions followed, recording the wonders of Yellowstone.

One group that came to verify the frontier stories was the Washburn-Langford-Doane expedition of 1870, a party of 19 organized by several influential Montana citizens. It was named for Henry D. Washburn, Surveyor-General of Montana; Nathaniel P. Langford; and Lieutenant Gustavus C. Doane, who commanded the small military escort. They spent almost four weeks investigating the area and naming many features, including Old Faithful. Most important, they sat around a campfire one evening to discuss the future of the fantastic place they had explored. According to H. M. Chittenden, the noted historian of Yellowstone, it was Judge Cornelius Hedges who insisted that no part of the region should ever be privately owned, but that it ought to be held by the government for the use of the people. The others agreed and charted the campaign to make Yellowstone a national park.

The writing and lecturing done by members of this expedition resulted in an official exploration in 1871 by the U.S. Geological Survey. The enthusiastic endorsement of F. V. Hayden, the leader, was buttressed by a superb set of photographs taken by William H. Jackson. From that came a recognition of the superlative nature of the Yellowstone "wonders." Representative William Horace Clagett, of Montana, introduced his famous Park Bill in 1871; it succeeded after one of the most formidable public-interest lobbying campaigns in history.

President Ulysses S. Grant signed the bill into law on March 1, 1872, placing—for the very first time—a parcel of the public domain under protection of the federal government as "a public park or pleasuring ground for the benefit and enjoyment of the people."

Fire has been part of Yellowstone since long before the park was established and long before the first explorer saw it. Fire swept through periodically, releasing the nutrients—such as nitrogen, calcium, phosphorus, and potassium—that come from burned wood. They mixed into the soil to act as a fertilizer. Fire also opened the cones of lodgepole pines, raining seeds on the ground. Most fire did not kill all the trees within a burn; those it left, free of competition for nutrients, light, and water, grew stronger and healthier.

Many Indian tribes considered fire a friend, just as primitive peoples in various parts of the world set fire to "green up the grass" and stimulate new growth. But as a consequence of wildfires devastating to valuable commercial timber forests, American public policy for the past century has been designed to suppress all fires. So the national parks were managed until 1972, when "natural regulation," or "let burn," became the policy, allowing natural fires, such as those caused by lightning, to run their course, except when threatening human life or property.

Research has shown the vast majority of wildfires die on their own, seldom burning more than 100 acres. In the 16 years before 1988, for example, 140 natural fires in Yellowstone burned an average of 240 acres.

Then came June of 1988. Lightning danced in the sky and sparked in the trees. A severe drought had turned trees into tinder. Dead litter on the forest floor, untouched during the years of fire suppression, made it worse. A carelessly tossed cigarette butt set off a new massive blaze in July.

In early September, when I was in the Grand Tetons, 50 miles south, I saw the first snow fall on Wyoming. It helped extinguish the fires, which involved about 400,000 acres. The following summer, I found that more than half of Yellowstone remained untouched. The landscape indeed has changed, stimulating a new perception of our first national park and of the natural forest at work in it.

## THE PRACTICAL GUIDE

**BACKGROUND.** A trip to Yellowstone deserves forethought and preparation. Pick your time carefully. Some 70 percent of the park's visitors come during July and August, when concessions and park facilities are hard-pressed; if you come during these months have a good idea of where you will stay. Study a map of the area. Major park campgrounds could be full, and no overflow camping is allowed. U.S. Forest Service campgrounds, reasonably convenient to major park features, are an alternative.

Allow three to five days to tour the highlights, not simply the one and a half days to do the Grand Loop. The park has five entrances: Gardiner, Montana (north); West Yellowstone, Montana (west); via Grand Teton National Park and Jackson, Wyoming (south); via Cody, Wyoming (east); and Cooke City, Montana (northeast).

Principal park roads normally are open from early May through October, depending on weather conditions. Early and late snowstorms can close the roads at any time. In winter, the only road open to automobiles is from the North Entrance at Gardiner, Montana, to Mammoth Hot Springs and on to Cooke City, Montana, near the Northeast Entrance.

**ACCESS.** During the summer, you can reach West Yellowstone by Greyhound and several airlines. TW Services, the park concessioner, operates buses daily during the summer from Bozeman, Livingston, and West Yellowstone, Montana; and Cody and Jackson, Wyoming, to Canyon Village in the park. (The Bozeman bus operates once weekly in the off-season as far as West Yellowstone.) Bozeman and Livingston are both served by Greyhound.

**VISITOR CENTERS.** Each of the five Visitor Centers interprets a different phase of the Yellowstone story. **Grant Village** features fire ecology, with video shows, three-dimensional displays, and relief models depicting the fires of 1988. **Mammoth** contains exhibits on Indians, early park history, and wildlife. **Fishing Bridge** describes birdlife, fish, and geology of the Yellowstone Lake area. **Old Faithful** explains hot spring and geyser activity, with probable erupting times of Old Faithful posted prominently. The other is at **Canyon Village.**

**Wildlife.** Not many visitors see a grizzly, for the bears are few in number. Though normally shy, grizzly bears can be a problem in the backcountry. Observe from a distance! Don't test your luck! Park officials have announced intention to close recreational facilities near Fishing Bridge—prime bear habitat—placing the facilities at Grant Village and elsewhere. Check with rangers for restricted or closed areas.

You will increase your chances of seeing wildlife if you fit your schedule to theirs: the early and late hours of the day are best. Many a meadow is dotted with elk in those periods, especially around Norris, but empty when the sun beats down and insects grow active. Best chances of finding moose are in Hayden Valley, near Fishing Bridge, Yellowstone Lake Lodge area, and Pelican Creek; bighorn sheep on Mount Washburn or near Soda Butte; bison along Nez Perce Creek south of Madison Junction; pronghorn near the north entrance; and coyote in both Lamor and Hayden Valley.

**TOURS.** TW Services, Inc. conducts tours of varying lengths. Package tours lasting two and three days start from Yellowstone and Grand Teton, featuring both national parks.

**ACTIVITIES. Sightseeing. Grand Loop** links the best-known park features on a 145-mile drive. Before you start, decide how much time you have available and which points interest you the most.

Starting from the north entrance (Gardiner), and going counterclockwise around the Grand Loop, the main features begin at **Mammoth Hot Springs,** near park headquarters. Well-marked trails enable close-range views of the brimming, terrace-like formations created by limestone deposits. **Norris Geyser Basin,** 21 miles south, is filled with exciting geysers and bubbling springs, including Steamboat, the most powerful geyser in the park. Be sure to see the new National Park Ranger Museum, opened in 1991 in the old soldier station dating from the early 1900s, when the military patrolled the park. **Madison Junction** is within view of National Park Mountain, at the foot of which the pioneering 1870 expedition camped. Drive along Firehole River, a stream warmed by the springs in its bed. **Old Faithful** is located in an area extensively burned during the 1988 fires, but it still erupts on schedule. Some of the most beautifully colored pools are found at **Black Sand Basin,** where vivid orange and yellow colors trace colonies of algae, water plants growing at the limits of life in the hot springs. **Geyser Hill Nature Trail** leads through a wonderland of scalding water and superheated steam. Old Faithful, the emblem of the park, has never missed an eruption during more than 80 years of observation, at intervals averaging about 90 minutes.

At **West Thumb,** after the Grand Loop twice crosses the Continental Divide, the gaudy mudpots operate against the backdrop of sparkling **Yellowstone Lake.** The road winds around the northwest shore of the lake, the largest body of water in North America at so high an elevation (7,733 feet). Its blue waters, 320 feet at its deepest, are fed by snow stored in forests above its 100-mile shoreline. Allow time for a stop at the museum, built in the early 1930s of logs and stone, restored and refurbished in the early 1980s. It contains mounted fish, birds, and mammals. Benches behind the museum overlook Yellowstone Lake, a choice spot to rest and observe. From the famous **Fishing Bridge** (no fishing allowed) at the outlet of the lake, you may see a variety of birds on the water, including white pelicans, gulls, mallards, and geese. North of Fishing Bridge, the road follows the **Grand Canyon of the Yellowstone,** 1,200 feet deep, a breathtaking spectacle from any vantage point along its twisting, 24-mile course. The dominant color of the walls is yellow, ranging in shade from pale lemon to brilliant orange. The most exciting way to see and hear the thundering **Lower Falls,** twice as high as Niagara, is to go by trail down to the brink, a rather strenuous walk. The **Upper Falls** are spectacular, too, and can be viewed without a climb. **Tower Fall,** named by the men of the 1870 expedition, is best seen from the observation platform. Along the canyon walls, one of the most interesting rock formations of basalt, a dark lava, looks as though it had been pressed into columns.

**Side Roads.** Take a pleasant detour off the main loop by traveling a secondary road. The **Virginia Cascade Drive,** between Norris and Canyon, provides a spectacular waterfall view. **Fountain Flats Drive,** from Madison Junction to Old Faithful, offers a dramatic view of Midway Geyser Basin and Grand Prismatic Spring.

**Naturalist Programs.** Plan your trip to include campfire programs, which are given each evening during the summer at the main areas. There is no television or commercial movie theater in the park, but these illustrated programs by park naturalists are much better, dealing with the wonders you came to enjoy.

**Field seminars** of one to several days are conducted each summer by the nonprofit Yellowstone Institute, combining scientific study, nature appreciation, and recreation. Subjects include fire ecology, wildlife, wildflowers, photography, and backpacking. The Institute also offers a series of courses in the winter of four and five days on winter camping, photography, and ecology, with field travel on skis (for information, write Yellowstone Institute, Box 117, Yellowstone National Park, WY 81290; 307/344-2294).

Don't miss the **National Park Ranger Museum,** commemorating National Park Service employees who have maintained, interpreted, and protected the parks over the years. Dedicated in 1991 on the 75th anniversary of the service, the museum houses exhibits tracing the colorful history of park rangers and other employees. It is located in the rustic Norris Soldier Station, built in 1908 as shelter for U.S. Army troops who first protected the park, before establishment of the park service in 1916.

**Hiking.** Yellowstone has more than 1,000 miles of well-marked, safe, backcountry trails. Some of the finest are explored on rewarding naturalist-conducted hikes. If you have but two hours to spend, try the easy **Storm Point Walk,** any morning from Fishing Bridge, to observe birds and plants along the shore of Yellowstone Lake. The **Clear Lake Walk,** afternoons from the Grand Canyon, explores the life of forest and meadow on the way to picturesque Clear Lake, a leisurely introduction to the wild country. If you're interested in seeing mudpots off the beaten path, join the three-hour hike to Pocket Basin, which leaves three mornings a week from Midway Geyser Basin.

An excellent, not-too-strenuous, all-day hike of 7.2 miles round-trip leads through forest and flowering alpine meadows on the slopes of Mount Washburn to the snowy 10,243-foot summit, an adventure capped by the breathtaking view of the whole park from the lookout tower. This trip is held three

mornings weekly from Canyon Village as soon after July 1 as snow conditions permit. A rewarding, but rigorous, naturalist hike leaves three times weekly from Lamar River Bridge, on the northeast entrance road, to **Specimen Ridge,** the setting of the many-layered fossil forest. The **Avalanche Peak Hike** takes you above the timberline to lofty summits; it leaves Fishing Bridge four times weekly, beginning July 1, or as soon as snow conditions permit.

**Backpacking.** Trails open the way to hot springs, choice fishing streams and wildlife summering in the high country. From the Bechler Ranger Station, in the southwest corner of the park (reached by car from Ashton, Idaho), the **Bechler Trail** leads past one waterfall after another. Sandhill cranes, rare trumpeter swans, ducks, and shore birds find an ideal home in meadows and swamps. Diagonally across the park, **Hellroaring Creek Trail** starts three miles west of the Tower Fall Ranger Station, leading down along Elk Creek and across the Yellowstone River on a high, narrow suspension bridge. Deer, elk, and moose are commonly seen here. Fishermen consider this a choice area. Careful study of a U.S. Geological Survey topographic map and a talk with a ranger will reveal the wide variety of trips to appeal to your own interest. Notify the ranger of your backcountry itinerary when you obtain a permit. All areas require permits for backcountry use. Four hundred backcountry campsites and 600 miles of trails struck by fire were to be spruced up as part of a two-year rebuilding program begun in 1989.

**Riding.** You can take good one-day guided trips from Mammoth Hot Springs, Canyon and Roosevelt Lodge near Tower Junction. Top outfitters are conveniently located around the park in Montana, Idaho, and Wyoming; they can arrange trips that last a week or a whole summer, during which you never cross a motor road or retrace your own tracks.

**Boating and Fishing.** For good fishing and nature enjoyment, take a trip to the South Arm or the Southeast Arm of Yellowstone Lake, where no roads reach and no power boats are permitted, but where a series of camps lines the shore. Though canoes are not rented, you can hire a good rowboat. Gear, equipment, and a boat can be hauled or towed by boat taxi from Bridge Bay to (and from) Plover Point, the gateway to the South Arm. Deep in the Southeast Arm, the Molly Islands are nesting grounds for white pelican, gull, cormorant, and tern. Around Peale Island in the South Arm, the trout fishing is celebrated. Abundant moose may be observed—from a safe distance—munching aquatic plants.

Another outstanding experience is the trip from **Lewis Lake** to **Shoshone Lake,** 7 miles in length but well worth the effort (average time about three hours), especially for backcountry camping. Travel here is restricted to hand-propelled craft. Shoshone, a sanctuary for animal and bird life, abounds in fish, with a geyser basin at the southwest corner. Canoeists and rowboaters must bear in mind that Yellowstone waters are icy cold, and that sudden winds can whip up a violent surf within minutes. Craft 16 feet or less in length and all canoes are well advised to stay within ¼ mile of shore. A boat permit is required for all boats used on park waters. Boats longer than 40 feet are not allowed in the park.

Fishing and Yellowstone are synonymous, though the best waters are in the backcountry. Heart, Grebe, and Shoshone lakes are recommended for combined hiking, camping, and fishing trips. Firehole River is a choice dry-fly trout stream, due to abundant aquatic insect life and the tempering influence of warm springs. Consider engaging a guide at one of the popular tackle shops near the park. You are required to obtain a fishing permit (free) to show you understand the regulations. Opening dates and catch limits vary throughout the park. "Fishing-for-fun" is encouraged.

To maintain native species despite a steady increase in fishing, many rivers and streams within park boundaries are on "catch-and-release" regulations. Fishing is no longer allowed on the famous Fishing Bridge near the outlet of Yellowstone Lake. Instead, fish-viewing—of trout coming to spawn on nearby gravel beds—has become popular.

**Photography.** Use fast shutter speed to

photograph geysers. Hot pools are best on warm days, when steam does not obscure the subjects. Clean your camera lens with a soft, lintless cloth after leaving each area, since silica residues stick to the surface once they dry.

**Birdwatching.** Yellowstone's checklist is a long one. The trumpeter swan, the park's largest bird (rescued from near extinction), stretches snow-white wings seven feet and squawks its low-pitched "beep" while gliding gracefully over streams, such as the Madison River, in search of food. Yellowstone Lake and its islands provide breeding grounds for the white pelican, gulls, double-crested cormorants, and terns.

**ACCOMMODATIONS.** Accommodations are extensive along the Grand Loop in the park. Many date from an earlier day and earlier modes of travel. They are operated today as a concession by TW Services, Inc., Yellowstone National Park, Wyoming 82190. For reservations call 307/344-7311. Lodgings are also available outside the park at Cooke City, Gardiner, and West Yellowstone, Montana; along US 191, the Island Park section of Idaho; and Cody and Jackson, Wyoming. Some visitors use facilities in Grand Teton for touring both parks.

Accommodations in the park come in 11 different classifications, including 1,200 cabins ranging from stylish deluxe "Western" to basic old-style "Frontier." These are spread over the following locations:

**Mammoth Motor Inn,** at the North Entrance. Rooms with bath, rooms without bath, cabins with bath, and cabins without bath. L to M.

**Roosevelt Lodge,** in the Tower Falls area. Cabins with bath, family cabins without bath, Rough Rider cabins (wood heat, showers nearby, bring your own towel), and rustic shelters (wood heat, showers nearby, bring your own towel and bedding). L.

**Lake Yellowstone Hotel/Cabins.** Oldest hotel in the park (1891), a showpiece in its day, renovated and restored in 1989. Summer reservations a must. Cabins with bath and family cabins without bath. M to H.

**Lake Lodge Cabins.** Modern cabins with bath and standard cabins with bath. L to M.

**Old Faithful Inn,** built early in the century, one of the first and finest examples of "appropriate architecture" with use of native materials; refurbished in 1993. A variety of room types. M to H.

**Old Faithful Lodge.** Cabins with bath, family cabins without bath, budget cabins with showers nearby, and budget shelters (showers nearby and bring your own towel and bedding). L.

**Old Faithful Snowlodge.** Cabins with bath, family cabins without bath, budget cabins with showers nearby, and budget shelters (showers nearby and bring your own towel and bedding). L.

**Canyon Village,** near the Grand Canyon of the Yellowstone River, a motel-type facility. A variety of rooms. M.

**Grant Village,** the newest facility, nearest to the South Entrance. Newest, modern rooms. M.

**CAMPING.** Consider staying in smaller campsites in or outside the park. During the summer peak, you may expect to find major campgrounds filled to capacity. Before leaving home, check Mistix for site reservations at Bridge Bay, initiated on a trial basis. Ask a ranger for suggestions about less crowded sites. Trailers are permitted, but there are no electrical or plumbing hookups. Scenic Forest Service campgrounds around the park perimeter include **Snake River,** near the south entrance; **Pahaska** and **Three Mile,** east entrance; **Chief Joseph** and **Colter,** near Cooke City; and **Bakers Hole** and **South Fork,** west entrance.

**SEASONS.** Lodgings and stores gradually start to open in May; all are in business from about June 20 to mid-September; some remain open through October, and two facilities are open in winter. Accommodations are always available in nearby communities. The northern portion of the park is open all year through the Gardiner entrance.

Flowers are in full bloom in the lowlands

around Mammoth Hot Springs in late May, when much of the park is still snowbound. Flowers appear on Mount Washburn in mid-July. The best periods to see animals and birds are May through June and September through October. In summer, animals spread over the high country range, while some birds move north and others become secretive around their nests. In autumn, snows on high ridges nudge animals to sites nearer the roads, and birds start moving south. The most memorable hour of any September visit involves the sound (and sometimes sight) of bull elk bugling their challenge. Flies and mosquitos can be troublesome in June. Summer temperatures average in the 70s, though nights are cool, with temperatures dropping to the 30s before sunrise. September is frequently as pleasant, though a little cooler.

Winter is a newly popular visitor season. The road from Gardiner at the north entrance through Mammoth Hot Springs to Cooke City at the northeast is open all winter, affording an excellent opportunity to see wildlife. Private snowmobiles are restricted to unplowed roads in the park. Snowcoaches leave from the west entrance, from Mammoth and from Flagg Ranch on the south side of the park, to Old Faithful, where winter accommodations are available. Old Faithful Visitor Center is the starting point of ski and snowshoe treks and of naturalist-led hikes around Geyser Hill Loop. All unplowed roads and trails are open to cross-country skiing and snowshoeing. Mammoth also remains open all year.

**NEARBY.** Due east through Sylvan Pass, the Buffalo Bill Highway (US 14/20) leads through **Shoshone National Forest,** the country's oldest forest reserve, a scenic region of lakes, glaciers, and camping areas, to Cody, location of the outstanding **Whitney Gallery of Western Art.** Northeast, through Silvergate and Cooke City, the Beartooth Highway (US 212) winds around snow-clad Granite Peak, the highest point in Montana (12,850 feet), and through Red Lodge to spectacular Beartooth Pass in **Custer National Forest** en route to Billings. **Madison River Canyon Earthquake Area,** north of West Yellowstone, scene of the 1959 earthquake, is interpreted in displays and by personnel of the **Gallatin National Forest.** South of West Yellowstone, the **Island Park** region of **Targhee National Forest** in Idaho offers streams and reservoirs for boating and fishing. Due south of Yellowstone lie the mighty **Grand Tetons,** a worthy companion park to Yellowstone.

**RECOMMENDED READING.** *Yellowstone Place Names,* by Lee Whittlesey; *The Yellowstone Story,* by Aubrey L. Haines; and *Fascinating Facts about Old Faithful and Other Hot Springs,* by Susan Scofield.

**FOR FURTHER INFORMATION.** Write to Yellowstone Library and Museum Association, Yellowstone National Park, WY 82190, for its complete literature list. 307/344-7381.

# YOSEMITE NATIONAL PARK

## CALIFORNIA

ESTABLISHED 1890

THE idea that in 1990 Yosemite National Park turned 100 years old makes me think of it as history. Even though they are designed to preserve nature, national parks embody history as well, perhaps none more so than Yosemite. Whenever I come to the park, I picture it as it once was, and the people who walked the trails before me.

Indians dwelled and traveled through the Yosemite country, giving many of the places names we use today. They, alas, were doomed by the gold rush that began in 1849. The Mariposa Battalion, dispatched by the governor of California in 1851, chased the Indians from Yosemite Valley, and subsequently spread the word of marvels to be seen: massive El Capitan, Half Dome, Bridalveil Falls, Yosemite Falls, the Merced River flowing through meadows and pines, and giant sequoias in the Mariposa Grove of Big Trees. Horace Greeley visited in 1859, and proclaimed, "I know of no single wonder of Nature on earth which can claim a superiority over the Yosemite."

Presently, the valley was well established as a tourist attraction, with trails and hotels. The concerns of a thoughtful few led Congress in 1864 to turn Yosemite Valley over to the state of California "to be held inalienable for all time," not the entire park as we know it now, but only the valley and the Mariposa Big Tree Grove. Frederick Law Olmsted, a pioneer of park principles, saw preservation of natural scenes as beneficial to the human spirit. So did John Muir, who made his first trip to Yosemite in 1868, the start of his 40 years of adventure, exploring, interpreting, and defending the country. He launched the campaign that led to the establishment of Yosemite as a national park.

I think of Muir while hiking and camping in Yosemite. He is the guide who is always there with his words illuminating the surrounding natural treasures. I listen to what he called "the most songful streams in the world"; and rejoice at the sight of "the noblest forests, the loftiest granite domes, the deepest ice-sculptured canyons, and snowy mountains soaring into the sky." The towering waterfalls sound at close range like roaring volcanoes, but from a distance appear like strands of silver. The granite spires and domes rising from the floor

of Yosemite Valley are softened by subtle shadows and the conifers growing beneath them. The giant sequoias are impressive as towering monarchs.

Few areas of this size (761,170 acres) have a wider variety of native plants and animals. From the warm foothills, at 2,000 feet above sea level, to the windy summit of 13,114-foot Mount Lyell, five of the seven continental life zones are represented. Between these two limits, bear, deer, and about 75 other species of mammals make their homes. Observers have noted about 220 kinds of birds, 25 kinds of reptiles, and nine kinds of amphibians. There are more than 1,200 species of flowering plants and many species of trees, including magnificent stands of pine and fir and enormous incense-cedars.

The natural history of Yosemite spans many millions of years, starting from the ancient age when a warm, shallow sea spread across what is now the Sierra Nevada and Great Valley of California. The first of at least three glaciers extended down the Merced River canyon as far as El Portal, while the last left a moraine of rock debris damming the Merced back into Yosemite Valley. Sediments that subsequently filled the lake form the level valley floor of today.

Muir studied the glaciers and proved their influence in shaping Yosemite. In 1892, he organized the Sierra Club to aid in the effort to secure federal administration of the entire Yosemite region. In 1905, California ceded the Valley and the Grove back to the federal government.

In 1903 President Theodore Roosevelt spent three days in the park with Muir. The first night they bedded down in fir boughs among giant trunks of the sequoias, listening to the hermit thrush and the waterfalls tumbling down the sheer cliffs. "It was like lying in a great solemn cathedral," wrote the president, "far vaster and more beautiful than any built by the hand of man."

New history is being written at Yosemite. In recent years visitation has risen sharply, especially to Yosemite Valley. Some steps have been taken to protect and restore the setting—including conversion of roads to one-way traffic, expansion of shuttle service, removal of a golf course—and more are likely.

Nature has a way of writing its own history. In 1990 major fires turned portions of the park inside the west boundary (along Big Oak Flat Road and Wawona Road) into a moonscape, but ecological regeneration soon began with wildflower regrowth, leading to new chapters in natural history.

## THE PRACTICAL GUIDE

**BACKGROUND.** Though some people mistakenly regard Yosemite Valley as the whole park, it actually occupies only 7 of the total 1,189 square miles. Do your best to visit the valley before Memorial Day or after Labor Day.

**ACCESS.** The park has five entrances. Four are open all year: Arch Rock Entrance (67 miles from Merced via El Portal); South Entrance 59 miles from Fresno), connecting with Wawona Road; Hetch Hetchy Entrance accessing the northwest region of the park; and North Entrance on Big Oak Flat Road (71 miles from Oakdale). The Tioga Road, which offers the only entrance from the east via Tioga Pass, traverses the park from the high country to a junction with Big Oak Flat Road, but is open only from about Memorial Day weekend to early November. For a different approach from the San Francisco Bay area, take State Highway 120 through the San Joaquin Valley, including Groveland, historic, colorful gold mining town about one hour from Yosemite valley.

Airlines, AMTRAK, and bus lines from Los Angeles and San Francisco serve Merced and Fresno, where rental cars are available. California Yosemite Tours offers daily bus service—by reservation only—between Merced AMTRAK Station and Yosemite Lodge; also between Fresno Air Terminal and Yosemite Valley. The Yosemite Transportation System (a unit of Yosemite Park and Curry Co.) operates daily during summer from both cities (and from Merced all year) to Yosemite Valley; the company also runs bus service from Lee Vining via Tioga Pass in summer. In the park, free shuttle buses travel between lodgings, campgrounds, and visitor facilities in Yosemite Valley. The buses usually run from 9 A.M. to 10 P.M., though frequency varies from season to season. Bicycles can be rented in Yosemite Valley.

**VISITOR CENTER.** Yosemite Valley Visitor Center has outstanding exhibits about the valley. During summer, demonstrations of Indian basketry and cooking are presented outdoors. Naturalists provide information on more than 750 miles of trails and answer a thousand questions a day about wildflowers in bloom and guided hikes, and still enjoy their work.

The **Indian Cultural Museum,** in the building west of the Visitor Center, is a recent major addition to the Yosemite scene. The collections include rare, unique objects loaned from museums throughout the country. They depict the cultural history of the Miwok and Paiute people from early times to the present.

**ACTIVITIES.** A focal point of the **naturalist program,** which began in 1920, is the Happy Isles Nature Center at the upper end of Yosemite Valley, with exhibits on plants and animals. Here also children 8 to 12 are invited to participate in the unique summer Junior Rangers Program. Interpretive facilities vary throughout the park. At Wawona the Pioneer Yosemite History Center displays old structures and conveyances associated with the early days of the area. Illustrated evening naturalist programs are conducted year-round in Yosemite Valley and during the summer campfire talks are offered at many of the campgrounds. Yosemite Field Seminars offers courses such as Family Backpack, Bird Banding, and Photographing Wildflowers of Yosemite; all involve some hiking but are not endurance trips. Write Box 230, El Portal, CA 95318. For more educational opportunities, and courses for school groups, write Box 487, Yosemite National Park, CA 95389.

**Sightseeing. Yosemite Valley.** The mile-wide valley is flanked with granite walls, domes, and peaks rising as high as 4,892 feet, and lovely waterfalls streaming down to feed the Merced River. Instead of driving, try the shuttle bus system that moves visitors on a loop in the eastern half of the valley—you'll enjoy the park more, ease congestion, and help lessen pollution. At the head of the valley from the west, the massive buttress of **El Capitan,** a geological wonder, has scarcely a fracture in its entire perpendicular wall. Other imposing formations are the **Three Brothers** (named for sons of Chief Tenaya, whose tribe lived in the mountains), **Sentinel Rock, Cathedral Spires,** and, at the end of the valley, mighty **Half Dome.** The famed waterfalls include **Upper Yosemite Fall,** dropping 1,430 feet, a height equal to nine Niagaras, and **Lower Yosemite Fall,** immediately below, dropping another 320 feet, as well as celebrated **Bridalveil, Ribbon, Vernal, Nevada,** and **Illilouette.**

From the stone lookout at **Glacier Point,** get a panoramic view from the crest of the Sierra Nevada down into Yosemite Valley. Hiking trails start here, including Four Mile Trail, leading to the valley 3,254 feet below.

Yosemite has three groves of giant sequoias (*Sequoiadendron giganteum*), a relative of the coastal redwood, *Sequoia sempervirens*. The largest stand in the park, the **Mariposa Grove** near the South Entrance, contains 200 trees exceeding 10 feet in diameter, and 500 mature sequoias, overall. The oldest, the Grizzly Giant, is estimated to be near 3,000 years of age and stands 209 feet tall. Park in a designated area at the edge of the Mariposa Grove and ride through Muir's "Columns of Heaven" on an open-air shuttle tram, subject to modest fee. Trams operate from mid-May until mid-October. Better yet, combine a walking and riding tour through the grove. The **Tuolumne Grove,** a group of 25 fine specimens, covers about 20 acres east of the Big Oak Flat entrance. Four miles south, the **Merced Grove** contains 20 large trees. In this same region is the **"Rockefeller Tract,"** one of the finest stands of sugar pine in the world, whose purchase price was contributed by John D. Rockefeller, Jr.

**Tuolumne Meadows** is the park's major wilderness threshold, an ideal camping place and starting point for fishing, hiking, and climbing trips across meadows flecked with wildflowers, tumbling streams, and along blue lakes in the shadow of glacial cliffs. It is the only one of the six permanent trail camps accessible by automobile. From this favorite region of John Muir, the **John Muir Trail** starts at Happy Isles, traverses Tuolumne, then winds its spectacular way along the Sierra Crest to Mount Whitney, 188 miles southeast, in Sequoia National Park.

Trips may be taken on foot or horseback to aptly named Waterwheel Falls, as well as to Glen Aulin, Muir Gorge, Tenaya Lake, and Soda Springs. During the summer months the park conducts a naturalist program, including nature walks and hikes.

**High Sierra by Muleback.** Saddle trips of six days start twice a week from Tuolumne Meadows, making a loop into the mountains. Overnight stops are made at the permanent trail camps, each set in an area of scenic beauty 7 to 10 miles apart. For instance, **Glen Aulin** is located at the foot of the White Cascade of the Tuolumne River, in the outer fringe of one of the finest stands of graceful mountain hemlock. Nearby is the spectacular series of falls made by the river in its drop to the Grand Canyon of the Tuolumne. **Merced Lake Camp,** at the head of one of the largest lakes bordering the western Sierra slopes, lies 13 miles from Yosemite Valley over a thrilling stretch of trail. The camps provide hot

showers, dormitory-style tent accommodations, and wholesome food served family style. Mules are really not stubborn, just sure-footed and mountain-wise. Besides the group trips, you can arrange for a guided saddle-horse-pack trip, or hire a pack burro to haul your gear while you hike. For information, write Yosemite Park and Curry Company, 5410 E. Home St., Fresno, CA 93727.

**Hiking the Loop.** Check at a ranger station. Use of the park's backcountry is regulated year-round with a limit of 4,000 visitors in the area at any one time. Permits are required for overnight backcountry use; reservations for backcountry camping are accepted from February through May; otherwise, permits are issued on a first-come, first-served basis. Tuolumne Meadows trailheads fill up most summer weekends.

**Fishing and Boating.** The Tuolumne and Merced Rivers, and tributary streams and lakes, all remarkably clear, offer many possibilities for dry fly and a variety of lures. A California fishing license with stamps is required. Boats (without motors) are permitted on only a few lakes.

**ACCOMMODATIONS.** Yosemite Park & Curry Co., the park concessioner, maintains varied accommodations and services throughout Yosemite. The company address, Yosemite National Park, CA 95389. The reservations number is 209/252-4848. Lodgings include the following:

**Ahwahnee Hotel.** The most celebrated (and luxurious) lodging in the park is a work of art of another day that has never gone out of style. Dinner reservations advisable year-round; dress code for dinner. Sunday brunch is a special treat. H.

**Yosemite Lodge.** Among the pines near the floor of Yosemite Falls; ranges from lodge rooms with bath to family rooms, cabins with bath and cabins without bath. Ask for one of the older units. They're attractive, with character, cost less. M to H.

**Wawona Hotel.** The oldest hotel in continuous service in the National Park system lies 4 miles inside the South Entrance. The rambling gingerbread wooden structures date from

1879. Tennis, 9-hole golf, and saddle trips. M.

**Curry Village.** Also a varied complex; hotel rooms, cabins with bath, cabins without bath, and more than 400 tent cabins. L to M.

**Curry Housekeeping Camp.** Along the Merced River, 300 tent cabins are rented unfurnished except for cots and stove. Bring or rent as much gear as needed. L.

**Tuolumne Meadows and White Wolf Lodges.** Cabins with bath and tent cabins offer uncrowded, pleasant experiences off the beaten path. L.

A number of lodges are nearby outside the park:

**Evergreen Lodge,** Evergreen Rd. Rustic cabins near the Hetch Hetchy entrance. Good restaurant. 209/379-2606. M.

**Yosemite Motels,** Box 1989, Mariposa, CA 95338. This company will make reservations for you at a number of motels and lodges in the communities outside the park. 209/742-7106 or in California 800/321-5261.

**CAMPING.** The 330-site **Tuolumne Meadows Campground** is the largest, most popular of eight Tioga Road campgrounds, a good base for hikes to 13,000-foot Mount Lyell. Half of the Tuolumne campground is on the Mistix system, and half is held aside for same-day arrivals—which means get there early. Narrow roads lead to more secluded campgrounds, including **Tamarack Flat** and **Yosemite Creek.** Check into the new backpackers' camp near O'Shaughnessy Dam. Two national forest campgrounds on Evergreen Road offer a small number of first-come sites; they fill quickly in summer but often have midweek vacancies in late spring and early fall. For information and campground data, call 209/372-0200. For campsite reservations, call 1-800/365-2267. Or write Mistix, Box 85705, San Diego, California 92186-5705.

**SEASONS.** Yosemite Lodge and Curry Villages are open all year. The Ahwahnee closes only briefly in late autumn. The Wawona Hotel runs mid-May to mid-October. Tuolumne Meadows Lodge and White Wolf Lodge close in early September. Two campgrounds in Yosemite Valley and one at Wawona are open all year, but others in the park open during summer only. Usually in May and early June, when snows are melting, the great falls are at their thunderous best; mariposa lilies and other wildflowers spread carpets of color across the lower meadows. By July, the upper meadows are bright with flowers and the short High Sierra season begins; by late summer, many of the falls practically disappear. To many, autumn is the finest time to see Yosemite Valley, particularly for the vista from Glacier Point, overlooking the coloring of oaks, willows, and cottonwoods. By the end of October, Big Oak Flat and Wawona roads are often in riotous display. In winter the high passes are snowed in, but the towering granite walls shelter the valley. Winter sports facilities include a large outdoor skating rink near Curry Village, ski slopes and school at Badger Pass, 20 miles away, and ski touring trails to the hut at Ostrander Lake. Join a ranger on a daily two-hour snowshoe walk or a five-hour Saturday cross-country ski tour (equipment available). Yosemite Mountaineering School offers daily classes in cross-country skiing and guided trips of two and three days.

**NEARBY.** An interesting approach to the park from the northwest is via California 49 and 120, through the **Mother Lode Country** and old gold mining communities like Amador City, Angels Camp, and Columbia. On the east side of the park, near Lee Vining, **Mono Lake** at 6,400 feet elevation harbors a protected gull rookery, with boat launching and campsites on the shore. **Devils Postpile National Monument,** in a magnificent lake and forest country southeast of the park, features an extraordinary formation of colored basalt columns. Flanking the park are four national forests: **Stanislaus,** on the west and northwest; **Toiyabe,** on the northeast; **Inyo,** on the east; and **Sierra,** on the south, all with fishing, swimming and camping.

**RECOMMENDED READING.** *Yosemite—The Embattled Wilderness,* by Alfred Runte.

**FOR FURTHER INFORMATION.** Write Superintendent, Box 577, Yosemite National Park, CA 95389. 209/372-0200.

M-9-ZM-896-S

**YOSEMITE
NATIONAL PARK
CALIFORNIA**

0  1  2  3      5                    10
ONE INCH EQUALS APPROXIMATELY 8.4 MILES

# ZION NATIONAL PARK

## UTAH

### ESTABLISHED 1919

IT TOOK me a little more than half a day to cover the five-mile round-trip hike from the trailhead on Zion Canyon Road to Angels Landing; parts of it were fairly tough going. It's almost 1,500 feet uphill, and the final stretch involves holding on to handrails along a steep, narrow path, but the time and energy were more than worth it. Every step of the way opened a new vista of the "Land of the Rainbow Canyons" in southern Utah. I traced the vertical walls of red sandstone as they gradually merged upward into white, while beneath them shales of purple, pink, orange, and yellow revealed what surely must be some of the most brilliantly colored rock in the world.

Zion's rich concentration of bold, multicolored features appeals to everyone—the color photographer, landscape artist, geologist (amateur or professional), trail rider, and hiker, with a special challenge awaiting the tested backcountry explorer in the aptly named "Narrows" of the Virgin River.

Through this strange land of high plateaus, deep canyons, and broad mesas, the Virgin River has cut its valley. The rock reveals that at times Zion was covered with water, oceans moving in and out as the region continued to rise, then subside. At other times broad, raging rivers traversed its surface. Most rock was laid as gravel, sand, mud, and limy ooze, which then consolidated and cemented. Across its six geologic epochs were periods of deserts with moving sand dunes, and of tropical lowlands with cycad and tree-fern forests. Embedded in the rock are fossilized seashells, fish, trees, and the bones and tracks of land animals. Thus it is known that immense reptiles and dinosaurs once wallowed in marshes and bayous in this area.

One of the most surprising discoveries was made in 1976 in a small park spring: a relict, or remnant, population of minute snails, believed to have survived for 10 to 15 million years. Totalling 10,000 to 15,000 in number, these snails likely comprise a distinctive species, found nowhere else on earth.

Zion Canyon, central feature of the 147,035-acre park, bespeaks the middle, or Mesozoic, period of geological history. It begins where the ancient record of the Grand Canyon leaves off, and it ends where the later history of Bryce Canyon begins. In these three parks, one can journey through a thousand million years of time, unfolding the story of this continent from one logical sequence to the next. Geologic forces, the water, wind, and ice—even the plants and animals—that shaped this narrow canyon in the Markagunt Plateau are still at play.

During spring runoff and after a sudden summer storm, the Virgin River, an important erosion force, may become a raging torrent, depositing debris at every turn—logs, rock, and other material from many miles distant.

Zion's "hanging gardens" in the cliffs are beautiful during spring and summer, with a cover of columbine, shooting-star, and cardinal flowers. The park's most interesting blossom, however, the sacred datura, grows on the canyon floor, reaching heights of two feet and more; its large, white, trumpet-shaped flowers open in the evening and wilt beneath the morning sun's rays.

In contrast to the desert vegetation and water-loving plants crowding the river bottoms are the deep-green forests of pine, Douglas fir, and white fir along the cool upper ledges and at the rim of the plateau. It takes time to see and appreciate the diverse parts that shape the whole landscape.

Human history in Zion, traced through crumbling ruins, reaches back to the Basketmakers, the earliest inhabitants of the Southwest, followed by the Pueblos, followed by the Paiutes, a peaceful people who claimed this region when the Spaniards arrived at the time of the American Revolution. It was the Mormons of the succeeding century who named it Zion, interpreted as the "heavenly city of God." They gave religious names to natural temples in the canyon, and when I reached the perch of Angels Landing, I felt they had named it well.

## THE PRACTICAL GUIDE

**BACKGROUND.** Many scenic attractions of Zion Canyon are visible from the roadway, but allow at least two days, even more if you want to take wonderful trips into the backcountry on foot or horseback.

**Zion–Mt. Carmel Highway,** the approach from US 89 and the east gate (elevation 5,725 feet), ranks among the spectacular drives of the country. In descending 11 miles and 1,800 feet from the entrance, the highway passes through mile-long Zion Tunnel, where window-like galleries gouged in the rock enable travelers to view the panorama of the canyon and scenic wonders like East Temple and the Great Arch. Then it zigzags over six huge switchbacks, dropping 800 feet in less than 4 miles. (Stopping is prohibited for safety reasons.) The **Kolob Canyons Road** is a 5.2-mile spur leading into the northeast corner of the park from 1-15.

**VISITOR CENTERS.** The **South Visitor Center**, an attractive, low building near the south entrance station on Utah 9, is an important stop. Besides observing the museum displays, check the schedule of naturalist-guided walks conducted several times each day during the summer. Illustrated evening programs are presented by naturalists nightly at park campgrounds and at Zion Lodge. Families should ask about the junior ranger program, which invites youngsters age 6 to 12 to learn about the park and to earn a Zion shoulder patch. **Kolob Canyons Visitor Center** is an excellent stop for local and regional information on the Grand Circle of southwest national parks, monuments, and recreation areas. It is conveniently located at the 1-15 exit into the northwest section of the park and is open daily all year.

**TOURS.** From May to October, Color Country Tours provides bus service from Cedar City and from St. George three times weekly. Zion Lodge provides one-hour narrated tram rides along the scenic drive. Horseback trips are conducted by the concessioner every day during the summer travel season from Zion Lodge on the Sand Bench Trail.

**ACTIVITIES. Sightseeing. Zion Canyon Scenic Drive,** a round trip of 12 miles, provides a constantly changing vista of varicolored cliffs rising above the valley floor. The dominant feature, beyond Twin Brothers, Mountain of the Sun, and Red Arch, is the towering 2,400-foot monolith called **Great White Throne**. The throne ranges in color from deep red at the base up through pale pink and gray to white at the top. North of the throne, the road and river make a wide swing past a splintered crimson formation called the Organ, with Angels Landing rising 1,500 feet behind it. As the canyon steadily narrows, the roadway reaches its end at the **Temple of Sinawava**, a huge natural amphitheater, with two large stone pillars, The Altar and The Pulpit, in the center.

**Weeping Rock Trail** is one of three easy, self-guiding nature trails. It takes only 45 minutes from the parking area at the foot of Cable Mountain, climbing gradually to the Weeping Rock, with a display of wildflowers along the way. The abundant vegetation is due to water-resistant qualities in the shale; downward percolation from the highlands is interrupted, so the water streams down the rock face and seemingly "weeps." Another self-guiding trail, **Canyon Overlook**, begins at the upper end of Zion Tunnel, following the rock ledges above Pine Creek Canyon through pinyon pine, juniper, yucca, and cactus to a point directly above the Great Arch.

**Gateway to the Narrows Trail** is the third

easy, popular trip (of two hours or less) starting from the Temple of Sinawava and following the Virgin River up the narrow canyon to a point where there is no longer room for both river and trail—only a few feet separate walls one-quarter mile high. This is a naturalist-guided walk, but you may take it on your own. The high cliffs, springs, and seeps offer a cool, moist environment for a large variety of plants and animals. Watch for mule deer along the trail, and for tracks of skunk, bobcat, gray fox, and ringtail. You may see the "blue-bellied lizard" and a few choice snakes, including the rare, beautiful, regal ringneck. Well-maintained trails of approximately 55 miles give access to other impressive features. Going to **Angels Landing** requires a fairly strenuous 5-mile round trip to the top, but you'll be rewarded with beautiful views of the canyon.

**Kolob Canyons Road** (or Taylor Creek Road) leads to the northwest section of the park near Kanarraville, with overlooks commanding spectacular views. It contains the red sandstone canyons of the Kolob, a deeper red than in Zion Canyon itself. Sheer walls form box canyons 1,500 feet deep. Hurricane Fault represents a displacement of rock caused by splitting of the earth's crust. Layers from the time of the Kaibab formation are clearly exposed by the fault.

**Backcountry Trails**. Among several routes, a choice, accessible one is the **West Rim Trail,** 12.3 miles long, good for two days of backpacking. The West Rim country, formed of deep, beautiful canyons and high, forested plateaus, is rich in wildlife, with a few cougars and such birds as swallows, nuthatches, bluebirds, and warblers. Hawks and golden eagles nest in the higher pinnacles. **LaVerkin Creek Trail** affords an opportunity to view the high, rugged wilderness at its best, with an excellent backpacking and horseback route and good campsites along LaVerkin Creek. The trail can be approached from Lee Pass on the west side, and a topographic map (available at the Visitor Centers) should be part of your equipment. An interesting side trip is **Kolob Arch**, 120 feet thick and 390 feet high, even higher

than the famed Rainbow Bridge. The Kolob Canyons constitute some of southern Utah's most scenic country. Routes starting on the headwaters of the Virgin River, north of the park, join the celebrated, unique **Narrows Trip**, which ends at the **Temple of Sinawava** in Zion Canyon. A three-day trip begins on Deep Creek in Dixie National Forest near Cedar Breaks National Monument. The most popular hike, 12 miles on the North Fork, starting from the vicinity of Chamberlain's Ranch, can be done in one day, but may be better in two. Much of the trip is negotiated by wading between sheer, sandstone walls. Sometimes the walls overhang the stream; at other times they widen into amphitheaters of sculptured cliffs where glens are carpeted with grass and wildflowers. Rocky bars and sandy banks in shoal areas provide campsites. Such was the way of travel of the Paiutes and the early explorers like Jedediah Smith, who named the river for a contemporary, Thomas Virgin. Weather conditions govern the trip season. It is dangerous in spring due to snow runoff from the mountains, and even more so during July and August when flash floods rise in the narrow gorge. The best months are June, September, and early October, but even then hiking parties should obtain a Narrows Permit and check for advice at the Visitor Centers. Permits are required for overnight backcountry use.

**Birdwatching**. Among almost 250 species, you are apt to see birds of the desert, like the roadrunner and spurred towhee, as they dart across canyon lowlands, or the western kingbird perching on a fence ready to pounce on insect prey. In the narrow, moist canyon of the Virgin River you can hear the shrill "cheep" of a canyon wren and catch sight of this lively bird flitting from rock to rock. Zion is known for southern birds at the northern limit of their range; these include the black hawk, gray vireo, and painted redstart. The Kolob Plateau is an excellent place to observe highland species during spring and summer.

**Photography** possibilities are unlimited with deep shadows and bright cliffs. Along with recording scenery, you can tell the story in pictures of Zion's intriguing geology. Start with the pattern of crossbedded deposits in Checkerboard Mesa near the east entrance. Shoot the East Rim trail for Navajo sandstone, the East Temple for Carmel limestone, the Chocolate Cliffs or Belted Cliffs of Moenkopi, ancient rock exposed to view—before long you'll find new meaning in photographs, and in your travels. During summer, midmorning is best to photograph Zion Canyon; midday is best in winter. Photography in the high country is best during morning and late afternoon.

**ACCOMMODATIONS.** In addition to a concession-operated lodge in the park, accommodations are available year-round at Springdale, just outside the south entrance.

**Zion Lodge,** c/o TW Services, Inc., 451 N. Main St., Cedar City, UT 84720. Motel, rustic cabins, and dining room with a view in the center of Zion Canyon (5 miles north of South park entrance). 801/586-7686. M.

**Flanigan's Inn and Restaurant,** Springdale, UT 84767. Shaded natural setting. Pool. 801/772-3244. L to M.

**Zion House Bed and Breakfast,** Springdale, UT 84767. Homey hospitality and home-cooked breakfast. 801/772-3281. M.

**CAMPING.** The park's two large campgrounds are the South and the Watchman, both just inside the South Entrance. Lava Point has a small campground with pit toilets and no water. All have 14-day limits.

**SEASONS.** The park is open all year, but accommodations are available only from early spring to late fall. The exact dates vary from year to year. Though winter is usually mild and snowfall is light in the canyon, the higher trails can become impassable. Colored cliffs stand out in contrast to snow-covered terraces and slopes. May is the time for violets, or-

chids, penstemons, and, in shady nooks, columbine and monkey flowers. Summers are hot (up to 100 degrees), except in the high country. Late summer is a blooming time, of asters, paintbrush, and cardinal flowers. September and October are excellent months to visit Zion, with clear skies, light crowds and mild climate.

**NEARBY.** The North Rim of the **Grand Canyon** lies 125 miles south, while **Bryce Canyon National Park** lies 89 miles northeast—a compact triumvirate of scenic and geological marvels. **Cedar Breaks National Monument**, 86 miles north on the Markagunt Plateau, contains a gigantic, multicolored natural amphitheater, the Pink Cliffs, a part of the Wasatch formation, at elevations as high as 10,700 feet in surrounding **Dixie National Forest**, Navajo Lake is a favored vacation spot with fishing, lodge, and choice campgrounds. **Strawberry Point**, southeast of the lake, affords panoramic views across the Zion Canyon country. **St. George**, just above the state line on the road to Lake Mead and Las Vegas, is the site of the first Mormon temple in Utah. Standing 175 feet high, it was built in 1877 of hand-quarried sandstone. In the center of town, the colonial-style winter home of Brigham Young contrasts with the rough pioneer dwellings of the period. At **Santa Clara,** 5 miles west of St. George, the 1862 house of Jacob Hamlin, Mormon scout and peacemaker among the Indians, still stands. Nearby **Snow Canyon State Park**, with its walls of red and yellow sandstone, has been the setting of numerous western films (and the hideout of early outlaws). Motel accommodations can be found in Springdale and nearby Cedar City, Glendale, Kanab, and St. George.

**FOR FURTHER INFORMATION.** Write Superintendent, Zion National Park, Springdale, UT 84767. 801/772-3256.

# ADDITIONAL NATIONAL PARK
# SERVICE AREAS

# IN AND AROUND WASHINGTON, D.C.

ALMOST ALL OF THE MAJOR MONUMENTS and shrines and nearly everything green in Washington, D.C., are administered as part of the National Park system. Activities and facilities range from concerts, nature walks and picnic areas, to jogging and bicycle trails, and countless scheduled events.

It's impossible to do it all in a weekend, or even in a week. I strongly advise starting with a ride on the concession-operated Tourmobile, which provides interpretive shuttle service to key sites in the heart of Washington, plus Arlington National Cemetery and Mount Vernon in Virginia. You can get on and off all you want at these locations without extra charge on the same day. You can also get guidance from Park Service personnel stationed at information kiosks in the monumental heart of the city.

Another helpful source: the information center in the Great Hall of the Smithsonian Institution at the heart of the Mall. Ask about fees and walking time from subway stops to Washington's attractions. The center is open 9 A.M. to 5:30 P.M. daily except Christmas.

Make a list of your own special points of interest. If this is your first visit, include the Jefferson and Lincoln memorials, Washington Monument, Vietnam Veterans Memorial, and the White House. Work with a map to conserve time and energy. If you've been here before, visit new points of interest, like the Vietnam Women's Memorial, dedicated in 1993; Korean War Veterans Memorial, scheduled for completion July 27, 1995; and Franklin Delano Roosevelt Memorial Park, scheduled for dedication in autumn, 1996. You'll do plenty of walking, so choose a few sitting activities, such as a boat trip on the Chesapeake & Ohio Canal or a concert at Wolf Trap Farm Park.

You'll get a new vista of the capital from the open-air observation level of the renovated Old Post Office Building, 12th and Pennsylvania N.W. Free tours are conducted to the clock tower. The Old Post Office is midway between the White House and the Capitol, with a variety of places to shop and eat. Other eating places worth mentioning are: the National Sculpture Garden; the National Gallery of Art; and cafeterias at the Capitol and most government buildings— some serve breakfast; for lunch, get in early.

More than 150 miles of bike path are administered by the National Capital Region. These include compacted gravel and asphalt trails, sidewalks, and side

*Thomas Jefferson National Memorial*

streets in the Mall area, East and West Potomac parks, the C & O towpath from Georgetown to Great Falls Park, Maryland, and the Virginia bikeway extending all the way to Mount Vernon.

A great deal has been done to make the parks and monuments accessible to physically disabled visitors. Sign language tours can be arranged at almost every National Park Service site, including Ford's Theatre and Frederick Douglass Home.

For daily schedules, special events, entry fees (where they apply) or further information on any of these areas, call Dial-a-Park (619-PARK) or National Capital Region (619-7222) or write National Capital Region, National Park Service, 1100 Ohio Drive, S.W., Washington, D.C. 20242.

## ARLINGTON HOUSE
### Virginia

Robert E. Lee married and lived here until he left for the Civil War. The house was occupied by Union troops, and in 1864 the surrounding estate was transformed into a cemetery. The stately mansion, now beautifully restored with original furnishings, faces the national capital as the frontispiece of Arlington National Cemetery, with the grave of John F. Kennedy on the knoll below. You can reach it by car via Memorial Bridge and park at Arlington Cemetery Visitor Center, but you don't really have to drive. Take the Tourmobile, which stops at the Visitor Center (a significant point of interest in itself). 703/557-3154.

## CATOCTIN MOUNTAIN PARK
### Maryland

This mountain retreat of 5,700 acres is near Thurmont, 65 miles north of Washington. Park Central, the main park road, begins at the Visitor Center off Maryland 77, winds through the park for 4.6 miles to its junction with the Foxville-Deerfield Road. Twenty-five miles of well-marked trails traverse the park, leading to outstanding views and natural features. The Owens Creek Campground is available from mid-April through October for family camping. Modern rest rooms, tables, and fireplaces are provided. Camping is limited to seven consecutive days and fourteen days per season; a nominal fee is charged. Due to the terrain, trailers more than 22 feet in length are not permitted. A full program of interpretive services, such as guided walks, talks, and campfire programs, is offered; a schedule is available at the Visitor Center, which houses a museum. The two camps you pass along Park Central Road—Greentop and Misty Mount—are now used primarily for Environmental Education. Greentop is available on spring and fall weekends to organized groups; Misty Mount, to the general public from May to the end of October. Camp David, the presidential retreat, is closed to the public. 301/663-9343.

## CHESAPEAKE AND OHIO CANAL NATIONAL HISTORICAL PARK
### District of Columbia–Maryland–West Virginia

Many canals were built in the age of westward movement, but this remains one of the longest and least altered. The canal was begun with enthusiasm in 1828, designed to link Georgetown, in the District of Columbia, with Pittsburgh, on the Ohio River. However, endless difficulty and adversity slowed things down so that by 1850 it extended only as far as Cumberland, in western Maryland, and by then the railroad obviously was becoming the dominant means of transportation. The canal lingered on until 1924, principally as a carrier of coal from Cumberland to the eastern market.

Had it not been for the care and concern of Justice William O. Douglas and other conservationists during the 1950s, the C & O Canal might have become a paved highway. Justice Douglas described the canal as a long stretch of quiet and peace "not yet marred by the roar of wheels and sound of horns." In 1977, Congress dedicated the park to him "in grateful recognition."

Mule-drawn barge trips travel three miles of the canal in 1½ hours. Interpreters in period dress describe daily barge life and perform music of the canal era. There are two barges from which to choose: the *Georgetown*, which leaves from 30th Street in the heart of Georgetown, and *Canal Clipper*, from the historic Great Falls Tavern, now a park museum, in Potomac, Maryland, about 15 miles northwest of Washington.

At its peak, during the 1870s, about 500 boats navigated the 185 miles from Georgetown to Cumberland, loaded with coal, flour, grains, and lumber. Each was pulled by two or three mules and raised and lowered through 75 locks along the way. All told, almost 500 structures have been left to represent the canal era.

The historic canal was placed under the National Park Service in 1938, then proclaimed a national monument in 1961; through congressional action the park was significantly enlarged in 1971 and given historical park status. In 1972 a hurricane caused severe damage. An extensive repair program was undertaken and now most is restored.

Along the towpath the National Park Service has installed a series of simple campsites, nicknamed "Hiker-Biker Overnighters," 10 miles apart, from Dam 3, opposite Harpers Ferry, to Cumberland. Antietam Creek Campground is the largest one, providing access to the towpath and to fishing (for bass, catfish, and sunfish) in the nearby Potomac.

**Attention, birdwatchers**. Mark early May as the time to see the famed spring eastern warbler migration from along the towpath. You'll see many other species, including cardinals, bluebirds, and wood ducks, even on the mule-drawn barge trip from Georgetown.

The Kiwanis Youth Hostel near Sandy Hook, Maryland, provides simple, inexpensive accommodations for American Youth Hostel members. Near Harpers Ferry, it is close to mile 58 on the Canal, where the Appalachian Trail crosses the Potomac River. 301/739-4200.

## CLARA BARTON NATIONAL HISTORIC SITE

### Maryland

Clara Barton, founder of the American National Red Cross (who lived from 1821 to 1912), built this large house in Glen Echo, Maryland, a suburb of Washington, D.C., in the 1890s. The 36 rooms and 38 large closets were designed to accommodate Red Cross workers and their emergency relief supplies. From 1897 to 1904 the house was national Red Cross headquarters. Miss Barton lived here her last twenty years. Reminders of her life and times, including her strong support of women's rights, are displayed throughout the house. 301/492-6246.

## FORD'S THEATRE NATIONAL HISTORIC SITE

### District of Columbia

Abraham Lincoln was fatally shot here by John Wilkes Booth on April 14, 1865. It has been authentically restored to its appearance of that period. Plays are presented usually from September through May. Some, but not all, are historic in nature. Prices are high for the average family, though children and groups are favored with special rates. The **Lincoln Museum** in the basement has reopened after a two-year renovation; it's open daily, and evenings to theater patrons. The **House Where Lincoln Died,** directly across the street, is restored to its original appearance. Here Secretary of War Stanton uttered his memorable words, "Now he belongs to the ages." 202/426-6924.

## FORT WASHINGTON PARK

### Maryland

The fort is across the Potomac River from Mount Vernon. This is an imposing bastion of another age. The first fort was built in 1809, designed by Pierre Charles L'Enfant (who laid out the city of Washington). It was destroyed by the British during the War of 1812, then subsequently rebuilt as an outer defense of the capital. Open 7:30 A.M. to dark. 301/292-2112.

## FREDERICK DOUGLASS HOME

### District of Columbia

The former slave who became a prominent statesman as well as America's leading African-American spokesman lived in this 14-room Victorian home, which he named "Cedar Hill," from 1877 until his death in 1895. This lovely home and its furnishings were saved through the years by organizations until they were added to the National Park system in 1962. The little one-room study he called the "Growlery" was reconstructed in 1981. Open 9 A.M. to 5 P.M. daily. 202/426-5960.

## GEORGE WASHINGTON MEMORIAL PARKWAY

### Virginia-Maryland

Landscaped with native plants, the 23-mile completed section of the parkway extends from the Capital Beltway (I-495) on the Virginia side of the Potomac River to the country's foremost mansion, George Washington's home at Mount Vernon. Since it opened, in 1932, the parkway has become a well-traveled route from the nation's capital to the shrine. Many walk or bicycle the paths along the Potomac, some fish, others watch birds. Picnic tables are popular.

The parkway includes important shrines and recreation areas. **Great Falls** offers spectacular views of the Potomac River gorge and falls on both sides of the river. On the Virginia side are picnic areas and remnants of an old canal started by George Washington; on the Maryland side, the old Great Falls Tavern, C & O Canal locks, and conducted walks during summer months.

At the U.S. Marine Corps War Memorial, popularly called the **Iwo Jima Memorial,** the American flag flies 24 hours a day; weekly sunset reviews are given by Marines during the summer. Nearby, the **Netherlands Carillon** represents an expression of appreciation from a small nation for help during World War II; carillon concerts are given Saturdays spring to fall, and on holidays. **Arlington House** (formerly Custis-Lee Mansion) is the frontispiece of Arlington Cemetery (see page 292) facing Washington. **Theodore Roosevelt Island,** reached by footbridge, is an 88-acre preserve in the Potomac River with forest and swamp trails (see page 296).

At the south end of the parkway the great reward is to stroll the grounds of Mount Vernon (administered by the Mount Vernon Ladies Association) and gaze over the Potomac to the opposite shore, where some parts are preserved today much as they looked years ago. Nearby points of interest associated with Washington's family and friends include Woodlawn Plantation, Gunston Hall, and Pohick Church. 703/285-2600.

## GREENBELT PARK

### Maryland

This 1,078-acre woodland park is 12 miles northeast of Washington on the Baltimore-Washington Parkway. It has 12 miles of marked trails, abundant wildlife, and facilities for hiking and camping. The 178 campsites are available for 5-day stays from June to Labor Day, 14 days the rest of the year. 301/344-3948.

## JOHN F. KENNEDY CENTER FOR THE PERFORMING ARTS

### District of Columbia

The Concert Hall, Opera Hall, Eisenhower Theater, Film Institute, and other facilities comprise a national cultural center in this overpowering structure on the banks of the Potomac River between Key and Memorial bridges. It opened in September 1971. The Park Service is responsible principally for maintenance and protection. It is one of the most heavily visited buildings in Washington, handsomely furnished with gifts of other nations. Regular tours are conducted daily 10 A.M. to 1:15 P.M. 202/416-7910.

## KENILWORTH AQUATIC GARDENS

### District of Columbia

Located in Anacostia Park, reached via Kenilworth Avenue, N.E., the gardens were started by a government employee as a hobby 80 years ago. Now they contain more than 100,000 water plants, including rare exotic species with immense leaves up to six feet in diameter. Best time to visit is in mid-June when thousands of plants are in bloom. In late July and August the tropical water lilies open. Many flowers close in the heat of day, so visit in the mornings. Open year-round. 202/619-7005.

## KOREAN WAR VETERANS MEMORIAL

### District of Columbia

In West Potomac Park, southeast of the Lincoln Memorial, the design of this new memorial includes 19 individual pieces of sculpture representing a squad of troops, and a granite wall depicting combat and support troops. President Bush broke ground for construction on Flag Day, June 14, 1992, before thousands of Korean veterans. Completion was scheduled for July 27, 1995, the 42nd anniversary of the signing of the Korean War armistice. For information, call the Korean War Memorial Advisory Board, 202/208-3561.

## LINCOLN MEMORIAL
### District of Columbia

The classical structure of dignity and beauty at the approach to Arlington Memorial Bridge is bordered by 36 columns, one for each state in the Union at the time of Lincoln's death. Within the chamber, the 19-foot marble statue of the emancipator, by Daniel Chester French, occupies the place of honor, while on flanking walls the Gettysburg Address and Second Inaugural Address are inscribed. On the wall behind the statue are these words: "In this temple as in the hearts of the people for whom he saved the Union, the memory of Abraham Lincoln is enshrined forever." The memorial is very impressive at night when the lights come on.

Ask about reservations for the guided tour

*Abraham Lincoln National Memorial*

called "Looking Under Lincoln," which is given periodically. It's the only spelunker's tour in Washington, going 45 feet below the surface into the memorial's cave-like foundation. You'll find stalagmites and stalactites, as in a natural cave, formed by water percolating through cracks in the memorial's limestone foundation. 202/426-6895.

## LINCOLN MUSEUM

See Ford's Theatre, page 293.

## LYNDON BAINES JOHNSON MEMORIAL GROVE ON THE POTOMAC
### Virginia

A grove of 500 white pine trees forms a living memorial to the late president. The 15-acre site, in Lady Bird Johnson Park, on the west bank of the Potomac River commands an imposing vista of the national capital. The park includes a mile of walking trails. A towering slab of Texas pink granite has been engraved with some of President Johnson's more significant statements. 202/619-7005.

## MARY McLEOD BETHUNE COUNCIL HOUSE NATIONAL HISTORIC SITE
### District of Columbia

The 19th century, 4-story Victorian townhouse on Logan Circle was the home of the famed educator from 1943 until her death in 1955. Born to slave parents in South Carolina, she was founder and president of Bethune-Cochran College in Florida, as well as an advisor to four presidents starting with Calvin Coolidge. The house contains the National Archives for Black Women's History and a memorial museum. 202/619-7005.

## NATIONAL MALL
### District of Columbia

The original 1790 plan of French architect Pierre de L'Enfant for the new capital city called for a formal park, the Mall, from the Capitol to the present Washington Monument. Now extended to the Lincoln Memorial, the Mall contains 145 acres of lawns, reflecting pools, hiking trails, and wooded glades. Units of the Smithsonian Institution and the National Gallery of Art are located on the Mall. 202/426-6720.

## OXON HILL FARM
### Maryland

The farm, which overlooks the Potomac River a few miles south of Washington, includes pens and pastures with common farm animals. Hay barn, feed room, equipment shed, and workroom are open; machinery and equipment are displayed and demonstrated. Open daily 8 A.M. to 5 P.M. 202/619-7005.

## PISCATAWAY PARK
### Maryland

Seven miles of riverfront across the Potomac River from Mount Vernon preserve the scenic view from Washington's home. The historic landscape of marshes, streams, forests, and open fields enhance fishing and picnicking. The **National Colonial Farm,** operated by the Accokeek Foundation, showcases agricultural techniques of the 1700s. Staple crops are raised without the use of insecticides. Tilling and planting are done by hand. Livestock include Devon cattle and Dorset sheep, types prevalent during colonial times, as an integral part of the farm. Each spring and fall the farm conducts sales of its goods and reenacts colonial life. 301/292-2112.

## PRINCE WILLIAM FOREST PARK
### Virginia

The forested parkland is located at Triangle, about 35 miles south of Washington, D.C. It is an excellent place to camp on a visit to the Washington area. Approximately 35 miles of trails and fire roads afford access to the wilder regions of the park. Parking areas along park roads provide convenient starting points for many hikes. Self-guiding nature trails begin and end at each picnic area and campground. There are also bike trails in the park and

rental bicycles available. Oak Ridge Campground has 113 family sites, each with a paved slip, available on a first-come, first-served basis. Turkey Run Ridge Campground has 12 group tent sites, for which reservations are required. Travel Trailer Village, operated by a concessioner, has 98 all-year sites for 7-day stays. 703/221-4706.

## ROCK CREEK PARK
### District of Columbia

James Bryce, the British statesman, said there is "nothing comparable" in Europe's capitals to Rock Creek Park. John Burroughs said "Rock Creek has . . . not only pleasing but wild and rugged scenery." This natural woodland in northwest Washington, some 4 miles long and a mile wide, is one of the country's larger urban parks, favored by hikers, bicyclists, and horseback riders. Its 1,754 acres contain: historic Pierce Mill; the Joaquin Miller Cabin; a superb nature center and planetarium; outdoor activity facilities; and the Carter Barron Amphitheater—an outdoor setting for musical and variety programs. 202/426-6833.

## SEWALL-BELMONT HOUSE NATIONAL HISTORIC SITE
### District of Columbia

The 2½-story red brick house is reputed to be one of the oldest on Capitol Hill. It stands as a memorial to the dedication of Alice Paul and her associates, who were leaders in the women's suffrage battle and founded the Congressional Union, later called the National Women's Party. 202/546-1210.

## THEODORE ROOSEVELT ISLAND
### District of Columbia

This island of plants and animals in a wild state is a living memorial to Theodore Roosevelt, who, while in the White House (1901–09), did more than any other president to preserve the nation's natural resources through establishment of the national forests and wildlife refuges. Even in Washington he loved to explore the outdoors. Roosevelt Island, one mile long and a half mile wide, lies south of Key Bridge in the Potomac. The woods and waters provide the habitat for raccoons, muskrats, and other small animals; you may see or hear a variety of birds from kingfishers to woodpeckers and wood thrushes. Interpretive programs are given frequently. The island is now accessible by footbridge from the Virginia shore. A highway crossing the southern tip of the island was constructed in the 1960s. There is no access to the park from that highway. 202/619-7005.

## THOMAS JEFFERSON MEMORIAL

### District of Columbia

Reflections of the circular colonnaded structure in the waters of Washington's Tidal Basin enhance its beauty, especially in early spring when Japanese cherry trees are in blossom. Jefferson's words, "I have sworn upon the altar of God eternal hostility against every form of tyranny over the mind of man," are inscribed above the 19-foot bronze statue of the man who wrote the Declaration of Independence and served as third president of the United States. Open daily, 8 A.M. to midnight. 202/426-6822.

## VIETNAM VETERANS MEMORIAL

### District of Columbia

This striking, simple monument evokes strong memories of those who lost their lives in America's most controversial war. Its simple geometric form, two gleaming walls of polished black marble in a landscaped setting, pointing to the nearby Lincoln Memorial and to the Washington Monument, makes it one of the most significant places of pilgrimage in Washington, D.C. A bronze life-sized sculpture of three servicemen faces the wall, as though looking for their own names, and in tribute to the women who served in Vietnam, an additional sculpture was dedicated in 1993. Almost every day visitors leave behind a single rose, a wreath, a religious object, or a small American flag. Park Service personnel are stationed at the memorial to assist in finding names. 202/619-7005.

## VIETNAM WOMEN'S MEMORIAL

### District of Columbia

The memorial, dedicated on Veterans Day, November 11, 1993, honors more than 10,000 women who served in the Vietnam conflict. An addition to the Vietnam Veterans Memorial, it features a heroic-size bronze sculpture by Glenna Goodacre depicting three Vietnam-era women and a wounded soldier. 202/619-7005.

## WASHINGTON MONUMENT

### District of Columbia

Construction began in 1848 but proceeded slowly, with delays and changes in design over the years. By 1884, the monument, a classic obelisk, was completed. It was the tallest structure in the world.

*Washington Monument*

A fitting monument to the father of his country, the granite shaft rises 555 feet from ground to apex. The elevator ride to the 500-foot-high observation room takes one minute. The observation windows afford the finest orientation view of the capital—on a clear day you can see everything within 20 miles. Open 9 to 5; summer, 8 A.M. to midnight. Prepare for long waiting lines in spring and summer. 202/426-6839.

## WHITE HOUSE
### District of Columbia

The grounds of the nation's foremost residence and office are administered by the National Park Service. Many of the trees are of historic interest; every president from James Madison through Ronald Reagan has planted a tree on the grounds. Mrs. Reagan planted a Magnolia Alba. The White House is open to visitors Tuesday through Saturday from 10 A.M. to 12:45 P.M. in summer; 10 A.M. to noon in winter. Summer tours are organized; free tickets are issued, starting at 8 A.M. Tickets are available the day of the tour only. Check with the office of your Congressman or Senator for tickets to "Congressional Tours," given 8:15 A.M. Tuesday through Saturday. 202/485-9836.

## WOLF TRAP FARM PARK FOR THE PERFORMING ARTS
### Virginia

The park, located near Vienna, about 14 miles from Washington, is a showcase for opera, jazz, modern dance, ballet, and symphony concerts. You can sit under cover in the 6,900-seat Filene Center, or bring a blanket and picnic and enjoy the lawn beyond it. 703/255-1800.

*The White House*

# ARCHAEOLOGICAL AREAS

MANY of the archaeological ruins of the Southwest were observed by the early Spanish explorers. Father Kino is believed to have discovered the Casa Grande ruin, in the Gila River Valley of Arizona, as early as 1694. Escalante, the Franciscan missionary, reported on finding extensive cliff dwellings and pueblos along his route. In 1805 the Spaniards massacred Navajos in Canyon del Muerto, a part of what is now Canyon de Chelly National Monument.

For the most part, the ruins were left as they had been lived in long before the dawn of recorded history on this continent. The aboriginal Indians had abandoned their dwellings in good condition, presumably driven out by a long period of drought in the 13th century. The Spaniards saw no promise of gold in these cities in the rock and caused little disturbance to them.

By the end of the 19th century, however, it was another story. The surge of migration into the Southwest brought with it a wave of uncontrolled vandalism. Wholesale commercial looting was conducted by "pot hunters" to meet increasing demands for artifacts. Probably no cliff dwelling in the Southwest was more thoroughly dug over in search of pottery and other objects for commercial purposes than Cliff Palace, in what is now Mesa Verde National Park. Parties of "curio seekers" camped on the ruins for several winters. Some of the treasures they carried out are now in museums, others are lost forever to science. Perhaps even worse, in the process of digging they thoughtlessly blew out walls with powder, mutilated the buried kivas, and used beams for firewood so that not a single roof was left.

In 1906, at last, Congress adopted the Act for the Preservation of American Antiquities, or the Antiquities Act, which made it a federal offense to injure, damage, or destroy antiquities on federal lands. It also provided for the establishment of national monuments by presidential proclamation. National monuments now can be established either by such proclamation or by congressional action, so long as they have national significance worth preserving—scientific, historic, or natural. All but one of the archaeological areas are national monuments.

Despite best intentions and legislation, the protection of antiquities remains a challenge. When you visit one of the archaeological areas, ask a ranger to bring you up to date.

## ALIBATES FLINT QUARRIES
### Texas

On this site, 35 miles northeast of Amarillo, the Alibates mines were found and used by ancient man more than 12,000 years ago—7,000 years before the pyramids were built in Egypt. The brightly colored flint was quarried for making tools and weapons. Use of Alibates flint continued into the modern period by the Plains Indians, until metal was obtained from the white man. The monument is reached by driving northeast of Amarillo on Texas 136, 35 miles to Alibates Road (7½ miles southwest of Fritch), then 5 miles to the Bates contact station. Guided tours are conducted by a historian twice daily (10 A.M. and 2 P.M.) from Memorial Day to Labor Day; off-season tours by reservation. The tours cover about 1 mile, round trip, including a walk up steep inclines to the Alibates site and a demonstration of shaping flint into weapons. Collecting samples is not permitted at the historic site, though one handful of flint is permitted from the Lake Meredith area.

Traces of pre-Pueblo culture have also been found at Palo Duro Canyon State Park (noted especially for the exposure of 200 million years of geological formations). The Panhandle-Plains Historical Museum, at Canyon, presents the panorama of life in the area from ancient to frontier times. Address: c/o Lake Meredith National Recreation Area, Box 1438, Fritch, Texas 79036. 806/857-3151.

## AZTEC RUINS
### New Mexico

Near Farmington and the Navajo Reservation in the Four Corners country, the monument preserves the stabilized ruins of a major prehistoric Indian town built of masonry and timber in the 12th century. The name is misleading, since the Aztecs of Mexico never lived in the area. The people here shared cultures of those at Chaco Canyon National Monument, 65 miles south, and Mesa Verde National Park, 100 miles northwest. Follow the self-guided trail through the west pueblo, site of the restored Great Kiva, to the Hubbard Ruin. Pottery, weapons, and jewelry are on display at the Visitor Center. Address: Box 640, Aztec, New Mexico 87410. 505/334-6174.

## BANDELIER
### New Mexico

This beautiful canyon country 46 miles west of Santa Fe contains many cliff and open-pueblo ruins of the late prehistoric period. The most accessible features are the ruins in Frijoles Canyon, houses of masonry one to three stories high with many cave rooms gouged out of the soft volcanic ash of the cliff. The Frijoles inhabitants grew corn, beans, and squash in their oasis in the dry country. They wove cotton cloth on a floor loom; they made black-on-gray, decorated pottery. The story of these people, where they came from and where they went, is gradually being brought to light through research. The monument was named to honor Adolph F. A. Bandelier, who carried on an extensive survey of prehistoric ruins and Pueblo Indians in the 1880s.

The monument has an excellent museum in the Visitor Center. A self-guiding walking tour of the principal ruins takes about an hour. The park staff conducts daily activities, including evening campfire programs in summer. Approximately 90 percent of its 32,737 acres is backcountry, accessible by 70 miles of trail leading through forests and steep-walled gorges. These trails unfold the geologic, as well as archaeological, interest in the Pajarito Plateau. During the spring Frijoles Canyon, with its abundant birdlife, holds special appeal.

The monument is open all year except Christmas Day. Weather is favorable and relative humidity generally low. A curio shop and snack bar operate all year. A campground is situated on the mesa above the canyon. Areas of interest nearby include: Los Alamos, the atomic city; Indian pueblos along the Rio Grande; Spanish-American settlements in the Sangre de Cristo Mountains; and the cultural centers of Santa Fe and Taos. Write Superintendent, Bandelier National Monument, Los Alamos, New Mexico 87544. 505/672-3861.

## CANYON DE CHELLY

### Arizona

About 300 Navajos have their summer homes on the floor of the canyons, while they pasture cattle between sheer red sandstone walls rising about 40 feet at the mouth and up to 1,000 feet at Spider Rock. Canyon de Chelly itself is joined by Canyon del Muerto, 35 miles long. Pictographs and petroglyphs on walls of cliffs and caves date to early prehistoric occupation. Cliffdweller ruins and natural formations like 800-foot Spider Rock make Canyon de Chelly one of the finest adventures in the Southwest. All inner-canyon visitors must be accompanied by a park ranger or authorized guide, except for those hiking the self-guiding trail from White House Overlook to the White House ruin.

Thunderbird Lodge operates jeep tours up the canyon floor daily from mid-April to November 1, depending on weather conditions. Navajo guides are available. The Visitor Center is open daily from 8 A.M. to 5 P.M., late fall to late spring, and 8 A.M. to 6 P.M. during the summer months. Thunderbird Lodge (Chinle, Arizona 86503) provides hotel accommodations and a cafeteria; it and the adjacent campground are open year-round, but winter can be very cold.

The 83,840-acre monument lies one mile east of Chinle Community and is reached either north from Gallup, New Mexico, or Holbrook, Arizona (near Petrified Forest), or south from Farmington, New Mexico. Combine your visit here with a stop at Hubbell Trading Post National Historic Site, a few miles south. Address: Box 588, Chinle, Arizona 86503. 602/674-5436.

## CASA GRANDE RUINS

### Arizona

This is the oldest archaeological monument in the national park system, first set aside as a federal reserve in 1982. In 1694 the Spanish missionary, Father Kino, discovered the ruins, a classic of Indian construction, and described them as "a four-story building as large as a castle." Self-guiding trail, ranger talks of 30 to 45 minutes; museum devoted to archaeology and ethnology. The ruins are on Arizona 87/287 at Coolidge, near the Coolidge exit of I-10. Address: Box 518, Coolidge, Arizona 85228. 602/723-3172.

## CHACO CULTURE NATIONAL HISTORICAL PARK

### New Mexico

Because Chaco Canyon embraces some of the most significant ruins in America, Congress in 1980 enlarged the former national monument and redesignated it as Chaco Culture National Historical Park. It also identified 33 outlying sites as Chaco Culture Archaeological Protection Sites, in light of extensive development of energy resources in the San Juan Basin. These sites constitute part of the 80 known prehistoric communities in the highly organized and far-reaching Pueblo culture centered at Chaco Canyon. To reach the park, located in the northwestern part of the state, take unpaved New Mexico 57 at Blanco Trading Post (which is 27 miles southeast of Bloomfield on New Mexico 44). From the trading post it is 30 miles to the Visitor Center. Or take New Mexico 57 from Thoreau on I-40 (near Gallup). From here it is 60 miles to the Visitor Center, the last 20 miles of which are unpaved road. Visitor Center hours are 8 A.M. to 5 P.M. A campground is maintained; but there is no gas, food, or lodging available in the park. Address: Chaco Culture National Historical Park, SR #4, Box 6500, Bloomfield, New Mexico 87413. 505/988-6716.

## EFFIGY MOUNDS
### Iowa

Effigy Mounds is a hidden gem of timber, trails, and prehistory, along the edge of sheer cliffs plunging to the Mississippi River. The park has been called "Iowa's Yellowstone." The 191 known mounds, most in the forms of bears and birds, were put in the earth thousands of years ago by native Americans. The North Unit, reached by easy trail from the Visitor Center, offers superlative Mississippi vistas. The South Unit contains effigies of birds in flight and the "Marching Bear Unit." Accommodations are available at nearby Marquette, with camping at Yellow River State Forest. Address: 151 Highway 76, Harpers Ferry, Iowa 52146. 319/873-3491.

## GILA CLIFF DWELLINGS
### New Mexico

These well-preserved, natural cavities in the face of an overhanging volcanic cliff were occupied more than 700 years ago (approximately 1280 to the early 1300s) by the Mogollon Culture people. In 1988, while exploring near the monument, a teenage youth discovered a cave containing three *ollas*, storage jars made in the coiled clay method by a master Mogollon craftsman; the site was named in honor of Mark Imhoff, who turned his find over to archaeologists. The monument is in rugged country of southwestern New Mexico, 44 miles north of Silver City on New Mexico 15. The ruins are open 4 A.M. to 6 P.M. Memorial Day through Labor Day; 9 A.M. to 5 P.M., rest of the year. The Visitor Center is open daily 8 A.M. to 5 P.M. Both facilities are closed January 1 and December 25. Address: Route 11, Box 100, Silver City, New Mexico 88061. 505/536-9461.

## HOPEWELL CULTURE NATIONAL HISTORICAL PARK
### Ohio

In the Scioto Valley of southern Ohio, the prehistoric Hopewell Indians reached their cultural zenith from about 200 B.C. to A.D. 500. They are best known for artistic achievements and for erecting burial mounds. The area was first designated as Mound City Group National Monument in 1923, then was renamed and expanded in 1992 to include tour areas of large, important earthworks. From the extraordinary wealth of ornaments, pottery, and other items found in the mounds, archaeologists have learned a great deal about these people. Marked trails provide a close view of the mounds; the Visitor Center displays the fine Hopewell handiwork. Lodging and camping facilities in Chillicothe, 3 miles south, and in nearby state parks. Address: 16062 State Route 104, Chillicothe, Ohio 45601-8694. 614/774-1126.

## HOVENWEEP
### Utah-Colorado

In the Four Corners region west of Mesa Verde National Park, six clusters of prehistoric towers, pueblos, and cliff dwellings (four in Colorado, two in Utah) are reached only via dirt and gravel road. They represent the northern, or Mesa Verde, branch of the prehistoric San Juan Anasazi Culture that occupied this arid land 700 years ago. There are camping facilities, but carry wood. Address: McElmo Route, Cortez, Colorado 81330. 303/529-4461.

## MONTEZUMA CASTLE
### Arizona

When driving north from Phoenix to the Grand Canyon, allow time to visit this five-story, 20-room "castle" in the Verde Valley. Built in a limestone cliff during the 12th and 13th centuries, it is still 90-percent intact, one of the best-preserved cliff ruins in the Southwest. It lies almost immediately accessible off the main highway (I-17), midway between Phoenix and Flagstaff. The self-guiding Sycamore Trail, starting from the Visitor Center, follows Beaver Creek through the heart of the monument. You can walk it easily in about 45 minutes. The castle, set in a cliff 100 feet above the valley floor, is a 19-room apartment house constructed with stone and wooden tools that has lasted 800 years. It was a perfect natural fortress, reached by ladders from above or below. Follow the full length of the trail to Castle A, where you may climb into some of the caves. The castle area includes a pleasant picnic spot. The monument also includes Montezuma Well, 7 miles northeast, a large limestone sinkhole rimmed with pueblos and cave houses. Address: Box 219, Camp Verde, Arizona 86322. 602/567-5276.

## NAVAJO

### Arizona

Three of the largest, most elaborate of known cliff dwellings are preserved in rugged country 31 miles west of Kayenta and 63 miles northeast of Tuba City, completely surrounded by the Navajo Reservation. The most accessible, 700-year-old Betatakin, or "Ledge House," once had almost 135 rooms. During the main summer season, guided tours to Betatakin are given three times daily; they accommodate up to 24 people on a first-come, first-served basis. Write for information about and reservations for the hike or horseback adventure to Keel Seel cliff dwelling (16 miles round trip). Displays and a slide show at the Visitor Center provide a helpful introduction to the Anasazi. Campgrounds are located in the monument. Address: Tonalea, Arizona 86044. 602/672-2366.

## OCMULGEE

### Georgia

Circular earthlodges and mounds of soil stand as monuments to the ancestors of the Creek Indians who lived along the Ocmulgee River of the Macon Plateau. The site covers 1,000 acres of woods, swamps, and grassland, with seven miles of trail. There is a museum that displays interpretive early lifeways on the plateau. You'll find a picnic area in the park, lodging and limited camping in nearby Macon. Address: 1207 Emery Highway, Macon, Georgia 31201. 912/752-8257.

## PIPESTONE

### Minnesota

This was a sacred place known to tribesmen of a large part of the continent. "It is not too much to say that the great Pipestone Quarry," wrote John Wesley Powell, founder of the Bureau of American Ethnology, "was the most important single location in aboriginal geography and lore." Walk the Circle Trail to see how the monument now conserves the remainder of the unusual red stone from which the Indians for at least three centuries fashioned their prized calumets, or ceremonial pipes. The material is now called catlinite, in honor of the artist-explorer, George Catlin, who entered the quarries in 1836 and then gave the first published description. The Visitor Center and connected Upper Midwest Indian Cultural Center provide a museum demonstration area for pipe making. Attractive pipes and other stone products made by local Indians are on sale. The monument lies near the town of Pipestone, in southwest Minnesota, near Sioux Falls, South Dakota. Address: Box 727, Pipestone, Minnesota 56164. 507/825-5464.

## RUSSELL CAVE

### Alabama

Excavated only as recently as 1953, the cave contained tools, weapons and other evidence showing a record of life from at least 6000 B.C. to about A.D. 1650. It lies near the town of Bridgeport, close to Chattanooga, Tennessee. Various activities performed by early inhabitants are demonstrated daily. These include fire making, flint knapping, use of the blow gun, and spear throwing using the atlatl. Visitor Center and archaeology exhibit. Address: Route 1, Box 175, Bridgeport, Alabama 35740. 205/495-2672.

## SALINAS
### New Mexico

This unique complex of original Pueblo Indian and Spanish ruins is located in central New Mexico, at the junction of New Mexico 14 and US 60. The name *Salinas* derives from the Spanish name for the region which contains salt lagoons, important both prehistorically and historically. Abandoned by Indians and Spaniards alike in the 1670s, the massive masonry ruins survived the centuries remarkably intact. The limestone ruins of Gran Quivira lie 26 miles south of Mountainair; the red sandstone ruins of Abo, 9 miles west; Quarai, 8 miles north. An orientation center is located in Mountainair; Gran Quivira and Quarai have small museums. Open daily all year. Address: Box 496, Mountainair, New Mexico 87036. 505/847-2585.

*Tuzigoot*

## TONTO
### Arizona

Reached via the thrilling Apache Trail above Roosevelt Lake, the well-preserved Pueblo cliff dwellings were occupied in the 14th and 15th centuries by Indians farming the Salt River Valley. Small museum and trail provide excellent perspectives. Trail closes at 4 P.M. daily. Address: Box 707, Roosevelt, Arizona 85545. 602/467-2241.

*Tonto*

## TUZIGOOT
### Arizona

In the Verde Valley near Clarkdale, the excavated ruins include a pueblo which housed 200 to 400 persons, with each unit individually designed—an outstanding example of late prehistoric pueblos. It's estimated that the community peaked around A.D. 1250 and disappeared by 1450. Museum has pottery, basketry, stone tools, and turquoise jewelry. Address: Box 68, Clarkdale, Arizona 86324. 602/634-5564.

## WALNUT CANYON
### Arizona

Cliff dwellings in shallow caves at the edge of Flagstaff were inhabited by Sinagua Indians about 800 years ago. Utilizing projecting limestone ledges as foundations, the houses apparently were built for separate families. Museum, observation building, and self-guiding trails. Address: Walnut Canyon Road, Flagstaff, Arizona 86004. 602/526-3367.

*Wupatki*

## WUPATKI

### Arizona

Red sandstone prehistoric pueblos about 45 miles northeast of Flagstaff were occupied from about A.D. 1100 to 1225 by farming Indians, from whom the Hopi are believed to be partly descended. After the late 11th-century eruption of nearby Sunset Crater made farming productive, this became one of the most densely populated sections of northern Arizona and a melting pot of Southwest cultures, until winds eventually removed or drifted the water-retaining cover of ash and cinders. Among the most impressive of more than 800 ruins are Wupatki, the "Tall House," and the Citadel, built at the edge of a limestone sinkhole. There are also earth lodges on the mesa tops and isolated field houses of one and two rooms, used by the Indians while tending crops. Visitor Center and museum at Wupatki ruin. Self-guiding trail through Wupatki and Citadel ruins. Limited space is available for a 14-mile, ranger-guided backpacking trip to Crack-in-Rock ruin to explore rock etchings at the mesa base; applications should be made well in advance for the trip, which is offered only on weekends in April and October. Address: H.C. 33, Box 444A, Flagstaff, Arizona 86004. 602/527-7040.

# HISTORICAL AREAS

MORE THAN ONE-HALF of all areas of the National Park system relate directly to the aspirations, inspirations, struggles, and achievements of humankind on the American soil.

These include national historical parks, national military parks, national battlefield parks, national historic sites, national battlefield sites, national memorials, and national cemeteries. The differences in nomenclature have to do more with size and legal origin than with purpose. Most battlefields, for instance, had been administered by the War Department until transferred in 1933 to the National Park Service. Two years later Congress adopted the Historic Sites Act, directing the Park Service "to preserve for public use historic sites, buildings and objects of national significance."

Prepare to find history entwined with nature. You may go to Gettysburg to view the battle scene, but you will also be treated to a rich variety and abundance of birds. Look also for art and architecture, the cultural story unfolding with history.

## ABRAHAM LINCOLN BIRTHPLACE NATIONAL HISTORIC SITE

### Kentucky

A granite memorial building encloses a log cabin symbolic of the one in which Abraham Lincoln was born near Hodgenville on February 12, 1809. The Lincoln family lived at this location for the first 2½ years of Abraham's life and then moved to another small farm 10 miles away. The park grounds include 100 acres of the family's Sinking Springs Farm. Address: 2995 Lincoln Farm Road, Hodgenville, Kentucky 42728. 502/358-3874.

Related points include the Lincoln Museum and statue in downtown Hodgenville; Lincoln Boyhood Home at Knob Creek, 10 miles northeast on US 31E; and the boyhood home of his father, Thomas, 53 miles northeast of Hodgenville in Lincoln Homestead Stae Park, at Springfield.

## ADAMS NATIONAL HISTORIC SITE

### Massachusetts

The home at 135 Adams Street in Quincy of the distinguished Adams family for four generations, beginning with the second president of the United States, is one of the country's finest historic houses. The beautiful garden was started by Mrs. John Adams. The site includes the birthplaces of John Adams, at 133 Franklin Street, and of John Quincy Adams, at 141 Franklin Street. It is easily reached from Boston, only eight miles away. A new Visitor

Center on Hancock Street in downtown Quincy offers information on the many historical sites in the area. A commuter train from Boston stops nearby. Address: Box 531, Quincy, Massachusetts 02269. 617/773-1177.

## ALLEGHENY PORTAGE RAILROAD NATIONAL HISTORIC SITE

### Pennsylvania

The Portage Railroad, built between 1831 and 1834, crossed a forested mountain divide to become the first railroad crossing of the Allegheny Mountains. It consisted of ten inclined planes and eleven level sections to connect the eastern and western divisions of the Pennsylvania Mainline Canal. Charles Dickens in 1842 found it an exciting trip, yet "not to be dreaded for its dangers."

The Visitor Center and Engine House Interpretive Shelter feature a movie, exhibits, and models depicting the history of the Portage Railroad and Mainline Canal. Ranger-conducted programs and costumed demonstrations are presented during the summer. Allow time for hiking and picnicking in the area. Address: Box 189, Cresson, Pennsylvania 16630.

## AMERICAN MEMORIAL PARK

### Saipan

A tribute to those who died in World War II in armed conflict far from home, the park consists of 133 scenic acres along the shoreline of Tanapag Harbor outside of Garapan. It includes a monument and museum, plus picnic facilities along the shoreline and swimming from Micro Beach. Limited boat dock facilities offer glass-bottomed and other boat tours for viewing the coral reef and for access to nearby Managha Island. Address: Box 198 CHRB, Saipan, Commonwealth of the Marianas 96950. 670/234-7207.

## ANDERSONVILLE NATIONAL HISTORIC SITE

### Georgia

In the quiet country above Americus, the town of Andersonville recalls how 45,000 Union prisoners were once imprisoned and 12,912 of them died. At the National Cemetery, ½ mile north of the town, Union prisoners are buried among magnolias and hardwoods, resting with men of other wars. Six graves isolated from the rest contain the remains of the Raiders, who were convicted of robbing and murdering fellow prisoners and were sentenced to hanging by the prisoners themselves. The cemetery and prison site are well maintained and interpreted by the National Park Service as a memorial to American prisoners of all wars. Portions of the prison wall have been reconstructed, giving a prisoner's view of life inside the stockade. Clara Barton, famous Civil War nurse, helped identify and mark the graves of those who died while confined at Andersonville.

The little town of Andersonville is worth exploring. Much of it has been restored to pre–Civil War appearance. The Visitor Center/Museum will get you started on a self-guiding driving or walking tour. The village and national historic site are on the Andersonville POW Memorial Trail, a 75-mile loop between Perry and Cordele, which includes Georgia's last operating river ferry. Address: Route 1, Box 800, Andersonville, Georgia 31711. 912/924-0343.

## ANDREW JOHNSON NATIONAL HISTORIC SITE

### Tennessee

The tailor shop where Johnson worked from 1831 until 1843, his last home (1851–1875), and his grave memorialize Lincoln's successor to the presidency. Impeached by the House and acquitted by one vote in the Senate, Johnson was somewhat vindicated with his return to the Senate in 1875. The site is open every day except Christmas; daily tours of the Homestead are offered, fee charged. A few miles north of the shop lies Davy Crockett Birthplace. Address: Box 1088, Greenville, Tennessee 37744. 615/638-3551.

## ANTIETAM NATIONAL BATTLEFIELD

### Maryland

The scene of the bloody battle on September 17, 1862, between 87,000 Union troops and 41,000 Confederates, that brought to an end Lee's first northern invasion, is marked by monuments, battlefield exhibits, and the Visitor Center. More than 23,000 of both sides were killed or wounded before the day was done; 4,000 men fell in three hours at Bloody Lane. Cannons denote the places where six generals lost their lives. Civil War burials in the National Cemetery number more than 5,000. In 1990 the Richard King Mellon Foundation announced it would donate three additional battlefield tracts, totalling 280 acres, to the park. Address: Box 158, Sharpsburg, Maryland 21782. 301/432-5124.

## APPOMATTOX COURT HOUSE NATIONAL HISTORICAL PARK

### Virginia

The village (20 miles east of Lynchburg) where General Lee surrendered the Confederate Army of Northern Virginia to General Grant on April 9, 1865, bringing the Civil War to an end, has been restored to present a moving and impressive picture of that day. When Grant told Lee, in the McLean House, that Confederate soldiers could keep their horses and mules to work their farms, his old foe replied, "It will be very gratifying and will do much toward conciliating our people." Within the restored village of Appomattox Court House are 27 historic structures, all in easy walking distance from the Visitor Center. Address: Box 218, Appomattox, Virginia 24522. 804/352-8987.

## ARKANSAS POST NATIONAL MEMORIAL

### Arkansas

The first European settlement in the lower Mississippi Valley, Arkansas Post was established in 1686 by Henri de Tonty, a French explorer. It is located 7 miles south of Gillett, 18 miles northeast of Dumas. Five different national governments have had jurisdiction over Arkansas Post. In 1819, the territorial capitol was established here, but its existence as a community came to an end in January 1863 with the Union victory at Fort Hindman and bombardment of the fort, virtually destroying the town. Address: Route 1, Box 16, Gillett, Arkansas 72055. 501/548-2432.

## ARLINGTON HOUSE

See page 292.

## BARTON, CLARA, NATIONAL HISTORIC SITE

See Clara Barton National Historic Site, page 293.

## BENJAMIN FRANKLIN NATIONAL MEMORIAL

### Pennsylvania

"The American people feel a deep debt of gratitude to Benjamin Franklin for his outstanding services to the Nation as a statesman and for his achievements as a scientist and inventor," Congress declared in designating this memorial in 1972. The Benjamin Franklin Institute has been a leader in scientific progress since its founding in 1824. The main institute building contains James Earle Frazer's 20-foot, 10½-inch marble statue of Franklin. Address: The Franklin Institute, 20th and Benjamin Franklin Parkway, Philadelphia, Pennsylvania 19103. 215/448-1000.

## BENT'S OLD FORT NATIONAL HISTORIC SITE

### Colorado

A principal outpost of civilization on the southern plains, this reconstructed fort on the banks of the Arkansas River, 8 miles from La Junta, was a rendezvous for Indians, trappers, traders, and troops. It played a key role in shaping the destiny of the Southwest between 1833 and 1849. Address: 35110 Highway 194 East, La Junta, Colorado 81050. 719/384-2596.

## BIG HOLE NATIONAL BATTLEFIELD

### Montana

Remains of shallow, grass-grown trenches and battle-scarred trees in a remote but scenic setting recall the fierce two-day battle in August 1877, when Indian women and children were slain, with their warriors, by U.S. troops. Led by valiant Chief Joseph, the Nez Perce were making their epic retreat from Idaho when they were trapped here. The Visitor Center offers a dramatic view high above the scene. It displays authentic artifacts from the period. Markers attest, despite defeat in the Big Hole Valley, that the Indians pressed on through Yellowstone, only to be captured 40 miles from Canada and freedom. Address: Box 237, Wisdom, Montana 59761. 406/689-3155.

## BOOKER T. WASHINGTON NATIONAL MONUMENT

### Virginia

The 224-acre monument, comprising most of the original plantation and replicas of buildings Washington might have known as a boy, is the only one in the park system that interprets life under slavery. The restored farm embraces buildings, tools, crops, animals, and, at times, people in period dress. A visit to Washington's earliest home demonstrates the challenges he faced to become an eminent educator, presidential advisor, and leader of black Americans. The park, near Burnt Chimney (about 20 miles southwest of Roanoke) is an easy side trip from the Blue Ridge Parkway. Address: Route 3, Box 310, Hardy, Virginia 24101. 703/721-2094.

## BOSTON AFRICAN-AMERICAN NATIONAL HISTORIC SITE

### Massachusetts

The African Meeting House (1806) on Beacon Hill is the oldest black church building standing in this country. The 1½-mile, easily walkable **Black Heritage Trail** connects the Meeting House with 14 other historic structures significant in the development of Boston's early black community. During peak visitor months, interpretive rangers along the Trail complement the self-guiding trail booklet. Address: 46 Joy Street, Boston, MA 02144. 617/720-0753.

## BOSTON NATIONAL HISTORICAL PARK

### Massachusetts

Eight sites in the heart of Boston, all closely identified with the early history of the United States, are the focal points of this park. All remain under public or private ownerships, but are operated and maintained in accord with National Park Service regulations.

Start from the park service **Visitor Center,** 15 State Street, directly across from the Old State House. It is an excellent source of information and literature and is starting point of various guided walking tours. Everyone will want to see the **Charlestown Navy Yard** (also known as the Boston Naval Shipyard). The first operating drydock in the nation was completed here in 1833 and the Navy Yard has built, outfitted, and launched ships for every American war since 1812. With its history and weathered old buildings, it attracts about one million visitors yearly. The most conspicuous sight in the Yard is the USS *Constitution*, or "Old Ironsides," most famous ship in American history, built in 1797 (though not in action until the unofficial war with the Barbary pirates at Tripoli in 1803). It appears as it did during its first full-scale sea battle, in the War of 1812, even staffed with sailors in period uniform. Near Old Ironsides is the USS *Cassin Young*, a World War II destroyer and the first and only warship managed by the National Park Service. Other sights in the Navy Yard: Rope Walk, a building almost a quarter-mile long where all the rope for the U.S. Navy was made until 1971; USS *Constitution* Museum, with displays on naval history; the Commandant's House, built in 1803. Also in Charlestown, **Bunker Hill** (or Breed's Hill), surrounded by the 19th-century town houses of Monument Square, preserves the battleground of June 17, 1775. On that morning British General Howe advanced up the hill in textbook style with a force of about 3,000 redcoats. The colonials, whose ammunition was low, obeyed Colonel Prescott's famous order not to fire "until you see the whites of their eyes." The 220-foot Bunker Hill Monument now dominates the scene.

Downtown, on Boston's well-marked Freedom Trail, **Faneuil Hall** is the historic marketplace built in 1740–42 that served as a political forum for Revolutionary leaders. By all means climb the stairs to the second-floor chamber where public meetings are still held, thus continuing a tradition over 250 years old. Faneuil Hall Marketplace is one of the liveliest spots in Boston. The centerpiece is Quincy Market, a 500-foot-long Greek Revival complex first opened in 1826. It has been restored and revitalized and is occupied by food merchants the way it used to be.

Then follow the Trail to the **Old State House**, built in 1713. Though engulfed by modern traffic you can still see the circle of cobblestones in front of the building commemorating the Boston Massacre of 1770. Note the balcony where the Declaration of Independence was first read to Bostonians on July 18, 1776. Climb the spiral staircase within

to the second-floor Council Chamber, where patriot James Otis argued against the Writs of Assistance, search warrants used by the British to track down smuggled goods. John Adams termed his speech "the first act of opposition to the arbitrary claims of Great Britain." Both Faneuil Hall and the Old State House have undergone detailed preservation work; bricks have been repaired and historic ornaments releafed in gold and aluminum. A new wheelchair lift has been installed at the Old State House, providing better access to the ground floor.

The **Old South Meeting House** is another venerable structure, built in 1729, then restored in 1783 after the interior had been gutted by the British in 1775. It was here that 5,000 citizens met in protest immediately preceding the Boston Tea Party of December 16, 1773.

At North Square, the **Paul Revere House** stands as the oldest wooden building in Boston—it predates the Revolution by a century. Revere purchased the house in 1770 and lived in it for about thirty years. If you leave North Square by way of Prince Street and walk one block left to Hanover, you will find yourself in a charming Italian neighborhood. This route leads to the Paul Revere Mall, or Prado, and to Christ Church, popularly known as **Old North Church**, the oldest church in Boston, built in 1723. Here the two lanterns (according to tradition) were hung from the belfry by the sexton Robert Newman, on April 18, 1775, to warn the patriots that the British were advancing by sea toward Concord to seize arms stored there. Meanwhile, Paul Revere made his way with muffled oars past British gunboats and began his famous ride.

At **Dorchester Heights** in South Boston a memorial tower and greensward mark the location of American batteries which threatened the British in Boston leading to their evacuation of the city on March 17, 1776. Here the Americans achieved their first real military success in the Revolution. Address: Charlestown Navy Yard, Boston, Massachusetts 02129. 617/242-5644.

## BRICES CROSS ROADS NATIONAL BATTLEFIELD SITE

### Mississippi

General Nathan Bedford Forrest led his cavalrymen in a brilliant tactical victory near Baldwyn over a large Union force on June 10, 1864. Sherman was so impressed that he ordered his commander in the field to "go out and follow Forrest to the death, if it costs ten thousand lives and breaks the Treasury." From the high ground of the one-acre site, a large part of the scene of action is within view, identified by marker and maps. Address: c/o Natchez Trace Parkway, Route 1, N.T. 143, Tupelo, Mississippi 38801. 601/842-1572.

## BROWN v. BOARD OF EDUCATION NATIONAL HISTORIC SITE

### Kansas

On a fall day in 1950, Linda Brown waited on the front steps of Sumner School in Topeka, Kansas. Her father, Reverend Oliver Brown, was inside trying to enroll her in the third grade. The school refused to admit her—Sumner School was a white school and Linda Brown was black. Thus began a four-year battle that led to the landmark Supreme Court decision: "Separate educational facilities are inherently unequal" and violate the Fourteenth Amendment. This site commemorates that struggle; it consists of the Monroe School, on the other side of town from Sumner, where Linda was sent to attend classes. Sumner School, still in operation, is a National Historic Landmark. Address: c/o National Park Service, Midwest Region, 1709 Jackson Street, Omaha, Nebraska 68102. 402/221-3481.

## CABRILLO NATIONAL MONUMENT

### California

The discovery of the coast of California by Juan Rodriguez Cabrillo in 1542 is commemorated near the scene of his landfall on Point Loma in San Diego Bay. The Cabrillo statue faces the actual landing spot, while the nearby Visitor Center interprets the discovery and subsequent events. Near the southern tip, the famous old lighthouse served from 1855 to 1891. The park is especially popular from mid-December to mid-February as an observation point for watching gray whales offshore heading to Baja California from the Arctic. Also, allow time to walk the nature trail, visiting some of the most scenic tide pools left in southern California. The Bayside Trail starts below the lighthouse as a paved road (once used for military patrol), but presently turns to gravel through coastal scrub and chaparral. Visit the tide pools during a minus tide, and you are apt to see crabs, starfish, and small colorful fish. Address: Box 6670, San Diego, California 92166. 619/557-5450.

## CARL SANDBURG HOME NATIONAL HISTORIC SITE

### North Carolina

Connemara, in the highland foothills in Flat Rock, where the noted writer and poet lived the last 22 years of his life, is preserved in the 264-acre National Historic Site. The unpretentious, white colonial-style house, with its floor-to-ceiling bookshelves in many rooms, was built in 1838 as a summer residence for Christopher G. Memminger, later to be Secretary of the Treasury of the Confederacy. While at Connemara, Sandburg wrote his autobiography, *Always the Young Strangers*. Tours are conducted through the home ($2). Trails lead to the pastures, ponds, and mountain area where Sandburg strolled. *The World of Carl Sandburg*, based on his poetry, humor, folk music, and philosophy, is presented during summer by performers of the Flat Rock Playhouse. The actors also present the *Rootabaga Stories*, Sandburg's own tales for children. Address: 1928 Little River Road, Flat Rock, North Carolina 28731. 704/693-4178.

## CARVER, GEORGE WASHINGTON, NATIONAL MONUMENT

See George Washington Carver National Monument, page 325.

## CASTILLO DE SAN MARCOS NATIONAL MONUMENT

### Florida

After the founding of St. Augustine in 1565, the wooden fortification built there became the northernmost outpost of the vast Spanish New World empire. It strengthened the title to Florida and protected the route of ships returning to Spain. The masonry fort erected in 1672–95 of native shellstone, called coquina, and mortar made from shell lime, continued the original purpose. The buff-plastered walls of the square-shaped, four-bastioned structure were 13 feet thick at the base and 30 feet high—a grim symbol of power and determination. Although it underwent major sieges in 1702 and 1740, it was never conquered. In the 18th century, modernization work gave the Castillo its present appearance, and transformed it into the core of a defense system that reached to the north, south, and west. In 1821 Spain ceded Florida to the United States. The fort's name was changed to Fort Marion and it was used as a military prison, gun battery, and storage. The massive well-preserved structure is the oldest masonry fortification in the country, as well as the most impressive sight of Spanish St. Augustine. The fort is open 8:45 A.M. to 4:45 P.M. year-round. Admission fee is $2 for adults. Children 17 and under and senior citizens 62 and older, free. Educational groups should make reservations. Address: 1 Castillo Drive, St. Augustine, Florida 32084. 904/829-6506.

## CASTLE CLINTON NATIONAL MONUMENT

### New York

Built in 1808 as a fort at the tip of Lower Manhattan, it served variously as civic garden festooned with shrubs and flowers; setting of fireworks, gala concerts, and an occasional balloon ascent; receiving depot for more than seven million immigrants following the Civil War; and, from 1896 to 1941, as a fabulous aquarium. It was completely refurbished in 1986 to serve both as a museum and an information center for National Park Service sites in metropolitan New York. Castle Clinton provides a view into military life at a time when the fort was quite new and guarding New York City from possible British invasion.

Stop at the Visitor Center for tickets for the Statue of Liberty Circle Line Ferry, operating between the Battery and Liberty Island. Also ask about the National Park Service program of free guided walking tours of six historic New York City neighborhoods: Brooklyn Heights, Chinatown–Lower East Side–Little Italy, Gramercy Park, Greenwich Village, SoHo, and the Wall Street financial district. These are available to groups by appointment at least two weeks in advance mid-May to mid-October. (212/264-8129). Address: Superintendent, Manhattan Sites, National Park Service, 26 Wall Street, New York, New York 10005. 212/344-7220.

## CHAMIZAL NATIONAL MEMORIAL

### Texas

A section of Cordova Island in the Rio Grande at El Paso has been chosen to commemorate friendship between the United States and Mexico and the peaceful settlement of a major boundary dispute. *Chamizal* is the Spanish name for the plants which once covered the area. The national memorial includes a museum, documentary films, and a cultural pavilion, managed by a bilingual staff and designed as a center for the exchange of Mexican and American cultural programs. The 500-seat auditorium and outdoor amphitheater are utilized for musical and dramatic events in both Spanish and English. Performances are scheduled most nights from September through July. Special events include the Border Folk Festival in October and the

International Siglo de Oro Drama Festival in March. The Mexicans have constructed a companion park across the Rio Grande in Ciudad Juarez, Mexico. Address: 800 S. San Marcial, El Paso, Texas 79905. 915/532-7273.

## CHARLES PINCKNEY NATIONAL HISTORIC SITE
### South Carolina

Located north of Charleston, the home and farm of Charles Pinckney, signer of the Declaration of Independence, governor of South Carolina, and member of the U.S. Senate, are now surrounded by housing subdivisions. In 1988 Congress authorized the new historic site to preserve a landmark of national value; in 1990 the Snee Farm, where Pinckney grew up in the house his father built in 1754, was conveyed to the Park Service. Facilities will be developed in time. Address: c/o Fort Sumter National Monument, 1214 Middle Street, Sullivans Island, South Carolina 29482. 803/883-3123.

## CHEROKEE STRIP LIVING MUSEUM
### Kansas

Located two miles north of the Oklahoma border, at Arkansas City, Kansas, the museum commemorates the famous "Cherokee Strip Run" of September 16, 1863. That was the date when 150,000 settlers lined up at high noon and joined the rush for land in the Oklahoma frontier. The museum displays contemporary newspapers, photographs, and artifacts associated with the Run, as well as Indian and local memorabilia. Address: Box 230, Arkansas City, Kansas 67005.

## CHESAPEAKE AND OHIO CANAL

See page 292.

## CHICAGO PORTAGE NATIONAL HISTORIC SITE
### Illinois

Here is a portion of the famous portage discovered by Marquette and Joliet and used by the pioneers to link the waters of the Great Lakes with the Mississippi. Address: c/o Cook County Forest Preserve, Cummings Square, River Forest, Illinois 60305. 402/221-3481.

## CHICKAMAUGA AND CHATTANOOGA NATIONAL MILITARY PARK
### Georgia-Tennessee

These fields and hills, now peaceful, witnessed some of the hardest fighting in the Civil War. The battlefields comprise the oldest and largest national military park in the U.S., and today over 1,400 monuments and markers commemorate the fighting of both North and South on sites in and around Chattanooga. **Chickamauga Battlefield**, 7 miles south of Chattanooga on US 27, contains more than 5,000 acres over which 120,000 men fought on September 19–20, 1863, for control of Chattanooga. A 7-mile, self-guided tour; slide program; tape tour; and Visitor Center/Museum display complement a full range of guided tours and demonstrations explaining the events of this major Confederate victory. One of the most complete collections of American shoulder arms is also on display in the Battlefield Visitor Center.

From **Point Park**, in the Lookout Mountain portion of the park, there is a sweeping view of the entire city, and the Moccasin Bend of the Tennessee River below. The Ochs Museum and Point Park Visitor Center interpret the siege and battles for Chattanooga in October and November 1863. Though the focal point of attention is the Civil War, Lookout Mountain is an interesting place to hike on paths through the beautiful hardwood forests.

Civil War buffs should not miss smaller sites that commemorate the battles of Wauhatchie and Missionary Ridge, and the site of General Grant's Chattanooga headquarters at Orchard Knob. Directions to these beautifully monumented areas, and further information on the park's varied units, may be obtained from the Point Park and Chickamauga Battlefield Visitor Centers. Both Visitor Centers are open 8 A.M. to 4:45 P.M. all year; later in the summer. Address: P.O. Box 2128, Ft. Oglethorpe, Georgia 30742. 615/752-5213.

## CHIMNEY ROCK NATIONAL HISTORIC SITE

### Nebraska

Towering 500 feet above the North Platte River Valley, this strange rocky spire of solitary grandeur was a celebrated prairie landmark on the Oregon Trail. Many of the passersby swam the river in order to climb "this great natural curiosity," and also probably to look ahead toward Scotts Bluff, which is 23 miles west. Chimney Rock lies southwest of Bayard, and can be reached in the pioneer style only, afoot. Stop at the interpretive trailer operated by the State of Nebraska on the main highway. Address: c/o Nebraska State Historical Society, 1500 R Street, Bayard, Nebraska 69334. 402/471-4758.

## CHRISTIANSTED NATIONAL HISTORIC SITE

### Virgin Islands

Three city blocks on the Christiansted waterfront preserve the colonial aura when "sugar was king" and St. Croix typified Danish plantation society in the New World. In this stimulating environment, Alexander Hamilton spent his youth. Fine architectural taste was reflected in buildings like the Customhouse, Steeple Building, and Government House. In the late 1980s, the site underwent major restoration to its mid–19th-century appearance, utilizing methods and material of the past. New exhibits interpret the plantation system,

architecture, and military history. Open daily 8 A.M. to 4 P.M. Other key historic points on the island are the Whim Greathouse, a restored sugar plantation; and Fort Frederik, in Frederiksted, dating from 1671, where the Danish governor in 1848 emancipated the slaves. Address: Box 160, Christiansted, Virgin Islands 00820. 809/773-1460.

## CLARK, GEORGE ROGERS, NATIONAL HISTORIC PARK

See George Rogers Clark National Historical Park, page 325.

## COLONIAL NATIONAL HISTORICAL PARK

### Virginia

On the Virginia Peninsula, three famous places between the York and James Rivers—Jamestown, Williamsburg, and Yorktown—form a triangle only 14 miles at the base, linked today by the Colonial Parkway. Each has a thrilling story of its own, starting from **Jamestown**, the first permanent English settlement in the New World, established in 1607. Jamestown Island in its entirety is a National Historic Site, jointly administered by the National Park Service and the Association for the Preservation of Virginia Antiquities. From the Visitor Center, a walking tour extends over the town site, along old streets and paths to the site of "James Fort," where Pocahontas was married, and the ruins of early houses, taverns, and shops. Also, visit the glass house, where costumed artisans demonstrate 17th-century glass-making. They sell attractive pieces at reasonable prices. A motor road loops the wildwood section of the island. Though not part of the national historical park, **Williamsburg**, capital of the Virginia colony after the decline of Jamestown, has been restored to its 18th-century appearance through the interest of the late John D. Rockefeller, Jr. More than 400 buildings stand in their colonial form; over half are original structures and the rest, faithful reproductions on original sites. From Williamsburg the parkway passes early plantation sites while following the York River to the final battleground of the American Revolution at **Yorktown**. The Siege Line Lookout on the roof deck of the Visitor Center affords a panoramic view over the strategic areas of the famous battle where Washington scored his great victory over Lord Cornwallis in 1781. A self-guided motor drive circles the battlefield, en- campment areas, and the old town. Along the tour are the famous redoubts, with cannons in place; the Nelson House, home of a colonial Virginia statesman; the Moore House, where terms of surrender were drawn; and the site of Washington's headquarters. You can rent bicycles at Williamsburg and use the parkway and tour roads at Jamestown and Yorktown. Peak visitor periods are April (gardens in bloom), summer, Thanksgiving, and Christmas through New Year's Day; so pick another time, or plan early. Address: Box 210, Yorktown, Virginia 23690. 804/898-3400.

## CORONADO NATIONAL MEMORIAL

### Arizona

Commemorating the first significant explorations by Europeans into the Southwest, the 4,976-acre memorial lies on the international boundary with Mexico, within sight of the valley through which Francisco Vasquez de Coronado and his expedition entered the present United States in 1540. From the parking area at Montezuma Pass, 30 miles west of Bisbee, a well-marked foot trail leads to Coronado Peak and a view of San Pedro Valley and the stark country through which the bold expedition marched. Another trail, about 3 miles long, follows Smugglers' Ridge to a picnic area. Coronado failed to find the golden cities, but he brought back knowledge of vast lands, paving the way for Spanish colonization. The annual International Borderlands Festival in April combines arts, crafts, music, and dance of Yaqui, Apache, English, and Spanish. Address: Route 2, Box 126, Hereford, Arizona 85615. 602/366-5515.

## CUMBERLAND GAP NATIONAL HISTORICAL PARK

### Kentucky-Tennessee-Virginia

A park of 20,305 acres in scenic hills where three states meet memorializes the westward adventure of Daniel Boone and his 30 axmen who blazed the "Wilderness Road" into Kentucky, and of pioneers who followed their paths in the trans-Allegheny migration. The Visitor Center, near the Middlesboro, Kentucky, entrance, houses paintings, pioneer tools, and weapons. Naturalist-historians answer questions.

**Pinnacle Mountain Overlook**, 2,440 feet above sea level, reached on an easy 4-mile scenic drive from the Visitor Center, affords a view of the historic notch in the mountain far below; the Tri-State Peak, where Kentucky, Virginia, and Tennessee meet; and a panorama of forested mountain and valley. **Hensley**, America's "last pioneer settlement," straddling the hilly Kentucky-Virginia line like an Inca fortress, is a restored mountaintop village of 28 buildings. You can see cabins made with hand-hewn logs, stone and wooden hinges, gun racks, plows, bee gums, and possum boards for drying skins. It is a good hike up the Cumberland Mountain to Hensley, but it is worth it.

Some 70 miles of trails lead to many interesting areas, such as **Goose Nest–Sink Sand Cave** (with an entrance 80 feet high), **White Rocks**, and **Hensley Settlement.** The 16-mile Ridge Trail, starting at the Pinnacle, follows the Cumberland crest along the Virginia-Kentucky border, presenting spectacular views of both states. Overnight trails involve fairly steep climbing; come prepared with good equipment. Wilderness Road Campground, accessible by car, offers 160 campsites and is the starting point for the Gibson Gap Trail. Three other campgrounds (Gibson Gap, Martins Fork, and White Rocks) are accessible only by foot. A backcountry permit serves as a campsite reservation for back-packers.

**The Iron Furnace,** reached on a remaining portion of the Wilderness Trail from the Gap, is one of many coldblast, charcoal-burning furnaces of pre-industrial America. Address: Box 1848, Middlesboro, Kentucky 40965. 606/248-2817.

## DAYTON AVIATION HERITAGE NATIONAL HISTORICAL PARK

Ohio

This park, authorized in 1992, preserves both the area's aviation heritage associated with Orville and Wilbur Wright and the life and works of poet Paul Laurence Dunbar, a friend and classmate of the Wright brothers. The park is not yet operational, but the Wrights' cycle shop and the Huffman Prairie Flying Field are open. A guidebook is available at area book shops. Address: Box 9280, Wright Brothers Station, Dayton, Ohio 45409. 513/223-0020.

## DE SOTO NATIONAL MEMORIAL

Florida

On May 30, 1539, Hernando De Soto set foot on the west coast of Florida. The 25-acre De Soto National Memorial commemorates that landing and the significance of his 4-year expedition throughout what is now the southeastern United States. Follow the boardwalk trail through the Mangrove Swamp for a picture of what conditions may have been like in De Soto's time. The Visitor Center offers exhibits of 16th-century arms and armor, as well as a historical documentary film from late December to early April, a living history camp, complete with costumed conquistadors firing the crossbow and arquebus (a matchlock gun), gives visitors a glimpse of the daily lives of Spanish soldiers. Address: Box 15390, Bradenton, Florida 34280. 813/792-0458.

## DOUGLASS, FREDERICK, HOME

See Frederick Douglass Home, page 293.

## EDGAR ALLAN POE NATIONAL HISTORIC SITE

Pennsylvania

Of the several houses where Poe lived at one time or another during his six years in Philadelphia, only this one—at 532 North Seventh Street—survives. It tells a great deal about the writer and his influence, opening doors to new approaches in mystery, adventure, and science fiction. Address: c/o Independence National Historical Park, 313 Walnut Street, Philadelphia, Pennsylvania 19106. 215/597-7120.

## EDISON NATIONAL HISTORIC SITE

New Jersey

Here are the laboratories where Thomas A. Edison and his coworkers spent 44 years in technological investigation and development. Guided tours (daily, 9 a.m. to 5 p.m.) include his office and library, and the "Black Maria," a reconstruction of Edison's motion picture studio. Here you'll see that classic pioneer film, "The Great Train Robbery," and an early "talkie" newsreel featuring Edison himself. In the visitors' lobby of the lab several hundred photos, models, and artifacts trace the genius of the man.

The site also includes Edison's home, "Glenmont," a 23-room Victorian mansion. The house is decorated with original furnishings, heirlooms, and family portraits. Guided tours are on the hour, 12 noon to 4 p.m., Wednesday through Sunday (except holidays). Make arrangements at the laboratory. Make your reservation as soon as you arrive at the laboratory. You won't be admitted to the residence without a pass and the number per tour is limited. Address: Main Street and Lakeside Avenue, West Orange, New Jersey 07052. 201/736-0550.

## EISENHOWER NATIONAL HISTORIC SITE

### Pennsylvania

Dwight D. Eisenhower loved his 230-acre Gettysburg farm adjoining the national military park and often said he wanted to "leave the place better than I found it." But leave it to whom? In 1967, Ike and Mamie made a gift of the property to the people of the United States, reserving the right of lifetime occupancy. He died in 1969, and she ten years later. The house has been open to the public since 1980, furnished much as when the former First Family occupied it—both a home for comfort and a showplace for entertaining. In order to visit the farm, stop early at the park service Visitor Center on Taneytown Road in Gettysburg, where tickets are distributed on a first-come, first-served basis for each day's scheduled tours. Off-season advance reservations can be made for groups only. A shuttle bus takes visitors to the farm and back. Address: Box 1080, Gettysburg, Pennsylvania 17325. 717/334-1124.

## ELEANOR ROOSEVELT NATIONAL HISTORIC SITE

### New York

This 180-acre estate of the First Lady includes Val-Kill, the stone cottage constructed in the mid-1920s for her by FDR. This site opened to the public on October 11, 1984, on the 100th anniversary of her birth. During the summer and fall tourist seasons, shuttle buses operate from the FDR Home National Historic Site to this site, two miles away. Private auto parking is allowed only during the off-season, except for visitors who are physically impaired. Address: Roosevelt-Vanderbilt National Historic Sites, Bellfield Headquarters, 249 Albany Post Road, Hyde Park, NY 12538. 914/229-9115.

## ELLIS ISLAND

See Statue of Liberty National Monument, page 351.

## EL MORRO NATIONAL MONUMENT

### New Mexico

Located 56 miles from Gallup and 42 miles from Grants (en route to Zuni Reservation). Principal feature is "Inscription Rock," a sandstone monolith bearing Indian petroglyphs, as well as inscriptions left by Spanish explorers and early western settlers. Trails are self-guiding; small picnic grounds, and campgrounds with water and pit toilets. Campground may be closed during off-season due to weather. Address: Ramah, New Mexico 87321. 505/783-4226.

## EUGENE O'NEILL NATIONAL HISTORIC SITE

### California

The genius of modern American tragic drama came to this wooded mountainside overlooking the San Ramon Valley in 1937. Here he wrote his last four great works, from *The Iceman Cometh* to *A Moon for the Misbegotten*. Tours of the home and grounds are regularly scheduled. The site, though in a growing San Francisco suburb, is perched on a remote mountain hideaway. Visitors may not access the site on their own. Tours are on a reservation basis, with transportation provided by Tours Are Us, Inc. For information write: c/o Eugene O'Neill National Historic Site, Box 280, Danville, California 94526. 510/943-5131.

## FATHER MARQUETTE NATIONAL MEMORIAL

### Michigan

Located in Straits State Park, 2 miles south of St. Ignace on US 2, the memorial pays tribute to the life and work of Father Jacques Marquette, the French Jesuit who came to the area in the 1600s. Address: c/o Straits State Park, St. Ignace, Michigan 49781. 906/643-8620.

## FEDERAL HALL NATIONAL MEMORIAL

### New York

On the corner of Wall and Nassau streets in downtown Manhattan, site of the present Federal Sub-Treasury Building, momentous events in American history took place. Here stood Federal Hall, where the first Congress met under the Constitution and where George Washington was inaugurated the first president. The stone on which he stood to take the oath of office is preserved in the rotunda, and one exhibit hall is set aside as a memorial to Peter Zenger, whose trial here marked a milestone in freedom of the press. New exhibits for the Museum of American Constitutional Government were dedicated in 1989 by President George Bush. You may see students who have come to "role play" Supreme Court arguments, as they learn how the Constitution influences their lives. Address: Superintendent, Manhattan Sites, National Park Service, 26 Wall Street, New York, New York 10005. 212/264-8711.

## FORD'S THEATRE

See page 293.

## FORT BOWIE NATIONAL HISTORIC SITE

### Arizona

Created as a military post in 1862 commanding Apache Pass in the northern foothills of the Chiricahua Mountains, the fort was the center of operations during the bloody campaigns against Cochise and Geronimo, the famed Chiricahua Apache leaders, and the taming of the Southwest. Some of the walls of the fort still stand. The area also includes sections of the Butterfield Overland Stage Route. Address: c/o Chiricahua National Monument, Dos Cabezas Route, Box 6500, Willcox, Arizona 85643. 602/847-2500.

## FORT CAROLINE NATIONAL MEMORIAL

### Florida

East of Jacksonville along the St. John's River, this 138-acre site commemorates the first permanent settlement in what became the United States. In 1565 the colony was wiped out by the Spanish, who established a settlement to the south. Although no vestige of the original fort and colony remains, the Visitor Center contains native Timucuan and European objects. A trail system leads to a scale model of the fort, passing through groves of pine and oak of the old Kingsley Plantation. Address: 13165 Mt. Pleasant Road, Jacksonville, Florida 32225. 904/221-5568.

## FORT CLATSOP NATIONAL MEMORIAL

### Oregon

Lewis and Clark enthusiasts will find a replica of the log fort in which the explorers spent the winter of 1805–06, after their epochal journey to the Pacific Coast. Trails from the fort replica, corresponding to those used by the explorers, lead to the canoe landing and to the camp spring. Allow time for the living history program and to visit the expanded Visitor Center, dedicated in 1991. Address: Route 3, Box 604FC, Astoria, Oregon 97103. 503/861-2471.

## FORT DAVIS NATIONAL HISTORIC SITE

### Texas

A key post in the defense system of West Texas from 1854 to 1891, Fort Davis guarded immigrants, freighters, and stages from Apaches and Comanches on the San Antonio–El Paso road. The stone and adobe structures, including officers row, barracks, and hospitals, are the most impressive of any Southwestern fort. The commanding officers' quarters and a kitchen have been furnished in period; in the summer women guides in costume are on duty. During this season a living history program presents officers on duty at the enlisted barracks and commissary. Any day of the year you can enjoy the recording of a sundown dress parade, complete with martial music and the sounds of a mounted review. You may also want to hike a trail to the ridge crest for another perspective of the fort. Adjacent is scenic Davis Mountain State Park (lodge, camping). Address: Box 1456, Fort Davis, Texas 79734. 915/426-3225.

## FORT DONELSON NATIONAL BATTLEFIELD

### Tennessee

The well-preserved earthen fort, rifle pits, and batteries, along with markers and tablets, trace the course of action near Dover in early 1862, when General U. S. Grant made bold use of the Tennessee River. He moved 17,000 men on transports, then marched them across a watershed between the Tennessee and Cumberland, and attacked. After intensive action Grant's demand for "unconditional surrender" resulted in the capture of some 14,000 Confederate troops and opened a river route into the heart of the Confederacy. Visitor Center contains exhibits and a slide program. Almost 700 Union war dead are buried in the national cemetery. Address: Box 434, Dover, Tennessee 37058. 615/232-5348.

## FORT FREDERICA NATIONAL MONUMENT

### Georgia

The ruins of the fort on St. Simons Island symbolize Great Britain's struggle to hold southeastern coastal lands against the Spanish. In its day this was the largest, most costly British fort in America, built of "tabby"—a mixture of oystershell, sand, and lime. In 1742 the Spanish fleet and army attacked, but James Oglethorpe, founder of the Georgia colony, scored a decisive victory in the Battle of Bloody Marsh fought nearby. Address: Route 9, Box 286-C, St. Simons Island, Georgia 31522. 912/638-3639.

## FORT LARAMIE NATIONAL HISTORIC SITE

### Wyoming

Near the confluence of the North Platte and Laramie River, this was a frontier center for trade, diplomacy, and warfare from 1834 to 1890. The fort was associated with Kit Carson, Jim Bridger, Buffalo Bill, Captain John C. Fremont, Red Cloud, and Spotted Tail, and countless wagon trains heading west. Today 11 original structures, including "Old Bedlam" (post headquarters) and the Sutler's Store, have been restored, surrounded by ruins of others. The 1889 commissary storehouse serves as the Visitor Center. Guided one-hour tours are conducted frequently during the day. Many special events are scheduled, including moonlight tours, art exhibits, and an old-fashioned July 4th. Visit Chimney Rock and Scotts Bluff in nearby Nebraska, then come here to picnic in the wooded grove and spend the rest of the day. Address: Box 86, Fort Laramie, Wyoming 82212-0086. 307/837-2221.

## FORT LARNED NATIONAL HISTORIC SITE

### Kansas

As a key frontier post established in 1859, this fort guarded the eastern part of the Santa Fe Trail and served as a base of operations against the Plains Indians. Nine original sandstone buildings frame the quadrangle parade ground with its restored 100-foot flagpole. The Visitor Center (in the enlisted men's barracks) contains a museum and an audiovisual program. Guided tours are available during the summer and on request the rest of the year. Make the most of the living history programs given on summer weekends. Address: Route 3, Larned, Kansas 67550-9733. 316/285-6911.

## FORT McHENRY NATIONAL MONUMENT

### Maryland

From a vessel offshore in the Patapsco River, Francis Scott Key, who had gone to secure the release of a friend from the British fleet, witnessed the 25-hour bombardment of this fort at the entrance to Baltimore's inner harbor. A barrage of 1,500 to 1,800 bombs, rockets, and shells were fired until after midnight. In the morning, when he saw the Stars and Stripes still waving, he began to write his immortal lines on the back of a letter. Thus the National Anthem was born.

The Visitor Center contains various exhibits, including a 16-minute film, on the history of the fort and the War of 1812. A weekend summer treat is provided by Fort McHenry Guard volunteers reenacting history in period uniforms. Programs begin at 1 p.m. each Saturday and Sunday. An island of green in the heart of industrial Baltimore, the park is bounded by water on three sides and is visited by a wide variety of birds during both spring and fall migrations. Congress approved $3 million to stabilize areas of the fort that are deteriorating, starting in 1992. Address: East Fort Avenue, Baltimore, Maryland 21230. 301/962-4290.

## FORT MATANZAS NATIONAL MONUMENT

### Florida

On the southern tip of Anastasia Island in 1565, a Spanish commander put to death two bands of French prisoners and eliminated the threat of continued French settlement in Florida. Later, in 1742, the Spaniards built Fort Matanzas on nearby Rattlesnake Island to protect St. Augustine's south entrance from enemy attempts to reach the city via the inland waterway. The small, historic fort sits on Rattlesnake Island across from the Visitor Center and museum. You can reach it aboard a small free ferry that operates daily 9 a.m. to 4:45 P.M. Address: c/o Castillo de San Marcos National Monument, 1 Castillo Drive, St. Augustine, Florida 32084. 904/471-0116.

## FORT NECESSITY NATIONAL BATTLEFIELD

### Pennsylvania

The battlefield surrounding the reconstruction of George Washington's 1754 fort is the park's principal unit and has been reconstructed faithfully. It is 11 miles east of Uniontown on US 40. Here George Washington engaged in his first major battle, signaling the start of the French and Indian War. For 200 years details of the fort were lost (the French burned it). Archaeological research has made possible the present replica of the fort, entrenchments, earthworks, and log cabin.

Include three nearby areas in your visit. Jumonville Glen, about 7½ miles away, was the scene of a wild preliminary skirmish after Washington had led a striking force of 40 men on an all-night march. Braddock's Grave, 1 mile west of the fort, marks the site where Major General Edward Braddock, commander of all British soldiers in the American colonies, was buried, in 1755, after being mortally wounded in the Battle of Monongahela. Note the monument erected to his memory by the Coldstream Guards in 1913. (His aide-de-camp, George Washington, had two horses shot from under him.) Mount Washington Tavern, overlooking Fort Necessity, typifies the sturdy stage stations built during the 1820s on the Old National Pike, when it was a mainstream of travel to the West. It is now a museum of the early pioneer period. Address: RD 2, Box 528, Farmington, Pennsylvania 15437. 413/329-5512.

## FORT POINT NATIONAL HISTORIC SITE

### California

In the Presidio under the south end of the Golden Gate Bridge is the massive brick fortification built by the Army between 1853 and 1861 to guard the entrance to San Francisco Bay.

The architecture of Fort Point is truly outstanding, incorporating many technical refinements into the masterwork of the Pacific Coast. It was used over a wide span of military history, from the Civil War down through the Indian Wars and the Spanish American War. Address: Box 29333, The Presidio of San Francisco, California 94129. 415/556-1693.

## FORT PULASKI NATIONAL MONUMENT

### Georgia

Built in the 19th century with an estimated 25 million bricks and walls 7.5 feet thick, it took 18 years to complete the massive structure on Cockspur Island commanding the mouth of the Savannah River, 15 miles east of Savannah. In the long casemated galleries are examples of some of the finest brickarch masonry in America. Surrounded by a moat, Pulaski was declared impregnable at a time when smoothbore guns would do little damage. And then came the Civil War.

The fort was seized first by the Confederates, but in 1862 Union forces on Tybee Island, a mile distant, unleashed a bombardment with the rifled gun. Within 30 hours the fort surrendered. This was the first site where rifled cannon were used successfully against a masonry fortification, ending the era of the moated medieval fortress. Fort Pulaski lies in a natural setting bordered by marsh and woodland; its moat, though a military failure, serves successfully as a rendezvous for birds like the heron, crane, and egret.

The best time for Pulaski is spring, and the ideal base is Savannah, a city distinguished by palmetto-shaded squares, small parks, and restored buildings. For further information write Superintendent, Fort Pulaski National Monument, Box 30757, Savannah, Georgia 31410. 912/786-5787.

## FORT RALEIGH NATIONAL HISTORIC SITE

### North Carolina

The restored fort occupies the site of the legendary "Lost Colony," the first attempted English settlement within the bounds of the present United States. The 150 men, women, and children sent by Sir Walter Raleigh arrived at Roanoke Island on the Outer Banks in July 1587. One month later the first child of English parentage in the New World, Virginia Dare, was born. But when Governor John White went to England and then returned to Roanoke Island in August 1590, he found the colony had disappeared. The only clue he found was the word "CROATAN" carved on a palisade post. The mystery of the "Lost Colony" has never been solved. This historic episode is the theme of an outdoor drama presented during summer evenings. Illustrated talks are given in the Visitor Center, which houses excavated artifacts.

The center is the starting place of the scenic Thomas Hariot Trail. Vegetation along the way is like that seen by the first settlers.

The nearby Outer Banks stretch 120 miles along the coast, forming a barrier between the Atlantic Ocean and the interior sounds and constantly undergoing changes caused by wind and wave. Cape Hatteras National Seashore and the Wright Brothers National Memorial should be visited. Address: c/o Cape Hatteras National Seashore, Route 1, Box 675, Manteo, North Carolina 27954. 919/473-5772.

## FORT SCOTT NATIONAL HISTORIC SITE

### Kansas

In 1842 two companies of the First Dragoons began building a fort 90 miles south of Kansas City to be part of a chain of outposts extending from Minnesota to Louisiana marking the boundary between U.S. and Indian lands. Following the Mexican War of 1846, the fort fell into disuse, but soon became a focal point of pre–Civil War conflicts between pro-slavery forces and followers of John Brown, the fabled abolitionist. It was the "Bloody Kansas" period. Then during the war the fort was activated again as a major supply center, with as many as 6,000 troops camped in the area, including two regiments of black soldiers—the First and Second Kansas Colored Volunteer Infantry. After the troops marched out for the last time, in 1873, the fort was forgotten for almost a century. Now the guard house, parade ground, officers quarters, hospital, and other buildings have been restored. Address: Old Fort Boulevard, Fort Scott, Kansas 66701-1471. 316/223-0310.

## FORT SMITH NATIONAL HISTORIC SITE

### Arkansas

Although one of the first U.S. military posts in the Louisiana Territory, three decades—from the 1870s through 1890s—represent Fort Smith's period of greatest fame. During that period it sheltered the famous court of Isaac C. Parker, the "Hanging Judge," who sentenced 160 men to the gallows while spreading law to the raw frontier. The site preserves the remains of two forts and Judge Parker's court. The nearby Belle Grove Historic District, covering 22 blocks, protects a variety of notable restored buildings, several of which serve new purposes as shops, restaurants, and apartments. Address: Box 1406, Fort Smith, Arkansas 72902. 501/783-3961.

## FORT STANWIX NATIONAL MONUMENT

### New York

The British built this fort in 1758 to protect a major Mohawk River portage in the French and Indian War. The 15-acre site is now in the center of the city of Rome, New York. The fort was completely reconstructed as it was, with logs, barracks, and cannon platform, for the 1976 Bicentennial. This followed archaeological excavation to locate the fort's features so they could be accurately restored. Recovered artifacts also shed light on the garrison life of the time. The original fort was lost through fire and leveling of the site. The fort was the scene in 1768 of the Indian Treaty of Fort Stanwix, in which the Iroquois ceded to the British a vast area east of the Ohio River. When the British attacked the colonies from Canada in August 1777, during the Revolution, the fort withstood a three-week siege. Address: 112 East Park Street, Rome, New York 13440. 315/336-2090.

## FORT SUMTER NATIONAL MONUMENT

### South Carolina

The five-sided fort, built on a small island in Charleston harbor as part of the chain of coastal fortifications, gained a place in history on April 12, 1861, when Confederate troops fired the opening shots of the Civil War at the small Federal garrison striving to hold it. For 34 hours the fort was defended until, as the commanding officer reported, "the quarters were entirely burned, the main gates destroyed by fire, the gorge walls seriously injured, the magazines surrounded by flames." After the Confederates occupied the fort, it became a symbol of their new nation. For nearly four years Federal forces were held at bay despite siege and bombardment, until the Confederates made their evacuation in February 1865. Today the fort is reached on regular two-hour boat tours from the City Marina in Charleston or Patriot's Point in Mt. Pleasant.

**Fort Moultrie,** a unit of the national monument accessible by car on Sullivans Island, preserves the scene of one of the first decisive victories of the American Revolution in 1776, and the burial place of the valiant Indian chief Osceola. The fort tells the story of seacoast defense from the Revolution to World War II.

Take the multilevel tour through underground powder magazines and installations covering five different time periods. While at the Visitor Center, don't miss the dramatic vistas from the observation deck—in one direction, of the fort with the Atlantic Ocean behind it and in the other direction, of Charleston harbor and the city. Address: 1214 Middle Street, Sullivans Island, South Carolina 29482. 803/883-3123.

## FORT UNION NATIONAL MONUMENT

### New Mexico

Located on the route of the Santa Fe Trail, where the mountains meet the plains, this fort was the largest military post guarding the 19th-century southwestern frontier. Kit Carson and General James H. Carleton were two of the illustrious figures who served here. Only adobe walls and chimneys rising starkly from the plains remain today, but a self-guiding trail leads through the ruins. The Visitor Center offers various displays that recall the drama and the adventure of yesterday's Southwest. During its 40 years in operation, the fort guarded the surrounding frontier and received shipments of materials for assignment to other forts in the Southwest. The monument is located 8 miles north of I-25, 26 miles north of Las Vegas, New Mexico. Camping facilities are nearby in Storrie Lake State Park and in the Santa Fe and Carson National Forests. Address: c/o Capulin Volcano National Monument, Capulin, New Mexico 88414. 505/425-8025.

## FORT UNION TRADING POST NATIONAL HISTORIC SITE

### North Dakota–Montana

As the principal fur-trading center on the upper Missouri River for four decades, Fort Union at Buford, N.D., became a stopping place for every important trailblazer, trapper, soldier, and traveler, from Jim Bridger to John J. Audubon and George Catlin. The Bourgeois House, once occupied by the fort manager, is the centerpiece of multimillion-dollar reconstruction completed in 1989. Other features include the trade house, palisade bastions, and 20-foot-high white wall surrounding the compound. Address: RR 3 Box 71, Williston, North Dakota 58801. 701/572-9083.

## FORT VANCOUVER NATIONAL HISTORIC SITE

### Washington

Established by the Hudson's Bay Company in 1825 and moved to this site in 1829, Fort Vancouver became the hub of fur-trading, political, social, and cultural activity. It was the symbol of Britain's claim to the Northwest when America was still in its expansion period. Much of the fort has been reconstructed. Events during the year include the annual tour by candlelight in October and living history demonstrations from April through October. Stop for lunch or dinner at the 1849 Grant House, now a restaurant serving continental fare. Along with Ulysses S. Grant, the fort (renamed Vancouver Barracks) housed at various times George Pickett, George C. Marshall, and Omar Bradley. To reach the park from I-5, turn off the Mill Plain Boulevard interchange; buses also run from downtown Portland. Address: Vancouver, Washington 98661. 206/696-7655.

## FRANKLIN, BENJAMIN, NATIONAL MEMORIAL

See Benjamin Franklin National Memorial, page 308.

## FREDERICK LAW OLMSTED NATIONAL HISTORIC SITE

### Massachusetts

Living and working here at "Fairsted" while developing plans for Boston's "Emerald Necklace" of parks, Olmsted was one of the foremost conservationists of the 19th century. His extensive papers are also housed here. Open only Friday through Sunday noon to 4:30 p.m. while restoration is continuing. Address: 99 Warren Street, Brookline, Massachusetts 02146. 617/566-1689.

## FREDERICKSBURG AND SPOTSYLVANIA COUNTY BATTLEFIELD MEMORIAL NATIONAL MILITARY PARK

### Virginia

No other area of comparable size on the American continent has witnessed such heavy and continuous fighting as this setting of four major Civil War battles within a 17-mile radius. The Visitor Centers near the southern edge of Fredericksburg and at Chancellorsville feature dioramas, pictorial displays, and maps, while narrative markers and monuments interpret the field of action with miles of original, well-preserved trench remains and gun pits. Fredericksburg, midway between the two capitals of Washington and Richmond, became the scene of fierce action in December 1862. Chatham Manor, privately occupied for about 200 years, played a key role as a Federal headquarters and hospital during the battle at the Rappahannock River. With its restored colonial garden, it is an attractive feature of the park. Other key tracts in the park boundaries have also been acquired. The site of a federal pontoon bridge that spanned the Rappahannock is nearby. You can see where Longstreet's men fired point-blank from Marye's Heights at charging Federals along the Sunken Road and forced them to retreat over the Rappahannock. In spring 1863 the Confederates won another signal victory at Chancellorsville, but Stonewall Jackson was accidentally wounded by his own men and died at Guiney Station (now Stonewall Jackson Shrine). At battles of the Wilderness and Spotsylvania Court House, in May 1864, a determined Union army under Grant began the

final drive that sealed the Confederacy. More than 15,000 Union soldiers are buried in the National Cemetery here, including 12,000 who are unidentified. The park also administers Old Salem Church, a 19th-century brick structure that was the scene of a sharp battle during the Chancellorsville Campaign. Bicycling is an excellent means to tour the individual battlefields. Address: 120 Chatham Lane, Fredericksburg, Virginia 22405. 703/373-4461.

## FRIENDSHIP HILL NATIONAL HISTORIC SITE

### Pennsylvania

This park preserves the country estate of Albert Gallatin, Secretary of Treasury under Presidents Jefferson and Madison, chief negotiator of the treaty ending the War of 1812, and U.S. envoy to both France and Great Britain. Gallatin built Friendship on the hill overlooking the Monongahela River near New Geneva in 1789. The house has recently undergone a major restoration, and is open daily, from 8:30 A.M. to 5:00 P.M.; closed December 25. Events include Festifall the last Sunday in September. Address: c/o Fort Necessity National Battlefield, RD 2, Box 528, Farmington, Pennsylvania 15437. 412/725-9190.

## GARFIELD, JAMES A., NATIONAL HISTORIC SITE

See James A. Garfield National Historic Site, page 332.

## GENERAL GRANT NATIONAL MEMORIAL

### New York

On a bluff overlooking the Hudson River (at Riverside Drive and 122nd Street) in Manhattan, the gray granite memorial to the great soldier who commanded the Union armies contains the sarcophagi of General Grant and his wife. Exhibits depicting the life of General Grant are displayed. Address: Superintendent, Manhattan Sites, National Park Service, 26 Wall Street, New York, New York 10005. 212/666-1640.

## GEORGE ROGERS CLARK NATIONAL HISTORICAL PARK

### Indiana

In the oldest city of the state, Vincennes, the imposing circular, columned memorial to George Rogers Clark celebrates his heroism in the winning of the Northwest. The 25 acres of formally landscaped grounds surround the stately memorial on the site of Fort Sackville, with the Wabash River flowing by the western boundary. Start at the Visitor Center to learn the full story from exhibits and motion pictures. As early as 1732 the French built the first fort here, but lost it in time to the English. Within the rotunda a bronze statue of Clark, the fiery young Virginian, is flanked by seven large murals depicting dramatic scenes in his expedition of 1778–79, when his little army swept the British out of the Northwest frontier. Near the memorial other historic structures are well worth visiting. These include: white-spired St. Francis Xavier Church, built in 1826; Grouseland, the home of William Henry Harrison; and the building that served as first capitol of the territory. The annual Spirit of Vincennes Rendezvous Memorial Day weekend at the park features historic re-enactments with 300 uniformed members of the North West Territorial Alliance. Address: 401 South Second Street, Vincennes, Indiana 47591-1001. 812/882-1776.

## GEORGE WASHINGTON BIRTHPLACE NATIONAL MONUMENT

### Virginia

A pastoral setting on the bank of Pope's Creek, 38 miles east of Fredericksburg, marks the ancestral plantation where George Washing-

ton was born. The original house burned in 1779; the present structure, designed to represent a typical planter's quarters, is carefully furnished in the period of Washington's boyhood. Young George spent the first three and one-half years of his life here, until 1735, when his family moved to Little Hunting Creek Plantation, later renamed Mount Vernon. George's half-brother, Augustine, inherited Pope's Creek upon his father's death, in 1743, and young George again spent several of his teen-age years on the plantation, as a companion to Augustine. On the grounds of the estate, the family burial plot contains the remains of his father, grandfather, and great-grandfather. The colonial "living farm" maintains livestock, poultry, and crops of old breeds and varieties common during colonial times. A few miles south along the Potomac is Stratford Hall, the ancestral estate of the Lees of Virginia and birthplace of Robert E. Lee. Address: RR 1, Box 717, Washington's Birthplace, Virginia 22443. 804/224-1732.

## GEORGE WASHINGTON CARVER NATIONAL MONUMENT

### Missouri

Birthplace of a slave who rose to fame as botanist, agronomist, and pioneer conservationist, the monument is located a few miles southeast of Joplin. The Visitor Center traces Carver's career and mighty achievements, including his developing new uses for Alabama clay, peanuts, sweet potatoes, and cotton. A self-guiding trail winds along the stream and through the woods of his youth. Address: Box 38, Diamond, Missouri 64840. 417/325-4151.

## GETTYSBURG NATIONAL MILITARY PARK

### Pennsylvania

Of more than 2,000 land engagements during the Civil War, Gettysburg ranks first in the memory of a nation. On the three days of July 1, 2, and 3, 1863, more men died than in any other battle ever fought on the soil of North America. Under terrible strains and sacrifices, the Confederate Army of 75,000 under Lee reached its high-water mark, but met its match in 97,000 Union troops under Meade and was turned back. Then, four months later, a portion of the battleground was dedicated as a burial ground by President Lincoln in a speech of 272 immortal words.

Gettysburg is one of the world's most monumented battlefields, veritably a museum of commemorative architecture and sculpture, with more than 400 memorials, many impressively large, plus 900 smaller markers. Your starting point should be the **Visitor Center**, which features the famed Electric Map orientation program and houses a large collection of Civil War relics. Within walking distance is the **Cyclorama Center,** where you can view museum exhibits, a 10-minute film, and the mammoth circular Cyclorama painting depicting Pickett's Charge. In the summer, an original copy of the Gettysburg Address is on display. Take your youngsters to the **Campfire Program** at the amphitheater in Pitzer's Woods, nightly at dusk during summer, where a National Park Service ranger conducts a program. There are several ways of touring the battlefield. The self-guided auto tour is outlined in a free park folder. The park also sponsors the **Licensed Battlefield Guide** program; dispatched from the Visitor Center, the guide provides a two-hour tour in your vehicle for a set fee. Bus tours, tape tours, and bicycles for rent are available at commercial locations near the Visitor Center. (For details on these programs contact the Gettysburg Travel Council, 35 Carlisle Street, Gettysburg, Pennsylvania 17325.) The use of bicycles in the park is encouraged on roads, and suggested routes are outlined in the park folder. There is no bike use of trails. Among monuments and memorials you will see are the **High Water Mark,** the climax of Gettysburg, where Pickett's Charge was halted; the **Pennsylvania Monument**, with statues of officers and the names of 35,000 Pennsylvanians who fought in the ranks; the **Virginia Memorial**, surmounted by a statue of General Robert E. Lee on his horse, Traveller; the spirited monuments of other states, possibly including your own; the **Eternal Light Peace Memorial,** dedicated to "peace eternal in a nation united"; and the **National Cemetery,** where Lincoln rose to his full height on November 19, 1863, and transformed the word Gettysburg from memorial to the dead into inspiration for the living.

**Winter scene.** The Visitor Center, in the heart of the park, is open year-round. Winter has become popular. Address: Gettysburg, Pennsylvania 17325. 717/334-1124.

## GOLDEN SPIKE NATIONAL HISTORIC SITE
### Utah

The ceremony on May 10, 1869, when the Union Pacific from the East met the Central Pacific from the West, is commemorated annually at the historic site of Promontory. About 1.7 miles of track have been relaid on the original roadbed where the rails were joined, with authentic working replicas of the original locomotives to recreate the emotion and excitement of the ceremony. Address: Box 897, Brigham City, Utah 84302. 801/471-2209.

## GRAND PORTAGE NATIONAL MONUMENT
### Minnesota

On the site of the old North West Company depot, bordering serene Grand Portage Bay, a newly reconstructed stockade (replacing an earlier one that burned) recalls the adventurous age when voyagers, seeking a treasure in furs, transferred supplies and trade goods from Lake Superior to the border lakes canoe route. The "great depot," established in 1778 near the Canadian boundary, was the first white settlement in Minnesota, a vital link in the 3,000-mile waterway extending from Montreal to Western Canada. Much of the charm of the 710-acre monument today is in the centuries-old trail—the 9-mile portage, with its lichen-covered rocks and reindeer moss. The trail offers an outstanding experience, but wear hiking shoes and expect encounters with mud, mosquitoes, and flies. Excursion boats operate from Grand Portage to Isle Royale National Park, 25 miles away in Lake Superior. If you're driving on the North Shore you'll find that Grand Portage is closely tied in with Old Fort William, the reconstruction of the bustling headquarters of a vast fur-trading empire at Thunder Bay, Ontario, at the western end of the Great Lakes. The old fort is like a living community, and has artisans who make things ranging from clothing to big-freight canoes. Grand Portage Rendezvous Days, in mid-August, revive old ways and traditions of Chippewa Indians and the British Northwest Company. Address: Box 668, Grand Marais, Minnesota 55604. 218/387-2788.

## GRANT-KOHRS RANCH NATIONAL HISTORIC SITE

### Montana

Located in the Deer Lodge Valley, north of Yellowstone, the headquarters of a 19th-century cattle kingdom—one of the giant "spreads" of the Old West—still preserves early log buildings and the main ranch house. The site commemorates the frontier cattle era of American history. Livestock, together with the ranch collection of saddles, tools, wagons, buggies, and other artifacts, complete the cattleman's saga. Allow time to observe the blacksmith and other artisans at work and the guided tour of the Victorian house. The town of Deer Lodge also has some fascinating public and private buildings, including the Territorial Prison. Address: Box 790, Deer Lodge, Montana 59722. 406/846-2070.

## GUILFORD COURTHOUSE NATIONAL MILITARY PARK

### North Carolina

In gentle rolling country in Greensboro, the battle fought here in March 1781 was part of the British campaign to subdue the southern colonies one by one while advancing north. Though the strategy had already backfired at Kings Mountain and Cowpens, Cornwallis won this battle over General Nathanael Greene's poorly equipped colonials. But he lost 25 percent of his troops, and when he advanced into Virginia, it was to the ultimate defeat at Yorktown. Graphic, colorful exhibits at the contemporary-style Visitor Center tell the story of the southern campaign, while memorials are located at various points on the battlefield. You can follow a one-way tour road by car; better yet, the bicycle trails or footpaths. Address: Box 9806, Greensboro, North Carolina 27429-0806. 919/288-1776.

## HAMILTON GRANGE NATIONAL MEMORIAL

### New York

The only home ever owned by Alexander Hamilton, a principal figure in shaping the Republic, and one of the few Federal-period structures surviving in New York City. Eventually the house will be restored to its appearance in Hamilton's time. Present programs are conducted around themes of drama, music, and colonial crafts. Address: Superintendent, Manhattan Sites, National Park Service, 26 Wall Street, New York, New York 10005. 212/283-5154.

## HAMPTON NATIONAL HISTORIC SITE

### Maryland

An elaborate Georgian mansion built with formal charm and elegance during the latter part of the 18th century lies on a 60-acre tract near

Towson. This once vast agricultural/industrial domain contains 28 separate structures and includes the 14-acre Hampton Farm complex, with overseer's house, slave quarters, granary, and barns. During the Revolution the Hampton ironworks supplied arms and ammunition to the patriots. Charles Ridgely, nephew of the builder, served as governor of Maryland from 1815 to 1818. It was he who developed the Ridgely empire, amassing a great estate that extended as far as the eye could see. The Ridgely family occupied Hampton from 1788 to 1948. Formal gardens and greenhouses still remain with geometric parterres and broad grass ramps. Adjacent to the mansion are the orangery, carriage house, stables, and outstanding trees. Within the mansion, obviously planned for elaborate entertaining, are period furnishings and portraits by such notable early artists as Sully and Peale. Open daily from 9 A.M. to 4 P.M.; closed Thanksgiving, Christmas, and New Year's Day. Address: 535 Hampton Lane, Towson, Maryland 21286-1397. 410/962-0688.

## HARPERS FERRY NATIONAL HISTORIC PARK

Virginia–West Virginia–Maryland

In the shadow of the Blue Ridge Mountains, where the Shenandoah and Potomac rivers meet, the hillside town became the scene of John Brown's ill-fated abolitionist raid in 1859, which forced the nation to realize the slavery issue was inescapable. The Visitor Center and museum are located in the paymaster's headquarters of the old arsenal that was the target of Brown's little band in its effort to arm the slaves and establish a free state in the mountains. Gun buffs will appreciate the breech-loading Hall rifles on display. Though Brown's men captured the arsenal, within two days they were driven to refuge in the little engine house known as "John Brown's Fort" and forced to surrender. When the Civil War broke out, two years after Brown's raid, the town was almost a continual battleground and finally was left in ruins. Follow the marked half-mile walking tour (about one hour) past restored old houses, shops, stores, and the "fort" returned to near its original site. Visit the restored blacksmith shop, where craftsmen produce articles for homes and shops of the town with 19th-century tools. Then walk to the heights of Jefferson Rock, for a view of the rivers favored by Thomas Jefferson. Take advantage of the large new visitor parking lot and shuttle bus to points of interest. Address: Box 65, Harpers Ferry, West Virginia 25425. 304/535-6224.

## HARRY S TRUMAN NATIONAL HISTORIC SITE

Missouri

This century-old Victorian house was home to President Truman from his marriage, in 1919, until his death, in 1972. It served as the "Summer White House" during his time in office, 1945 to 1953. The first floor was opened to visitors for the Truman Centennial in May 1984. Reservations for guided tours (small fee) are available the day of the tour only, at the Information Center, Truman Road and Main Street. The Truman Presidential Library is a few blocks away. In addition, several homes in the surrounding historic district are included in the park, preserving the early–20th century air. In 1994 the Truman Farm Home at Grandview was added to the historic site. Truman often said his respect for hard work and common sense took root at the farm. Address: 223 North Main Street, Independence, Missouri 64050-2804. 816/254-2720.

## HERBERT HOOVER NATIONAL HISTORIC SITE

Iowa

At West Branch, the 31st president of the United States was born August 10, 1874, in a simple two-room cottage that still stands and forms the nucleus of this attractive, landscaped area. A National Park Service employee greets visitors and chats about Herbert

Hoover's childhood, while pointing out such family items as the cradle and high chair used by the Hoover children. On the north side of Penn Street, across from the birthplace, the reconstructed blacksmith shop is similar to the one operated by the President's father. During spring and summer blacksmiths demonstrate their crafts. Here, too, are the grave where Mr. Hoover was buried in 1964 while 75,000 mourners stood in silent tribute, and the limestone Hoover Presidential Library-Museum, a museum full of mementos of a life of humanitarianism and public service. Address: Box 607, West Branch, Iowa 52358. 319/643-2541.

## HOME OF FRANKLIN D. ROOSEVELT NATIONAL HISTORIC SITE

### New York

The house at the edge of a gently rolling plateau overlooking the Hudson River where the "Squire of Hyde Park" was born and reared was ample for the large family, but scarcely reflects elegance or opulence. The mood is set by the surrounding woodlands he loved and helped to plant, and by the burial place where he and his wife lie beneath a plain white marble monument within a garden where roses bloom. Oil portraits, gifts of crystal, gold, and brocade, tokens sent by emperors and everyday people—these are housed with 30,000 volumes and vast correspondence in the adjacent Franklin D. Roosevelt Library, a source of learning for scholars and schoolchildren for generations to come. Visiting hours 9 a.m. to 5 p.m., but crowds are heavy during summer and on weekends, so arrive early. Address: Bellfield Headquarters, 249 Albany Post Road, Hyde Park, New York 12538. 914/229-9115.

## HOMESTEAD NATIONAL MONUMENT

### Nebraska

A T-shaped quarter section of prairie and woodland, 160 acres, near Beatrice (due south of Lincoln), is on the site of the claim of one Daniel Freeman, an Illinois farmer, who became one of the first to file for free land under the Homestead Act. This law, signed by Abraham Lincoln in 1862, was an epochal advance in democracy, enabling more than one million citizens to become landholders. The Visitor Center displays trace development of the Homestead movement. The adjacent cabin is furnished to the finest details with remnants of the belongings of the people who once called it home. The restored one-room Freeman School is west of the cabin on Nebraska 4. Displayed behind the center are farm implements and carriages. History touches everything, even to the 1½-mile-long nature trail. The path winds through native prairie and wooded areas, reaching its high point at the graves of Freeman and his wife, Agnes, high on a hill. More than 130 species of birds have been sighted, showing the richness of the tall-grass prairie. Address: RFD 3, Box 47, Beatrice, Nebraska 68310. 402/223-3514.

## HOPEWELL FURNACE NATIONAL HISTORIC SITE

### Pennsylvania

The cold-blast ironworks symbolize the industrial techniques of the nearly self-sufficient "iron plantations" that were once a way of life. Founded about 1770, Hopewell Village supplied cannon and shot for the Revolutionary War effort and produced cast iron until 1883. Many of the structures beyond the Visitor Center are the originals—the "Big House," or Ironmaster's Mansion, blacksmith shop, charcoal house, furnace, and tenant homes. Others, like the waterwheel, bridge house, barn, and store, have been handsomely restored to complete the walk into America's yesterday. During July and August the village comes "alive" with the costumed interpretation program reflecting the 1820–1840 period. Hopewell is open daily 9 A.M. to 5 P.M. except Thanksgiving Day, December 25, and January 1. French Creek State

Park, immediately adjacent, provides facilities for camping, picnicking, and swimming. Address: 2 Mark Bird Lane, Elverson, Pennsylvania 19520. 215/582-8773.

## HORSESHOE BEND NATIONAL MILITARY PARK

### Alabama

Near the present site of Dadeville, on March 27, 1813, Major General Andrew Jackson's army of Tennessee soldiers and Indian allies defeated the Creek Indian warriors of Chief Menawa at the Battle of Horseshoe Bend. This ended the Creek Indian War and opened large portions of the present states of Alabama and Georgia to settlement by European-Americans. The battle is interpreted at the museum and a free audio tape is available at the Visitor Center for those interested in taking the automobile tour. Enjoy the parks' picnic area and explore the hiking trails. Address: Route 1, Box 103, Daviston, Alabama 36256. 205/234-7111.

## HUBBELL TRADING POST NATIONAL HISTORIC SITE

### Arizona

His name was John Lorenzo Hubbell, but he was known as "Don Lorenzo," champion of Indians, and especially of Indian craftspeople. He established his trading business about 1878. The sprawling adobe home appears as it did at the turn of the century, displaying his valuable collection of paintings and Indian crafts. The trading post is open to all as a living remnant of the old days.

The rug room has been famous for decades. Mr. Hubbell influenced the Navajo women to produce well-made rugs with native patterns and bright red, black, and white colors, products that would find ready acceptance in the east- and west-coast markets. Today stacks of beautiful rugs are available for inspection and sale. Collections of firearms, books, and other memorabilia further enhance the southwestern atmosphere of the room.

The Park Service maintains the live atmosphere of the home just as in the operation of the trading post. There are no protective covers on the original furnishings or the Navajo floor rugs—a type of textile that absolutely defies wear. Visitors are not admitted to the home except during conducted tours. At sheep-shearing time visitors may see wool being weighed, purchased, and sacked for shipment to the mills as in Don Lorenzo's day.

The trading post is located 1 mile west of Ganado within the boundaries of the Navajo Reservation, and 55 miles from Gallup, New Mexico. From the east it is on the way to Grand Canyon National Park, Canyon de Chelly National Monument, and the Hopi mesas. Address: Box 150, Ganado, Arizona 86505. 602/755-3475.

## ILLINOIS & MICHIGAN CANAL NATIONAL HERITAGE CORRIDOR

### Illinois

This unusual and new type of national park unit was established through legislation signed by President Reagan in Chicago on August 24, 1984. The heritage corridor extends from Chicago south and west for a hundred miles along three parallel canals that cut across the prairie in the valleys of the Des Plaines and Illinois rivers to the small cities of La Salle and Peru. The common factor tying the region together is the now-abandoned Illinois & Michigan Canal, a great feat of manual labor and engineering, which operated from 1848 to 1900 as the first commercial transportation link between the Great Lakes and Great Plains.

The heritage corridor can be reached almost anywhere along I-55 southwest from Chicago to Joliet, then along I-80 to the west. Address: 15701 South Independence Boulevard, Lockport, Illinois 60441-6584. 815/740-2047.

# INDEPENDENCE NATIONAL HISTORICAL PARK

## Pennsylvania

The principles of self-government by men and self-determination by nations are memorialized in the heart of Philadelphia, in an area properly called "the most historic square mile in America." Here lie the sites where Congress met during the bitter, trying days of the American Revolution, where the Declaration of Independence and Constitution were conceived and adopted, and where, starting in 1790, Congress and the Supreme Court conducted their affairs for 10 years before moving to the new capital city, Washington.

You will find this historical park the most extensive and complex restoration ever undertaken by government in the United States—a combined federal, state, and city effort. In block after block, the visitor can see historic and architectural monuments that figured in the flowering of America's independence.

To avoid crowds, try to arrive early. Most buildings are open 9 to 5 daily, but hours are extended at some during summer. From early May to Labor Day, waiting times for tours of Independence Hall range from 15 minutes to an hour. Because of school groups, Thursday and Friday are peak days of April, May, and June, so plan your visit for other weekdays. Picnicking is allowed throughout the park; street vendors provide a wide range of fare. Leave your car elsewhere, even though two Philadelphia Parking Authority garages are located in the park. The park can be easily reached by bus, subway, or taxi.

The place to begin is the **Visitor Center,** at Third and Chestnut streets, which provides orientation to the park through displays and a film shown in twin 300-seat cinemas. The development of the 20-acre historical park has involved demolishing 100 worn and faded structures, including one 10-story building, and replacing them with 18th-century–style plantings and landscape features between historic buildings. This restoration tells a story of Philadelphia as well as the nation. The city stepped in to rescue the hall and square in 1818, when it was proposed to parcel out land for building lots, and it continues to hold title to them.

The main building to visit, of course, is **Independence Hall.** Once, as the capitol of Pennsylvania, it was the most impressive building in the colonies; now it has been pieced together anew after precarious years when ceilings sagged and walls neared collapse. In the interior, the first floor has been returned to its appearance of 1774–87. Toward this end skilled technicians performed patient, minute work and historians examined four million manuscripts in this country and in Great Britain. The Assembly room has been refurnished with authentic period items and originals, and it appears substantially the same as the day when delegates adopted the Declaration of Independence. In 1979, Independence Hall was designated a World Heritage Site, in recognition of its role in national and international historic events.

Cross Chestnut Street to the **Liberty Bell,** originally ordered in 1751 as a memorial to William Penn's "Charter of Privileges," but which became in time a worldwide symbol of liberty. In the early hours of 1976, the National Park Service moved the 2,000-pound bell from Independence Hall to its new $900,000 pavilion of glass and stone 100 yards away. The bell was moved from a crowded location to permit easier viewing.

**Congress Hall** next door looks the way John Adams found it for his inauguration, and as Congress knew it at the time that the members formally added the Bill of Rights to the Constitution. Other buildings in this cluster harmonious in style are **Philosophical Hall**, headquarters of America's oldest learned society, founded by Benjamin Franklin; and **Library Hall**, a reconstruction of the original, housing major historical collections.

As one of several major restorations for the Bicentennial, the Park Service opened the unique **Franklin Court** area in 1976. Though Franklin's home is long gone, the site on the south side of Market Street is outlined by a large steel frame, with a ramp leading to an underground museum, featuring sophisticated displays and devices that would have intrigued Old Ben himself. In addition, five bordering row houses on Market Street (three of which he owned) have been restored and adapted to interpret various phases of Franklin's life. At 316 Market Street, a post office now commemorates Franklin's role as the first Postmaster of the United States. Stop in to buy stamps and mail letters—they'll carry the famous postmark: "B. FREE FRANKLIN."

The **Second Bank of the United States,** one of two National Portrait Galleries in the U.S., houses 185 portraits of individuals from American history; the majority were painted from real life by artist Charles Willson Peale during the years 1776–1800. Visitors may gaze upon the likenesses of Thomas Jefferson, John Quincy Adams, and other prominent Philadelphians of the period. The building itself was designed and built in the 1800s by William Strickland, modeled after the Parthenon of Greece; it is now considered one of the finest examples of Greek Revival design in America.

Other restored focal points of the Revolutionary era are **Old City Hall,** first meeting place of the Supreme Court; the three-story reconstructed **Declaration (Graff) House,** where Thomas Jefferson stayed while writing the Declaration of Independence; and the house once occupied by General Thaddeus Kosciuszko. Walk two blocks from Independence Hall to **Washington Square,** burial ground for about 2,000 Revolutionary War soldiers. It will become part of the park after improvements are completed.

Among other notable buildings in the park are: **Christ Church,** where Franklin, Washington, and other statesmen worshipped; Gloria Dei Church, a privately owned National Historic Site and the oldest church in Pennsylvania; and the house where Dolley Todd Madison lived with her first husband. You can walk to **Mikveh Israel Cemetery,** ancient Jewish burial ground, where Haym Salomon, patriot of the Revolution, is interred. Evening makes an ideal time for a walking tour, particularly in summer, when Philadelphia's daytime tends to be humid.

Best of all is the pleasure of browsing along little streets like Delancey, Pine, or Lombard, in the Society Hill section, where the environment of another era pervades. Not all the houses are old, or even simulated antique, but the most modern are in scale. Try not to drive into downtown Philadelphia. If you can't stay at nearby hotels (like the Holiday Inn), then stay at the outskirts and take public transportation. Address: 313 Walnut Street, Philadelphia, Pennsylvania 19106. 215/597-8974.

## JAMES A. GARFIELD NATIONAL HISTORIC SITE
### Ohio

Lawnfield, the home of the twentieth president of the United States, is located on US 20 at Mentor, northeast of Cleveland. The first two floors are furnished with original Garfield possessions. Also on the site are the small building used as headquarters in the 1880 campaign and the log-cabin replica of Garfield's birthplace. Address: 8095 Mentor Avenue, Mentor, Ohio 44060. 216/526-5256.

## JEAN LAFITTE NATIONAL HISTORICAL PARK
### Louisiana

This area, authorized by Congress in 1978, is emerging as an exciting public facility in the Mississippi River Delta. Make your first stop the Visitor and Folklife Center in historic Jackson Square, in the heart of New Orleans. See exhibits on diverse cultures of the area, then start on walking tours of the French Quarter, a national historic district.

The former Chalmette National Historical Park, another unit of the new park, is located 6 miles from New Orleans and commemorates the last major battle of the War of 1812. The decisive American victory on January 8, 1815, led to General Andrew Jackson's rise to national prominence. The Visitor Center and battle museum are in the historic Beauregard

House, starting place for touring the battlefield.

The Baratarie Marsh Unit, 15 miles south of New Orleans, comprises freshwater swamp and marsh laced with bayous and canals. It was struck by Hurricane Andrew in 1992, exposing marshlands to wave erosion and saltwater intrusion. Barataria was frequented by Jean Lafitte, the celebrated privateer-smuggler, in bringing contraband into New Orleans. Bayou des Familles and Bayou Coquille are parts of a canoe trail completed in 1984. From the Visitor Center you can walk the Bayou Coquille Trail, less than a mile long, bordered by freshwater marsh and cypress–tupelo gum swamp, or the longer Ring Levee Trail. Address: 423 Canal Street, New Orleans, Louisiana 70130. 504/589-3882.

## JEFFERSON MEMORIAL

See Thomas Jefferson Memorial, page 297.

## JEFFERSON NATIONAL EXPANSION MEMORIAL NATIONAL HISTORIC SITE

### Missouri-Illinois

Commemorating the territorial growth of the United States, this national historic site covers 91 acres at the "Gateway to the West," the original site of St. Louis. The dominant feature, a 630-foot-high stainless steel arch on the shore of the Mississippi River designed by Eero Saarinen, contains an elevator system— really a five-passenger train—enabling the visitor to reach a lofty observatory. At the base of the arch, a Museum of Westward Expansion depicts adventures in shaping the western heritage. The Old Courthouse, high above the river, is also part of the memorial. Dating from 1839, it served as setting of the famous Dred Scott case. The Old Cathedral, begun in 1831, has also been preserved and included in the park. In August 1984, President Reagan signed legislation expanding the park to include a portion of the waterfront in East St. Louis, Illinois, opposite the Gateway Arch. A national museum of ethnic culture ultimately may be constructed on the site. Address: 11 North Fourth Street, St. Louis, Missouri 63102-1882. 314/425-4468.

## JIMMY CARTER NATIONAL HISTORIC SITE

### Georgia

In 1975, when Jimmy Carter began his campaign for the presidency, the small south Georgia town he called home became the focus of national attention. Following his election, little Plains overflowed with curiosity seekers, as well as media, Secret Service agents, and government officials. Plains will never be the same again, but the National Historic Site (including the Carter residence, boyhood home, and high school) and the 650-acre preservation district reflect rural southern heritage and culture. The residence is definitely private, protected by the Secret Service, but by all means stop at the railroad depot, in the downtown area, which served as Carter campaign headquarters and is now the park's visitor center. Tie in a visit to Andersonville, the Civil War prison, a few miles north, and Westville, a fascinating restored community in which the Jimmy Carter family has long been interested, outside Lumpkin, a few miles west. Address: c/o Andersonville National Historic Site, Route 1, Box 800, Andersonville, GA 31711. 912/924-0343.

## JOHN FITZGERALD KENNEDY NATIONAL HISTORIC SITE

### Massachusetts

At 83 Beals Street, Brookline, the late president of the United States was born on May 29, 1917. The family lived here until 1921. Mrs. Rose Kennedy, the late President's mother, supervised restoration and refurnishing of the two-story house. Address: 83 Beals Street, Brookline, Massachusetts 02146. 617/566-7937.

## JOHN MUIR NATIONAL HISTORIC SITE
### California

The apostle of national parks lived in this rambling house in Martinez from 1890 to 1914, while writing some of his most important works. The study, or "scribble den," where he wrote many of his books and articles, is the most important room in the house. During this period he founded the Sierra Club, a great conservation organization which carries on in his tradition throughout the country. The house actually was built by Muir's father-in-law, Dr. John Strentzel, often called the father of California horticulture. After viewing the interior, walk through the orchard to the historic Martinez Adobe, home of his eldest daughter and her husband. Address: 4202 Alhambra Avenue, Martinez, California 94553. 415/228-8860.

## JOHNSON, ANDREW, NATIONAL HISTORIC SITE

See Andrew Johnson National Historic Site, page 307.

## JOHNSON, LYNDON B., NATIONAL HISTORIC SITE

See Lyndon B. Johnson National Historical Park, page 337.

## JOHNSTOWN FLOOD NATIONAL MEMORIAL
### Pennsylvania

The valley town of Johnstown has been hit by three major floods during the past 100 years. The memorial park honors the 2,209 victims of the most severe flood, which occurred in 1889. On May 31st of that year, the South Fork Dam collapsed, sending a 40-foot wall of water 14 miles down the valley to Johnstown. Within ten minutes the town was destroyed. The Visitor Center features exhibits and displays, and lectures by rangers are presented during spring and summer. The site also includes hiking trails and a picnic area. Address: c/o Allegheny Portage Railroad National Historic Site, Box 189, Cresson, Pennsylvania 16630. 814/886-6100.

## KALAUPAPA NATIONAL HISTORICAL PARK
### Hawaii

On the north shore of the island of Molokai, at the base of 2,000-foot cliffs, and virtually isolated from the rest of the island, except by plane, Kalaupapa has long attracted world attention and admiration. Here in 1866 a leper colony was established, designed to isolate patients who might spread the disease if left "at large." The work of the legendary Father Damien (from his arrival in 1873 until his death in 1889) in due course focused interest in leprosy, or Hansen's Disease, concern for its victims, and hope for therapy. The establishment of the national park in 1980 marks a landmark in human learning and tolerance, while also safeguarding the settlement and its residents.

Access is limited by geography and regulation. Kalaupapa is jointly managed by the National Park Service and Hawaii State Department of Health. A visitor permit (required to protect privacy and lifestyle of residents rather than for medical reasons) is available through either one of two tour companies locally owned and operated. For details and costs, write Damien Tours or Ike's Scenic Tours, c/o Kalaupapa Settlement, Kalaupapa, Hawaii 96742. The bonus for coming is in observing the spectacular north shore cliffs, rising 3,000 feet from the ocean. Remote areas of the 10,726-acre park include lush rain forests and abundant stone structures and other ancient features that make Kalaupapa a rich archaeological preserve. Address: Kalaupapa, Hawaii 96742. 808/567-6729.

## KALOKO-HONOKOHAU NATIONAL HISTORICAL PARK

### Hawaii

Authorized by Congress in 1978, this park on the Kona Coast of the "Big Island" of Hawaii will preserve a complex of structures and sites representing Hawaiian culture before contact with Europeans. At present, all lands remain in private ownership and the area is closed to the public. Contact nearby Pu'uhonua Ō Honaunau National Historical Park. Address: 73-4786 Kanalani Street 14, Kailua, Kona, Hawaii 96740. 808/329-6881.

## KENNESAW MOUNTAIN NATIONAL BATTLEFIELD PARK

### Georgia

Kennesaw Mountain National Battlefield Park commemorates the entire Atlanta Campaign of the Civil War. Union forces led by General William Sherman made a direct assault on the entrenched Confederates under General Joe Johnston. When the battle was over, there were nearly 3,000 Union casualties compared to 800 Confederate losses. The mountaintop offers a sweeping view of the well-preserved battlefield. Exhibits at the Visitor Center interpret the entire campaign; 16 miles of interpretive trails afford close-up views of the battle lines. Address: 900 Kennesaw Mountain Dr., Kennesaw, Georgia 30144-4854. 404/427-4686.

## KEWEENAW NATIONAL HISTORICAL PARK

### Michigan

The heritage of copper mining on the Keweenaw Peninsula is commemorated in this innovative historical site, established in 1992. A large portion of the property within the park will remain in private ownership. Although in the early stages of development, a number of attractions already tell the stories of America's first mineral rush. Brochures are available from the Keweenaw Tourism Council, Box 336, Houghton, Michigan 49931 (1-800/338-7982) or Keweenaw National Historical Park, Box 471, Calumet, Michigan 49913. 614/774-1126.

## KINGS MOUNTAIN NATIONAL MILITARY PARK

### South Carolina

On a quiet, stony crest in the foothills just below North Carolina, visitors can walk in the footsteps of backcountry men of Appalachia who struck an overwhelming blow against British forces on October 7, 1780, during the darkest period of the Revolutionary War in the South. The 900 "ragged" men advanced with their long rifles against the steel bayonets and disciplined ranks of Provincial Regulars and Tories who held the mountaintop. They screamed and hooted, charging through tangled brush and wooded ravines, stirring autumn leaves and driving birds to flight. "Face to the hill!" shouted Major William Chronicle when his troops wavered; even as he was struck and killed they moved ahead, destroying the Tory force of 1,100. At the Visitor Center and along the trails lined with memorial stones, you will learn how the tide was turned at Kings Mountain into the advance toward victory at Yorktown. Since the battle occurred during October, autumn is especially appropriate for photography. Address: Box 40, Kings Mountain, North Carolina 28086. 803/936-7921.

## KLONDIKE GOLD RUSH NATIONAL HISTORICAL PARK

### Washington

This unit of the park depicts Seattle's historic role as main supply center for stampeders heading north to Alaska and the Klondike gold fields in 1897–98, and complements the unit of Klondike Gold Rush National Historical Park in Skagway, Alaska. (See under Alaska Parks, page 403.) Mining exhibits, artifacts, photomurals, and audiovisual programs relate the gold rush drama. History pervades the surrounding Pioneer Square neighborhood. Address: 117 South Main, Seattle, Washington 98104. 206/553-7220.

## KNIFE RIVER INDIAN VILLAGES NATIONAL HISTORIC SITE
### North Dakota

The sites of three Hidatsa and Mandan Indian villages at the confluence of the Knife and Missouri rivers are rich in history and valuable evidence of the lifestyle of the Plains Indians. Sacajawea, the Indian guide of the Lewis and Clark expedition, lived here.

The site covers about 1,300 acres, recalling the period when the villages were centers of a social order built on buffalo hunting, agriculture, and fur trading. The last village was abandoned in 1845, following decimation of the Hidatsa by smallpox. Address: Box 168, Stanton, North Dakota 58571. 701/745-3300.

## KOSCIUSZKO, THADDEUS, NATIONAL MEMORIAL

See Thaddeus Kosciuszko National Memorial, page 353.

## LINCOLN, ABRAHAM, BIRTHPLACE

See Abraham Lincoln Birthplace National Historic Site, page 306.

## LINCOLN BOYHOOD NATIONAL MEMORIAL
### Indiana

Lincoln's boyhood home and the burial site of his mother, this 200-acre wooded park contains a memorial Visitor Center and museum, built of native limestone connected by a semicircular cloistered walk. At the Lincoln Living Historical Farm, normal farming activities provide visitors the chance to try pioneer skills. Try to use the froe and wooden beatle to rive shingles for the cabin roof the way Abe did. Lake with camping facilities at nearby Lincoln State Park. Address: Highway 162, Lincoln City, Indiana 47552-1816. 812/937-4541.

## LINCOLN HOME NATIONAL HISTORIC SITE
### Illinois

To Abraham Lincoln, Springfield was home. Here he moved his family into the only house he ever owned, where he lived from 1844 to 1861. In 1988, following three years of extensive renovation and restoration costing $2.2 million, the house was reopened to the public, returned to its appearance of 1860, with furniture and furnishings of that day. When the Lincolns left for Washington on a rainy Monday in February 1861, the president told a gathered crowd, "Here I have lived a quarter of a century, and have passed from a young to an old man. I now leave, not knowing when, or whether ever, I may return." The historic site covers four city blocks and preserves twelve homes of Lincoln's neighbors. Address: 413 South Eighth Street, Springfield, Illinois 62701-1905. 217/492-4241.

## LINCOLN MEMORIAL

See page 295.

## LITTLE BIGHORN BATTLEFIELD NATIONAL MONUMENT
### Montana

The Sioux and Cheyenne, in the Battle of the Little Bighorn, destroyed the flamboyant Lt. Col. George A. Custer and his troopers of the Seventh Cavalry during two hot days in June, 1876, but it was the final victory in their defense of an independent way of life. The field of "Custer's Last Stand" is in southeastern Montana, near Hardin, on the route between the Black Hills and Yellowstone. The monument preserves only 765 acres of a battlefield that stretched six miles long and more than a mile wide. Park archaeologists have excavated human bones and everyday items (nails, buckles, and rivets) from the monument and from adjacent private land. Their findings will help establish Indian and cavalry battle positions, and fill in gaps about the battle. Start at the Visitor Center to see maps and dioramas of the battle, then drive the loop road over the frontier ridges. Guided bus tours (modest fee) and interpretive programs are offered daily mid-June through Labor Day. Address: Box 39, Crow Agency, Montana 59022. 406/638-2622.

## LONGFELLOW NATIONAL HISTORIC SITE

### Massachusetts

Henry Wadsworth Longfellow wrote "Evangeline," "Hiawatha," and other literary works here. The mansion at 105 Brattle Street in Cambridge, Massachusetts, was the poet's residence from his appointment as a professor of modern languages at Harvard University in 1837 till his death in 1882. Built in 1759 by a wealthy Royalist, the house is a prime example of Georgian architecture. Starting in mid-July 1775, General George Washington made it his Continental Army headquarters. The property, covering almost two acres, includes a carriage house and formal gardens, all of which have been maintained by the Longfellow House Trust since 1913. Chamber music concerts are given on the lawn on Sunday afternoons during summer. Address: 105 Brattle Street, Cambridge, Massachusetts 02138. 617/876-2100.

## LOWELL NATIONAL HISTORICAL PARK

### Massachusetts

Established in 1978, this park commemorates the birth of the industrial revolution in America and what is sometimes called "the first planned community for mass production." The majority of the early work force here was composed of young women from all over New England, attracted by the chance to leave the farm and earn steady wages. In time the textile industry went elsewhere and Lowell suffered decades of decline. The park along with Lowell Heritage State Park has sparked its resurgence as one of the liveliest places in New England. The Visitor Center is located in the former Bigelow Carpet Company mill at 171 Merrimack Street. Don't miss the Boott Cotton Mills Museum, opened in 1991—it's the first major museum on industrial history in the National Park System. Reservations are required for the guided tours conducted daily late May through Labor Day. Tours on turn-of-the-century trolleys run daily late May through mid-October. Address: 169 Merrimack Street, Lowell, Massachusetts 01852. 508/459-1000.

## LYNDON B. JOHNSON NATIONAL HISTORICAL PARK

### Texas

This park is divided into two units located 15 miles apart. The **LBJ Ranch Unit** includes ranch, Texas White House, family cemetery, and reconstructed birthplace. Nearby is Lyndon B. Johnson State Historical Park. A free 90-minute bus tour from the state park features Johnson landmarks. Tours available daily except January 1 and December 25. The **Johnson City Unit** includes Johnson Settlement where the president's grandparents lived and the Visitor Center. Open daily except January 1 and December 25. Also in Johnson City, the vacant LBJ Memorial Hospital was transferred to the National Park Service in 1990; it has been refurbished for use as a visitor center. The new facility will open this year. Reservations available for groups of 15 or more for both units of the park. Address: Box 329, Johnson City, Texas 78636. 512/868-7128.

## LYNDON BAINES JOHNSON MEMORIAL GROVE ON THE POTOMAC

See page 295.

## MAGGIE L. WALKER NATIONAL HISTORIC SITE

### Virginia

The residence in Richmond of this pioneer black civic leader became a national park unit through Congressional action in 1978. "Miss Maggie" was the first American woman known to establish and head a bank (in 1903). She was also an early supporter of voter registration for blacks. Most furnishings at the 18-room red brick home at 110½ E. Leigh Street have been left intact. The surrounding area of 19th-century row houses is an historic district. Address: c/o Richmond National Battlefield Park, 3215 East Broad Street, Richmond, Virginia 23223. 804/226-1981.

## MANASSAS NATIONAL BATTLEFIELD PARK

### Virginia

The opening field battle of the Civil War was fought July 21, 1861, about 26 miles southwest of Washington, the first test of strength between two armies. Henry House Hill, the most significant site within the park, is where General Stonewall Jackson arrived at the crucial hour. Another officer striving to rally his disorganized men pointed to Jackson's line and shouted: "There stands Jackson like a stone wall! Rally behind the Virginians!" Jackson had won his immortal name, and before the day was done, the desperate Confederate defense changed into an attack, routing the Union army back to Washington. The following summer, the Second Battle of Manassas (Bull Run, it was called in the North) was fought between 73,000 Union troops and 55,000 Confederates under Robert E. Lee. After two fierce days the Confederates scored a decisive victory, and Lee prepared to invade Maryland. At the Visitor Center, an electric map traces the troop movements. Two driving tours follow paths of significance throughout the park. In 1980 Congress voted to extend the boundaries of the 3,000-acre national battlefield. Additions include Stone Bridge and the Brawner Farm, where Jackson ordered the charge for the Second Battle. In 1988 Congress voted again to expand the park, authorizing addition of a site where Lee established his field headquarters. Address: 12521 Lee Highway, Manassas, Virginia 22110. 703/754-1861.

## MANZANAR NATIONAL HISTORIC SITE

### California

Congress early in 1992 designated Manzanar as a national historic site—shortly after the 50th anniversary of Executive Order 9066, the decree signed by President Franklin D. Roosevelt that forced Japanese-Americans from their homes on the West Coast. More than 100,000 were rounded up and moved to ten "war relocation centers," actually little more than concentration camps. Manzanar, in a scrubby desert valley on the east side of the Sierra Nevada mountains, was the first of the camps; at its peak it held more than 10,000 people in discomfort and shame.

The presidential decree was motivated by fear, following the attack on Pearl Harbor, of a Japanese strike on the West Coast and by widespread anti-Asian racism. But forty years later the government conceded an abuse of civil rights. On August 10, 1988, President Ronald Reagan signed a bill providing an apology as well as payment of $20,000 to each individual imprisoned under the executive order.

The national historic site, covering 550 acres, is located off Route 395 north of Lone Pine in the Owens Valley between Sequoia–Kings Canyon National Parks and Death Valley National Park. The only buildings still standing are a sentry post, guard post, and combined auditorium and gymnasium, but streets that separated the barracks and traces of former rock gardens are still visible. Development of park facilities is underway. Water is unavailable, so be sure to bring your own. Sturdy walking shoes are essential. The annual pilgrimage of former residents is held the last Saturday in April. The Eastern California Museum, 5 miles north of Manzanar, has a collection of photographs and artifacts from the camp. Address: c/o Death Valley National Monument, California 92328. 619/786-2331.

## MARTIN LUTHER KING, JR., NATIONAL HISTORIC SITE

### Georgia

Within several blocks of the juncture of Auburn Avenue and Boulevard in Atlanta are the birthplace, boyhood home, church, and grave site of Dr. Martin Luther King, Jr., civil rights leader and advocate of social change through nonviolent action. Guided tours are conducted of the King home; open daily except January 1 and December 25; large groups should call for reservations. The national historic site, authorized by Congress in 1980, and surrounding Preservation District include such structures as the 1895 Fire Station; Our Lady of Lourdes Catholic Mission; the King home; Ebenezer Baptist Church; and commercial buildings. These are among approximately 300 historic structures within 95 acres located several blocks from the heart of Atlanta. Many homes have been owned by the same families since the early 1900s. In early 1996 a visitor center and museum are scheduled to open on the site. For now, an information station and bookstore are open daily. The 1996 Summer Olympics will bring many visitors to Atlanta. The Park Service and the local community are working to complete a number of other improvements. Address: c/o National Park Service, 522 Auburn Avenue N.E., Atlanta, Georgia 30312. 404/331-5190.

## MARTIN VAN BUREN NATIONAL HISTORIC SITE

### New York

The eighth president of the United States lived here at Lindenwald, his estate 25 miles south of Albany, from the time he left the presidency in 1841 till his death in 1862. Born in nearby Kinderhook, in 1782, Van Buren became a leader in the emergence of Jacksonian democracy, served as Andrew Jackson's vice president, then ran successfully as Jackson's choice to succeed him in 1836. While serving as president, he purchased this house, a 2½-story Federal-style brick structure built in 1797. After his reelection defeat by William Henry Harrison, Van Buren turned his attention to Lindenwald. He installed a ballroom, added a rear wing, a four-story brick tower, and Victorian front porch. The cream-painted house with slate roof appears much as it did in Van Buren's day. Extensive renovations have kept the building closed except for weekends. The 42-acre site includes 13 acres adjacent to the original Lindenwald grounds. Address: Box 545, Route 9H, Kinderhook, New York 12106. 518/758-9689.

## McLOUGHLIN HOUSE NATIONAL HISTORIC SITE

### Oregon

One of the few remaining pioneer dwellings in the region once known as the "Oregon Country" was built in 1845–46 by Dr. John McLoughlin, who won enduring fame by aiding American settlers in establishing their homes. Federal, state, and private funds have combined to restore and refurnish the house. Address: c/o Fort Vancouver National Historic Site, Vancouver, Washington 98661. 206/696-7655.

## MINUTE MAN NATIONAL HISTORICAL PARK

### Massachusetts

The celebrated "Battle Road of the Revolution" has been reclaimed from long years of neglect. The park (authorized in 1959 and officially established as a major event of the 1976 Bicentennial) embraces portions of the route in Lexington, Lincoln, and Concord, along which armed citizens declared their right to be free. Original stone walls, boulders, and important landmarks are still in place west of Massachusetts 128 (I-95). About dawn on April 19, 1775, almost 70 militia men faced a force of 700 British soldiers at Lexington Green. Four hours later at Old North Bridge, in Concord, the first British soldier fell and, by Emerson's poetic testimony, "the embattled farmers stood, and fired the shot heard round the world."

Try to start at the **Visitor Center** on Massachusetts 2A, between Lexington and Concord, completed for the 1976 Bicentennial. Then go to Lexington Green. The heroic statue represents minuteman Captain Parker facing the line of British approach. The Revolutionary monument, on the southeast corner, commemorates the eight Americans killed here; they were the first fatalities of the war. The British continued their march—but would return later in the day defeated.

From the center of Lexington drive to Fiske Hill, start of the preserved 4-mile section of the **Battle Road** on which the famous running battle took place. This was the scene of some of the heaviest fighting. Walk the 1-mile, self-guiding trail to the site of the 18th-century Fiske Farm.

Entering **Concord,** you'll want to visit at least a few of the homes of illustrious 19th-century literary figures. By all means include the Wayside (associated with the Alcotts, Nathaniel Hawthorne, and Margaret Sidney), which is administered by the National Park Service.

North Bridge, over the Concord River, is a key focal point. On one side of the bridge you'll see the graves of two British soldiers, the first of the king's men to fall in the American Revolution, and on the opposite side the famous Minute Man statue by Daniel Chester French.

Volunteers dressed as minutemen, farm wives, soldiers, and craftsmen often present special programs on summer weekends near the Buttrick Mansion. The first floor of the mansion serves as both information center and exhibit hall.

Visitors with disabilities should note that reservations can be made for "In Touch with the Past," an entire touch-and-feel tour of the Buttrick Mansion (the red-brick 1911 house), complete with spinning wheels, furniture, and tools. A one-day program designed for visitors on motorcoach tours provides a quick look at Minute Man and Lowell National Historical Parks, recalling how the American Revolution and the Industrial Revolution changed the country. Address: Box 160, Concord, Massachusetts 01742. 617/484-6156.

## MONOCACY NATIONAL BATTLEFIELD

### Maryland

This park, still under development, is designed to preserve a vital link in efforts of the Union Army to block a Confederate dash into Washington in July 1864. General Jubal Early, one of the boldest rebel leaders, brushed aside outer defenses and was leading his men down the Georgetown Pike near Rockville. On July 9, Union forces slowed Early down in the bloody battle on the Monocacy River, but did not stop him. Meanwhile, hundreds of rugged veterans were rushed by steamboat from the James River and Hampton Roads, in southern Virginia, to the defense of the capital. Early made a brief flurry on July 11, but had lost the edge and retreated. Address: 4801 Urbana Pike, Frederick, Maryland 21701. 301/662-3515.

## MOORES CREEK NATIONAL BATTLEFIELD

### North Carolina

A brief but decisive battle between Loyalists and Revolutionists was fought about 20 miles northwest of Wilmington, North Carolina, in an opening phase of the Revolution—an engagement often called "the Lexington and Concord of the South." It was on February 27, 1776, when 1,600 Loyalist militia attacked a patriot force of about 1,000 entrenched on

Moores Creek. The Revolutionists turned back the assault, and captured or dispersed the invaders.

At the Visitor Center, just inside the park entrance, you can learn the full significance of the battle. A trail leads past monuments and to the Negro Head Point Road, where the focal point is the reconstructed bridge. As the Loyalists stormed over, they were met by withering musket fire. The victory discouraged the growth of Loyalist sentiment and spurred Revolutionary fervor throughout the colonies. A good time to visit the park is in May, when magnolias and spring wildflowers are in full bloom. Address: Box 69, Currie, North Carolina 28435. 919/283-5591.

## MORRISTOWN NATIONAL HISTORICAL PARK

### New Jersey

Barely 30 miles from New York, Americans may experience the richest single source spot of the Revolution. In a little state where over 100 battles and skirmishes were fought, this was the site of Washington's military headquarters and the main encampment of his ragged army during the toughest winters of the war.

The park became federal property in 1933, when the Department of the Interior took it over from the Washington Association of New Jersey, which had operated the Ford Mansion since the 1870s.

The place to begin is the **Historical Museum,** in the heart of Morristown. It has one of the most extensive collections of military pieces in the country. Exhibits in this modern structure consist of weapons, military equipment, paintings, and old prints. Dioramas depict the Revolutionary events.

Adjacent to the museum, facing Morris Street, the **Ford Mansion** served as Washington's headquarters, where he reorganized his weary and depleted forces almost within sight of British lines in New York. It was here that Lafayette brought the welcome word that a French army was on its way to aid in the struggle. Inside, much of the furniture now displayed was there when Washington occupied it, while the remaining furnishings date from the Revolutionary period or earlier. Few preserved kitchens of the period are so completely furnished with colonial utensils and cooking equipment.

From the south end of Court Street, a road leads upward into the **Fort Nonsense** area, a key orientation point overlooking Morristown. Jockey Hollow, 4 miles south of Morristown, with rolling woodlands and open fields, closely resembles the setting at the time the main Continental army of 10,000 encamped here during the winter of 1779–80. Many of the campgrounds have remained relatively undisturbed, and physical evidence of army occupation can still be seen. You can photograph reconstructed log huts, chinked with clay and held together with nails and wooden pegs; the originals were built to hold 10 to 12 soldiers each. The **Wick House,** standing along the road to Menham, represents an architectural complement to the **Ford Mansion,** one typifying the elegance of town life, the other the solid qualities of the colonial rural scene. The kitchen garden of the Wick House is a feature in itself, with its herbs and rows of quince, gooseberry, and currant shrubs before the background of fruit trees, the whole ensemble recreating an 18th-century scene. Nature, both cultivated and wild, is much a part of this park. More than 100 species of birds, some 20 species of mammals and over 300 species of shrubs, trees, and wildflowers have been identified in Jockey Hollow. A walk over the Primrose Brook Nature Trail affords the opportunity to see many such elements of the park landscape.

Morristown is a park of all seasons. Winter is the time to see the bare trees and white carpet before the Ford Mansion and the snow nestling in the chinks of the little log huts. Standing there you can feel the same chill breeze that swept over the encampment. Address: Washington Place, Morristown, New Jersey 07960. 201/539-2016.

# MOUNT RUSHMORE NATIONAL MEMORIAL

## South Dakota

On the solid granite face of 5,725-foot Mount Rushmore, about 20 miles south from Rapid City in the Black Hills, colossal carved figures represent the heads of four great presidents—Washington, Jefferson, Lincoln, and Theodore Roosevelt. Work began under the direction of Gutzon Borglum in 1927 and was completed in 1941 under the guidance of his son, Lincoln. It was dedicated in 1991 by President George Bush. The heads are best seen under morning light; they are also visible by floodlight for a scheduled period each evening. Programs are presented in conjunction with the floodlighting each evening during summer at 9 P.M. in the Memorial Amphitheatre. A similar program is presented at the Visitor Center, at the same time, for persons with handicaps. The avenue leading to a view of the sculptures is lined with flags of each of the 50 states. Food services are provided during the summer by a concessioner. Camp in nearby Black Hills National Forest, Custer State Park, and local communities. Address: Box 268, Keystone, South Dakota 57751-0268. 605/574-2523.

# NATCHEZ NATIONAL HISTORICAL PARK

## Mississippi

Melrose Estate in Natchez provides a glimpse back in time to the planter society that flourished in the South before the Civil War. The mansion was built for John T. McMurran, a wealthy planter and attorney; today it is the heart of the historical park. Tour the house, explore the 80-acre park grounds and outbuildings, visit the bookstore, and enjoy special events such as living history weekends and ranger-guided programs. Recent additions to the park are the William Johnson House, built in the 1840s by the noted African-American diarist, and Fort Rosalie, located on the bluffs above the Mississippi River. They are currently undergoing restoration and are not open to the public. Address: Box 1208, Natchez, Mississippi 39121. 601/442-7047.

# NEZ PERCE NATIONAL HISTORICAL PARK

## Idaho

From northeastern Washington and Oregon across Idaho into Montana, 37 sites interpret the history and culture of the Nez Perce Indians and their valiant struggle for freedom under legendary Chief Joseph. The park was established in 1965 with 24 sites in or near the Nez Perce Indian Reservation in north-central Idaho. In 1992, key additions were made, including the grave of Chief Joseph at Nespelem, on the Colville Reservation in northeastern Washington; the Wallowa Valley grave site and monument of his father, outside Joseph, Oregon; and Big Hole National Battlefield in Montana, scene of fierce action in 1877 during the Indians' ill-fated flight to Canada (see separate listing, page 309).

An outstanding National Park Service Visitor Center is located at Spalding, near Lewiston, Idaho. Note the inscribed words of Too-Hool-Hool-Zute: "The earth is part of my body. I belong to the land out of which I came. The earth is my mother." Visit nearby wayside exhibits at Kamiah and White Bird Battlefield. Address: Spalding, Idaho 83551. 208/843-2261.

# NINETY SIX NATIONAL HISTORIC SITE

## South Carolina

The site of hard-fought skirmishes and battles during the Revolutionary War, Ninety Six was incorporated into the National Park system by congressional action during the Bicentennial, in 1976. The village of Ninety Six began as a frontier colonial outpost and became a key trading center and seat of justice for much of upcountry South Carolina beyond Charleston. Its curious name derived from the fact that it was located ninety-six miles from the principal Cherokee village of Keowee. A fort was built at Ninety Six during the bloody Cherokee War of 1759–1760. Like much of the rest of South Carolina, the village was predominantly Tory in sentiment as the Revolution came on. It became the scene of several confrontations between Loyalists and Patriots from the early months of the war until shortly before Cornwallis's surrender at Yorktown. The most notable was a month-long siege conducted by about 1,000 Patriot troops under General Nathanael Greene in May and June, 1781, which ended when Greene was forced to withdraw by the arrival of British reinforcements. Soon after, the British burned the village of Ninety Six, their last important base in the interior, and returned to Charleston. The archaeological remains of the frontier trading post and Indian fort, the colonial courthouse village and its Revolutionary War earthworks, and the post-war rural town form the basis of the park. Address: Box 496, Ninety Six, South Carolina 29666. 803/543-4068.

## PALO ALTO BATTLEFIELD NATIONAL HISTORIC SITE

### Texas

Civil War sites have long been well identified, but here, north of Brownsville, is the only unit of the National Park system related to the Mexican-American War. Fought on May 8, 1846, the battle of Palo Alto was the first major engagement of the war. It and another encounter at Resaca de la Palma the next day resulted in resounding defeat for the vaunted Mexican army. The war continued when American forces invaded lands that ultimately became New Mexico and California, as well as Mexico. The 1848 Treaty of Guadalupe-Hidalgo secured for the United States an enormous land mass, including all or parts of present states of California, New Mexico, Arizona, Colorado, Nevada, and Utah. The historic site first was authorized in 1978, but in 1992 Con-

gress voted to enlarge it from 50 to 3,400 acres. Address: Drawer 1832, Brownsville, Texas 78522. 210/548-2788.

## PEA RIDGE NATIONAL MILITARY PARK

### Arkansas

A hard-fought battle of the Civil War took place 30 miles northeast of Fayetteville (or 10 miles from Rogers) in March 1862. A Confederate force of 16,000 under Major General Earl Van Dorn marched northward planning to sweep across Missouri and capture St. Louis. At the same time, Brigadier General Samuel R. Curtis pushed his 10,500 Union soldiers southward to rid Missouri of enemy secessionists. The two armies collided at Pea Ridge, just south of the Missouri border, and the roar of battle could be heard for miles across the Ozark hills. Casualties were high on both sides. The outcome was of importance, for it secured Missouri for the Union. The events are interpreted at the modern stone Visitor Center beside US 62. For the best overall view of the battlefield, take the scenic 7-mile tour road along the old Telegraph Road (part of the route of the Butterfield Overland Mail Line from St. Louis to San Francisco). Stop along the way at the overlooks atop Pea Ridge and at the restored Elk Horn Tavern. Address: Pea Ridge, Arkansas 72751. 501/451-8122.

## PECOS NATIONAL HISTORICAL PARK

### New Mexico

The remains of an ancient Indian pueblo and a large Spanish colonial mission are located 25 miles southeast of Santa Fe off I-25, in what formerly was Pecos National Monument. When the Spaniards arrived in 1540, they found a five-story communal house with 2,000 inhabitants; the following year Coronado left from here on his expedition into the Great Plains. The first mission was established in the early 1600s by the Franciscans.

After the pueblo revolt of 1680, a second mission was established, the ruins of which are seen today. The attractive Visitor Center, worthy of the setting, is the gift of film star Greer Garson and her late husband, Buddy Fogelson. Visit the ruins on a 1¼ mile self-guiding trail.

In 1990 Congress expanded 365-acre Pecos National Monument to include 5,500 acres of The Fogelsons' Forked Lightning Ranch, and designated it a national historical park. The ranch land was officially transferred to the federal government in 1992, adding other historical dimensions to the park, including sites associated with early Spanish settlement, the Santa Fe Trail, and the Civil War Battle of Glorieta. Address: Drawer 418, Pecos, New Mexico, 87552-0418. 505/757-6414.

## PERRY'S VICTORY AND INTERNATIONAL PEACE MEMORIAL

### Ohio

"We have met the enemy and they are ours," reported Oliver Hazard Perry after his dramatic victory in the Battle of Lake Erie during the War of 1812. The imposing pink granite memorial, commemorating that victory and the enduring peace between the United States and Canada, is located at Put-in-Bay on South Bass Island, 4 miles from the mainland. It is served during summer by car ferries from Scott Point on Catawba Island and from Port Clinton, and by plane both summer and winter from Port Clinton. From the observation deck (open April to October), near the top of the 352-foot-high memorial, you can see the battle scene between the shorelines of Canada and the United States. Address: Box 549, Put-in-Bay, Ohio 43456-0549. 419/285-2184.

## PETERSBURG NATIONAL BATTLEFIELD

### Virginia

Due south of Richmond, Petersburg was the scene of nine and one-half months of grim siege and warfare, beginning in the summer of 1864 and ending with the Confederate retreat toward surrender at Appomattox in April 1865. Throughout the siege Grant's huge army continually hammered at Lee's veterans stubbornly protecting their capital and the Petersburg rail center, adding new chapters to the heroism and suffering that was the Civil War. The park's Visitor Center is the start of the one-way, 4-mile auto tour to many points of interest. Battery 5, from which Grant shelled Petersburg with "The Dictator," a 17,000-pound seacoast mortar, is the first stop. Then comes Battery 9, with a trail leading to Meade's Station, which Lincoln visited during the fighting, and Fort Stedman, the site of Lee's "Last Grand Offensive." The most engrossing part of this battlefield surrounds the section called the Crater. Here Union troops from Pennsylvania, former coal miners, dug a tunnel under Confederate lines and exploded four tons of gunpowder on July 30, 1864. The explosion killed 278 men and created an immense crater. In fighting that followed, the Confederates recaptured the crater, while the Union Army lost 4,000 men—killed, wounded, or captured. Daily throughout the summer the park's Living History program interprets the lives of a Union regiment in camp, a Confederate gun crew, and other military and civilian events during the siege. The park has 6 miles of marked bike trail. It is open year-round from 8 A.M. to dusk; the Visitor Center operates from 8 A.M. to 5 P.M., and 8 A.M. to 7 P.M. in the summer. While in the area, also visit City Point, Grant's headquarters during the siege. It lies at the confluence of the Appomattox and James rivers, in nearby Hopewell. Address: Box 549, Petersburg, Virginia 23804. 804/732-3531.

## PETROGLYPH NATIONAL MONUMENT

### New Mexico

Along the volcanic cliffs of Albuquerque's West Mesa a fascinating gallery of rock art, or petroglyphs, reveals an ancient culture. The first simple petroglyphs, mostly circles and lines, were created sometime between 1000 B.C. and A.D. 500 by hunter-gatherers. Anasazi Indians, farming the area between 700 and 1300, added a few more figures. After 1300, when villages crowded along the Rio Grande, the petroglyph gallery thrived—birds, animals, lizards, humans, horned serpents, star beings, flute players, and kachina masks were carved and pecked into the rock by Pueblo artists. Later Spanish settlers inscribed crosses. Over centuries, these artists created more than 15,000 petroglyphs. Congress designated the monument in 1990; necessary lands are being acquired and management plans developed so it may fully open to the public. In the meantime, visit Petroglyph State Park, managed by the city within the monument boundary. Address: c/o National Park Service, Box 728, Santa Fe, New Mexico, 87504. 505/988-6387.

## PIPE SPRING NATIONAL MONUMENT

### Arizona

The well-preserved Mormon fort, nestled at the base of the colorful vermillion cliffs near Fredonia in northwestern Arizona, was settled by the hardy followers of Brigham Young, who were determined to make their way in a harsh land. Within sturdy high sandstone walls and heavy gates, two houses face each other, sharing the benefits of a spring. Two mirrorlike pools of water and large shade trees enhance the area. A recently developed feature is the "living history ranch," with working cattle branding, baking of cookies, quilting, spinning, and weaving. The Visitor Center has displays interpreting both the Kaibab Paiutes, native Indians of the region, and the Mormon settlers. Gifts and food service are available. Address: HC 65, Box 5, Fredonia, Arizona 86022-1099. 602/643-7105.

## PU'UHONUA Ō HONAUNAU NATIONAL HISTORICAL PARK

### Hawaii

On the Kona coast of the "Big Island," the ancient place of refuge on a 20-acre lava shelf dipping into the ocean at the village of Honaunau was a guaranteed sanctuary to vanquished warriors and taboo breakers. Here you can see prehistoric house sites, royal fish ponds, coconut groves, and spectacular shore scenery along the coves, cliffs, and tidal pools. Demonstrations are given in ancient carving and weaving by park personnel. You can also picnic, swim, and snorkel. The nearby "Painted Church," gable-roofed St. Benedict's, is one of Hawaii's unusual sights, the work of a Belgian priest who wanted to bring his parishioners the splendors of medieval Europe—he painted walls, ceilings, and pillars with copies of religious works in Hawaiian motif. A new unit of the national historical park, Puukohola Heiau National Historic Site, is located at Kawaihae Bay, on the northwestern shore. Address: Box 129, Kona, Hawaii 96726. 808/328-2326.

## PUUKOHOLA HEIAU NATIONAL HISTORIC SITE

### Hawaii

The fourth unit of the National Park system on the "Big Island" protects the famous temple built by Kamehameha the Great and closely associated with the founding of the Kingdom of Hawaii, as well as remnants of the homesite of John Young, English adviser to the king. Hawaiians constructed the massive platform in 1791 of water-worn lava rocks and boulders, without use of mortar. None of the structures that once stood within the wall now remain. The park is located at Kawaihae Bay, on the beautiful northwestern shore. From the lovely setting here on the Kona Coast, you can see Mauna Kea, Mauna Loa, Hualalai, and the Koala Mountains.

To learn more about Hawaii's fascinating

history, be sure to schedule a visit to nearby Lapakahi State Historical Park, which depicts life in an ancient fishing village. Plan to swim (or snorkel) at Spencer Beach Park. Address: Box 4963, Kawaihae, Hawaii 96743. 808/882-7218.

## RICHMOND NATIONAL BATTLEFIELD PARK
### Virginia

This park preserves remnants of eleven separate Civil War sites that recount four embattled years of war. In the last nine months of the war, Richmond saw Union and Confederate forces wearily engaged in smaller actions, particularly near Chaffin's Farm. These earthen fortifications helped prevent capture of the Confederate capital until finally abandoned on April 2, 1865. At the Chimborazo Visitor Center exhibits and audio visual programs explain wartime Richmond. Maps, tapes, and literature are also available for touring each battlefield. Short trails at Gaines' Mill, Fort Harrison, Fort Brady, Malvern Hill, and Drewry's Bluff lead past historical features. Exhibit shelters at Fort Harrison and Cold Harbor offer displays and maps. Interpretive programs including historical talks, bus tours, and living history encampments are presented throughout the year. The Visitor Center is open daily except Christmas, New Year's and Thanksgiving. Address: 3215 East Broad Street, Richmond, Virginia 23223. 804/226-1981.

## ROGER WILLIAMS NATIONAL MEMORIAL
### Rhode Island

At the site of the old town spring, at North Main and Alamo Lane, in the heart of Providence, this memorial commemorates the contributions of Roger Williams to civil and religious liberty. Displays and an audiovisual presentation at the Visitor Center recall his advocacy of freedom of conscience. One mile north from Market Square on US 1, the North Burial Ground contains the grave of Roger Williams. Address: 282 North Main Street, Providence, Rhode Island 02903. 401/528-5385.

## ROOSEVELT CAMPOBELLO INTERNATIONAL PARK
### New Brunswick, Canada

Jointly owned and administered by the United States and Canada, this unique memorial covering 2,600 acres was established in 1964. It lies 80 miles north of Bangor, Maine, just across the Canadian border. The Franklin D. Roosevelt Memorial Bridge links Campobello Island, part of the little archipelago clustered about the mouth of Passamaquoddy Bay, with Lubec, Maine. Franklin D. Roosevelt spent all his summers here until stricken with polio in 1921. He described it as a place of "rest, refreshment, and freedom from care." The focal point of the park is the 34-room Dutch colonial summer home, the center of a 10½-acre landscaped estate, restored and furnished as it was in the 1920s, when FDR lived here. The park is open late May to mid-October seven days a week, 9 A.M. to 5 P.M., to 6 P.M. during July and August. Also on the island (but not in the park) are the Campobello Library and St. Anne's Anglican Church, where Roosevelt prayed. Three motels are located on Highway 774 at Wilsons Beach. Camping facilities are at Herring Cove Park. Crossing the Canadian border presents no difficulty, but be sure to carry identifying papers or proof of citizenship, just in case. Address: Box 97, Lubec, Maine 04654. 506/752-2922.

## ROOSEVELT, HOME OF FRANKLIN D.

See Home of Franklin D. Roosevelt National Historic Site, page 329.

## ROOSEVELT, THEODORE, BIRTHPLACE

See Theodore Roosevelt Birthplace National Historic Site, page 353.

## ROOSEVELT, THEODORE, INAUGURAL NATIONAL HISTORIC SITE

See Theodore Roosevelt Inaugural National Historic Site, page 353.

## SAGAMORE HILL NATIONAL HISTORIC SITE

### New York

The home of Theodore Roosevelt from 1885 until his death in 1919 lies at the end of Cove Neck Road in historic Oyster Bay, Long Island. The rambling Victorian structure, the summer White House for eight years, is furnished with original Roosevelt pieces extensively restored in 1993. Trophies of a crowded life pack the North Room. His gun collection is on the top floor. On every hand are crowded bookshelves, reflecting his wide interests. Also included in the site is the Old Orchard Museum, which features exhibits and regularly scheduled documentary films on Teddy Roosevelt. Open all year except Thanksgiving, Christmas, and New Year's Day, but only 15 visitors are allowed into the house at a time. Space sells out early on summer weekends. Open 9 A.M. to 6 P.M. in summer; 9 A.M. to 5 P.M. in winter. Address: 20 Sagamore Hill Road, Oyster Bay, New York 11771. 516/922-4447.

## ST. CROIX ISLAND INTERNATIONAL HISTORIC SITE

### Maine

On this island in the St. Croix River, which forms the boundary between Maine and New Brunswick, Canada, the French attempted to found a permanent settlement in 1604; from here Champlain continued his journey to the coast and traveled through the area of present-day Acadia National Park. Address: c/o Acadia National Park, Route 1, Box 1, Bar Harbor, Maine 04609. 207/833-3131.

## SAINT-GAUDENS NATIONAL HISTORIC SITE

### New Hampshire

The home (called Aspet), studio, and gardens of the celebrated sculptor Augustus Saint-Gaudens are preserved, with many of his portraits, busts, and casts on view, at Cornish, 18 miles south of Hanover and 2 miles from the Windsor, Vermont, covered bridge. Within the formal garden note especially the copy of the renowned Adams Memorial; the original is in Washington, D.C. Each summer the Saint-Gaudens Memorial sponsors concerts and art exhibitions. Address: Route 2, Box 73, Cornish, New Hampshire 03745. 603/675-2175.

## ST. PAUL'S CHURCH NATIONAL HISTORIC SITE

### New York

Nearly a century after Anne Hutchinson fled to the area to escape religious tyranny in Massachusetts Bay Colony, St. Paul's became a focal point in the freedom-of-the-press trial of John Peter Zenger. The site includes the restored church, adjacent village green, churchyard, and a Bill of Rights Museum. The grounds are open dawn to dusk. Free tours of the church are by appointment Monday through Friday, all year; also special weekend tours. Address: 897 South Columbus Avenue, Mount Vernon, New York 10550. 914/667-4116.

## SALEM MARITIME NATIONAL HISTORIC SITE

### Massachusetts

The long Derby Wharf once was the busiest of more than 50 wharves that lined the Salem waterfront. In the early days, when foreign trade was at the heart of the nation's economy, Salem was a gateway to the world (and sixth-largest city in the United States). Most of it is gone, but in nine waterfront acres preserved in the national historic site, you can still walk on the wharves where cargoes were unloaded from around the world. Central Wharf, built in several stages, retains the brick foundation of Capt. Simon Forrester's 1790s warehouse. Derby Wharf, the largest, was crowded with vessels laden with silk from India, tea from China, coffee from Arabia. Just east of the wharf, the brick Derby House, built in 1762, represents the beginning of Salem's tenure as mistress of the seas. It was owned by Elias "King" Derby, the coastal magnate called "America's first millionaire," and contains some of the most elegantly carved woodwork found anywhere. Adjacent to it stands the largest vestige of Salem's seaport glory, the Custom House, erected in 1819, where Nathaniel Hawthorne worked as a book-keeper in 1846. He described the scene and mood of the wharf, as viewed through his office window, in *The Custom House*. Address: Custom House, Derby Street, Salem, Massachusetts 01970. 508/744-4323.

## SALT RIVER BAY NATIONAL HISTORICAL PARK AND ECOLOGICAL PRESERVE

### St. Croix, Virgin Islands

The forested hills, mangrove stands, and reef coral of Salt River Bay bring to mind the scene Columbus may have encountered when he anchored here on his second voyage to the Western Hemisphere in 1493. The archaeological remains of the site, including a ceremonial plaza from the 13th or 14th century where the Taino Indians played ritual games, remind the visitor of earlier peoples as well.

Added to the National Park system in 1992, the 912-acre park preserves stands of black, white, and red mangroves said to be the largest in the Virgin Islands. Green, leatherback, and hawksbill sea turtles, all endangered, gather in the area. The bay is refuge for 24 bird species listed federally or locally as endangered. Salt River Bay was originally declared a national historic landmark in 1960 and a natural landmark in 1980. Address: c/o Christiansted National Historic Site, Box 160, Christiansted, St. Croix, Virgin Islands 00820.

## SAN ANTONIO MISSIONS NATIONAL HISTORICAL PARK

### Texas

Four missions of the 18th century and an historic irrigation system are preserved along a 7-mile section of the San Antonio River at San Antonio. They comprise the greatest concentration of Spanish missions in the United States. The missions still serve active parishes. **Mission Concepcion** originally was established in 1716. After several moves, in 1731 it was located in its present site on the banks of the San Antonio River. The stone church, noted for its twin towers and cupola, has never fallen into ruins and is the oldest unchanged and unrestored edifice of its kind in the United States. **Mission San Jose,** founded in 1720, is admired as "The Queen of the Missions." At one point, it was inhabited by 350 Indians, many proficient in some craft, as evidenced by their carvings on the facade and paintings on the walls of the church. During the 19th century, the mission fell into disuse and the church dome and roof caved in. **Mission San Juan** was established on the San Antonio River in 1731. The present church, with its walls made of filled-in arches and side-facing bell towers, is believed to be a converted granary used as a temporary church, while the permanent church was under construction. Beginnings of the massive walls and oddly shaped octagon sacristy are still visible. **Mission Espada,** founded in 1690 as San Francisco de los Tejas, was the first Spanish mission in Texas. It was moved several times before ending up as the southernmost of the San Antonio missions. Although only the church facade has not been reconstructed, this most rural of the missions demonstrates the most complete Spanish colonial irrigation system, in continuous use, in the United States.

A fifth San Antonio mission of note, **Mission San Antonio de Valero,** the celebrated Alamo, is not part of the park, but well worth visiting. So is the Spanish governor's palace, an aristocratic mansion of the southwest frontier. Missions of the park are open daily. Address: 2202 Roosevelt Avenue, San Antonio, Texas 78210. 512/229-5701.

## SANDBURG, CARL, HOME NATIONAL HISTORIC SITE

See Carl Sandburg Home National Historic Site, page 311.

## SAN FRANCISCO MARITIME NATIONAL HISTORICAL PARK

### California

Board historic ships at the San Francisco waterfront and visit the National Maritime Museum to explore seafaring history. The best way to reach the park is via public transit, including the Powell & Hyde cable car. The oldest of the ships, the *Balclutha*, a square-rigger launched in 1886, is moored at Pier 43, largely restored to her original appearance. The *Jeremiah O'Brien*, the last Liberty Ship of World War II, in June 1994 returned to the beaches of Normandy for the 50th anniversary of the D-Day landing it made in 1994. Start at the museum, at the foot of Polk Street, where guided tours are offered daily. Get your bearings, learn the schedule of living history demonstrations, films, and tours of the ships. Allow time to enjoy the vistas of Aquatic Park. Golden Gate Promenade begins here, follow-

ing the shoreline 3½ miles to Fort Point under the Golden Gate Bridge. Address: Building 204, Fort Mason, San Francisco, California 94123. 415/556-1659.

## SAN JUAN ISLAND NATIONAL HISTORICAL PARK

### Washington

Historic sites of American and English camps on San Juan Island, the third largest island in Puget Sound, associated with the Oregon Territory boundary dispute, are protected in this park. Both camps were fortified in the so-called "Pig War" of 1859, but there was no fighting before the final settlement by arbitration in 1872 sustained the American claim to the San Juan, and the last British flag was lowered within territorial United States.

The island is reached by ferry from Anacortes, Washington, or Sidney, British Columbia. Commercial flights keep regular schedules from Seattle and Bellingham, Washington, to Friday Harbor. Address: Box 429, Friday Harbor, Washington 98250. 206/378-2240.

## SAN JUAN NATIONAL HISTORIC SITE

### Puerto Rico

These masonry fortifications are the centerpiece of a massive restoration in San Juan. The site includes most of the City Walls that ring Old San Juan and the Spanish colonial forts of El Morro, San Cristóbal, and El Cañuelo.

El Morro was built by the Spanish in the 16th century to protect the entrance to strategic San Juan Harbor. The fort was enlarged between continual attacks by the English, French, and Dutch.

San Cristóbal, larger than El Morro, was completed in 1773 and protected the land approaches to Old San Juan.

The stout defenses have had a colorful history, associated with four major attacks by the English and Dutch in colonial times. The first was in 1595, when Sir Francis Drake assaulted San Juan with a fleet of 23 ships and 3,000 men but was driven off with heavy casualties. The last was in 1898 during the Spanish American War. The U.S. Army continued to post troops and cannons in the old forts until the late 1960s, when these historic landmarks were transferred to the National Park Service.

Examine massive City Walls by walking along the shoreline between El Morro and La Fortaleza, home of the governors of Puerto Rico for over 400 years. Many other sites of historic interest, such as San Juan Cathedral of Casa Blanca, home of the Ponce de León family, are within comfortable walking distance of the forts. Address: Box 712, San Juan, Puerto Rico 00902. 809/729-6777.

## SARATOGA NATIONAL HISTORICAL PARK

### New York

Thirty miles north of Albany, where the Hudson River narrows to flow through wild forest and field, a ragtag rebel army dug in behind fortifications designed by the Polish Volunteer Colonel Thaddeus Kosciuszko. The Crown Forces (British and German) had advanced from Canada, reaching the area within the park in mid-September of 1777. From the Visitor Center and museum on Fraser Hill, you can see most of the battleground, where Burgoyne's "Redcoats" and blue-coated Germans were fought to a standstill by Continental soldiers and American militia from all over New England and New York. This was one of the most decisive series of battles in world history, the victory here earning support for the rebels from France, Holland, and Spain.

The park is extremely well laid out. It is best to enter from New York 32 or US 4, where your first stop is at the Visitor Center and museum, overlooking the battlefield from the highest hill in the park. Battle maps, dioramas, and exhibits tell the story of the two Battles of Saratoga in a first-hand approach.

The combination auto-walking tour route, which begins at the Visitor Center, has 10 marked stops in the heart of the action.

During the summer season park employees, both men and women, in period dress, are stationed at various stops along the tour road. They engage in such 18th-century activities as baking waffles and foods of the period, dressmaking, demonstrating the use of muskets and rifles, and playing military music. Special events of various types are held each season, such as lectures by noted scholars on different aspects of the Burgoyne Campaign.

Eight miles north of the park, at Schuylerville (Old Saratoga), New York, the General Philip Schuyler House is a separate portion of the park. The fine country house, the third on the site, was built in late 1777 to replace one the British burned. Address: RFD 2, Box 33, Stillwater, New York 12170. 518/664-9822.

## SAUGUS IRON WORKS NATIONAL HISTORIC SITE

### Massachusetts

A meticulous reconstruction of America's first well-sustained iron works came into being in 1954 as the result of six years of work by historians, architects, archaeologists, and builders financed by the American Iron and Steel Institute. Excavations produced over five tons of artifacts left by the original works, which operated from 1648 to about 1670. The old Ironmaster's House stands complete with 10-foot fireplaces and original hand-hewn beams. The ironworks contain the reconstructed Blast Furnace, Forge, and Rolling and Slitting Mill. The Warehouse and Wharf recapture when iron and iron products were shipped to colonies along the coast and to overseas customers. A blacksmith demonstrates early methods of iron working, producing nails, and other hand-wrought items. Address: 244 Central Street, Saugus, Massachusetts 01906. 617/233-0050.

## SCOTTS BLUFF NATIONAL MONUMENT

### Nebraska

The rocky promontory, rising 800 feet above the North Platte Valley, served as landmark and camping area for thousands crossing the treeless plains in the westward migrations between 1843 and 1869 over the Oregon and Mormon trails. You can easily spend several enjoyable hours here, with Fort Laramie National Historic Site nearby in Wyoming as your next stop en route west. The Oregon Trail Museum tells the story of early fur traders, the wagon trains, and Pony Express, and displays paintings by William Henry Jackson, the pioneer photographer-artist. A paved road and foot trail lead to the summit of the bluff and outstanding views of the North Platte River Valley. Address: Box 27, Gering, Nebraska 69341-0027. 308/436-4340.

## SEWALL-BELMONT HOUSE NATIONAL HISTORIC SITE

See page 296.

## SHILOH NATIONAL MILITARY PARK
### Tennessee

In the first major battle of the western campaign, General U. S. Grant opened his drive to control the Mississippi River. By victories on the Tennessee River, Grant paved the way for Union advances into Mississippi and Alabama. Federal control of the Mississippi River was completed the following year with the fall of Vicksburg. From the park Visitor Center, where battle relics, exhibits, and maps are displayed, the 10-mile self-guiding auto tour begins. You can also walk the battlefield on foot trails and take advantage of picnic areas. At Pittsburg Landing, Grant's 40,000 troops established their base after steaming up the Tennessee River from Fort Henry and Fort Donelson. At the Reconnoitering Road and Fraley Field, the two-day battle began April 6, 1862, when Confederate armies under General Albert Sidney Johnson attacked the Union forces. The Hornet's Nest was the site of deadly fighting around a natural fortress of dense woods, and at the Bloody Pond soldiers

of both sides came to drink and bathe their wounds. About 3,700 war dead are buried at the National Cemetery; virtually all remains of Confederate dead lie in burial trenches throughout the park. Nearby Pickwick Landing State Park offers camping and a modern resort inn. Address: Shiloh N.M. Park, Box 67, Tennessee 38376. 901/689-5275.

## SPRINGFIELD ARMORY NATIONAL HISTORIC SITE
### Massachusetts

The Armory Museum shows how for almost two centuries the Springfield Armory produced a stream of military small arms almost legendary in quality and quantity. From its beginning in the American Revolution, the Armory went on to become the small arms center of the world. Grounds are shared with Springfield Technical Community College. Other museums and historic restorations are in downtown Springfield. Address: 1 Armory Square, Springfield, Massachusetts 01105. 413/734-6477.

## STATUE OF LIBERTY NATIONAL MONUMENT
### New York–New Jersey

The colossal copper statue on Liberty Island, New York harbor, is a universal symbol of freedom and democracy. "The New Colossus," as Emma Lazarus called it in her celebrated poem, was the work of Frederic Bartholdi, and a gift of the French people in 1884, commemorating the alliance of France and America during the American Revolution.

The "Lady with a Lamp" has lately been restored to her original glory; the refurbished statue was dramatically unveiled on July 4, 1986. The $30 million project included replacement of the original gold leaf torch with a replica plated with gold to make it shine in the sun. During 1985, French craftsmen at the statue's base hammered out copper sheets using the same painstaking technique their countrymen did in building the statue.

The monument is reached by ferry, a delightful trip starting from the slip at the Battery next to Castle Clinton (every hour on the hour, every half-hour in summer). This trip has been called "the shortest cruise in the world"—it takes 15 minutes. Now you can take another trip into history from the Battery (or from Liberty State Park in Jersey City) to nearby Ellis Island, gateway to the New World for more than 12 million American immigrants. Call Circle Line Statue of Liberty Ferry for fares and schedules (212/269-5755); for the Jersey City boat call 201/435-9499.

Liberty State Park, on the New Jersey banks of the Hudson, offers dramatic views of the Statue of Liberty, Ellis Island, and the skyline of lower New York City. At the north end of the park, close to Ellis Island, the Central Railroad passenger station has been reconstructed to reflect the days when it was used by immigrants.

At the Statue of Liberty, an elevator runs to the balcony level, and a spiral stairway leads to the observation platform in the lady's head, affording thrilling views of ships and shoreline. The American Museum of Immigration in the base of the statue has been dedicated as a memorial to the millions who chose to start a new life in this country. Displays, posters, dioramas, photographs—all tell the dramatic story of the life and times of the immigrant.

Ellis Island served as an immigration reception center from 1892 until 1954. In its peak years—1900 to 1914—as many as 5,000 immigrants a day entered the country though this gateway, escaping poverty, persecution, and pogroms. After a $156 million restoration, Ellis Island opened in 1990 as a major museum of immigration. Allow time to see three floors of exhibits in the refurbished main building. They include "Treasure from Home," artifacts the immigrants brought with them; the Registry Room, where immigrants were inspected and processed; and the film, *Island of Hope, Island of Tears*. The Wall of Honor is known as the "world's longest wall of names." Address: Liberty Island, New York, New York 10004. 212/363-8828.

## STEAMTOWN NATIONAL HISTORIC SITE

### Pennsylvania

The steam railroad in American history is memorialized appropriately in what once was a major freight yard, roundhouse, and locomotive repair shop of the Delaware, Lackawanna, and Western Railroad. The park was established in 1986, two years after the Steamtown Foundation had moved from Vermont to Scranton, complete with its collection of steam locomotives and rolling stock. Reconstruction of the roundhouse and turntable began in 1990, the first major project in a $60 million rehabilitation plan. Railroad enthusiasts should combine a visit here with a call at Allegheny Portage Railroad National Historic Site, at Johnstown, in western Pennsylvania (see page 307). And keep in mind the Golden Spike National Historic Site, in Utah, which preserves the site of completion of the first transcontinental railroad (see page 326). Address: 150 South Washington Avenue, Scranton, Pennsylvania 18503-1280. 717/961-6062.

## STONES RIVER NATIONAL BATTLEFIELD AND CEMETERY

### Tennessee

A stubbornly fought three-day midwinter battle which started December 31, 1862, a short distance from Murfreesboro, began the Federal offensive to split the Confederacy in three parts. The Hazen Brigade Monument, erected in 1863, is one of the oldest memorials of the Civil War. The decisive turn of events came the third day with a 58-gun concentration of Union artillery roaring out more than 100 rounds a minute on advancing Confederates. In a matter of minutes, 1,800 Confederates fell—killed or wounded. Under the pall of this overwhelming disaster, General Braxton Bragg ordered the withdrawal of his decimated army.

The national cemetery contains approximately 7,000 burials, with about one-third of the bodies unidentified. Address: 3501 Old Nashville Highway, Murfreesboro, Tennessee 37129. 615/893-9501.

## TAFT, WILLIAM HOWARD, NATIONAL HISTORIC SITE

See William Howard Taft National Historic Site, page 357.

## THADDEUS KOSCIUSZKO NATIONAL MEMORIAL

### Pennsylvania

This small row house at 301 Pine Street, Philadelphia, is the country's only surviving residence of General Thaddeus Kosciuszko, Polish patriot and hero of the American Revolution. While living here in 1797–98, Kosciuszko was visited frequently by Vice President Thomas Jefferson, who asked him to serve as a peace emissary to France. An old friend, Jefferson had described Kosciuszko during the Revolution "as pure a son of liberty as I have ever known." Kosciuszko wrote his will in this house and gave it to Jefferson, bequeathing his fortune to the cause of freedom of slaves. Kosciuszko volunteered his services to the colonies in 1776. He was appointed chief engineer of the Army in the South, where his logistical planning was instrumental in the campaign's success. Address: c/o Independence National Historical Park, 313 Walnut Street, Philadelphia, Pennsylvania 19106. 215/597-7120.

## THEODORE ROOSEVELT BIRTHPLACE NATIONAL HISTORIC SITE

### New York

In the four-story brownstone at 28 East 20th Street, Manhattan, currently amid an area of commercial building and craft centers near Gramercy Park, the 26th president was born, in 1858. He lived his formative years here—until he was 15—beset by ailments. Furnished in period style, with museum, audiovisual programs, and a guided tour. Address: Superintendent, Manhattan Sites, National Park Service, 26 Wall Street, New York, New York 10005. 212/260-1616.

## THEODORE ROOSEVELT INAUGURAL NATIONAL HISTORIC SITE

### New York

Theodore Roosevelt took the oath of office as President of the United States here at the Ansley Wilcox House in Buffalo on September 14, 1901, within hours after the death of President McKinley. Roosevelt had been sidetracked into the vice presidency by the political bosses, but once he assumed command he became the "Apostle of Energy" in the domestic and foreign policies of the nation. Address: 641 Delaware Avenue, Buffalo, New York 14202. 716/884-0095.

## THOMAS STONE NATIONAL HISTORIC SITE

### Maryland

This area, authorized by Congress in 1978, includes the mansion house known as "Habre de Venture" and a 325-acre plantation once owned by Thomas Stone, a signer of the Declaration of Independence, at Port Tobacco, in southern Maryland. The house is being reconstructed and is not yet open to the public. Address: c/o George Washington Birthplace National Monument, Washington's Birthplace, Virginia 22575. 804/224-0196.

## TIMUCUAN ECOLOGICAL AND HISTORIC PRESERVE

### Florida

Named for the Timucuan (tee-MOO-kwon) Indians who once lived here, this 46,000-acre preserve features coastal marshes, islands, mudflats, and meandering tidal creeks and estuaries. Key sites provide traces of the Timucuans, remains of European colonial ventures, southern plantation life, and 19th-century military activities. Still under development, the preserve has three National Park Service operational areas: Fort Caroline National Memorial (see separate listing, page 318); the Theodore Roosevelt Area, a 540-acre natural area; and Kingsley Plantation, the oldest existing plantation in Florida. Address: 13165 Mt. Pleasant Road, Jacksonville, Florida 32225. 904/221-5568.

## TOURO SYNAGOGUE NATIONAL HISTORIC SITE

### Rhode Island

The most significant and most exquisitely designed building in Newport is the oldest house of Jewish worship in the United States, founded by 15 families responding to Roger Williams's declaration of religious liberty. The plans were made by Peter Harrison, known as America's first professional architect, who is also responsible for several great Boston churches. Features include Windsor benches, massive bronze candelabra, fine examples of 18th-century silversmithing—and the memory of George Washington's appearance in 1790. It continues as the place of worship for Congregation Jeshuat Israel, while the Society of Friends of Touro Synagogue conducts efforts toward fulfilling the 18th-century appearance.

From the synagogue it is only a short walk to the old burial ground, a small plot which served as inspiration for Longfellow's poem, *The Jewish Cemetery at Newport*. Address: Touro Synagogue, 85 Touro Street, Newport, Rhode Island 02840. 401/847-4794.

## TUMACACORI NATIONAL HISTORIC PARK

### Arizona

San Jose de Tumacacori was a northern outpost of a mission chain built in Spanish Sonora. With the charm of culture planted in the desert, this church was built in 1822, abandoned in 1848. The Park Service has conserved its stately remains, in which you may study interesting structural elements of the neo-classic architecture and the faded but original colors which Indian workmen applied. The museum contains dioramas and ar-

tifacts that bring the frontier mission age to life. You can take self-guiding walks about the grounds. Plan to visit other historic sites added to the park in 1990: the ruins of Calabazas mission, eight miles south, and the ruins of Los Santos Angeles de Guevavi, Arizona's oldest Jesuit mission, 15 miles south. Tumacacori is located 43 miles south of Tucson on I-19, just 19 miles north of Nogales and the Mexican border. Open daily, except December 25, from 8 a.m. to 5 p.m. Early each December several thousand visitors gather for the annual fiesta. It features food, entertainment, and booths in which native craftspeople—Apache, Yaqui, and Papago Indians and Mexican-Americans—demonstrate pottery making, woodcarving, basketweaving, and leather tooling. Address: Box 67, Tumacacori, Arizona 85640. 602/398-2341.

## TUPELO NATIONAL BATTLEFIELD

### Mississippi

A granite marker serves as a memorial to soldiers of both armies and interpretive maps are within a one-acre tract in Tupelo where Federal forces fought in July 1864, to protect Sherman's supply line while he was moving on Atlanta. Address: c/o Natchez Trace Parkway, Route 1, NT 143, Tupelo, Mississippi 38801. 601/842-1572.

## TUSKEGEE INSTITUTE NATIONAL HISTORIC SITE

### Alabama

Founded by Booker T. Washington in 1881, Tuskegee Institute (now Tuskegee University) became a major force in launching black Americans into higher education. Students built most of the early structures on the campus. From two or three buildings near Tuskegee, the school has expanded to 161 buildings on 5,000 acres, with 3,500 students. The historic site includes the founder's home, The Oaks, restored to its early 20th-century appearance, and the Carver Museum, a museum-laboratory established by George Washington Carver, the famous scientist, in 1938. A 50-acre historic district is maintained under agreement with the National Park Service, though retained by the university. Address: 399 Old Montgomery Road, Tuskegee, Alabama 36083. 205/727-6390.

## ULYSSES S. GRANT NATIONAL HISTORIC SITE

### Missouri

The White Haven estate where Grant and his family lived from 1854 to 1860 is a tribute to the life of the 18th President and Commander-in-Chief of the Union Army. Grant purchased the childhood home of his wife, Julia Dent Grant, during the Civil War. The 9.65 acres preserves the main White Haven house, out-buildings, woods, and lawns related to Grant's pre–Civil War and presidential years. The site is presently undergoing restoration and is open by appointment only. Address: 7400 Grant Road, St. Louis, Missouri 63123-1659. 314/842-1867.

## U.S.S. *ARIZONA* MEMORIAL AND BOWFIN PARK

### Hawaii

Spanning the width of the sunken battleship *Arizona* is a memorial to the men who lost their lives during the Japanese attack on Pearl Harbor in December 1941, especially those whose bodies are buried with their ship. The memorial, established by the navy, is now administered by the National Park Service through a cooperative agreement authorized by Congress in 1978. A shore-side Visitor Center provides for visitors; be sure to see the memorial on the waterside lawn, honoring victims of the attack who were not on the *Arizona*. The museum and a film portray the Pacific naval war and the action at Hawaii. A canopied launch operated by the navy, carrying 150 passengers at a time, ferries visitors across the harbor to "battleship row," where

the hull of the *Arizona* lies in 38 feet of water. The National Park Service Tour is the only Pearl Harbor tour that allows you to land on the memorial; commercial tours pass, but do not have permission to land. In all, 19 warships were sunk or damaged in the Japanese attack. All but two have been raised by salvage efforts. A large marble wall in the memorial bears the names of 1,177 sailors and marines who perished with the ship.

Half a block from the *Arizona* memorial at Bowfin Park, you can tour the sub U.S.S. *Bowfin*, which was active during World War II, recommissioned during the Korean War, then used as a training sub in Seattle from 1960 to 1970. Address: 1 Arizona Memorial Place, Honolulu, Hawaii 96818. 808/422-2771.

## VALLEY FORGE NATIONAL HISTORICAL PARK

### Pennsylvania

No name in American history conveys more of suffering, sacrifice, and triumph than Valley Forge, where 12,000 ragged, hungry men went into camp on December 19, 1777, endured a harsh winter and emerged in the spring as a trained, disciplined army. General Washington himself selected this location, named for a small iron forge on Valley Creek, because of its defensive position and his ability to watch the approaches to Philadelphia, 20 miles to the east. You'll find a great deal to see and do at the 3,000-acre park. The Visitor Center houses the original tent used by Washington in the field and the priceless Neumann collection of muskets, rifles, swords, and other Revolutionary weapons. On leaving the Visitor Center for the tour route, you can see where some 2,000 log huts were raised during the encampment. About 40 have been reconstructed in recent years. Tour other key sites, including the Grand Parade, Artillery Park, and the forts and earthworks built up to protect the camp and command nearby roads and rivers. Visit the stone colonial house used by Washington as his headquarters. The National Memorial Arch, a dominant feature of the park, is dedicated to the "incomparable patience and fidelity of the soldiery"—the men who departed here in spring of 1778 as a toughened fighting force. Buildings are open 9 A.M. to 5 P.M. daily. Address: Superintendent, Valley Forge National Historical Park, Box 953, Valley Forge, Pennsylvania 19481. 215/783-1000.

## VAN BUREN, MARTIN, NATIONAL HISTORIC SITE

See Martin Van Buren National Historic Site, page 339.

## VANDERBILT MANSION NATIONAL HISTORIC SITE

### New York

The 54-room country home was built at Hyde Park in 1898 by Frederick W. Vanderbilt, grandson of Cornelius Vanderbilt, "the Commodore." This "monument to an era," with Italian marble, Flemish tapestry, a 300-year-old Persian carpet and French Renaissance furniture, is in marked contrast to the stately Victorian home of Franklin D. Roosevelt nearby. Address: Bellfield Headquarters, 249 Albany Post Road, Hyde Park, New York 12538. 914/229-9115.

## VICKSBURG NATIONAL MILITARY PARK

### Mississippi

General U. S. Grant, striving to split the Confederacy with daring, large-scale movements across the heartland of America, moved against Vicksburg in the spring of 1863. On May 19, one of Grant's three corps launched an attack. It was repulsed. Three days later his whole army moved. Failure to capture the heavily defended city, despite bloody fighting, compelled Grant to start siege operations, aided by the Union navy, to cut off communications and blast the city from the river. After 47 days of tightening the grip from three

sides, Grant took Vicksburg and control of the Mississippi. You can see the main defensive fortifications (along Confederate Avenue) and the main part of the investment line (along Union Avenue) in the semicircular park. About 1,400 monuments, memorials, and tablets have been erected to mark positions of the armies. The equestrian statue of General Grant stands in the area where the general maintained his headquarters. The national cemetery, at the north end of the park, contains the graves of 17,000 Union soldiers, including many who died in other actions nearby. The Confederate dead are buried in the city cemetery. The Visitor Center, adjacent to the entrance near US 80, contains life-size exhibits. An 18-minute film relates the events of the campaign. In late 1980, the park opened the USS *Cairo* Museum, which houses thousands of artifacts—including bottles, tools, weapons, cooking, and eating utensils—recovered from the ill-fated Union gunboat. A Confederate "electric" mine sent the *Cairo* to the bottom of the Yazoo River in 1862, where it lay mired in mud for almost 100 years until discovered by historians. While in Vicksburg, see the old Court House Museum, with an exhibit of relics from the campaign. Address: 3201 Clay Street, Vicksburg, Mississippi 39180. 601/636-0583.

## WAR IN THE PACIFIC NATIONAL HISTORICAL PARK

### Guam

Authorized by Congress in 1978, this park commemorates the bravery and sacrifices of people of all nations involved in the Pacific Theater of World War II. The park provides a center of information of operations involving Japan, Australia, New Zealand, Great Britain, France, Canada, the Netherlands, the Soviet Union, China, the Pacific Islands people, and the United States. The park consists of six separate units. The T. Stell Newman Visitor Information Center houses exhibits on Pacific operations, an audiovisual program, and interpretive information about Guam, the Mariana Islands, and Micronesia. Numerous historic structures are found throughout the park, both on the land and offshore areas. Several trails lead to Japanese pillboxes and gun installations. Sites in park waters protect the remains of the invasion of Guam in July 1944. These areas are accessible to scuba divers. Additional park areas will be opened as they are developed. Address: Box FA, Agana, Guam 96910. 671/477-9362.

## WASHINGTON, BOOKER T. NATIONAL MONUMENT

See Booker T. Washington National Monument, page 309.

## WASHINGTON, GEORGE, BIRTHPLACE

See George Washington Birthplace National Monument, page 325.

## WASHINGTON MONUMENT

See page 297.

## WEIR FARM NATIONAL HISTORIC SITE

### Connecticut

Julian Alden Weir bought this farm in 1882 for $10 and one of his own still-life paintings. Considered a founder of American Impressionism, Weir lived on the farm, entertaining friends who came to visit and to paint, until his death in 1919. The farm has since been owned and inhabited by artists and, in 1990, became the first national park unit dedicated to the legacy of an American painter. Long-range planning for the park, which includes Weir's farmhouse, two studios, and other farm buildings, is under way. Visitors are invited to explore the farm, starting with an introduction at Burlingham House, near the southern end. Because the Weir house and studios are still in use by working artists, visitors are asked to confine excursions to the

public areas. Address: 735 Nod Hill Road, Wilton, Connecticut 06897. 203/834-1896.

## WHITMAN MISSION NATIONAL HISTORIC SITE

### Washington

Near Walla Walla, Marcus and Narcissus Whitman, the first family of white settlers to cross the Rocky Mountains, established a mission for the Cayuse Indians and a haven for travelers on the Oregon Trail, which they operated from 1836 until the couple were slain by Indians in 1847.

Start at the Visitor Center to see the orientation film and exhibit on Indian tribes and cultures. Then walk the easy trail past foundation ruins of mission buildings and a trace of the historic Oregon Trail. The Memorial Monument, erected on a high bluff in 1897, overlooks the Walla Walla Valley and faces the Blue Mountains to the east. Address: Route 2, Box 247, Walla Walla, Washington 99362. 509/522-6360.

## WILCOX, ANSLEY, HOUSE

See Theodore Roosevelt Inaugural National Historic Site, page 353.

## WILLIAM HOWARD TAFT NATIONAL HISTORICAL SITE

### Ohio

The 27th president was born in September 1857 in this three-story brick home on Auburn Avenue in Cincinnati. His father had been Secretary of War and Attorney General under President U. S. Grant, but this did not prevent young William and his four brothers from enjoying a typical boyhood and active neighborhood life, including swimming, skating, and baseball. After studying at Yale, he returned home in 1878 to complete his studies at Cincinnati Law School. Then he began his advance on the national scene, reaching the double pinnacle, as President (1909–1913) and Chief Justice (1921–1930). A major restoration of the house was completed in 1989. The site is open daily 10 A.M. to 6 P.M., Memorial Day through Labor Day; to 4:30 P.M., rest of year. Address: 2038 Auburn Avenue, Cincinnati, Ohio 45219-3025. 513/684-3262.

## WILLIAMS, ROGER, MEMORIAL

See Roger Williams National Memorial, page 346.

## WILSON'S CREEK NATIONAL BATTLEFIELD PARK

### Missouri

At a site 10 miles southwest of Springfield, Union and Confederate forces engaged in a bitter struggle during the first year of the Civil War (August 10, 1861) for control of Missouri. Though the Southerners won the battle of Wilson's Creek, they were too badly crippled to follow through in pursuit. Thus, Missouri was secured for the Union. Starting from the Visitor Center, wayside exhibits and restored historic structures show the effect of the battle on soldiers and civilians. The Ray House, used as a Confederate field hospital, is the only house of the war period still standing. Address: Route 2, Box 75, Republic, Missouri 65738-9514. 417/732-2662.

## WOMEN'S RIGHTS NATIONAL HISTORICAL PARK

### New York

On July 9, 1848, five reform-minded women met at a private home near Seneca Falls, New York, planning a strategy that marked the beginning of the women's rights movement. The story of the movement and of its founders is the focus of this park. Tours are conducted from the Visitor Center on Fall Street to significant sites, including the homes and offices of Elizabeth Cady Stanton, Amelia Jenks Bloomer, and other notable early women's rights activists. The park includes the Wesleyan Methodist Chapel, the site of the 1848 Women's Rights Convention. Address: Box 70, Seneca Falls, New York 13148. 315/568-2991.

## WRIGHT BROTHERS NATIONAL MEMORIAL

### North Carolina

The site of the first sustained flight by a heavier-than-air machine, made by Wilbur and Orville Wright at Kill Devil Hills in December 1903, is marked by a granite pylon monument in the dunes. The Visitor Center contains a replica of their famous plane, *The Flyer*. Address: Route 1, Box 675, Manteo, North Carolina 27954. 919/441-7430.

## ZUNI-CIBOLA NATIONAL HISTORICAL PARK

### New Mexico

South of Gallup, New Mexico, near the Arizona border, the Zuni pueblo has nurtured native American cultures for over 1,700 years. It was visited by Coronado during his gold-searching expedition of 1540, believed to be the first European contact with the people of what is now known as the southwestern United States. In 1988, Congress moved to cooperate with the Zuni government in preserving and protecting the pueblo's abundant nationally significant resources through this new national historical park. The new park will become operational on completion of a leasehold agreement and management plan designed to protect fragile archaeological sites and the Zuni community from being overrun. The park will feature house ruins, kivas, pictographs, and petroglyphs of prehistoric villages, a mission church, and convents, all registered national historic landmarks. Stop at El Morro National Monument (see page 317) for guidance and latest information. Address: Pueblo of Zuni, Box 339, Zuni, New Mexico 87327. 505/988-6387.

# NATURAL AND RECREATIONAL AREAS

WHETHER THEY ARE CALLED NATIONAL PARKWAYS; national seashores, lakeshores, or riverways; national monuments; or national recreation areas—these are all national treasures. All of the natural and recreation areas administered by the National Park Service offer unlimited opportunities for education, recreation, and travel enjoyment.

National monuments are the oldest category in this section. Devils Tower, Wyoming, was established as a national monument by presidential proclamation in 1906. National monuments include prehistoric cliff dwellings, caverns, an underwater marine garden, fortresses, landmarks of early settlement, spectacular canyons and desert wilderness, virgin stands of redwood and cactus. National monuments devoted to nature are described in this section of the guide. (Monuments relating to archaeology are described in Archaeological Areas, pages 299 to 305; monuments of historical significance are included in Historical Areas, pages 306 to 358.)

National seashores, lakeshores, riverways, and wild and scenic rivers, on the other hand, are among the newest categories in the National Park System. All have been established since 1953. For many years the nation has protected representative portions of other natural environments, such as virgin forest, glacial wilderness, and inland marsh. Now the value of the native seashores, lakeshores, and rivers has been recognized as well.

In this section you will read about some of the largest units of the National Park System (the National Recreation Areas) and the most heavily visited (National Parkways). Parkways are parks too, designed for leisurely motoring, rather than for transportation from one point to another.

The natural and recreation areas offer an infinite variety of outdoor experience; each one of the areas detailed on this and following pages is worth a visit.

## AGATE FOSSIL BEDS NATIONAL MONUMENT

### Nebraska

The major fossil beds are located in University Hill (named for the University of Nebraska) and Carnegie Hill (for Carnegie Institute), near the eastern end of the monument. Follow the self-guiding foot trail to the two hills to view exposed fossils. You'll see the fossil bones of Miocene mammals where they have been buried for 20 million years. Be on the alert for rattlesnakes, which are present in the area. The Visitor Center museum has excellent exhibits. The terrain of the prairie landscape slopes gradually upward from the Niobrara River, flowing quietly on its journey to the Missouri. The land is covered with bluestem, grama, buffalo, and other grasses. In spring and summer a variety of wildflowers adds color to the scene. In May and June creamy white flowers of yucca add particular beauty. Follow Nebraska 29 to the monument, 34 miles north of Mitchell, 22 miles south of Harrison. Address: c/o Scotts Bluff National Monument, Box 27, Gering, Nebraska 69341-0027. 308/436-4340.

## AMISTAD NATIONAL RECREATION AREA

### Texas

A joint project of the United States and Mexico, this major international recreational facility in the warm, dry Southwest comprises nearly 63,000 acres of land and water.

Indian pictographs, 8,000 to 10,000 years old, are found along the walls of Lake Amistad; the only way to see them is by boat. One of the most popular sites, Panther Cave, is about 7 miles south of the Pecos River boat landing, just inside Seminole Canyon. The park has provided a boat dock here, where you can tie up and climb the hill to visit the cave. Don't expect to get close enough to touch—a fence has been erected by the Texas Historical Foundation to avert vandalism. There are 9 ramps on Lake Amistad. To reach pictographs on foot, take a walking tour to the Fate Bell Shelter in Seminole Canyon State Historical Park, which abuts the recreation area.

Water sports are the main activity through most of the year, but lands bordering the reservoir can be used for camping, backcountry hiking, bird watching, picnicking, and nature study. The tawny desert and scrubby grassland above the Rio Grande have a charm all their own. Mammals in the area include coyote, whitetailed deer, peccary, raccoon, ringtail, squirrel, and jackrabbit.

Many islands at various reservoir levels lend themselves to use by boating parties. The shoreline especially is an angler's delight, with hundreds of pockets, caves, and canyons branching off the main bodies of water. There is no reciprocal license arrangement with Mexico; a license must be obtained before fishing its portion of the lake. One may be purchased in Ciudad Acuna, Del Rio's sister city across the Rio Grande. A Texas license is required for the U.S. side. Hunting is good, particularly for whitetail, mourning dove, and waterfowl. Numerous RV parks and motels are located in Del Rio and along US 90, adjacent to the lake. Address: Box 420367, Del Rio, Texas 78842-0367. 512/775-7491.

## APOSTLE ISLANDS NATIONAL LAKESHORE

### Wisconsin

They were thought to number only 12 by the early missionaries who named them, but there are actually 22 islands in the cluster off the Bayfield Peninsula in Lake Superior ranging in size from tiny islets to one of 14,000 acres. Some of the earliest fur traders and French explorers came this way. Established as the core of a new national lakeshore in 1970, the breezy Apostles are among the delights of the Great Lakes region. Some are inhabited only by deer, bear, and birds. Biting insects are common early June to mid-September, so come prepared. The spring months are especially good for bird-watching. Hawks, shorebirds, and waterfowl can be seen from several of the islands.

The national lakeshore consists of 68,500 acres, including 21 of the islands and 11 miles of the mainland shore. Start at the Visitor Center in the Old Courthouse Building at Bayfield. See the displays and slide programs and pick up a copy of the weekly schedule of activities. Opportunities include the Raspberry Island Lighthouse Adventure and Historic Hokenson Fishery Tour. Camping permits are issued here.

A mainland unit of the lakeshore adjoins the Red Cliff Indian Reservation, with secluded sand and pebble beaches and vistas of rock cliffs. The Little Sand Bay Information Center provides information and camping permits. Visit ranger stations on Rocky, South Twin, Stockton, Manitou, Raspberry, and Oak Islands; personnel are glad to provide guidance and current information.

**Winter beauty** draws increasing numbers of visitors for cross-country skiing, snowshoeing, and camping. With heavy snow and temperatures well below freezing, weather can be harsh on the unwary and unprepared.

**Bayfield,** the gateway town, has an attractive boat basin shared by commercial and sport fishermen. From here campers can travel by regular excursion boat to the islands. Then take in interpretive programs and hiking trails, and explore agate beaches, caves, and rock outcrops.

Narrated cruises are offered by the park concessioner during the summer season. The 3-hour "Grand Tour" leaves Bayfield daily at 10 a.m. and passes several islands and lighthouses, while on Saturday evenings the Sunset Cruise passes the Squaw Bay Cliffs. Cruises also provide scheduled camper service to many of the islands. Call Apostle Islands Cruise Service, 715/779-3925.

**Madeline Island,** the largest of the Apostles (though not included in the National Lakeshore), is reached from Bayfield on a 30-minute ferry ride. At the historical museum opposite the dock you can learn about the activities of John Jacob Astor's American Fur Company. Fifty miles of road lead to small resorts, white beaches, and rock caves. Address: Route 1, Box 4, Bayfield, Wisconsin 54814-9599. 715/779-3397.

# ASSATEAGUE ISLAND NATIONAL SEASHORE

## Maryland-Virginia

Named by Indians, roamed by the legendary Chincoteague ponies, Assateague is a low barrier island, 37 miles, with 19,000 acres of land stretching along the Atlantic Ocean. It is connected by bridges to the mainland at both the northern and southern ends and lies about 90 miles from Norfolk, Virginia. Regular conventional two-wheel drive vehicles can presently travel on the island a distance of 3½ miles from the Maryland Bridge and approximately 4 miles from the Assateague Island Bridge in Virginia. No communities exist on the island, the largest undeveloped seashore between Massachusetts and North Carolina. Assateague and the other national seashores are different in that their purpose is to protect and restore coastal wilderness.

**Bird and Wildlife Watching.** Birds flock to the area, which is on the Atlantic flyway, to occupy varying habitats of sea, beach, pine woods and thicket, marsh, and bay. More than 275 kinds of birds have been identified, and each season has its own coterie of species. Approximately 11 miles of the southern part of the island form the Chincoteague National Wildlife Refuge, where enormous flocks of shore birds are seen in migration during September and October, and where large flocks of ducks, geese, and swans are at home all winter. To fully enjoy the shore birds, tramp the wild beach from the parking area at the southern end through the wildlife refuge. The Chincoteague ponies, whose ancestors came here centuries ago, roam wild, living off the marsh grass. The last week in July is "Pony Penning Week," time of the annual sale of the Virginia herd's colts following the traditional roundup.

The exotic small Sika deer (released on the island by a Boy Scout troop in 1923) can be glimpsed occasionally, along with foxes, raccoons, muskrats, and otters.

**The north end** is fascinating with ever-changing sand dunes and washover areas, marsh grasses, pools, nesting terns and skimmers, as well as shore birds. Assateague State Park, directly across the bridge from the mainland, provides a protected beach, bathhouse, food services, and 311 modern campsites on hardtop loop roads. North Beach, inside the national seashore, has lifeguard protection for swimmers, and two primitive family campgrounds. Three hike-in campsites are located behind the primary dune, and four canoe-in campsites are located on the bay side; these backcountry sites are quite primitive, and all water and shelter must be packed in. Four-wheel-drive, over-sand vehicles are permitted to run as far south as the Virginia line. However, the Park Service has imposed a permit system with stringent restrictions on use of the 16 miles of beach open to vehicles.

**At the southern tip,** called Tom's Cove Hook, the Park Service operates a 5-mile-long day-use recreation area. This area includes bathhouse and lifeguard protection. During summer both the Park Service and Fish and Wildlife Service offer interpretive nature walks and lectures; the wildlife refuge also offers an open bus ride into the refuge and a boat ride into the bay.

Light cartop boats can be launched at mainland ramps and used in most of the shallow bay, though heavier boats are restricted to bay channels or the ocean.

Marinas are available in nearby towns of Chincoteague, Virginia, and Ocean City, Maryland. Nearly all of the island beaches can be traversed by foot, providing for excellent beachcombing during winter; summer beachcombing is rarely good except near the two inlets at either end, or after a heavy storm. The shallow bay offers many places to find hardshell clams and blue crabs.

National Park Service Visitor Centers at both ends will help visitors to understand the ecology of a true barrier beach. Address: Route 611, 7206 National Seashore Lane, Berlin, Maryland 21811. 410/641-1441.

## BIG CYPRESS NATIONAL PRESERVE

### Florida

Comprising 729,000 acres of watershed directly northwest of Everglades National Park, Big Cypress was hit but not badly damaged by Hurricane Andrew in 1992. It provides a freshwater supply essential to the park. It also preserves subtropical plant and animal life. Rare and endangered species here include the Florida panther, manatee, brown pelican, Everglades kite, and roseate spoonbill. Visitors can enjoy primitive camping at designated sites, hiking, and sightseeing; hunting, fishing, and trapping are authorized in accordance with state law.

Stop at Big Cypress Visitor Center, 55 miles east of Naples on US 41 for guidance. The interest in the area is primarily natural, but there are historical and cultural values as well. Following the Seminole Wars in Florida, the Big Cypress became the last stronghold of these Indians, and Miccosukee villages still dot the area. Collier-Seminole State Park, 6,423 acres of swampland and uplands, serves as both a recreation area and informal memorial to the Indians and to Barron Collier, who at one time owned the surrounding Collier County. The park entrance lies off US 41, 17 miles south of Naples. This state park includes camping and picnic areas. The Preserve is in a remote section. Limited services are available at access areas. There are no gas stations or food services in the Preserve. Fringing the western edge of the state park, a boat basin, ramp, and marina provide access to the Blackwater River. Address: HCR 61, Box 110, Ochopee, Florida 33943. 813/695-2000.

## BIG SOUTH FORK NATIONAL RIVER AND RECREATION AREA

### Tennessee–Kentucky

The Big South Fork flows north into Kentucky from its source on the Cumberland Plateau. En route, its gorges and the adjacent ridges provide outstanding scenery and unparalleled opportunities for outdoor recreation. This is a major new territory to explore. The area covers more than 105,000 acres of rugged terrain 65 miles northwest of Knoxville, Tennessee, and within 50 miles of two interstate highways, I-40 and I-75. Trails lead to jewels like Honey Creek and Yahoo Falls. Several hundred miles of trails and old logging roads are available to hikers, mountain bikers, and riders. More than 80 miles of choice canoe waters range from easy floats to challenging white-water runs through rapids. Get a copy of the river guidebook at park headquarters.

Or sign up with an outfitter like Cumberland Outdoor Adventures, Inc., Route 6, Box 372B, Corbin, Kentucky 40701. **Bandy Creek** complex is a major activities center on the Tennessee side, with trailer and tent camping, canoe rental, and access to trails. **Blue Heron,** named for an abandoned mining community in the Kentucky portion, includes a small campground on the bluffs above the Big South Fork, facilities for hiking, swimming, fishing, and canoeing, plus a program on life in the mining town. **Charit Creek Hostel** on Station Creek provides full meal service as well as hostel accommodations at low cost. Call 615/879-3625. Be sure to visit historic **Rugby,** on State Route 52, the restoration of a 19th-century utopian village. Lodging and meals are available. Primary north-south access routes are I-75 and US 27 and 127. Address: Route 3, Box 401, Oneida, Tennessee 37841. 615/879-4890.

## BIG THICKET NATIONAL PRESERVE

### Texas

As a crossroads of ecological zones, this 84,550-acre preserve in southeast Texas embraces eight different biological habitats, ranging from savanna to bald-cypress swamp to uplands of beech, magnolia, white oak, and loblolly pine. Included are almost 300 bird species; mammals ranging from foxes and otter to mountain lions, armadillo, and occasional black bear; 3 kinds of insect-eating plants, and 27 species of wild orchids. Because of this diversity, Big Thicket is recognized by the United Nations as an International Biosphere Reserve.

The old, primitive Big Thicket stretched roughly from the Sabine River on the east to past Trinity River on the west. Less than one-tenth remains in wilderness today. The 12 units of the preserve are scattered as far as 50 miles apart; they range in size from 25,024 acres in the Lance Rosier Unit to 550 acres in the Loblolly Unit, a pocket of enormous pines glimmering in spongy swamps. Development of public-use facilities is steady but slow.

Visit the **Visitor Information Station** located on FM 420, 2½ miles east of US 69 (about 7½ miles north of Kountze), for orientation and detailed information. Ask about the cruise on the *Big Thicket Queen* up the Neches River to Cook's Lake. Hike the adjacent 1.7-mile loop **Kirby Nature Trail** for a leisurely introduction to the thicket and a view of lovely Village Creek, a favorite canoeing waterway. Or take the 9.2-mile **Turkey Creek Trail,** which is said to contain the greatest concentrated plant diversification in the preserve. The trail winds through pine plateaus, creek bottoms with huge hardwoods, cathedral-like beech-magnolia-loblolly glades, and fascinating acid bog "baygalls." Ask about them.

Trails are also available in the **Beech Creek Unit, Hickory Creek Savannah Unit,** and **Big Sandy Creek Unit,** each offering different views of the diverse Big Thicket.

**Big Thicket Museum,** at Saratoga, makes a choice starting point of a visit to the area. Operated by the nonprofit Big Thicket Association, the museum features displays on flora, fauna, and history. Canoe explorations are scheduled throughout the year. Big Thicket Day is conducted annually the first Saturday in June. Write Big Thicket Museum, Box 198, Saratoga, Texas 77585.

Accommodations in the Big Thicket region cover a wide spectrum. The Alabama-Coushatta Indians have developed campgrounds with a fishing lake. Chain-O-Lakes Campground, on Daniel Ranch Road, Romayor, covers 175 acres, with many of the trees, plants, flowers, and vines of the area, including wild orchids growing in the swimming pond. The 250 campsites range from full hookups to wilderness sites. The Triple D Guest Ranch is an excellent base for hiking and riding in the Big Thicket. And Double Lake Recreation Area, 5 miles from Coldspring in Sam Houston National Forest, offers boating, swimming, and fishing, as well as camping. State parks provide camping areas in Steinhagen, Sam Rayburn, Livingston, and Toledo Bend reservoirs. Address: 3785 Milam, Beaumont, Texas 77701. 409/839-2689.

## BIGHORN CANYON NATIONAL RECREATION AREA

### Wyoming–Montana

Flanked by the Pryor Mountains on the west and the Bighorn Mountains on the east, the Bighorn River cuts a chasm between the mountains. The national recreation area was established in 1966 following completion of the 525-foot-high Yellowtail Dam, which produced the 71-mile-long Bighorn Lake.

Bighorn Canyon offers year-round recreation. Pleasure boating, water skiing, and lake fishing on Bighorn Lake and the afterbay, and stream fishing below the dam are summer activities, while the Horseshoe Bend area offers ice fishing in winter. Fishing regulations follow state laws, and fishing in either Montana or Wyoming requires the appropriate fishing license. The recreation area offers more than water-oriented activities. Visit the **Bighorn Canyon Visitor Center** outside Lovell, Wyoming, or the **Fort Smith Visitor Information Station** near Fort Smith, Montana, for orientation through exhibits, films, and brochures.

Camping comes in a variety of environments. The RV and tent campground at Horseshoe Bend and the boat-in/hike-in campground at Medicine Creek are in arid land. Riparian habitat camping can be found at Barry's Land and Afterbay campgrounds; a pine forest, lakeside campsite is at the boat-in-only campground in Black Canyon.

Hikers experience a diversity of cross-country hiking. Obtain free backcountry permits at either Visitor Center. For the less adventuresome, the Crooked Creek Nature Trail at Horseshoe Bend and the Om-Ne-A Trail at the dam are well marked.

The scenic drive along Ok-A-Beh Road through short-grass prairie is highlighted by wildflowers from May through July. The wildflower display along Bad Pass Road in the south district is somewhat shorter due to drier conditions. Don't miss the magnificent canyon view offered from Devil Canyon Overlook, looking down near-vertical cliffs to the ribbon of a lake 976 feet below. Bad Pass Road from Horseshoe Bend to Barry's Landing passes through a portion of Pryor Mountain Wild Horse Range.

Access to the north end of the recreation area is from Hardin, Montana, on Montana 313. US 14A in Wyoming provides access to the south end. The north and south ends of the recreation area are not connected by a direct route. Address: Box 458, Fort Smith, Montana 59035-0458. 406/666-2412.

## BLACK CANYON OF THE GUNNISON NATIONAL MONUMENT

### Colorado

Sunlight sparkles on dark-colored ancient rock, opened to view in the narrow gorge cut by the Gunnison River east of Montrose to a maximum depth of 2,700 feet. The narrowest width at the top is 1,100 feet, and at one point in the bottom the river channel narrows to only 40 feet. A backcountry permit is needed for the descent into the canyon, which is arduous and hazardous. On each rim there is a highway that leads to spectacular observation points over the shadowed depths. Campgrounds on both of the rims are open June to October. Address: 2233 East Main Street, Montrose, Colorado 81401. 303/249-7036.

## BLUE RIDGE PARKWAY

### North Carolina–Virginia

This highly popular area attracts more than 20 million visitors a year. And little wonder. The parkway is the longest scenic drive in the world, providing quiet, leisurely travel, free of commercial congestion, for 469 miles through the forested mountains of Virginia and North Carolina. It is much more than a road: it is a *garden* of flowering trees, shrubs, and herbs; a *park* with nature trails, picnic grounds, and camping; a *museum* of the southern highlands culture, expressed at restored mills, weathered cabins, and farms bordered by split-rail fences; a *wildlife sanctuary* for deer, bear, bobcat, skunk, and possibly

200 species of birds; and a center of beautiful, authentic mountain handicrafts. It is *not* a high-speed freeway.

In some sections the parkway runs along the very crest of the mountains. Breathtaking vistas unfold from overlooks 2,000 to 6,000 feet high. Many miles of excellent hiking trails are available, from short leg-stretchers to steep climbs. The Appalachian Trail roughly parallels the parkway north of Roanoke. High spots in the Virginia portion include: **Humpback Rocks,** near Waynesboro, the northern end of the parkway, where the self-guiding trail weaves among a cluster of log buildings of pioneer days; **Peaks of Otter,** near Roanoke, a high valley sheltered by the towering triple peaks, popular as a mountain retreat since Jefferson's day; and **Mabry Mill,** where you can see a genuine water-powered gristmill in operation grinding corn.

Across the border in North Carolina: **Brinegar Cabin** offers weaving demonstrations on an old mountain loom. **Linville Falls,** a wilderness beauty spot around a mighty gorge, was presented to the park system by John D. Rockefeller, Jr. **Museum of North Carolina Minerals,** near Spruce Pine, is a special delight to rockhounds with a display of gemstones and minerals found nearby. **Mount Mitchell** (6,680 feet), in a state park bordering the parkway, is the highest mountain in the East. **Craggy Gardens,** north of Asheville, is a favorite spot to walk among flowering rhododendrons of late spring. **Devils Courthouse,** a rocky summit, affords a 360-degree view across the mountains of the Carolinas, Tennessee, and Georgia.

**Shopping Guide.** Craft demonstrations at key points and the finest souvenir shops in the entire National Park system help visitors to appreciate native skills and to purchase worthwhile travel mementos. **Northwest Trading Post,** near West Jefferson, North Carolina, features everything from homemade cheeses and jellies to fine quilts and carvings. At the **Folk Art Center,** east of Asheville at Milepost 382, members of the Southern Highlands Handicraft Guild are seen making rugs and baskets and weaving. A series of workshops in Appalachian crafts, open to all at modest fees, is conducted here by the guild.

**Birdwatching.** Late September and early October are prime for observing southerly migration of many birds and butterflies from overlooks along the parkway. From Milepost 92, near the Peaks of Otter, in Virginia, hundreds of hawks can often be observed in a single day, gliding on billows of air that rise from the Blue Ridge valleys. Depending on the weather conditions, some birds fly so high that they appear to be mere specks in the sky, whereas spiraling flight patterns of other birds bring them into high-level view. The roadside exhibit depicts patterns of various hawks, eagles, ospreys, and vultures.

**Seasons and Accommodations.** In early spring migrant birds, including many warblers, grace forests and fields. Dogwood and wildflowers open the flowering season late in April. Flame azalea blazes in the hills from mid-May, reaching a peak in the high mountains around Asheville in June. Mountain laurel and snowy-white rhododendron continue the flower show until late July. Autumn brings a new set of colors in the spectacular hardwoods of the eastern forests. The parkway is excellent for cross-country skiing because it receives a dependable amount of snow. Lodges and housekeeping cabins provide accommodations for visitors. Advance reservations are recommended at all facilities. Some parkway campgrounds remain open all year, weather and road conditions permitting. Other campgrounds are in national forests, state parks, and private areas all along the parkway. Historic Hotel Botetourt in Buchanan is now a member of American Youth Hostel's network of low-cost accommodations. So is Blue Ridge Country AYH-Hostel, 100 feet off the parkway, 10 miles east of Galax, "capital of old-time mountain music." From mid-June through Labor Day, naturalists and historians lead guided walks and give evening programs at major visitor use areas. Visitor Centers at Humpback Rocks, James River, Rocky Knob, Peaks of Otter, and Craggy Gardens are open May through October. The Museum of North Carolina Minerals and the Folk Art Center are open year-round. The parkway is open all year; however, some sections are closed in icy or snowy weather. Address: 200 BB&T Building, Asheville, North Carolina 28801. 704/259-0718.

## BUCK ISLAND REEF NATIONAL MONUMENT

### Virgin Islands

Off the northeast coast of St. Croix, the prime attraction of this uninhabited island is the lush coral reef—a marine garden of coral, grottoes, sea fans, gorgonias, and myriad tropical fish. Here the Park Service has established the underwater Buck Island Reef nature trail, complete with informational signs on the ocean floor to guide snorkelers. You can swim the trail—an outstanding snorkeling opportunity—in about 30 minutes. Day trips in small boats are conducted by captains operating from Christiansted, 6 miles away, and they will furnish the snorkel gear. There is also ample time to walk the nature trail through the tropical vegetation covering the island, and while on the trail you may get the chance to see the rookery of pelicans and Caribbean birds. The island is also the habitat of several species of sea turtles. Address: c/o Christiansted National Historic Site, Box 160, Christiansted, St. Croix, Virgin Islands 00820. 809/773-1460.

## BUFFALO NATIONAL RIVER

### Arkansas

Massive bluffs and deeply entrenched valleys give the Buffalo River a striking setting as it winds 132 miles through the Ozarks of northwest Arkansas to its mouth on the White River at the hamlet called Buffalo City. The Buffalo is undoubtedly one of America's most beautiful streams, with countless rapids, cliffs, caves, hills, mountains, and scenic side canyons, many with waterfalls and sinkholes, along its course. Bordering lands support 1,500 varieties of plants and many types of small animals. Just over 95 percent of the land is in federal ownership at this time. Eventually the park will include 95,730 acres for fishing, hiking, boating, hunting, camping, and nature study. One of the park's highlights, Hemmed-in Hollow (which can be reached only by foot), contains the largest free-leaping waterfall between the southern Appalachians and the Rockies. For a display of autumn colors from the dogwoods, hickories, red and white oaks, and maples, visit the park around mid-October. Adjacent Ozark National Forest offers an annual bus tour when the fall colors are at their peak; call 501/446-5122 in early October for the exact date.

**Canoeing** is the main activity. Except for extreme dry periods, the Lower River (east of Silver Hill) can be floated almost any time. The Upper River, however, is usually too low after June 1. Buffalo Point (formerly Buffalo River State Park) is the principal center. Located 17 miles south of Yellville, via Arkansas 14 and 268, facilities include 106 campsites, 14 housekeeping cottages, dining room, and picnic areas. During summer, park rangers conduct nature walks across wild and beautiful terrain. Lost Valley (formerly Lost Valley State Park) lies in the heart of the most rugged section of the Ozarks, with primitive campsites for those who enjoy roughing it. Steel Creek primitive camp is located just downstream from the Ponca low-water bridge and offers spectacular scenery. It is an excellent put-in point for canoeists when water permits. Both Lost Valley and Steel Creek are reached via Arkansas 43 from Harrison or Arkansas 74 from Jasper. Outfitters outside the park offer canoe rentals and guide service if desired. Along the river, camps are made on innumerable gravel bars edging the stream. Primitive float camps have been established, offering minimal facilities. Canoeists are asked to respect the rights of private landowners when selecting a campsite. Maps and additional information are available at Buffalo Point, Silver Hill, and Pruitt Stations. Address: Box 1173, Harrison, Arkansas 72602. 501/741-5443.

# CANAVERAL NATIONAL SEASHORE
## Florida

One of the last major wild areas on Florida's Atlantic coast is preserved in this national seashore and its companion, **Merritt Island National Wildlife Refuge.** Canaveral was established in 1975 from what had been the northern portion of Kennedy Space Center and a Florida state park; it covers 57,627 acres, including 25 miles of beachfront.

**Apollo Beach,** at the north end, lies about 10 miles south of New Smyrna on Florida A1A. A paved road provides about 6 miles of vehicle access. **Playalinda Beach,** at the south end, is 12 miles east of Titusville on Florida 402. An information booth is open 9 A.M. to 4:30 P.M. A paved road parallels the ocean for about 5 miles behind the tall dunes. It's a good place for swimming, surfing, and beach walking. Summer weekends are apt to be crowded and visitors may be turned away when the limited parking spaces are filled.

The central portion of the seashore, measuring about 14 miles along the coast, is managed as a roadless area where nature comes first. Scrub vegetation, including saw palmetto, covers most of the land, with the exception of the marsh. In spring and summer, giant loggerhead and green turtles crawl up on the beach at night to lay their eggs. The seashore is wintering ground for thousands of birds of many species. Bald eagles nest in tall pine trees. Brown pelicans occupy a mangrove rookery island in the heart of the seashore. More than 280 species of birds have been sighted along the shore and in the interior. The Merritt Island National Wildlife Refuge provides special opportunities for birdwatching and wildlife observation. The major attraction in this region, of course, is the Kennedy Space Center, which offers excellent displays for visitors and a guided tour of its installations. Camping is available within the central section of the seashore. A permit is required. Address: 308 Julia Street, Titusville, Florida 32796. 407/267-1110.

# CAPE COD NATIONAL SEASHORE
## Massachusetts

The slender, bent arm of land thrust 70 miles into the ocean from the mainland was settled within two decades after colonists established Plymouth, to be lived on by fishermen, sea captains, and whaling men. For generations it was a remote place of heath, marsh, pine forest, and lakes, and its principal visitors were millions of birds en route between Canada and the South. The national seashore was established in 1961, preserving the old heritage on 44,600 acres. Thus was rescued from development a 40-mile ribbon, where the life-community of the land—plants like milkwort, sandwort, and seaside goldenrod—can still steal to the ocean's edge to meet incoming jellyfish, kelp, clam, and rockweed.

**Attention, birdwatchers.** The beauty and variety of Cape Cod birds reflect different environments to which they have adapted. Some are fishers of the deep sea, while others are waders, scratchers, wood borers, seed eaters, and scavengers. Try to match birds with habitats as you go along. Join illustrated evening bird talks and other programs.

**Nauset Area.** Start at the Salt Pond Visitor Center, easily reached just off Route 6 in Eastham. It features spectacular views of Salt Pond and Nauset Marsh, plus a wealth of information about seashore attractions and programs. The museum portion, renovated and expanded in 1989, is a showcase of 19th-century and early-20th-century Cape Cod artifacts. These include the Clark collection of scrimshaw, one of the largest and most impressive in New England, recalling the age when whaling voyages lasted two years or more and sailors hand-carved elaborate designs into scraps of whalebone. One of the finest features in the park is the Buttonbush Trail for the Blind; Fort Hill and Nauset Marsh Trails are also very worthwhile. For swimming, head for Coast Guard Beach and Nauset Light Beach (both have lifeguards); for surf fishing for striped bass, Great Beach. A popular bike trail runs through the area. Birders should take advantage of the excellent observation point at Nauset Beach, where thousands of sea birds and shore birds congregate during summer.

**Attention, bicyclists.** The Cape Cod Rail Trail, created from an abandoned Cape Cod Central Railroad line, will give you access to hidden scenic treasures. Seven ponds border the trail, and most are open for swimming.

**Province Lands.** Some of the most spectacular dunes along the Atlantic Coast are at the tip of the Cape in a 4,400-acre area set aside ever since 1670, when the "Plimoth Colony" undertook an early conservation action. Swimming beaches (lifeguards on duty) at Race Point and Herring Cove are open 9 A.M. to 5 P.M. Guided walks are conducted through the beech forest and marshland. Eight miles of bicycle trails run through the dunes. Behind the "hook of the cape," the visitor looks at Provincetown on Cape Cod Bay, where the *Mayflower* made its first landfall in 1620.

**Pilgrim Heights.** Self-guiding trails lead along heath-covered slopes bordering the Atlantic and to a spring where the Pilgrims may have found their first fresh drinking water after leaving England. Picnic tables, guarded swimming are at Head-of-the-Meadow Beach, Truro.

**Marconi Station.** Overlooking the ocean from high, sandy bluffs near the village of Wellfleet, a shelter house stands near the site of the first wireless station in the United States, and contains a scale model of the original from which Guglielmo Marconi successfully transmitted a message to England in 1903. The views are spectacular, particularly of the Great Beach, which was given its name by Thoreau. ("A man may stand there and put all America behind him," he wrote.) Guided walks. A swimming beach is available at Marconi.

**Accommodations and Seasons.** Resort accommodations ranging from hostels and simple cottages to deluxe hotels and motels are located in towns adjoining the seashore. Privately operated campgrounds are within the authorized boundaries, and several are nearby. For complete listings, write the Cape Cod Chamber of Commerce, Hyannis, Massachusetts 02601. Several hostels in the area offer dormitory-style accommodations, with separate men's and women's rooms and self-service kitchens for low cost. Some are open summer only. Write for a Cape Cod Hostels brochure to American Youth Hostels, Dept. CC, Box 37613, Washington, D.C. 20013-37613. The Cape is a popular place; advance reservations, for rooms and campsites, should be made for the summer months. Address: South Wellfleet, Massachusetts 02663. 508/349-3785.

# CAPE HATTERAS NATIONAL SEASHORE
## North Carolina

A 70-mile slender strand, only 3 miles at its widest, the Cape Hatteras seashore area lies between foaming ocean surf and broad, shallow sounds. One should not come here anticipating the usual seaside vacation, but rather a *different* experience, where the main activities are apt to be watching thousands of snow geese, or the bottle-nosed dolphin rolling and playing offshore, or vivid sunsets over the sea and sand.

This is the first of the national seashores, established in 1953. It covers 28,500 acres from Nags Head, on Bodie Island, southward to include Hatteras and Ocracoke Islands, now connected by bridge and ferry. An asphalt road leads through villages like Rodanthe, Salvo, and Buxton, which date to colonial days. From parking turnouts visitors can walk to the beach to fish, swim, or explore the wreckage of ships that ran aground in the "Graveyard of the Atlantic."

These storied Outer Banks, where the English first tried to establish colonies in 1585, and where Blackbeard was tracked down and killed, are no longer isolated—but they offer a spirit of isolation.

**Bodie Island Visitor Center** is the best place to start; exhibits focus on U.S. Lighthouse Services. Other Visitor Centers are at Cape Hatteras and Ocracoke. From mid-June to Labor Day guided walks along the beach and illustrated evening talks are held.

**Pea Island National Wildlife Refuge,** at the north end of Hatteras Island, is a key way station on the Atlantic flyway, and it helps to make the national seashore a birder's delight. Throngs of snow geese winter here, as do large numbers of whistling swans, Canada geese, and ducks. More than 300 species of birds have been recorded.

**Cape Hatteras Lighthouse,** the tallest lighthouse in the country, reopened in 1993 after a $950,000 renovation. It's 268 steps to the top, but don't miss it.

**Ocracoke Village** is well worth a visit, though it lies at the southern tip of the national seashore. The small fishing fleet at harbor, gnarled live oaks, the oldest lighthouse of the Outer Banks, sandy lanes, and Teach's Hole, where Blackbeard may have met his end, are among its attractions. A tiny cemetery, bordered by a white picket fence, marks the burial place of four British sailors whose bodies washed ashore in 1942 after their ship was sunk by a German submarine southeast of Hatteras. The cemetery, leased by North Carolina to the British government in 1976, is maintained by the U.S. Coast Guard.

Besides the free ferry across Hatteras Inlet, Ocracoke can be reached by the Cedar Island ferry from the mainland (it makes several round trips daily) via the town of Atlantic on North Carolina 70, and from Swan Quarter, off US 264.

**Sport fishing** is celebrated: surf casting from the ocean beach; trolling from boats in the inland sounds and bays and in the deep waters of the Gulf Stream 20 miles offshore. Best periods for channel bass are April 15 to June 15 and September 20 to November 20; cobia, June and July; blues and mackerels, July and August. However, fish may be caught every month. Charter boats available.

**Swimming** is best where lifeguard service is provided in summer. Strong currents make swimming at unguarded beaches hazardous. Funding permitting, guarded beaches may be found at Coquina Beach, Salvo Campground, Cape Point Campground, Frisco Campground, and Ocracoke. Water is too cold for swimming before late May. Surfing is popular but restricted from areas near swimming beaches, hotels, and fishing piers.

**Accommodations and Seasons.** Hotels, motels, and cottages are found in communities just north of the seashore and in villages within the boundaries, including Hatteras and Ocracoke, and Manteo, on Roanoke Island. For a complete list, write Dare County Tourist Bureau, Manteo, North Carolina 27954. Five campgrounds for tents and trailers (no utility connections) are located in the seashore park, generally on flat, shadeless areas; awnings and long tent stakes are advised. Bring mosquito netting and repellent. Reservations through Ticketron June through Labor Day: limit 14 days. Facilities are crowded in summer. Ocracoke, Oregon Inlet, and Cape Point campgrounds are open mid-April to mid-October. Address: Route 1, Box 675, Manteo, North Carolina 27954. 919/473-2111.

## CAPE LOOKOUT NATIONAL SEASHORE

### North Carolina

This National Seashore, established in 1976, encompasses 55 miles of ocean shore south of Ocracoke Inlet on Portsmouth Island, Core Banks, and Shackleford Banks. The combination of Hatteras and Lookout National Seashores gives North Carolina the greatest length of continuous protected shoreline on the U.S. east coast. The area is a wintering ground for loons, mergansers, cormorants, gannets, geese, swans, and, occasionally, Arctic birds. In summer, terns, pelicans, egrets, herons, and various shore birds take over. Large, 20-foot-high dunes characterize Cape Lookout Bight and Shackleford Banks, while a forest of live oak, cedar holly, and pine backs up the banks at Shackleford. Present use includes sport fishing and waterfowl hunting. Programs are given daily during summer at the lighthouse, North Carolina Maritime Museum, and North Carolina Aquarium. Dolphins are a familiar sight.

**Ferry service** is available from Harkers Island (reached by road from Beaufort) to the Cape Lookout Bight area and from Davis and Atlantic off US 70 to points on the Core Banks. You can reach Portsmouth Village by charter ferry from Ocracoke, at the southern tip of Cape Hatteras National Seashore; from Ocracoke the Cedar Island ferry connects with US 70 south to Beaufort. There are rustic overnight accommodations at the seashore. If you intend to camp, be sure to bring tents with mosquito netting, suntan lotion, insect repellent, food, and water. Address: 3601 Bridges St., Suite F, Morehead City, North Carolina 28557. 919/240-1409.

## CAPULIN VOLCANO NATIONAL MONUMENT
### New Mexico

Ever wanted to walk into a volcano? You can at Capulin Volcano. A 2-mile road spirals to the summit parking lot. Two self-guiding trails tour the summit: short trail to the vent; 1-mile trail circles the rim. The monument lies near the northeast corner of the state off US 64/87, between Raton and Clayton, New Mexico. The Visitor Center and picnic area are open all year. Address: Capulin, New Mexico 88414. 505/278-2201.

## CATOCTIN MOUNTAIN PARK
See page 292.

## CEDAR BREAKS NATIONAL MONUMENT
### Utah

A huge natural coliseum, eroded into the Pink Cliffs, lies between Zion and Bryce National Parks. The rim of the amphitheater, whose amazing colors change with the sun's rays, averages over 10,000 feet in elevation. Mule deer often graze meadows and slopes in morning and evening. Campground and Visitor Center; recreation facilities in surround-

ing Dixie National Forest. Address: Box 749, Cedar City, Utah 84720. 801/586-9451.

## CHATTAHOOCHEE RIVER NATIONAL RECREATION AREA
### Georgia

This area, authorized by Congress in 1978, consists of 14 noncontiguous parcels of land along 48 miles of the Chattahoochee River between Lake Sidney Lanier and Atlanta. The Park Service now manages about 4,100 acres along the river. The most popular activities are picnicking, hiking, fishing, and rafting along gentle stretches of the waterway.

The Chattahoochee derives its name from the Cherokee word for "flowering rock," denoting the many waterfalls tumbling in the Appalachian highlands, the source of the river. Nearby is the Kennesaw Mountain National Battlefield Park. There are campgrounds near Lake Sidney Lanier, north of Atlanta. Address: 1978 Island Ford Parkway, Dunwoody, Georgia 30350. 404/399-8070.

## CHICKASAW NATIONAL RECREATION AREA
### Oklahoma

This new area combines the lands of the former Platt National Park and Arbuckle National Recreation Area to form, in the words of Congress, "a fitting memorialization of the Chickasaw Indian Nation." The combined area contains cold mineral springs, freshwater springs, woods, and waterfalls in the Arbuckle Mountains of southern Oklahoma, adjacent to the town of Sulphur, south of Oklahoma City.

The Arbuckle Reservoir provides fishing, boating, and swimming. Stream fishing and hiking are features of Upper Rock Creek. Camping and picnicking are also available. So are nature trails through a woodland of oaks, persimmon, osage-orange, hickory, walnut, cedar, and juniper; and shrubs such as sumac, elder, plum, and redbud.

Students have come from great distances to study the unusual geology of the ancient Arbuckle Mountains, which have been uplifted, deformed, and worn down to their roots. Within a few miles of the reservoir are unusual outcrops, rugged slopes and gorges, an outstanding fossil-bearing site, waterfalls, and a dramatic geologic array (along US 77) known locally as the "gravestones."

**Visitor Center.** Travertine Nature Center, in the eastern end of the area, contains interpretive displays featuring live snakes, frogs, lizards, insects, plants, and fish native to the area. The center is the main visitor information point and start of several nature trails through the Environmental Study Area, an outdoor classroom. During summer, guided walks, movies, a children's program, and evening talks are given each day. The center is open every day of the year except Christmas and New Year's Day.

**Perimeter Road,** a 7-mile circuit drive, offers motorists a scenic view of the area. Sixteen miles of trail provide access to all points of interest in the recreation area.

**Bromide Hill,** a steep, wooded bluff easily reached by road or trail, offers a fine panoramic view.

**Mineral spring waters** may be used by all visitors, but should not be taken in quantity except on a physician's advice. The mud from some sulfur-water pools is said to help in treating certain skin diseases. In the eastern end of the recreation area, Buffalo and Antelope springs were named because herds of these animals used to come from the surrounding prairies to drink.

Of the area's six campgrounds, two are open all year. Address: Chickasaw National Recreation Area, Box 201, Sulphur, Oklahoma 73086. 405/622-3161.

## CHIRICAHUA NATIONAL MONUMENT

### Arizona

A wilderness of unusual rock shapes, gigantic monoliths eroded by wind and water, with strata telling the story of nearly 30 million years of the earth's forces, lies high in the Chiricahua Mountains, near the old stronghold of Cochise and his Apache braves. The "wonderland of rocks" lies between Willcox on I-10 and Douglas on the Mexican border. A paved road leads to an overlook, with horseback and foot trails reaching all parts of the monument, Visitor Center and campgrounds. Nearest lodgings are in Willcox.

Chiricahua comprises one of the country's truly choice birding spots. Shady glens in the canyon bottoms provide haven for unique species, including many closely associated with Mexico. The wide range of climate and vegetation attracts a wide spectrum of southwest mountain birds. The bridled titmouse and painted redstart are two of the most unusual. At times the elusive Montezuma quail is fairly common here. Some of the most interesting species are best seen in the canyon near the Visitor Center. Address: Dos Cabezas Route, Box 6500, Willcox, Arizona 85643. 602/824-3560.

## CITY OF ROCKS NATIONAL RESERVE

### Idaho

Striking granite spires and sculptured rock formations, almost due south of Burley, Idaho, just north of the Utah border, have long made the City of Rocks a special place, with both geological and historical value. Not until 1988, however, did Congress act, designating 14,320 acres (including City of Rocks State Park) for federal protection. Visitors see ruts of wagon wheels left by settlers heading for Oregon, and something more—inscriptions of the pioneers, many applied with axle grease, still legible on the rocks. Camp Rock provides easy access to some of the old writing, a choice spot to reflect on the environment of glaciated mountains, wild rivers, thundering waterfalls, lakes and streams, grassland prairie, and desert. Take time to hike or climb among the rocks; the massive granite formations are thought to be the oldest rocks in western North America. City of Rocks, in fact, is known as one of the best climbing places in Idaho, rewarding to climbers of all skill levels. However, avoid climbing on rocks bearing old inscriptions or where birds of prey may nest. Address: c/o Hagerman Fossil Beds National Monument, 963 Blue Lakes Boulevard, Suite 1, Twin Falls, Idaho 83301. 208/733-8398.

## COLORADO NATIONAL MONUMENT
### Colorado

Steep canyon walls, towering monoliths and rounded domes, red-streaked and patterned with the bright green of juniper and pinon pine—these are the uplifted and eroded sandstones of the Uncompaghre Plateau. Rim Rock Drive follows the canyon rims and overlooks along the way provide views of the magnificent rock sculpture. Many trails reward hikers with superb vistas and close-up views of the rock formations. Spring and summer wildflowers add splashes of color to the juniper-pinon forest of the semiarid desert. Exploring this harsh and beautiful environment leaves a feeling of cleansing—all the city dirt is burned away. A backcountry permit is required for camping in the area; lodgings and private campgrounds are available in and near Grand Junction. Address: Fruita, Colorado 81521. 303/858-3617.

## CONGAREE SWAMP NATIONAL MONUMENT
### South Carolina

This unique flood plain contains a rare remnant of southern river bottomland forest barely 20 miles south of Columbia. It includes deciduous hardwoods, huge loblolly pines, bald cypress, and tupelos. Elsewhere in the Southeast, lumbering has all but wiped out such forest stands. Congress approved establishment of the national monument in 1976. Reach the monument via South Carolina 48, southeast from Columbia. Enjoy guided tours,

25 miles of walking trails, fishing, primitive camping, and canoeing on Cedar Creek. Note the uprooted and snapped trees left by Hurricane Hugo in 1989. Nearby are Manchester State Forest and Poinsett State Park. There is a campground in the state park. No fee is charged, but a camping permit is required. Only primitive camping is available. The visitor center is open from 8:30 a.m. to 5:00 p.m. Address: 200 Caroline Sims Rd., Hopkins, South Carolina 29061. 803/776-4396.

## COULEE DAM NATIONAL RECREATION AREA
### Washington

The area centers on Franklin D. Roosevelt Lake, a reservoir extending 151 miles along the Columbia River from Grand Coulee Dam north to the Canadian border. It offers many outdoor activities: fishing, water skiing, swimming, boating, and camping in quiet coves. In addition, it holds interest in the immense dam, rolling hills, varied plants, and wildlife. On the north and west shores are Indian lands, the dwelling place of a dozen tribes, including the descendants of Chief Joseph's Nez Percé, who made their valiant, futile struggle for freedom in 1877.

The best place to gain an impression of the lake's dimensions is the high **lookout point** at the west end of the dam. The dam was completed in 1941 by the U.S. Bureau of Reclamation to provide irrigation water for the Columbia River Basin. The powerhouse is open to visitors during summer. The lake has 660 miles of shoreline, with 13 developed beaches and 26 recreation areas providing camping, boat launching, picnicking, and bathhouses. Camping sites range from highly organized to primitive.

The travel season extends from May to November. Water in the reservoir reaches maximum level in late June or early July and remains full all summer. Illustrated programs are presented at major campgrounds to interpret the geology and plant and animal life, as well as human history, of the Columbia River

Valley. For more on the dam and geologic history of the Columbia Basin, watch "Water and Life," a laser light show visible summer evenings from a large area downstream of the dam; tune your car radio or listen at the visitor center at the base of the dam for the accompanying audio program. A choice is boating from Coulee Dam to the beautiful Arrow Lakes of Canada, a distance of 300 miles. A popular scenic drive leads from Coulee Dam to Fort Spokane, then to Kettle Falls.

Hunting is permitted within the recreation area subject to state regulations. Upland birds are common, and chukars have been introduced. Address: Box 37, Coulee Dam, Washington 99116. 509/633-9441.

## CRATERS OF THE MOON NATIONAL MONUMENT

### Idaho

This is an astonishing landscape of vast lava fields studded with cinder cones. Although the last eruptions occurred about 2,000 years ago, volcanic activity in the area dates back over a million years. The repeated floods of massive rivers of liquid rock destroyed all vegetation in their paths. Barren and sterile, the surface presented a harsh environment which at first only the hardiest plants could invade; but in time 200 species of plants and many animals have successfully established themselves in this seemingly desolate area that resembles the craters on the moon.

The national monument covers 53,545 acres. Many features are readily accessible by car and trail. Start at the **Visitor Center,** which contains exhibits explaining the volcanic formations, plants, animals, and history. Then take the 7-mile loop drive and side trips leading from it. Look for "bombs" scattered about the cinder slopes, curious objects formed from ejected blobs of frothy lava that hardened into globular shape while in the air.

In spring, wildflower displays are spectacular in the cinder gardens. You can see them closely on one of the several trails that range from a 20-minute walk in the formation called **Devils Orchard** to a two-hour hike to the **Tree Molds.** For the veteran explorer, who checks first with a ranger, a vast lava wilderness lies waiting in the southern section. From mid-June to Labor Day illustrated programs are presented in the campground.

The national monument campground provides water, tables, grills, restrooms, but no electrical or sewage hookups. Fee charged; no reservations. It lies 18 miles west of Arco, which provides the nearest facilities for gas or food. For further information write Superintendent, Craters of the Moon National Monument, Box 29, Arco, Idaho 83213. 208/527-3257.

## CUMBERLAND ISLAND NATIONAL SEASHORE

### Georgia

This national seashore, with its Spanish moss-draped forests and 18 miles of golden beach, is open to the public for day use and limited overnight camping. The island is reached via a National Park Service ferry that leaves twice a day, five days a week, from St. Marys, Georgia. Reservations are advisable for the tour boat, which holds 140 passengers. Call 912/882-4315. With the installation of a 135-foot floating dock, small boaters are able to tie up at the island. The dock is located on a channel off the Intracoastal Waterway with 8 feet of water alongside (measured at low tide). Large boats are asked to anchor out to avoid taking up most of the space.

You are welcome to join naturalist-conducted tours covering key aspects of the island. Then strike out on your own with an official Backcountry Map to discover wonders lying along marked trails. Wear long trousers and broad-brimmed hat. Carry sunscreen, sunglasses, mosquito and tick repellent, and snakebite kit; check frequently for ticks.

**Where to Stay.** Greyfield Inn, at the edge of Cumberland Sound, has nine rooms much in demand in Spring and Fall. Make reservations far in advance; it is expensive. Greyfield provides ferry service from Fernandina Beach, Florida 32034; telephone 904/261-6408.

**Camping** at the park is limited to a total of 120 persons per night. Sea Camp, accommodating 60, is the only developed camp. Four other camping areas have drinking water only. Reservations are required; specific sites are assigned and backcountry use permits issued on arrival. Campers must carry all equipment and supplies to the campsite on foot. Water and comfort facilities are available for day-use visitors, as well as campers. There is no food service on the island.

The island is the southernmost of the **Golden Isles,** which have been inhabited continuously for 10,000 years. The live oak–palmetto and longleaf-pine forests add a rare dimension to the National Park system's plant communities, including many species heretofore not represented. Deer, raccoon, numerous birds, and nesting loggerhead turtles dwell on the island. Reservations may be made by calling 912/882-4335. Address: Cumberland Island National Seashore, Box 806, St. Marys, Georgia 31558. 912/882-4337.

## CURECANTI NATIONAL RECREATION AREA

### Colorado

In the heart of Colorado's western slope—an area of rugged high country, open mesas, and rushing mountain streams—a chain of three dams and reservoirs form the Curecanti Unit of the Colorado River Storage Project. **Blue Mesa Dam,** completed in 1965, backs up the largest body of water in Colorado, 20-mile-long Blue Mesa Lake, the major storage feature of the Curecanti Unit.

Blue Mesa is popular for camping, fishing, boating, sailing, and waterskiing. You'll find launching ramps, marinas with rental boats, equipment, and some grocery items. Three major campgrounds border the lake: Elk Creek (16 miles west of Gunnison on US 50); Lake Fork (near Blue Mesa Dam); and Stevens Creek (4 miles east of Elk Creek). Blue Mesa

offers choice fishing for Kokanee salmon, and rainbow, brown, and Mackinaw trout.

Stop at **Elk Creek Visitor Center** for interpretive programs and to see the fishpond. Join summer hikes and bird walks that start here and evening campfire programs at the Campground Amphitheater.

Access for anglers and boaters to **Morrow Point Lake** is provided along the east side over the Pine Creek Trail. Even if you're just sightseeing, take advantage of the 2-hour summer boat tours on the lake, in a deep fjordlike canyon (fees are charged). A 30-passenger boat takes visitors on a two-hour, 18-mile round-trip tour. A park naturalist explains various natural features of geology, botany, and wildlife. Seats are reserved at the Elk Creek Marina or by calling 303/641-0403. At **Cimarron** (20 miles east of Montrose), a narrow-gauge railroad exhibit includes locomotive, coal tender, freight car, and caboose that once ran through the narrow canyon before it was flooded by the reservoir. Beyond the railroad exhibit there is a viewpoint that overlooks Morrow Point Dam.

The surrounding high mountain country at the Gunnison and San Isabel National Forests to the north and east, and the San Juan Mountains to the south and southwest add a greater dimension to the enjoyment of this recreation area. The **Black Canyon of the Gunnison National Monument,** to the west, is one of the scenic highlights of western Colorado. Address: 102 Elk Creek, Gunnison, Colorado 81230. 303/641-2337.

## CUYAHOGA VALLEY NATIONAL RECREATION AREA

### Ohio

In legislation signed by President Ford on December 27, 1974, Congress authorized this park of 32,400 acres. The early Indians had a word for this river: *ka-ih-ogh-ha.* It meant crooked, or twisting. Through many variations, explorers in the 18th century settled on Cuyahoga as the spelling for the winding stream which comes from the northeast, drops swiftly through a deep glacial-carved gorge, then meanders northward to its outlet at Lake Erie. Miraculously, a 20-mile stretch of the valley between heavily populated metro areas of Cleveland and Akron remains open meadows and wooded hillsides, with remnants of the Ohio and Erie Canal paralleling the river.

More than 20,000 acres are open and available as public parklands, much of it long protected by Cleveland and Akron. Make the most of your trip by starting at either **Happy Days Visitor Center,** on Ohio 303 two miles east of Peninsula, or **Canal Visitor Center,** in Valley View. The centers are open daily.

The **Virginia Kendall Unit,** operated by the park service, has a notable trail network leading to a major geological feature, the Ritchie Ledges. Other areas include Brecksville and Bedford reservations in Cuyahoga County; and Deep Lock Quarry, Furnace Run, O'Neil Woods, and Hampton Hills in Summit County. Each park has recreation and picnic facilities and its own well-marked hiking trails. From almost the northern extremity to the south, the **Buckeye Trail** follows near the river and canal, often on the old towpath. This is the walking trail extending from Mentor Headlands on Lake Erie to Cincinnati on the Ohio River. Blue blazes mark the route.

**Bird watchers,** note the varying habitats that attract different species. The overgrown canal is a busy spot for waterfowl and other water birds. The Deep Lock Quarry area is particularly good for viewing warblers during migration. Pick up a bird list at Happy Days Visitor Center or Canal Visitor Center.

For **rail fans,** the Cuyahoga Valley Scenic Railroad, utilizing rolling stock of the Midwest Railway Historical Foundation from the 1930s, '40s, and '50s, operates weekends June through October and each Friday in September and October. The Polar Bear Limited train begins operation the Friday after Thanksgiving and runs weekends through Christmas. The train leaves from Independence at 10:30 A.M., following the century-old valley route

along the Cuyahoga River to Hale Farm, then to Quaker Square in Akron.

The area is rich in historic values. In fact, you can stay overnight at the Inn at Brandywine Falls, a bed-and-breakfast inn formerly the James Wallace Farm, adjoining two other historic properties, leased by the government under the historic property leasing program. On Oak Hill Road, the **Hale Farm and Village** complex stands as one of the outstanding restorations of the rural scene in the Middle West. The village, a venture of the Western Reserve Historical Society, typifies a crossroads of the 19th century, complete with working farm, general store, land survey office, blacksmith shop, gristmill, and homes. Other sites include Peninsula Village, with several restored buildings of the middle 1800s; Twelve Mile Lock and Fourteen Mile Lock on the Ohio and Erie Canal; the Frazee/Hynton House, built as a stagecoach stop in 1806; and Moneyshop, the lair of early counterfeiters. Address: 15610 Vaughn Road, Brecksville, Ohio 44141. 216/526-5256.

## DEATH VALLEY NATIONAL MONUMENT

See Death Valley National Park, p. 90.

## DELAWARE WATER GAP NATIONAL RECREATION AREA

### Pennsylvania–New Jersey

The famous gap—a break in the Kittatinny Ridge of the Blue Ridge Mountains, threaded by the Delaware River—is a forested canyon and a real beauty spot astride the Pennsylvania–New Jersey border near Stroudsburg, Pennsylvania. Highways I-80 and US 611 now pass through the gap, but it was rather remote until recent years, for all its proximity to the eastern megalopolis. The National Recreation Area was originally conceived as part of the proposed Tocks Island dam and reservoir project. In the face of strong citizen opposition, the dam may never be built.

Points of interest are found throughout the park. Activities range from fishing, swimming, and canoeing, to hiking, hunting, and scenic driving. The area excels for birdwatching, especially during spring migration before leaves are on the trees and again during fall migration. Tremendous flocks of blackbirds use the Delaware Valley on their migration route. Spring is colorful, with passing warblers and other perching birds. August marks the beginning of the migration of hawks and eagles. The best vantage points for observing the fall phenomenon are along Kittatinny Mountain.

From the overlook near the **Kittatinny Point Visitor Center,** between I-80 and the Delaware, you get a wonderful view of the river flowing between the rocky walls of the gap. The Appalachian Trail passes here and leads to glacial Sunfish Pond, a mountain lake atop Kittatinny Ridge on the New Jersey side. It has remained unchanged down through the time of the Indians, who came into the valley 12,500 years ago, and the time of the European settlers. At **Dingmans Falls Visitors Center,** one mile west of Route 209, walk on a half-mile nature trail through rhododendrons and hemlocks to two waterfalls.

**Slateford Farm,** off Pennsylvania 611 near Portland, Pennsylvania, affords a unique opportunity to learn about slate quarrying. In Millbrook, 12 miles from I-80 on New Jersey's Old Mine Road, park personnel give tours and demonstrations of 19th-century crafts from mid-June to Labor Day. Another 12 miles north of Millbrook, **Peters Valley Crafts Village,** near Walpack, enables visitors to take contemporary craft courses in blacksmithing, ceramics, fine metals, textiles, and wood. Studios are open daily during the summer, as are the crafts store and gallery.

**Grey Towers** is the family home of Gifford Pinchot—pioneer forester, conservationist, and two-time governor of Pennsylvania. On a high knoll above Milford, Pennsylvania, this unusual 41-room mansion, styled like a French chateau, overlooks the river and the Delaware Valley. The U.S. Forest Service conducts free tours.

The Pocono Environmental Education Center, located inside the park, teaches thousands of school children each year about the natural world. For information, write RD 2, Box 1010, Dingmans Ferry, Pennsylvania, 18328.

Accommodations of wide variety are found in resort centers such as Stroudsburg, East Stroudsburg, and the Poconos. Public campgrounds are located in Worthington State Forest, Stokes State Forest, and High Point State Park, New Jersey. Old Mine Road Youth Hostel, at Hainesville, New Jersey, provides low-cost lodgings to young people and family groups. Address: Box 172, Layton, New Jersey 07851 (201/948-6750). Park address: Bushkill, Pennsylvania 18324. 717/588-2435.

## DEVILS POSTPILE NATIONAL MONUMENT
### California

In the eastern part of the Sierra Nevada, near the resort community of Mammoth Lakes and Yosemite National Park, symmetrical blue-gray columns rise as high as 60 feet, fitting closely together, a remnant of basaltic lava flow. Trails lead to the top and to the Rainbow Fall on the Middle Fork of the San Joaquin River. Situated at an elevation of 7,600 feet, the monument is open approximately July to October. Campgrounds are at the northern end and in surrounding Inyo National Forest. Address: c/o Superintendent, Sequoia-Kings Canyon National Park, Three Rivers, California 93271. 619/934-2289.

## DEVILS TOWER NATIONAL MONUMENT
### Wyoming

The first national monument, established in 1906, encompasses the most conspicuous landmark in northeast Wyoming, an 865-foot tower of columnar rock, the remains of a molten formation born of volcanic activity. The sides are symmetrical, almost perpendicular, while the small top, high above the Belle Fourche River, has a growth of sagebrush and grass. A prairie-dog colony is located near the monument entrance. A marked trail from the Visitor Center encircles the monument; there are nightly summer programs at the campground. The campground, accommodating both trailers and tents, makes it a good stop en route from the Black Hills of South Dakota to Yellowstone National Park, in Wyoming. Address: Box 8, Devils Tower, Wyoming 82714-0008. 307/467-5283.

# DINOSAUR NATIONAL MONUMENT

## Utah–Colorado

This monument contains the world's most concentrated deposit of petrified bones of dinosaurs, crocodiles, and turtles. In addition, the folded and tilted rock layers show the results of tremendous forces of earth movement; weird and fascinating contours of the land tell the story of wind and rain erosion; the deep canyons of the Green and Yampa rivers have a haunting wilderness beauty about them. Dinosaur is a large area of 211,141 acres; the place to begin is the **Dinosaur Quarry Visitor Center,** 7 miles north of Jensen, Utah. One wall is formed by the quarry face, enabling you to watch workmen with jackhammer and chisel cutting away barren rock to expose fossil bones, more than a thousand of which are embedded here. From the **Headquarters Visitor Center** near Dinosaur, Colorado, a 31-mile paved scenic drive leads to the heart of a spectacular canyon country. At Harpers Corner, above the confluence of the Green and Yampa rivers, you can watch the stream swirl and plunge, almost 3,000 feet below, around the base of Steamboat Rock and through Whirlpool Canyon. The area called Echo Park became the focus of nationwide attention when reclamation engineers proposed to construct a dam; the resulting controversy reached culmination in the 1950s when Congress upheld the principle of park values. Commercial river outfitters offer float trips of one to six days through the wilderness of cliff-bordered rapids. The one-day trip, designed for those with limited time, travels through Split Mountain Gorge. Longer trips originate at Gates of Lodore, on the Green River, and Deerlodge Park, on the Yampa. For hiking, try the Harpers Corner Trail (2 miles) or Purple Point Trail (8 miles) from Island Park Overlook. Better yet, try both. Campgrounds are at Split Mountain, Green River, and Echo Park. Visit the Field Museum (open till 9 p.m. in summer) inspired by the late Arthur Nord as a great showcase of "Dinosaurland." Address: Box 210, Dinosaur, Colorado 81610. 303/374-2216.

# EL MALPAIS NATIONAL MONUMENT

## New Mexico

Established by Congress early in 1988, El Malpais lies 75 miles west of Albuquerque and south of the city of Grants. It protects nationally significant lava flows, volcanic craters, lava tubes, and cultural resources like the Las Ventanas Culture Archaeological Protection Site adjacent to I-40 and along the west side of NM Route 117. El Malpais (Spanish for "badlands"), once a land of fire, is a land of unusually striking beauty—especially when scarlet blooms of cactus dot the black lava. The legislation provides for two special management units, the 114,000-acre national monument, administered by the National Park Service, and 262,000-acre conservation area, a protective buffer zone administered by the Bureau of Land Management. It also includes ancient sites sacred to native Americans of Acoma pueblo, which the federal agencies have pledged to protect. Two Visitor Centers are being established: one at Grants next to I-40, and the other near Bandera, on NM Route 53, on the northern edge of El Malpais. The New Mexico Welcome Center at Gallup can provide more information. Address: Box 939, Grants, New Mexico 87020. 505/988-6387.

## FIRE ISLAND NATIONAL SEASHORE
### New York

Located within 60 miles of Manhattan, this national seashore protects the largest remaining barrier beach off the south shore of Long Island, extending 32 miles, with a changing tableau of high thickets and forests, salt marshes, grassy wetlands, and rolling swales.

**Fishing and Wildlife Watching.** On the ocean side, along the Great South Beach, you can catch striped bass, bluefish, mackerel, weakfish, and fluke; in the shallow bay, bluefish, fluke, winter flounder, and blowfish. From October to March, the sheltered waters are alive with waterfowl. Small populations of ducks and geese remain to breed. Night herons nest in the bayside forests. Deer are best seen along the eastern portion of the national seashore. **Swimming** at protected beaches is available at the Watch Hill recreational site and at Sailor's Haven. Visitor Centers are located at both areas. Nature walks and illustrated talks are given during the summer seasons. You also will find a network of foot and bicycle **trails**—a relief from motorways. One of the highlights of any visit is a walk through the Sunken Forest, adjacent to Sailor's Haven, a secluded woodland with gnarled American holly, sassafras, black gun, and serviceberry. The extensive tidal marshes of East Fire Island provide some of the seashore's best waterfowl habitats and excellent sites for birdwatching. Migrating hawks reach their peak in late September and early October. Limited camping, by reservation only (telephone: 516/377-6455). Weekdays are definitely the best bet.

Most of the national seashore is roadless. You can reach the island near its eastern end by driving over William Floyd Parkway and Smith Point Bridge, or take the Long Island Railroad to ferry connections. Ferry lines (foot passengers only) operate from Bayshore, Sayville, and Patchogue to the island. Address: 120 Laurel Street, Patchogue, Long Island, New York 11772. 516/289-4810.

## FLORISSANT FOSSIL BEDS NATIONAL MONUMENT
### Colorado

The area contains geologic remains of some 35 million years ago. Within the ancient mudflows are sequoia stumps as large as 14 feet in diameter and 12 feet tall, and well-preserved insect and leaf fossils. These beds have been the subject of scientific study since their discovery, in 1874. A museum containing about 500 specimens is open daily, and there is a nature walk to the petrified sequoia stumps. Address: Box 185, Florissant, Colorado 80816. 719/748-3253.

*Florissant Fossil Beds*

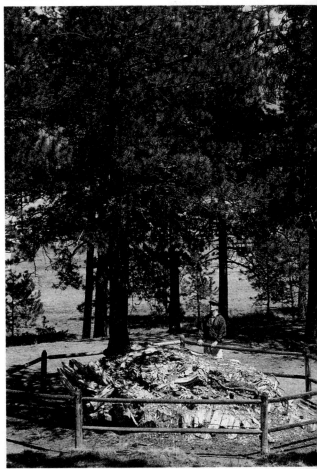

## FOSSIL BUTTE NATIONAL MONUMENT

### Wyoming

Fish that were swimming in western Wyoming waters 50 million years ago are visible in fossil form in this 8,178-acre area set aside by Congress in 1972. Fossil Butte contains some of the world's best known and most significant aquatic fossils of the Eocene epoch. Fossilized freshwater life is rare. "No other fossil-bearing formation in North America," says paleontologist Curtis Julian Hesse, "has produced so many and such characteristic fossils as this great series of lakebeds." Perch, paddlefish, garpike, stingray, and herring which once plied the waters of Fossil Butte are preserved here by the thousands. In no other National Park system area is this important chapter in the history of life represented. The monument also contains outstanding examples of lake, shoreline, and tributary-river floodplain deposits. The fine-bedded layers of the Green River formation make up much of the rugged landscape. The richest fossil deposits are in limestone layers three feet thick and 30 to 300 feet below the butte surface. Plant remains—from fossil palm and fern leaves to pollen—are also numerous. The Visitor Center, open 8 to 5:30 daily in summer, includes a 14-foot-long fossil crocodile replica, displays of deep- and shallow-water prehistoric fish, and displays showing how paleontologists work. Try the 2½-mile Quarry Loop Trail, which climbs 600 feet to the site of an old fossil quarry, or the less steep, 1½-mile Fossil Lake Loop Trail. Address: Box 592, Kemmerer, Wyoming 83101. 307/877-4455.

## GATEWAY NATIONAL RECREATION AREA

### New York–New Jersey

The 26,000 acres of this area surrounding New York Harbor are divided into four units—**Sandy Hook,** on the New Jersey shore; **Staten Island,** across New York Harbor from Manhattan; **Breezy Point,** on the Rockaway Peninsula in Brooklyn; and **Jamaica Bay,** also in Brooklyn. The Jamaica Bay unit contains a 6,000-acre wildlife refuge, one of the few reserves of its kind accessible by subway and bus. The refuge's white poplars, blooming bayberries, extensive saltwater marsh, and calm waters protect more than 200 species of birds and small animals. Dotting the periphery of the bay are recreational areas—Canarsie Pier, Frank Charles Memorial Park, and Floyd Bennett Field.

Exciting times at Jamaica Bay are spring nesting season and fall migration, when thousands of ducks and geese on the Atlantic flyway stop over on the refuge ponds. Other choice birdwatching areas are Sandy Hook (where the near-extinct population of osprey shows signs of coming back), Breezy Point on the Rockaway Peninsula, and Great Kills Park on Staten Island.

**Fort Tilden,** a major defense unit during World War I (with the largest guns protecting New York harbor), is located in the Breezy Point unit. Park rangers lead visitors on explorations of the site and along bays and beaches with fascinating marine life. A short drive from Fort Tilden is Floyd Bennett Field, New York's first important airport. Amelia Earhart, "Wrong Way" Corrigan, and Wiley Post began their adventures here. Now it is the headquarters of the recreation area and of **Ecology Village,** where thousands of young people camp out and learn about nature. **Jacob Riis Park,** 220 acres at the western end of the Rockaways Peninsula, is an excellent example of 1930s municipal park design.

Sandy Hook, long a military area containing old Fort Hancock, has 7 miles of beach ideal for swimming, surfing, and surf fishing. **Sandy Hook Lighthouse,** constructed in 1764 to guide merchant ships into New York harbor, is the oldest lighthouse in the country. Address: Floyd Bennett Field, Building 69, Brooklyn, New York 11234. 718/338-3575.

## GAULEY RIVER NATIONAL RECREATION AREA

See New River Gorge National River, page 390.

## GLEN CANYON NATIONAL RECREATION AREA

### Arizona-Utah

This is more than a water playground astride the desert boundary of Arizona and Utah; it is an immense 1,200,000 acres, superlative in beauty. Lake Powell, formed behind Glen Canyon Dam, extends 186 miles, with 1,900 miles of shoreline, including vividly colored fjordlike side canyons.

Glen Canyon Dam, a major engineering achievement built across the Colorado River by the Bureau of Reclamation, rises 710 feet above the riverbed. The graceful **Glen Canyon Steel Arch Bridge,** even higher, supports US 89 as a link between Flagstaff (and the South Rim of the Grand Canyon) and Kanab, southern gateway to Utah's national parks. Adjacent to the dam are many scenic viewpoints, an impressive lakeshore drive and the extensive development at **Wahweap.** Here the National Park Service provides complete camping facilities, concession-operated Wahweap Lodge, and a large marina, offering boat rentals and guided boat tours of the lake. One outstanding destination by water (an all-day tour) is **Rainbow Bridge National Monument,** containing the largest known natural stone arch. Another is Hole-in-the-Rock, the famous and seemingly impossible crossing of the Colorado River used by Mormons in 1879–80. A party of 236 men, women, and children drove several hundred cows, sheep, and 80 wagons to Hole-in-the-Rock, then blasted a gap in the slim, impassable crevice that blocked their path. They lowered the wagons by rope, built a boat on the shore, and crossed the river to what is now called Register Rock. Facilities are also available at **Hite Crossing, Halls Crossing,** and **Bullfrog Basin**—good road access to Bullfrog is now available on Utah 95 and Utah 276. The Bullfrog Resort and Marina features a lodge with commanding view, housekeeping units, RV facilities, rental houseboats, and power boats. For reservations, call ARA Leisure Services, 800/528-6154. A ferry, the *John A. Burr*, operates between Bullfrog Basin and Halls Crossing, a 20-minute trip covering 3.1 miles. The distance by road between Bullfrog Basin and Halls Crossing is 130 miles. A boat ride on the river above Lees Ferry is a delightful cruise between towering, rust-colored sandstone walls. The twisting channel, now flowing with cold crystal-clear water, is a trout fisherman's paradise. Access to this area, about 55 miles by road from Wahweap, is from US 89A at Marble Canyon, Arizona.

**Fishing for bass** rates with the best in the West. Lake Powell is currently undergoing the period of a "blossoming" new reservoir when fish population multiplies. In addition, warm weather of late spring and early fall combines with hot summer weather to produce a long growing period. Choice fishing occurs on the Escalante and San Juan rivers from late September through October, when fish migrate into canyons and coves in search of shallower layers of water.

**Boating and swimming** can be enjoyed even in the hottest weather, but anyone in an open boat needs protection from the sun. Between mid-June and early September days are hot, and physical activity for most people is limited. (Temperatures at Wahweap sometimes reach 106 degrees.) Nevertheless, hiking or walking in the early morning or twilight hours can be delightful. Many interesting plants can be studied, including several species of cactus and bayonet-tipped yuccas. Because most desert animals are nocturnal travelers and feeders, footprints and tracks become as intriguing as the sight of animals themselves. Look for rounded pad marks of bobcat, doglike tracks of coyote, sharp-pointed tracks of mule deer at drinking places.

**Indian ruins** dot the lakeshore in several places to attract the attention of hiker, explorer, and photographer. Two of the most interesting are located in **Iceberg Canyon** and off the **Escalante River.** These dwellings, remnants of the Anasazi people, are protected from the elements by huge cliff overhangs which prevent all but the most direct wind and rain from reaching the ruins. Address: Box 1507, Page, Arizona 86040. 602/645-2471.

## GOLDEN GATE NATIONAL RECREATION AREA

### California

This major park complex extends along 28 miles of California coastline, from Tomales Point above Point Reyes in Marin County south to Sweeney Ridge in San Mateo County, embracing the largest blocks of open space in the San Francisco Bay area and the last fragments of undisturbed bayfront. Besides its natural landscapes, the park includes diverse fascinating historic sites.

**Fort Point, Maritime National Historical Park,** and **Muir Woods,** administered as separate units of the National Park system, are covered elsewhere in the *Guide;* suffice for the moment to say they complement interpretive themes and recreation opportunities of other units of the park. These include:

**The Presidio,** one of the country's oldest and most beautiful military installations, newly transformed (October 1, 1994) to national park. Long the guardian of the Golden Gate, the Presidio served under Spanish and Mexican flags before being transferred by treaty to the United States in 1848. Now, under the National Park Service, it faces a new role in American life. You can easily spend a full day or more exploring its features. Make the Main Post the starting point for hiking and biking tours. For information and guidance, check the National Park Service Presidio Resource Center on Montgomery Street. Key points include the Presidio Army Museum, Coastal Defense Batteries, and San Francisco National Military Cemetery. More than 10 miles of trail crisscross the Presidio. Walk along coastal bluffs for spectacular vistas of the Golden Gate and Marin headlands.

**Alcatraz,** never meant to be a showpiece, but "the Rock" certainly is one now. Reach it via Red and White Fleet ferry, then start with the slide show introduction, outlining the federal penitentiary years, 1934–1963, when Al Capone and the "Birdman" were here. Rent a headset for the 35-minute recorded tour of the cellhouse guided by the voices of former inmates and guards. Join a ranger-led natural history walk. **Note:** Alcatraz may be the most popular tourist site in San Francisco, so make your ferry reservations at least one day in advance (415/546-2700).

**Sweeney Ridge,** a rugged crest in Pacifica, south of San Francisco, surrounding the site where Gasper de Portola in 1796 first saw San Francisco Bay. Enjoy magnificent panoramic views from the summit. **Land's End,** excellent for birdwatching, particularly during the fall hawk migration. For the loop trail along cliffs above coast and sea, park at the Palace of the Legion of Honor Museum.

**Fort Mason Center,** year-round cultural center, site of the Western Regional Folklife Festival, the last weekend in September. Have a meal of natural foods at the Zen Center restaurant, Greens, one of San Francisco's favorite restaurants.

**Marin Headlines,** across the Golden Gate Bridge, with miles of trail affording excellent opportunities for hiking and riding, with views of the oceanic entrance to San Francisco harbor. Start at the Marin Headlines Visitor Center. Golden Gate Youth Hostel is located here, 4 miles from the north end of Golden Gate Bridge. The San Francisco Hostel at Fort Mason is even more centrally located.

Golden Gate NRA is easy to reach, whether by car or public transportation. Combining bus, street car, subway and ferry can be fun in itself. Address: Building 201, Fort Mason, San Francisco, California 94123. 415/556-0560.

## GREAT SAND DUNES NATIONAL MONUMENT
### Colorado

In a remote corner of the San Luis Valley in south-central Colorado, hikers can climb to the top of the tallest dunes in North America. Deposited over thousands of years by southwesterly winds, they rise to heights of nearly 700 feet on the western slopes of the lofty Sangre de Cristo Mountains. Summer days dawn clear and calm, but the best hiking is early and late, since midday sand temperature can reach 140°F. A round-trip walk from the picnic area takes about three hours. Watch for interesting hardy plants and small mammals that have adapted to this desert-like environment. The Visitor Center offers excellent exhibits, belied by its exterior. There is a campground, and supplies are available four miles south or at Alamosa, 36 miles to the southwest. Address: 11500 Highway 150, Mosca, Colorado 81146. 719/378-2312.

## GULF ISLANDS NATIONAL SEASHORE
### Florida-Mississippi

President Nixon signed the bill creating the eighth national seashore on January 8, 1971, at a critical time when coastal islands and their marshes were falling more rapidly than any other land type before the bulldozers of "progress." The seashore includes a series of history-rich offshore islands and keys stretching 150 miles from Gulfport, Mississippi, to Destin, Florida. The outstanding recreation resources consist of more than 50 miles of sparkling white sand beaches, developed primitive camping areas, and facilities for fishing, swimming, and birdwatching.

*Great Sand Dunes*

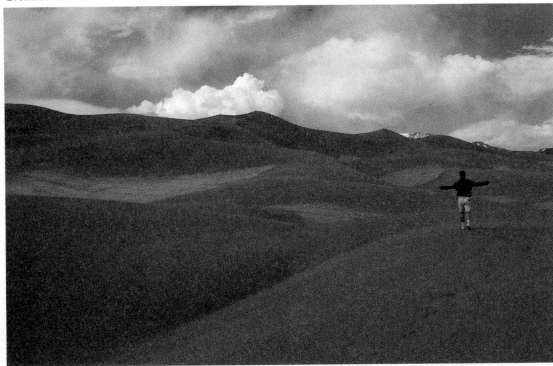

The national seashore covers 139,776 acres—73,959 in Mississippi and 65,817 in Florida. In the **Mississippi section,** Ship Island, the key island in the barrier chain, was held at various times by France, Britain, Spain, and the Confederacy. It was later used as a prison for captured Confederate soldiers, and old **Fort Massachusetts** still stands in remarkably good condition. Until Gulfport's harbor was completed in 1902, the harbor at Ship Island was filled for years with 20 to 30 ships at a time, loading southern lumber for export to all parts of the world, a process requiring four to eight weeks a ship. The old ocean-going supply ships have been replaced with fishing boats today. Daily and weekend excursions (March to November) are available aboard the *Pan American, Island Clipper, Pan American Clipper,* and *Gulf Islander* from Biloxi and Gulfport. The trip covers 14 miles; snack bars operate on the boats. Lower decks are enclosed, but passengers usually ride on the sun deck above. On arrival, there are ranger-led tours of the fort. There are beaches and surf for swimmers and picnic shelters with tables for picnickers.

On the mainland, Davis Bayou offers nature trails, picnic area, and campground at 3500 Park Road, outside Ocean Springs, Mississippi. The Visitor Center is open daily.

The other two Mississippi islands, Horn and Petit Bois, comprise the **Gulf Islands Wilderness.** Their brackish inland ponds, lagoons, and marshes provide ideal habitat for wintering migratory waterfowl and nesting places for permanently residing shore birds. Horn Island is believed to support the largest nesting population of ospreys on the Gulf Coast, as well as a sizable population of alligators and ocean turtles. With its many different habitats, Horn Island supports a variety of wildlife, including nutria, rabbits, raccoons, and various snakes. Wild plants and flowers grow in and around the dunes.

**Attention, birdwatchers.** More than 280 species have been identified in the dunes, marshes, woodland, and open beaches of Gulf Island National Seashore. Large numbers of birds congregate during spring and fall migrations. From late September through October migratory flights of hawks can be seen moving westward across Gulf Breeze Peninsula. Look for bald eagles, especially in Mississippi, flying over the barrier islands. Their population has been successfully restored after an absence of more than 40 years.

The **Florida section** of the seashore embraces portions of Santa Rosa Island, part of Perdido Key, the old Naval Live Oaks Reservation and the historic forts located at the Pensacola Naval Air Station. History and military buffs will find this section especially appealing. Santa Rosa offers **Fort Pickens,** on which construction was begun in 1829, as well as coastal defense structures of later periods up to World War II. An entrance fee is charged. Bicyclists will enjoy the flat terrain of Santa Rosa, especially in less crowded fall and spring seasons. The Live Oaks Reservation was set aside in 1828 to assure the navy of timber for its sailing vessels—probably the first federal conservation measure. Pensacola's forts include Battery San Antonio, built by the Spanish, and two later American additions, Fort Barrancas and Advanced Redoubt of Fort Barrancas. Campgrounds and picnic areas are available at the Fort Pickens area. Beach facilities are available at Perdido Key, Santa Rosa, and Okaloosa areas. Address: 1801 Gulf Breeze Parkway, Gulf Breeze, Florida 32561 or 3500 Park Road, Ocean Springs, Mississippi 39564. 904/934-2604.

## HAGERMAN FOSSIL BEDS NATIONAL MONUMENT

### Idaho

For hundreds of miles, the Snake River winds through deep gorges and broad plains of southern Idaho. In the Hagerman Valley, near the town of Hagerman, southeast of Boise, between Mountain Home and Twin Falls, a canyon wall alongside the river reveals the remains of animals and plants of 3½ million years ago, the Pliocene period. These are considered among the largest and best preserved sites of their kind in the world.

The 4,394-acre national monument was established in 1988 to protect 310 registered paleontological sites. Most of the land involved was formerly administered by the Bureau of Land Management. The fossil beds are along a spectacular bluff on the west side of the Snake River. Birdlife of the Hagerman Valley includes golden eagles, songbirds, and waterfowl. Monument displays in due course will interpret species now largely extinct—zebra-like horses, saber-toothed cats, mastodons, and smaller animals—living in the ancient ecosystem of an aquatic lake or marshland. Address: 963 Blue Lakes Boulevard, Suite 1, Twin Falls, Idaho 83301. 208/733-8398.

## ICE AGE NATIONAL SCIENTIFIC RESERVE

### Wisconsin

Nowhere in the United States is the effect of glacial action more evident or more impressive than in Wisconsin. This scientific reserve, administered by the state of Wisconsin with development assistance from the National Park Service, is designed to consist of nine units preserving landforms shaped by the last great glacial period. These are being joined by the new **Ice Age National Scenic Trail.** The trail traverses land administered by different public and private interests. Look for Ice Age Trail markers and interpretive displays.

Key units of the reserve include: **Kettle Moraine State Forest,** 50 miles north of Milwaukee, famed for the abundant kettles, formed by the melting of buried blocks of ice, and conical hills called moulin kames. The Kettle Moraine Scenic Highway provides access, and the Glacial Hiking Trail a close-up of significant and unusual features. **Horicon Marsh Wildlife Refuge,** west of Kettle Moraine via Route 28, the Wild Goose Parkway, features an extinct glacial lake and choice wildlife observation. **Devils Lake State Park,** less than 50 miles north of Madison (3 miles from Baraboo), lies in the heart of glacial action that shifted the flow of the Wisconsin

River. Guided naturalist hikes focus on geology, birdwatching, plants, and flowers (including remnant species of preglacial days). At **Mill Bluff,** hiking trails wind among towering rocky buttes, affording choice views of the ancient lake bed and driftless area. **Interstate,** the westernmost unit, has ancient lava flows and the gorge of the St. Croix River, once a main glacial drainage. Address: Department of Natural Resources, Division of Tourism and Information, Box 7921, Madison, Wisconsin 53707. 608/266-7616.

## INDIANA DUNES NATIONAL LAKESHORE

### Indiana

Along the southern shore of Lake Michigan, between Gary and Michigan City, the clean sandy beaches backed by huge sand dunes have long attracted interest. "The Dunes," Carl Sandburg wrote, "are to the Midwest what the Grand Canyon is to Arizona and Yosemite is to California. They constitute a signature of time and eternity." A national park was proposed here as early as 1916. Authorized 50 years later, through the untiring efforts of the Save the Dunes Council and Senator Paul Douglas of Illinois, the unit preserves remaining dunes, bogs, and marshes and provides recreational opportunities. The national lakeshore was enlarged in 1976, 1980, and again in 1992 to protect dunes and wetlands. Facilities at **Indiana Dunes State Park** include camping, picnicking, swimming, bathhouse, pavilion, and naturalist tours. Cowles Bog, immediately south of Dune Acres, and Pinhook Bog, six miles south of Michigan City, are of special interest for their variety of plants and animals. This habitat includes the northern range of many birds and plants as well as bogs representative of cooler climates. It provides resting, nesting, or wintering areas for at least 223 species of birds. Miller Woods, a composition of open beach, dunes, and oak forest, provides an ideal setting for the Paul H. Douglas Center for Environmental Education. Other major visitor attractions include West Beach, with a bathhouse and a parking area, the Chellberg Farm, and the restored **Bailly Homestead,** built by a French-Canadian trader who settled near the Calumet River in 1822. Park open all year. Address: 1100 North Mineral Springs Road, Porter, Indiana 46304-1299. 219/926-7561.

## JEWEL CAVE NATIONAL MONUMENT
### South Dakota

This beautiful cave in the Black Hills, 14 miles west of Custer, is particularly noted for its lining of sparkling calcite crystal. In the 1960s and early 1970s, a local couple, Herbert and Jan Conn, explored over 60 miles of passage, a bewildering maze that made Jewel Cave the fourth longest explored cave in the world. Many spectacular cave formations were discovered, including several of a type found in Jewel Cave and nowhere else. In some locations cementations of quartz and calcite—called scintillite—cover walls or floors with deep red encrustation of sparkling jewels. At other locations, hoary gypsum "beards" grow over a foot long from limestone walls, fragile beauty swaying in the cave breeze. Tours of varying lengths are conducted May 1 to September 30, with tickets sold on a first-come, first-served basis. A guide fee is charged. Cave tours are strenuous, not recommended for those with heart or respiratory ailments. Cave temperature is 47 degrees Fahrenheit, so dress accordingly. Visitor Center open all year. Address: RR 1, Box 60AA, Custer, South Dakota 57730. 605/673-2288.

## JOHN DAY FOSSIL BEDS NATIONAL MONUMENT
### Oregon

At three sites in north-central Oregon, both plant and animal fossils reveal a classic panorama of earth history. The Clarno Unit in Wheeler County preserves evidence of sub-tropical growth. The Painted Hills Unit, near Mitchell, has volcanic ash deposits with leaf remnants of a temperate hardwood forest. At Sheep Rock, near Dayville, fossils show progressively drier and more seasonal climates. Along the trails you'll find unusual exhibits depicting the region as it was 28 to 35 million years ago. Stop at the Cant Ranch bunkhouse, now housing the fascinating Fossil and Fossil Hunters Exhibit. For more fossils, contact Hancock Field Station, which offers educational programs for junior high and high school students, and week-long June programs designed mostly for teachers (but others may also enroll); write Hancock Field Station, Fossil, Oregon, 97830. Picnic areas are in all three units of the monument. Address: 420 West Main Street, John Day, Oregon 97845. 503/575-0721.

## JOHN D. ROCKEFELLER, JR. MEMORIAL PARKWAY
### Wyoming

Named in honor of the philanthropist whose gifts of land and money were instrumental in establishment of several national parks, the parkway extends the full length of Grand Teton National Park to West Thumb in Yellowstone National Park, a distance of 82 miles. It includes a 23,777-acre section between the two parks now administered as a recreation area. Camping facilities are provided at the Snake River campground and at the concession-operated facilities at Flagg Ranch. Address: c/o Grand Teton National Park, Drawer 170, Moose, Wyoming 83012. 307/733-2880.

## JOSHUA TREE NATIONAL MONUMENT
See Joshua Tree National Park, p. 169.

## LAKE CHELAN NATIONAL RECREATION AREA

See North Cascades National Park, page 203.

## LAKE MEAD NATIONAL RECREATION AREA

### Arizona-Nevada

Nearly 1,500,000 rugged acres of far-reaching tawny deserts, deep canyons, and lofty plateaus spread across Arizona and Nevada from Grand Canyon National Park almost to the edge of lively Las Vegas and southward past Davis Dam. Within these boundaries, Lake Mead and Lake Mohave, vast reservoirs, provide water sports centers in the midst of cactus country.

**Boulder City,** Nevada, the main gateway, was established in the early 1930s to house personnel building Hoover Dam, eight miles away. In some ways it still looks like the town of that day. There are no high rises, no gambling. The restored Boulder Dam Hotel, opened in 1932, is the only hotel in town. (Overnighters will find a dozen motels.) The Alan Bible Visitor Center, located midway between town and dam at 601 Nevada Highway, is information headquarters for the national recreation area.

**Hoover Dam** spans the Colorado River, its crescent top serving as a highway. You can park at either side and join a tour of the power plant in the heart of the dam, descending by elevator 528 feet—the equivalent of a 44-story building. The power plant alone, with its turbines and generators, equals the height of a 20-story building. Nearby Boulder Beach is the most developed of six main recreation centers around **Lake Mead's** 550-mile shoreline. It has a modern lodge, marina, and swimming pool. One-hour boat trips operate daily to Hoover Dam, the colorful Paint Pots, and Fortification Hill. Boulder Beach has a swimming beach; all centers have launching ramps, camping facilities, boat rentals, lodgings, restaurants, and trailer courts; Las Vegas Wash, however, does not have lodgings. Evening illustrated programs about the area are presented seasonally at Boulder Beach.

The most developed of three recreation areas on **Lake Mohave,** a long, narrow lake extending 67 miles south from Hoover Dam, is at Katherine, near Davis Dam (35 miles west of Kingman, Arizona). Naturalist programs are given in an amphitheater here, too. Fishing is popular on both lakes all year—rainbow trout and bass are the chief catches in Lake Mohave; bass, striped bass, crappie, and catfish in Lake Mead. Seven Crowns Resorts offers houseboat vacations on both lakes; for information and reservations, call 800/752-9669.

Although water is the focal point for outdoor sports, the region is rich in natural, historical, and archaeological resources which should not be overlooked. About 60 species of mammals have been identified, including wild burros along the lakeshores, desert bighorn, coyotes, cougars, and bobcats. Over 200 miles of secondary road lead into the backcountry, where fossilized bones of mammoths, camels, ground sloths, and giant beavers in soft silt of ancient lake basins are part of the patterns of geology. Two roads are of special interest. One leads from Las Vegas to Callville Bay, Echo Bay, and Overton Beach, on the north shore of Lake Mead, with access to **Valley of Fire State Park,** a fantastic desert area with ancient petroglyphs left by primitive Americans amid brilliant sandstone formations. The other cuts across the desert from US 93 along the Grand Wash Cliffs and through a forest of Joshua trees to Pearce Ferry, at the western edge of the Grand Canyon. Pick up a copy of *Flowering Plants of the Lake Mead Region*, or some other good guidebook, so you can learn to identify the many species growing here and to appreciate the marvel of natural survival and beauty in a tough environment. Address: 601 Nevada Highway, Boulder City, Nevada 89005. 702/293-8920.

## LAKE MEREDITH NATIONAL RECREATION AREA

### Texas

This scenic lake, surrounded by grasslands and steep canyons, answered a long-felt need in the High Plains of the Texas Panhandle near Amarillo. It was created behind **Sanford Dam,** the principal structure in the Canadian River reclamation project, and is bordered by seven developed areas providing boating, fishing, picnicking, semi-improved and primitive campsites, and access to hunting. Fish include bass, crappie, walleye, and catfish. Among the animals and birds of the Canadian River country are deer, pronghorn, coyotes, turkeys, and quail, with throngs of ducks and geese. The uplands vegetation typifies the High Plains, with mixed grasses, mesquite, and yucca, while bottomland trees include cottonwoods, hackberries, and salt cedar (or tamarisk). On the south side of the lake, the Alibates Flint Quarries National Monument contains quarries used by prehistoric people 12,000 years ago. Address: Box 1438, Fritch, Texas 79036. 806/857-3151.

## LAVA BEDS NATIONAL MONUMENT

### California

Great cinder cones, deep chasms, and more than 200 caves spreading across rugged terrain below the Oregon border, midway between Crater Lake and Lassen Volcanic National Parks, are the products of a shield volcano which has spewed masses of molten lava for a million years. The monument is pleasantly uncrowded. Interpretive programs are offered Memorial Day through Labor Day when conducted walks and talks are regularly scheduled along with evening programs on caves, volcanos, and more. Rangers encourage a "do it yourself" approach to exploration of the caves. They hand you a flashlight and a map and wish you well. Some caves of the 46,239-acre monument, like Merrill Cave, contain permanent ice. In contrast, some caves are carpeted by ferns and mosses, while others bear Indian pictographs on their walls. In a detached northeast section, petroglyphs are carved on the bluffs near Tule Lake, where the national wildlife refuge attracts throngs of ducks, geese, and other birds during spring and fall migration. The lava beds served as principal theater of the Modoc Indian War of 1872–73, when the Indians entrenched themselves in the natural lava fortifications. Campgrounds near park headquarters; lodgings at Tulelake and in Klamath Falls and Merrill, Oregon. Address: Box 867, Tulelake, California 96134. 916/667-2282.

## LOWER ST. CROIX NATIONAL SCENIC RIVERWAY

See St. Croix National Scenic Riverway, page 397.

## MISSISSIPPI NATIONAL RIVER AND RECREATION AREA

### Minnesota

Eighty miles of the Mississippi River and about 50,000 acres of shoreline in the Twin Cities metropolitan area were designated by Congress in 1988 for addition to the National Park system. A commission was established to prepare within three years a coordinated federal/state/local plan for managing the corridor, which extends from the mouth of the Crow River at Dayton downstream past Minneapolis and St. Paul to the mouth of the St. Croix River near Hastings. Address: 175 East Fifth Street, St. Paul, Minnesota 55101-2901. 612/290-4160.

## MUIR WOODS NATIONAL MONUMENT

### California

In a mountain valley just north of San Francisco, at the foot of Mount Tamalpais, the cathedral-like grove of redwoods was given in 1908 by Congressman William Kent and his wife, in honor of John Muir.

The area covers less than one square mile near San Francisco along a beautiful forested canyon, where redwoods grow in full splendor. The main trail winds among these giant trees, interspersed with other trees of the western forest—Douglas fir, bigleaf maple, California buckeye, tanbark oak, and madrona. The last named is a beautiful broadleaf evergreen related to eastern rhododendron; its bright orange-colored bark and shiny leaves make it seem, as John Muir wrote, "like some lost wanderer from the magnolia groves in the South." Listen closely along the trails bordering Redwood Creek to hear when the water is full or at low ebb, and also when it's dusk and time to leave (from the sound of the great horned owl, of course). The 553-acre monument is reached easily from San Francisco via the Golden Gate Bridge by car or tour bus. Neither picnicking nor camping is permitted in Muir Woods, but there is a campground in adjacent Mount Tamalpais State Park which is a treat in its own right. The canyons and coastal mountains comprise fabulous hiking country. Loops of almost any length are possible. Climb the ridge crest on the Dipsea Trail overlooking the Pacific, perhaps going all the way to Stinson Beach. Weather is often cool or wet, so carry a jacket. Be sure to stop at the new visitor center opened in 1990; see exhibits funded by Save-the-Redwoods League. Address: Mill Valley, California 94941. 415/388-2595.

## NATCHEZ TRACE PARKWAY

Tennessee-Alabama-Mississippi

The parkway commemorates the storied Indian and pioneer trail between Nashville and Natchez called the Natchez Trace. Along the roadside, the forest, meadows, and fields present a continually changing landscape, with many flowering plants and lush semitropical vegetation. The route is pleasantly free of commercialism. When complete, it will cover 445 miles through the three states. Nearly 420 miles are finished and open.

A number of recreation areas and vestiges of the old trace lend interest to the trip. In middle **Tennessee,** near Hohenwald, **Meriwether Lewis Site** marks the spot where the great trailblazer died. Nearby **Metal Ford** and **Napier Mine** offer a look at iron mining and smelting of the early 1800s, when the trace was the most heavily traveled road in the Old Southwest, linking the Union with the remote lower Mississippi Valley.

In **Alabama, Colbert Park,** at Pickwick Lake, provides water-oriented activities including swimming, boating, fishing, and waterskiing. The lake is administered by the Tennessee Valley Authority and formed by Pickwick Landing Dam in Tennessee.

In **Mississippi,** stop at the **Visitor Center** at park headquarters north of Tupelo to see the film and exhibits that explain how the ancient trail evolved into a post road and highway. Beginning about 1785, farmers from as far up as the Ohio River floated crops down to Natchez or New Orleans, then hiked homeward along the trace. It was used by boatmen, bandits, settlers, and soldiers until the steamboat and better-roads era of the 1830s. Markers, trails, and exhibits like those at **Chickasaw Village** and **Bynum Mounds** remind you that this was the land of the Choctaw, Chickasaw, and prehistoric Indians. **Emerald Mound,** an ancient ceremonial earthwork covering eight acres, is among features on the southernmost section leading past Port Gibson to Natchez. Here **Mount Locust** has been restored to its 1810 appearance when it served as one of 50 inns like it along the Old Trace. Uniformed interpreters provide talks about the parkway, Old Trace, and Mount Locust.

**Bicycling.** Called one of the best bicycling routes in the country, the parkway features smooth, paved road and terrain varying from lowlands to ridges and rolling hills. Dry, mild weather makes May and early June the best cycling time.

**Seasons and Accommodations.** In spring nature trails are at their best in areas like the

Tupelo–Bald Cypress Swamp. Camellias and azaleas bloom in March in parkway communities like Natchez and Vicksburg, where semiannual garden pilgrimages are held. Fall foliage provides the background for the annual two-day Meriwether Lewis Country Fair and Arts Festival near **Hohenwald,** Tennessee, in mid-October. An interesting campground is located on the trace at **Jeff Busby,** a high wooded area near French Camp, Mississippi. Another splendid campground is located at **Rocky Springs,** northeast of Port Gibson. A third campground is located at the **Meriwether Lewis Site** in Tennessee. All operate on a first-come, first-served basis. Address: Route 1, NT 143, Tupelo, Mississippi 38801. 601/680-4000.

# NATIONAL PARK OF AMERICAN SAMOA

## American Samoa

This new unit (established by Congress in 1988) on an island trust territory in the South Pacific is not a national park in the usual sense. For one thing, the land involved is not and will not be federally owned. For another, it's comparatively small—only 8,500 acres. But these factors do not deny its significance. The primary feature consists of two undisturbed tropical rain forests (2,800 acres above Pago Pago harbor on the island of Tutuila and 5,400 acres on the nearby island of Ta'u), especially choice at a time when rain forests are being lost the world over. The Samoan rain forests comprise five distinct plant communities with hundreds of different plant species—plus two species of native flying foxes, striking animals with wing spans of up to four feet.

The park also includes beautiful coral beaches, coves, reefs, and islets alive with seabird colonies. Because of Samoan traditions of communal land ownership, park legislation provides for long-term leasing from local villages. Visiting American Samoa National Park will be easier when these agreements are completed. But anyone with patience and respect for Samoan courtesies can enjoy a visit now. The three units of the park are as follows. **Tutuila,** the most accessible, has good examples of the park landscape seen on the paved road from Pago Pago to the village of Vatia. Tutuila has some hotels, restaurants, and rental cars. **Ta'u,** remote and pristine, is reached by a 40-minute flight from Tutuila, followed by travel on a dirt road to the village of Fitiuta, and hike along the sea. A small motel has opened at Fitiuta, but rental cars and restaurants don't exist. Plan on patience to hire a guide and arrange a place to stay. **Ofu,** a small unit, mostly beach and reef, is also reached by plane. The park is easily accessible on foot (with permission) from the airstrip. A small motel is located next to the strip. Address: Pago Pago, American Samoa 96799. 684/633-7082.

# NATURAL BRIDGES NATIONAL MONUMENT

## Utah

In a land of brilliantly colored cliffs, tortuous box canyons, sandstone pinnacles, and arches, the three major natural bridges of this monument are outstanding for both their proportions and height. The largest, Sipapu, rises 220 feet above the stream bed, with a span of 268 feet and width of 31 feet. Owachomo, representing the oldest stage of bridge formation, is only 9 feet thick and has a span of 180 feet. Anasazi Indian people lived in the area some 800 years ago. Facilities have been improved, including an 8-mile paved loop road with viewpoints for the major bridges, a Visitor Center, campground-picnic area, and a museum with historical and geological exhibits. The monument's solar power system is becoming an independent attraction. The monument lies 45 miles west of Blanding and can easily be visited on an itinerary that includes Arches, Canyonlands, Monument Valley, and Glen Canyon. Address: Box 1, Lake Powell, Utah 84533-0101. 801/259-5174.

## NEW RIVER GORGE
## NATIONAL RIVER
### West Virginia

This unit of the park system, a 53-mile stretch of the winding New River, in the southern part of the state, ensures protection of a spectacular portion of one of the oldest rivers in the world. The steep-walled gorge measures from 700 to 1,300 feet deep and exposes ancient rock dating to the Mesozoic era. It is generally considered one of the finest white-water streams in the East because of challenging rapids in the lower 15-mile section from Thurmond to Fayette Station and because usually reliable waters flow the entire summer season. The 23-mile section from Hinton to Prince offers calmer water for canoeing and leisurely float trips. In 1988, Congress established the Gauley River National Recreation Area, covering 10,300 acres along a 25-mile stretch of the twisting, scenic Gauley River and five miles of the Meadow River. A 10-mile segment of the Bluestone is also protected as Bluestone National Scenic River. Both areas are administered in conjunction with the New River. Commercial outfitters in the vicinity offer varied services from early April to late October. Pick up details at the Canyon Rim Visitor Center on US 19 near Fayetteville and the New River Gorge Bridge, open all year, or the Visitor Centers at Hinton, Grandview, and Glen Jean. During two weekends in October the New River Train operates all-day excursions through the gorge; the trip is considered one of the most exciting train rides in America and sells out in advance every year. State parks in the gorge provide lodges and campgrounds. For information, call 800/CALL-WVA. Address: Box 246, Glen Jean, West Virginia 25846. 304/465-0508.

## NIOBRARA/MISSOURI NATIONAL
## SCENIC RIVERWAYS
### Nebraska

In 1991, 70 miles of the Niobrara were designated a national scenic river. As the meeting place of the great eastern deciduous forests and the western ponderosa pine forests, the valley of the Niobrara is biologically unique. The 98 miles of the Missouri Recreational River include 20 miles of the Niobrara and eight miles of Verdigre Creek from the town of Verdigre to the confluence with the Niobrara. Both rivers played important roles for homesteaders on the Great Plains and are still important to farmers in the region. The Park facilities will be developed. Write Box 591, O'Neill, NE 68763. 402/336-3970.

## OBED WILD AND SCENIC RIVER
### Tennessee

On the Cumberland Plateau, this park area, established in 1976, will preserve scenic river gorges comprising some of the most striking scenery in the Southeast. The Obed, and its principal tributaries, Clear Creek and Daddy Creek, are bordered by bluffs reaching 200 to 500 feet high. These multicolored canyon walls are pockmarked by shallow caves—some deep enough to offer shelter. Rapids alternate with deep, long pools amid huge boulders. The Obed system provides highly technical white-water canoeing during the period from December to April or May. Water flow is usually too low during the remainder of the year for canoeing, but the pools provide opportunities for swimmers and fishermen. This country can't support heavy use; facilities are limited and primitive. Address: Box 429, Wartburg, Tennessee 37887. 615/346-6294.

## OREGON CAVES NATIONAL MONUMENT

### Oregon

Joaquin Miller, celebrated poet of the Sierra, did much to attract attention to this area in the Siskiyou Mountains, 20 miles from Cave Junction, by calling the caves the "Marble Halls of Oregon." Columns, stalactites, and canopies of marble formation line passageways and hang from vaulted domes. Crews have worked for several years to restore the caves to their original condition, removing old asphalt trails and other facilities introduced to help tourists, but harmful to the cave environment. Guided tours; nursery for small children. Oregon Caves Chateau and cottages at monument entrance; campgrounds in adjacent Siskiyou National Forest. Address: 19000 Caves Highway, Cave Junction, Oregon 97523. 503/592-2100.

## ORGAN PIPE CACTUS NATIONAL MONUMENT

### Arizona

A segment of the Sonoran desert, complete with stark mountains, sweeping *bajadas*, or outwash plains, rocky canyons, flats, and dry washes, is preserved within the 330,688-acre monument in southwestern Arizona at the Mexican border. The desert is a fascinating life-community of plants and animals. Some 30 species of cactus have been identified within the monument, notably the organpipe, this country's second largest cactus, which produces a cluster of stems that can reach a height of 20 feet. Desert ironwood, giant saguaro, palo verde, and ocotillo are among other plants that survive in the arid region. Animals, too, have adapted to the harsh environment, including the Gila monster—the only poisonous lizard native to the United States—desert bighorn sheep, pronghorn, coyote, and a variety of birds.

The monument presents what is likely the finest display of Sonoran desert birdlife north of Mexico. For some species, such as lark bunting and white-crowned sparrow, this is a winter home; for others, including white-winged dove and nighthawk, it is a summer home. Many species are year-round residents. Quitobaquito, a spring-fed pond near the Mexican border, offers an excellent opportunity to see regular desert species and migrants.

The life of the desert is interpreted at the **Visitor Center,** the starting point for two graded scenic loop drives. The Ajo Mountain loop covers 21 miles (about two hours) and the Puerto Blanco Drive, 51 miles (half a day). Organ Pipe's campground hugs the gentle southeast slope of the Puerto Blanco Mountains. Camping is limited to 14 days mid-January to mid-April; 30-day limit, remainder of year. The popular season extends from November until May, when temperatures are comfortable. Summer daytime temperatures frequently reach 100 degrees Fahrenheit, or higher. Follow a few simple precautions for walking or hiking in this country. Wear clothing suitable for rough terrain and strong sun. Carry fresh drinking water. Watch your step around cactus—spines can be painful. Keep an eye out for rattlesnakes, and let them be. Address: Route 1, Box 100, Ajo, Arizona 85321. 602/387-6849.

## OZARK NATIONAL SCENIC RIVERWAYS

### Missouri

In the heart of the steep, wooded hills south of Rolla are preserved about 140 miles of the unpolluted, natural, free-flowing Current River and its tributary, the Jacks Fork, both noted for fine fishing and camping on gravel bars. Canoes are available from local outfitters. The headwaters of the Current are formed at an immense spring in **Montauk State Park,** adjoining the north end of the riverways. Principal campgrounds, picnic areas, and other visitor facilities are found at Big Spring near Van Buren; Alley Spring near Eminence; and Owls Bend. Each center has its own attractions and activities: Alley Spring, a gristmill grinding cornmeal and morning classes at Story's Creek Schoolhouse throughout the summer; Big Spring, johnboat and paddle-making through summer; Owls Bend, working blacksmith shop. Special programs feature Ozark music and canoe demonstrations. At a popular fishing spot on the Current River known as Gooseneck, 27 miles southwest of Van Buren, archaeologists have unearthed the remains of a 1,200-year-old Indian village, considered a major find. Summers on the Ozark rivers are hot; spring and fall are ideal seasons. Address: Box 490, Van Buren, Missouri 63965-0490. 314/323-4236.

## PADRE ISLAND NATIONAL SEASHORE

Texas

An offshore barrier dune island paralleling the south Texas coast in the Gulf of Mexico is separated from the mainland by the Laguna Madre. This very shallow body of water is part of the Intracoastal Waterway, a dredged canal system along the Texas Coast.

The 113-mile-long island has an endless sweep of broad beaches, grass-topped dunes, and windswept sand formations. It is developed for several miles at both ends, but the boundaries of the national seashore embrace 69 miles of the middle section (up to 3 miles in width).

There are two approaches from the north; one leads from Corpus Christi over a modern causeway to Padre Island and Nueces County Park; the other leads from Port Aransas, historic and scenic seaport, down Mustang Island via Park Road 53. The south end of the island is reached by causeway from Port Isabel to Cameron County Park.

Padre Island National Seashore is a biological showcase. More than 380 species of plants grow here and more than 300 species of birds are either permanent residents, part-time residents, or pass through on migration. These include the rare peregrine falcon. The national seashore contains the only marine nesting colony of white pelicans on the gulf coast of the United States. Commonly seen birds include herons, egrets, ibis, gulls, terns, and more than 30 species of shorebirds. Ducks and geese are abundant in fall and winter, attracting hunters to Laguna Madre. Coyotes are heard at night and occasionally seen in the daytime, but most mammals spend the daylight hours underground to avoid the hot sun, coming out to forage for food in the cool of evening. A major international effort is now being made to establish a nesting population of the endangered Ridley sea turtle. The plan involves transplanting eggs, imprinted in Padre Island sand, from the turtles' primary nesting site at Rancho Nuevo, Tamaulpais, Mexico.

**Shelling** is a popular winter pastime. Some beaches abound with marine snails, clams, and other mollusks. The struggle and survival of humble plants and grasses in the dunes are a marvel of their own.

**Swimming and surf fishing** are year-round activities. Redfish, sea trout, and black drum are the most commonly caught fish. A Texas fishing license is required. Guides and boats for deep-sea fishing are available in Port Aransas.

**Seasons and Accommodations.** Winters are generally mild; however cold snaps ("northers") sometimes drop temperatures to uncomfortable levels for short periods. Summers are most popular, but can be hot and windy. Spring and fall are pleasant. There are no overnight accommodations in the national seashore. The closest motels are in the Corpus Christi area, to the north, or the Port Isabel area, to the south.

Malaquite Beach Campground, near the northern entrance of the seashore, has modern restrooms with showers and a dump station. Primitive camping is permitted year-round in the north and south beach areas, with a 14-day limit. Chemical toilets are provided.

Nueces County Parks on North Padre Island and at Port Aransas provide trailer facilities. For information on rates and facilities, write to Nueces County Parks, 10901 South Padre Island Drive, Corpus Christi, Texas 78418. For information on camping on South Padre Island, write to Cameron County Parks, Box 666, Port Isabel, Texas 78578.

National Seashore address: 9405 South Padre Island Drive, Corpus Christi, Texas 78418. 512/937-2621.

## PICTURED ROCKS NATIONAL LAKESHORE

### Michigan

The multicolored sandstone cliffs called the pictured rocks, rising perpendicularly to heights of 200 feet, stretch approximately 15 miles along the shore of Lake Superior, the largest freshwater lake in the world. They make the national lakeshore on Michigan's Upper Peninsula a place of beautiful landscapes and vistas. Begin with a boat tour (leaving daily from Munising, June to mid-October) to observe the expanse of forest-topped rocks bearing such names as Miners Castle, Indian Head, and Battleship Rock. Then plan to hike at least a portion of the Lakeshore Trail running along the shore the entire length of the park between Munising and **Grand Marais.** Stop at the Visitor Center to get a list of interpretive programs, including the historic walks on "Lighthouse and Shipwrecks." Near the Visitor Center, enjoy Munising Falls, which drop nearly 50 feet over the sandstone bluff; walk along the natural cavity *behind* the falls and you won't get wet! New trails and old logging roads provide a variety of hiking opportunities. Don't miss the Grand Sable Dunes and Au Sable Light Station near Grand Marais. The park has three campgrounds—Little Beaver Lake, Twelvemile Beach, and Hurricane River—accessible by car, plus additional sites spaced along the Lakeshore Trail. Overnight lodgings are available at Munising and picturebook Grand Marais. Address: Box 40, Munising, Michigan 49862-0040. 906/387-2607.

## PINELANDS NATIONAL RESERVE

### New Jersey

The unit was established to preserve and enhance the distinctive tract of 1,100,000 acres in southern New Jersey composed of pine-oak forest, cedar swamps, and streams. Located within 50 miles of Philadelphia and 100 miles of New York City, it is one of the largest open space areas on the east coast. Congress established this national reserve in 1978. Sphagnum moss, cattails, pinecones, blueberries, and cranberries are among the abundant products of nature. The area is underlaid by an important natural aquifer, or watershed. Though there are no National Park Service facilities, Batsto Mansion, part of a former iron-making community, serves as a Visitor Center within Wharton State Forest. Batsto Village is a prime spot, with guided tours of the old gristmill, blacksmith shop, sawmill, and other structures. It makes a good starting point for hiking and canoeing. Wharton State Forest has 400 miles of sand roads, mostly unmarked but well suited for naturalist hikes. The 40-mile Batona Trail starts at the village and runs north through the pinelands to New Lebanon State Forest. Four of south New Jersey's popular canoe streams are located within the state forest. Address: c/o Regional Office, National Park Service, 143 South Third Street, Philadelphia, Pennsylvania 19106 or Pinelands Commission, Box 7, New Lisbon, New Jersey 08064. 617/223-3769.

## PINNACLES NATIONAL MONUMENT

### California

Here is a real discovery for the off-beat outdoors explorer. The last remnants of an ancient volcano, carved by erosion into spectacular pinnacles and spires, many over 1,000 feet high, contrast strikingly with the surrounding chaparral of west-central California—a chaparral cover considered the finest in the National Park system. There are two entrances to the park: on the east side, south of Hollister off California 25; on the west, via Soledad, which is on US 101. It is not possible to drive across the monument. Climbers have long been attracted to the Pinnacles, but unstable rock surfaces are hazardous and require specialized gear. Self-guiding trails are outstanding, particularly in spring, when wildflowers carpet the hills. Fill your canteen; no water is available on the trail. Bring a flashlight to see the Balconies Caves, formed by earthquakes and running water. Park headquarters and Visitor Center are on the east side, but sites for tent camping (without utility connections) are available on the west side. Address: Paicines, California 95043. 408/389-4485.

## PISCATAWAY PARK

See page 296.

## POINT REYES NATIONAL SEASHORE
### California

A peninsula noted for its long beaches, sand dunes, and lagoons, backed by tall cliffs, forested ridges, grassland, and brushy slopes, lies barely 35 miles northwest of San Francisco. It escaped private development, perhaps because most of the peninsula was cattle and dairy ranch land, or because the promontory experiences more wind and fog than any other part of the California coast.

The national seashore was authorized in 1962. Almost half of its acreage remains in ranching as a pastoral zone. Its newest feature, the imposing $1.5-million **Bear Valley Interpretive Center,** is set among historic barns and ranch buildings of Bear Valley, 1 mile west of Olema on famous California 1, the Coastal Highway. More than 250 exhibits and 140 specimens of native plants and wildlife are on display, including two 25-foot trees (a Douglas fir and a Bishop pine), specially preserved for exhibit. You can also see a working seismograph measuring earth movements along California's San Andreas Fault and elsewhere. Just beyond the center you can walk to

a replica of a Miwok Indian Village and the Morgan Horse Ranch and explore the Earthquake Trail, a seven-tenths-mile, paved route where tilted trees, broken fences, and interpretive signs portray the earthquake phenomenon. Take the trail on your own or join a ranger on Sundays at 2 P.M. for a guided walk.

**Hiking trails** start from Bear Valley and from the Palomarin Trailhead, near the Point Reyes Bird Observatory, off Mesa Road. The trail system, including old ranch roads, covers more than 140 miles of backcountry, but if you're bicycling, the Bear Valley and Coast trails are the only ones suitable. You can rent bikes at Point Reyes Station. Traveling on foot, you can take the Sky Trail to the summit of Mount Wittenberg (1,407 feet), 5 miles round-trip, or continue on the Ridge Trail to Drake's Bay on the coast. Those with time should take the 11-mile complete loop, with a hike through the Bear Valley area. It cuts through a natural break in the Inverness Ridge covered with Douglas fir. Little pocket beaches at the base of cliffs along Drake's Bay are reached only by trail. Beaches are great for hiking, but not for swimming. Even wading can be dangerous in the surf off Point Reyes and McClure's Beaches. Swimming is safe at Limantour and Drake's Beaches, but water stays at 55 degrees year-round.

**Birdwatching and wildlife watching** are outstanding, with over 300 species of birds ranging from sea voyagers to dwellers of the dense forest. Limantour Estero and its mudflats are famous for concentrations of shore birds. Abbott's Lagoon is an important wintering ground for waterfowl. Point Reyes also provides sanctuary to a living fossil, the mountain beaver.

**Sir Francis Drake Highway** leads across the pastoral zone of canyons and arroyos, freshwater lakes, and grassy lowlands, with access roads to Pacific beaches. Some views are not unlike those that greeted Sir Francis Drake in 1579, when he presumably stopped here on his global voyage, and the 19th-century traders, whalers, and fur hunters who frequented Drake's Bay. Near the end of the highway, visit the century-old lighthouse, once a primary landfall beacon for incoming ships. Built in Paris in 1867, it was first illuminated by a flickering oil lamp and then by electricity. In 1975 an automated light just down the cliff replaced it. You can climb down a steep staircase to the lighthouse at the very tip of Point Reyes and examine its clockwork mechanism.

**Point Reyes Beach** is a beautiful coastal wilderness, a beachcomber's paradise, but it receives the full brunt of the Pacific—prepare for fog and high wind. **Drake's Beach,** on the sheltered side, has facilities for day use (no camping). **McClure's Beach** is near the north end of the peninsula off Drake Highway.

**Seasons and Seminars.** Each season brings distinctive pleasures. Winter is the time to watch whales in migration between the Bering Sea and Baja California. March and April bring out the wildflowers. Summer means warm weather and autumn clear, fog-free days. Field seminars of one to four days are offered through most of the year in natural history, art, and "biophotography." Participants are welcome to stay at the Environmental Education Center dormitory, youth hostel, motels, or campground. Write Point Reyes Field Seminars, Point Reyes, California 94956.

**Camping.** Hikes to four backpacking campgrounds along the trail system—Sky, Coast, Glen, and Wildcat—go from 3 to 8 miles. These are in great demand and should be reserved four weeks in advance for winter weekends, six to eight weeks in advance for summer. Telephone the Visitor Center (415/663-1092) for reservations; there is no charge for use of the site. Olema Ranch Campground, a private facility, is located near the Visitor Center on California 1. Other camping facilities are at Samuel P. Taylor State Park, 6 miles from park headquarters on the road to San Rafael. Laguna Ranch Holiday Hostel (Box 59, Point Reyes, California 94956; phone 415/669-9985) provides year-round low-cost accommodations near the end of Limantour Beach Road, 7 miles from park headquarters. Address: Point Reyes, California 94956. 415/663-8522.

## POVERTY POINT NATIONAL MONUMENT

Louisiana

Established by Congress in 1988, this 900-acre archaeological site in West Carroll Parish, in northeastern Louisiana, preserves the largest and most complex geometrical earthwork in North America, quite possibly by native people dating to 1700 B.C. The site is expected to be transferred from the State of Louisiana to the National Park Service. Address: Box 248, Epps, Louisiana 71237. 505/988-6387.

## PRINCE WILLIAM FOREST PARK

See page 296.

## RAINBOW BRIDGE NATIONAL MONUMENT

Utah

In the semidesert just north of the Arizona-Utah border, the monument embraces the greatest known natural bridge in the world. With a 278-foot span, the symmetrical arch of salmon-pink sandstone curves gracefully upward to a height of 309 feet. You can reach it by special boating trips on Lake Powell to the Bridge Canyon landing, then walking about 1 mile, or by horse trail from Rainbow Lodge (14 miles), or Navajo Mountain Trading Post (24 miles). There are no facilities within the monument. The nearest town, Page, Arizona, is 60 miles away. Address: c/o Glen Canyon National Recreation Area, Box 1507, Page, Arizona 86040. 602/645-2471.

## RIO GRANDE WILD AND SCENIC RIVER

Texas

This area will preserve a segment on the U.S. side of the Rio Grande from mile 842.3 above Mariscal Canyon within Big Bend National Park, to river mile 651.1 at the Terrell–Val

Verde County Line. No land has been purchased yet on portions of the scenic river lying outside Big Bend National Park. Address: c/o Big Bend National Park, Texas 79834. 915/477-2251.

## ROOSEVELT, THEODORE, ISLAND

See page 296.

## ROSS LAKE RECREATION AREA

See North Cascades National Park, page 207.

## SAGUARO NATIONAL MONUMENT

### Arizona

A forest of giants dominates the Sonoran desert east and west of Tucson. Studding this country are thousands of stately saguaros, *Cereus giganteus*, which may live 200 years and reach heights of 35 feet, occasionally higher. The saguaros produce beautiful creamy-white flowers, most profuse in late May. The plant, unique to southern Arizona and Mexico, serves as a nesting site for flickers, Gila woodpeckers, elf and screech owls, and other birds. Huge picture windows of the **Rincon Mountain Unit Visitor Center** (east of Tucson) face the desert and Santa Catalina Mountains. From the center you can start the 8-mile loop drive, with nature trails along the way. A permit is required for overnight backcountry use in the Rincon Mountain Unit. The Tucson Mountain Unit, west of the city, includes a 9-mile scenic loop drive from the **Red Hills Visitor Center,** nature walks, hiking trails, and choice picnic sites. Address: 3693 South Old Spanish Trail, Tucson, Arizona 85730. 602/670-6680.

*Saguaro National Monument*

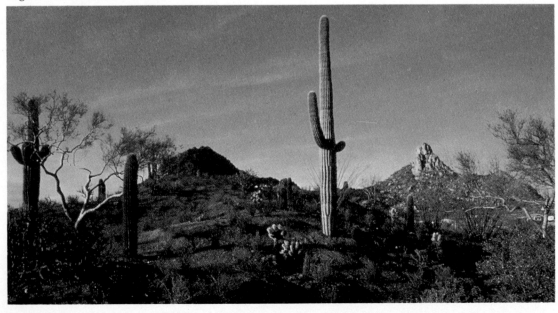

## ST. CROIX NATIONAL SCENIC RIVERWAY

### Minnesota–Wisconsin

More than 250 miles of the Namekagon and St. Croix rivers, flowing through scenic, undeveloped portions of Wisconsin and Minnesota, have been designated as part of the National Wild and Scenic River System through federal legislation of 1968 and 1972. The **upper St. Croix and Namekagon** offer choice canoeing through wilderness-like stretches with rapids, alternating with lake-like stretches, or flowages, formed by dams. The **lower St. Croix** extends 52 miles from St. Croix Falls dam to Prescott, Wisconsin, where it joins the Mississippi River. The river plunges through the spectacular high cliffs of the Dalles, then becomes wider and shallower, with many islands, sloughs, and backwaters, allowing for sailboating and powerboating. Stop at the Riverway Visitor Center located in St. Croix Falls, Wisconsin. Allow time to visit the St. Croix–Taylors Falls area, historical communities atop the high bluffs of the river gorge. Information stations open in season near Grantsburg (on the upper St. Croix) and in Trego (on the Namekagon). The two largest picnic areas are in Earl Park, near Trego, and near Osceola (the lower St. Croix). Camping along most of the riverway is limited to primitive sites accessible only by canoe; developed campgrounds are located in the nearby Chequamegon National Forest, and state parks and forests in both Minnesota and Wisconsin. Snowmobiles are permitted to cross the riverway on approved trails; groomed cross-country ski trails are maintained near Trego and Grantsburg, Wisconsin. North Country National Scenic Trail (cross-country hiking) traverses the riverway from Gordon to Danbury, Wisconsin. Address: Box 708, St. Croix Falls, Wisconsin 54024-0708. 715/483-3287.

## SANTA MONICA MOUNTAINS NATIONAL RECREATION AREA

### California

The Santa Monica Mountains stretch almost 50 miles westward from Griffith Park, in downtown Los Angeles, to Point Mugu, on the Pacific Coast. In 1978, following 15 years of effort, this national recreation area was established by Congress as a cooperative project to preserve, protect, and wisely use 150,000 acres of mountains and seashore, a legendary domain utilized by ancient Indians and glamorized in our time by moviemakers who used it as natural stage sets to represent landscapes of the world.

Follow famous **Mulholland Drive** and Highway westward from the Hollywood Freeway. It leads 50 winding miles through the national recreation area to Leo Carrillo State Beach. Visit **Paramount Ranch,** near Mulholland on Cornell Road, open daily, where guided hikes of the ranch and tours of the movie set are conducted weekends. **Diamond X Ranch,** off Mulholland east of Las Virgenes, is an outdoor education center. **Peter Strauss Ranch,** 5 minutes from the Ventura Freeway, offers opportunities for hiking and picnicking in a natural setting.

For hiking, **Castro Crest** (reached from Corral Canyon Road) is part of the Blackbone Trail stretching along the Santa Monica Crest. **Rancho Sierra Vista,** north of Point Mugu State Park, is open for hikes and ranger-led interpretation.

**Point Mugu State Park** itself includes 70 miles of hiking and riding trails and 5 miles of ocean shoreline. Point Mugu, Malibu Creek, and Topanga State Parks, plus 9 state beaches, already are available within the park. Address: 30401 Agoura Road, Suite 100, Agoura Hills, California 91301. 818/597-1036.

## SLEEPING BEAR DUNES NATIONAL LAKESHORE

### Michigan

This area protects 31.5 miles of shoreline on Lake Michigan on the northwest section of Michigan's lower peninsula, together with the two Manitou islands, bearing sand dunes, forests, and inland lakes of their own. The most prominent feature of the lakeshore is a towering mass of sand that looks from a distance like the profile of a bear at rest. The dunes are fed by sands from wind-eroded headlands and stretch in a shifting pattern across great plateaus. The mile-long Old Grade Trail passes through marsh, meadow, and woodland habitat, providing interesting birding activity. Bird walks are offered periodically. The Park Service administers campgrounds on the mainland and South Manitou Island. Backcountry camping is permitted on North Manitou. The Platte River campground on the mainland has electrical hook-ups and hot showers.

To reach South Manitou take the passenger ferry offering service from Leland during spring and summer. The island, 3 miles across and 12 miles around, is rimmed with long, wide sandy beaches, but Lake Michigan is too chilly for all but hardy swimmers. On the mainland, climbing the dunes is a popular activity. The Pierce Stocking Drive, 7.6 miles through forest and across dunes, provides magnificent views of Glen Lake, Sleeping Bear, and Lake Michigan shoreline. Address: Box 277, 9922 Front Street, Empire, Michigan 49630. 616/326-5134.

## SUNSET CRATER VOLCANO NATIONAL MONUMENT

### Arizona

About 900 years ago the last of a long series of eruptions occurred amid the peaks of the San Francisco Mountains north of Flagstaff. The massive, 1,000-foot-high volcanic cinder cone of Sunset Crater, whose crater-pocked summit is tinted with reddish-orange hues, probably appears much as it did after the eruption. The trail to the rim was closed in 1973 due to excessive erosion. However, the ½-mile self-guiding Lava Flow Nature Trail is open year-round. Easy to visit while driving north to Grand Canyon (with a stop also at nearby Wupatki National Monument). Only on Christmas and New Year's Day is the Visitor Center closed. Address: c/o Wupatki National Monument, 2717 North Steve's Boulevard, Suite 3, Flagstaff, Arizona 86001. 602/527-7042.

## TIMPANOGOS CAVE NATIONAL MONUMENT

### Utah

A series of small underground limestone chambers, ornamented with beautiful mineral deposits, is situated on the northern slope of snowcapped Mount Timpanogos, between Salt Lake City and Provo, easily reached along Utah 92. Much of the cave interior is covered by a filigree of pink and white translucent crystals. It is noted especially for its delicate and unusual helictites. Open May 15 to October 15 (weather permitting). Walk the 1.5-mile trail along the forested canyon of the American Fork River. It's steep, but interesting in its own right, with numbered stops along the way. Allow at least three hours for the round trip, including the cave tour. Wear comfortable shoes and take a jacket to wear inside the cave. Address: Route 3, Box 200, American Fork, Utah 84003. 801/756-5239.

## UPPER DELAWARE SCENIC AND RECREATIONAL RIVER

### New York–Pennsylvania

The 73-mile stretch of the Upper Delaware River (northwest of Port Jervis, New York, between Sparrow Bush and Hancock) flows through forested and rolling country, dotted with farms and small towns. Its values appeal to canoeists, fishermen, and swimmers; expert canoeists will find special challenge in the white-water rapids. The area is rich in historic sites, which include vestiges of Indian settlements, remains of the Delaware and Hudson Canal (including the Delaware Aqueduct Bridge) and the house, at Lackawaxen, Pennsylvania, where Zane Grey wrote some of his many adventure novels about the West. In 1987, Congress appropriated $300,000 to purchase and restore the Zane Grey house. Some portions of the Upper Delaware have changed little over the years. The river corridor is one of the few places in the eastern United States where you can see eagles, ospreys, herons, and vultures in their natural surroundings.

Summer is the most popular season, but autumn colors compare with New England at its best. Rural communities complement the park. Several private campgrounds and a few resorts are located in the river valley. The National Park Service operates several information centers at key public access sites. For daily reports on river and boating conditions, call the Information Line at 914/252-7100. If you don't bring your own canoe, you can easily arrange to rent one. The degree of difficulty does not exceed Class II under normal conditions, even at Skinners Falls (but don't get hurt by taking foolish chances). Lower stretches, from Narrowsburg south, usually are crowded on weekends. A good full-day canoe trip in little-spoiled surroundings is the 20 miles from Hancock to Hankins. Address: Box C, Narrowsburg, New York 12764. 717/729-7135.

## WHISKEYTOWN-SHASTA-TRINITY NATIONAL RECREATION AREA

### California

High in the northern mountains, the area is located near Redding, within one day's drive of San Francisco and Sacramento, and Portland, Oregon. It is a three-unit area, with the 42,503-acre Whiskeytown unit being administered by the National Park Service, and the Shasta unit and the Clair Engle–Lewiston

unit under the jurisdiction of the Forest Service. Whiskeytown Reservoir, with 5 miles of open water, extensive shoreline, and numerous coves, was formed by the Whiskeytown Dam, dedicated by President John F. Kennedy in 1963 as a part of the Central Valley Project of the Bureau of Reclamation. It is an excellent area for boating, waterskiing, scuba diving, and swimming. The shallows begin to warm by late May or early June, although deeper waters are always cold.

Fishing is permitted all year on the reservoir. Stream fishing opens the last Saturday in April and closes November 15. California regulations apply in the area. The California Department of Fish and Game and the U.S. Fish and Wildlife Service stock the lake with trout, bass, and Kokanee salmon. Hunting is permitted during autumn in compliance with California regulations.

Campgrounds, picnic areas, marinas, and boat ramps have been constructed and are available for use.

Shasta Bally, the most prominent landmark within the recreation area, rises 6,029 feet in the midst of rolling woodlands and clear streams. Below Whiskeytown Dam, Clear Creek winds through gorges and rocky hills. Address: Box 188, Whiskeytown, California 96095. 916/241-6584.

## WHITE SANDS NATIONAL MONUMENT

### New Mexico

In the wide Tularosa Basin of south-central New Mexico lies the world's largest deposit of gypsum dunes. Displays in the Visitor Center explain the story of sediments deposited by receding prehistoric seas and how these gypsum sediments were concentrated into the lowest portion of the Tularosa Basin. Evaporation left gypsum crystals called selenite, which over thousands of years have weathered into sand-grain size by wind and weather and piled into a dune field nearly 30 miles in length and 10 miles in width. A scenic 16-mile round-trip-loop drive leads to the heart of the dune field, with the final portion on pure, hard-packed gypsum with many pullouts for your convenience. Daytime hours, all year; evening hours, summer only.

Visitors are welcome to climb the dunes for an exhilarating view and choice picture-taking. Extended summer hours from Memorial Day to Labor Day allow visitors to attend naturalist-conducted walks, talks, and illustrated slide programs in the dune field or summertime full-moon programs with guest speakers. Moonlight programs begin at 8:45 p.m. A picnic area in the dunes is available with shelters and rest rooms, but no drinking water. Lodgings and meals are available in nearby Las Cruces, 53 miles southwest, and Alamogordo, 15 miles northeast. Address: Box 458, Alamogordo, New Mexico 88310. 505/479-6124.

# ALASKA MONUMENTS, PRESERVES, AND HISTORICAL PARKS

THE 15 UNITS NOW ADMINISTERED by the National Park Service in Alaska cover more land than all units—parks, monuments, historic sites, seashores, and rivers—administered by the service in the rest of the nation.

Ten of these parklands were established by the Alaska Lands Act of 1980. You may not find the same kinds of facilities you know in other parks. Remember that the parklands are vast in size and that dangers of the wilds are apt to rise. Consider going with an outfitter, guide, or outdoors group, at least on your first trip or two.

Travel within Alaska is different from elsewhere. There are fewer than 3,500 miles of public highway, much of it concentrated near population centers like Fairbanks and Anchorage. But scheduled and charter planes fly virtually anywhere. Cruise vessels, state-operated ferries, and the railroad provide fascinating alternatives.

Summer is the favorite time to visit Alaska. Days are long, so you can see and do more. But prepare for mosquitoes, usually at their worst in June, then tapering off in July, and gone by late August or September. May, September, and October can be attractive times. Certainly they are less crowded. Fall starts early, around mid-August, with an alluring panorama of birch and aspen turning to gold, the dwarf forest of the tundra changing to yellow and red, and fresh snow whitening the mountains. Days are sunny and clear.

Climate varies widely and defies prediction. Travel light but carry wool clothing, rubber boots, and raingear. Prepare to peel off or add on layers of garments.

Besides the National Park Service areas, other public areas are well worth including in your itinerary. Misty Fiords and Admiralty Island, in southeastern Alaska, are two major national monuments administered by the Forest Service. Wood-Tikchik and Kachemak Bay are among the state parks with wide interest and appeal.

Guidebooks worth reading include *The Milepost*, the annually revised highway guide, indispensable for driving the Alaska Highway. For general background and spirit of the land, read *Two in the Far North*, by Margaret Murie, and

*A Naturalist in Alaska*, by Adolph Murie. Write the Alaska Tourism Marketing Council (Box E-501, Juneau, AK 99811) for a copy of the *Vacation Planner*.

To help visitors get their bearings, Public Lands Information Centers have been opened in Alaska's two largest cities, Anchorage and Fairbanks, and at Tok on the Alaska Highway. Stop in for guidance. By touching the screen of a video monitor, you can tell the computer which part of Alaska you want to visit, the type of recreation you want, and how you're traveling to get there. The computer will respond with a choice of recreational opportunities from state and federal lands.

For details and further information, write National Park Service, 2525 Gambell St., Anchorage, AK 99503. Another valuable source is the State Division of Tourism, Pouch E, Juneau, AK 99811.

## ANIAKCHAK NATIONAL MONUMENT AND PRESERVE

### Alaska

Aniakchak encompasses more than 600,000 acres on the Alaska Peninsula, which extends from the mainland of Alaska westward toward the Aleutians between the Pacific Ocean and the Bering Sea. In a land of tundra, lakes, rivers, and volcanic peaks, the focal point of the national monument, Aniakchak Caldera, is one of the largest calderas (or cones with collapsed summits) in the world.

Often shrouded by fog and rain, Aniakchak remained unknown until 1922. Relatively few people have seen it even now, and fewer still have walked across the floor. This requires careful preparation and physical fitness.

Aniakchak lies about 400 miles from Anchorage. The most practical gateway, **King Salmon,** lies about 150 miles from the monument and is reached on scheduled airline service; guides and charter flights are available from that point for a trip into the monument. The caldera is subject to violent windstorms and rain, which can make hiking and camping difficult.

Father Bernard R. Hubbard, the "Glacier Priest," led a party into Aniakchak overland in 1930. They entered during a raging storm, but once the torrents subsided, they found a walled world of lush plant and animal life, including ferns growing in areas moderated by subterranean heat. Walls 2,000 feet high lend a feeling of isolation and enclosure. Vent Mountain rises 2,200 feet as a secondary cone inside the caldera, while ancient lava flows spread out across the floor. The world around the caldera is occupied by brown bear, moose, caribou, numerous smaller mammals and birds—somewhat reminiscent of the famed Ngorongoro Crater in Africa. **Surprise Lake,** the favorite landing place for seaplanes, covers 2½ square miles. The Aniakchak, a challenge to white-water rafters, also is included in the National Wild and Scenic Rivers System. Address: Box 7, King Salmon, Alaska 99614. 907/246-3305.

## BERING LAND BRIDGE NATIONAL PRESERVE

### Alaska

Just below the Arctic Circle, the preserve covers 2.7 million acres of the **Seward Peninsula**—the gateway to the New World, where human history of the Americas began. This area contains immense deposits of remains directly related to the Bering Land Bridge, where the prehistoric hunters are believed to have migrated from Asia. These remains include vestiges of mammoths, horses, giant bison, and a few traces of early people as well.

Eskimo villages are scattered across the flat

landscape of western Alaska, facing the Bering Sea between Kotzebue and Nome. For thousands of years, ancestors of the villagers have lived off the land and sea. A part of the attraction of the national preserve is to observe Eskimos pursuing subsistence lifestyles, managing reindeer herds, and producing handicrafts and art objects.

This preserve is a delight for the adventurous birdwatcher and wildlife watcher. Waterfowl, shore birds, and songbirds swarm to the Arctic to breed in summer. Clear lakes, streams, and lagoons make choice habitat for water birds and fish.

Travelers coming this way must do so equipped with their own food, shelter, and proper clothing. There are no facilities available, though primitive campgrounds are planned for the future. Insects are most active mid-June to early August, the heart of the short summer. Air travel is the principal means of access to and within Alaska's remote country. Nome and Kotzebue are both served by scheduled jet service, and it's possible to charter light planes from either place into **Serpentine Hot Springs** or to the beaches of the preserve. Address: Box 220, Nome, Alaska 99762. 907/443-2522.

## CAPE KRUSENSTERN NATIONAL MONUMENT

### Alaska

Touching the Chukchi Sea above the Arctic Circle, Cape Krusenstern reveals a long and fascinating history of nature at work and of human survival. Here it is possible to trace back to the melting of the Wisconsin glaciers, when the ocean level rose and submerged the Bering Land Bridge that had connected what is now Alaska with the Asian land mass.

The national monument embraces 560,000 acres of Arctic coastal lowland above Kotzebue Sound. Where Cape Krusenstern—about 35 miles from the gateway town of Kotzebue—bends eastward, the gravel driven by west winds accumulates offshore. Every 50 years or so, the winds shift to the southwest in the springtime, when the sea ice is breaking up. Giant ice floes then gouge out the gravel and drive it onshore above tideline, where it forms a new beach. This sequence has occurred repeatedly for 5,000 years, as evidenced by 114 beach ridges from the newest beachline to Ingitkalik Mountain. The mountain, which is located far inland, is known to be the ancient frontier of the Chukchi Sea.

There are no facilities within the monument. The determined visitor, however, will find rewarding adventure. Migratory birds are in abundance throughout the summer months. These include such species as the yellow wagtail shuttling back and forth from Siberia. Pods of beluga whales and spotted seals are often seen offshore.

**Kotzebue,** which lies at the end of a one-hour flight from Anchorage (and even less from Fairbanks) may be one of the oldest communities on the continent. Historians estimate it began more than 6,000 years ago as a foothold in the migrations from Asia over the Bering Land Bridge. The population of 2,500 is currently about 80 percent Eskimo. Seals, whales, and walrus are still hunted. Salmon that are caught in summer are hung and dried and then stored to be eaten in winter. In an age of changing traditions, the setting is not picturesque. Kotzebue's showpiece, the **Living Museum of the Arctic,** however, is a most worthy representation of ancient ways and of the new National Park system units in the region: Bering Land Bridge, Cape Krusenstern, Kobuk Valley, and Noatak. Address: Box 1029, Kotzebue, Alaska 99752. 907/442-3890.

## KLONDIKE GOLD RUSH NATIONAL HISTORICAL PARK

### Alaska

This park, authorized in 1976, memorializes the heyday of the 1897–1898 gold rush, when thousands of miners (adventurers, really) streamed over the trails from Dyea and Skagway, Alaska, to the Yukon Territory in Canada. The 13,271-acre park includes the rugged Chilkoot Trail (extending 33 miles from Dyea, Alaska, to Bennett, British Columbia); the White Pass Trail; and more than a dozen historic buildings in Skagway, which grew in a few months from a wilderness trading post to a brawling city of more than 10,000. Many buildings still retain their original appearance, enhancing Skagway's attraction to visitors aboard cruise ships and Alaska state ferries plying the Inland Passage. Several buildings owned by the National Park Service are being restored. The new Visitor Center, in the Mascot Saloon, is open daily June to September. Stop in for information and orientation to the park, Chilkoot Trail conditions, films, guided tours of the Skagway Historic District, and evening programs. The Chilkoot Trail is a tough climb of 3-5 days, with the prospect of severe weather en route. Consult the rangers about your gear. Allow time for one of the great rail trips of the continent, aboard the narrow-gauge White Pass and Yukon Railroad, built for the Klondike gold rush, operating from late May through late September. It has 1890s parlor cars, a 1947 steam engine and diesel locomotive for steep grades through White Pass. Write White Pass and Yukon Route, Box 435, Skagway, Alaska 99840, or call 800/343-7373 or 907/983-2217. Another unit of this park is in Seattle, Washington, jumping-off point for the treasure hunters of 1898. It is listed separately in the Historical Areas section of this book, page 335. Address: Box 517, Skagway, Alaska 99840. 907/983-2921.

## NOATAK NATIONAL PRESERVE

Alaska

A major portion of the largest untouched river basin in America lies within this 6.5-million acre national preserve above the Arctic Circle. It is bordered on three sides by two national parks and a national monument—Gates of the Arctic, Kobuk Valley, and Cape Krusenstern, respectively—to comprise a vast complex of protected lands.

River travel is easier than walking and the

*Noatak National Preserve*

first 300 miles of the Noatak, starting from the headwaters, rank with the finest wild stretches of river anywhere. The chief obstacle to walking is the almost impenetrable brush, mostly various types of willow. Walking is a little easier with higher elevation, but the only reasonable routes of travel are rivers and large streams.

The DeLong and Baird Mountains form the river basin, including the steep-walled stretch known as the Grand Canyon of the Noatak, and are reminiscent of the American Southwest. Migratory birds by the thousands breed on the river and the lakes that dot the basin. Moose are commonly seen, and there always are chances of spotting bear, Dall sheep, caribou, and wolves.

West of the canyon region, the village of **Noatak** is the only permanent settlement in the basin. It lies 50 miles from Kotzebue. The Igichuk Hills, westernmost edge of the Baird Mountains, are the final gate through which the Noatak flows on its course to the Arctic. It becomes a large river, sometimes half a mile wide, influenced by tides.

There are no public facilities within the preserve, but guide and outfitting services are increasing. At **Kiana,** within easy reach from Kotzebue, arrangements can be made to float and fish the Noatak or the Squirrel, which flows south from the Baird Mountains. Address: Box 1029, Kotzebue, Alaska 99752. 907/442-3890.

## SITKA NATIONAL HISTORICAL PARK
### Alaska

Adjoining the town of Sitka in southeastern Alaska, the park centers around the site of the battle for Sitka where the Tlingit Indians made their last stand against the Russians in 1804. In a forested setting of spruce and hemlock stand 19 totem poles of the finest native craftsmanship. The Visitor Center here is one of the finest historical showcases in Alaska, housing in one wing the Southeast Alaska Indian Cultural Center. It provides an interpretive program of teaching and demonstration to students and visitors. In late 1978 the rebuilt Saint Michael's Orthodox Cathedral was consecrated in Sitka, more than a decade after the original burned to the ground in 1966. The historic structure had been standing on the site since 1848, when it was built by the first Russian Orthodox congregation in North America. Sitka residents were able to save most of the icons and other treasured pieces, which had come from Czarist Russia. In a recent and ambitious project, the Russian Bishop's House, on Crescent Harbor, has been restored to its 1852 appearance. After 15 years of work (completed in 1988), the first floor has been converted into an impressive museum of

*Sitka National Historical Park*

Russian colonial days, while the second floor appears as it did when the Bishop lived here. Climb the stairs and step into the last century. Address: Box 738, Sitka, Alaska 99835. 907/747-6281.

## YUKON-CHARLEY RIVERS NATIONAL PRESERVE
### Alaska

In the uplands of interior Alaska, this national preserve of 2.5 million acres preserves a 128-mile-long segment of the corridor of the fabulous Yukon River, the central artery of a vast Canadian-Alaskan frontier, known at times as the "Mississippi of the North," and the entire Charley River drainage, a little-disturbed watershed with wilderness atmosphere.

This is one national park area in Alaska with gateways readily accessible by motor vehicle. You can take either the Steese Highway from Fairbanks to Circle, in the northwest area, or the Taylor Highway, which begins at Tetlin Junction (near Tok) on the Alaska Highway, to Eagle, in the southeast area. Both towns are reminiscent of the gold rush, riverboat travel, and military days.

At **Circle** you will be only 50 miles south of the Arctic Circle. Old log cabins and assorted items of yesteryear recall when the only sure way to travel was on the Yukon, which flows 2,000 miles from its source in Canada in a great northwest arc across Alaska to empty in the Bering Sea. Lodgings are available in **Circle, Circle Hot Springs,** and **Central.**

**Eagle,** once the main port of entry from Canada, was the trading center for Klondike miners and prospectors. A post office was established here in 1898; a military post, Fort Egbert, one year later; and Eagle became the first incorporated city of interior Alaska in 1901. You can take a walking tour, conducted by the Eagle Historical Society, of the town and fort, much of which are restored. The **Eagle Museum** features displays on Roald Amundsen, the polar explorer who arrived in Eagle in 1905. Lodging facilities are not highly developed, but a campground is maintained and there are stores that sell provisions. Float trips and guide service can be arranged.

Going downstream from Eagle to Circle, a distance of 160 miles, shows a large portion of the preserve. Drifting with the current and camping on bars and shorelines, you will see wildlife such as golden eagles, falcons, water birds, bear, and moose.

The **Charley River** and its corridor demand experienced wilderness river runners, hikers, and campers. The Charley is ideal for canoeing. It flows between Twin Mountain and Mount Sorenseon, 100 miles from mountain headwaters to its rendezvous with the Yukon, bounded in places by gentle slopes and in others with bluffs. White-water rapids dominate a part of the course. Address: Box 167, Eagle, Alaska 99738. 907/547-2233.

# INDEX

# ABOUT THE AUTHOR

Michael Frome has enjoyed a colorful and creative career as writer, activist, and educator, which he continues to pursue with enthusiasm and unflagging energy. National parks are very much a part of his life. Michael has explored them in the United States and the rest of the world, often as camper, backpacker, canoer and kayaker. He has been to the areas included in this guidebook over and over again, always learning new things about the parks.

Born in New York City, he served as a World War II navigator, flying to distant corners of the world. He has been a newspaper reporter, a successful travel writer, outdoorsman, and eloquent conservationist. He has been called "the voice of the wilderness" and "the conscience of the national parks." Senator Gaylord Nelson of Wisconsin declared in Congress: "No writer in America has more persistently and effectively argued for the need of national ethics of environmental stewardship than Michael Frome."

As Ph.D. he serves as a professor at Huxley College of Environmental Studies, Western Washington University (Bellingham, Washington), where he directs a program in environmental journalism and writing. He and his students utilize the resources of nearby national parks and national forests in the North Cascades and Olympics. He has lectured at many colleges and universities.

In 1986 he received the Marjorie Stoneman Douglas Award from the National Parks and Conservation Association for his many years of work on behalf of national parks. In 1993 he received the Award of Merit from the Desert Protective Council and in 1994 the Jade of Chiefs, the highest conservation award of the Outdoor Writers Association of America. As a tribute to him, the University of Idaho, where he taught for four years, established the Michael Frome Scholarship for Excellence in Conservation Writing.

His latest book is *Regreening the National Parks*. Others include *Strangers in High Places—The Story of the Great Smoky Mountains, Conscience of a Conservationist, Promised Land—Adventures and Encounters in Wild America*, and the *National Park Guide* (now in its twenty-ninth annual edition).

Your comments about the *National Park Guide* and reports on your trips to the parks are helpful and always welcome. Write Michael Frome, c/o Macmillan, 15 Columbus Circle, New York, NY 10023.